Rick Steves

BEST OF
ITALY

Contents

Post-Pandemic Travels: Expect a Warm Welcome...and a Few Changes
Research for this guidebook was limited by the COVID-19 outbreak, and the long-term impact of the crisis on our recommended destinations is unclear. Some details in this book will change for post-pandemic travelers. Now more than ever, it's smart to reconfirm specifics as you plan and travel. As always, you can find major updates at RickSteves.com/update.

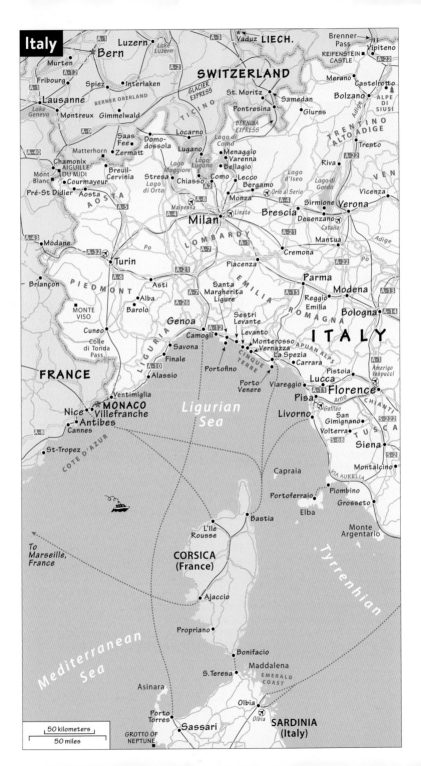

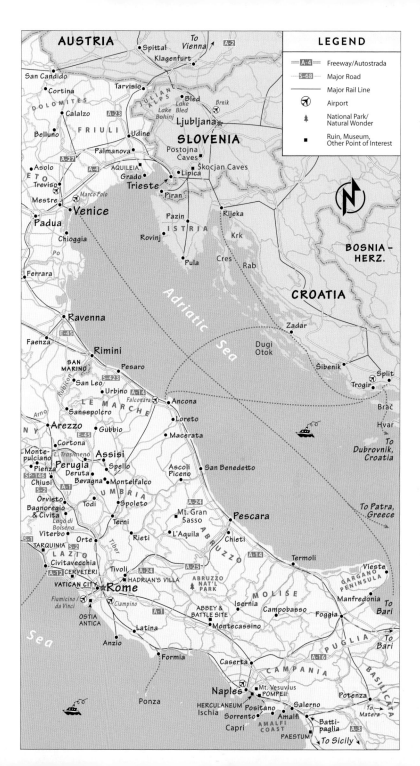

Introduction

Bella Italia! Italy has Europe's richest, craziest culture. It bubbles with emotion, traffic jams, strikes, crowds, and irate ranters shaking their fists at each other one minute and walking arm-in-arm the next. Accept Italy as a package deal—from the exquisite to the exasperating. It's the sum of its amazing parts that makes it my favorite country.

Italy is the cradle of European civilization—established by the Roman Empire and carried on by the Roman Catholic Church. Here you'll stand face-to-face with some of the world's most iconic images from this 2,000-year-plus history: Rome's ancient Colosseum and gleaming Trevi Fountain, Florence's Renaissance masterpieces (Michelangelo's towering *David*, Botticelli's perfect Birth of *Venus*), and the elegantly decaying island-city of Venice.

Beyond such famous sights, simple traditions endure within a country that is modern, vital, and passionate. Join the locals for their ritual evening stroll—the *passeggiata*. Seek out homemade gelato, dodge motor scooters and pickpockets, and make time for *il dolce far niente* (the sweetness of doing nothing). Ramble through ancient rubble and mentally resurrect the timeless stones. Write a poem over a glass of wine in a sun-splashed village. Italy is for romantics.

THE BEST OF ITALY

This book focuses on Italy's top destinations, from its thriving cities to its authentic towns. The biggies on everyone's list are Venice, Florence, and Rome. But no visit to Italy is complete without seeing the countryside, from the coastal villages of the Cinque Terre to the hill towns of the central heartland. For a dose of southern Italy, dip down past Rome to gritty Naples, seaside Sorrento, historic Pompeii, and the scenic Amalfi Coast.

Beyond the major destinations, I also cover the Best of the Rest—great destinations that don't quite make my top cut, but are worth seeing if you have more time: Milan, Varenna on Lake Como, and Pisa. When interesting sights or towns are near my recommended destinations, I cover them briefly.

To help you link the top sights, I've designed a two-week itinerary (see page 26), with tips for tailoring it to your interests.

LIECH.

AUSTRIA

SLOVAKIA

SWITZERLAND

F
R
A
N
C
E

SLOVENIA

CROATIA

Lake
Maggiore

Varenna
Lake
Como

Milan

Verona

Padua

Venice

BOSNIA-
HERZ.

Monterosso al Mare
Vernazza
Corniglia,
Manarola &
Riomaggiore

The Cinque Terre

Pisa

Florence

Ligurian Sea

Siena

Hill Towns

Adriatic Sea

Montalcino &
Montepulciano

Assisi

Corsica
FR.

Orvieto

Civita

Rome

**Naples & the
Amalfi Coast**

Sardinia

Pompeii
Positano
Sorrento

Capri

Tyrrhenian
Sea

100 Kilometers

N

100 Miles

Sicily

Mediterranean
Sea

THE BEST OF VENICE

Frozen in time, speckled with fanciful domes and spires, the island-city of Venice still looks much as it did centuries ago. It's a place of museums and churches, sensuous paintings, powdered-wig Vivaldi concerts, faded grandeur, and eternal romance.

❶ Explore the **back lanes and canals** to find a Venice without tourists.

❷ Ascend the **Campanile** bell tower for a sky-high view of Venice.

❸ Hiring a **gondolier** can be worth the splurge. You'll pay more at night, but the experience is dreamy.

❹ Long an emblem of the city, fanciful masks capture the anything-goes spirit of **Carnevale,** celebrated with gusto in Venice.

❺ Exotic inside and out, **St. Mark's Basilica** sports bulbous domes topping a church slathered with gold mosaics inside.

❻ Ride a vaporetto water bus down the **Grand Canal**—Venice's grandest thoroughfare—passing gondolas, water taxis, and a parade of palaces.

❼ Spanning the Grand Canal with style, the **Rialto** is Venice's signature bridge.

THE BEST OF THE CINQUE TERRE

This string of five villages dotting the coast of the Italian Riviera is a marvelous place to take a vacation from your vacation. The villages, each with a distinct and engaging personality, are connected by trains, hiking trails, and boats. There's no checklist of sights—just scenic hikes, succulent seafood, hidden beaches, and sparkling Mediterranean views.

❶ *Vernazza, the cover-girl town of the Cinque Terre, has long been my favorite.*

❷ *Seek out the* **regional specialties:** *tegame (fresh anchovies with potatoes and tomatoes), pesto, and antipasti frutti di mare (mixed seafood).*

❸ *Manarola poses for your picture.*

❹ *Enjoy a stroll along Vernazza's breakwater at* **sunset,** *when colors deepen and glow.*

❺ *Splash!*

❻ *Cinque Terre kids use their* **town squares** *as backyards.*

❼ *Spend a day* **hiking** *trails that connect the towns.*

❽ *The most resort-like town of the Cinque Terre,* **Monterosso** *has the longest beach and best nightlife.*

THE BEST OF FLORENCE

Florence hosts the Uffizi Gallery's world-class collection of Renaissance art, Brunelleschi's dome-topped cathedral, and Michelangelo's *David*. Its compact core offers the greatest hits of the Renaissance against a lively urban backdrop of high fashion, zippy Vespa scooters, and Italy's best gelato.

❶ *Florence's cathedral, the **Duomo,** is topped with a strikingly graceful dome—thanks to architect Brunelleschi.*

❷ *Michelangelo's David, in the Accademia Gallery, symbolizes the Renaissance.*

❸ *Palazzo Vecchio, on Florence's main square, has a soaring tower you can climb.*

❹ *The wide Arno River is spanned by the historic **Ponte Vecchio,** with central Florence on the left and the unvarnished Oltrarno neighborhood on the right.*

❺ *The city is famous for having Italy's finest **gelato.** "Artigianale" means it's made from scratch.*

❻ *You can reserve ahead for the **Uffizi Gallery's** wonderful collection of Renaissance art, starring Botticelli's beautiful Birth of Venus.*

THE BEST OF THE HILL TOWNS

The top towns of Italy's central region are proud Siena, saintly Assisi, and classic Orvieto. Siena has the most sights, with its magnificent red-brick Il Campo square, towering City Hall, and massive cathedral; in summer, it hosts the thrilling, medieval-style Palio horse race. Serene Assisi is graced by the fresco-covered Basilica of St. Francis. Orvieto and its tiny neighbor, the village of Civita, are small, cute, and perched on pinnacles.

❶ Adorable **Civita di Bagnoregio,** high atop a hill, is reachable only by a footbridge.

❷ Pilgrims and art lovers come to **Assisi's Basilica of St. Francis,** drawn by the saint's divine message and Giotto's expressive frescoes.

❸ **Tuscan cuisine** is reason alone to visit. This chef serves cheese with tasty toppings.

❹ **Orvieto** is famous for its ceramics, Classico wine, and cathedral (interior pictured here).

❺ The **Tuscan countryside** offers sublime views.

❻ During Siena's **Palio horse race,** each neighborhood waves its flag and cheers wildly for its horse to win.

❼ Conversation flows with **Classico wine.**

❽ The facade of Siena's **Duomo** is lively and colorful.

THE BEST OF ROME

Rome, Italy's capital, is studded with ancient ruins and floodlit-fountain squares. From the Vatican to the Colosseum, with crazy traffic in between, Rome is wonderful, huge, and exhausting. The crowds, the heat, and the weighty history of the Eternal City where Caesars walked can make tourists wilt. Recharge by taking siestas, gelato breaks, and after-dark walks, strolling from one atmospheric square to another in the refreshing evening air.

❶ *The much-admired* **Pantheon**—*which had the world's largest dome until the Renaissance—is nearly 2,000 years old (and doesn't look a day over 1,500).*

❷ *Raphael's* School of Athens *in the* **Vatican Museums** *embodies the humanistic spirit of the Renaissance.*

❸ *In the* **Colosseum**, *gladiators fought wild animals and one another, entertaining crowds of up to 50,000.*

❹ *Smiles are free at this Rome* **ristorante.**

❺ *Brightly garbed guards at* **St. Peter's Basilica** *take their work seriously.*

❻ *At the* **Trevi Fountain**, *toss in a coin and make your wish to return to Rome. It's always worked for me.*

❼ *Michelangelo's dome tops* **St. Peter's Basilica.**

THE BEST OF NAPLES AND THE AMALFI COAST

This region south of Rome is rich in contrasts, from cities to beaches, and from rugged to glamorous. The colorful port of Naples, with its impressive Archaeological Museum (containing Pompeii's best artifacts), makes a fascinating stop between Rome and Sorrento. The seaside resort of Sorrento serves as a fine home base, with connections to nearby sights: ancient Pompeii, the island of Capri, and the Amalfi Coast—Italy's Coast with the Most.

❶ *Naples has a vibrant street scene.*

❷ *Enjoy **pizza** in its birthplace—Naples.*

❸ *Along the **Amalfi Coast**, picturesque villages spill down toward the Mediterranean.*

❹ *Three generations straddle one **motorbike**.*

❺ *Explore ancient **Pompeii**, the Roman town buried and preserved in volcanic ash for centuries.*

❻ ***Mount Vesuvius** looms over Naples and the surrounding region.*

THE BEST OF THE REST

With extra time or interest, splice any of these destinations into your itinerary. You might fly into or out of modern Milan, which has historic highlights that include Europe's third-largest cathedral and Leonardo da Vinci's *Last Supper*. The laid-back village of Varenna on Lake Como is scenic, relaxing, and romantic. In Pisa, the tipsy Leaning Tower floats over the green grass of the Field of Miracles.

❶ *In **Milan**, Leonardo's Last Supper is compelling, even as it fades.*

❷ *The peaceful village of **Varenna on Lake Como** whispers honeymoon.*

❸ ***Pisa's famous tower** leans out from behind the cathedral.*

TRAVEL SMART

Approach Italy like a veteran traveler, even if it's your first trip. Design your itinerary, get a handle on your budget, make advance arrangements, and follow my travel strategies on the road. For my best advice on sightseeing, accommodations, restaurants, and transportation, see the Practicalities chapter.

Designing Your Itinerary

Decide when to go. Italy's best travel months are May, June, September, and October. Crowds aside, these months combine the convenience of peak season with pleasant weather. The heat in July and August can be grueling, especially in the south. Between November and April, expect cool weather, shorter hours at sights, and fewer crowds and activities.

Choose your top destinations. My itinerary (on page 26) gives you an idea of how much you can reasonably see in 14 days, but it's easy to adapt it to fit your interests and timeframe. Romantics linger in Venice. The Cinque Terre is tops for hikers and beach fun. Art lovers are drawn to Florence and Rome. If rolling hills,

charming towns, and wine tastings sound like paradise, you'll find it heavenly to spend a week exploring Italy's hill towns. Pilgrims make tracks to Assisi, while honeymooners hide out at Lake Como. Historians could marvel at Rome's sights for days. Stretching out a southern loop from Rome—from a few days to a week or more—offers a lot of variety: Naples (Italy in the extreme), ancient Pompeii, jet-setting Capri, friendly Sorrento, and the wildly scenic Amalfi Coast, with the beach village of Positano.

Draft a rough itinerary. Figure out how many destinations you can comfortably fit in the time you have. Don't overdo it—few travelers wish they'd hurried more. Allow enough days per stop: Figure on at least two or three days for major destinations.

Staying in a home base—like Florence or Sorrento—and making day trips can be more time-efficient than changing locations and hotels. Minimize one-night stands, especially consecutive ones; it can be worth taking a late-afternoon train ride or drive to get settled into a town for two nights.

Connect the dots. Link your destinations into a logical route. Determine which cities

you'll fly into and out of; begin your search for transatlantic flights at Kayak.com.

Decide if you'll travel by car, take public transportation, or use a combination. A car is particularly helpful for exploring the hill-town region, where public transportation can be spotty. But a car is useless in cities, and it's not necessary for connecting far-apart destinations (easier by train), unless you plan to make a lot of stops along the way.

If relying on public transit, you'll probably use a mix of trains and buses. Trains are faster, but buses can reach a few places that trains can't.

Allot sufficient time for transportation in your itinerary. Whether you travel by train, bus, or car, it'll take a half-day to get between most destinations. To determine approximate travel times between your destinations, study the driving chart on page 499 and check online train schedules at Trenitalia.it. Compare the cost of any long train ride with a budget flight; check Skyscanner.com for intra-European flights.

Plan your days. Fine-tune your itinerary; write out a day-by-day plan of where you'll be and what you want to see. To help you make the most of your time, I've suggested day plans for each major destination. But

take sight closures into account: Avoid visiting a town on the one day a week that its must-see sights are closed. Check if any holidays or festivals fall during your trip—these attract crowds and can close sights (for the latest, visit Italy's tourist website, Italia.it). Give yourself some slack. Every trip, and every traveler, needs downtime for doing laundry, picnic shopping, relaxing, people-watching, and so on. Pace yourself. Assume you will return.

Ready, set... You've designed the perfect itinerary for the trip of a lifetime.

Trip Costs

Run a reality check on your dream trip. You'll have major transportation costs in addition to daily expenses.

Flight: A round-trip flight from the US to Milan or Rome costs about $900-1,500, depending on where you fly from and when.

Public Transportation: For a two-week trip, allow about $350 for second-class trains and buses. You'll usually save money by buying train tickets in Italy rather than purchasing a rail pass. In some cases, a short flight can be cheaper than taking the train.

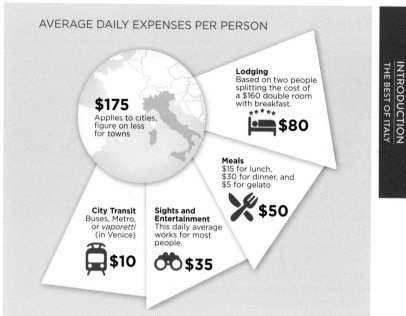

AVERAGE DAILY EXPENSES PER PERSON

$175
Applies to cities, figure on less for towns

Lodging
Based on two people splitting the cost of a $160 double room with breakfast.
$80

Meals
$15 for lunch, $30 for dinner, and $5 for gelato
$50

City Transit
Buses, Metro, or *vaporetti* (in Venice)
$10

Sights and Entertainment
This daily average works for most people.
$35

Car Rental: Allow roughly $250 per week, not including tolls, gas, parking, and insurance (theft insurance is mandatory in Italy).

Budget Tips: You can cut your daily expenses by taking advantage of the deals you'll find throughout Italy and mentioned in this book.

City transit passes (for multiple rides or all-day usage) decrease your cost per ride. Avid sightseers buy combo-tickets or passes that cover multiple museums. If a town doesn't offer deals, visit only the sights you most want to see, and seek out free sights and experiences (people-watching counts).

Some businesses—especially hotels and walking-tour companies—offer discounts to my readers (look for the RS% symbol in the listings in this book).

Book your rooms directly with the hotel. Some hotels offer discounts if you pay in cash and/or stay three or more nights (it pays to check online or ask).

Rooms cost less outside of peak season (roughly November through March). And

even seniors can stay in hostels (some have double rooms) for about $30 per person. Or check Airbnb-type sites for deals.

It's no hardship to eat cheap in Italy. You can get tasty, inexpensive meals at delis, bars, takeout pizza shops, ethnic eateries, and Italian restaurants, too. Cultivate the art of picnicking in atmospheric settings.

When you splurge, choose an experience you'll always remember, such as a gondola ride or a food-tasting tour. Minimize souvenir shopping—how will you get it all home? Focus instead on collecting wonderful memories.

Before You Go

You'll have a smoother trip if you tackle a few things ahead of time. For more info on these topics, see the Practicalities chapter and RickSteves.com, which has helpful travel tips and talks.

Make sure your travel documents are valid. If your passport is due to expire within six months of your ticketed date of

THE BEST OF ITALY IN 2 WEEKS

Here's an itinerary for an unforgettable two-week trip that'll show you the very best that Italy has to offer. It's geared for Italy's good public transportation system (mainly trains and a few buses), but can be supplemented by car: For example, you could rent a car when leaving Siena to more fully explore the hill-town region, then drop it off in Orvieto, which has good train connections with Rome.

DAY	PLAN	SLEEP
	Arrive in Venice	Venice
1	Sightsee Venice	Venice
2	Venice	Venice
3	Travel to the Cinque Terre (6 hours by train)	Cinque Terre
4	Cinque Terre	Cinque Terre
5	More Cinque Terre, then travel to Florence (2.5-3 hours by train)	Florence
6	Florence	Florence
7	More Florence, then travel in the evening to Siena (1.5 hours by bus or train)	Siena
8	Siena	Siena
9	Travel to Assisi (2 hours by bus)	Assisi
10	More Assisi, then travel to Orvieto (2-3 hours by train)	Orvieto
11	Orvieto and Civita	Orvieto
12	Travel in the morning to Rome (1-1.5 hours by train)	Rome
13	Rome	Rome
14	Rome	Rome
	Fly home	

Adding Naples, Sorrento, and the Amalfi Coast

To add these southern destinations (and lengthen your trip), insert them after Orvieto. After your southern loop, enjoy a grand finale in Rome, which has good flight connections to the US.

DAY	PLAN	SLEEP
12	Travel in the morning from Orvieto to Sorrento, with a midday stop in Naples (total of 5 hours by train)	Sorrento
13	Sightsee the Amalfi Coast (by bus or minibus) or Capri (by boat). Or add a day and do both.	Sorrento
14	Visit Pompeii en route to Rome (3 hours by train)	Rome
15	Rome	Rome
16	Rome	Rome
17	Rome	Rome
	Fly home	

Alternatively, to fit this southern loop into a 14-day trip, drop whichever destinations (such as sleepy hill towns or weather-dependent coastal towns) aren't a must-see for you.

Rick's Free Video Clips and Audio Tours

Travel smarter with these free, fun resources:

Rick Steves Classroom Europe, a powerful tool for teachers, is also useful for travelers. This video library contains more than 400 short clips excerpted from my public television series. Enjoy these videos as you sort through options for your trip and to better understand what you'll see in Europe. Check it out at Classroom.RickSteves.com (just enter a topic to find everything I've filmed on a subject).

Rick Steves Audio Europe, a free app, makes it easy to download and lis-

ten to my audio tours offline as you travel. For this book, these audio tours (look for the 🎧) cover sights and neighborhoods in Venice, Florence, Siena, Assisi, Rome, Naples, and Pompeii. The app also offers insightful interviews from my public radio show with experts from Europe and around the globe. Find it in your app store or at RickSteves.com/AudioEurope.

return, you need to renew it. Allow six weeks or more to renew or get a passport (www.travel.state.gov). Check for current Covid entry requirements, such as proof of vaccination or a negative Covid-19 test result..

Arrange your transportation. Book your international flights. It's worth thinking about buying essential train tickets in advance, renting a car, or booking cheap European flights. (You can wing it once you're there, but it may cost more.) Drivers: Consider bringing an International Driving Permit (sold at AAA offices in the US, www.aaa.com) along with your US license.

Book rooms well in advance, especially if your trip falls during peak season or any major holidays or festivals.

Reserve or buy tickets in advance for major sights. In Florence, reserve ahead for the Uffizi Gallery (Renaissance paintings), Accademia (Michelangelo's *David*), and to climb the cathedral dome (mandatory). For Pisa, you can book a time to climb the Leaning Tower. For Milan, reserve three months ahead for Leonardo's *Last Supper.* For Padua, book

at least two days in advance for Giotto's Scrovegni Chapel. In Rome, book several days ahead for the Borghese Gallery (Bernini sculptures). Reservations are essential for the Vatican Museums (Sistine Chapel) and for quick entry into the Colosseum and Forum.

Consider travel insurance. Compare the cost of the insurance to the cost of your potential loss. Check whether your existing insurance (health, homeowners, or renters) covers you and your possessions overseas.

Call your bank. Alert your bank that you'll be using your debit and credit cards in Europe. Ask about transaction fees, and get the PIN number for your credit card. You don't need to bring euros for your trip; you can withdraw euros from cash machines in Europe.

Use your smartphone smartly. Sign up for an international service plan to reduce your costs, or rely on Wi-Fi in Europe instead. Download any apps you'll want on the road, such as maps, translators, transit schedules, and Rick Steves Audio Europe (see sidebar).

A little Italian goes a long way.

Takeaway sandwiches save time and money.

Pack light. You'll walk with your luggage more than you think. I travel for weeks with a single carry-on bag and a daypack. Use the packing checklist in Practicalities as a guide.

Travel Strategies on the Road

If you have a positive attitude, equip yourself with good information, and expect to travel smart, you will.

Read—and reread—this book. To have an "A" trip, be an "A" student. As you study up on sights, note opening hours, closed days, crowd-beating tips, and whether reservations are required or advisable. Check the latest at RickSteves .com/update.

Be your own tour guide. As you travel, get up-to-date info on sights, reserve tickets and tours, reconfirm hotels and travel arrangements, and check transit connections. Visit local tourist information offices. Upon arrival in a new town, lay the groundwork for a smooth departure; confirm the train, bus, or road you'll take when you leave.

Give local tours a spin. Your appreciation of a city or region and its history can increase dramatically if you take a walking tour or even hire a private guide. If you want to learn more about any aspect of Italy, experts are happy to teach you.

Outsmart thieves. Pickpockets abound in crowded places where tourists congregate. Treat commotions as smokescreens for theft. Keep your cash, cards, and passport secure in a money belt tucked under your clothes; carry only a day's spending money in your front pocket. Don't set valuable items down on counters or café tabletops, where they can be quickly stolen or easily forgotten.

Minimize potential loss. Keep expensive gear to a minimum. Bring photocopies or take photos of important documents (passport and cards) to aid in replacement if they're lost or stolen. Back up photos and files frequently.

Beat the summer heat. If you wilt easily, choose a hotel with air-conditioning, start your day early, take a midday siesta at your hotel, and resume your sightseeing later. Churches offer a cool haven (though dress modestly—no bare shoulders or shorts). Take frequent gelato breaks. Join in the *passeggiata,* when locals stroll in the cool of the evening.

Guard your time and energy. Taking a taxi can be a good value if it saves you a long wait for a bus or an exhausting walk across town. To avoid long lines at sights, follow my crowd-beating tips, such as making advance reservations, or sightseeing early or late. Buy combo-tickets

at less-visited sights to quickly get into popular ones.

Be flexible. Even if you have a well-planned itinerary, expect changes, closures, sore feet, sweltering weather, and so on. Your Plan B could turn out to be even better.

Attempt the language. Many Italians—especially those in the tourist trade and in big cities—speak English, but if you learn even just a few Italian phrases, you'll get more smiles and make more friends. Practice the survival phrases near the end of this book, and even better, bring a phrase book.

Connect with the culture. Interacting with locals carbonates your experience. Enjoy the friendliness of the Italian people. Ask questions—most locals are happy to point you in their idea of the right direction. Set up your own quest for the best piazza, bell tower, or gelato. When an unexpected opportunity pops up, say *"Si!"*

Hear the gondolier singing? Taste the pasta and chianti? Your next stop...Italy!

Welcome to Rick Steves' Europe

Travel is intensified living—maximum thrills per minute and one of the last great sources of legal adventure. Travel is freedom. It's recess, and we need it.

I discovered a passion for European travel as a teen and have been sharing it ever since—through my tours, public television and radio shows, and travel guidebooks. Over the years, I've taught millions of travelers how to best enjoy Europe's blockbuster sights—and experience "Back Door" discoveries that most tourists miss.

This book offers you a balanced mix of Italy's lively cities and cozy towns, from brutal but *bella* Rome to *tranquillo,* traffic-free coastal villages. And it's selective—rather than listing dozens of hill towns, I recommend only the best ones. My self-guided museum tours and city walks give insight into the country's vibrant history and today's living, breathing culture.

I advocate traveling simply and smartly. Take advantage of my money- and time-saving tips on sightseeing, transportation, and more. Try local, characteristic alternatives to expensive hotels and restaurants. In many ways, spending more money only builds a thicker wall between you and what you traveled so far to see.

We visit Italy to experience it—to become temporary locals. Thoughtful travel engages us with the world, as we learn to appreciate other cultures and new ways to measure quality of life.

Judging from the positive feedback I receive from readers, this book will help you enjoy a fun, affordable, and rewarding vacation—whether it's your first trip or your tenth.

Buon viaggio! Happy travels!

Rick Steves

Venice

Venice is a world apart. Built on a hundred islands, its exotic-looking palaces are laced together by graceful bridges over sun-speckled canals. Romantics revel in the city's atmosphere of elegant decay, seeing the peeling plaster as a metaphor for beauty in decline. And first-time visitors are often stirred deeply, waking from their ordinary lives to a fantasy world unlike anything they've ever seen.

Those are strong reactions, considering that Venice today, frankly, can also be an overcrowded tourist trap. While there are about 270,000 people in greater Venice (counting the mainland, not counting tourists), the old town has a small-town feel. To see Venice away from the touristic flak, escape the Rialto-San Marco tourist zone and savor the town early and late. At night, when the hordes of day-trippers have gone, another Venice appears. Glide in a gondola through quiet canals. Dance across a floodlit square. Pretend it's Carnevale, don a mask—or just a clean shirt—and become someone else for a night.

VENICE IN 2 DAYS

Venice's greatest sight is the city itself, easily worth two days. It can be Europe's best medieval wander if you make time to stroll and explore.

Day 1: In the morning, take the slow vaporetto #1 from the train station down the Grand Canal to St. Mark's Square. Stop off midway at the Rialto market (Rialto Mercato) to grab an early lunch. Resume your ride down the Grand Canal to St. Mark's Square. Spend the afternoon on the square, visiting your choice of St. Mark's Basilica, Doge's Palace, Bridge of Sighs, the Correr Museum, and Campanile bell tower (open late in summer).

On any evening: Do a *cicchetti* (appetizer) crawl for dinner (except on Sun, when most bars are closed), or dine later at a restaurant. Enjoy a gondola ride (or, the budget version, a moonlit vaporetto. Catch a Vivaldi concert. Hum along with the dueling orchestras on St. Mark's Square, whether you get a drink or just stroll.

Day 2: Spend the morning shopping and exploring as you make your way over the Rialto Bridge to the Frari Church for the art. Afterward, head to the Dorsoduro neighborhood for lunch, then devote the afternoon to more art—select from the Accademia (Venetian art), Peggy Guggenheim Collection (modern art), and Ca' Rezzonico (18th-century palace).

Too many museums? Go on a photo safari through back streets and canals. Or take a short vaporetto trip to the San Giorgio Maggiore island for a sublime skyline view of Venice.

With extra time: Visit the lagoon islands of Murano, Burano, and Torcello. For beach time, it's the Lido (across the

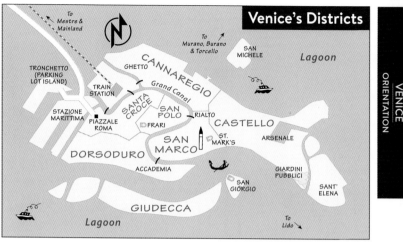

lagoon via vaporetto). The nearby towns of Padua (with Giotto's frescoed Scrovegni Chapel—reserve ahead) and Verona (with a Roman amphitheater) make great day trips or stops to or from Venice.

ORIENTATION

The island city of Venice is shaped like a fish. Its major thoroughfares are canals. The Grand Canal winds through the middle of the fish, starting at the mouth where all the people and food enter, passing under the Rialto Bridge, and ending at St. Mark's Square (Piazza San Marco). Park your 21st-century perspective at the mouth and let Venice swallow you whole.

Venice has six districts known as *sestieri*: San Marco (from St. Mark's Square to the Accademia Bridge), Castello (the area east of St. Mark's Square—the "tail" of the fish), Dorsoduro (the "belly," on the far side of the Accademia Bridge), Cannaregio (between the train station and the Rialto Bridge), San Polo (west of the Rialto Bridge), and Santa Croce (the "eye" of the fish, across the canal from the train station).

The easiest way to navigate is by landmarks. Many street corners have a sign pointing you to *(per)* the nearest major landmark, such as San Marco, Accademia, Rialto, and Ferrovia (train station). Obedient visitors stick to the main thoroughfares as directed by these signs...and miss the charm of back-street Venice.

Beyond the city's core there are several other islands, including San Giorgio (with great views of Venice), Giudecca (more views), San Michele (old cemetery), Murano (famous for glass), Burano (lacemaking), Torcello (old church), and the skinny Lido (with Venice's beach).

Rick's Tip: *Don't worry about **getting lost**—in fact, get as lost as possible. When it comes time to find your way, **follow the arrows** on building corners or simply ask a local, "Dov'è San Marco?" ("Where is St. Mark's?") Or, if you're lost, pop into a hotel and ask for their business card—it probably comes with a map and a prominent "You are here."*

Tourist Information

With this chapter, a city map, and the events schedule on the TI's website, there's little need to make an in-person visit to a Venice TI. To check or confirm something, try phoning the TI information line at 041-2424 or visit VeneziaUnica.it.

If you must visit a TI, you'll find four convenient branches (all are open daily):

VENICE AT A GLANCE

▲▲▲**St. Mark's Square** Venice's grand main square. See page 52.

▲▲▲**St. Mark's Basilica** Cathedral with mosaics, saint's bones, treasury, museum, and viewpoint of square. **Hours:** Mon-Sat 9:30-17:00, Sun 14:00-17:00 (Sun until 16:30 Nov-Easter). See page 54.

▲▲▲**Doge's Palace** Art-splashed palace of former rulers, with prison accessible through Bridge of Sighs. **Hours:** Sun-Thu 8:30-21:00, Fri-Sat until 23:00, Nov-March daily until 19:00. See page 58.

▲▲▲**Rialto Bridge** Distinctive bridge spanning the Grand Canal, with a market nearby. **Hours:** Market—souvenir stalls open daily, produce market closed Sun, fish market closed Sun-Mon. See page 63.

▲▲**Correr Museum** Venetian history and art. **Hours:** Daily 10:00-19:00, Nov-March 10:30-17:00. See page 59.

▲▲**Accademia** Venice's top art museum. **Hours:** Tue-Sun 8:15-19:15, Mon until 14:00. See page 61.

▲▲**Peggy Guggenheim Collection** Popular display of 20th-century art. **Hours:** Wed-Mon 10:00-18:00, closed Tue. See page 62.

▲▲**Frari Church** Franciscan church featuring Renaissance masters. **Hours:** Mon-Sat 9:00-18:00, Sun from 13:00. See page 63.

▲▲**Scuola San Rocco** Tintoretto's "Sistine Chapel." **Hours:** Daily 9:30-17:30. See page 64.

▲▲**Ca' Rezzonico** Posh Grand Canal palazzo with 18th-century Venetian art. **Hours:** Wed-Mon 10:00-18:00, Nov-March until 17:00, closed Tue year-round. See page 63.

▲**Campanile** Dramatic bell tower on St. Mark's Square with elevator to the top. **Hours:** Daily 8:30-21:00, Sept-mid-Oct until sunset, mid-Oct-April 9:30-17:30. See page 60.

▲**Bridge of Sighs** Famous enclosed bridge, part of Doge's Palace, near St. Mark's Square. **Hours:** Always viewable. See page 60.

▲**La Salute Church** Striking church dedicated to the Virgin Mary. **Hours:** Daily 9:30-12:00 & 15:00-17:30. See page 62.

▲**T Fondaco dei Tedeschi View Terrace** Rooftop terrace atop luxury mall, with views over the Grand Canal. **Hours:** Daily 10:15-19:30, June-Aug until 20:15, Nov-March until 19:15. See page 63.

Nearby Islands

▲▲**Burano** Sleepy island known for lacemaking and lace museum. **Hours:** Museum open Tue-Sun 10:30-17:00, Nov-March until 16:30, closed Mon year-round. See page 66.

▲**San Giorgio Maggiore** Island facing St. Mark's Square, featuring dreamy church and fine views back on Venice. **Hours:** Daily 9:00-19:00, Nov-March 8:30-18:00. See page 61.

▲**Murano** Island famous for glass factories and glassmaking museum. **Hours:** Glass Museum open daily 10:30-18:30, Nov-March until 16:30. See page 65.

▲**Torcello** Near-deserted island with old church, bell tower, and museum. **Hours:** Church open daily 10:30-18:00, Nov-Feb 10:00-17:00, museum closed Mon. See page 66.

St. Mark's Square (in the far-left corner with your back to the basilica), airport, bus station (inside the huge white Autorimessa Comunale parking garage), and train station (across from track 2).

Maps: Venice demands a good map. Hotels give away freebies. TIs and vaporetto ticket booths sell decent maps—but you can find a wider range at bookshops, newsstands, and postcard stands. If you spend €5, you'll get a map that shows all the tiny alleys. It may be the best money you spend in Venice. But know you'll still spend some time "exploring" (read: lost). Also consider a mapping app for your mobile phone. (City Maps 2Go and Google Maps cover Venice well.)

Helpful Hints

Sightseeing Tips: Venice offers plenty of sightseeing passes, but only a few—like the Doge's Palace and Correr Museum combo-ticket—are worth the money. For more on passes and other sightseeing advice, see page 52.

Theft Alert: The dark, late-night streets of Venice are generally safe. Even so, pickpockets (often elegantly dressed) work the crowded main streets, docks, and vaporetti. Your biggest risk of pickpockets is inside St. Mark's Basilica, near the Accademia or Rialto bridges, or on a tightly packed vaporetto.

Dress Modestly: When visiting St. Mark's Basilica or other major churches, men, women, and even children must cover their shoulders and knees. Remove hats when entering a church.

Public Toilets: Handy pay WCs are near major landmarks, including St. Mark's Square (behind the Correr Museum and at the waterfront park, Giardinetti Reali), Rialto, and the Accademia Bridge.

Laundry: These laundry places are near St. Mark's Square (see page 74 for locations): Self-service **Effe Erre** is off Campo Santa Maria Formosa (daily 6:30-23:30, on Ruga Giuffa, Castello 4826, mobile 349-058-3881). **Lavanderia Gabriella** offers

full-service laundry, a few streets north of St. Mark's Square (drop off Mon-Fri 8:00-12:30, closed Sat-Sun; pick up 2 hours later or next working day, on Rio Terà de le Colonne, San Marco 985, tel. 041-522-1758, friendly Elisabetta).

Tours
WALKING TOURS
Avventure Bellissime Venice Tours offers small-group tours, including a basic two-hour St. Mark's Square introduction (€25, includes church entry) and a 65-minute boat tour of the Grand Canal (€48, RS%—10 percent discount, contact before booking for promo code, www.tours-italy.com, tel. 041-970-499, info@tours-italy.com).

Alessandro's Classic Venice Bars Backstreets Tours introduce Venetian *bacari*—classic old bars serving wine and traditional *cicchetti* snacks in two-hour evening tours (€40/person). His 1.5-hour Backstreets Tour gets you into offbeat Venice (€20/person, book via email at alessandro@schezzini.it or by phone at 335-530-9024; www.schezzini.it).

Venice Bites Food Tours is run by two expats who enjoy sharing their love for *cicchetti* culture. Their 3.5-hour food tours include lots of walking, noshing, and fun insights (€105-112/person, RS%—€15 off if you book online with discount code "RICKSTEVES"; tel. 800-656-0713, www.venicebitesfoodtours.com).

Venicescapes offers private, themed tours of Venice that are intellectually demanding, intertwining history, art, politics, economics, culture, and religion (2 people—$280-320 or the euro equivalent, $60/person after that, admissions and transport extra, tel. 041-850-5742, mobile 349-479-7406, www.venicescapes.org, info@venicescapes.org).

LOCAL GUIDES
Figure about €75/hour with a 2-hour minimum for most local guides: **Walks Inside Venice** is enthusiastic about

Is Venice Sinking?

Venice has battled rising water levels since the fifth century. Several factors, both natural and man-made, cause Venice to flood dozens of times a year—usually from October until late winter—a phenomenon called the *acqua alta*.

Venice sits atop sediments deposited at the ancient mouth of the Po River. Early industrial projects, such as offshore piers and the railroad bridge to the mainland, affected the sea floor and tidal cycles in ways that made the city more vulnerable to flooding. Twentieth-century industry worsened things by pumping massive amounts of groundwater out of the aquifer beneath the lagoon for nearly 50 years before the government stopped the practice in the 1970s. In the last century, Venice has sunk by about nine inches.

Meanwhile, the waters around Venice are rising. The notorious *acqua alta* happens when an unusually high tide combines with strong sirocco winds and a storm, causing a surging storm tide. Add to that the worldwide sea-level rise caused by climate change, and a high sea gets much higher.

If the *acqua alta* appears during your visit, you'll see the first puddles in the center of paved squares, pooling around the limestone grates at the square's lowest point. These grates cover cisterns that long held Venice's only source of drinking water. For centuries, residents carried water from the mainland with much effort and risk. In the ninth century, they devised a way to collect rainwater by using paved, sloped squares as catchment systems, with limestone filters covering underground clay tubs. Hundreds of cisterns provided the city with drinking water until 1884, when an aqueduct was built to bring in water from nearby mountains. Now the wells are capped, the clay tubs are rotted out, and rain drains from squares into the lagoon—or up from it.

So, what is Venice doing about the flooding? In 2003, engineers began construction on the MOSE Project. Underwater "mobile" gates are being installed on the sea floor at the three inlets where the open sea enters Venice's lagoon. When the seawater rises above a certain level, air will be pumped into the gates, causing them to rise and shut out the Adriatic. The first gates are already installed. But, a corruption scandal has stranded the entire project for the foreseeable future.

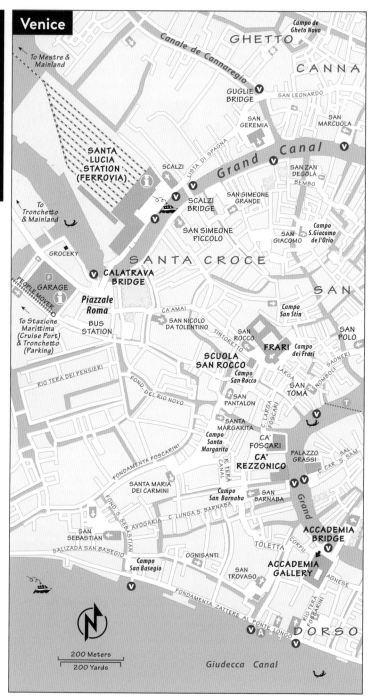

Venice

GHETTO

Campo de
Gheto Novo

CANNA

Canale de Cannaregio

To Mestre &
Mainland

GUGLIE
BRIDGE

SAN LEONARDO

SAN
GEREMIA

SAN
MARCUOLA

SANTA
LUCIA
STATION
(FERROVIA)

SCALZI

LISTA DI SPAGNA

Grand Canal

SAN ZAN
DEGOLÀ
BEMBO

To
Tronchetto
& Mainland

SCALZI
BRIDGE

SAN SIMEONE
GRANDE

SAN
GIACOMO

Campo
S.Giacomo
de l'Orio

SAN SIMEONE
PICCOLO

GROCERY

SANTA CROCE

SAN

CALATRAVA
BRIDGE

PEOPLE MOVER

GARAGE

Piazzale
Roma

CA'AMAI

Campo
San Stin

To Stazione
Marittima
(Cruise Port)
& Tronchetto
(Parking)

BUS
STATION

SAN NICOLÒ
DA TOLENTINO

SAN
ROCCO

TINTORETTO

FRARI

Campo
dei Frari

SAN
POLO

RIO TERA DEI PENSIERI

FOND. DEL RIO NOVO

SCUOLA
SAN ROCCO

Campo
San Rocco

LARGA

SAN
TOMÀ

NOMBOLI

SAONERI

SAN
PANTALON

SANTA
MARGARITA

C. LARGA
FOSCARI

FONDAMENTA FOSCARINI

Campo
Santa
Margarita

R. TERÀ
CANAL

CA'
FOSCARI

CA'
REZZONICO

PALAZZO
GRASSI

SAL. CAR. S SAM

SANTA MARIA
DEI CARMINI

Campo
San Barnaba

SAN
BARNABA

Grand

FOND. S. SEBASTIAN

AVOGARIA

C. LUNGA S. BARNABA

SAN
SEBASTIAN

SALIZADA SAN BASEGIO

Campo
San Basegio

OGNISANTI

ACCADEMIA
BRIDGE

TOLETTA

CORFU

ACCADEMIA
GALLERY

AGNESE

SAN
TROVASO

FONDAMENTA ZATTERE AI PONTE LONGO

RIO TERA
FOSCARINI

DORSO

N

200 Meters
200 Yards

Giudecca Canal

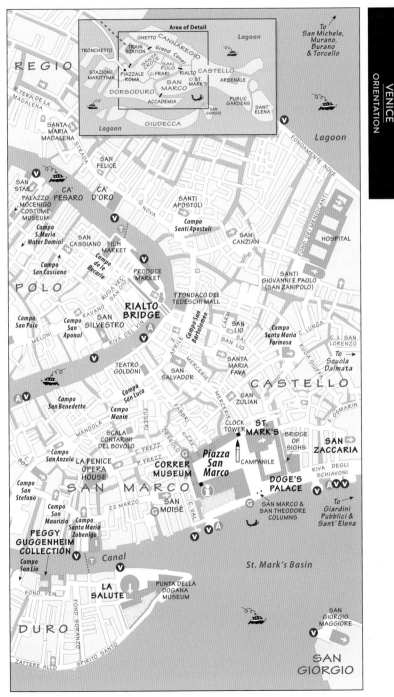

teaching (€280/3 hours per group of up to 6, RS%; Roberta: mobile 347-253-0560; Sara: mobile 335-522-9714; www.walksinsidevenice.com, info@walksinsidevenice.com). **Elisabetta Morelli** and **Corine Govi,** who run **2Guides4Venice,** are informative and reliable (Elisabetta: mobile 328-753-5220, bettamorelli@inwind.it; Corine: mobile 347-966-8346, corine_g@libero.it; www.2guides4venice.com). **Venice with a Guide** is a co-op of eight good Venetian guides (€75/hour, www.venicewithaguide.com). **Best VeniceGuides.it** offers an online catalog of about 100 local guides, with information to help you pick the right one (family-friendly guides, shared group tours available, most guides about €75/hour, www.bestveniceguides.it).

GRAND CANAL CRUISE

Take a joyride and introduce yourself to Venice by boat, an experience worth ▲▲▲. Cruise the Canal Grande all the way to St. Mark's Square, starting at the train station (Ferrovia) or the bus station (Piazzale Roma). Consider topping it off with my self-guided tour of St. Mark's Basilica (later, under "Sights in Venice"). Or, to avoid daytime vaporetto crowds, ride at night. With nearly empty boats and chandelier-lit palace interiors viewable from the Grand Canal, this cruise can be a highlight of your Venetian experience.

This 45-minute tour, organized by boat stop, is designed to be done on **slow boat #1.** Express boat #2 travels the same route, but skips many stops, making this tour hard to follow and hop-on/hop-off sightseeing impossible.

You can break up the tour by hopping on and off at various sights—but remember, a single-fare vaporetto ticket is good for just 75 minutes (passes let you hop on and off all day).

Tours: ⍨ Download my free Grand Canal Cruise **audio tour.**

Seating Strategies: As the vaporetti can be jammed, strategize about where to sit—then, when the boat pulls up, make a beeline for your preference. You're more likely to find an empty seat if you catch the vaporetto at Piazzale Roma—the stop *before* Ferrovia.

Grand Canal

Vaporetto stop at the train station

Calatrava Bridge

A few remaining older vaporetti have seats in the bow (in front of the captain's bridge), the perfect vantage point for spotting sights left, right, and forward. With a standard boat and normal crowds, I'd head for the open-air section in the stern and grab the middle seat. If it's not crowded, you can hang out in the middle (loading zone) and bop from side to side (especially easy after dark). Your worst option is sitting inside and trying to look out the window.

Overview

The Grand Canal is Venice's "Main Street." At more than two miles long, nearly 150 feet wide, and nearly 15 feet deep, it's the city's largest canal. It's the remnant of a river that once spilled from the mainland into the Adriatic. The sediment it carried formed barrier islands that cut Venice off from the sea, forming a lagoon.

Venice was built on the marshy islands of the former delta, sitting on wood pilings driven nearly 15 feet into the clay. About 25 miles of canals drain the city, dumping like streams into the Grand Canal. Technically, Venice has only three canals: Grand, Giudecca, and Cannaregio. The 45 small waterways that dump into the Grand Canal are referred to as rivers (e.g., Rio Novo).

Venice is a city of palaces, dating from the days when the city was the world's richest. The most lavish palaces formed a grand architectural cancan along the Grand Canal. Once frescoed in reds and blues, with black-and-white borders and gold-leaf trim, they made Venice a city of dazzling color. This cruise is the only way to truly appreciate the palaces, approaching them at water level, where their main entrances were located. Today, strict laws prohibit any changes in these buildings, so while landowners gnash their teeth, we can enjoy Europe's best-preserved medieval/Renaissance city—slowly rotting.

◑ Self-Guided Cruise

Start at the Ferrovia vaporetto stop (at **Santa Lucia train station**). The #1 boat to San Marco generally leaves from dock E (far to the right).

❶ Ferrovia

This site has been the gateway into Venice since 1860, when the first train station was built. The Santa Lucia station, one of the few modern buildings in town, was built in 1954. The "F.S." logo above the entry stands for "Ferrovie dello Stato," the Italian state railway system. Consider that before the causeway was built in the mid-1800s, Venice was an island with no road or train access and no water system. With the causeway the city got a train line, an aqueduct, and a highway.

More than 20,000 people a day commute in from the mainland, making this the busiest part of Venice during rush hour. The nearby **Calatrava Bridge,** spanning the Grand Canal between the train station and Piazzale Roma upstream,

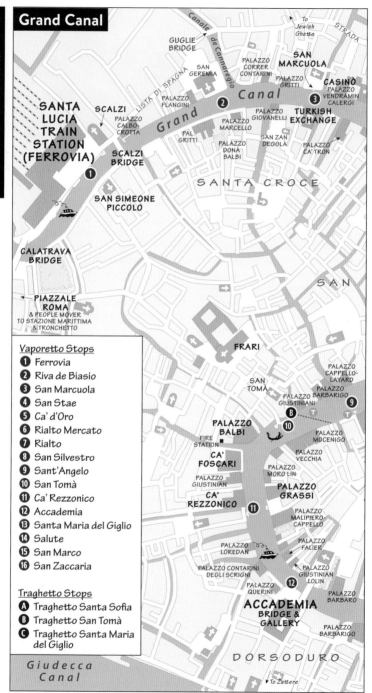

Grand Canal

GUGLIE BRIDGE

Canale de Cannaregio

To Jewish Ghetto

STRADA

SAN GEREMIA

PALAZZO CORRER CONTARINI

SAN MARCUOLA

PALAZZO GRITTI

CASINÒ

PALAZZO VENDRAMIN CALERGI

LISTA DI SPAGNA

PALAZZO FLANGINI

Canal

2

SANTA LUCIA TRAIN STATION (FERROVIA)

SCALZI

PALAZZO CALBO-CROTTA

Grand

PALAZZO GIOVANELLI

TURKISH EXCHANGE

3

PALAZZO MARCELLO

PAL. GRITTI

PALAZZO DONÀ BALBI

SAN ZAN DEGOLA

PALAZZO CA'TRON

SCALZI BRIDGE

1

SAN SIMEONE PICCOLO

SANTA CROCE

CALATRAVA BRIDGE

PIAZZALE ROMA
& PEOPLE MOVER
TO STAZIONE MARITTIMA
& TRONCHETTO

SAN

FRARI

PALAZZO CAPPELLO-LAYARD

SAN TOMÀ

PALAZZO BARBARIGO

PALAZZO GIUSTINIANI

9

B

PALAZZO BALBI

FIRE STATION

10

PALAZZO MOCENIGO

CA' FOSCARI

PALAZZO VECCHIA

PALAZZO GIUSTINIAN

PALAZZO MORO LIN

CA' REZZONICO

11

PALAZZO GRASSI

PALAZZO MALIPIERO-CAPPELLO

PALAZZO LOREDAN

PALAZZO FALIER

PALAZZO CONTARINI DEGLI SCRIGNI

PALAZZO GIUSTINIAN LOLIN

PALAZZO QUERINI

12

PALAZZO BARBARO

ACCADEMIA
BRIDGE & GALLERY

PALAZZO BARBARIGO

DORSODURO

Giudecca Canal

To Zattere

Vaporetto Stops

1 Ferrovia
2 Riva de Biasio
3 San Marcuola
4 San Stae
5 Ca' d'Oro
6 Rialto Mercato
7 Rialto
8 San Silvestro
9 Sant'Angelo
10 San Tomà
11 Ca' Rezzonico
12 Accademia
13 Santa Maria del Giglio
14 Salute
15 San Marco
16 San Zaccaria

Traghetto Stops

A Traghetto Santa Sofia
B Traghetto San Tomà
C Traghetto Santa Maria del Giglio

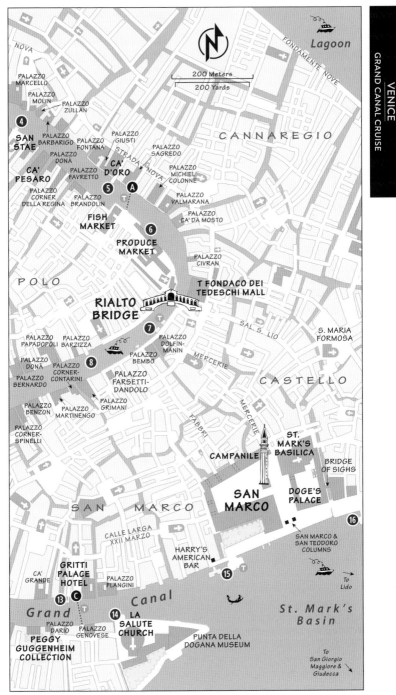

Lagoon

NOVA

FONDAMENTE NOVE

PALAZZO MARCELLO

PALAZZO MOLIN

PALAZZO ZULIAN

4

SAN STAE

PALAZZO BARBARIGO

PALAZZO FONTANA

PALAZZO GIUSTI

CANNAREGIO

PALAZZO DONÀ

STRADA NOVA

PALAZZO SAGREDO

CA' PESARO

PALAZZO FAVRETTO

CA' D'ORO

PALAZZO MICHIEL COLONNE

PALAZZO CORNER DELLA REGINA

PALAZZO BRANDOLIN

5

A

PALAZZO VALMARANA

FISH MARKET

PALAZZO CA' DA MOSTO

6

PRODUCE MARKET

PALAZZO CIVRAN

POLO

T FONDACO DEI TEDESCHI MALL

RIALTO BRIDGE

SAL. S. LIO

S. MARIA FORMOSA

PALAZZO PAPADOPOLI

PALAZZO BARZIZZA

7

PALAZZO DOLFIN-MANIN

PALAZZO BEMBO

MERCERIE

CASTELLO

PALAZZO DONÀ

8

PALAZZO CORNER-CONTARINI

PALAZZO FARSETTI-DANDOLO

PALAZZO BERNARDO

PALAZZO BENZON

PALAZZO MARTINENGO

PALAZZO GRIMANI

MERCERIE

PALAZZO CORNER-SPINELLI

FABBRI

ST. MARK'S BASILICA

CAMPANILE

BRIDGE OF SIGHS

SAN MARCO

DOGE'S PALACE

SAN MARCO

16

CALLE LARGA XXII MARZO

SAN MARCO & SAN TEODORO COLUMNS

HARRY'S AMERICAN BAR

GRITTI PALACE HOTEL

CA' GRANDE

PALAZZO FLANGINI

15

To Lido

Canal

St. Mark's Basin

13

C

14

LA SALUTE CHURCH

Grand

PALAZZO DARIO

PALAZZO GENOVESE

PEGGY GUGGENHEIM COLLECTION

PUNTA DELLA DOGANA MUSEUM

To San Giorgio Maggiore & Giudecca

200 Meters

200 Yards

was built in 2008 to alleviate some of the congestion.

❷ Riva de Biasio

About 25 yards past the Riva de Biasio stop, look left down the broad **Cannaregio Canal** to see what was the **Jewish Ghetto.** The twin, pale-pink, six-story "skyscrapers"—the tallest buildings you'll see at this end of the canal—are reminders of how densely populated the world's original ghetto was. Set aside as the local Jewish quarter in 1516, this area became extremely crowded—one of the most closely knit business and cultural quarters of all the Jewish communities in Italy—and gave us our word "ghetto" (from *geto*, the copper foundry located here).

❸ San Marcuola

At this stop, facing a tiny square just ahead, stands the unfinished Church of San Marcuola, one of only five churches fronting the Grand Canal. Centuries ago, this canal was a commercial drag of expensive real estate in high demand by wealthy merchants. About 20 yards ahead on the right (across the Grand Canal) stands the stately gray **Turkish Exchange (Fondaco dei Turchi),** one of the oldest houses in Venice. Its horseshoe arches and roofline of triangles and dingle balls are reminders of its Byzantine heritage. Turkish traders in turbans docked here, unloaded their goods into the warehouse on the bottom story, then went upstairs for a home-style meal and a place to sleep. Venice in the 1500s was very cosmopolitan, welcoming every religion and ethnicity, so long as they carried cash. (Today the building contains the city's Museum of Natural History.)

Just 100 yards ahead on the left (the tallest building with the red canopy), Venice's **Casinò** is housed in the palace where German composer Richard (*The Ring*) Wagner died in 1883. See his strong-jawed profile in the white plaque on the brick wall. In the 1700s, Venice was Europe's

Vegas, with casinos and prostitutes everywhere. Today casinos are run by the state to keep Mafia influence at bay. Notice the fancy front porch, rolling out the red carpet for high rollers arriving by taxi or hotel boat.

❹ San Stae

The San Stae Church sports a delightful Baroque facade. Opposite the San Stae stop is a little canal opening—on the second building to the right of that opening, look for the peeling plaster that once made up **frescoes** (you can barely distinguish the scant remains of little angels on the lower floors). Imagine the facades of the Grand Canal at their finest. Most of them would have been covered in frescoes by the best artists of the day. As colorful as the city is today, it's still only a faded, sepia-toned remnant of a long-gone era, a time of lavishly decorated, brilliantly colored palaces.

Just ahead (on the right, with blue posts) is the ornate white facade of **Ca' Pesaro** (which houses the International Gallery of Modern Art). "*Ca*'" is short for *casa* (house).

In this city of masks, notice how the rich marble facades along the Grand Canal mask what are generally just simple, no-nonsense brick buildings. Most merchants enjoyed showing off. However, being smart businessmen, they only decorated the sides of the buildings that would be seen and appreciated. But look back as you pass Ca' Pesaro. It's the only building you'll see with a fine side facade. Ahead (about 100 yards on the left) is Ca' d'Oro, with its glorious triple-decker medieval arcade (just before the next stop).

❺ Ca' d'Oro

The lacy **Ca' d'Oro** (House of Gold) is the best example of Venetian Gothic architecture on the canal. Its three stories offer different variations on balcony design, topped with a spiny white roofline. Venetian Gothic mixes traditional Gothic (pointed arches and round medallions stamped with a four-leaf clover) with Byzantine styles (tall, narrow arches atop thin columns), filled in with Islamic frills. Like all the palaces, this was originally painted and gilded to make it even more glorious than it is now. Today the Ca' d'Oro is an art gallery.

Look at the Venetian chorus line of palaces in front of the boat. On the right is the arcade of the covered **fish market,** with the open-air **produce market** just beyond. It bustles in the morning but is quiet the rest of the day. This is a great scene to wander through—even though European Union hygiene standards have made it cleaner and less colorful than it once was.

Find the *traghetto* gondola ferrying shoppers—standing like Washington crossing the Delaware—back and forth. While once much more numerable, today only three *traghetto* crossings survive along the Grand Canal, each one marked by a classy low-key green-and-black sign. Piloting a *traghetto* isn't the normal day job of these gondoliers. As a public service, all gondoliers are obliged to row a *traghetto* a few days a month. Make a point to use them. At €2 a ride, *traghetti* offer the cheapest gondola ride in Venice (but at this price, don't expect them to sing to you).

❻ *Rialto Mercato*

This stop serves the busy market. The long, official-looking building at the

stop is the Venice courthouse. Directly ahead (on the left), is the **T Fondaco dei Tedeschi**—the former German Exchange (a trading center for German merchants in the 16th century). Later the central post office, it's now a luxury shopping mall with great rooftop views. Rising above it is the tip of the Campanile (bell tower), crowned by its golden-angel weathervane at St. Mark's Square, where this tour will end.

You'll cruise by some trendy and beautifully situated wine bars on the right, but look ahead as you round the corner and see the impressive Rialto Bridge come into view.

A major landmark, the **Rialto Bridge** is lined with shops and tourists. Constructed in 1588, it's the third bridge built on this spot. Until the 1850s, this was the only bridge crossing the Grand Canal. With a span of 160 feet and foundations stretching 650 feet on either side, the Rialto was an impressive engineering feat in its day. Earlier bridges here could open to let big ships in, but not this one. By the time it was completed in the 16th century, Venetian trading power was ebbing. After that, much of the Grand Canal was closed to shipping and became a canal of palaces.

When gondoliers pass under the fat arch of the Rialto Bridge, they take full advantage of its acoustics: *"Volare, oh, oh..."*

Ca' d'Oro—the House of Gold

The lively Rialto market

Rialto Bridge

❼ Rialto

A separate town in the early days of Venice, Rialto has always been the commercial district, while San Marco was the religious and governmental center. Today, a winding street called the Mercerie connects the two, providing travelers with human traffic jams and shopping temptations. Boats unloaded the city's basic necessities here: oil, wine, charcoal, iron. Today, the quay is lined with tourist-trap restaurants.

Venice's sleek, black, graceful **gondolas** are a symbol of the city. With about 500 gondoliers joyriding amid the churning vaporetti, there's a lot of congestion on the Grand Canal. Pay attention—this is where most of the gondola and vaporetto accidents take place. While the Rialto is the highlight of many gondola rides, gondoliers understandably prefer the quieter small canals. Watch your vaporetto driver curse the better-paid gondoliers.

❽ San Silvestro

We now enter a long stretch of important **merchants' palaces,** each with proud and different facades. Because ships couldn't navigate beyond the

Rialto Bridge, the biggest palaces—with the major shipping needs—line this last stretch of the navigable Grand Canal.

Palaces like these were multifunctional: ground floor for the warehouse, offices and showrooms upstairs, and living quarters above, on the "noble floors" (with big windows to allow in maximum light). Servants lived and worked on the very top floors (with the smallest windows). For fire-safety reasons, kitchens were also located on the top floors. Peek into the noble floors to catch a glimpse of their still-glorious chandeliers of Murano glass.

The **Palazzo Grimani** (across from the San Silvestro dock) sports a heavy white Roman-style facade—a reminder that the Grimani family included a cardinal and had strong Roman connections. The **Palazzo Papadopoli,** with the two obelisks on its roof (50 yards beyond the San Silvestro stop on the right, with the blue posts), is the very fancy Aman Hotel where George and Amal Clooney were married in 2014.

❾ Sant'Angelo

Notice how many buildings have a foundation of waterproof white stone (*pietra d'Istria*) upon which the bricks sit high and dry. Many canal-level floors are abandoned as the rising water level takes its toll.

The **posts**—historically painted gaily with the equivalent of family coats of arms—don't rot underwater. But the wood at the waterline, where it's exposed to oxygen, does. On the smallest canals, little "no motorboats" signs indicate that these canals are for gondolas only (no motorized craft, 5 kph speed limit, no wake).

⑩ San Tomà

Fifty yards ahead, on the right side (with twin obelisks on the rooftop) stands **Palazzo Balbi,** the palace of an early-17th-century captain general of the sea. This palace, like so many in the city, flies three flags: Italy (green-white-red), the European Union (blue with ring of stars), and Venice (a lion on a field of red and gold). Today it houses the administrative headquarters of the regional government.

Just past the admiral's palace, look immediately to the right, down a side canal. On the right side of that canal, before the bridge, see the traffic light and the **fire station** (the 1930s Mussolini-era building with four arches hiding fireboats parked and ready to go).

The impressive **Ca' Foscari,** with a classic Venetian facade (on the corner, across from the fire station), dominates the bend in the canal. This is the main building of the University of Venice, which has about 25,000 students. Notice the elegant lamp

on the corner—needed in the old days to light this intersection.

The grand, heavy, white **Ca' Rezzonico,** just before the stop of the same name, houses the Museum of 18th-Century Venice. Across the canal is the cleaner and leaner **Palazzo Grassi,** the last major palace built on the canal, erected in the late 1700s. It was purchased by a French tycoon and now displays part of Punta della Dogana's contemporary art collection.

⑪ Ca' Rezzonico

Up ahead, the Accademia Bridge leads over the Grand Canal to the **Accademia Gallery** (right side), filled with the best Venetian paintings. There was no bridge here until 1854, when a cast-iron one was built. It was replaced with this wooden bridge in 1933.

⑫ Accademia

From here, look through the graceful bridge and way ahead to enjoy a classic view of **La Salute Church,** topped by a crown-shaped dome supported by scrolls. This Church of St. Mary of Good Health was built to ask God to deliver Venetians from the devastating plague of 1630 (which had killed about a third of the city's population).

The low, white building among greenery (100 yards ahead, on the right, between the Accademia Bridge and the church) is the **Peggy Guggenheim Collection.** The

A Venetian water taxi

Ca' Foscari

Best Views in Venice

- A slow vaporetto ride down the **Grand Canal**—ideally very early or just before sunset—is a shutterbug's delight.
- On St. Mark's Square, enjoy views from the soaring **Campanile** or the **balcony of St. Mark's Basilica** (both require admission).
- The **Rialto and Accademia bridges** provide expansive views of the Grand Canal, along with a cooling breeze.
- The luxury mall **T Fondaco dei Tedeschi,** just north of the Rialto Bridge, has even better views, especially around sunset (free but book a reservation; see details on page 63).
- Get off the main island for a view of the Venetian skyline: Ascend **San Giorgio Maggiore's bell tower** (admission fee), or venture to Giudecca Island to visit the swanky bar of the **Molino Stucky Hilton Hotel** (the free-to-"customers" shuttle boat leaves from near the San Zaccaria-B vaporetto dock).

American heiress "retired" here, sprucing up a palace that had been abandoned in mid-construction. Peggy willed the city her fine collection of modern art.

Two doors past the Guggenheim, Palazzo Dario has a great set of characteristic **funnel-shaped chimneys.** These forced embers through a loop-the-loop channel until they were dead—required in the days when stone palaces were surrounded by humble wooden buildings, and a live spark could make a merchant's workforce homeless. Three doors later is the **Salviati building,** which once served as a glass-works. Its fine Art Nouveau mosaic, done in the early 20th century, features Venice as a queen being appreciated by the big shots of society.

⓭ Santa Maria del Giglio

Back on the left stands the fancy **Gritti Palace hotel.** Hemingway and Woody Allen both stayed here.

Take a deep whiff of Venice. What's all this nonsense about stinky canals? All I smell is my shirt.

⓮ Salute

The huge **La Salute Church** towers overhead as if squirted from a can of Catholic Reddi-wip.

As the Grand Canal opens up into the lagoon, the last building on the right with the golden ball is the 17th-century **Customs House,** which now houses the Punta della Dogana contemporary art museum. Its two bronze Atlases hold a statue of Fortune riding the ball. Arriving ships stopped here to pay their tolls.

⓯ San Marco

Up ahead on the left, the green pointed tip of the Campanile marks **St. Mark's**

La Salute Church

The Campanile and Doge's Palace dominate the view of Venice from San Giorgio Maggiore.

Square, the political and religious center of Venice...and the final destination of this tour. You could get off at the San Marco stop and go straight to St. Mark's Square. But I'm staying on the boat for one more stop, just past St. Mark's Square (it's a quick walk back).

Survey the lagoon. Opposite St. Mark's Square, across the water, the ghostly white church with the pointy bell tower is **San Giorgio Maggiore,** with great views of Venice. Next to it is the residential island Giudecca, stretching from close to San Giorgio Maggiore past the Venice youth hostel (with a nice view, directly across) to the Hilton Hotel (good nighttime view, far right end of island).

Still on board? If you are, as we leave the San Marco stop look left and prepare for a drive-by view of St. Mark's Square. First comes the bold white facade of the old mint (in front of the bell tower) marked by a tiny cupola, where Venice's golden ducat, the "dollar" of the Venetian Republic, was made. Then come the twin columns topped by St. Theodore standing on a crocodile and the winged lion of St. Mark, who've welcomed visitors since

the 15th century. Between the columns, catch a glimpse of two giant figures atop the **Clock Tower**—they've been whacking their clappers every hour since 1499. The domes of **St. Mark's Basilica** are soon eclipsed by the lacy facade of the **Doge's Palace.** Next you'll see many gondolas with their green breakwater buoys, the **Bridge of Sighs** (leading from the palace to the prison—check out the maximum-security bars), and finally the grand harborside promenade—the **Riva.**

Follow the Riva with your eye, past elegant hotels to the green area in the distance. This is the largest of Venice's few **parks,** which hosts the annual Biennale festival. Much farther in the distance is the **Lido,** the island with Venice's beach. Its sand and casinos are tempting, though given its car traffic, it lacks the medieval charm of Venice.

⓰ *San Zaccaria*

OK, you're at your last stop. Quick—muscle your way off this boat! (If you don't, you'll eventually end up at the Lido.)

At San Zaccaria, you're right in the thick of the action. A number of other vaporetti depart from here (see page 91). Otherwise, it's a short walk back along the Riva to St. Mark's Square. Ahoy!

SIGHTS

Sightseeing Strategies
Avoiding Lines and Crowds

The city is inundated with cruise-ship passengers and tours from mainland hotels daily from 10:00 to about 16:00. Major sights are busiest in the late morning, making this a smart time to explore the back lanes.

To avoid the worst of the crowds at St. Mark's Basilica, go early or late. To bypass the ticket line, reserve a time online—or if you have a large day bag, you can usually avoid the line by checking it (see the St. Mark's Basilica listing). For the Doge's Palace, purchase your ticket at the Correr Museum across St. Mark's Square (see next). You can also visit later in the day, when crowds thin out. For the Campanile, ascend first thing in the morning or go late, or skip it entirely if you're going to the similar San Giorgio Maggiore bell tower.

Free Days: Some state museums in Italy (including Venice's Accademia) are free to enter once or twice a month, usually on a Sunday. Free days are actually bad news—they attract crowds. Check sight websites in advance.

Sightseeing Passes

Venice offers a dizzying array of combo-tickets and sightseeing passes. For most people, the two best options are the combo-ticket for the Doge's Palace and Correr Museum or the Museum Pass (which covers those two plus more). Note that many of the most visit-worthy sights in town (the Accademia, Peggy Guggenheim Collection, Scuola San Rocco, Campanile, and the three sights within St. Mark's Basilica that charge admission) are not covered by any pass.

All the passes described here are sold at the TI (except for the combo-ticket). Most are also available at participating sights.

Doge's Palace/Correr Museum Combo-Ticket: A €25 combo-ticket covers both of these sights. To bypass the long line at the Doge's Palace, buy your combo-ticket at the never-crowded Correr Museum (or online—€1 surcharge). The two sights are also covered by the Museum Pass.

Museum Pass: Busy sightseers may prefer this more expensive pass, which covers these city-run museums: the Doge's Palace; Correr Museum; Ca' Rezzonico (Museum of 18th-Century Venice); Palazzo Mocenigo Costume Museum; Casa Goldoni (home of the Italian playwright); Ca' Pesaro (modern art); Museum of Natural History in the Santa Croce district; the Glass Museum on the island of Murano; and the Lace Museum on the island of Burano. At €35, this pass is the best value if you plan to see the Doge's Palace, Correr Museum, and one or two of the other covered museums. You can buy it at any participating museum or via their websites (€1 surcharge).

Rolling Venice: If you're under 30, this youth pass offers discounts at dozens of sights and shops, but its best deal is for transit. It lets you buy a 72-hour transit pass for just €22—about half price (€6 pass for ages 6-29; sold at TIs, vaporetto ticket offices, and VèneziaUnica shops).

San Marco District
▲▲▲ST. MARK'S SQUARE (PIAZZA SAN MARCO)

This grand square is surrounded by splashy, historic buildings and sights: St. Mark's Basilica, the Doge's Palace, the Campanile bell tower, the Clock Tower, and the Correr Museum. It's your private rendezvous with the Venetian past late at night, when it becomes Europe's most magnificent dance floor.

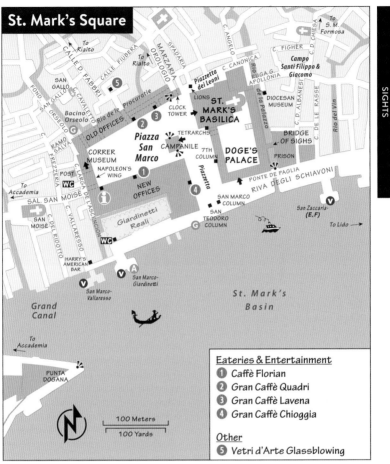

St. Mark's Square

Eateries & Entertainment

1. Caffè Florian
2. Gran Caffè Quadri
3. Gran Caffè Lavena
4. Gran Caffè Chioggia

Other

5. Vetri d'Arte Glassblowing

Rick's Tip: *If you're bombed by a pigeon, resist the initial response to wipe it off immediately—it'll just smear into your hair. Wait until it dries, and it should flake off cleanly. But if the poop splatters on your clothes, wipe it off immediately to avoid a stain.*

St. Mark's Basilica dominates the square with its Eastern-style onion domes and glowing mosaics. Mark Twain said it looked like "a vast warty bug taking a meditative walk." To the right of the basilica is its 325-foot-tall Campanile. Behind the Campanile, you can catch a glimpse of the pale pink Doge's Palace.

With your back to the church, survey one of Europe's great urban spaces. Lining the square are the former government offices (procuratie) that administered the Venetian empire's vast network of trading outposts, which stretched all the way to Turkey. On the right are the "old offices" (16th-century Renaissance). At left are the "new offices" (17th-century High Renaissance). Napoleon called the piazza "the most beautiful drawing room in Europe," and added to the intimacy by building the final wing, opposite the

The ornate exterior of St. Mark's Basilica

basilica, that encloses the square.

🎧 For more on the square, the Clock Tower, the Campanile, and other sights on the square, download my free St. Mark's Square **audio tour.**

▲▲▲ST. MARK'S BASILICA (BASILICA DI SAN MARCO)

Built in the 11th century, this basilica's distinctly Eastern-style architecture underlines Venice's connection with Byzantium (which protected it from the ambition of Charlemagne and his Holy Roman Empire). It's decorated with booty from returning sea captains—a Venetian trophy chest. The interior glows mysteriously with gold mosaics and colored marble. Since about AD 830, the saint's bones have been housed on this site. The San Marco Museum within holds the original bronze horses (copies of these overlook the square), and a balcony offering a remarkable view over St. Mark's Square.

Cost and Hours: Basilica entry is free, though you can pay €3 for an online reservation that lets you skip the line (see next). Three separate exhibits within the church charge admission: **Treasury**-€3, **Golden Altarpiece**-€2, and **San Marco**

Museum-€5. Church and all exhibits open Mon-Sat 9:30-17:00, Sun 14:00-17:00 (Sun until 16:30 Nov-Easter), interior brilliantly lit Mon-Sat 11:30-12:45. Tel. 041-270-8311, www.basilicasanmarco.it.

Avoiding Lines: There's almost always a long line to get into St. Mark's, but you can avoid it by reserving an entry time online, even for the same day (€3, April-Oct only, book at www.venetoinside.com). Or, if you have a large day bag (bigger than a purse), you can check it and skip the line (larger bags and backpacks are not allowed inside the church). Check above-limit bags for free for up to one hour at Ateneo San Basso church, 30 yards to the left of the basilica, down narrow Calle San Basso (see the map; daily 9:30-17:00). Take your claim tag to the basilica's tourist entrance. Keep to the left of the railing where the line forms and show your tag to the gatekeeper.

Tours: Free, hour-long English **tours** (heavy on the mosaics' religious symbolism) are offered many days at 11:00 (meet in atrium, schedule varies, see schedule board just inside entrance). Audioguides are on sale as you enter.

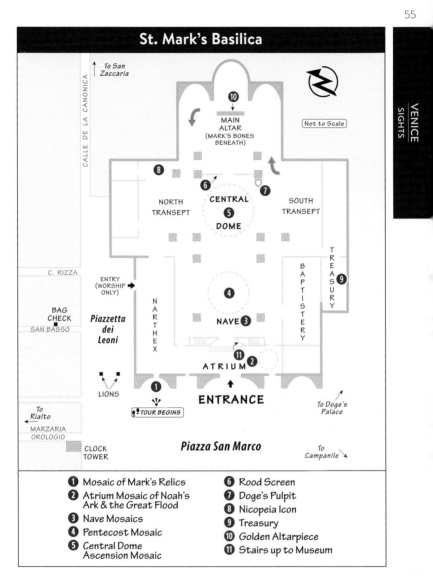

St. Mark's Basilica

❶ Mosaic of Mark's Relics
❷ Atrium Mosaic of Noah's Ark & the Great Flood
❸ Nave Mosaics
❹ Pentecost Mosaic
❺ Central Dome Ascension Mosaic
❻ Rood Screen
❼ Doge's Pulpit
❽ Nicopeia Icon
❾ Treasury
❿ Golden Altarpiece
⓫ Stairs up to Museum

🎧 Download my free St. Mark's Basilica **audio tour.**

⊙ SELF-GUIDED TOUR

Start outside in the square, far enough back to take in the whole facade. It's a riot of domes, columns, and statues, completely unlike the towering Gothic churches of northern Europe or the heavy Baroque of much of the rest of Italy.

Inside is a decor of mosaics, colored marbles, and oriental treasures that's rarely seen elsewhere. The Christian symbolism is unfamiliar to Western eyes, done in the style of Byzantine icons and even Islamic designs. Older than most of Europe's churches, St. Mark's feels like a remnant of a lost world.

The church is encrusted with materials looted from buildings throughout the Venetian empire. Their prize booty was the four bronze horses that adorn the balcony, stolen from Constantinople during the Fourth Crusade (these are copies). Now zero in on the details.

❶ Exterior—Mosaic of Mark's Relics: The mosaic over the far left door shows two men (in the center, with crooked staffs) entering the church bearing a coffin with the body of St. Mark.

Eight centuries after Mark's death, his holy body was in Muslim-occupied Alexandria, Egypt. In AD 829, two visiting Venetian merchants "rescued" the body from the "infidels" and spirited it away to Venice.

• Enter the atrium of the basilica and find a golden arch overhead with scenes of Noah's Ark.

❷ Atrium Mosaic of Noah's Ark and the Great Flood: Of all the famous mosaics of St. Mark's, this is one of the oldest (13th century) and finest. The scenes show Noah and his sons sawing logs to build the Ark. Below that are scenes of Noah putting all species of animals into the Ark. Then the Flood hits in full force, drowning the wicked. Noah sends out a dove twice to see whether there's any dry land where he can dock. He finds it, leaves the Ark with a gorgeous rainbow overhead, and offers a sacrifice of thanks to God.

• Climb a few steps, and into church. Just inside the door, step out of the flow and survey the church.

❸ The Nave—Mosaics Above and Below: These golden mosaics are in the Byzantine style, though many were designed by artists from the Italian Renaissance and later. The often-overlooked lower walls are covered with green-, yellow-, purple-, and rose-colored marble slabs, cut to expose the grain, and laid out in geometric patterns. Even the floor is mosaic, with mostly geometrical designs. It rolls like the sea. Venice is sinking and shifting, creating these cresting waves of stone.

• Find the chandelier in the nave (in the shape of a cathedral space station) and run your eyes up the support chain to the dome above. This has one of the church's greatest mosaics.

❹ Pentecost Mosaic: In a golden heaven, the dove of the Holy Spirit shoots out a pinwheel of spiritual lasers, igniting tongues of fire on the heads of the 12 apostles below, giving them the ability to speak other languages without a Rick Steves phrase book. One of the oldest mosaics in the church (c. 1125), it has distinct "Byzantine" features: a gold background and apostles with halos, solemn faces, almond eyes, delicate blessing hands, and rumpled robes, all facing forward.

• Shuffle along with the crowds up to the center of the church.

❺ Central Dome Ascension Mosaic: Gape upward into the central dome, the very heart of the church. Christ—having lived his miraculous life and having been crucified for man's sins—ascends into the starry sky on a rainbow. In Byzantine churches, the window-lit dome represented heaven, while the dark church below represented earth—a microcosm of the hierarchical universe.

Under the Ascension Dome: Look around at the church's furnishings and imagine a service here. The ❻ rood screen (like the iconostasis in a Greek church), topped with 14 saints, separates the congregation from the high altar, heightening the "mystery" of the Mass. The ❼ pulpit (the purple one on the right) was reserved for the doge, who led prayers and made important announcements.

• In the north transept (left of the altar), is an area usually reserved for prayer. The worshippers are facing a big stone canopy, which houses a small painting of the Virgin Mary.

❽ Nicopeia (North Transept): Venetians then and now pray to a painted wooden icon of Mary and Baby Jesus known as Nicopeia, or Our Lady of Victory. For centuries, Nicopeia was venerated by the Byzantines, who asked

Ⓐ *The altar and tomb of St. Mark*

Ⓑ *Mosaic showing St. Mark's body being carried into the church*

Ⓒ *Noah's Ark mosaic*

Ⓓ *Central dome and the Ascension mosaic*

Mary to protect them in battle. When Venetian Crusaders captured it, the icon came to protect Venice.

Additional Sights: The ❾ **Treasury** (Tesoro) and ❿ **Golden Altarpiece** (Pala d'Oro) are the easiest ways to see the glories of the Byzantine Empire outside of Istanbul or Ravenna. The treasury is a beautiful collection of chalices, reliquaries, and jewels, most of them stolen from Constantinople. As you view these treasures, remember that some are nearly 2,000 years old. Beneath the high altar lies the body of St. Mark ("Marce") and the Golden Altarpiece, made of 250 blue-backed enamels with religious scenes, all set in a gold frame and studded with 15 hefty rubies, 300 emeralds, 1,500 pearls, and assorted sapphires, amethysts, and topaz.

Upstairs, in the ⓫ **San Marco Museum** (Museo di San Marco) you can see an up-close mosaic exhibition, more religious objects that once adorned the church, a fine view of the church interior, a view of the square from the balcony with bronze horses, and (inside, in their own room)

the original horses. The staircase up to the museum is in the atrium, near the basilica's main entrance.

▲▲▲DOGE'S PALACE (PALAZZO DUCALE)

The seat of the Venetian government and home of its ruling duke, or doge, this was the most powerful half-acre in Europe for 400 years. The Doge's Palace was built to show off the power and wealth of the Republic. The doge lived with his family on the first floor up, near the halls of power. From his once-lavish (now sparse) quarters, you'll follow the one-way tour through the public rooms of the top floor, finishing with the Bridge of Sighs and the prison. The place is wallpapered with masterpieces by Veronese and Tintoretto.

Cost and Hours: €25 combo-ticket includes Correr Museum, also covered by Museum Pass; Sun-Thu 8:30-21:00, Fri-Sat until 23:00, Nov-March daily until 19:00; café, next to St. Mark's Basilica, just off St. Mark's Square, vaporetto stops: San Marco or San Zaccaria, tel. 041-271-5911, http://palazzoducale.visitmuve.it.

Doge's Palace

Avoiding Lines: If the line is long at the Doge's Palace, buy your combo-ticket at the Correr Museum across the square; then you can go directly through the Doge's turnstile without waiting in line. Or, you can buy your ticket online. Crowds tend to diminish after 16:00.

Tours: The fine **Secret Itineraries Tour** follows the doge's footsteps through rooms not included in the general admission ticket. Though the tour skips the palace's main hall, you're welcome to visit the hall afterward on your own. Three 75-minute English-language tours run each morning. Reserve ahead, as tours can fill up several weeks in advance—although you can try just showing up at the information desk (€28, includes Doge's Palace admission but not Correr Museum, €15 with combo-ticket; reserve over the phone or online: tel. 041-4273-0892, http://palazzoducale.visitmuve.it, €1 online surcharge). Don't confuse this with the Doge's Hidden Treasures Tour, which isn't worth its fee.

The **audioguide** is dry but informative (€5, 1.5 hours, need ID for deposit).

Visiting the Doge's Palace: You'll see the restored facades from the **courtyard.** Notice a grand staircase (with nearly naked Moses and Paul Newman at the top). Even the most powerful visitors climbed this to meet the doge. This was the beginning of an architectural power trip.

In the **Senate Hall,** the 120 senators met, debated, and passed laws. Tintoretto's large *Triumph of Venice* on the ceiling (central painting, best viewed from the top) is an allegory of the city in all her glory. Lady Venice is up in heaven with the Greek gods, while barbaric lesser nations swirl up to give her gifts and tribute.

The **Armory**—a dazzling display originally assembled to intimidate potential adversaries—shows remnants of the military might that the empire employed to keep the East-West trade lines open (and the local economy booming).

The giant **Hall of the Grand Council** (175 feet by 80 feet, capacity 2,600) is

Tintoretto, Triumph of Venice

where the entire nobility met to elect the senate and doge. It took a room this size to contain the grandeur of the Most Serene Republic. Ringing the top of the room are portraits of the first 76 doges (in chronological order). The one at the far end that's blacked out (in the left corner) is the notorious Doge Marin Falier, who opposed the will of the Grand Council in 1355. He was tried for treason, beheaded, and airbrushed from history.

On the wall over the doge's throne is Tintoretto's monsterpiece, *Paradise,* the largest oil painting in the world. Christ and Mary are surrounded by a heavenly host of 500 saints. The painting leaves you feeling that you get to heaven not by being a good Christian, but by being a good Venetian.

Cross the covered **Bridge of Sighs** over the canal to the **prisons.** Circle the cells. Notice the carvings made by prisoners—from olden days up until 1930—on some of the stone windowsills of the cells, especially in the far corner of the building.

Cross back over the Bridge of Sighs, pausing to look through the marble-trellised windows at all the tourists.

More Sights on the Square

▲▲CORRER MUSEUM (MUSEO CORRER)

This uncrowded museum gives you a good overview of Venetian history and art. The doge memorabilia, armor, banners, statues (by Canova), and paintings (by

Canova, Daedalus and Icarus

bricks in 1902, a thousand years after it was built. Ride the elevator 325 feet to the top of the bell tower for one of the best views in Venice (especially at sunset). For an ear-shattering experience, be on top when the bells ring. The golden archangel Gabriel at the top always faces into the wind. Beat the crowds and enjoy the crisp morning air at 9:00 or the cool evening breeze at 18:00. Go inside to buy tickets; the kiosk in front only rents audioguides and is operated by a private company.

Rick's Tip: *Lines at the Campanile can be long. For* **shorter lines and a view** *that's just as impressive, head across the lagoon to the similar San Giorgio Maggiore bell tower.*

Cost and Hours: €8; daily 8:30-21:00, Sept-mid-Oct until sunset, mid-Oct-April 9:30-17:30, last entry 45 minutes before closing; may close during thunderstorms, audioguide-€3, tel. 041-522-4064, www.basilicasanmarco.it.

the Bellini family and others) re-create the festive days of the Venetian Republic. And it's all accompanied—throughout the museum—by English descriptions and views of St. Mark's Square. But the Correr Museum has one more thing to offer, and that's a quiet refuge—an elegant Neoclassical space—in which to rise above St. Mark's Square when the piazza is too hot, too rainy, or too overrun with tourists.

Cost and Hours: €25 combo-ticket includes Doge's Palace, also covered by Museum Pass; daily 10:00-19:00, Nov-March 10:30-17:00; bag check free and mandatory for bags bigger than a large purse, elegant café, enter at far end of square directly opposite basilica, tel. 041-240-5211, http://correr.visitmuve.it.

▲CAMPANILE (CAMPANILE DI SAN MARCO)

This dramatic bell tower replaced a shorter tower, part of the original fortress that guarded the entry of the Grand Canal. That tower crumbled into a pile of

Behind St. Mark's Basilica
▲BRIDGE OF SIGHS

This much-photographed bridge connects the Doge's Palace with the prison. Travelers popularized this bridge in the Romantic 19th century. Supposedly, a condemned man would be led over this bridge on his way to the prison, take one last look at the glory of Venice, and sigh. Though overhyped, the Bridge of Sighs is undeniably tingle-worthy—especially after dark, when the crowds have dispersed and it's just you and floodlit Venice. In the middle of the day, however, being immersed in the pandemonium of global tourism (and selfie sticks) can be a fascinating experience in itself.

Getting There: The Bridge of Sighs is around the corner from the Doge's Palace. Walk toward the waterfront, turn left along the water, and look up the first canal on your left. You can walk across the bridge (from the inside) by visiting the Doge's Palace.

Bridge of Sighs

San Giorgio Maggiore

Across the Lagoon from St. Mark's Square

▲SAN GIORGIO MAGGIORE

This is the dreamy church-topped island you can see from the waterfront by St. Mark's Square. The striking church, designed by Palladio, features art by Tintoretto, a bell tower, and good views of Venice.

Cost and Hours: Church—free, open daily 9:00-19:00, Nov-March 8:30-18:00; bell tower elevator—€6, runs until 20 minutes before the church closes, does not run during Sun services; tel. 041-522-7827.

Getting There: To reach the island from St. Mark's Square, take the one-stop, five-minute ride on vaporetto #2 from San Zaccaria (€5 special vaporetto ticket, runs every 12 minutes from dock B, direction: Piazza Roma).

Dorsoduro District

▲▲ACCADEMIA
(GALLERIA DELL'ACCADEMIA)

Venice's top art museum, packed with highlights of the Venetian Renaissance, features paintings by the Bellini family, Titian, Tintoretto, Veronese, Tiepolo, Giorgione, Canaletto, and Testosterone. It's just over the wooden Accademia

Bridge from the San Marco action.

Cost and Hours: €15; Tue-Sun 8:15-19:15, Mon until 14:00, last entry one hour before closing; dull audioguide-€6, vaporetto: Accademia, tel. 041-522-2247, www.gallerieaccademia.it.

Avoiding Lines: Just 400 people are allowed into the gallery at one time, so you may have to wait. It's most crowded on Tue mornings and whenever it rains; it's least crowded Wed, Thu, and Sun mornings (before 10:00) and late afternoons (after 17:00). While it's possible to book tickets in advance (€2/ticket surcharge; either book online or call 041-520-0345), it's generally not necessary if you avoid the busiest times.

Renovation: The museum is nearing the end of a major expansion and renovation. If you can't find paintings in the rooms listed below, ask a museum guard to point you in the right direction.

Visiting the Accademia: The Accademia offers a good overview of painters whose works you'll see all over town. Venetian art is underrated and, I think, misunderstood. It's nowhere near as famous today as the work of the florescent Florentines, but—with historical slices of Venice, ravishing nudes, and very

Veronese, Feast in the House of Levi, *at the Accademia*

human Madonnas—it's livelier, more colorful, and simply more fun. The Venetian love of luxury shines through in this collection, which starts in the Middle Ages and runs to the 1700s.

Medieval highlights include elaborate altarpieces and golden-haloed Madonnas, all painted at a time when realism, depth of field, and emotion were considered beside the point. Medieval Venetians, with their close ties to the East, borrowed techniques such as gold-leafing, frontal poses, and "iconic" faces from the religious icons of Byzantium (modern-day Istanbul).

Among early masterpieces of the Renaissance is Mantegna's studly *St. George* (Room 4). As the Renaissance reaches its heights, so do the paintings, such as Titian's magnificent *Presentation of the Virgin* (Room 24). It's a religious scene, yes, but it's really just an excuse to display secular splendor (Titian was the most famous painter of his day—perhaps even more famous than Michelangelo). Veronese's sumptuous *Feast in the House of Levi* (Room 10), pictured below, also has an ostensibly religious theme (in the middle, find Jesus eating his final meal)—but it's outdone by the luxury and optimism of Renaissance Venice. Life was a good thing and beauty was to be enjoyed. (Veronese was hauled before the Inquisition for painting such a bawdy Last Supper...so he fine-tuned the title.)

End your tour in the largest room in the museum, Room 23. This giant hall is the upper half of an old Gothic church. The nave was divided under Napoleon's rule, and this became the fine arts academy—the Accademia. It's now home to fine temporary exhibitions, and where art displaced by the gallery's ongoing renovation often ends up.

▲▲PEGGY GUGGENHEIM COLLECTION

The popular museum of far-out art, housed in the American heiress' former retirement palazzo, offers one of Europe's best reviews of the art of the first half of the 20th century. Stroll through styles represented by artists whom Peggy knew personally—Cubism (Picasso, Braque), Surrealism (Dalí, Ernst), Futurism (Boccioni), American Abstract Expressionism (Pollock), and a sprinkling of Klee, Calder, and Chagall.

Cost and Hours: €15; Wed-Mon 10:00-18:00, closed Tue; audioguide-€7, pricey café, 5-minute walk from the Accademia Bridge, vaporetto: Accademia or Salute, tel. 041-240-5411, www.guggenheim-venice.it.

▲LA SALUTE CHURCH (SANTA MARIA DELLA SALUTE)

This impressive church with a crown-shaped dome was built and dedicated to the Virgin Mary by grateful survivors of the 1630 plague.

Cost and Hours: Church-free; Sacristy-€4; both open daily 9:30-12:00 & 15:00-17:30; 10-minute walk from the Accademia Bridge, at vaporetto: Salute, tel. 041-274-3928, www.basilicasalutevenezia.it.

▲▲CA' REZZONICO (MUSEUM OF 18TH-CENTURY VENICE)

This Grand Canal palazzo offers the most insightful look at the life of Venice's rich and famous in the 1700s. Wander under ceilings by Tiepolo, among furnishings from that most decadent century, enjoying views of the canal and paintings by Guardi, Canaletto, and Longhi.

Cost and Hours: €10; Wed-Mon 10:00-18:00, Nov-March until 17:00, closed Tue year-round; ticket office closes one hour before museum, audioguide-€5 or €6/2 people, café, at vaporetto: Ca' Rezzonico, tel. 041-241-0100, http://carezzonico.visitmuve.it.

San Polo District

▲▲▲RIALTO BRIDGE

One of the world's most famous bridges, this distinctive and dramatic stone structure crosses the Grand Canal with a single confident span. The arcades along the top of the bridge help reinforce the structure... and offer some enjoyable shopping diversions, as does the market surrounding the bridge (produce market closed Sun, fish market closed Sun-Mon).

▲T FONDACO DEI TEDESCHI (GERMAN EXCHANGE) VIEW TERRACE

In the Middle Ages, Venice was the world's trading center, hosting scores of nationalities, each with its own caravanserai-like center. The most famous is the home of the Tedeschi (German) traders, just off the Rialto Bridge. It was recently purchased by the Benetton family and turned into a luxury mall. The ground floor features gourmet food shops and ritzy cafés.

The mall's top floor terrace offers a unique perspective over the roofs of Venice and an unforgettable view of the big bend in the Grand Canal. Four times an hour, 80 people are allowed onto the roof for 15 minutes. As you ride the red-carpet elevator to the top floor, notice how the old architectural bones of the structure survive.

Cost and Hours: The terrace is free but access requires a reservation (15-minute timeslots, book online at www.dfs.com/en/info/t-fondaco-rooftop-terrace; you can attempt to show up and reserve, but no guarantees). Terrace open daily 10:15-19:30, June-Aug until 20:15; east side of Rialto Bridge, tel. 041-314-2000.

▲▲FRARI CHURCH (BASILICA DI SANTA MARIA GLORIOSA DEI FRARI)

My favorite art experience in Venice is seeing art in the setting for which it was designed—as it is at the Frari Church. The Franciscan "Church of the Brothers" and the art that decorates it are warmed by the spirit of St. Francis. It features the work of three great Renaissance masters: Donatello, Giovanni Bellini, and Titian—each showing worshippers the glory of God in human terms.

Cost and Hours: €3; Mon-Sat 9:00-18:00, Sun from 13:00; audioguide-€2, modest dress recommended, on Campo dei Frari, near San Tomà vaporetto and *traghetto* stops, tel. 041-272-8611, www.basilicadeifrari.it.

Tours: You can rent an **audioguide** for €2, or download my free ∩ Frari Church **audio tour.**

Visiting the Church: In **Donatello's wood statue of St. John the Baptist** (in the first chapel to the right of the high altar), the prophet of the desert—emaciated from his breakfast of bugs 'n' honey and dressed in animal skins—announces the coming of the Messiah. Donatello was a Florentine working at the dawn of the Renaissance.

Bellini's *Madonna and Child with Saints and Angels* painting (in the sacristy farther to the right) came later, done by a Venetian in a more Venetian style—soft

Frari Church

Titian, Assumption of the Virgin

focus without Donatello's harsh realism. While Renaissance humanism demanded Madonnas and saints that were accessible and human, Bellini places them in a physical setting so beautiful that it creates its own mood of serene holiness. The genius of Bellini, perhaps the greatest Venetian painter, is obvious in the pristine clarity, rich colors (notice Mary's clothing), believable depth, and reassuring calm of this three-paneled altarpiece.

Finally, glowing red and gold like a stained-glass window over the high altar, **Titian's** *Assumption of the Virgin* sets the tone of exuberant beauty found in the otherwise sparse church. Titian the Venetian—a student of Bellini—painted steadily for 60 years...you'll see a lot of his art. As stunned apostles look up past the swirl of arms and legs, the complex composition of this painting draws you right to the radiant face of the once-dying, now-triumphant Mary as she joins God in heaven.

▲▲SCUOLA SAN ROCCO

Sometimes called "Tintoretto's Sistine Chapel," this lavish meeting hall (next to

the Frari Church) has some 50 large, colorful Tintoretto paintings plastered to the walls and ceilings. The best paintings are upstairs in the grand Chapter Room and especially in an adjacent smaller room, with Tintoretto's *Crucifixion.* View the neck-breaking splendor with the mirrors available in the Chapter Room.

Cost and Hours: €10, daily 9:30-17:30, tel. 041-523-4864, www.scuolagrandesanrocco.org.

Venice's Lagoon

With more time, venture to some nearby islands in Venice's lagoon. While still touristy, they offer an escape from the crowds, a chance to get out on a boat, and some enjoyable diversions for fans of glassmaking, lace, and sunbathing.

LAGOON TOUR

The islands of San Michele (cemetery), Murano (glass), Burano (lace), and Torcello (oldest church in Venice) make a good, varied, and long day trip that you can do on your own.

The Plan: You can travel to any of the

four islands by vaporetto. Since single vaporetto tickets (€7.50) are only valid for 75 minutes, getting a vaporetto pass for a lagoon excursion makes more sense (for details on tickets and passes, see page 89). Confirm vaporetto times by downloading the latest schedule from www.actv.it.

Start your journey at the **Fondamente Nove** vaporetto stop, on Venice's north shore (the "back" of the fish). Fondamente Nove is a pleasant 15-minute walk from Rialto or St. Mark's. Alternatively, you could reach Fondamente Nove by vaporetto: From San Zaccaria (near St. Mark's), take the #4.1 (35 minutes). From the train or bus station, take #4.2 (30 minutes).

From Fondamente Nove, take the #4.1 or #4.2 vaporetto for Murano (about every 10 minutes). On the way, get off at the Cimitero stop on the island of San Michele to see the cemetery (6-minute ride). Continue on to Murano, arriving at the Murano-Colonna stop (3-minute ride). Sightsee Murano as you make your way to the Murano-Faro stop, where you board vaporetto #12 for the trip to Burano (30-40 minutes). From Burano, you can side-trip to Torcello (on the #12, 5-minute trip each way). To return to Venice from Burano, take vaporetto #12 all the way back to Fondamente Nove (45 minutes). For a longer, more scenic return past even more lagoon islands, take the #14 from Burano to the San Zaccaria dock near St.

Mark's Square (70 minutes).

Note that during summer, slightly faster express vaporetti go directly to Murano-Colonna (if you're OK with skipping the cemetery on San Michele): From San Zaccaria, catch the #7, or from the train/bus stations catch the #3.

SAN MICHELE (A.K.A. CIMITERO)

This island is the final resting place of Venetians and a few foreign VIPs, from poet Ezra Pound to composer Igor Stravinsky. It's also full of flowers, trees, scurrying lizards, and birdsong, and has an intriguing chapel (cemetery open daily 7:30-18:00, Oct-March until 16:30).

▲MURANO

Famous for its glassmaking, this island is home to several glass factories and the Glass Museum. From the Colonna vaporetto stop, skip the glass shops in front of you, walk to the right, and wander up the street along the canal, **Fondamenta dei Vetrai** (Glassmakers' Embankment). The Faro district of Murano, on the other side of the canal, is packed with factories (*fabriche*) and their furnaces (*fornaci*). You'll pass dozens more glass shops, including the high-class **Venini** shop, with glass that's a cut above much of what else is on offer here, and with an interior showing off the ultimate in modern Venetian glass design (at #47, closed Sun). Murano's **Glass Museum** (Museo del Vetro)

Murano's Fondamenta dei Vetrai

Firing up the glass furnace on Murano

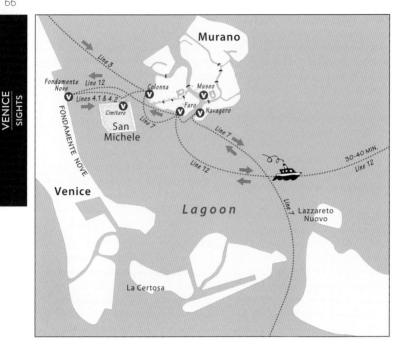

Murano

Line 3

Fondamente
Nove   Line 12

Lines 4.1 & 4.2

Colonna   Museo

Cimitero

San
Michele

Faro   Navagero

Line 7

Line 7

Line 12

30-40 MIN.
Line 12

Venice

Line 7   Lazzareto
Nuovo

Lagoon

La Certosa

traces the history of this delicate art (€14, daily 10:30-18:30, Nov-March until 16:30, tel. 041-739-586, http://museovetro.visit muve.it).

▲▲BURANO

This island's claim to fame is lacemaking, and (along with countless lace shops) it offers a delightful pastel village alternative to big, bustling Venice. The tight main drag is packed with tourists and lined with shops, some of which sell Burano's locally produced white wine. Its **Lace Museum** *(Museo del Merletto di Burano)* shows the island's lace heritage (€5, Tue-Sun 10:30-17:00, Nov-March until 16:30, closed Mon year-round, tel. 041-730-034, http://museomerletto.visitmuve.it).

▲TORCELLO

The birthplace of Venice, Torcello is where the first mainland refugees settled, escaping the barbarian hordes. Yet today, it's the least-developed island (pop.

Colorful Burano

Burano lace is prized.

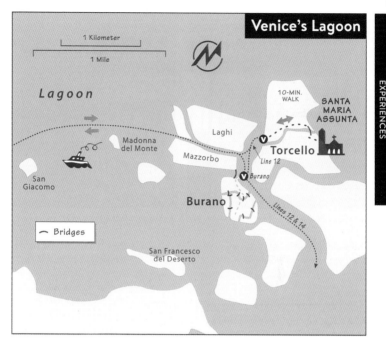

Inside the map:

Venice's Lagoon

1 Kilometer

1 Mile

Lagoon

10-MIN. WALK

SANTA MARIA ASSUNTA

Laghi

Madonna del Monte

Mazzorbo

Torcello

Line 12

San Giacomo

Burano

Burano

Lines 12 & 14

~ Bridges

San Francesco del Deserto

---

20) in the most natural state, marshy and shrub-covered. There's little for tourists to see except the **Santa Maria Assunta Church,** the oldest in Venice, which still sports some impressive mosaics, a climbable bell tower, and a modest museum of Roman sculpture and medieval sculpture and manuscripts (10-minute walk from dock, €12 combo-ticket covers museum, church, and bell tower; museum only-€3; church and bell tower-€5 each; church open daily 10:30-18:00, Nov-Feb 10:00-17:00, museum and bell tower close 30 minutes earlier, museum closed Mon year-round; museum tel. 041-730-761).

LIDO BEACH

Venice's nearest beach is across the lagoon on an island connected to the mainland (which means car traffic). The sandy beach is pleasant, family-friendly, and good for swimming. You can rent an umbrella, buy beach gear at the shop, get food at the self-service café, or have a drink at the bar. Everything is affordable and in the same building (vaporetto: Lido S.M.E., walk 10 minutes on Gran Viale S. Maria Elisabetta to beach entry).

EXPERIENCES

Gondola Rides

Riding a gondola in Venice is simple, expensive, and one of the great experiences in Europe. Gondoliers hanging out all over town are eager to have you hop in for a ride. While this is a rip-off for some, it's a traditional must for romantics.

The price for a gondola starts at €80 for a 35-minute ride during the day. You can divide the cost—and the romance—among up to six people per boat, but only two get the love seat. Prices jump to €100 after 19:00—when it's most romantic and relaxing. Adding a singer and an accordionist will cost an additional €120. If you value budget over romance, you can save money by recruiting fellow travelers to split a gondola. Prices are standard and

A gondola station

A gondola ride at night is worth the price.

listed on the gondoliers' association website (go to www.gondolavenezia.it, click on "Using the Gondola," and look under "charterage").

Rick's Tip: *For* **cheap gondola thrills** *during the day, stick to the one-minute ferry ride on a Grand Canal traghetto. At night, vaporetti are nearly empty, and it's a great time to cruise the Grand Canal on the slow boat #1.*

Dozens of gondola stations (*servizio gondole*) are set up along canals all over town. Because your gondolier may offer narration or conversation during your ride, talk with several and choose one you like. You're welcome to review the map and discuss the route. Doing so is also a good way to see if you enjoy the gondolier's personality and language skills. Establish the price, route, and duration of the trip before boarding, enjoy your ride, and pay only when you're finished. Most gondoliers honor the official prices, but a few might try to scam you out of some extra euros, particularly by insisting on a tip. (While not required or even expected, if your gondolier does the full 35 minutes and entertains you en route, a 5-10 percent tip is appreciated; if he's surly or rushes through the trip, skip it.)

If you've hired musicians and want to hear a Venetian song (*un canto Veneziano*), try requesting "Venezia La Luna e Tu." Asking to hear "O Sole Mio" (which comes from Naples) is like asking a Chicago lounge singer to sing "Swanee River."

Glide through nighttime Venice with your head on someone's shoulder. Follow the moon as it sails past otherwise unseen buildings. Silhouettes gaze down from bridges while window glitter spills onto the black water. You're anonymous in the city of masks, as the rhythmic thrust of your striped-shirted gondolier turns old crows into songbirds. This is extremely relaxing (and, I think, worth the extra cost to experience at night).

Festivals

Venice's most famous festival is **Carnevale,** the celebration Americans call Mardi Gras (February; www.carnevale.venezia. it). In Carnevale's heyday—the 1600s and 1700s—you could do pretty much anything with anybody from any social class if you were wearing a mask. These days, tourists and Venetians gather for 18 days of parades, parties, and masquerade balls.

Every year, the city hosts the Venice **Biennale International Art Exhibition,** alternating between art in odd years (the main event) and architecture in even years (much smaller). The exhibition

Carnevale is a masked extravaganza.

spreads over the Arsenale and Giardini park (take vaporetto #1 or #2 to Giardini-Biennale; for details and an events calendar, see www.labiennale.org). The actual exhibition usually runs from June through November, but other events loosely connected with the Biennale—film, dance, theater—are held throughout the year in various venues on the island.

Shopping

Popular souvenirs and gifts include Murano glass, Burano lace, Carnevale masks, prints of Venetian scenes, traditional stationery (pens and marbled paper products of all kinds), calendars with Venetian scenes (and sexy gondoliers), and plenty of goofy knickknacks.

In touristy areas, shops are typically open from 9:00 to 19:30 (sometimes with a break at midday), and some stores are open on Sunday. If you're buying at a market, bargain—it's accepted and almost expected. In shops, you may save by offering to pay cash.

Popular **Venetian glass** is available in many forms: vases, tea sets, decanters, glasses, jewelry, lamps, mod sculptures, and on and on. Shops will ship your glass home for you, but it's expensive, and you may have to pay duty on larger purchases. Make sure the shop insures its merchandise (*assicurazione*), or you're out of luck if it breaks.

You'll want to avoid the cheap glass you'll see—most of it is imported. Genuine, high-end Venetian glass comes with the signature of the artist etched directly into the glass, along with a number if it's a limited edition piece (for example, 14/30—number 14 of a total of 30 pieces made).

If you're serious about glass, visit the island of Murano, its glass museum, and its many shops—you'll find greater variety on the island. Or, consider a free glass-blowing demo at the **Vetri d'Arte** showroom in Palazzo Rota. From Gran Caffè Quadri on St. Mark's Square, Sottoportico dei Dai leads over a bridge and, 30 yards later, directly into a lobby (it's unsigned, look for the ATM) where stairs lead up to the showroom (RS%—20 percent dis-

A Dying City?

Venice's population (fewer than 55,000 in the historic city) is half what it was just 30 years ago, and a thousand people leave every year. Of those who stay, 25 percent are 65 or older.

Sad, yes, but imagine raising a family here: Apartments are small and expensive. Humidity and occasional flooding make basic maintenance a pain. Home-improvement projects require navigating miles of red tape, and you must follow regulations intended to preserve the historical ambience. Everything is expensive because it must be shipped in from the mainland. Running errands involves lots of walking and stairs—imagine crossing over arched bridges while pushing a child in a stroller and carrying a day's worth of groceries.

With millions of visitors a year (150,000 a day at peak times), on any given day Venetians are likely outnumbered by tourists. Despite government efforts to subsidize rents and build cheap housing, the city is losing its residents. The economy itself is thriving, thanks to tourist dollars and rich foreigners buying second homes. But the culture is dying.

Locals happily rent apartments to tourists a few times a month rather than affordably to local families, and shopkeepers sell trinkets to tourists before pots and pans to the local population. Even the most hopeful city planners worry that in a few decades Venice will not be a city at all, but a museum, a cultural theme park, a decaying Disneyland for adults.

count on glass with this book, daily 8:30-17:00, San Marco 834—see the map on page 53 for location, tel. 041-241-2664).

Nightlife

You must experience Venice after dark. The city is quiet at night, as many tour groups (not mine) stay in the cheaper hotels of Mestre on the mainland, and the masses of day-trippers return to their beach resorts and cruise ships.

Check at the TI or the TI's website (www.veneziaunica.it) for listings of events, church concerts, festivals, and entertainment. The free monthly *Un Ospite di Venezia* lists all the latest happenings in English (free at fancy hotels, or check www.unospitedivenezia.it).

Concerts

Venice is a city of the powdered-wig Baroque era. For about €25, you can take your pick of traditional Vivaldi concerts in churches throughout town. You'll find

frilly young Vivaldis hawking concert tickets on many corners. Most shows start at 20:30 and generally last 1.5 hours. Hotels sell tickets at face value. Tickets can usually be bought the same day as the concert, so don't bother with websites that sell tickets with a surcharge. Musicians in wigs and tights offer better spectacle; musicians in black-and-white suits are better performers.

The **Interpreti Veneziani orchestra,** considered the best group in town, generally performs 1.5-hour concerts nightly at 21:00 inside the sumptuous San Vidal Church (€28, church ticket booth open daily 9:30-21:00, north end of Accademia Bridge, tel. 041-277-0561, www.interpreti veneziani.com).

Musica a Palazzo is a unique evening of opera at a Venetian palace on the Grand Canal. You'll spend about 45 delightful minutes in each of three sumptuous rooms (about 2.25 hours total) as seven musicians (generally three instruments

The evening café scene on St. Mark's Square

and four singers) perform. With these kinds of surroundings, and under Tiepolo frescoes, you'll be glad you dressed up. As there are only 70 seats, you must book by phone or online in advance (€85, nightly at 20:30, Palazzo Barbarigo Minotto, Fondamenta Duodo o Barbarigo, vaporetto: Santa Maria del Giglio, San Marco 2504, mobile 340-971-7272, www.musicapalazzo.com).

St. Mark's Square

Streetlamp halos, live music, floodlit history, and a ceiling of stars make St. Mark's magic at midnight. Just being here after dark is a thrill, as **dueling café orchestras** entertain.

You can wander around the square listening to the different orchestras, or take a seat at a café. At any place with live music, it's perfectly acceptable to nurse a drink for an hour—you're paying for the music with the cover charge. The prices are clearly posted. If you sit outside and get just an espresso (your cheapest option), expect to pay €12.50—€6.50 for the coffee and a €6 cover charge when the orchestra is playing (which is most of the day). Service is included (no need to tip).

Caffè Florian (on the right as you face the church) is the most famous Venetian café and was one of the first places in Europe to serve coffee. The outside tables are the main action, but walk inside through the richly decorated, old-time rooms where Casanova, Lord Byron, Charles Dickens, and Woody Allen have all paid too much for a drink. The café's orchestra—the most serious on the square—plays daily from 10:00 to 24:00. Each hour comes with a musical theme (operetta, Latin, Romantic, jazz, Venetian, and so on—you can ask for the program; open daily 9:00-24:00, shorter hours in winter, www.caffeflorian.com).

Gran Caffè Quadri, opposite the Florian and established in 1780, has another illustrious roster of famous clientele.

Gran Caffè Lavena, near the Clock Tower, is less storied—although it dates from 1750 and counts composer Richard Wagner as a former regular—so it's less intimidating than the more formal cafés here. Drop in to check out its dazzling but politically incorrect chandelier.

Gran Caffè Chioggia, on the Piazzetta facing the Doge's Palace, charges no cover and has one or two musicians playing— usually a pianist (€7 cocktails, music from 10:30 to 23:00—jazz after 21:00).

Rick's Tip: *You'll hear about the famous* **Harry's American Bar,** *which sells overpriced food and cocktails, but* **it's a tourist trap**...*and the last place Hemingway would drink today. It's cheaper to get a drink at any of the hole-in-the-wall bars just off St. Mark's Square.*

SLEEPING

I've listed rooms in these areas: St. Mark's bustle, the Rialto action, the quiet Dorsoduro area behind the Accademia art museum, and near the train station.

Hotels in Venice can be tricky to locate. The website Venicexplorer.net allows you to search using a hotel's address number and district, which I've included in my listings (click "Venice Civic Number" on the website to open the search window).

Near St. Mark's Square

To get here from the train station or Piazzale Roma bus station, ride the slow vaporetto #1 to San Zaccaria or the fast #2 (which also leaves from Tronchetto parking lot) to San Marco.

East of St. Mark's Square

Located near the Bridge of Sighs, just off the Riva degli Schiavoni waterfront promenade, these places rub drainpipes with Venice's most palatial five-star hotels.

$$$ Hotel Campiello, lacy and bright, was once part of a 19th-century convent. Ideally located 50 yards off the waterfront on a tiny square, its 16 rooms offer a tranquil, friendly refuge (RS%, air-con, elevator, just steps from the San Zaccaria vaporetto stop, Castello 4647; tel. 041-520-5764, www.hcampiello.it, campiello@hcampiello.it; family-run for four generations, currently by Thomas, Nicoletta, and Monica). They also rent three modern, upscale, and quiet family apartments for up to six people, under rustic timbers just steps away from the hotel.

$$$$ Hotel Fontana, two bridges behind St. Mark's Square, is a pleasant family-run place with 15 sparse but classic-feeling rooms overlooking a lively square (RS%, several rooms with terraces, family rooms, air-con, elevator, closed Jan, on Campo San Provolo at Castello 4701, tel. 041-522-0533, www.hotelfontana.it, info@hotelfontana.it, cousins Diego and Gabriele).

$$$ Locanda al Leon, which feels a little like a medieval tower house, is conscientiously run and rents 12 rooms just off Campo Santi Filippo e Giacomo (RS%, some view rooms, family rooms, air-con, one- and two-bedroom apartments, Campo Santi Filippo e Giacomo, Castello 4270, tel. 041-277-0393, www.hotelalleon.com, leon@hotelalleon.com, Giuliano and Marcella). Their annex down the street,

B&B Ca' Marcella, has three newer, classy, and spacious rooms for the same rates (check in at main hotel).

$$ Albergo Doni, situated along a quiet canal, is dark and quiet. This time-warp—with creaky floors and 13 well-worn, once-classy rooms—is run by friendly Tessa and her two brothers, Barnaba and (now "retired") Italian stallion Nikos (RS%, cheaper rooms with shared bath, family rooms, ceiling fans, a few rooms have air-con, Wi-Fi in common areas, on Fondamenta del Vin at Castello 4656, tel. 041-522-4267, albergodoni@hotmail.it). The hotel also has three nice overflow apartments at the same prices (but without breakfast).

North of St. Mark's Square

$$$$ Hotel Orion rents 21 simple, welcoming, pricey rooms in the center of the action (you're paying a premium for the location). Steep stairs (there's no elevator) take you from the touristy street into a peaceful world high above (RS%—use code RSTEVES, air-con, 2 minutes inland from St. Mark's Square, 10 steps toward St. Mark's from San Zulian Church at Calle Spadaria 700a, tel. 041-522-3053, www.hotelorion.it, info@hotelorion.it).

$$$ Hotel al Piave, with 25 rooms above a bright, tight lobby and breakfast room, is comfortable and cheery, and you'll enjoy the neighborhood (RS%, family rooms, lots of narrow stairs, air-con, on Ruga Giuffa at Castello 4838, tel. 041-528-5174, www.hotelalpiave.com, info@hotelalpiave.com; Mirella, Paolo, Ilaria, and Federico).

$$$ Locanda Silva is a well-located hotel with a functional 1960s feel and a small terrace. It rents 23 simple rooms with small bathrooms (RS%, a few cheaper rooms with shared bathrooms, closed Dec-Jan, family rooms, air-con, lots of stairs, on Fondamenta del Remedio at Castello 4423, tel. 041-522-7643, www.locandasilva.it, info@locandasilva.it; Sandra and Katia).

Near Campo Santa Maria Formosa

Farther north, the quiet Castello area lies beyond inviting Campo Santa Maria Formosa.

$$$ Locanda la Corte is perfumed with elegance without being snooty. Its 14 attractive, high-ceilinged, wood-beamed rooms—Venetian-style, done in earthy pastels—circle a small, sun-drenched courtyard and a ground-level restaurant (RS%, family rooms, air-con, on Calle Bressana at Castello 6317, tel. 041-241-1300, www.locandalacorte.it, info@locandalacorte.it).

West of St. Mark's Square

These more expensive hotels are solid choices in a more elegant neighborhood.

$$$$ Hotel Flora sits buried in a sea of fancy designer boutiques and elegant hotels almost on the Grand Canal. It's formal, with uniformed staff and grand public spaces, yet the 40 rooms have a homey warmth and the garden oasis is a sanctuary for well-heeled, foot-weary guests (RS%, air-con, elevator, great family-size apartment, on Calle Bergamaschi at San Marco 2283a, tel. 041-520-5844, www.hotelflora.it, info@hotelflora.it).

$$$$ Hotel Bel Sito offers pleasing Old World character, 34 smallish rooms, generous public spaces, a peaceful courtyard, and a picturesque location—facing a church on a small square between St. Mark's Square and the Accademia (RS%, some view rooms, air-con, elevator; near Santa Maria del Giglio vaporetto stop—line #1, on Campo Santa Maria Zobenigo/del Giglio at San Marco 2517, tel. 041-522-3365, www.hotelbelsitovenezia.it, info@hotelbelsitovenezia.it, graceful Rossella).

Near the Rialto Bridge

These places are on opposite sides of the Grand Canal, within a short walk of the Rialto Bridge. Express vaporetto #2 brings you to the Rialto quickly from the train station, the Piazzale Roma bus station, and the parking-lot island of Tronchetto, but you'll need to take the "local" vaporetto #1 to reach the minor stops closer to the last two listings.

$$$$ Hotel al Ponte Antico is exquisite, professional, and small. With nine plush rooms, a velvety royal living/breakfast room, and its own dock for water taxi arrivals, it's perfect for a romantic anniversary. Because its wonderful terrace overlooks the Grand Canal, Rialto Bridge, and market action, its rooms without a canal view may be a better value (air-con, 100 yards from Rialto Bridge at Cannaregio 5768, use Rialto vaporetto stop, tel. 041-241-1944, www.alponteantico.com, info@alponteantico.com, Matteo).

$$$ Pensione Guerrato, right above the colorful Rialto produce market and just two minutes from the Rialto Bridge, is run by friendly, creative, and hardworking Roberto, Piero, Monica, and Matilde. Their 800-year-old building—with 22 spacious, charming rooms—is simple, airy, and wonderfully characteristic. It's a great value considering the location and charm (RS%, cheaper rooms with shared bath, family rooms, air-con, on Calle drio la Scimia at San Polo 240a, take vaporetto #1 to Rialto Mercato stop to save walk over bridge, tel. 041-528-5927, www.hotelguerrato.com, info@hotelguerrato.com). They also rent family apartments in the old center (great for groups of 4-8).

$$$ Hotel al Ponte Mocenigo is off the beaten path—a 10-minute walk northwest of the Rialto Bridge—but it's a great value. This 16th-century Venetian palazzo has a garden terrace and 15 comfy, beautifully appointed, and tranquil rooms (RS%, air-con, take vaporetto #1 to San Stae stop, head inland along right side of church and find Santa Croce 1985, tel. 041-524-4797, www.alpontemocenigo.com, info@alpontemocenigo.com, Sandro and Valter).

Near the Accademia Bridge

As you step over the Accademia Bridge, the commotion of touristy Venice is

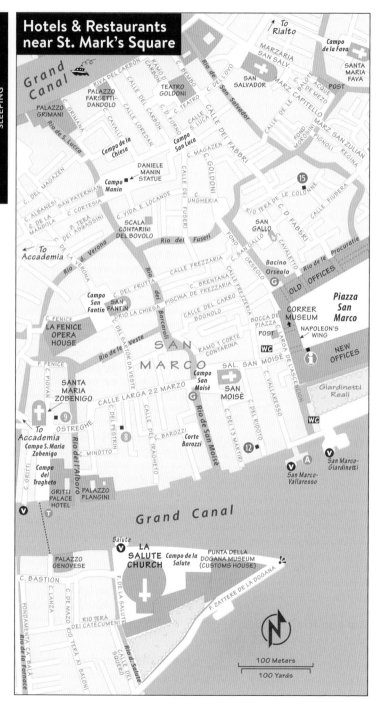

Hotels & Restaurants near St. Mark's Square

Grand Canal

To Rialto

Campo de la Fava

SANTA MARIA FAVA

MARZARIA SAN SALV.

POST

MARZ. CAPITELLO

C. BADE ACQUE

SAN SALVADOR

RIVA DEL CARBON

RAMO P. CARBON

C. BEMBO

CALLE DEL CARBON

Rio de l'Oyo

CALLE DE LA BISSA

FOND. MARZ SAN ZULIAN

MOROSINI PIGNOLI REGINA

PALAZZO FARSETTI-DANDOLO

TEATRO GOLDONI

C. TEATRO

C.D. FORNO

CALLE S. LUCA

CALLE DEI FABBRI

PALAZZO GRIMANI

C. GRIMANI

CAVALLI

CALLE LOREDAN

Campo San Luca

C. MAGAZEN

Rio de S. Lucca

Campo de la Chiesa

DANIELE MANIN STATUE

GOLDONI

C. D FABBRI

CALLE FIUBERA

RIO TERA DE LE COLONNE

15

C. DEL MAGAZEN

Campo Manin

C. UNGHERIA

C. ALBANESI

SAN PATERNIAN

C. DE LA MANDOLA

C. CORTESIA

C. VIDA E LOCANDE

SAN GALLO

C. D FABBRI

C. DE LA

C. TERA DEI ASSASSINI

SCALA CONTARINI DEL BOVOLO

CALLE DEI FUSERI

C. D FABBRI

CAVALETTO

To Accademia

Rio V. Verona

Rio del Fuseri

FOND. SAN GALLO

Bacino Orseolo

Rio de le Procuratie

OLD OFFICES

CALLE FREZZARIA

G

C. DEL FRUTTA

C. BRENTANA

PISCINA DE FREZZARIA

CALLE FREZZERIA

Campo San Fantin

SAN FANTIN

DRIO LA CHIESA

CALLE DEL CARRO BOGNOLO

BOCCA DE PIAZZA

CORRER MUSEUM

Piazza San Marco

LA FENICE OPERA HOUSE

CALLE DEI BARCAROLI

POST

NAPOLEON'S WING

NEW OFFICES

F. FENICE

Rio de le Veste

RAMO 1 CORTE CONTARINA

SAN MARCO

C. PIOVAN

Rio de le SARTOR DA VESTE

SAL. SAN MOISÈ

WC

i

SANTA MARIA ZOBENIGO

CALLE LARGA 22 MARZO

Campo San Moisè

SAN MOISÈ

CALLE LARGA DE L'ASCENSION

Giardinetti Reali

C. VALLARESSO

To Accademia

OSTREGHE

9

C. DEL PESTRIN

G

Rio de San Moisè

C. DEL RIDOTTO

WC

Campo S. Maria Zobenigo

Rio del l'Alboro

8

C. BAROZZI

Corte Barozzi

C. DEL 13 MARTIRI

12

Campo del Tragheto

C. MINOTTO

CALLE DEL TRAGHETO

San Marco-Giardinetti

C. GRITTI

GRITTI PALACE HOTEL

PALAZZO FLANGINI

A

V

V

San Marco-Vallaresso

T

Grand Canal

PALAZZO GENOVESE

Salute

V

LA SALUTE CHURCH

Campo de la Salute

PUNTA DELLA DOGANA MUSEUM (CUSTOMS HOUSE)

C. BASTION

C. LANZA

C. DE MAZO

F. DE LA SALUTE

RIO TERA DEI CATECUMENI

F. ZATTERE DE LA DOGANA

FONDAMENTA CA' BALA

Rio de la Fornace

RIO TERA AI SALONI

CALLE DEL

Rio de Salute

N

100 Meters

100 Yards

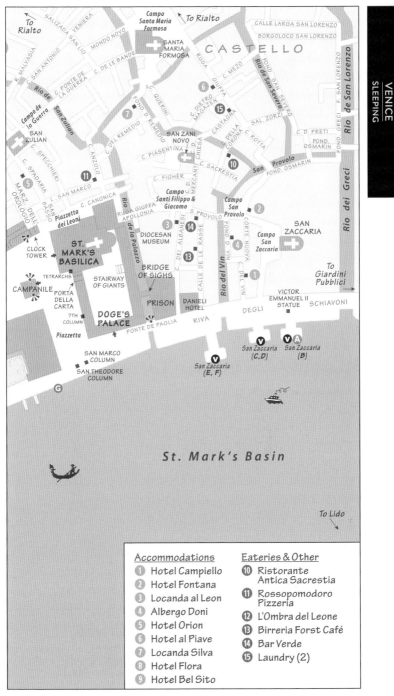

Accommodations
1. Hotel Campiello
2. Hotel Fontana
3. Locanda al Leon
4. Albergo Doni
5. Hotel Orion
6. Hotel al Piave
7. Locanda Silva
8. Hotel Flora
9. Hotel Bel Sito

Eateries & Other
10. Ristorante Antica Sacrestia
11. Rossopomodoro Pizzeria
12. L'Ombra del Leone
13. Birreria Forst Café
14. Bar Verde
15. Laundry (2)

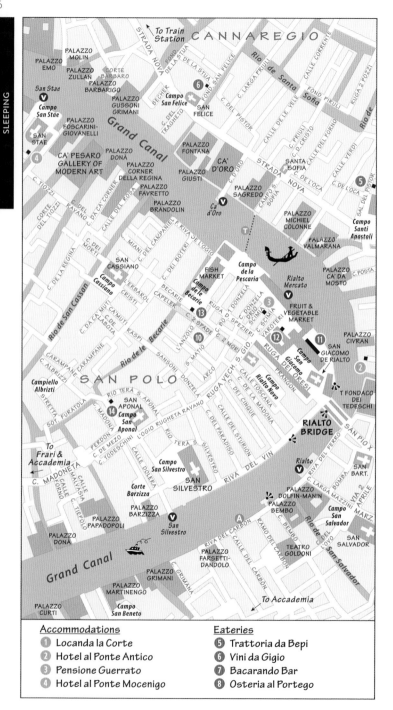

CANNAREGIO

To Train Station

STRADA NOVA

FOND. DE LA STUA

PALAZZO MOLIN

PALAZZO EMO

PALAZZO ZULLAN

CORTE BARBARO

PALAZZO BARBARIGO

San Stae

V Campo San Stae

FOND. SAN FELICE

C. LARGA PRIULI

Rio di Santa Sofia

CALLE CORRENTE

FOND. PIRULI

RUGA 2 POZZI

Rio de

BECHER

Campo San Felice

C. DEL TRAGHETO

PALAZZO GUSSONI GRIMANI

SAN FELICE

C. DEL PISTOR

C. DE LE VELE

C. PRIULI

C. DEL FORNO

C. DO CRISTO

SANTA SOFIA

C. DE L'OCA

C. VERDI

Grand Canal

PALAZZO FOSCARINI-GIOVANELLI

SAN STAE

CA' PESARO GALLERY OF MODERN ART

PALAZZO DONÀ

PALAZZO FONTANA

CA' D'ORO

STRADA NOVA

C. DE L'OCA

C. DE L'OCA

5

SAL DEL PISTOR

PALAZZO CORNER DELLA REGINA

PALAZZO GIUSTI

PALAZZO SAGREDO

Campo S. SOFIA

PALAZZO MICHIEL COLONNE

Campo Santi Apostoli

C. TIOZZI

C. DEL RAVANO

C. DA CA' CORNER

PALAZZO FAVRETTO

PALAZZO BRANDOLIN

V Ca' d'Oro

T

PALAZZO VALMARANA

PALAZZO CA' DA MOSTO

C.POSTA

CORTE DEL TIOZZI

C. DE LA REGINA

C. DEI MORTI

C. MIANI DEL CAMPANIEL

C. DEI BOTERI

RIVA DE L'OGIO

Campo de la Pescaria

Rialto Mercato

SAN CASSIANO

Campo Cassiano

SERBOLI

CRISTI

CAPELER

FISH MARKET

Campo de le Becarie

RUGA D. DONZELA

C. DO. SCIMIA

3

FRUIT & VEGETABLE MARKET

PALAZZO CIVRAN

Rio de San Cassan

C. DA CA' MUTI

C. DE CLABOIA

RASPI

13

C. 2 SPADE

C. 2 MORI

VANZOLO

RUGA D. SPEZIERI

VAROTERI

12

Campo San Giacomo DEI DRESI

11

SAN GIACOMO DE RIALTO

2

Rio de le Becarie

CARAMPANE

C. ALBRIZI

SANSONI

MATIO

DONZELA

ARGO

RUGA D. ORESI

Campo Rialto Novo

PRAGION

T FONDACO DEI TEDESCHI

Campiello Albrizti

STRETTA

SOT. FURATOLA

SAN POLO

RIO TERA S. APONAL

C. MADONA

SAN APONAL

14 Campo San Aponal

RUGA VECH.

C. DEI CINQUE

C. DE LA MADONA

RIALTO BRIDGE

SAN PIO X

To Frari & Accademia

C. MADONETA

PERDON

C. DE MEZO

C. TODESCHINI

RIO TERA S. SILVESTRO

CALLE DEL PARADISO

CALLE DELLO STURION

Rialto

RIVA DEL VIN

SAN BART.

RIVA DEL FERRO

C. LARGA MAZZINI

VIA 2 APRILE

Campo San Silvestro

SAN SILVESTRO

PALAZZO DOLFIN-MANIN

PALAZZO BEMBO

Campo San Salvador

Corte Barzizza

PALAZZO BARZIZZA

V San Silvestro

A

RAMO DEL CARBON

C. BEMBO

TEATRO GOLDONI

SAN SALVADOR

PALAZZO PAPADOPOLI

PALAZZO DONÀ

RIVA DEL CARBON

CALLE DEL CARBON

Rio de bel...

Grand Canal

PALAZZO GRIMANI

PALAZZO MARTINENGO

PALAZZO CURTI

Campo San Beneto

PALAZZO FARSETTI-DANDOLO

To Accademia

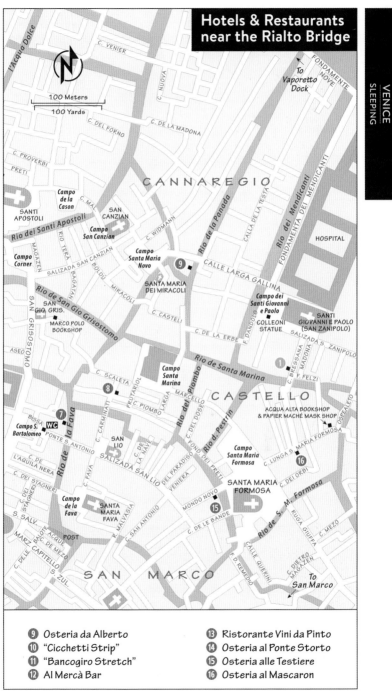

Hotels & Restaurants
near the Rialto Bridge

9 Osteria da Alberto
10 "Cicchetti Strip"
11 "Bancogiro Stretch"
12 Al Mercà Bar

13 Ristorante Vini da Pinto
14 Osteria al Ponte Storto
15 Osteria alle Testiere
16 Osteria al Mascaron

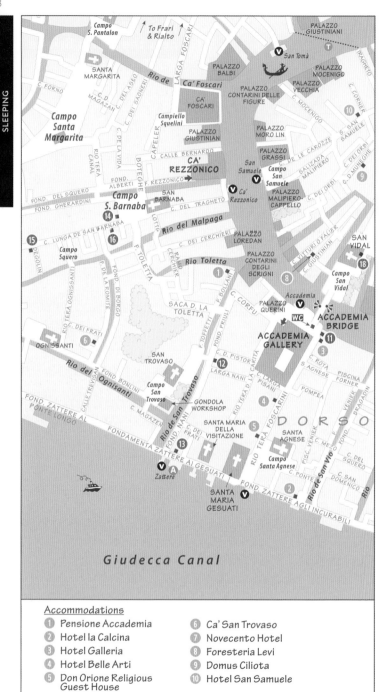

Accommodations

1 Pensione Accademia
2 Hotel la Calcina
3 Hotel Galleria
4 Hotel Belle Arti
5 Don Orione Religious
Guest House

6 Ca' San Trovaso
7 Novecento Hotel
8 Foresteria Levi
9 Domus Ciliota
10 Hotel San Samuele

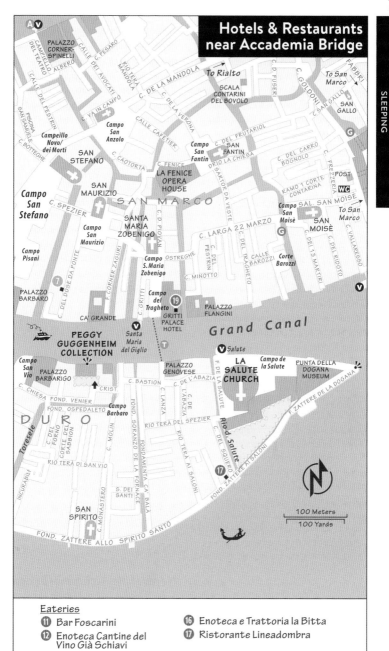

Hotels & Restaurants near Accademia Bridge

Eateries

- ⑪ Bar Foscarini
- ⑫ Enoteca Cantine del Vino Già Schiavi
- ⑬ Terrazza dei Nobili
- ⑭ Ristoteca Oniga
- ⑮ Pizzeria al Profeta
- ⑯ Enoteca e Trattoria la Bitta
- ⑰ Ristorante Lineadombra

Nightlife

- ⑱ Interpreti Veneziani Concerts
- ⑲ Musica a Palazzo

replaced by a sleepy village laced with canals. This quiet area, is a 15-minute walk from the Rialto or St. Mark's Square. The fast vaporetto #2 to the Accademia stop is the typical way to get here from the train station, Piazzale Roma bus station, Tronchetto parking lot, or St. Mark's Square (early and late, #2 terminates at the Rialto stop, where you change to #1). For hotels near the Zattere stop, vaporetto #5.1 or the Alilaguna speedboat from the airport are good options.

South of the Accademia Bridge, in Dorsoduro

$$$$ Pensione Accademia fills the 17th-century Villa Maravege like a Bellini painting. Its 27 comfortable, elegant rooms gild the lily. You'll feel aristocratic gliding through its grand public spaces and lounging in its wistful, breezy gardens (family rooms, air-con, no elevator but most rooms on ground floor or one floor up, on Fondamenta Bollani at Dorsoduro 1058, tel. 041-521-0188, www.pensione accademia.it, info@pensioneaccademia.it).

$$$$ Hotel la Calcina, the home of English writer John Ruskin in 1876, maintains a 19th-century formality. It comes with three-star comforts in a professional yet intimate package. Its 25 nautical-feeling rooms are squeaky clean, with nice wood furniture, hardwood floors, and a peaceful waterside setting facing Giudecca Island (some view rooms, air-con, no elevator and lots of stairs, rooftop terrace, buffet breakfast outdoors in good weather on platform over lagoon, near Zattere vaporetto stop at south end of Rio de San Vio at Dorsoduro 780, tel. 041-520-6466, www.lacalcina.com, info@ lacalcina.com).

$$$$ Hotel Galleria has nine old-fashioned and velvety rooms, half with views of the Grand Canal. Some rooms are quite narrow, but you can open your window to watch boats pass by at any time. It's run with a family feel by Luciano (one cheaper room with detached private bath, breakfast in room, ceiling fans, 30 yards from Accademia art museum, next to recommended Foscarini pizzeria at Dorsoduro 878a, tel. 041-523-2489, www. hotelgalleria.it, info@hotelgalleria.it).

$$$$ Hotel Belle Arti, with a stiff, serious staff, lacks personality but has a grand entry, an inviting garden terrace, and 67 heavily decorated rooms (air-con, elevator, 100 yards behind Accademia art museum on Rio Terà A. Foscarini at Dorsoduro 912a, tel. 041-522-6230, www.hotelbellearti.com, info@hotelbellearti.com).

$$$$ Don Orione Religious Guest House is a big cultural center dedicated to the work of a local man who became a saint in modern times. With 80 rooms filling an old monastery, it feels cookie-cutter-institutional, but is also classy, clean, and peaceful. It's beautifully located, comfortable, and supports a fine cause: Profits go to mission work in the developing world (family rooms, groups welcome, air-con, elevator, on Rio Terà A. Foscarini, Dorsoduro 909a, tel. 041-522-4077, www.donorione-venezia.it, info@ donorione-venezia.it).

$$$ Ca' San Trovaso rents six pleasant rooms in a little three-floor, formerly residential building. The location is peaceful, on a small, out-of-the-way canal (RS%, some view rooms, breakfast in your room, tiny roof terrace, apartments available with 3-night minimum, near Zattere vaporetto stop, off Fondamenta de le Romite at Dorsoduro 1350, tel. 041-241-2215, mobile 349-125-3890, www.casan trovaso.com, info@casantrovaso.com, Anna and Alessandra).

North of the Accademia Bridge

These places are between the Accademia Bridge and St. Mark's Square.

$$$$ Novecento Hotel rents nine plush rooms on three floors, complemented by a big, welcoming lounge, an elegant living room, and a small breakfast garden. This boutique hotel is nicely located and has a tasteful sense of style, mingling Art Deco with North African and Turkish decor (air-con, lots of stairs, on Calle del Dose, off Campo San Maurizio at San Marco 2684, tel. 041-241-3765, www.novecento.biz, info@novecento.biz).

$$$$ Foresteria Levi, run by a foundation that promotes research on Venetian music, offers 32 quiet, institutional yet comfortable and spacious rooms—some are loft quads, a good deal for families (RS%, air-con, elevator, on Calle Giustinian at San Marco 2893, tel. 041-277-0542, www.foresterialevi.it, info@foresterialevi.it). From the base of the Accademia Bridge, it's just over the tiny Ponte Giustinian.

$$$ Domus Ciliota is a big, efficient, and sparkling-clean place—well-run, well-located, church-owned, and plainly furnished—with 30 dorm-like rooms and a peaceful courtyard. If you want industrial-strength comfort with no stress and little character, this is a fine value. During the school year, half the rooms are used by students (air-con, elevator; just off Campo San Stefano at San Marco 2976; tel. 041-520-4888, www.ciliota.it, info@ciliota.it).

$$$ Hotel San Samuele rents 10 tidy rooms in an old *palazzo* near Campo San Stefano. Antique furniture and restored original floors give this place a homey feel. It's in a great locale, and the rooms with shared bath can be a good deal (RS%, no breakfast, fans, some stairs, on Salizada San Samuele at San Marco 3358, tel. 041-520-5165, www.hotelsansamuele.com, info@hotelsansamuele.com, Judith).

EATING

While touristy restaurants are the norm in Venice, my recommended places are popular with locals and respect the tourists who happen by. First trick: Walk away from triple-language menus or laminated pictures of food. Second trick: For freshness, eat fish. Many seafood dishes are the catch-of-the-day. Third trick: Eat later. A place may feel touristy at 19:00, but if you come back at 21:00, it can be filled with locals...or, at least, Italian visitors.

Eating Tips: Unique to Venice, *cicchetti* bars specialize in finger foods and appetizers that combine to make a speedy and tasty meal. *Cicchetti* (the Venetian version of tapas) was designed as a quick meal for working people. The selection and ambience are best on workdays—Monday

Cicchetti *bars in Venice offer tasty snacks.*

through Saturday for lunch or early dinner (see "The Stand-Up Progressive Venetian Pub-Crawl Dinner" sidebar, later).

Sandwiches are sold fast and cheaply at bars everywhere (order a *panini, piadini,* or *tramezzini*). You can eat your sandwich at the bar or take it with you.

A favorite Italian tradition is the *aperitivo* (predinner drink). The dominant *aperitivo* among Venetians is the *spritz* (white wine, soda, and ice with a liquor of your choice). When you order, you'll be asked if you'd like your *spritz con Campari* (bitter) or *con Aperol* (sweeter). Another popular drink is the Bellini—a cocktail of prosecco and white-peach puree, invented at the pricey Harry's American Bar near St. Mark's Square.

Near the Rialto Bridge
North of the Bridge

These restaurants and wine bars are located near or beyond Campo Santi Apostoli, on or near the Strada Nova, the main drag going from Rialto toward the train station.

$$$ Trattoria da Bepi, bright and alpine-paneled, feels like a classic, where Loris carries on his mother's passion for good, traditional Venetian cuisine. Ask for the seasonal specialties: The seafood appetizer plate and crab dishes are excellent. There's good seating inside and out (Fri-Wed 12:00-14:30 & 19:00-22:00, closed Thu, reservations recommended, a half-block off Campo Santi Apostoli on Salizada Pistor, Cannaregio 4550, tel. 041-528-5031, www.dabepi.it).

$$$$ Vini da Gigio, a more expensive option, has a traditional Venetian menu and a classy but unsnooty setting that's a pleasant mix of traditional and contemporary (Wed-Sun 12:00-14:30 & 19:00-22:30, closed Mon-Tue, 4 blocks from Ca' d'Oro vaporetto stop on Fondamenta San Felice, behind the church on Campo San Felice, Cannaregio 3628a, tel. 041-528-5140, www.vinidagigio.com).

East of the Rialto Bridge

The next few places hide away in the twisty lanes between the Rialto Bridge and Campo Santa Maria Formosa. Osteria da Alberto is a tad farther north of the others.

$ Bacarando Bar has a youthful feel, with clearly marked and priced little dishes at the counter and table seating (daily 11:00-24:00, tel. 342-800-3823). It's behind Campo San Bartolomeo (if the statue turned around, walked to the far right-hand corner, and explored the back lanes there, he'd find Bacarando in Corte dell'Orso).

$$ Osteria al Portego is a small and popular neighborhood eatery near Campo San Lio. Carlo serves good meals, bargain-priced house wine, and excellent €1-3 *cicchetti*—best enjoyed around 18:00 (picked over by 21:00). The *cicchetti* here can make a great meal, but consider sitting down for a dinner from their menu. From 12:00-14:30 & 17:30-21:30, their six tables are reserved for those ordering from the menu; reserve ahead if you want a table (daily 11:30-15:00 & 17:30-22:00, on Calle de la Malvasia, Castello 6015, tel. 041-522-9038, Federica). From Campo San Bartolomeo, continue over a bridge to Campo San Lio, turn left, and follow Calle Carminati straight 50 yards over another bridge.

$$ Osteria da Alberto, up near Campo Santa Maria Novo, is one of my standbys, with locals at lunch and tourists at dinner. They offer up excellent daily specials: seafood dishes, pastas, and a good house wine in a woody and characteristic interior. It's smart to reserve at night—I'd request a table in front (daily 12:00-15:00 & 18:30-22:00; on Calle Larga Giacinto Gallina, midway between Campo Santi Apostoli and Campo San Zanipolo/Santi Giovanni e Paolo, and next to Ponte de la Panada bridge, Cannaregio 5401; tel. 041-523-8153, www.osteriadaalberto.it, run by Graziano and Giovanni).

The Stand-Up Progressive Venetian Pub-Crawl Dinner

My favorite Venetian dinner is a pub crawl (*giro d'ombra*)—a tradition unique to Venice. (*Giro* means stroll, and *ombra*—slang for a glass of wine—means shade, from the old days when a portable wine bar scooted with the shadow of the Campanile bell tower across St. Mark's Square.)

Venice's residential back streets hide plenty of characteristic bars (*bacari*), with countless trays of interesting toothpick munchies (*cicchetti*) and wines served by the glass. The *cicchetti* selection is best early, so start your evening by 18:00. Many bars are closed on Sunday. For a guided pub crawl, consider a tour with charming Alessandro Schezzini (see page 38).

Cicchetti bars have a social stand-up zone and a cozy gaggle of tables where you can generally sit down with your *cicchetti* or order from a simple menu. Look for a place that's more "bar" than "restaurant." Make sure they have *cicchetti* on display. Bar-hopping Venetians enjoy an *aperitivo,* a before-dinner drink (try a Bellini, a *spritz con Aperol,* or a prosecco).

While you can order a plate, Venetians prefer going one-by-one...sipping their wine and trying this...then one of those...and so on. Try deep-fried mozzarella cheese, gorgonzola, calamari, artichoke hearts, and anything ugly on a toothpick. Crostini (small toasted bread with a topping) are popular, as are marinated seafood, olives, and prosciutto with melon. Meat and fish (*pesce;* PESH-ay) munchies can be expensive; veggies (*verdure*) are cheap, at about €3 for a meal-sized plate. There's usually a set price per food item (e.g., €1.50). To get a plate of assorted appetizers for €8, ask for *"Un piatto classico di cicchetti misti da €8"* (oon pee-AH-toh KLAH-see-koh dee chee-KET-tee MEE-stee dah OH-toh eh-OO-roh). Bread sticks (*grissini*) are free.

An *ombra rosso* (red) or *ombra bianco* (white), or a small beer (*birrino*) costs about €1. *Vin bon,* Venetian for fine wine, is €2-6 per little glass. A good last drink is *fragolino,* the local sweet wine—*bianco* or *rosso*. It often comes with a little cookie (*biscotto*) for dipping.

Rialto Market Area

The north end of the Rialto Bridge is a great area for menu browsing, bar-hopping, drinks, and snacks; it also has fine sit-down restaurants. You'll find lots of hard-working holes-in-the-wall with a line on the freshest of ingredients and catering to local shoppers needing a quick, affordable, and tasty bite. It's crowded by day, nearly empty early in the evening, and packed with trendy Venetians later.

My listings include a stretch of dark and rustic pubs serving *cicchetti* (Venetian tapas), a strip of trendy places fronting the Grand Canal, and several places at the market and nearby.

The Cicchetti Strip: The 100-yard-long stretch starting two blocks inland from the Rialto Market (along Sotoportego dei Do Mori and Calle de le Do Spade) is beloved for its delightful bar munchies, good wine by the glass, and fun stand-up conviviality. These four $ places serve food all day, but the spread is best at around noon (unless otherwise noted, generally open daily 12:00-15:00 & 18:00-20:00 or 21:00). Scout these places in advance (listed in the order you'll reach

Venetian Cuisine

Even more so than the rest of Italy, Venetian cuisine relies heavily on fish, shellfish, risotto, and polenta. For more on Italian food, see the "Eating" section of the Practicalities chapter.

Antipasti (Appetizers)

Venetians often start a meal with some *cicchetti*—finger-food appetizers. For tips on eating in Venice's *cicchetti* bars, see page 81.

Antipasto di mare: Marinated mix of chilled fish and shellfish

Asiago cheese: Cow's-milk cheese that's either *mezzano* (young, creamy) or *stravecchio* (aged, pungent)

Sarde in saor: Sardines marinated with onions

Rice, Pasta, and Polenta

Bigoli in salsa: Long, fat, whole-wheat noodle in anchovy sauce

Pasta alla buzzara: Pasta in a seafood-tomato sauce, generally with shrimp

Pasta al pomodoro: Pasta in a simple tomato sauce

Pasta al vongole: Pasta with clams

Pasta e fagioli: Bean-and-pasta soup

Polenta: Thick cornmeal porridge served soft or cut into firm slabs and grilled

Risi e bisi: Rice and peas

them, if coming from the Rialto Bridge) to help decide which ambience is right for the experience you have in mind.

At each place, look for the list of snacks (around €2) and wine by the glass (€1-3) at the bar or on the wall. **Bar all'Arco,** a bustling one-room joint, is particularly enjoyable for its *cicchetti* (Mon-Sat 10:00-17:00, closed Sun, San Polo 436; Francesco, Anna, Matteo). **Cantina Do Mori** has been famous with locals (since 1462) and savvy travelers (since 1982) as a convivial place for wine and *francobolli* (a spicy selection of 20 tiny, mayo-soaked sandwiches nicknamed "stamps"). Go here to be abused in

a fine atmosphere—the frowns are part of the shtick—and be aware that prices can add up quickly (closed Sun, can be shoulder-to-shoulder, San Polo 430).

Osteria ai Storti is more of a sit-down place (tables inside and on street). It's run by Alessandro, who speaks English and enjoys helping educate travelers (around the corner from Cantina Do Mori on Calle San Matio, San Polo 819). **Cantina Do Spade** is run by Francesco and is also good for sit-down restaurant-style meals (30 yards down Calle de le Do Spade from Osteria ai Storti at San Polo 860, tel. 041-521-0583).

Risotto: Short-grain rice simmered in broth with seafood, meat, or veggies. *Risotto al nero*—black risotto—is made with squid ink.

Frutti di Mare (Seafood)

Baccalà: Preserved Atlantic salt cod that's rehydrated and served with polenta; also mixed with mayonnaise as a *cicchetti* topping called *baccalà mantecato*

Branzino: Sea bass, grilled and served whole

Calamari: Squid, often cut into rings and deep-fried or marinated

Cozze: Mussels, often steamed in an herb broth with tomato

Gamberi: Shrimp—*gamberetti* are small, and *gamberoni* are large.

Moleche col pien: Fried soft-shell crabs

Orata: Sea bream, a white fish

Pesce fritto misto: Deep-fried seafood, often calamari and prawns

Pesce spada: Swordfish

Rombo: Turbot, a flatfish similar to flounder

Rospo: Frogfish, a small fish that's often grilled

Salmone: Salmon

Seppia: Cuttlefish, a squid-like creature. *Nero di seppia* is the squid served in its own ink, often over spaghetti.

Sogliola: Sole, served poached or oven-roasted

Vitello di mare: "Sea veal," like swordfish—firm, mild, and grilled

Vongole: Clams, often steamed with fresh herbs and wine, or served as *spaghetti alle vongole*

Zuppa di pesce: Seafood stew

Canalside Seating: What I call the "Bancogiro Stretch," just past the Rialto Bridge, between Campo San Giacomo and the Grand Canal, has some of the best canalside seating in Venice. Unless otherwise noted, all are open daily and serve drinks, *cicchetti,* and somewhat pricey sit-down meals. But between mealtimes you can enjoy a drink or a snack at fine prices. After dinner hours, the Bancogiro Stretch—especially in the surrounding alleys that house low-rent bars—becomes a trendy nightspot. Here's the rundown (in the order you'll reach them from the Rialto Bridge): **$$$ Bar Naranzaria** serves Italian dishes with a few Japanese options. **$$ Caffè Vergnano** is your cheapest option (vegetarian dishes and a busy microwave oven). **$$$ Osteria al Pesador** has a friendly staff and serves local specialties. **$$$ Osteria Bancogiro** has the best reputation for dinner, a passion for the best cheese, and good *cicchetti* options at the bar (nice cheese plate, closed Mon, tel. 041-523-2061). The more modern **$$ Bar Ancòra** seems to be most popular with the local bar crowd, with a live piano player crooning lounge music during busy times (*cicchetti* at the bar).

At the Market: A few steps away and off the canal, **$ Al Mercà Bar** ("At the Market") is a lively little nook with a happy crowd. The price list is clear, and the youthful crowd seems to enjoy connecting with curious tourists (stand at bar or in square—there are no tables and no interior, Mon-Sat 10:00-14:30 & 18:00-21:00, closed Sun, on Campo Cesare Battisti, San Polo 213).

$$ Ristorante Vini da Pinto is a tourist-friendly eatery facing the fish market, with a large menu and relaxing outdoor seating (and easily confused with the restaurant next door). Owner Giorgio visits the market each morning to select the day's best catch. Enjoy the lunch-only, fixed-price, three-course seafood meal for €18, including a pasta, seafood sampler plate, veggies, and dessert. Rick Steves readers receive a welcoming prosecco and a farewell *limoncello* and homemade cookie (daily 11:00-23:00, Campo de le Becarie, San Polo 367a, tel. 041-522-4599).

Farther Inland, off Campo San Aponal: A little family-run place, **$$ Osteria al Ponte Storto** is on a quiet canalside corner a block off the main drag and worth seeking out for its good-value main dishes, daily specials, and peaceful location (Tue-Sun 12:00-15:00 & 18:00-21:45, closed Mon, down Calle Bianca from San Aponal church, San Polo 1278, tel. 041-528-2144, Nicola is the chef/owner).

Near St. Mark's Square

$$$$ Ristorante Antica Sacrestia is a classic restaurant where the owner, Pino, greets you personally. His staff serves creative fixed-price meals (€35, €55, or €80), a humdrum *menù del giorno,* and wonderful pizzas. You can also order à la carte; their antipasto spread looks like a lagoon aquarium spread out on a plate. My readers are welcome to a free *sgroppino* (lemon vodka after-dinner drink) upon request (Tue-Sun 11:30-15:00 & 18:00-

23:00, closed Mon, behind San Zaninovo/Giovanni Novo Church on Calle Corona, Castello 4463, tel. 041-523-0749, www.anticasacrestia.it). There's no wine by the glass. Order carefully. Pizza is your only budget escape.

$$ Rossopomodoro Pizzeria is a big, fun, and practical pizzeria offering top quality, good prices, and a very handy location. They cook Naples-style pizzas in their wood oven and offer a selection of hearty salads and pastas (long hours daily, Calle Larga San Marco 404, tel. 041-243-8949).

$$$ L'Ombra del Leone is a modern and classy bar (with attached restaurant) featuring an outdoor terrace right on the Grand Canal. It's in the Biennale offices and is popular with gondoliers. Its bar menu of salads and sandwiches has reasonable prices for the elegance and location (long hours daily, in Ca' Giustinian, behind San Moisè Church at the end of Calle Ridotto, tel. 041-241-3519).

Sandwich Row: On Calle de le Rasse, just steps away from the tourist intensity at St. Mark's Square, is a handy strip lined with several **$ sandwich bars.** It's the closest place to St. Mark's to get a decent sandwich at an affordable price with a place to sit down (most places open long hours daily, about €1 extra per item to sit; from the Bridge of Sighs, head down the Riva and take the second lane on the left). They all sell the *tramezzino* local-style sandwiches. Try **Birreria Forst** (daily 9:30-23:00, air-con, rustic wood tables, Castello 4540, tel. 041-523-0557) or **Bar Verde** (also splittable salads, fresh pastries, at the end of Calle de le Rasse facing Campo Santi Filippo e Giacomo, Castello 4526).

Rick's Tip: *Though you* **can't picnic on St. Mark's Square,** *you can take your snacks to the* **nearby Giardinetti Reali,** *the small park along the waterfront west of the Piazzetta.*

North of St. Mark's Square, near Campo Santa Maria Formosa

For a (marginally) less touristy scene, walk a few blocks north to the inviting Campo Santa Maria Formosa.

$$$$ Osteria alle Testiere is my top dining splurge in Venice. Hugely respected, Luca and his staff are dedicated to quality, serving up creative, artfully presented market-fresh seafood (there's no meat on the menu), home-made pastas, and fine wine. With only 22 seats, it's tight and homey, with the focus on food and service. They have daily specials, 10 wines by the glass, and one agenda: a great dining experience. They're open for lunch (12:00-15:00), and reservations made via email only are a must for their two dinner seatings: 19:00 and 21:30 (plan on spending €60 for dinner, closed Sun-Mon, on Calle del Mondo Novo, just off Campo Santa Maria Formosa, Castello 5801, tel. 041-522-7220, www.osterialletestiere.it, info@osterialletestiere.it

$$$ Osteria al Mascaron is a rustic little bar-turned-restaurant where Gigi, Momi, and their food-loving band of ruffians dish up rustic-yet-sumptuous pastas with steamy seafood. The *antipasto misto* fish-and-vegetable plate and two glasses of wine make a terrific light meal (Mon-Sat 12:00-15:00 & 18:00-23:00, closed Sun, reservations smart Fri-Sat; on Calle Lunga Santa Maria Formosa, a block past Campo Santa Maria Formosa, Castello 5225; tel. 041-522-5995, www.osteriamascaron.it).

Dorsoduro

These recommendations are within a 10-minute walk of the Accademia Bridge and well worth the walk.

Near the Accademia Bridge

$$ Bar Foscarini, next to the Accademia Bridge and Galleria, offers decent pizzas and *panini* in a memorable Grand Canal-view setting. The food is forgettable and drinks are pricey. But you're paying a premium for this premium location. They also serve breakfast (daily 8:00-23:00, Nov-April until 20:30, on Rio Terà A. Foscarini, Dorsoduro 878c, tel. 041-522-7281, Paolo and Simone).

$ Enoteca Cantine del Vino Già Schiavi, with a wonderfully characteristic *cicchetti*-bar ambience, is much loved for its inexpensive *cicchetti,* sandwiches (order from list on board), and wine. You're welcome to enjoy your wine and finger food at the bar, in the back room surrounded by wine bottles, or out on the sidewalk (specify *"fuori"* to sit outside and they'll provide plastic cups; please don't sit on the bridge). This is primarily a wine shop with great prices for bottles to go (Mon-Sat 8:30-20:30, closed Sun, 100 yards from Accademia art museum on San Trovaso canal; facing the Accademia, take a right and then a forced left at the canal to the second bridge—it's at Dorsoduro 992, tel. 041-523-0034; they have no WC).

Zattere

The far south side of Dorsoduro has a wide promenade along the canal that, on warm summer evenings, has a special charm.

$$$ Terrazza dei Nobili takes full advantage of the warm, romantic evening sun. They serve regional specialties and pizza at tolerable prices. The breezy and beautiful seaside seating comes with formal service and the rumble of vaporetti from the nearby stop. The interior is bright and hip (daily 12:00-24:00; at the Zattere vaporetto stop, turn left to Dorsoduro 924; tel. 041-520-6895).

On or near Campo San Barnaba

This small square is a delight—especially in the evening. Reservations may be necessary to dine later in the evening.

$$$ Ristoteca Oniga has an eclectic yet cozy interior, great tables on the square, and is run by the enthusiastic Raffaele. The menu has a few vegetarian and meat dishes but focuses on fresh fish and other

Splurging on a Great View

A meal with a view generally comes with lower quality and/or higher prices. But if you're determined to take home a canalside memory, these places are worth the splurge.

Overlooking the Giudecca Canal: Immediately behind La Salute Church, **$$$$ Ristorante Lineadombra** has commanding lagoon views of the Giudecca Canal. The gorgeously presented dishes are both local and modern. Reserve ahead and choose seating inside or on their terrace (daily 12:00-15:00 & 19:00-22:00, closed Tue off-season, directly across the island from the Salute vaporetto stop, Dorsoduro 19, tel. 041-241-1881, www.ristorantelineadombra.com).

On Fondamente Nove, with a Lagoon View: $$$$ Ristorante Algiubagiò is a good place for quality, creative Venetian cuisine with a view over the northern lagoon. Reserve a waterside table or sit in their classy dining room (daily 12:00-15:00 & 19:00-22:30, between the two sets of vaporetto docks on Fondamente Nove, Cannaregio 5039, tel. 041-523-6084, www.algiubagio.net).

On St. Mark's Square: At **$$$$ Gran Caffè Quadri** (a.k.a. Bistro ABC Quadri), you'll enjoy a traditional and accessible menu and prices that won't ruin your appetite. While its 15 tables are all inside, the orchestra is just out the window (daily 12:00-15:00 & 19:00-22:30, reservations smart, San Marco 121, tel. 041-522-2105, www.alajmo.it/grancaffe-quadri).

sea creatures, highlighted by their specialty, *bucintoro*—a pan full of mussels, clams, prawns, calamari, and spaghetti (daily 12:00-14:30 & 19:00-22:30, reservations smart, Campo San Barnaba, Dorsoduro 2852, tel. 041-522-4410, www.oniga.it).

$$ Pizzeria al Profeta is a casual place popular with tourists for great pizza. Its sprawling interior seems to stoke conviviality, as does its leafy garden out back (daily 12:00-14:30 & 19:00-23:30; from Campo San Barnaba, a long walk down Calle Lunga San Barnaba to #2671; tel. 041-523-7466).

$$$ Enoteca e Trattoria la Bitta is dark and woody, with a soft-jazz bistro feel, tight seating, and a small back patio. They serve beautifully presented, traditional Venetian food with—proudly—no fish. Their helpful wait staff and small, handwritten daily menu are focused on local ingredients (including rabbit) and a "slow food" ethic. They offer two dinner seatings (19:00 and 21:00) and require res-ervations (dinner only, closed Sun, cash only, just off Campo San Barnaba on Calle Lunga San Barnaba, Dorsoduro 2753a, tel. 041-523-0531, Debora and Marcellino).

TRANSPORTATION

Getting Around Venice

Narrow pedestrian walkways connect Venice's docks, squares, bridges, and courtyards. To navigate, look for signs on street corners pointing you to (*per*) the nearest major landmark. Determine whether your destination is in the direction of a major, signposted landmark, then follow the signs through the maze.

Every building in Venice has a house number. The numbers relate to the district (each with about 6,000 address numbers), not the street. If you need to find a specific address, it helps to know its district, street, house number, and nearby landmarks.

Some helpful street terminology:

Campo means square, a campiello is a small square, calle (pronounced "KAH-lay" with an "L" sound) means "street," and a ponte is a bridge. A fondamenta is the embankment along a canal or the lagoon. A rio terà is a street that was once a canal and has been filled in. A sotoportego is a covered passageway. Salizzada literally means a paved area (usually a wide street). The abbreviations S. and SS. mean "saint" and "saints" respectively. Don't get hung up on the exact spelling of street and square names, which may sometimes appear in Venetian dialect (which uses de la, novo, and vechio) and other times in standard Italian (which uses della, nuovo, and vecchio).

By Vaporetto

These motorized bus-boats work like city buses except that they never get a flat, the stops are docks, and if you jump off between stops, you might drown. You can purchase tickets and passes at docks and from ACTV affiliate VèneziaUnica (ACTV—tel. 041-2424, www.actv.it; VèneziaUnica—www.veneziaunica.it).

TICKETS AND PASSES

Individual Vaporetto Tickets: A single ticket costs €7.50 (kids under 6 travel free). Tickets are good for 75 minutes; you can hop on and off at stops and change boats during that time. Your ticket (a paper ticket embedded with a chip) is refillable—you can put more money on it at the kiosks and avoid waiting in line at the ticket window. It's also smart to keep your receipt (in case you're checked and your ticket is faulty).

Vaporetto Passes: You can buy a pass for unlimited use of vaporetti: €20/24 hours, €30/48 hours, €40/72 hours, €60/7-day pass (the clock starts ticking the first time you use it). Because single tickets are pricey, these passes pay for themselves in a hurry. Think through your Venice itinerary before you step up to the ticket booth to pay for your first vaporetto trip. The 48-hour pass pays for itself with five rides (for example: to your hotel on your arrival, on a Grand Canal joyride, into the lagoon and back, to the train station...and that spur-of-the-moment moonlight cruise). Some smaller and outlying stops are

Helpful signs direct you toward (per) your destination in maze-like Venice.

unstaffed—another reason to buy a pass.

Travelers between ages 14-29 can get a 72-hour pass for €22 if they also buy a **Rolling Venice** discount card for €6 (see page 52).

Passes are also valid on some of ACTV's mainland buses, including bus #2 to Mestre (but not the #5 to the airport nor the airport buses run by ATVO, a separate company). Pass holders get a discounted fare for all ACTV buses that originate or terminate at Marco Polo Airport (see page 95).

Buying and Validating Tickets and Passes: Purchase tickets and passes from the machines at most stops (English-language option, major credit cards accepted), from ticket windows (at larger stops), or from the VèneziaUnica offices at the train station, bus station, and Tronchetto parking lot.

Before you board, validate your ticket or pass by touching it to the small white pad on the dock until you hear a pinging sound. With passes, you need to touch the pass each time you board. The machine readout shows how long your ticket is valid—and inspectors often check tickets. If you're unable to purchase a ticket before boarding, seek out the conductor immediately to buy a single ticket (or risk a €60 fine).

IMPORTANT VAPORETTO LINES

For most travelers, only two vaporetto lines matter: **line #1** and **line #2**. These lines leave every 10 minutes or so and go up and down the Grand Canal, between the "mouth" of the fish at one end and St. Mark's Square at the other. Line #1 is the slow boat, taking 45 minutes and making every stop along the way. Line #2 is the fast boat that zips down the Grand Canal in 25 minutes, stopping only at Tronchetto (parking lot), Piazzale Roma (bus station), Ferrovia (train station), Rialto Bridge, San Tomà (Frari Church), San Samuele (opposite Ca' Rezzonico), Accademia Bridge, and San Marco (west end of St. Mark's Square, end of the line).

Study the maps at docks before you board. Some boats run on circular routes, in one direction only (for example, lines #5.1 and #5.2, plus the non-Murano sections of lines #4.1 and #4.2). Line #2 runs in both directions and is almost, but not quite, a full loop. The #2 boat leaving from the San Marco stop goes in one direction (up the Grand Canal), while from the San Zaccaria stop—just a five-minute walk away—it goes in the opposite direction (around the tail of the "fish").

To clear up any confusion, ask a ticket-seller or conductor for help (sometimes they're stationed on the dock). Get a copy of the most current ACTV map and timetable (download from www.actv.it, theoretically free at ticket booths but often unavailable). System maps are posted at stops, but it's smart to print out your own copy of the map from the ACTV website before your trip.

BOARDING AND RIDING

Many stops have more than one departure platform. At these larger stops, check the electronic departure board to see which boats are coming next, when, where they're going, and from which platform they leave (for example, "Line 2 to San Marco, from platform B"). At smaller stops without electronic displays, signs on each platform show the vaporetto lines that stop there and the direction they are headed. Be aware that other boats may

A traghetto *crossing*

Handy Vaporetti from San Zaccaria, near St. Mark's Square

Several vaporetti leave from the San Zaccaria docks, located 150 yards east of St. Mark's Square. The four docks are spaced about 70 yards apart, with six different berths, lettered A to F. Check the big electronic board (next to the C/D dock), which indicates the departure time, line number, destination, and berth letter of upcoming vaporetti. Once you've figured out which boat you want, go to that letter berth and hop on.

- **Line #1:** This vaporetto goes up the Grand Canal, making all the stops, including San Marco, Rialto, Ferrovia (train station), and Piazzale Roma (but it does not go as far as Tronchetto). In the other direction, it goes from San Zaccaria to Arsenale and Giardini before ending on the Lido (dock E).
- **Line #2:** This vaporetto zips over to San Giorgio Maggiore, the island church across from St. Mark's Square (5 minutes, €5 ride). From there, it continues on to stops on the island of Giudecca, the parking lot at Tronchetto, and then down the Grand Canal (dock B). Note: You cannot ride the #2 up the Grand Canal (for example, to Rialto or the train station) directly from this stop—you'll need to walk five minutes along the waterfront, past St. Mark's Square, to the San Marco-Giardinetti dock and hop the #2 from there.
- **Line #4.1:** This boat goes to San Michele and Murano (45 minutes, dock D).
- **Line #7:** This is the summertime express boat to Murano (25 minutes, dock D).
- **Molino Stucky Shuttle Boat:** This takes even non-guests to the Hilton Hotel, with its popular view bar (20-minute ride, 3/hour, from its own dock near the San Zaccaria-B dock).
- **Lines #5.1** and **#5.2:** These are the *circulare* (cheer-koo-LAH-ray) lines, making a loop around the perimeter of the island, with a stop at the Lido—perfect if you just like riding boats. Line #5.1 goes counterclockwise, and #5.2 goes clockwise. Both run less frequently in the evenings (#5.1 leaves from dock D, #5.2 from dock C).
- **Alilaguna Shuttle Boat:** This runs to and from the airport (dock D).

also be leaving from your same platform. When your boat arrives, confirm the direction posted on the bow ("Line 2, San Marco"). To double-check, ask the conductor when you board ("San Marco?").

By Traghetto

Only four bridges cross the Grand Canal, but *traghetti* (shuttle gondolas) ferry locals and in-the-know tourists across the Grand Canal at three additional locations. Just step in, hand the gondolier €2, and enjoy the ride. Some *traghetti* are seasonal, some stop running as early as 12:30,

and all stop by 18:00. *Traghetti* are not covered by any transit pass.

By Water Taxi

Venetian taxis hang out at busy points along the Grand Canal. Prices are regulated: €15 for pickup, then €2 per minute; €5 per person for more than four passengers (boats can carry around 10 people); and €10 between 22:00 and 6:00. If you have more bags than passengers, the extra ones cost €5 apiece. Despite regulation, prices can be soft; negotiate before stepping in. For travelers with lots of luggage or small

Vaporettos ply the busy Grand Canal.

groups who can split the cost, taxi boat rides can be a worthwhile and time-saving convenience—and skipping across the lagoon in a classic wooden motorboat is a cool indulgence. For about €120 an hour, you can have a private, unguided taxi-boat tour. You may find more competitive rates if you prebook through the Consorzio Motoscafi water taxi association (tel. 041-522-2303, www.motoscafivenezia.it).

Arriving and Departing

A two-mile-long causeway (with highway and train lines) connects Venice to the mainland. Mestre, the sprawling mainland section of Venice, has fewer crowds, cheaper hotels, and plenty of inexpensive parking lots, but zero charm. Don't stop in Mestre unless you're changing trains, parking your car, or sleeping there.

By Train

All trains to "Venice" stop at Venezia Mestre (on the mainland). Most continue on to **Santa Lucia Station** (a.k.a. Venezia S.L.) on the island of Venice itself. If your train happens to terminate at Mestre, you'll need to buy a €1.25 Mestre-Santa Lucia ticket and validate it before hopping any nonexpress, regional train (with an R or RV prefix) for the ride across the causeway to Venice (6/hour, 10 minutes).

Santa Lucia train station is right on the Grand Canal, an easy vaporetto ride or fascinating 45-minute walk (with a number of bridges and steps) to St. Mark's Square.

The station has a **baggage check** (daily 6:00-23:00, no lockers; along track 1). Pay **WCs** are at track 1 and in the back of the big bar/cafeteria area inside the station. You'll find the **TI** across from track 2.

Getting from the Train Station to Central Venice: It's best by **vaporetto.** Walk straight out of the station to the canal, where you'll see five vaporetto docks (A, B, C, D, and E), each serving different boats. Electronic signboards show which boats are leaving when and from which dock (for example, boat #2 to San Marco, from dock B). Most tourists want the fast boat #2 down the Grand Canal to Rialto and San

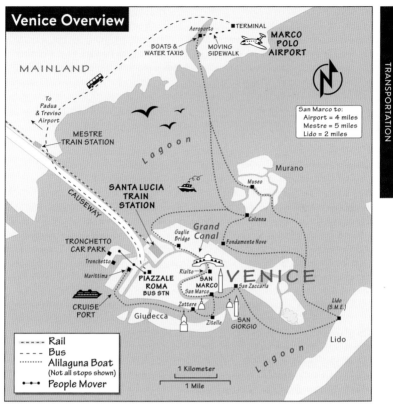

Marco (generally from dock B) or the slow boat #1 down the Grand Canal, making every stop all the way to Rialto and San Marco. A **water taxi** from the train station to central Venice costs about €60-80 (the taxi dock is straight ahead).

TRAIN CONNECTIONS

For general information on train travel in Italy, see page 491.

When taking the train from Venice to nearby cities such as Padua or Verona, prices and journey times can vary greatly, depending on whether the train is express or regional.

From Venice by Train to: Padua (30 minutes, Trenitalia: 2/hour, Italo: hourly), **Verona** (1.5 hours, Trenitalia: 2/hour, Italo: 7/day), **Florence** (Trenitalia: hourly, 2-3 hours, may transfer in Bologna, often crowded—reserve ahead; Italo: 4/day, 2 hours, reservations required), **Milan** (Trenitalia: 2/hour, most direct on high-speed ES trains, 2.5 hours; Italo: 7/day, 2.5 hours), **Cinque Terre/Monterosso** (5/day, 6 hours, change in Milan), **Rome** (Trenitalia: hourly, 4 hours; direct night train, 7 hours, reserve ahead; Italo: 4/day, 3.5 hours, reservations required), **Naples** (Trenitalia: almost hourly, 5.5 hours, some change in Bologna or Rome, reserve ahead; Italo: 3/day, 5.5 hours, reservations required).

By Bus

Venice's "bus station" is an open-air parking lot called **Piazzale Roma.** The square itself is a jumble of different operators, platforms, and crosswalks over busy lanes of traffic. But bus stops are well-signed. The ticket windows for ACTV (including #5 to Marco Polo Airport) are in a building near the modern Calatrava Bridge and the vaporetto stop. The ATVO ticket office (express buses to Marco Polo and Treviso airports and to Padua) is at #497g in the big, white building, on the right side of the square as you face away from the canal (office open daily 6:45-19:30).

Piazzale Roma also has two big **parking garages** and the **People Mover monorail** (€1.50, links to the cruise port and then the parking-lot island of Tronchetto). **Baggage storage** is next to the monorail at #497m (€7/24 hours, daily 6:00-21:00).

Getting from the Bus Station to Central Venice: Find the vaporetto docks (just left of the modern bridge) and take #1 or the faster #2 down the Grand Canal to reach the Rialto, Accademia, or San Marco (St. Mark's Square) stops.

By Car

The freeway dead-ends after crossing the causeway to Venice. At the end of the road you have two parking-garage choices: Tronchetto or Piazzale Roma. As you drive into the city, signboards with green and red lights indicate which lots are full.

Parking at Tronchetto: This big garage is a bit farther out, but it's a little cheaper and well-connected by vaporetto (€3-5/ hour, €21/24 hours, tel. 041-520-7555, www.veniceparking.it).

From the garage, cross the street to the brick building and go right to the vaporetto dock (not well-signed, look for *ACTV*), where you can catch vaporetto #2 in one of two directions: via the Grand Canal (more scenic, stops at Rialto, 40 minutes to San Marco), or via Giudecca (around the city, faster, no Rialto stop, 30 minutes to San Marco).

Don't be waylaid by aggressive water-taxi boatmen. They charge €100 to take you where the vaporetto will for far less. Also avoid the travel agencies masquerading as TIs; deal only with the ticket booth at the vaporetto dock or the VèneziaUnica public transport office.

If you're staying near the bus or train station, you can take the €1.50 **People Mover** monorail, which brings you from Tronchetto to the bus station at Piazzale Roma. From there, it's a five-minute walk across the Calatrava Bridge to the train station (buy tickets with cash or credit card from machine, 3-minute trip).

Parking at Piazzale Roma: The two garages here are more convenient but a bit more expensive and likelier to be full. Both face the busy Piazzale Roma, where the road ends. The big white building on your right is the **Autorimessa Comunale** city garage (€26/24 hours, TI office in payment lobby open daily 7:30-19:30, tel. 041-272-7211, www.avmspa.it). In a back corner of the square is the private **Garage San Marco** (€32/24 hours, tel. 041-523-2213, www.garagesanmarco.it). At either, you'll have to give up your keys. Near the Garage San Marco, avoid the Parcheggio Sant'Andrea, which charges higher rates.

By Plane

MARCO POLO AIRPORT

Venice's surprisingly large, modern airport is on the mainland shore of the lagoon, six miles north of the city (code: VCE, tel. 041-260-9260, www.veniceairport.it). There's one sleek terminal, with a TI (daily 9:00-20:00), car-rental agencies, ATMs, a bank, and plenty of shops and eateries.

Getting Between the Airport and Venice: You can get between the airport and central Venice in any of four ways: by Alilaguna boat, water taxi, airport bus, or land taxi.

Alilaguna boats reach most of my recommended hotels very simply, with no changes. Both Alilaguna boats and water taxis leave from the airport's boat dock, an eight-minute walk from the terminal, following signs along a sleek series of (indoor) moving sidewalks. Ticket offices are at the docks.

Transport	Speed	Cost	Notes
Alilaguna boat	Slow	Moderate	No transfer
Water taxi	Fast	Expensive	No transfer
Airport bus to Piazzale Roma	Medium	Cheap	Transfer to vaporetto
Land taxi to Piazzale Roma	Medium	Moderate	Transfer to vaporetto

When flying out of Venice, allow plenty of time to get to the airport. From your hotel to the airport can take two hours. Alilaguna boats are small and can fill up. In an emergency, you can always hop in a water taxi and get to the airport in 30 minutes.

Alilaguna Airport Boats: These boats shuttle across the lagoon between the airport and the island of Venice (€15, €27 round-trip, €1 surcharge if bought on boat, includes 1 suitcase and 1 piece of hand luggage, additional bags–€3 each, roughly 2/hour, 1-1.5-hour trip depending on destination). Alilaguna boats are not covered by city transit passes, but they do use the same docks and ticket windows as the regular vaporetti. You can buy Alilaguna tickets online for a slight discount, but it does not ensure a reservation as you must still exchange the voucher for a ticket (www.alilaguna.it or www.venicelink.com).

There are three key Alilaguna lines for reaching St. Mark's Square. From the airport, the **orange line** (linea arancio) runs down the Grand Canal, reaching Guglie (handy for Cannaregio hotels, roughly 2/hour, 45 minutes), Rialto (1 hour), and San Marco (1.25 hours). The **blue line** (linea blu) heads first to Fondamente Nove (40 minutes), then loops around to San Zaccaria and San Marco (roughly 2/hour, about 1.5 hours) before continuing to Zattere and the cruise terminal (almost 2 hours). In high season, the **red line** (linea rossa) runs to St. Mark's (1/hour, just over an hour). It circumnavigates Murano and then runs parallel to the blue line, ending at Giudecca Zitelle. For a full schedule, see www.alilaguna.it.

Water Taxis: Luxury taxi speedboats

zip directly between the airport and the closest dock to your hotel in about 30 minutes. The official price is €110 for up to four people; add €10 for every extra person (10-passenger limit). You may get a higher quote—politely talk it down.

From the airport, arrange your ride at the water-taxi desk or with the boat captains at the dock. From Venice, book your taxi trip the day before your departure, either through your hotel or directly with the Consorzio Motoscafi water taxi association (tel. 041-522-2303, www.motoscafivenezia.it).

Airport Shuttle Buses: Buses between the airport and Venice are fast, frequent, and cheap. They drop you at Venice's bus station, at the square called Piazzale Roma. From there, you can catch a vaporetto down the Grand Canal—convenient for hotels near the Rialto Bridge and St. Mark's Square.

Two bus companies serve this route: ACTV and ATVO. ATVO buses take 20 minutes and go nonstop. ACTV buses make a few stops en route and take slightly longer (30 minutes), but you get a discount if you buy a Venice vaporetto pass at the same time (see page 89). The service is equally good (either bus: €8 one-way, €15 round-trip; ACTV bus with transit-pass discount: €6 one-way, €12 round-trip; runs about 5:00-24:00, 2/hour, drops to 1/hour early and late, check schedules at www.atvo.it or www.actv.it). Double-check the destination; you want Piazzale Roma. If taking ACTV, you want bus #5.

Land Taxi or Private Minivan: A **land taxi** can get you from the airport to Piazzale Roma for about €50 (20 minutes). To reserve a private minivan, contact **Treviso Car Service** (minivan—€55, seats up to 8; car—€50, seats up to 3; mobile 338-204-4390 or 333-411-2840, www.trevisocarservice.com).

TREVISO AIRPORT

Several budget airlines use Treviso Airport, 12 miles northwest of Venice (code: TSF, tel. 042-231-5111, www.trevisoairport.it). The fastest option into Venice (Tronchetto parking lot; convenient if taking vaporetto line #2) is on the **Barzi express bus,** which does the trip in just 40 minutes (€12, buy tickets on board, every

1-2 hours, www.barziservice.com). From Tronchetto, hop on a vaporetto, or take the People Mover monorail to Piazzale Roma for €1.50. **ATVO buses** are a bit more frequent and drop you right at Piazzale Roma (saving you the People Mover ride), but take nearly twice as long (€12 one-way, €22 round-trip, about 2/hour, 70 minutes, www.atvo.it; buy tickets at the ATVO desk in the airport and stamp them on the bus). **Treviso Car Service** offers minivan service to Piazzale Roma (minivan-€75, seats up to 8; car-€65, seats up to 3; for contact info, see listing earlier).

NEAR VENICE

If you want low-key Italian towns that have just enough sights and more than enough ambience, Padua and Verona make good stops. Art lovers head to Padua for Giotto's celebrated Scrovegni Chapel (reservations required). History buffs enjoy Verona's impressive Roman ruins. The town is also the pick for star-crossed lovers retracing Romeo and Juliet's steps.

The towns are nearly next-door neighbors. Connected by frequent trains (2/hour), Verona and Padua are only 40-80 minutes apart (depending on the speed of your train). Either town makes a fine day trip or a pleasant overnight. They're easy stops on the Milan-Venice train line.

Padua

Despite the fact that Padua's museums and churches hold their own in Italy's artistic big league, the city doesn't feel touristy. Padua's Old Town center is elegantly arcaded, filled with students, and sprinkled with surprises, including some of Italy's most inviting squares for lingering over an *aperitivo* as the sun slowly dips low in the sky.

Day Plan

Your entry time to see Giotto's Scrovegni Chapel (reservation required) will dictate the order of your sightseeing. I'd do it this way: 9:00—market action and sightseeing in town center, 11:00—Basilica of St. Anthony, 13:00—lunch, 15:00—Scrovegni Chapel tour.

Orientation

Padua's main tourist sights lie on a north-south axis through the heart of the city, from the train station to Scrovegni Chapel to the market squares (the center of town) to the Basilica of St. Anthony. It's roughly a 10-minute walk between each of these sights. Padua's wonderful single tram line makes lacing things together quick and easy.

Tourist Information: Padua has two TIs, both open daily—in the **center** (in the alley behind Caffè Pedrocchi at Vicolo Cappellatto Pedrocchi 9) and at the **train station** (tel. 049-520-7415, www.turismopadova.it).

Sightseeing Pass: The **Padova Card** includes entry to all my recommended sights plus unlimited tram rides (€16/48

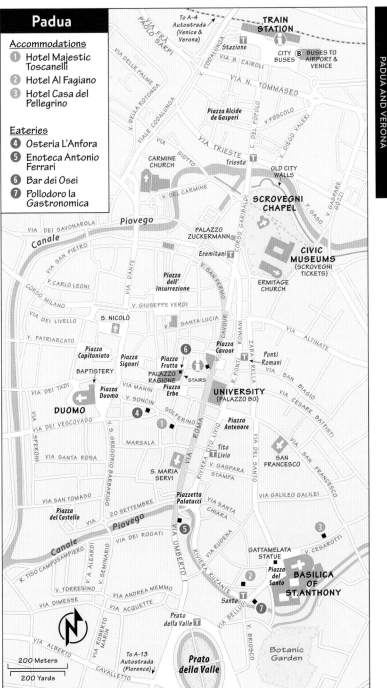

Padua

Accommodations

1 Hotel Majestic Toscanelli
2 Hotel Al Fagiano
3 Hotel Casa del Pellegrino

Eateries

4 Osteria L'Anfora
5 Enoteca Antonio Ferrari
6 Bar dei Osei
7 Pollodoro la Gastronomica

hours, €21/72 hours; buy at either TI, the Scrovegni Chapel, or online at www.padovacard.it).

Local Guide: Charming **Cristina Pernechele** is a great teacher (€120/half-day, mobile 338-495-5453, cristina@pernechele.eu).

Getting There

Trains from Venice are cheap, take 30 minutes, and run frequently (2/hour). Baggage check is available at Padua's station. To get downtown, simply hop on Padua's handy **tram** (purchase ticket inside station or from booth out front). A **taxi** into town costs €8-10.

If you arrive **by car,** Padua has a smart park-and-ride system near each end of the tram line.

Sights

Padua's two main sights (Basilica of St. Anthony and Scrovegni Chapel) are, respectively, at the southern and northern reaches of downtown. But its atmospheric, cobbled core—with bustling markets and inviting sun- and café-speckled piazzas—is its own ▲▲▲ attraction.

▲▲**MARKET SQUARES**

The stately Palazzo della Ragione provides a dramatic backdrop for Padua's produce market, which fills the surrounding squares—**Piazza delle Erbe and Piazza della Frutta**—each weekday morning and all day Saturday (closed Sun). This market has been renowned for centuries for its selection of fresh herbs, fruits, and vegetables.

Don't miss the indoor market zone on the ground floor of the Palazzo della Ragione, where you'll find butchers, *salumerie* (delicatessens), cheese shops, bakeries, and fishmongers at work. **Piazza dei Signori,** just a block away, is a busy clothing market in the morning and a popular gathering place in the evening.

▲▲▲**SCROVEGNI CHAPEL (CAPPELLA DEGLI SCROVEGNI)**

Wallpapered with Giotto's beautifully preserved cycle of nearly 40 frescoes, the glorious Scrovegni Chapel holds scenes depicting the lives of Jesus and Mary. To protect the paintings from excess humidity, only 25 people are allowed in the chapel at a time. Every 20 minutes, a new group is admitted for a 15-minute video

Scrovegni Chapel

presentation, followed by 20 minutes in the chapel.

After making a name for himself in Assisi by painting frescoes of the life of St. Francis, Giotto di Bondone (c. 1267-1337) painted this entire chapel in 200 working days over two years, from 1303 to 1305. A sign of the Renaissance to come, Giotto placed real people in real scenes, expressing real human emotions. These frescoes were radical for their 3-D nature, lively colors, light sources, and humanism.

Cost and Hours: €14 (also covers Civic Museums). The chapel is open daily 9:00-19:00; special evening visits are available in peak season (go to the Scrovegni website and choose "Giotto Under the Stars").

Reservations: Prepaid reservations are required. Reserve your ticket well in advance at www.cappelladegliscrovegni.it or by calling 049-201-0020. If you opt for the Padova Card (see earlier), make your chapel reservation when you buy the card online.

Rick's Tip: *If you packed* **binoculars,** *bring them along for a better—and more comfortable—view of the* **uppermost frescoes.**

Getting In: The chapel is within the Eremitani museum complex (at Piazza Eremitani 8), which also includes Padua's museums of archaeological, medieval, and modern art. To reach the chapel, enter through the Eremitani building (nearest tram stop: Eremitani), where you'll find the ticket office and a free, mandatory bag check. Be at the chapel doors at least five minutes before your scheduled visit. If you're even a minute late, you'll forfeit your spot.

Visiting the Chapel: At your appointed time, you'll enter an anteroom to watch an instructive 15-minute video (with English subtitles) and to establish humidity levels before continuing into the chapel. The story of Mary and Jesus spirals clockwise around the chapel, from top to bottom.

Although you have only a short visit inside the chapel, it is divine. You're inside a Giotto time capsule, looking back at an artist ahead of his time.

The Scrovegni frescoes break ground by introducing nature—rocks, trees, animals—as a backdrop for religious scenes. Giotto's people, with their voluminous, deeply creased robes, are as sturdy and massive as Greek statues, throwbacks to the Byzantine icon art of the Middle Ages. But these figures exude stage presence. Their gestures are simple but expressive: A head tilted down says dejection, an arm flung out indicates grief, clasped hands indicate hope. Giotto created his figures not just by drawing outlines and filling them in with single colors; he filled the outlines in with subtle patchworks of lighter and darker shades, and in doing so pioneered modern modeling techniques. Giotto's storytelling style is straightforward, and anyone with knowledge of the episodes of Jesus' life can read the chapel like a comic book.

▲▲▲BASILICA OF ST. ANTHONY (BASILICA DI SANT'ANTONIO)
Construction of this impressive Romanesque/Gothic church (with its Byzantine-style domes) started immediately after St. Anthony's death in 1231. As a mark of his universal appeal and importance in the medieval Church, he was sainted within a year of his death. For nearly 800 years, his remains and this glorious church have attracted pilgrims to Padua. A modest dress code is enforced.

Cost and Hours: The basilica and chapel are free and open daily 6:20-19:45 (closes at 18:45 Mon-Fri off-season; chapel closes at lunchtime year-round), Via Orto Botanico 11, www.santantonio.org. The nearest tram stop is Santo.

Visiting the Basilica: Guarding the church is Donatello's life-size equestrian statue of a Venetian general. Though it looks like a thousand other man-on-a-

Padua's Basilica of St. Anthony and Donatello's equestrian statue

horse statues, it was a landmark in Italy's budding Renaissance—the first life-size, secular, equestrian statue cast from bronze in a thousand years.

Inside, gaze through the incense haze to Donatello's glorious crucifix and statues gracing the high altar. Late in his career, the great Florentine sculptor spent more than a decade in Padua.

The gleaming marble masterpiece on the left side of the nave is the tomb of St. Anthony. Pilgrims file slowly through this chapel, touching his tomb or kneeling in prayer. You can skirt around the side of the queue for a closer look at the magnificent 16th-century panels, which show scenes and miracles from St. Anthony's life.

Behind the altar is the Chapel of the Reliquaries. The most prized relic is in the glass case at center stage—Anthony's tongue. When Anthony's remains were exhumed 32 years after his death (in 1263), his body had decayed to dust, but his tongue was found miraculously unspoiled and red in color. How appropriate for the great preacher who, full of the Spirit, couldn't stop talking about God.

Exit out into the cloisters (of the four, you can wander in three).

Sleeping

$$$ Hotel Majestic Toscanelli is old-fashioned, ornate, and conveniently located (RS%, Via dell'Arco 2, www.toscanelli.com). **$$ Hotel Al Fagiano** feels like a modern-art gallery (RS%, Via Antonio Locatelli 45, www.alfagiano.com). The bare-bones **$ Hotel Casa del Pellegrino** is owned by the friars of St. Anthony (Via Melchiorre Cesarotti 21, www.casadelpellegrino.com).

Eating

Colorful **$$ Osteria L'Anfora** serves classic dishes in an informal, fun space (closed Sun, reservations smart for dinner, tel. 049-656-629, Via dei Soncin 13). Bright and youthful **$$$ Enoteca Antonio Ferrari** is a top-end wine bar serving meat and cheese boards (Via Umberto 1). **$ Bar dei Osei** is a sandwich place with some of the best outdoor seats in town (Piazza della Frutta 1). **$ Pollodoro la Gastronomica** is my pick of the takeout delis near the basilica (Via Belludi 34).

If you're here in the early evening, get a **spritz** (an aperitif generally made with Campari, white wine or prosecco, and sparkling water) at a bar on Piazza dei Signori or Piazza della Erbe. Grab a table, become part of the scene, and enjoy a discussion with smart, English-speaking students.

Verona

Romeo and Juliet made Verona a household word. Though these star-crossed lovers were fictional, two real feuding families, the Montecchi and the Cappellos, were the models for Shakespeare's Montagues and Capulets. Fiction aside, Verona's main attractions are its Roman ruins, its pedestrian-only ambience, and its world-class opera festival. If you like Italy but don't need blockbuster sights, this town is a joy.

Day Plan

For a good day in Verona, take my self-guided walk, beginning with a visit to the Roman Arena.

Orientation

The vibrant and enjoyable core of Verona lies along Via Mazzini between Piazza Brà (pronounced "bra") and Piazza Erbe, Verona's market square since Roman times.

Tourist Information: Verona's helpful TI is just off Piazza Brà (open daily, Via degli Alpini 9, tel. 045-806-8680, www.turismoverona.eu). Ask about their weekend walking tours.

Sightseeing Passes: The **Verona Card** covers city transportation and entry to all recommended sights (€20/24 hours, sold at TI and at participating sights, www.turismoverona.eu).

Local Guides: Three enthusiastic Verona guides give private tours of the town and region: **Marina Menegoi** (mobile 328-958-1108, www.marina menegoi.com), **Valeria Biasi** (mobile 348-903-4238, www.aguideinverona.com), and **Franklin Baumgarten** (mobile 347-566-6765, franklin_baumgarten@web.de).

Getting There

Every hour, at least two trains connect Verona with Venice (and Padua). To save money, choose a cheaper regional train (R or RV, 1.5 hours) instead of the slightly faster but more expensive Italo or Frecce express trains.

From Verona's Porta Nuova train station (baggage check available), catch a **bus** to Piazza Brà, the city center (#11, #12, #13, #51, and #52 run Mon-Sat until 20:00; #90, #92, and #98 run after 20:00 and all day Sun; buy ticket from station tobacco shop). **Taxis** to the center of town cost €10-12. The Old Town center is closed to traffic: **Drivers** can park in well-marked lots and garages just outside the center.

Rick's Tip: *From mid-June through early September,* **Verona's opera festival** *brings the city to life, with music fans filling the Roman Arena. Cheap day-of-show tickets are often available at the box office at Via Dietro Anfiteatro 6B (www.arena.it).*

---

❷ Verona Walk

Allow two hours for this walk covering the essential sights in the town core, starting at Piazza Brà and ending at the cathedral.

If you're wondering about the name ❶ **Piazza Brà,** it means "big open space." The broad, marble sidewalk was built by 17th-century Venetians, who made it big and wide so that promenading socialites could see and be seen.

The ❷ **Roman Arena,** dating from the first century AD, looks great in its pink marble (most of it original). Over the centuries, crowds of up to 25,000 spectators have cheered Roman gladiator battles, medieval executions, rock concerts, and modern plays, all taking advantage of the arena's famous acoustics. This is where the popular opera festival is held every summer. Inside, if you climb to the top, you'll enjoy great city views (€10, skip

Verona's Roman Arena on Piazza Brà

combo-ticket with unimpressive Maffei Museum; Tue-Sun 8:30-19:30, Mon from 13:30, closes earlier during opera season).

To the right as you exit the arena, find the ❸ **devotional column** that blessed a marketplace held here in the Middle Ages. A **bronze plaque** in the sidewalk shows the Roman city plan—a town of 20,000 placed strategically in the bend of the Adige River.

With your back to the arena, head down Via Oberdan (bearing left at the fork). Continue a couple of blocks until you see an ancient gate to your right, ❹ **Porta Borsari.** You're standing before the main entrance to Roman Verona; back then, this gate functioned as a tollbooth (*borsari* means purse). Outside the adjacent Caffè Rialto, the stone on the curb is from a tomb: In Roman times, the roads outside the walls were lined with tombstones, because burials were not allowed within the town itself.

Cross under the Roman gate into the ancient city. As you walk down **Corso Porta Borsari,** discover bits of the town's illustrious past—chips of Roman columns, medieval reliefs, fine old facades, and fossils in marble. On the right, you'll pass

the recommended Osteria del Bugiardo, a good place to take a break. Or detour right down Vicolo San Marco in Foro to #7, and you'll find the funky ❺ **Enoteca Oreste.** This historic wine and grappa bar was once the private chapel of the archbishop of Verona.

Continue on Corso Porta Borsari until you hit ❻ **Piazza Erbe,** a bustling market square corralled by pastel buildings. In Roman times, this was a forum. In medieval times, the stone canopy in the center of the square held the scales where merchants measured goods.

At the far end of Piazza Erbe is a market column featuring St. Zeno, the patron of Verona, who looks at the crowds flushing into the city's silly claim to touristic fame: the ❼ **House of Juliet** (100 yards down Via Cappello to #23, on the left).

The tiny, admittedly romantic courtyard is a spectacle: Tourists from all over the world pose on the balcony (free, gates open roughly 8:30-19:30; "museum" not worth the entry fee). The red mailbox is for love letters to Juliet (they're reviewed by a Juliet Club, which awards the author of the sweetest letter a free vacation to Verona).

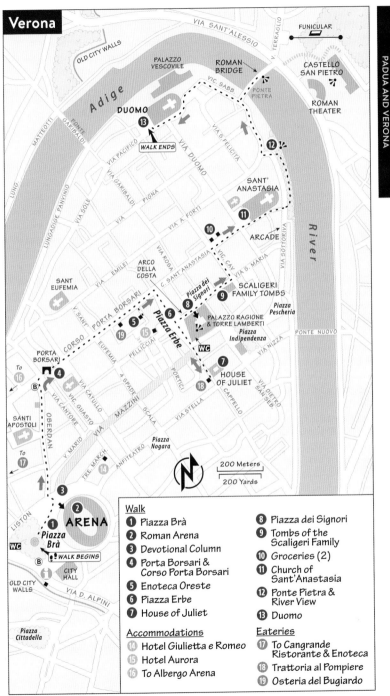

Verona

VIA SANT'ALESSIO

FUNICULAR

OLD CITY WALLS

PALAZZO
VESCOVILE

ROMAN
BRIDGE

CASTELLO
SAN PIETRO

A d i g e

DUOMO

PONTE
PIETRA

ROMAN
THEATER

WALK ENDS

SANT'
ANASTASIA

R i v e r

ARCADE

ARCO
DELLA
COSTA

SANT
EUFEMIA

Piazza dei
Signori

SCALIGERI
FAMILY TOMBS

Piazza
Pescheria

PONTE NUOVO

PALAZZO RAGIONE
& TORRE LAMBERTI

Piazza
Indipendenza

PORTA
BORSARI

To
16

PORTA BORSARI

WC

HOUSE
OF JULIET

SANTI
APOSTOLI

To
17

Piazza
Nogara

N

200 Meters
200 Yards

LISTON

ARENA

Piazza
Brà

WC

WALK BEGINS

CITY
HALL

OLD CITY
WALLS

VIA D. ALPINI

Piazza
Cittadella

Walk
1. Piazza Brà
2. Roman Arena
3. Devotional Column
4. Porta Borsari &
   Corso Porta Borsari
5. Enoteca Oreste
6. Piazza Erbe
7. House of Juliet
8. Piazza dei Signori
9. Tombs of the
   Scaligeri Family
10. Groceries (2)
11. Church of
    Sant'Anastasia
12. Ponte Pietra &
    River View
13. Duomo

Accommodations
14. Hotel Giulietta e Romeo
15. Hotel Aurora
16. To Albergo Arena

Eateries
17. To Cangrande
    Ristorante & Enoteca
18. Trattoria al Pompiere
19. Osteria del Bugiardo

Return to Piazza Erbe, and head right on Via della Costa to ❽ **Piazza dei Signori** ("Lords' Square"). Locals call the square Piazza Dante for the statue of the Italian poet **Dante Alighieri** that dominates it. Dante was expelled from Florence when that city sided with the pope, who didn't appreciate Dante's writing. Verona and its ruling Scaligeri family were at odds with the pope and granted Dante asylum.

At Dante's two o'clock is the 12th-century Romanesque **Palazzo della Ragione.** Peek into its courtyard to see the only surviving Renaissance staircase in Verona. Within the palazzo you can climb the 13th-century **Torre dei Lamberti** for a grand city view (€8, Mon-Fri 10:00-18:00, Sat-Sun 11:00-19:00).

Continuing downhill, you'll find the 14th-century Gothic ❾ **tombs of the Scaligeri family,** behind original, wrought-iron protective cages. The Scaligeri were to Verona what the Medici family was to Florence. They changed the law so that they could be buried in town and built their tombs atop pillars so they would be looked up to even in death.

At the next corner, turn left on Vicolo Cavalletto, then turn right along Corso Sant'Anastasia. For a tasty diversion, pop into ❿ **two classic grocery stores:** Salumeria Caliari (at #33, closed Sun afternoon) and Salumeria Albertini (#41).

Straight ahead is the big, unfinished brick facade of the ⓫ **Church of Sant'Anastasia** (€3, open daily except closed for Mass Sun morning). It's worth stepping inside to see the delightful way this region's medieval churches were painted. Don't miss Pisanello's fresco of *St. George and the Princess of Trebizond* (1438).

Leaving the church, walk along the right side to Via Sottoriva and turn left. You'll reach a small riverfront area with stone benches and a ⓬ **Ponte Pietra and river view.** The white stones of the footbridge are from the original Roman bridge that stood here. After the bridge was bombed in World War II, the Veronese fished the

marble chunks out of the river to rebuild it. From here, you can see across the river to an ancient Roman theater, built into the hillside. Way above the theater (behind the cypress trees) is a fortress, Castello San Pietro.

Continue up the river toward the tall white spire of the ⓭ **Duomo** (€3, open daily except closed for Mass Sun morning). Started in the 12th century, this church was built over a period of several hundred years. Inside, in the last chapel on the left, is Titian's 16th-century *Assumption of the Virgin.* Mary calmly rides a cloud—direction up—to the shock and bewilderment of the crowd below.

Adjacent to the church is a **baptistery** with clean Romanesque lines, a hanging 14th-century crucifix, and a fine marble font. On the left side of the Duomo is a peaceful Romanesque **cloister** (*chiostro*) with exposed mosaics from a fifth-century Christian church.

Sleeping

The stylish **$$$ Hotel Giulietta e Romeo** is on a quiet street behind the Roman Arena (Vicolo Tre Marchetti 3, tel. 045-800-3554, www.hotelgr.it). **$$ Hotel Aurora** has a welcoming terrace with wonderful piazza views (Piazzetta XIV Novembre 2, tel. 045-594-717, www.hotelaurora.biz). **$$ Albergo Arena** is basic and a good value (Stradone Porta Palio 2, tel. 045-803-2440, www.albergoarena.it).

Eating

$$$$ Cangrande Ristorante & Enoteca offers fine dining a block off Piazza Brà (Via Dietro Liston 19D). **$$$ Trattoria al Pompiere** is a favorite of local foodies (closed Sun, Vicolo Regina d'Ungheria 5, reservations recommended, tel. 045-803-0537). The hip **$$ Osteria del Bugiardo** offers a buffet of little sandwiches, plates of top-quality cheeses, and good pasta (Corso Porta Borsari 17a).

BEST OF THE REST

Milan

For every church in Rome, there's a bank in Milan. Italy's second city and the capital of the Lombardy region, Milan is a hard-working, time-is-money center of fashion, industry, banking, TV, publishing, and conventions.

The city has several noteworthy sights: the Duomo and the Galleria Vittorio Emanuele II arcade, La Scala Opera House, Michelangelo's last pietà sculpture (in Sforza Castle), and Leonardo da Vinci's *The Last Supper.*

Many tourists come to Italy for the past. But Milan is today's Italy. In this city of refined tastes, window displays are gorgeous and even the cheese comes gift-wrapped. Yet, thankfully, Milan is no more expensive for tourists than any other Italian city.

For those with a round-trip flight into Milan: I'd recommend starting your journey softly by going first to Lake Como (one-hour train ride to Varenna). Then, with jet lag under control, dive into Milan.

Day Plan

On a short visit, tour the Duomo, hit any art you like (reserve ahead to see *The Last Supper*), browse elegant shops and the Galleria Vittorio Emanuele II, and try to see an opera. To maximize your time in Milan, use the Metro to get around.

A practical way to make the most of a quick visit is to use my free 🎧 Duomo neighborhood **audio tour**—see page 28.

Orientation

Most sights are within a 15-minute walk of the cathedral (Duomo), which is a straight eight-minute Metro ride from the Centrale train station.

Tourist Information: Milan's TI is at the La Scala end of the Galleria Vittorio Emanuele II (open daily, tel. 02-884-55555, www.turismo.milano.it).

Local Guides: These guides know their city's history: **Lorenza Scorti** (€160/3 hours, mobile 347-735-1346, lorenza. scorti@libero.it), **Sara Cerri** (€195/3 hours, mobile 380-433-3019, www.walkingtour milan.it), and **Valeria Andreoli** (highlights tour-€60/hour, €180/half-day, mobile 338-301-2220, www.bellamilanotours.com).

Getting There

By Air: Most international flights land at **Malpensa Airport** (MXP; www.milanair ports.com). Ride the **Malpensa Express train** into the city (€13, www.malpensa express.it): Take the Cadorna line to reach downtown (2/hour, 40 minutes) or the Centrale line to Milano Centrale train station (2/hour, 50 minutes). Airport **shuttle buses** cost about €8 for the one-hour trip downtown (www.malpensashuttle.it, www.terravision.eu, or www.autostradale. it). **Taxis** charge a fixed rate of €95.

Most European flights land at **Linate Airport** (LIN; www.milanairports.com), which is connected to downtown Milan by **shuttle bus** (€5, 35 minutes, www.air portbusexpress.it), **taxi** (about €30), and **public bus** #73 (€1.50, about 50 minutes).

Some budget airlines use Bergamo Airport (BGY; www.milanbergamoairport. it), linked to Milano Centrale train station by bus (€7, 5/hour, 1 hour): Autostradale (www.airportbusexpress.it), Terravision (www.terravision.eu), and Orio Shuttle (www.orioshuttle.com).

By Train: Common connections are **Venice** (2/hour, 2.5 hours), **Florence** (Trenitalia: hourly, 2 hours; Italo: 2/hour, 2 hours), **Rome** (Trenitalia: 1-3/hour, 3.5 hours; Italo: 11/day nonstop, 3 hours, more with stops), **Cinque Terre/Monterosso al Mare** (8/day, 3 hours), **Varenna** on Lake Como (nearly hourly, 1 hour), and **Naples** (Trenitalia: 2/hour, 4-5 hours, more with change in Rome; Italo: 11/day, 4-5 hours).

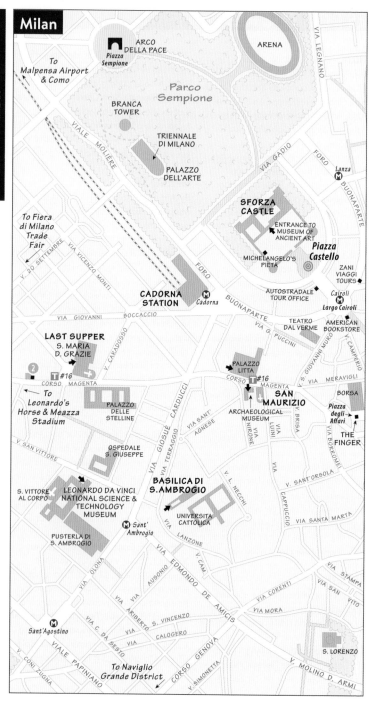

Milan

To Malpensa Airport & Como

ARCO DELLA PACE

Piazza Sempione

ARENA

VIA LEGNANO

Parco Sempione

BRANCA TOWER

TRIENNALE DI MILANO

PALAZZO DELL'ARTE

VIALE MOLIERE

VIA GADIO

FORO BUONAPARTE

Lanza

To Fiera di Milano Trade Fair

V. 20 SETTEMBRE

VIA VICENZO MONTI

V. GIOVANNI MONTI

FORO BUONAPARTE

SFORZA CASTLE

ENTRANCE TO MUSEUM OF ANCIENT ART

MICHELANGELO'S PIETA

Piazza Castello

ZANI VIAGGI TOURS

CADORNA STATION

Cadorna

AUTOSTRADALE TOUR OFFICE

Cairoli

Largo Cairoli

VIA GIOVANNI BOCCACCIO

VIA CARADOSSO

VIA G. PUCCINI

TEATRO DAL VERME

AMERICAN BOOKSTORE

V. CAMPERIO

LAST SUPPER

S. MARIA D. GRAZIE

#16

CORSO MAGENTA

PALAZZO LITTA

CORSO MAGENTA

#16

SAN MAURIZIO

V.S. GIOVANNI MURO

VIA MERAVIGLI

BORSA

To Leonardo's Horse & Meazza Stadium

PALAZZO DELLE STELLINE

ARCHAEOLOGICAL MUSEUM

VIA NIRONE

VIA LUINI

V. BRISA

Piazza degli Affari

THE FINGER

VIA BORROMEI

V. SAN VITTORE

OSPEDALE S. GIUSEPPE

VIA GIOSUE CARDUCCI

VIA SANT'AGNESE

VIA TERRAGGIO

VIA SANT'ORSOLA

S. VITTORE AL CORPO

LEONARDO DA VINCI NATIONAL SCIENCE & TECHNOLOGY MUSEUM

Sant' Ambrogio

BASILICA DI S.AMBROGIO

UNIVERSITA CATTOLICA

V. L. NECCHI

CAPPUCCIO

VIA SANTA MARTA

PUSTERLA DI S. AMBROGIO

VIA LANZONE

V. CAM.

V. OLONA

Sant'Agostino

VIA C. DA SESTO

VIA ARIBERTO

VIA

S. VINCENZO

VIA CALOGERO

AUSONIO

EDMONDO DE AMICIS

VIA CORENTI

VIA MORA

VIA STAMPA

VIA SAN VITO

V. CONI ZUGNA

VIALE PAPINIANO

To Naviglio Grande District

CORSO GENOVA

V. SIMONETTA

S. LORENZO

V. MOLINO D. ARMI

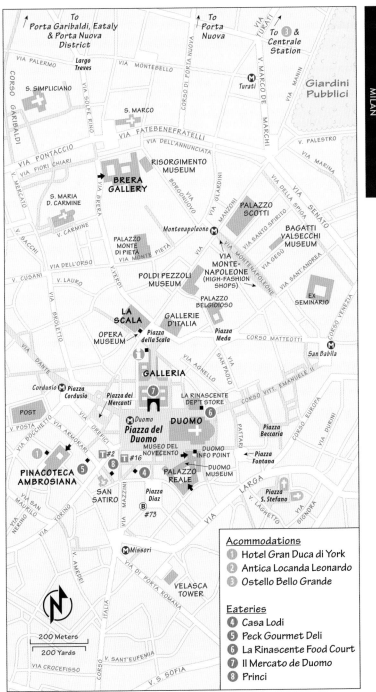

To Porta Garibaldi, Eataly & Porta Nuova District

To Porta Nuova

To ③ & Centrale Station

VIA PALERMO

Largo Treves

VIA MONTEBELLO

CORSO GARIBALDI

S. SIMPLICIANO

VIA SOLFERINO

VIA MARCO DE MARCHI

Turati Ⓜ

Giardini Pubblici

S. MARCO

VIA FATEBENEFRATELLI

V. PALESTRO

VIA DELL'ANNUNCIATA

VIA PONTACCIO

VIA FIORI CHIARI

CORSO DI PORTA NUOVA

VIA MARINA

RISORGIMENTO MUSEUM

BRERA GALLERY

VIA BORGONUOVO

VIA DELLA SPIGA

VIA DELLA SENATO

S. MARIA D. CARMINE

V. MERCATO

VIA BRERA

VIA GIARDINI

VIA MANZONI

PALAZZO SCOTTI

V. SACCHI

Montenapoleone Ⓜ

VIA SANTO SPIRITO

BAGATTI VALSECCHI MUSEUM

PALAZZO MONTE DI PIETA

VIA MONTE PIETA

VIA MONTENAPOLEONE

VIA GESÙ

VIA SANT'ANDREA

VIA DELL'ORSO

V. CUSANI

V. LAURO

V. VERDI

POLDI PEZZOLI MUSEUM

VIA MONTE-NAPOLEONE (HIGH-FASHION SHOPS)

EX SEMINARIO

PALAZZO BELGIOIOSO

CORSO VENEZIA

LA SCALA

GALLERIE D'ITALIA

Piazza Meda

CORSO MATTEOTTI

San Babila Ⓜ

OPERA MUSEUM

Piazza della Scala

VIA AGNELLO

VIA SAN PAOLO

VIA DANTE

GALLERIA

CORSO VITT. EMANUELE II

Cordusio Ⓜ Piazza Cordusio

⑦

Piazza dei Mercanti

LA RINASCENTE DEP'T STORE

⑥

CORSO EUROPA

POST

V. POSTA

VIA BOCCHETTO

VIA ARMORARI

VIA OREFICI

Ⓜ Duomo

Piazza del Duomo

DUOMO

Piazza Beccaria

VIA DURINI

VIA POSTA

①

#2

#16

MUSEO DEL NOVECENTO

DUOMO INFO POINT

Piazza Fontana

PINACOTECA AMBROSIANA

⑤

⑧

④

PALAZZO REALE

DUOMO MUSEUM

PATTARI

LARGA

VIA SAN MAURILIO

SAN SATIRO

Piazza Diaz

Ⓑ #73

Piazza S. Stefano

V. LAGHETTO

VIA SIGNORA

VIA SAN NERINO

VIA TORINO

VIA MAZZINI

Ⓜ Missori

VIA AMEDEI

VIA DI PORTA ROMANA

VELASCA TOWER

Ⓝ

200 Meters

200 Yards

VIA CROCEFISSO

ITALIA

CORSO

V. SANT'EUFEMIA

V. S. SOFIA

Acommodations
① Hotel Gran Duca di York
② Antica Locanda Leonardo
③ Ostello Bello Grande

Eateries
④ Casa Lodi
⑤ Peck Gourmet Deli
⑥ La Rinascente Food Court
⑦ Il Mercato de Duomo
⑧ Princi

Most trains arrive at the **Milano Centrale** station; to get downtown, follow signs for Metro yellow line 3 (direction: San Donato), go four stops to the Duomo stop, surface, and you'll be facing the cathedral. If you arrive at **Milano Cadorna** (served by the Malpensa Express from the airport), take Metro red line 1 to the Duomo. **Milano Porta Garibaldi** (used by high-speed trains from some international destinations and a few domestic trains) is on Metro green line 2, two stops from Milano Centrale, and on purple line 5.

By Car: Use the park-and-ride lots at suburban Metro stations (see www.atm.it).

Public Transit in Milan: A **single ticket,** valid for 90 minutes, can be used for one ride, including transfers, on all forms of transport (€2; www.atm.it). Tickets must be run through the machines at Metro turnstiles when you enter and again when you leave the station.

Sights

Milan's core sights—the Duomo, Duomo Museum, and Galleria Vittorio Emanuele II—cluster within easy walking distance. Also in the Duomo area are the Piazza della Scala and La Scala Opera House.

The city's other main sights—*The Last Supper,* Basilica di Sant'Ambrogio, Sforza Castle, and Brera Art Gallery—are scattered farther afield. It's easiest to reach them by public transportation.

▲▲▲DUOMO (CATHEDRAL)

The city's centerpiece is the third-largest church in Europe (after St. Peter's Basilica in Rome and Sevilla's cathedral). At 525 by 300 feet, the place is immense, with more than 2,000 statues inside (and another thousand outside) and 52 100-foot-tall pillars representing the liturgical calendar. The church was built to hold 40,000 worshippers.

Cost and Hours: Cathedral-€3, museum-€3, rooftops by elevator-€14. The archaeological area is free with any ticket. The best combo-ticket is the €17 Duomo Pass Lift, which includes the cathedral, rooftop terraces by elevator, archaeological area, and Duomo Museum. Cathedral open daily 8:00-19:00, archaeological area and rooftop from 9:00; Duomo Museum Thu-Tue 10:00-18:00, closed Wed; last entry one hour before closing. Recommended audioguide-€6.

Milan's Piazza del Duomo is home to the Galleria (left) and the lacy Duomo.

Information: Church tel. 02-7202-3375, museum tel. 02-3616-9351, www.duomomilano.it.

Buying Tickets: Timed-entry tickets are sold online. On-site, there are two ticket booths: the big ticket center with info office (on the south side of the cathedral) and at the Duomo Museum.

Rick's Tip: *Avoid long ticket lines by buying your tickets online; if buying on-site, the* museum often has shorter lines *than the cathedral. You can* avoid a long church security line *by doing the rooftop first and descending from there directly into the church.*

Visiting the Duomo: A visit here has several elements. First, take in the overwhelming **exterior** from various angles, admiring its remarkable bulk and prickly spires topped with statues. The style, Flamboyant Gothic, means "flame-like," and the church seems to flicker toward heaven with flames of pink-white marble.

Inside, the church is lit by glorious stained glass, some from the 15th century. At the far end, beneath the dome, is the dramatic Baroque altar where Napoleon crowned himself king of Italy in 1805. In the south (right) transept you'll find a unique, grotesque 16th-century statue of St. Bartolomeo, a first-century martyr skinned alive by the Romans.

The **archaeological area** beneath the church is a maze of ruined brick foundations of earlier churches. The artifacts date from the time of the Edict of Milan (AD 313), when Emperor Constantine made Christianity legal in the Roman Empire.

The ▲▲ **Duomo Museum** fills in the story of Milan's cathedral and lets you see its original art and treasures up close.

Strolling the cathedral's ▲▲ **rooftop terraces** is the most memorable part of a Duomo visit. You'll loop around through a fancy forest of spires with great views of the city, the square, and—on clear days—the crisp and jagged Alps to the north.

▲▲**GALLERIA VITTORIO EMANUELE II**
This breathtaking glass-domed arcade, next to Piazza del Duomo, is a symbol of Milan. The iron-and-glass shopping mall (built during the age of Eiffel and the heady days of Italian unification) showcased a new, modern era. It was the first building in town to have electric lighting, and since its inception it's been an elegant and popular meeting place.

At the venerable **Bar Camparino** (at the Galleria's Piazza del Duomo entry), turn an expensive cup of coffee or glass of Campari into a good value by enjoying some of Europe's best people-watching (Tue-Sun 7:30-20:00, closed Mon and Aug).

▲**LA SCALA OPERA HOUSE AND MUSEUM**
Milan's famous Teatro alla Scala opened in 1778 with an opera by Antonio Salieri (Mozart's wannabe rival). Today, opera buffs can get a glimpse of the theater and tour the adjacent museum's extensive collection. The collection features Verdi's top hat, Rossini's eyeglasses, Toscanini's baton, Fettuccini's pesto, original scores, diorama stage sets, busts, portraits, and death masks of great composers and musicians. But the main reason to visit the museum is the opportunity to peek into the theater. Take in the ornate red-velvet seats, white-and-gold trim, huge stage and orchestra pit, and massive chandelier made of Bohemian crystal.

Cost and Hours: €9, daily 9:00-17:30, Piazza della Scala, tel. 02-8879-7473, www.teatroallascala.org.

Performances: The show goes on at the opera house every month except August. Online tickets go on sale two months before performances (www.teatroallascala.org). On performance days, 140 low-price, restricted-view tickets are offered at the box office. Show up at 13:00 with an official ID to put your name on a list.

La Scala Opera House

▲▲BRERA ART GALLERY (PINACOTECA DI BRERA)

Milan's top collection of Italian paintings (13th-20th century) was established in 1809 to house Napoleon's looted art. Highlights are Antonio Canova's nude *Napoleon with Tinkerbell,* Andrea Mantegna's iconic foreshortened Christ, Raphael's *Marriage of the Virgin,* and Caravaggio's gritty yet intimate *Supper at Emmaus.*

Cost and Hours: €12, free first Sun of month; Tue-Sun 8:30-19:15, closed Mon, last entry 45 minutes before closing; audioguide-€5 (useful, but museum has excellent English descriptions), free lockers, Via Brera 28, Metro: Lanza or Montenapoleone, tel. 02-722-631, www.pinacotecabrera.org.

▲▲PINACOTECA AMBROSIANA

This oldest museum in Milan, inaugurated in 1618, features paintings by Botticelli, Caravaggio, and Titian—and, most important, a huge-scale sketch by Raphael and a rare oil painting by Leonardo da Vinci. The 17th-century **library** *(biblioteca)* hosts a revolving display of Leonardo sketches and notes, from the precious Codex Atlanticus, giving us a peek into his amazing mind.

Cost and Hours: €15; Pinacoteca open Tue-Sun 10:00-18:00, closed Mon; Biblioteca open Mon-Fri 9:00-17:00, closed Sat-Sun; last entry one hour before closing, audioguide-€3, near Piazza del Duomo at Piazza Pio XI 2, Metro: Duomo or Cordusio, www.ambrosiana.eu.

▲▲LEONARDO DA VINCI'S *THE LAST SUPPER (L'ULTIMA CENA/CENACOLO VINCIANO)*

Decorating the former dining hall of the Church of Santa Maria delle Grazie, this remarkable fresco by Leonardo da Vinci is one of the ultimate masterpieces of the Renaissance.

Hired by Milan's leading family, the Sforzas, Leonardo worked on the project from about 1494 until 1498. This gift was essentially a bribe to the Dominican monks so that the Sforzas could place their family tomb in the church. Ultimately, the French drove the Sforzas out of Milan, they were never buried here, and the Dominicans got a great fresco for nothing.

Deterioration began within six years of *The Last Supper's* completion because Leonardo painted on the wall in layers, as he would on a canvas, instead of applying pigment to wet plaster in the usual fresco technique. A 21-year restoration project peeled away 500 years of touch-ups, leaving Leonardo's masterpiece faint but vibrant.

Leonardo da Vinci, The Last Supper

Leonardo captures the psychological drama as the Lord says, "One of you will betray me," and the apostles huddle in stressed-out groups of three, wondering, "Lord, is it I?" Some are scandalized. Others want more information. Simon (on the far right) gestures as if to ask a question that has no answer. In this agitated atmosphere, Judas (fourth from left, with his face in shadow) clutches his 30 pieces of silver and looks pretty guilty.

The perspective is mathematically correct, with Jesus' head as the vanishing point where the converging sight lines meet. In fact, restorers found a tiny nail hole in Jesus' left eye, which anchored the strings Leonardo used to establish these lines.

Before stepping out, from the back of the room look one last time at Leonardo's masterpiece and imagine this room filled with 60 monks immersed in devotion.

Cost and Hours: €15 (includes €2 reservation fee), four time slots include a tour and cost an extra €3.50 (9:30 and 15:30 in English; 10:00 and 16:00 in Italian); open Tue-Sun 8:15-18:45 (last entry), closed Mon,; Piazza Santa Maria delle Grazie 2; tel. 02-9280-0360, http://cenacolovinciano.org.

Reservations: Tickets for each calendar month go on sale about three months ahead. For peak season tickets, be ready to book the moment they're released (Milan time). To book **online,** go to http://cenacolovinciano.vivaticket.it. If your time slot includes a tour, you must add the €3.50 tour supplement when you check out (you won't be able to buy a ticket without it). If you book by **phone,** you'll have more days and time slots to choose from (no same-day tickets, tel. 02-9280-0360, from the US dial 011-39-02-9280-0360, office open Mon-Sat 8:00-18:30, closed Sun).

Getting There: The church is a seven-minute walk from Metro: Conciliazione. Or take tram #16 from the Duomo (direction: San Siro or Piazzale Segesta).

Rick's Tip: *If you* **can't get a reservation** *for* The Last Supper, *consider joining a walking tour that includes a* **guided visit to Leonardo's masterpiece.** *Veditalia (www.veditalia.com) and City Wonders (www.citywonders.com) offer €65-80 tours (usually 3 hours) that also cover other top sights. Ideally book a week or more in advance.*

▲▲SFORZA CASTLE (CASTELLO SFORZESCO)

The castle of Milan features a sprawling museum and a chance to see Michelangelo's final, unfinished pietà.

Cost and Hours: €10; museum open Tue-Sun 9:00-17:30, closed Mon; castle grounds open daily 7:00-19:30; Metro: Cairoli or Lanza, tel. 02-8846-3700, www.milanocastello.it.

Visiting the Museum: The castle houses an array of exhibits, but I'd concentrate on the Michelangelo pietà and the Museum of Ancient Art.

Michelangelo died while still working on the so-called "Rondanini pietà," his fourth sculptural representation of a dead Christ with a sorrowful Virgin Mary. While unfinished and seemingly a mishmash of corrections and reworks, it's a thought-provoking work by a genius at nearly 90 years of age.

In the Museum of Ancient Art you'll find an extensive collection of interesting medieval armor, furniture, early Lombard art, and tapestries, as well as a ballroom painted by Leonardo and his followers.

Sleeping

$$$$ Hotel Gran Duca di York, three blocks from the Duomo, is modern and bright (Via Moneta 1, www.ducadiyork.com). **$$$ Antica Locanda Leonardo,** just down the street from *The Last Supper,* has a romantic, Old World vibe (Corso Magenta 78, www.anticalocandaleonardo.com). **¢ Ostello Bello Grande,** near the train station, is a hostel with hipster flair and some private rooms (Via Lepetit 33, www.ostellobello.com).

Eating

$$ Casa Lodi celebrates local ingredients (closed midday and for dinner on Mon, Via Cappellari 3). **$$ Peck Gourmet Deli** serves delectable food for a superb though pricey picnic dinner (Via Spadari 9). The seventh floor of **La Rinascente** department store, alongside the Duomo, has a crowded and upscale **$$$** food court. **$$ Il Mercato del Duomo** has four floors of eateries (daily 11:00-22:00, Piazza del Duomo 1). Crowded **$ Princi** is popular for its focaccia and luscious pastries (Via Speronari 6).

BEST OF THE REST

Varenna

At Lake Como (Lago di Como)—lined with elegant 19th-century villas, crowned by snowcapped mountains, and busy with boats—it seems like half the travelers you'll meet have tossed their itineraries into the lake and are actually relaxing. The village of Varenna, with its romantic promenade, tiny harbor, and narrow stepped lanes, is just the right place to savor a lakeside cappuccino or *aperitivo.* There's wonderfully little to do here.

Day Plan

Spend time exploring Varenna, then take a ferry to admire the scenery and lakeside villas, or to poke around in the picturesque town of Bellagio.

Orientation

Some say Lake Como is shaped like a man. The head is the north end, Varenna is the left hip (to the east), Menaggio (across the lake) is the right hip, and Bellagio is the crotch—or, more poetically, Punta Spartivento ("Point That Divides the Wind"). Across the lake, the farthest high ridges mark the border of Switzerland.

Tourist Information: The TI is near the **main square** (closed Mon, Via IV Novembre 7, tel. 0341-830-367, www.varennaturismo.com). The Tivano travel agency in the **train station** also operates as a TI and sells train tickets (daily, www.tivanotours.com).

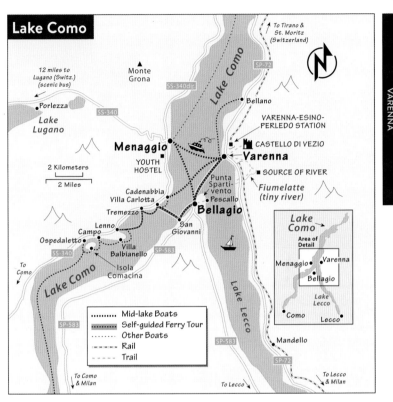

Lake Como

Getting There

By **train,** you'll reach Lake Como via Milan. At Milano Centrale station, catch a train (at :20 past most hours; trip takes 1 hour) heading for Sondrio or Tirano and get off at Varenna-Esino-Perledo. For a less convenient, slower, but more scenic trip by **boat,** take the train from Milan to the town of Como (2/hour, 45 minutes), walk 10 minutes to the dock, and catch either the speedy hydrofoil or the leisurely *battello* (boats leave about every 2 hours).

Varenna is small, and pretty much everything is within a 15-minute walk. A **taxi** from the train station costs about €10. **Drivers** should park in the multilevel lot at the south end of town.

Sights and Activities

PASSERELLA

A generation ago, Varenna built this elegant lakeside promenade, which connects the ferry dock with the Old Town center. Arcing past aristocratic 19th-century villas and gardens, it's romantic. After dark, it's adorned with caryatid lovers pressing silently against each other in the shadows.

▲HIKE TO VEZIO CASTLE (CASTELLO DI VEZIO)

A steep and stony trail leads to Varenna's ruined hilltop castle, in the peaceful hamlet of Vezio. Hike 20 steep minutes up Via per Vezio, the small road near Hotel Montecodeno. Arriving in Vezio, follow *castello* signs to a bar that serves as the castle's ticket desk. Follow the little loop trail on the lake side of the castle for vistas down on Varenna's rooftops, and climb

Varenna on Lake Como

the 60 steps of the castle tower to earn 360 degrees of Lake Como panoramas. The castle hosts low-key falconry shows, usually around 15:00—but check the website or call in the morning for times.

Cost and Hours: €4, Mon-Fri 10:00-18:00, Sat-Sun until 19:00, June-Aug stays open one hour later, March and Oct closes one hour earlier, closed Nov-Feb and in bad weather, www.castellodivezio.it, mobile 333-448-5975.

GARDENS

Two separate manicured lakeside gardens sit next door to each other just a short distance from Varenna's main square. The first are the small but lush terraces of Villa Cipressi. Just beyond are the more interesting grounds of Villa Monastero, which also admits visitors into the former residence of the De Marchi family, now a museum filled with overly ornate furnishings from the late 1800s. It offers the handiest look inside one of the old villas that line the lakeshore.

Cost and Hours: Villa Cipressi—€6, €11 combo-ticket includes Villa Monastero gardens but not museum; daily 8:00-sunset, closed Dec-April, www.hotelvillacipressi.it. Villa Monastero—

gardens-€6, gardens and museum-€9; gardens open daily 9:30-19:00, closed Nov-Feb; museum open Fri-Sun 9:30-19:00, closed Mon-Thu except open daily in Aug; www.villamonastero.eu.

SWIMMING

There are three spots to swim in Varenna: the free little beach behind the Hotel Royal Victoria off Piazza San Giorgio, the central lakefront area by Nilus Bar, and the lido (best-equipped for swimmers). Just north of the ferry dock, the lido has showers, bathrooms, a restaurant, a bar, and lounge chairs and umbrellas for rent (€3 entry).

BOAT TOURS (OR RENT YOUR OWN)

The best simple day out on Lake Como is to take the **mid-lake ferry** *(battello naveta)* on its entire 50-minute Varenna-Bellagio-Villa Carlotta-Tremezzo-Lenno route (€9.20 without stops, or buy the €15 one-day pass and make it hop-on, hop-off). On the return trip, hop off at any sights that interest you: the beautiful Villa del Balbianello and its gardens (in Lenno, www.visitfai.it/villadelbalbianello), the impressive museum and gardens of Villa Carlotta (www.villacarlotta.it), and/or Bellagio (see next).

Taxi Boat Varenna organizes hour-long central-lake tours (€30/person), plus a 2.5-hour version that adds a stop at Villa Balbianello (€60/person, price includes villa tour, www.taxiboatvarenna.com). **Nautica Varenna** allows you to be your own skipper (motorboats from €70/hour, up to 6 people; kayaks €10/hour; at harbor in front of Nilus Bar, www.varenna boatrental.com). **Varenna Rent a Boat** is a more serious boat-rental shop just beyond the ferry dock (from €80/hour, www.varennarentaboat.com).

BELLAGIO SIDE TRIP

A classy combination of tidiness and Old World elegance, Bellagio is easily reached by boat from Varenna. If you don't mind that "tramp in a palace" feeling, it's a fine place to surround yourself with posh travelers. Heavy curtains between the harborfront arcades create welcome shade and keep visitors and their poodles from sweating.

Boats go about every 30-45 minutes between Varenna and Bellagio (€4.60/hop, cash only, 15-minute ride, daily approximately 7:00-22:30). Because boats are frequent and the schedule is hard to read, I just show up, buy a ticket for the next boat, and wait. When you depart Bellagio, be sure you're at the right dock: One serves slow boats and hydrofoils, and the other is for faster car ferries. Ask when you buy your ticket (boat info: tel. 031-579-211, www.navigazionelaghi.it).

The Bellagio TI, at its slow boat/hydrofoil dock, has free brochures for several walking tours, varying from one to three hours. Nearby, Bellagio Water Limousines offers boat tours (www.bel-lagiowaterlimousines.com). A 15-minute walk away, on Pescallo Bay, Bellagio Water Sports offers kayaking tours (www.bellagiowatersports.com).

For wine tasting, step into the vaulted stone cellar of the funky **Enoteca Cava Turacciolo** to taste three regional wines with a sampling of cheeses, meats, and breads (€19 for Rick Steves readers,

open long hours but closed Wed, Salita Genazzini 3).

For dining in the Old Town, **$$ Trattoria San Giacomo** is a high-energy place with traditional North Italian cuisine (closed Tue, Salita Serbelloni 45). After your meal, climb to the top of town to **Gelateria del Borgo** for the best gelato (Via Garibaldi 46).

Picnickers can stock up at Butti Macelleria e Salumeria (closed Mon, Via Garibaldi 42). Good picnic spots are the benches along the waterfront in town and lining the promenade south of town.

An excellent viewpoint (that also works for a picnic) is Punta Spartivento, a park a few minutes' walk north of town. Its Renoir atmosphere comes complete with the inviting **$$$ La Punta Ristorante,** a little harbor, and a chance to sit on a park bench and gaze north past the end of the lake to the Swiss Alps.

Sleeping

$$$$ Villa Cipressi is a sprawling, centuries-old lakeside mansion (RS%, www.hotelvillacipressi.it); the romantic **$$$ Albergo Milano** has extravagant views (www.varenna.net); and **$$$ Albergo del Sole** rents eight simple, comfortable rooms right on the town square (www.solevarenna.altervista.org).

Eating

With a terrace overlooking the town and lake, **$$$$ Ristorante la Vista** is hard to beat (closed Tue, reservations required, tel. 0341-830-298, Via XX Settembre 35). **$$$ Ristorante il Cavatappi** is a classy little place with only seven tables (closed Wed and Oct-March, reserve for dinner, tel. 0341-815-349, Via XX Settembre 10). Two simple eateries beautifully situated along the waterfront in Varenna's old section are **Bar il Molo** and **Nilus Bar.** Varenna's two little grocery stores (at Via IV Novembre 2 and Via Venini 6) have all you need for a tasty picnic. **Gelateria Riva,** on the harborfront, prepares its gelato fresh every day.

The
Cinque Terre

Along a six-mile stretch of the Riviera lies the Cinque Terre (CHINK-weh TAY-reh), gently carving a good life out of difficult terrain. With a traffic-free charm—a happy result of their natural isolation—these five (cinque) towns are the rugged alternative to the glitzy resorts nearby. With sun, sea, sand (well, pebbles), and wine, this is pure, unadulterated Italy.

Each addictively photogenic village fills a ravine with a lazy hive of human activity—calloused locals and sunburned travelers enjoying a unique mix of culture and nature. Enjoy swimming, hiking, and evening romance in one of God's great gifts to tourism. While the Cinque Terre is now discovered and can get jam-packed, I've never seen happier, more relaxed tourists. Most of the crowds are day-trippers, so make a point to get the most out of those cool, relaxed, and quiet hours early in the day and in the evening.

I cover the five towns in order from north to south—from Monterosso to Riomaggiore. Choose a home base according to just how cut off you'd like to be from the outer world: resorty Monterosso, cover-girl Vernazza, hilltop Corniglia, photogenic Manarola, or amiable Riomaggiore. Avoid visiting in winter, when tall, crashing waves batter the charm out of the Cinque Terre.

THE CINQUE TERRE IN 2 DAYS

This string of five villages dotting the Italian Riviera makes an idyllic escape from the obligatory museums of turnstile Italy. The ideal stay is two or three full days; my recommended minimum is two nights and an uninterrupted day. It's easiest to arrive and depart by train. Don't bring a car to the Cinque Terre; you won't need it.

Within the Cinque Terre, you can connect the towns in three ways: by train, boat, or foot. Trains are cheap, boats are more scenic, and hiking lets you enjoy more pasta. Consider supplementing the often frustratingly late trains with the sometimes more convenient boats.

Study your options, and piece together your best visit, mixing hiking, swimming, trains, boat rides, and a search for the best focaccia.

You could spend one day hiking from town to town (or take a boat or train partway, or as the return trip). For the best light, coolest temperatures, and fewest crowds,

The Cinque Terre

To A-12 Autostrada (Brugnato Exit)
To Genua
A-12
SP-1
SP-566
To A-12 Autostrada (Carrodano Exit)
2 Kilometers
Beverino
To La Spezia & Pisa
To Sestri Levante, Santa Margherita, Bonassola & Genoa
2 Miles
Pignone
SP-1
SP-370
Levanto
To Monterosso's Old Town
SP-38
Pian di Barca
To New Town (Fegina)
SP-1
Monterosso al Mare
SANDY BEACH
SP-63
To La Spezia & A-12
Vernazza
Punta Mesco
Corniglia
SP-51
Volastra
CORNIGLIA STATION
Manarola
VIA LITORANEA
To La Spezia & A-12
Ligurian Sea
Riomaggiore
SP-370
To Porto Venere

start your hike early in the morning (or late afternoon). Cool off at a beach. Spend a second day visiting any towns you've yet to see, comparing main streets, beaches, and gelato. And fit in another hike, if you like.

In the evenings, linger at a restaurant, enjoy live music at a low-key club, stroll any of the towns, or take a glass of your favorite beverage out to the breakwater to watch the sun slip into the Mediterranean.

Getting Around the Cinque Terre

Within the Cinque Terre, you can connect towns by train, boat, or foot. Trains are the cheapest, fastest, and most frequent option. In calm weather, boats connect the towns nearly as frequently—and more scenically.

By Train: The five towns are just a few minutes apart by train. You must buy a new **individual ticket** for every train ride (€4), and tickets are valid only on the day of purchase. You can buy tickets and check schedules online (www.trenitalia.

com), at train-station windows or ticket machines, or at Cinque Terre park desks. The €16 **Cinque Terre Treno Card** pays for itself if you take four rides in one day, but its value comes more from convenience than economy (https://card. parconazionale5terre.it).

In peak season, trains connecting the five towns generally run two to three times hourly in each direction, but less frequently after about 20:00. Note that some trains do not stop at all five towns. Check schedules in advance (shops, hotels, and restaurants often post the current schedule). Trains from Levanto, Monterosso, Riomaggiore, or La Spezia sometimes skip lesser stations, so confirm that the train will stop at the town you need. (Train numbers starting with 21 or 24 generally stop at all five towns.) Northbound trains (using the tracks closest to the water) are going to Levanto, Genova, or Sestri Levante; southbound trains are headed for La Spezia. Know your train's number and final destination.

THE CINQUE TERRE AT A GLANCE

▲▲**Monterosso al Mare** Resorty, flat, and spread out, with a charming old town, a modern new town, and the Cinque Terre's best beaches, swimming, and nightlife. See page 124.

▲▲▲**Vernazza** The region's gem, crowned with a ruined castle above and a lively harborfront cradling a natural harbor below. See page 135.

▲**Corniglia** Quiet hilltop village with cooler temperatures, fewer tourists, and a tradition of fine wines. See page 146.

▲▲**Manarola** Mellow, hiking-focused waterfront village wrapped in vineyards and dotted with picturesque shops and cliff-climbing houses. See page 149.

▲▲**Riomaggiore** The most workaday of the five villages, with nightlife, too. See page 153.

By Boat: From Easter through October, a daily boat service connects Monterosso, Vernazza, Manarola, Riomaggiore, Porto Venere, and beyond. Though they can be very crowded, these boats provide a scenic way to get from town to town (operated by 5 Terre-Golfo dei Poeti, tel. 0187-732-987, www.navigazionegolfodeipoeti. it). Because tourists disembark onto little more than a plank, even just a small chop can cancel some or all of the stops.

The ticket price depends on the length of the boat ride (€7-18, €27 all-day pass, €35 adds Porto Venere). Buy tickets at the little stands at each town's harbor. Boats depart about hourly; schedules are posted online and at docks, harbor bars, Cinque Terre park offices, and hotels.

---

*Rick's Tip: To escape the crowds—or for a scenic splurge—**hire a captain** to ferry you between towns on a **private boat**. Split the cost among a few fellow travelers, and you have an affordable water taxi. Captains offer their services at the harbors in Monterosso, Vernazza, Manarola, and Riomaggiore.*

By Shuttle Bus: ATC shuttle buses (which locals call *pulmino*) connect each Cinque Terre town with its closest parking lot and various points in the hills (but they don't connect the five towns to each other). Buy tickets and get bus schedules at park info offices or TIs, or check times posted at bus stops (also online at www.atcesercizio.it). As you board, it's smart to tell the driver where you want to go. Some shuttles go beyond the parking lots and high into the hills—often terminating at the town's sanctuary church. To soak in the scenery, you can ride up and hike down.

Helpful Hints

Book in Advance: It's essential to reserve rooms well in advance for May, June, September, October, all summer weekends, and holidays (including Easter and April 25). Many accommodations in the Cinque Terre (especially in Vernazza) are *affittacamere,* or private rooms for rent. You get a key and come and go as you like, rarely seeing your landlord. Plan on paying cash. Some places have strict cancellation policies.

Pickpocket Alert: The Cinque Terre can be notoriously crowded and pickpockets (often groups of teens, frequently dressed as tourists), aggressively and expertly work the most congested areas. Be on guard, especially in train stations, on platforms, and on trains—particularly when getting on or off with a crush of people.

Money: You'll find ATMs and banks throughout the region.

Markets: Market days perk up the Cinque Terre from around 8:00 to 13:00 on Tuesday in Vernazza and on Thursday in Monterosso.

Booking Services: Arbaspàa, based in Manarola, sets up wine tastings, cooking classes, fishing trips, and more (www. arbaspaa.com). **Cinque Terre Riviera,** based in Vernazza, books rooms and apartments throughout the region, Vernazza opera tickets, cooking classes, and more (www.cinqueterreriviera. com). **BeautifuLiguria,** run by Anna Merulla, offers various excursions (www. beautifuliguria.com).

Local Guides: These guides are knowledgeable, a delight to be with, and charge from €125/half-day and €210/day: **Andrea Bordigoni** (mobile 393-133-9409, bordigo@inwind.it) and **Marco Brizzi** (mobile 328-694-2847, marco_brizzi@ yahoo.it).

Baggage Storage and Delivery: You can pay to store bags at or near the train stations in Monterosso, Vernazza, and Riomaggiore. To transfer luggage from the station to your accommodations, call ahead and arrange with **Roberto Pecunia** (mobile 370-375-7972).

HIKING THE CINQUE TERRE

The five Cinque Terre towns are connected by a main coastal trail and a web of trails higher up. The main coastal trail has four sections—two that are open (Monterosso to Vernazza, and Vernazza to Corniglia) and two that are closed due to trail conditions (Corniglia to Manarola, and Manarola to Riomaggiore—the famed "Via dell'Amore"). Also closed is the alternate Riomaggiore-Manarola trail (via "La Beccara"). Visitors hiking on the main coastal trail must buy a trail pass (see below).

Navigation: Trails are marked with red-and-white paint, white arrows, and some signs (*sentiero* means trail). The main coastal trail is variously indicated as "SVA," "the Blue Trail," or #592. Maps aren't necessary for the basic coastal hikes. But for the more challenging routes up high, pick up a good hiking map (about €5, sold everywhere).

Hiking Conditions: In general, trails are narrow, steep, rocky, and come with lots of challenging steps. I get many emails from readers who say the trails were tougher than they'd expected. The rocks and metal grates can be slippery in the rain. Don't venture up on these rocky cliffs without sun protection, water, and proper shoes (no flip-flops).

When to Go: The coastal trail can be extremely crowded and very hot at mid-day. For the best light, coolest temperatures, and fewer crowds, start your hike early (by 8:00) or late (16:00 or 17:00). Before setting out for an evening hike, find out when the sun will set, and leave plenty of time to arrive at your destination before then; there's no lighting on the trails.

Rick's Tip: *ATC* **shuttle buses** *can make hiking easier, connecting coastal villages to trailheads higher up.* **Locals know all the options**—*and shuttle bus schedules—so ask around. Be aware that shuttles heading into the high country only run in summer, and just once or twice a day.*

Cinque Terre Park Cards

The Cinque Terre—villages and all—is a national park. Each town's train station has a Cinque Terre national park infor-

The trail views are worth the effort.

mation office, which generally also serves as an all-purpose town TI and gift shop. They can answer questions about trails (including conditions and closures), shuttle bus schedules, and so on. Or, check the park's website, www.parconazionale5 terre.it, and the blog CinqueTerreInsider. com, written by American expat Amy Inman—it has up-to-date practicalities for visitors to this always-in-flux region.

Visitors using the main coastal trail must buy a park card. (Cards are not needed to hike on higher trails.) Cards can be purchased on the park website, above, or at train stations, TIs, and trailheads, and are good for 24 or 48 hours after validation. Some area hotels sell discounted park cards to guests.

The **Cinque Terre Trekking Card** costs €7.50 for one day of hiking or €14.50 for two days (covers trails, free use of WCs, park Wi-Fi, and ATC shuttle buses, but not trains).

The **Cinque Terre Treno Card** covers what the Trekking Card does, but also includes local trains connecting all Cinque Terre towns, plus Levanto and La Spezia (€16/24 hours, €29/48 hours, validate card at train station by punching it in the machine). Even if you're not planning to hike, this card can be worth it just to save you time on buying train tickets.

Top Three Hikes

These three hikes each give the quintessential Cinque Terre hiking experience. The first two are part of the main coastal trail (and require the national park card); the third takes you much higher (and is free).

▲▲▲ **Vernazza-Monterosso** (2 hours, 2 miles): The scenic up-and-down-a-lot trek from Vernazza to Monterosso is both challenging and rewarding. The trail is narrow, steep, and crumbly in spots, with a lot of steps but easy to follow. The views just out of Vernazza, looking back at the town, are spectacular. From there you'll gradually ascend to 550 feet, passing some scenic waterfalls populated by croaking

frogs. As you approach Monterosso, you'll descend steeply through vineyards—on very deep, knee-testing stairs—and eventually follow a rivulet to the sea. The last stretch is along a pleasant, paved pathway clinging to the cliff. You'll pop out right at Monterosso's refreshing old-town beach.

▲▲▲ **Corniglia-Vernazza** (1.5 hours, 2 miles): The hike from Corniglia to Vernazza—the wildest and greenest section of the coast—is very rewarding but very hilly. From the Corniglia train station, zigzag up to the town (via the steep stairs, the longer road, or the shuttle bus). From Corniglia, you'll reach the trailhead on the main road, past Villa Cecio. You'll hike through vineyards toward Vernazza. After about 10 minutes, you'll see a faded sign to Guvano beach, far beneath you (formerly a nude beach—now closed). The scenic trail continues through lots of fragrant and flowery vegetation into Vernazza. If you need a break before reaching Vernazza, stop at Bar la Torre, with a strip of amazingly scenic and delightfully shady tables perched high above the town.

▲▲ **Manarola-Corniglia via Volastra** (2.5 hours, 4 miles): This challenging hike from Manarola leads up to the village of Volastra, then north through high-altitude vineyard terraces, and steeply down through a forest to Corniglia. You can shave the two steepest miles off this route by taking the ATC shuttle bus from Manarola up to Volastra (about hourly, 15-minute trip).

If you'd rather hike to Volastra, you have two options: The national park's official route (trail #506) cuts up through the valley. Locals have cleared a more scenic but rougher alternate route that begins with the vineyard hike on my self-guided walk for Manarola (page 150); partway along this walk, where you reach the wooden religious scenes scampering up the hillside, take a sharp right and walk uphill, following signs for *Panoramico Volastra (Corniglia)*. While steeper than the official route, this trail follows the ridge at the top of the vineyard, with wonderful sea views.

Either way, in Volastra (where the shuttle bus drops off), look for *Corniglia* signs. From the front door of the church, directly across the piazza, find the trailhead (marked by an iron cross) for trail #586 to Case Pianca.

Here begins one of the region's finest hikes, tightroping along narrow trails tucked between vineyard terraces, with spectacular bird's-eye views over the entire Cinque Terre. You'll cut up and down the terraces a bit—just keep following the red-and-white markings and arrows. High above Corniglia, you'll reach a fork, where you turn left to proceed downhill on trail #587 to Corniglia.

Sanctuary Trails

Each of the five towns has its own sanctuary (with a chapel or church dedicated to the Virgin Mary), hovering in the hills a mile or two above town, and accessible by a long, steep hike (quiet and uncrowded).

Villagers feel deeply connected to these spiritual retreats, where they remember lost relatives and feel part of a timeless community. A network of "sanctuary trails" (no park card required) crisscrosses the hills above the main coastal route. There's no single path, but with a good map you can link up these moderately difficult trails.

In most towns, the shuttle bus can take you from the town center to the sanctuary—you could ride up and hike down. This works particularly well from Manarola and Vernazza. Or you can ride both ways (50 minutes round-trip, covered by one ticket).

MONTEROSSO AL MARE

Monterosso al Mare—the only Cinque Terre town with some flat land—has two parts: a new town (called Fegina) with a parking lot, train station, and TI; and an old town (Centro Storico), which cradles Old World charm in its small, crooked lanes. In the old town, you'll find hole-in-the-wall shops, rustic pastel townscapes, and a new generation of creative business owners eager to keep visitors happy. A handy pedestrian tunnel connects the old with the new.

This is a resort town with a few cars and lots of hotels, rentable beach umbrellas, and crowds. Strolling the waterfront promenade, you can pick out each of the Cinque Terre towns decorating the coast. After dark, they sparkle.

Orientation

Tourist Information: The TI, called Proloco Monterosso, is on the street below the train station (daily 9:00-18:30, longer hours in summer, shorter hours off-season, baggage storage, exit station and go left a few doors, tel. 0187-817-506, www.prolocomonterosso.it). Upstairs in the station is a Cinque Terre park info desk and a ticket office near platform 1 (usually daily 8:00-20:00, shorter hours off-season).

Arrival in Monterosso: Trains arrive in the new town. To reach most of my recommended hotels in the new town, turn right from the station. To get to the old town, turn left from the station—it's a scenic, flat 10-minute stroll.

Taxis usually wait outside the train station, or you can call one (€10 from station to old town, mobile 335-616-5842, 335-616-5845, or 335-628-0933). ATC **shuttle buses** also go to the old town and are cheaper, but only run about once an hour.

For **drivers,** Monterosso is 30 minutes off the freeway (exit: Carrodano-Levanto). About three miles above Monterosso, at an intersection, you must choose either *Monterosso Centro Storico* (old town) or *Monterosso Fegina* (new town and beachfront parking). You can't drive directly between the new town and old center. Parking is easy (except July-Aug and weekends in June) in the new town in the huge beachfront guarded lot. In the old town, find the Loreto parking garage on Via Roma, from which it's a 10-minute downhill walk to the main square.

Helpful Hints

Baggage Storage: The **TI** will store bags (€6/day—confirm closing time).

Laundry: For full-service, same-day laundry in the new town, try **Wash and Dry Lavarapido.** They'll pick up at your hotel, or you can drop it at their shop. Ask your hotelier to arrange the details (daily 9:00-19:00, Via Molinelli 17, mobile 339-484-0940, Lucia and Ivano). In the old town, head to **Luètu Lavanderia,** uphill on Via Roma and across from the post office (daily 8:00-20:00, tel. 328-286-1908).

Monterosso Walks

These self-guided walks will introduce you to Monterosso. The first one, focusing on the mostly level town center, takes about 30 minutes. For the second one, you'll summit the adjacent hill—allow an hour or so.

➊ Monterosso Harbor and Town Walk

• *Hike out from the dock in the old town and stand atop the concrete breakwater. (If you're arriving by boat, you'll disembark here.)*

Breakwater: From this point you can survey Monterosso's old town (straight ahead) and new town (stretching to the left, with train station and parking lot). Looking to the right, you can see all *cinque* of the *terre* from one spot: Vernazza, Corniglia (above the shore), Manarola, and a few buildings of Riomaggiore beyond that.

The partial breakwater is designed to save the beach from washing away. While old-timers remember a vast beach, their grandchildren truck in sand each spring to give tourists something to bask on. (The Nazis liked the Cinque Terre, too—find two of their bomb-hardened bunkers embedded in the bluff.)

The fancy four-star Hotel Porto Roca (the pink building high on the hill, on the far right of the harbor) marks the trail to Vernazza. High above, you see an example of the costly roads built in the 1980s to connect the Cinque Terre towns with the freeway over the hills.

Monterosso al Mare

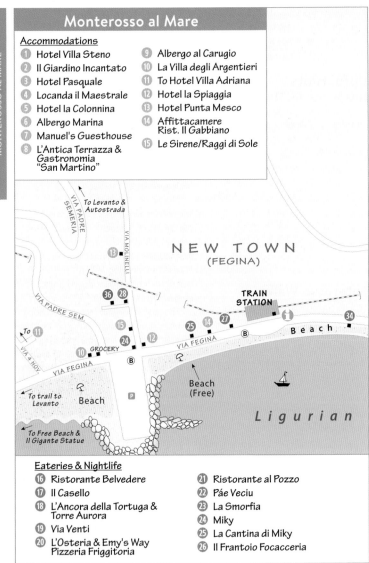

Monterosso al Mare

Accommodations

1. Hotel Villa Steno
2. Il Giardino Incantato
3. Hotel Pasquale
4. Locanda il Maestrale
5. Hotel la Colonnina
6. Albergo Marina
7. Manuel's Guesthouse
8. L'Antica Terrazza & Gastronomia "San Martino"
9. Albergo al Carugio
10. La Villa degli Argentieri
11. To Hotel Villa Adriana
12. Hotel la Spiaggia
13. Hotel Punta Mesco
14. Affittacamere Rist. Il Gabbiano
15. Le Sirene/Raggi di Sole

Eateries & Nightlife

16. Ristorante Belvedere
17. Il Casello
18. L'Ancora della Tortuga & Torre Aurora
19. Via Venti
20. L'Osteria & Emy's Way Pizzeria Friggitoria
21. Ristorante al Pozzo
22. Páe Veciu
23. La Smorfia
24. Miky
25. La Cantina di Miky
26. Il Frantoio Focacceria

The two prominent capes (Punta di Montenero to the right, and Punta Mesco to the left) define the Cinque Terre region. The closer Punta Mesco is part of a protected marine sanctuary and home to a rare sea grass that provides an ideal home for fish eggs. Buoys keep fishing boats away. The cape was once a quarry,

providing employment to locals who chipped out the stones used to build the local towns (the greenish stones making up part of the breakwater are from there).

On the far end of the new town, marking the best free beach around, you can just see the statue named *Il Gigante* (hard to spot because it blends in with the gray

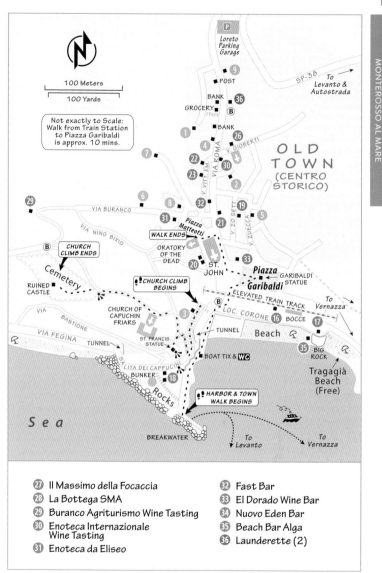

rock). It's 45 feet tall and once held a trident. Made of reinforced concrete, it dates from the early 20th century, when it supported a dancing terrace for a *fin de siècle* villa. A violent storm left the giant holding nothing but memories.

• *From the breakwater, walk toward the old town and under the train tracks. Then venture right into the square and find the statue of a dandy holding what looks like a box cutter (near the big playground).*

Piazza Garibaldi: The statue honors Giuseppe Garibaldi, the dashing firebrand revolutionary who, in the 1860s, helped unite the people of Italy into a modern nation. Facing Garibaldi, with your back

Church of St. John the Baptist

taller than it really is. Note the lacy, stone rose window above the entrance—considered one of the finest in northern Italy.

Step inside for more Ligurian Gothic: original marble columns and capitals with pointed arches to match. The octagonal baptismal font (in the back of the church) was carved from Carrara marble in 1359. Imagine the job getting that from the quarries, about 40 miles away. The fine Baroque altar was crafted with various marbles from around Italy in the 1700s. The church itself dates from 1307—the proud inscription on the left-middle column reads "MilloCCCVII."

• *Leaving the church, turn left and go to church again.*

Oratory of the Dead (Oratorio dei Neri): During the Counter-Reformation, the Catholic Church offset the rising influence of the Lutherans by creating brotherhoods of good works. These religious Rotary clubs were called "confraternities." Monterosso had two, nicknamed White and Black. This building is the oratory of the Black group, whose mission—as the macabre interior indicates—was to arrange for funerals and take care of widows, orphans, the shipwrecked, and the souls of those who ignore the request for a €1 donation. It dates from the 16th century, and membership has passed from father to son for generations. Notice the fine, carved pews (c. 1700) just inside the door, and the haunted-house chandeliers. Look up at the ceiling to find the symbol of the confraternity: a skull-and-crossbones and an hourglass...death awaits us all.

• *On that cheery note, you can end your walking tour here to enjoy strolling, shopping, gelato-licking, a day at the beach...or all of the above. But if you're up for a hike, read on.*

to the sea, you'll see (on your right) the orange City Hall. You'll also see A Ca' du Sciensa restaurant, which has historic town photos inside and upstairs; you're welcome to pop in for a look.

Just under the bell tower (with your back to the sea, it's on your left), a set of covered arcades facing the sea is where the old-timers hang out. The crenellated bell tower marks the church.

• *Go to church.*

Church of St. John the Baptist (Chiesa di San Giovanni Battista): First, walk along the right side the church. Near the second side door, find the high-water mark *(altezza massima)* from an October 1966 flood—which also famously devastated Florence. Nearby, a second (higher) plaque commemorates a 2011 flood that swept through Monterosso and Vernazza, taking the lives of four villagers.

Now hook left, around the church—and appreciate its black-and-white-striped main facade. With white marble from Carrara and green marble from Punta Mesco, the church is typical of the region's Gothic style. The church's marble stripes get narrower the higher they go, creating the illusion that the church is

◗ Capuchin Church and Climb

The hill that separates the old town from the new rewards anyone who climbs up with a peaceful church, a cemetery in the clouds, and a panoramic view.

St. Francis keeps an eye on Monterosso from above.

• *From the old town's beachfront, find the brick steps squeezed between Hotel Pasquale and its restaurant, and start climbing. The lane is signed* Salita dei Cappuccini *(nicknamed* Zii di Frati*), or...*

Switchbacks of the Friars: Follow the yellow brick road (OK, it's orange...). Partway up, detour left to the terrace above the seaside castle at a statue of St. Francis and a wolf taking in a grand view. Enjoy an opportunity to see all five of the Cinque Terre towns. Then backtrack 20 yards to the switchback and continue uphill.

• *When you reach a gate marked* Convento e Chiesa Cappuccini, *you have arrived at the...*

Church of the Capuchin Friars: The former monastery is now manned by a single caretaker friar. (If you meet Father Renato, take a moment to speak with him—he's a joyful soul.) Before stepping inside, notice the church's striped Romanesque facade. It's all fake. Tap it—no marble, just cheap 18th-century stucco. Go inside and sit in the rear pew. The high altarpiece painting of St. Francis can be rolled up on special days to reveal a statue of Mary behind it.

The fine painting of the **Crucifixion (on the left)** recalls how, when Jesus died, the earth went dark. Notice the eclipsed sun in the painting, just to the right of the cross. Do the electric candles work? Pick one up, pray for peace, and plug it in. (Leave an offering, or unplug it and put it back.)

• *Leave and turn left through another gate to hike 100 yards uphill to the cemetery filling the ruined castle. Reaching the cemetery's gate, look back and enjoy the view over the town.*

Cemetery in the Ruined Castle: In the Dark Ages, the village huddled behind this castle. You're looking at the oldest part of Monterosso, tucked behind the hill, out of view of 13th-century pirates.

Respectfully explore the cemetery. On the headstones, *Q.R.P.* is *Qui Riposa in Pace* (a.k.a. *R.I.P.*). Climb to the very summit—the castle's keep, or place of last refuge. Priests are buried in a line of graves closest to the sea, but facing inland, looking toward the town's holy sanctuary high on the hillside (its triangular steeple just peeking above the trees). Each Cinque Terre town has a lofty sanctuary, dedicated to Mary and dear to the village hearts.

• *Your tour is over—any trail leads you back into town.*

Experiences
Beaches
Monterosso's **new town** has easily the Cinque Terre's best—and most crowded—

beach (immediately in front of the train station). Most of the beach is private, where (at Stella Marina) you'll pay €20 to rent two chairs and an umbrella for the day (prices get soft in the afternoon). Light lunches are served by beach cafés to sunbathers at their lounge chairs. Various outfits rent kayaks and stand-up paddleboards (look for signs at the west end of the beach). If there are no umbrellas on a stretch of beach, it's public (free). A free beach is at the far west end, near the Gigante statue.

The **old town** also has a predominantly private beach; rent umbrellas, chairs, kayaks, and paddleboats from Beach Bar Alga, which is also a scenic spot for a drink. Tucked just beyond the private beach—under the Il Casello restaurant at the east end of town—is the free public beach called Tragagià, which is gravelly and generally less crowded (showers).

Wine Tasting

Buranco Agriturismo welcomes visitors to tastings on their expansive terrace with views over the vineyards. You'll taste some of their wines plus grappa (firewater) and *limoncino,* while snacking on bruschetta, olives, and the like. Call or email ahead (€20-30/person, tastings usually daily 12:00-18:00, follow Via Buranco uphill to path, 10 minutes above town, mobile 349-434-8046, www.burancocinqueterre.it, info@buranco.it).

Enoteca Internazionale is a good place in town to sample local wines. Mario is knowledgeable and serves five wines for €20 (his bruschetta makes a fine light meal as you're sipping, open daily until late, Via Roma 62, tel. 0187-817-278).

Boat Rides

In addition to the regularly scheduled big boats (see page 121), you can hire your own captain for transfers to other towns or for a lazy sightseeing cruise. **Stefano** has two six-person boats: the *Matilde* and the *Babaah* (about €100/hour, mobile

333-821-2007, www.matildenavigazione. com). **Diego** offers half-day, daylong, and sunset excursions for up to seven on his cushy boat (group tours–€70, daily 10:30-13:30 & 17:30-20:30, best to email or call to confirm and reserve; mobile 339-233-9297, www.cinqueterreboat.com). **Sea Breeze Boat Tours** arranges day and *aperitivo* sunset tours, and will shuttle you to any of the coastal towns (€85-140/person, mobile 328-824-6889 or 338-809-9278, www.seabreezeboattours.com).

Nightlife

Enoteca da Eliseo, my favorite wine bar in town, comes with operatic ambience. Taste wine by the glass (*bicchiere*) or select a bottle, then enjoy the wine, a few included nibbles, and views of the village action. They also stock more than a hundred varieties of *grappa* (Wed-Mon 14:00-23:30, closed Tue, Piazza Matteotti 3, a block inland behind church, tel. 0187-817-308).

Fast Bar is the best bar in town for young travelers and night owls. Customers mix travel tales with big, cold beers, and the crowd (and the rock 'n' roll) gets noisier as the night rolls on (cheap *panini,* salads, and other light meals usually served until midnight, open 9:30-late, in the old town at Via Roma 13).

La Cantina di Miky, in the new town just beyond the train station, is a trendy bar-restaurant with an extensive cocktail and *grappa* menu. Try the fun "five villages" wine tasting or top-end Italian microbrews (Thu-Tue until late, closed Wed, Via Fegina 90, tel. 0187-802-525).

El Dorado Wine Bar is the old-town nighttime hangout, offering music, drinks, and people-watching (Piazza Garibaldi 22, daily 10:00-2:00 in the morning, tel. 331-475-9611).

Beach Bars: In the new town, try **Nuovo Eden Bar,** overlooking the beach by the big rock (drinks come with a light snack, good ice cream). In the old town, **Beach Bar Alga** has an island ambience (all outside, daily until 20:00).

Sleeping

Rooms in Monterosso are a better value than similar rooms in crowded Vernazza, and the proprietors seem more genuine and welcoming.

In the Old Town

$$$$ Hotel Villa Steno is lovingly managed and features great view balconies, panoramic gardens, and a roof terrace with sun beds. Of their 16 rooms, 14 have view balconies (RS%, family rooms, air-con, hearty buffet breakfast, elevator, laundry service, ask about pay parking when you reserve, hike up to their panoramic terrace, closed Nov-March, Via Roma 109, tel. 0187-817-028 or 0187-818-336, www.villasteno.com, steno@pasini.com). It's a 15-minute climb (or €10 taxi ride) from the train station to the top of the old town. My readers get a free Cinque Terre info packet and a glass of local wine at check in—ask for it.

$$$$ Il Giardino Incantato ("The Enchanted Garden") is a charming, comfortable four-room B&B with impressive attention to detail in a tastefully renovated 16th-century Ligurian home in the heart of the old town. Sip their homemade *limoncino* at *aperitivo* time, and have breakfast under lemon trees in the delightful hidden garden (air-con, free minibar and tea-and-coffee service, laundry service, Via Mazzini 18, tel. 0187-818-315, mobile 333-264-9252, www.ilgiardinoincantato.net, giardino_incantato@libero.it).

$$$$ Hotel Pasquale is modern and comfortable with 15 seaview rooms. It's just a few steps from the beach, boat dock, and tunnel to the new town. While there is some train noise, the soundtrack is mostly a lullaby of waves (RS%, family room, air-con, elevator, laundry service, closed Nov-March, Via Fegina 4, tel. 0187-817-550 or 0187-817-477, www.hotelpasquale.it, pasquale@pasini.com).

$$$ Locanda il Maestrale rents six stylish rooms in a sophisticated and peaceful little inn. Although renovated with modern comforts, it retains its centuries-old character under frescoed ceilings. The peaceful sun terrace overlooking the old town and Via Roma action is a delight. Guests enjoy complimentary drinks and snacks each afternoon (air-con, Via Roma 37, tel. 0187-817-013, mobile 338-4530-531, www.locandamaestrale.net, maestrale@monterossonet.com).

$$$ Hotel la Colonnina has 22 big rooms, generous and meticulously cared-for public spaces, a cozy garden, and an inviting shared seaview terrace with sun beds. It's buried in the town's fragrant and sleepy back streets (family rooms, all but one room has a private terrace, cash preferred but cards accepted, air-con, fridges, elevator, a block inland from main square at Via Zuecca 6, tel. 0187-817-439, www.lacolonninacinqueterre.it, info@lacolonninacinqueterre.it).

$$$ Albergo Marina has 23 pleasant rooms and a garden with lemon trees. They serve a filling breakfast buffet and host a happy hour most days on the terrace (RS%, family rooms, elevator, air-con, fridges, free kayak and snorkel equipment, Via Buranco 40, tel. 0187-817-613, www.hotelmarina5terre.com, marina@hotelmarina5terre.com).

$$$ Manuel's Guesthouse, perched high above the town among terraces, is a garden getaway with six big, artfully decorated rooms and a grand view. After climbing the killer stairs from the town center, their killer terrace is hard to leave—especially after a few drinks (cash only, air-con, up about 100 steps behind church—you can ask them to carry your bags up the hill, Via San Martino 39, mobile 333-439-0809, www.manuelsguesthouse.com, manuelsguesthouse@libero.it).

$$ L'Antica Terrazza rents four tight, classy rooms right in town. With a pretty terrace overlooking the pedestrian street, it's a good deal (single room with private bath down the hall, air-con, Vicolo San

Martino 1, mobile 347-132-6213, www.anti caterrazza.com, post@anticaterrazza.com).

$ Albergo al Carugio has nine practical rooms in a big apartment-style building with a small patio at the top of the old town. It's quiet, comfy, and a fine budget value; one room has a private terrace (no breakfast, air-con, fridges, Via Roma 100, tel. 0187-817-453, www.alcarugio.it, info@ alcarugio.it).

In the New Town

$$$$ La Villa degli Argentieri offers 11 spacious rooms, many with balconies, from a choice position at the quiet end of the new town's beachfront street. The inviting rooftop terrace with sunbeds has panoramic views (air-con, elevator, Via Fegina 120, tel. 0187-818-963, www.lavilla degliargentieri.it, info@lavilladegli argentieri.it).

$$$$ Hotel Villa Adriana is big, con-temporary, and bright, with a peaceful gar-den, a pool, free parking, and a no-stress style. They rent 55 sterile rooms—some with terraces and/or sea views—ask for one when you reserve (family rooms, air-con, refrigerators, elevator, free loaner bikes, affordable dinners, Via IV Novem-bre 23, tel. 0187-818-109, www.villaadriana. info, info@villaadriana.info).

$$$$ Hotel la Spiaggia, facing the beach, has 19 rooms (half with sea views) and a quiet garden retreat (cash only, air-con, elevator, free parking—reserve in advance, Via Lungomare 96, tel. 0187-817-567, www.laspiaggiahotel5terre.com, laspiaggiahotel@gmail.com, Maria). They also rent four pricey, ultra-mod rooms on the seafront promenade.

$$$ Hotel Punta Mesco is a tidy, well-run little haven renting 17 quiet, casual rooms at a good price. Most rooms have small terraces backed up to the building next door (family room, air-con, parking, Via Molinelli 35, tel. 0187-817-495, www.hotel puntamesco.it, info@hotelpuntamesco.it).

$$ Affittacamere Ristorante il Gab-biano, a touristy restaurant on the beach-front road, rents five basic, dated, but affordable rooms upstairs. Three face the sea (two with small balconies); two have terraces overlooking a garden. Check in at the restaurant (big family rooms, cash only, no breakfast, air-con, Via Fegina 84, tel. 0187-817-578, www.affittacamere ristorante-ilgabbiano.com, lella-v71@ hotmail.it).

$ Le Sirene/Raggi di Sole, with nine simple rooms in two humble buildings, is a decent budget choice in this pricey town. It's run from a hole-in-the-wall reception desk a block from the station. I'd request the Le Sirene building, which has no train noise (RS%, family rooms, fans, Via Molinelli 1A, mobile 331-788-1088 or 329-595-1063, www.sirenerooms.com, sirene rooms@gmail.com).

Eating
With a Sea View

$$ Ristorante Belvedere, big and sprawl-ing, serves good-value meals indoors or outdoors on the harborfront. Their huge €49 *anfora belvedere*—mixed seafood stew dumped dramatically at the table into your bowl—feeds four. Their *misto mare* plate (2-person minimum, €16/person), a fishy treat, nearly makes an entire meal (Wed-Mon 12:00-14:30 & 18:00-22:00, closed Tue, on the harbor in the old town, tel. 0187-817-033).

$$ Il Casello offers outdoor terrace seating on a little bluff overlooking the old town beach when the weather's nice. It's a pleasant spot for pasta, seafood, or a drink (daily 12:00-22:00, mobile 333-492-7629).

$$$ L'Ancora della Tortuga is a top option in Monterosso for seaview ele-gance, with gorgeous outdoor seat-ing high on a bluff and a white-table-cloth-and-candles interior fit for an admiral. The food and service can be three-star, but the setting is five-star. Consider their €40 tasting *menu* (Tue-Sun 12:30-15:30 & 18:30-21:30, closed Mon and when stormy; at the tip of the point between the old and new towns—just

Cinque Terre Cuisine

Hanging out at a seaview restaurant while sampling local specialties could become one of your favorite Cinque Terre memories. For more on Italian food, see the "Eating" section of the Practicalities chapter.

The key staple is **anchovies** (*acciughe;* ah-CHOO-gay)—ideally served the day they're caught. If you've always hated anchovies, try them fresh here. They're prepared in a dizzying variety of ways: marinated, salted, drenched in lemon juice, butterflied and deep-fried (sometimes with a tasty garlic/vinegar sauce called *giada*), and so on. ***Tegame alla vernazzana*** is the most typical main course in Vernazza: a layered, casserole-like dish of whole anchovies, potatoes, tomatoes, white wine, oil, and herbs.

Seafood is plentiful. You'll often see ***muscoli ripieni*** (stuffed mussels) on menus. And, while **antipasto** means cheese and salami in Tuscany, here you'll get ***antipasti frutti di mare*** (or simply *antipasti misti*): a plate of mixed "fruits of the sea." For two diners, splitting one of these and a pasta dish can be plenty.

This region is the birthplace of **pesto.** You'll see it on gnocchi or on pasta that's either *trenette* (ruffled on one side) or *trofie* (short, dense twists).

Pansotti are ravioli with ricotta and a mixture of greens, often served with a walnut sauce (*salsa di noci*).

Focaccia—pillowy, flat, salty, olive-oily bread—also originates here. Focaccia comes plain or with onions, sage, or olives. Bakeries sell it in rounds or slices by weight (a portion is about 100 grams, or *un etto*).

Farinata, a humble flatbread snack sold at pizza and focaccia places, is made from chickpea flour, water, oil, and pepper and baked on a copper tray in a wood-burning stove. It's dense, filling, and less flavorful than focaccia.

The region also loves its locally grown lemons. The popular lemon liqueur is called **limoncino** (a.k.a. *limoncello*).

Vino delle Cinque Terre flows cheap and easy throughout the region. It's a white wine—crisp, refreshing, and great with seafood. Local wines are typically blends, predominantly using the bosco grape, found only here. For a sweet but potent dessert wine, ***sciacchetrà*** (shah-keh-TRAH) is worth a try (18 percent alcohol, often served with dunkable cookies).

outside the tunnel; tel. 0187-800-065, mobile 333-240-7956).

$$$$ Torre Aurora is a top-end restaurant where you'll dine outside (wrapped in a blanket if it's cold) around the medieval tower with commanding views while enjoying simple yet creative dishes. Reservations are smart (daily in good weather, mobile 366-145-3702, www.torreauroracinqueterre.com). They serve cocktails outside of mealtime.

In the Old Town

$$$ Via Venti is a quiet little trattoria, hidden in an alley deep in the heart of the old town, serving imaginative seafood dishes. Be tempted by their gnocchi with crab, ravioli stuffed with fresh fish, and pear-and-pecorino pasta. The outdoor seating is as humdrum as the interior—but you're here for the food (Fri-Wed 12:00-14:30 & 18:30-22:30, closed Thu, Via XX Settembre 32, tel. 0187-818-347).

$ Gastronomia "San Martino" is a tiny, humble combination of takeaway and sit-down café with surprisingly affordable, quality dishes. Eat at one of the few tables—inside or out on a pleasant street—or find a driftwood log for a feast-to-go (Tue-Sun 12:00-15:00 & 18:00-22:00, closed Mon, next to recommended L'Antica Terrazza hotel at Vicolo San Martino 3, mobile 346-109-7338).

$$ L'Osteria is a delightful little family-run place serving "cuisine with passion" at wonderful prices. Their Possa wine, from vineyards close to the sea, is the oyster of local wines (Tue-Sun lunch served 12:00-14:30, evening seatings at 19:00 and 21:00, closed Mon, Via Vittorio Emanuele 5, tel. 0187-819-224).

$$$ Ristorante al Pozzo is a favorite among locals. They have one of the best wine lists in town, serve only homemade pasta, and are known for their raw fish and wonderful seafood *antipasti misti* (Fri-Wed 12:00-15:00 & 18:30-22:30, closed Thu, Via Roma 24, tel. 0187-817-575).

$$ Páe Veciu, tucked away from the hubbub, has a short, creative menu of well-prepared seafood, pastas, and a few meat dishes. Eat inside in view of the kitchen or at one of the few streetside tables. Run by the folks from the recommended Buranco Agriturismo, it features a good selection of local wines (daily 11:30-15:00 & 18:30-22:00, Via Vittorio Emanuele 69, mobile 327-941-0430).

$ La Smorfia—a local favorite—cooks up good pizza in a sloppy setting that somehow seems to say, "Great pizza enjoyed here." Their large pizzas can feed three (Fri-Wed 11:00-24:00, closed Thu, Via Vittorio Emanuele 73, tel. 0187-818-395).

In the New Town

$$$$ Miky is packed with a well-dressed clientele who know their seafood. For elegantly presented, top-quality food that celebrates local ingredients and traditions, it's worth the steep prices. Their "pizza pasta" is served in a bowl topped with a thin pizza crust dome, then flambéed at your table (Wed-Mon 12:00-15:00 & 19:00-23:00, closed Tue, reservations wise, 100 yards from train station at Via Fegina 104, tel. 0187-817-608, www.ristorantemiky.it).

$$$ La Cantina di Miky, a few doors down from the station, is more youthful and informal than Miky, yet serves artfully crafted Ligurian specialties. Sit downstairs, in the garden, or on the promenade overlooking the sea (creative desserts, large selection of Italian microbrews, Thu-Tue 12:00-24:00, closed Wed, Via Fegina 90, tel. 0187-802-525). This place doubles as a cocktail bar in the evenings.

Light Meals and Takeout Food

In the Old Town: Lots of shops and bakeries sell pizza and focaccia to eat in or take out for an easy picnic. **$ Il Frantoio Focacceria** serves tasty pizza and focaccia (Fri-Wed 9:00-14:00 & 16:30-20:00, closed Thu, just off Via Roma at Via Gioberti 1). **$ Emy's Way Pizzeria Friggitoria** offers pasta, thick-crust pizza (whole and by the slice), and deep-fried seafood in to-go cones (daily 11:00-20:00, later in summer, along the skinny street next to the church, tel. 331-788-1088, Emiliano).

In the New Town: For a quick bite right at the train station (or on the beach), try **$ Il Massimo della Focaccia** for quiche-like tortes, sandwiches, focaccia pizzas, and desserts with a sea view (Thu-Tue 9:00-19:00, closed Wed except June-Aug, Via Fegina 50 at the station). **La Bottega SMA** is a smart minimart with fresh produce, *antipasti*, deli items, pay-by-the-weight sandwiches, and other picnic fare (daily 8:00-13:00 & 16:30-19:30 except closed Sun afternoon, shorter hours off-season, near Lavarapido at Vittoria Gianni 21).

VERNAZZA

With the closest thing to a natural harbor—overseen by a ruined castle, a stout stone church, and a pastel canyon of fisherfolk homes—Vernazza is the jewel of the Cinque Terre. Only the regular, noisy train reminds you of the modern world.

Proud of their Vernazzan heritage, the town's 500 residents like to brag: "Vernazza is locally owned. Portofino has sold out." Fearing change, proponents of keeping Vernazza small stopped the construction of a major road into the town and region. Families are tight and go back centuries; you'll notice certain surnames (such as Basso and Moggia) everywhere.

The action is at the harbor, where you'll find outdoor eateries ringing a humble piazza, a restaurant hanging on the edge of the castle, and a breakwater with a promenade, corralled by a natural amphitheater of terraced hills. Join (or watch) the locals devoting their leisure time to the *passeggiata*—strolling lazily together up and down the main street. Learn—and live—the phrase *"la vita pigra di Vernazza"* (the lazy life of Vernazza).

Orientation

Tourist Information: At the train station, you can get answers to basic questions at the gift shop/park office (daily 8:00-20:00, closed in winter, tel. 0187-812-533, WCs just down the track; see "Helpful Hints," below, for baggage storage).

Boats are a way of life in Vernazza.

Vernazza

Trail to Monterosso

Cliffs

Rocks

50 Meters
50 Yards

SUNNING & SWIMMING

TRAIN TRACKS & ALCOVES

ORIGINAL TRAIN STATION

Harbor

WALK BEGINS

ORATORY (OPERA)

SANTA MARGHERITA CHURCH

SUNNING

ELEMENTARY SCHOOL

Breakwater

Beach

Piazza Marconi

23 7

3

5

SASSO DEL SEGO

22

VIA VISCONTI

BOAT DOCKS HERE

14

13

11

15

22

TUNNEL

4

V. SAN GIOVANNI BATTISTA

24

CASTLE

12

1

Rocks and Cliffs

TUNNEL

Ligurian Sea

Accommodations

1. La Malà & La Marina Rooms
2. Vernazza sul Mare
3. Nicolina Rooms Reception & Ristorante Pizzeria Vulnetia
4. Monica Lercari Rooms
5. Francamaria Reception & Albergo Barbara Rooms
6. Vernazza Rooms Reception
7. Martina Callo Rooms & Trattoria del Capitano
8. Casa Cato
9. Giuliano Basso Rooms
10. Camere Fontanavecchia
11. Gianni Franzi Reception/Ristorante
12. Gianni Franzi Rooms

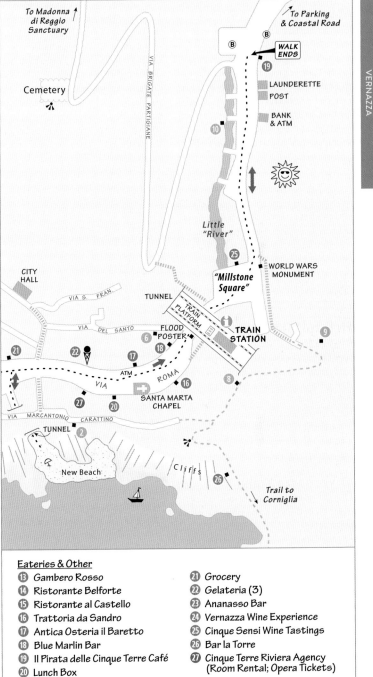

Eateries & Other

13 Gambero Rosso
14 Ristorante Belforte
15 Ristorante al Castello
16 Trattoria da Sandro
17 Antica Osteria il Baretto
18 Blue Marlin Bar
19 Il Pirata delle Cinque Terre Café
20 Lunch Box

21 Grocery
22 Gelateria (3)
23 Ananasso Bar
24 Vernazza Wine Experience
25 Cinque Sensi Wine Tastings
26 Bar la Torre
27 Cinque Terre Riviera Agency
   (Room Rental; Opera Tickets)

Arrival in Vernazza: The town's **train station** is only about three train cars long, so most cars come to a stop in a long, dimly lit tunnel. Get out anyway, and walk through the tunnel—heading for the light—to reach the station. From there the main street flows through town right down to the harbor. If you're sleeping here, many locals who rent rooms will meet you at the station and walk you to your place (call ahead to tell them which train you're on).

Rick's Tip: A steep 10-minute hike in either direction from Vernazza gives you a **classic village photo op.** *For the best light, head toward Corniglia in the morning—best views are just before the ticket booth for the national park—and toward Monterosso in the evening—best views are after the ticket booth.*

Helpful Hints

Baggage Storage: You can pay to leave your bags at the train station TI/gift shop (daily 9:00-19:00, closed in winter). The staff will also happily haul your luggage between the train station and your accommodations (€4/piece).

Laundry: A small self-serve launderette is at the top of town next to the post office (daily 9:00-22:00).

⊙ Vernazza Walk

This self-guided walk gives you a quick overview of the town and starts out on its breakwater.

• *From the train station, walk downhill and all the way out onto the breakwater. Find a comfortable and safe place to sit and get to know Vernazza.*

The Town: Before the 11th century, pirates made this coast uninhabitable, so the first Vernazzans lived in the hills above. The town's towers, fortified walls, and hillside terracing date mostly from the 12th through 15th century.

In the Middle Ages, there was no beach or square. The water went right up to the buildings, where boats would tie up, Venetian-style. Buildings had a water gate (facing today's square) and a front door on the higher inland side.

Vernazza has two halves. *Sciuiu* (Vernazzan dialect for "flowery") is the sunny side on the left, and *luvegu* (dank) is the shady side on the right. Houses below the castle were connected by an interior arcade—ideal for fleeing attacks. The "Ligurian pastel" colors of the buildings are regulated by the regional government's commissioner of good taste. The square before you is known for some of the area's finest restaurants.

Above Town: The small, **round tower** above the red building is another part of the city fortifications, reminding us of the town's importance in the Middle Ages. Back then, Genoa's enemies (rival maritime republics) were Vernazza's enemies.

Vineyards fill the mountainside beyond the town. Notice the many terraces. For six centuries, the economy was based on wine and olive oil. Then came the 1980s—and the tourists. Locals turned to tourism to make a living, and stopped tending the land, though many still maintain their small plots and proudly serve their family wines.

Church, School, and City Hall: Vernazza's Ligurian Gothic **church,** built with black stones quarried from Punta Mesco (the distant point between Monterosso and Levanto), dates from 1318. Note the gray stone (on the left) that marks the church's 16th-century expansion. The gray-and-red house above the spire is the **elementary school** (about 25 children attend). Older students go to the "big city," La Spezia. The red building on the hill to the right of the schoolhouse is the **City Hall.** Finally, on the top of the hill, is the **town cemetery.** It's only fair that hardworking Vernazzans—who spend their lives climbing up and down the hillsides—are rewarded with a world-class view from their eternal resting place.

• *Look high on your right to the castle.*

Castle (Castello Doria): The castle, which is now just stones and a grassy park with super views, still guards the town (€1.50, daily 10:00-20:00, summer until 21:00, closed Nov-March; from harbor, take stairs by Trattoria Gianni and follow *Ristorante al Castello* signs, the tower is a few steps beyond). This was the town's watchtower back in pirate days.

Ristorante Belforte, in the squat tower below the castle overlooking the water, is a great spot for a glass of wine or a meal. From the breakwater, you could follow the rope to the restaurant and pop inside, past an actual submarine door. A photo of a major storm showing the entire tower under a wave (not uncommon in the winter) hangs near the bar.

Harbor: In a moderate storm, you'd get soaked, as waves routinely crash over the *molo* (breakwater, built in 1972). Waves can rearrange the huge rocks—depositing them from the breakwater onto the piazza and its benches. Freak waves have even washed away tourists squinting excitedly into their cameras.

Vernazza's **fishing fleet** is down to just a few boats with net spools, but Vernazzans are still more likely to own a boat than a car. Boats are moored on buoys, except in winter or when the red storm flag indicates rough seas (see the pole at the start of the breakwater). When the red flag flies, boat owners are permitted to pull them up onto the square—which is usually reserved for restaurant tables.

• *Stroll from the breakwater to the harbor square. Look for a small historic stone just before the narrow stairway on the right.*

Harbor Square (Piazza Marconi): Vernazza, with the Cinque Terre's only natural harbor, was established as the sole place boats could pick up the fine local wine. The two-foot-high square **stone** at the foot of the stairs is marked *Sasso del Sego* (stone of tallow). Workers crushed animal flesh and fat in its basin to make tallow, which drained out from the tiny hole below. The tallow was then used to waterproof boats or wine barrels.

Take some time to appreciate the medieval stonework and chestnut timbers of the restaurant interiors facing the harbor. From here steps lead to your right up to the castle.

Towns along this coast were designed as what's called a "Ligurian Palazzata"—an interlinked series of buildings intended to provide protection from seaborne attacks. Vernazza's harborfront retains its thousand-year-old "stockade" of buildings, connected with tiny and easy-to-defend staircases leading from the vulnerable harbor higher into the community.

• *Cross to the church side of the harbor, and peek into the tiny street leading away from the water with its commotion of arches.*

Vernazza's harbor and breakwater

Castle at Vernazza

Vernazza's most characteristic side streets (caruggi) lead up from here.

Vernazza's Church: Vernazza's harborfront church sits on the tiny piazza, decorated with a river-rock mosaic. This popular hangout spot is where the town's older ladies soak up the last bit of sun, and kids enjoy a patch of level ball field. The church, nestled awkwardly into the rocks, is unusual for its east-facing (rather than the standard west-facing) entryway. With relative peace and prosperity in the 16th century, the townspeople doubled the size of their church, extending it west over what was the little piazza that faced it.

• *Now walk back across the harbor square and head left into town. After the lane opens up on the right, hike through the cave to the...*

"New Beach": This is where the town's stream used to hit the sea back in the 1970s. When a massive flood hit in 2011, it deposited landslide material here from the hills above. In the flood's aftermath, Vernazza's main drag and harbor were filled with mud and silt. Workers used the debris to fill in even more of this beach. But as time goes on, the forces of nature are once again taking it away.

• *Back on the main drag, continue uphill to...*

Vernazza's "Main Street": You're now strolling through Vernazza's "commercial center": souvenir shops, wine shops, the Blue Marlin Bar (a good nightspot), and so on. The small stone chapel with iron grillwork over the window (on the right) is the tiny **Chapel of Santa Marta,** where Mass is celebrated on special Sundays. You'll walk by a *gelateria,* bakery, pharmacy, grocery, and another *gelateria.* There are plenty of fun and cheap food-to-go options here. While it's easy to get distracted by all the tourists, try to see through them to notice locals going about their business.

On the right, just before the train tracks, study the big **poster,** which shows photos of the 2011 flood (*alluvione*) and the shops it devastated. Imagine this street from here to the harbor buried under 13 feet of mud.

• *Hike a few steps under and above the tracks to the little square.*

"Millstone Square": The **millstones** set on the square are a reminder that the town stream (which goes underground here and which you've been walking over ever since leaving the harbor area) once powered Vernazza's water mill. (You can still see its tiny "river" if you follow this road up a few steps.) Until the 1950s, the river ran openly through the center of town. Old-timers recall the days before the breakwater, when the river cascaded down, charming bridges spanned the ravine, and the surf sent waves rolling up Vernazza's main drag.

On the wall ahead at the bend in the road, notice the **World Wars Monument**—dedicated to those killed in World Wars I and II. Not a family in Vernazza was spared. Listed on the left are soldiers *morti*

Santa Margherita Church

Sunbathing in Vernazza

in combattimento who died in World War I; on the right is the WWII section. Some were deported to *Germania;* others—labeled *Part* (for *partigiani,* or partisans)—were killed while fighting Mussolini.

The path to Corniglia begins here (behind and above the monument). Even if you don't plan to hike its entire length, you don't have to go far to find fine views over Vernazza's stony peninsula.

• *To see a more workaday part of Vernazza, head a couple of minutes uphill from here to the...*

Top of Town; First you'll pass the **ambulance barn** (on the left, at #7, with big brown garage doors and a *croce verde Vernazza* sign), where a group of volunteers is always on call for a dash to the hospital, 40 minutes away in La Spezia. Farther up, you'll come to a functional strip of modern apartment blocks facing the river. In this practical zone—the only place in town that allows cars—are a bank, the post office, a launderette, and the popular bar/café called Il Pirata delle Cinque Terre. The parking lot fills a square called **Fontana Vecchia,** named for an "old fountain" that's so old, it's long gone. Shuttle buses run from here to hamlets and sanctuaries in the hills above. (Check the schedule post if you want to enjoy the scenic shuttle bus up to the sanctuary, described next.)

Experiences
Sanctuary Shuttle Bus Joyride and Hike

For a cheap and scenic joyride to the **Madonna di Reggio sanctuary,** worth ▲▲, hop on an ATC shuttle bus that loops from the top of Vernazza to sanctuaries and hamlets high in the hills—including the Madonna di Reggio and San Bernardino sanctuaries—and back again (50 minutes, €1.50; for times, check schedule posted at the bus stop, ask at the TI, or check online at www.atceser-cizio.it). Look for the bus to *Madonna di Reggio via Fornacchi.*

The bus ride is absolutely stunning. I prefer to stay on for three-quarters of the loop (to Madonna di Reggio, then hike back to Vernazza from there; see below), or you can ride all the way to complete the scenic circle. You'll see tiny settlements that predate the Cinque Terre villages, built back when people were afraid to live on the coast for fear of pirates. These hamlets and their terraces go back a thousand years.

For a delightful (if steep) half-hour **hike into Vernazza,** ask the driver to let you out at the stop for *Santuario Nostra Signora di Reggio.*

First, walk two minutes below the bus stop to the sanctuary, which dates from 1248 and has a Romanesque facade. Inside, interesting votives fill the rear corner—gifts from sailors who survived storms and soldiers who survived wars. A volunteer staffs the church selling coffee, water, and snacks.

From here signs direct you to trail #508. You'll be walking on thousand-year-old cobbles through abandoned olive groves and past the Stations of the Cross, which have inspired generations of processions trudging up from Vernazza. You'll descend through the cemetery, then either take the stairs down to the train station, or continue to the left down the lane to the square called Fontana Vecchia, where you caught the shuttle bus.

Beaches

The harbor's sandy cove has sunning rocks and showers by the breakwater. The sunbathing lane directly under the church has a shower. A ladder on the seaside of the breakwater aids deep-water swimmers. Vernazza's "new beach" can be accessed through a hole halfway along the town's main drag.

Boat Rides

In addition to the regularly scheduled big boats that depart from Vernazza's harbor (see page 121), hiring your own boat can be handy for intertown transport. From Vernazza, figure around €50 one-way to boat to the other towns (for up to six passengers in an outboard). At Vernazza's breakwater you'll find **Nord Est,** run by Vincenzo, the best-established option (mobile 338-700-0436, info@nordest-vernazza.com). **Vernazza Water Taxi,** run by Pietro, is another choice (mobile 338-911-3869, info@vernazzawatertaxi.it).

Wine Tasting

Vernazza Wine Experience hides out at the top of town just under the castle. Run by Alessandro, a sommelier, it's romantic, with mellow music and a hardwood, ship-deck ambience. Tastings start at €15/person and can be matched up with meat-and-cheese small plates. While the bill can add up, the quality is excellent and the view is unforgettable (cash only, daily 17:00-20:00, hike from harborfront and turn left before castle, Via S. Giovanni Battista 31, tel. 331-343-3801). Or, drop by his place behind the train station called **Cinque Sensi** (similar prices, Via Roma 71, daily 12:00-24:00).

A Little Taste of Opera

A favorite Cinque Terre evening memory for many is Vernazza's summer opera. A big-name maestro from Lucca brings talented singers to town twice weekly. Performances fill the small oratory, a medieval building with fine acoustics that was beautifully restored for this purpose (just up the steps from the church). Performances begin at 19:00 and last just over an hour (€18 in advance, €20 at the door, May-Oct Wed and Fri at 19:00, book tickets at Cinque Terre Riviera office at #24 on the main street, tel. 0187-812-123, info@cinqueterreriviera.com).

Nightlife

The town's nightlife centers on the bars on its waterfront piazza. The **Blue Marlin Bar** dominates the late-night scene with a mix of locals and tourists, good drinks, and an open piano (for more, see "Eating," later). **Ananasso Bar** offers early evening happy-hour fun and cocktails (*aperitivi*). Its harborfront tables get the last sunshine of the day (Fri-Wed 8:00-late, closed Thu, on Piazza Marconi).

Sleeping

Vernazza lacks any real hotels, and almost all of my listings are *affittacamere* (private rooms for rent). I favor hosts who rent multiple rooms and speak just enough English, have email, and are reliable. Most places accept only cash, promise free Wi-Fi (often spotty), and don't include breakfast unless noted. Some have killer views, and some come with lots of stairs. Expect noise at night: trains, church bells (7:00-22:00), crashing waves, cars in the upper town. Communicate your arrival time to your host and get clear instructions on where to meet and pick up the keys. They'll usually offer to meet you at the train station if they know when you're coming.

Rooms for Rent (Affittacamere)

The **Cinque Terre Riviera** agency, based in Vernazza, rents rooms here and throughout the region (www.cinqueterreriviera.com).

$$$$ **La Malà** is the town's jet-setter pad. Four crisp, pristine white rooms boast fancy-hotel-type extras and a shared seaview terrace. It's a climb—way up to the top of town—but they'll carry your bags to and from the station. Book early; this place fills up quickly (includes breakfast at a bar, family rooms, air-con, mobile 334-287-5718, www.lamala.it, info@lamala.it). They also rent two rooms at the simpler $ **"Armanda's Room"** nearby—a great value, since you get their attention to detail and amenities without paying for a big view (includes simple breakfast, air-con).

$$$$ **Vernazza sul Mare** rents two view, luxury apartments (one- and two-bedroom, sleeping 4-6) that overlook the sea and town from private, spacious

terraces. The light-filled, airy units come with sea breezes and a crashing-waves soundtrack. These are great for families and can be connected (both with air-con, fully equipped kitchens, climb steps up to Via Carattino 12, mobile 345-363-6118, www.vernazzasulmare.com, info@vernaz zasulmare.com).

$$$ Nicolina Rooms consists of seven rooms and one apartment in three buildings. Two cheaper rooms are in the center over the pharmacy, up a few steep steps; another, pricier studio with a terrace is on a twisty lane above the harbor; and four more rooms are in a building beyond the church, with great views and church bells (all include breakfast, Piazza Marconi 29—check in at Pizzeria Vulnetia, tel. 0187-821-193, mobile 333-842-6879, www. camerenicolina.it, info@camere nicolina.it).

$$$ La Marina Rooms is run by hard-working Christian, who speaks English and happily meets guests at the station to carry bags. There are five well-tended, airy, and renovated units, most high above the main street: One single works as a (very) tight double, and three doubles have fine oceanview terraces; he also has two apartments—one with terrace and sea views, and the other on the harbor-front square (rooms have fridges, mobile 338-476-7472, www.lamarinarooms.com, mapcri@yahoo.it).

$$$ Monica Lercari rents several rooms with modern comforts, perched at the top of town (more for seaview terrace, includes breakfast, air-con, tel. 0187-812-296, mobile 320-025-4515, monimarimax@gmail.com). Monica and her husband, Massimo, run the recommended Ristorante al Castello, in the old castle tower that overlooks the town.

$$ Francamaria and her husband Andrea rent 10 sharp, comfortable, and creatively renovated rooms. Their reception desk is on the harbor square (on the ground floor at Piazza Marconi 30), but the rooms are all over town (family rooms, some with air-con, mobile 328-711-9728, www.francamaria.com, francamariareservation@gmail.com). They also rent a room in Manarola.

$$ Vernazza Rooms rents 14 rooms: Four are above the Blue Marlin Bar looking down on the main street; another seven are a steep climb higher up, just under the City Hall (big family apartments, a few with air-con and others with fans, refrigerators, arrange check-in time in advance and meet your host at Via del Santo 9, mobile 351-918-3164, www. vernazzarooms.com, info@vernazza rooms.com).

$$ Martina Callo's four old-fashioned, spartan rooms overlook the harbor square; they're up plenty of steps near the silent-at-night church tower. While the rooms are simple, guests pay for and appreciate the views (family rooms, cheaper nonview room, air-con, ring bell at Piazza Marconi 26, tel. 0187-812-365, mobile 329-435-5344, www.roomartina.it, roomartina@roomartina.it).

$ Albergo Barbara rents nine tidy, Ikea-chic top-floor rooms overlooking the square with an attic communal lounge. Most have small windows and small views; view rooms are more expensive. It's a good value in a nice location (cheaper rooms with shared bathroom, lots of stairs, reserve online with credit card but pay cash, Piazza Marconi 30, tel. 0187-812-398, www.albergobarbara.it, info@ albergobarbara.it).

Above the Train Station:
$$$$ Casa Cato offers six modern, tight but well-outfitted rooms, some with private balconies and all with access to an inviting shared terrace overlooking the sea and town (RS%, air-con, fridge, expect some train noise, mobile 334-123-8579, www.casacatocinqueterre.com, info@ casacatocinqueterre.com, Lisa). They also rent an apartment in the center of town.

$$$ Giuliano Basso's four carefully crafted, well-appointed rooms form a cozy little compound with a common lounge and view terrace, straddling a ravine among orange trees. Giuliano—the town's last stone-layer—proudly built the place himself (2 rooms have air-con, more train noise than others; follow the main road up above the station, take the ramp up toward Corniglia just before Pensione Sorriso, follow the path, and watch for a sharp left turn—or ask Giuliano to meet you at the station; mobile 333-341-4792, www.cameregiuliano.com, giuliano@cdh.it).

$$ Camere Fontanavecchia, at the top of the town, is run by Annamaria, with eight bright and cheery rooms (three with terraces) overlooking a ravine and its rushing river (Via Gavino 15, tel. 0187-821-130, mobile 333-454-9371, www.cinqueterrecamere.com, m.annamaria@libero.it). She also rents an apartment.

Guesthouse (Pensione)

$$$ Gianni Franzi, a busy restaurant on the harbor square, runs the closest thing to a big hotel in Vernazza. There are 25 small rooms scattered across three buildings a hundred tight, winding stairs above the harbor square. Some rooms are funky and decorated à la shipwreck, with tiny balconies and grand sea views. The comfy, newer rooms lack views. All guests have access to a super-scenic cliff-hanging garden and panoramic terrace (where breakfast is served in season). Steely Marisa requires check-in before 16:00 or a phone call to explain when you're coming (RS%, closed Jan-Feb, Piazza Marconi 1, tel. 0187-812-228, mobile 393-9008-155, www.giannifranzi.it, info@giannifranzi.it). Pick up your keys at the restaurant, but on Wed, when the restaurant is closed, call ahead to make other arrangements.

Eating

Vernazza's restaurants work hard to win your business. Wander around at about 20:00 and compare the ambience. To get an outdoor table on summer weekends, reserve ahead. Harborside restaurants and bars are easygoing. You're welcome to grab a cup of coffee or glass of wine and disappear somewhere on the breakwater, returning your glass when you're done.

Rick's Tip: *If you dine in Vernazza but are staying in another town, be sure to* **check train schedules before sitting down to eat,** *as trains run less frequently in the evening.*

Harborside

$$$ Gianni Franzi is an old standby for well-prepared seafood and pastas and friendly service. The outdoor seating is under an arcade, while the indoor setting is big and classy (check their *menù cucina tipica Vernazza,* Thu-Tue 12:00-15:00 & 19:00-22:00, closed Wed except in Aug, tel. 0187-812-228).

$$$ Trattoria del Capitano feels unpretentious and serves breakfast and a short menu of straightforward local dishes, including *spaghetti allo scoglio*—pasta entangled with various types of seafood (Wed-Mon 8:00-22:00, closed Tue except in Aug, on Piazza Marconi, tel. 0187-812-201).

$$$ Ristorante Pizzeria Vulnetia has a jovial atmosphere and serves regional specialties and thin-crust pizzas—making this a good choice for those on a budget and families (Tue-Sun 12:00-22:00, closed Mon, Piazza Marconi 29, tel. 0187-821-193).

$$$$ Gambero Rosso is reliably good, and has a fine interior and great outdoor tables on the piazza (Fri-Wed 12:00-15:00 & 19:00-22:00, closed Thu and Dec-Feb, Piazza Marconi 7, tel. 0187-812-265).

By the Castle

$$$$ Ristorante Belforte is a cut above the rest, serving traditional and creative cuisine at tables embedded in four levels of the old castle. For the ultimate seaside perch, reserve a table on the *terrazza con vista* (view terrace) or request the "lovers'

table" on its own little terrace (Wed-Mon 12:00-15:00 & 19:00-22:00, closed Tue and Nov-March, tel. 0187-812-222).

$$$ Ristorante al Castello is just below the castle and offers commanding views. Reserve one of the dozen romantic cliffside seaview tables for two—where you'll feel like you're eating all alone with the Mediterranean. With this book get a free *sciacchetrà* or *limoncello* with biscotti by request (Thu–Tue 12:00–15:00 & 19:00–22:00, closed Wed and Nov–April, tel. 0187-812-296).

On or near the Main Street

$$ Trattoria da Sandro, on the main drag, mixes quality Genovese and Ligurian cuisine—including award-winning stuffed mussels—with friendly service (Wed-Mon 12:00-15:00 & 18:30-22:00, closed Tue, Via Roma 62, tel. 0187-812-223).

$$ Antica Osteria il Baretto is a solid bet for homey, reasonably priced traditional cuisine that's favored by locals (Tue-Sun 12:00-22:00, closed Mon, indoor and outdoor seating in summer, Via Roma 31, tel. 0187-812-381).

$$ Blue Marlin Bar, on the main street, busts out a short, creative menu of more casual dishes (pizzas, salads). It's a good choice if you want to grab something basic (Italian breakfast from 7:30, eggs and bacon 8:30-11:30). If you're awaiting a train, enjoy the outdoor seating with a prepaid drink in view of the tracks (Thu-Tue 7:30-23:00, closed Wed).

$$ Il Pirata delle Cinque Terre, a huge hit for breakfast, also attracts travelers

for lunch and dinner. While you're eating at the parking lot at the top of town, the food, service, and energy are great. And many are charmed by the Cannoli twins, who entertain while they serve. The menu is aimed squarely at American taste buds (reserve ahead for dinner from 18:00, daily 7:00-24:00, Via Gavino 36, tel. 0187-812-047).

$ Lunch Box serves *panini,* salads, and fresh fruit juices from a clever and flexible menu, with a couple of tables overlooking the main drag (daily 7:00-22:00, Via Roma 34, mobile 338-908-2841).

Rick's Tip: Drop by one of Vernazza's many little bakeries, focaccia shops, or grocery stores to assemble a **picnic breakfast** *to eat on the breakwater. Top it off with a coffee in a nearby bar.*

Pizzerias, Sandwiches, and Groceries: Vernazza's main-street eateries offer a fine range of quick meals. Several bakeries and creative little takeaway joints sell sandwiches and pizza by the slice. **Pino's grocery store** at #19 makes inexpensive sandwiches to order (generally Mon-Sat 8:00-13:00 & 17:00-19:30, closed Sun).

Gelato

Gelateria Il Porticciolo uses fresh ingredients to create intense flavors (try their *cannella*—cinnamon, or *nocciola*—hazelnut). **Gelateria Vernazza,** near the top of the main street, also takes its gelato seriously. **Gelateria Amore Mio** (midtown) has great people-watching tables.

CORNIGLIA

If you think of the Cinque Terre as The Beatles, Corniglia is Ringo. This tiny, sleepy town is the only one of the five not directly on the water. Locals claim that its ancient Roman residents produced a wine so widely exported that vases have been found at Pompeii stamped with the town name. Wine remains Corniglia's lifeblood today.

Corniglia has fewer tourists, cooler temperatures, a laid-back main square, a few restaurants, a windy overlook on its promontory, and plenty of private rooms for rent. From the town center, signs for *al mare* or *Marina* point to where a stepped path leads steeply down to sunning rocks by the water.

Orientation

Hill-capping Corniglia is connected with its train station far below by a long set of stairs (385 zigzagging steps), and much easier, by a hardworking little shuttle bus (schedule posted at the station and in town; buy ticket at station).

Tourist Information: A TI/park information office is down at the train station (likely daily 8:00-20:00, shorter hours off-season). A kiosk may also be open up in town on Ciappà square.

Hiking: From Corniglia, you can hike on the coastal trail to **Vernazza.** Also consider the challenging but rewarding "high road" to **Manarola via Volastra.** For details, see "Hiking the Cinque Terre" on page 122.

◉ Corniglia Walk

This self-guided walk might take 30 minutes...but only if you let yourself browse, sample the wine, or lick a gelato cone.
• *Begin near the shuttle bus stop located at a...*

Town Square: The gateway to this community is Ciappà square, with an ATM, old wine press, bus stop, and sometimes a TI kiosk in summer.
• *Look for the arrow pointing to the centro. Stroll along Via Fieschi, the spine of Corniglia. In the fall, the smell of grapes becoming wine wafts from busy cellars. Along this main street, you'll see...*

Corniglia's little lanes invite exploration.

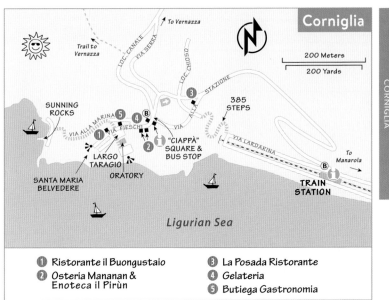

Corniglia

Trail to Vernazza

To Vernazza

200 Meters
200 Yards

SUNNING ROCKS

385 STEPS

"CIAPPÀ" SQUARE & BUS STOP

LARGO TARAGIO

ORATORY

SANTA MARIA BELVEDERE

VIA ALLA MARINA
VIA FIESCHI

LOC. CANALE
VIA SERRA
LOC. CHIOSO
STAZIONE
VIA ALLA

VIA LARDARINA

To Manarola

TRAIN STATION

Ligurian Sea

① Ristorante il Buongustaio
② Osteria Mananan & Enoteca il Pirùn
③ La Posada Ristorante
④ Gelateria
⑤ Butiega Gastronomia

Corniglia's Enticing Shops: As you enter Via Fieschi, a trio of neighboring gelato shops jockeys for your business. My favorite is the last one you come to (at #74, on the right), **Alberto's Gelateria** (open late). Before ordering, get a free taste of Alberto's *miele di Corniglia,* made from local honey.

Farther along, on the left, **Enoteca il Pirùn**—named for an oddly shaped wine pitcher designed to give the alcohol more kick as you squirt it into your mouth—is in a cool cantina at Via Fieschi 115. Try some local wines (small tastes generally free, €3/glass). If you order wine to drink from the *pirùn,* Mario will give you a bib (rookies tend to dribble).

Butiega Gastronomia (#142) is an old-fashioned grocery store/deli where Vincenzo sells organic local specialties (daily 8:00-19:30). For picnickers, they offer €5 made-to-order ham-and-cheese sandwiches and a fun *antipasti misti* (priced by weight). You'll find good places to picnic along on this walk.

• *Following Via Fieschi, you'll end up at the mellow...*

Main Square (Largo Taragio): On the square, tables from two bars and a trattoria spill around a WWI memorial and the town's old well. What looks like a church is the **Oratory of Santa Caterina**—a kind of spiritual clubhouse for a service group doing social work in the name of the Catholic Church. Up the stairs and behind the oratory, you'll find a terrace that children have made into a soccer field. The stone benches and viewpoint make this a peaceful place for a picnic.

• *Opposite the oratory, notice how steps lead steeply down on Via alla Marina to sunning rocks and a small deck. From the square, continue up Via Fieschi to the...*

End-of-Town Viewpoint: The Santa Maria Belvedere, named for a church that once stood here, marks the scenic end of Corniglia. This is a super picnic spot. From here, look high to the west (right), where the village and sanctuary of San Bernardino straddle a ridge. Way down below are the local swimming hole and huge sunning rocks.

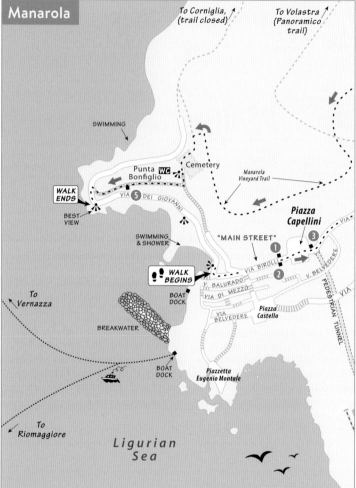

Manarola

To Corniglia,
(trail closed)

To Volastra
(Panoramico
trail)

SWIMMING

Cemetery

Punta
Bonfiglio **WC**

Manarola
Vineyard Trail

**WALK
ENDS**

VIA **5** DEI GIOVANNI

BEST
VIEW

Piazza
Capellini

VIA

3

"MAIN STREET"

1

SWIMMING
& SHOWER

**WALK
BEGINS**

VIA BIROLI

2

V. BELVEDERE

VIA

To
Vernazza

BOAT
DOCK

V. BALURADO

VIA DI MEZZO

Piazza
Castello

VIA
BELVEDERE

PEDESTRIAN TUNNEL

VIA

BREAKWATER

BOAT
DOCK

Piazzetta
Eugenio Montale

To
Riomaggiore

_Ligurian
Sea_

Eating

$$$ Ristorante il Buongustaio is a good bet for dinner on the square, serving _cucina casalinga_ (home cooking) and good seafood pasta and risotto (nice tables on the square, daily 12:00-21:15, Via Fieschi 164, tel. 0187-821-424).

$$ Osteria Mananan—between the Ciappà bus stop and the main square at Via Fieschi 117—has tasty dishes and a small, elegant interior (Tue-Sun 12:30-14:30 & 19:30-22:00, closed Mon, no outdoor seating, tel. 0187-821-166).

$$ Enoteca il Pirùn, on Via Fieschi, has a small restaurant above the wine bar serving typical local dishes (Fri-Wed 12:00-16:00 & 19:00-23:30, closed Thu, tel. 0187-812-315).

$$ La Posada Ristorante offers dinner in a garden under trees, overlooking the Ligurian Sea. To get here, stroll out of town to the top of the stairs that lead down to the station (daily 12:00-16:00 & 19:00-23:00, closed Nov-March, tel. 0187-821-174, mobile 338-232-5734).

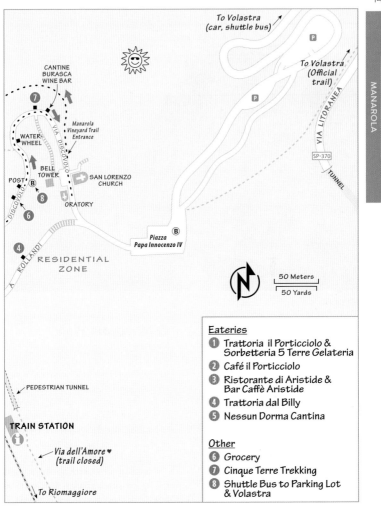

Eateries
1. Trattoria il Porticciolo & Sorbetteria 5 Terre Gelateria
2. Café il Porticciolo
3. Ristorante di Aristide & Bar Caffè Aristide
4. Trattoria dal Billy
5. Nessun Dorma Cantina

Other
6. Grocery
7. Cinque Terre Trekking
8. Shuttle Bus to Parking Lot & Volastra

MANAROLA

Mellow Manarola fills a ravine, bookended by its wild little harbor to the west and a diminutive hilltop church square inland to the east. The village hits a fine balance, giving it the "just right" combination of Cinque Terre qualities. The touristy zone squeezed between the train tracks and the harbor can be stressfully congested, but head just a few steps uphill and you can breathe again.

Manarola, which has hillsides that are blanketed with vineyards, also provides the easiest access to the Cinque Terre's remarkable dry-stone terraces. The trail ringing the town's cemetery peninsula, adjacent to the main harbor, provides some of the most strikingly beautiful town views anywhere in the region.

Orientation

Tourist Information: The TI/national park information office is in the train station (likely daily 8:00-20:00, shorter hours off-season).

Manarola

Arrival in Manarola: From the **train station,** walk through a 200-yard-long tunnel that's lined with interesting photos. To reach the busy harbor—with touristy restaurants, boat dock, and the start of my self-guided walk, head left (downhill) when you come out of the tunnel.

The ATC **shuttle bus** runs from near the old waterwheel (halfway up Manarola's main street), stopping at the parking lots above town, and then going all the way up to Volastra (about 2/hour except for afternoon breaks).

Drivers are better off parking in La Spezia. Or, park your car in one of the two pay lots just before town, then walk down the road to the church, and downhill to the main piazza.

Rick's Tip: *To get to the* **boats that connect Manarola** *with the other Cinque Terre towns, find the steps to the left of the harbor view—they lead down to the ticket kiosk. Continue around the left side of the cliff (as you face the water) to the dock.*

◐ Manarola Walk

From the harbor, this 45-minute self-guided walk shows you the town and surrounding vineyards and ends at a fantastic viewpoint.

• *Start down at the waterfront. Belly up to the wooden banister overlooking the rocky harbor, between the two restaurants.*

Harbor: Manarola is tiny and picturesque, a tumble of buildings bunny-hopping down its ravine to the fun-loving waterfront. The **breakwater**—which attempts to make this jagged harbor a bit less dangerous—was built (with reject marble from Carrara) just over a decade ago.

Facing the water, look up to the right, at the hillside Punta Bonfiglio **cemetery** and park. The trail running around the base of the point—where this walk ends—offers magnificent views back on this part of town.

The town's **swimming hole** is just below you. Manarola has no sand, but offers the best deep-water swimming in the area. The first "beach" has a shower, ladder, and wonderful rocks. The second has tougher access and no shower, but feels more remote and pristine (follow the paved path toward Corniglia, just around the point).

• *Go inland up the town's main drag—you'll climb a steep ramp that leads to Manarola's "new" square, which covers the train tracks.*

Piazza Capellini: Built in 2004, this square is an all-around great idea, giving the town a safe, fun zone for kids. Locals living near the tracks also enjoy a little less train noise. The mosaic in the middle of the square depicts the varieties of local fish in colorful enamel.

• *Go down the stairs at the upper end of the square. On your right, notice the tunnel that leads to Manarola's train station (and the closed Via dell'Amore trailhead). Head up...*

Via Discovolo: Manarola's main street twists up through town, lined by modest shops and filled with pooped hikers. About 100 yards up, just before the road bends sharply right, watch (on the right) for a **waterwheel.** Mills like this once powered the local industry. As you continue up, you'll hear the rushing waters of Manarola's stream. The rivulet was covered over after World War II. Before that time, romantic bridges arched over its ravine. You can peek below the concrete street in several places to see the stream surging below your feet.

Across the street from the waterwheel and a bit farther up, notice the **Cinque Terre Trekking** shop on your left, which outfits hikers. Around the corner is **Cantine Burasca** wine bar, a good place for a little wine tasting (closed Wed, Via Discovolo 86, mobile 339-807-1261).

• *Keep climbing until you come to the square at the...*

Top of Manarola: The square is faced by a church, an oratory—now a religious and community meeting place—and a bell tower, which served as a watchtower when pirates raided the town. To the right of the oratory, a stepped lane leads to the town's tourist-free residential zone.

The **Parish Church of St. Lawrence**

Church of St. Lawrence, Manarola

(San Lorenzo) dates from "MCCCXXX-VIII" (1338). Step inside to see two altarpiece paintings from the unnamed Master of the Cinque Terre, the only painter of any note from this region (left wall and above main altar). Note the humble painted stone ceiling, which features Lawrence, patron saint of the Cinque Terre, with his grill—the symbol of his martyrdom (he was roasted on it).

• *With the bell tower on your left, head about 20 yards back down the main street below the church and find a wooden railing on the right. It marks the start of a delightful stroll around the high side of town, and back to the seafront. This is the beginning of the...*

Manarola Vineyard Trail: Don't miss this experience. Simply follow the wooden railing, enjoying lemon groves and great views. Along the path, which is primarily flat, you'll get a close-up look at the region's famous dry-stone walls and finely crafted vineyards (with dried-heather thatches to protect the grapes from southwest winds). Smell the rosemary. Pick out the scant remains of an old fort.

Vineyards above Manarola

Manarola's cemetery

Notice the S-shape of the Manarola's main road—once a riverbed. The town's roofs are traditionally made of locally quarried slate and held down by rocks during windstorms.

Halfway along the lip of the ravine, a path marked *Panoramico Volastra (Corniglia)* leads steeply up into the vineyards (a challenging route that leads to the tiny hamlet of Volastra and then to Corniglia—see page 146).

Stick with your level path, passing a variety of simple wooden religious scenes, the work of local resident Mario Andreoli. Before his father died, Mario promised him he'd replace the old cross on the family's vineyard. Mario has been adding figures ever since. High above, notice ancient terraces that line the terrain like a topographic map.

• *Continue down to the cemetery (closed to the public). Stop by the gate for a peek inside.*

Cemetery: Ever since Napoleon—who was king of Italy in the early 1800s—decreed that cemeteries were health risks, Cinque Terre's burial spots have been located outside the towns. The result: The dearly departed generally get first-class sea views. Each cemetery—with evocative photos and finely carved Carrara marble memorial reliefs—is worth a look.

• *From the cemetery follow the steep and narrow stairs (through the green gate immediately below) and walk out onto the bluff.*

Punta Bonfiglio: This point offers some of the most commanding **views** of the entire region. For the best vantage point, walk out toward the water through a park. An inviting and recommended bar, **Nessun Dorma,** fills a long narrow terrace with people enjoying the vista.

Your Manarola finale is the bench at the tip of the point. Pause and take in the view.

• *From here steps go down and the path winds scenically back to the harbor, where we started.*

Experiences
Hikes

One of my favorite easy hikes is to head up into the **vineyards above Manarola,** then drop down into the town cemetery, enjoying great views on the way. This route is outlined in my "Manarola Walk," earlier.

For a longer hike, consider taking the **high route to Corniglia via Volastra** (much easier if you ride the shuttle bus, rather than hike, up to Volastra). For details, see "Hiking the Cinque Terre" on page 122.

Hiking Gear and Tips: A wonderful resource for hikers, **Cinque Terre Trekking** is near the top of the main street (halfway up to the church). If you're serious about hiking, stop in here to confirm your plans and to gear up (daily 11:00-13:00 & 14:00-19:00, shorter hours off-season, Via Discovolo 108, tel. 0187-920-834, www. cinqueterretrekking.com).

Pesto Making

Entrepreneurial Simone at the Nessun Dorma cantina (perched next to the cemetery at the most scenic edge of Manarola) leads a pesto-making workshop for up to 30 people at 10:30, followed by lunch at noon. The setting is unforgettable, and you get to eat what you make (€50/person, includes wine, no class on Tue, reserve ahead at www.nessundormacinqueterre.com or call mobile 340-888-4133, class cancelled in bad weather).

Eating

Via Discovolo, the main street climbing up through town from Piazza Capellini to the church, is lined with simple places and some small grocery stores. **Bar Caffè Aristide** is the busiest for breakfast. And the most enticing *gelateria* in town is **Sorbetteria 5 Terre Gelateria** (a couple of doors away).

Touristy restaurants are concentrated between Piazza Capellini and the harbor. The Scorza family works hard at **$$ Trattoria il Porticciolo** (Thu-Tue 12:00-21:30, closed Wed, Via Birolli 92, tel. 0187-920-083) and at their contemporary **cafè,** cheap and fast, across the way.

$$$ Ristorante di Aristide, right on Piazza Capellini, offers a trendy atmosphere and a pleasant outdoor setting (Fri-Wed 12:00-22:30, closed Thu, Via Discovolo 290, tel. 0187-920-000).

$$ Bar Caffè Aristide, next door, has indoor and streetside seating and a lighter menu (Fri-Wed 8:00-11:30 & 12:00-16:00, closed Thu).

$$$ Trattoria dal Billy, in the residential zone high above the touristy action, is top-notch. It's worth the climb for homemade black pasta with seafood and squid ink, green pasta with artichokes, and homemade desserts. Outdoor terraces offer commanding views over Manarola, while across the street an elegant, glassy dining room is carved into the rock. Reservations are a must (Fri-Wed 12:00-15:00 & 18:00-22:00, closed Thu, Via Aldo Rollandi 122, tel. 0187-920-628, www.trattoriabilly.com).

$$ Nessun Dorma Cantina is scenically perched under the cemetery and above the harbor, keeping the masses happy with bruschetta, cold cuts, salads, and lots of drinks (Wed-Mon 12:00-21:00, closed Tue, Localita Punta Bonfiglio, mobile 340-888-4133).

RIOMAGGIORE

Riomaggiore is a more real and laid-back town than its more touristy neighbors. The main drag, while traffic-free, feels more urban than "village," and surrounding the harbor is a fascinating tangle of pastel homes leaning on each other like drunken sailors. The views back on its harbor from the breakwater—especially at sunset—are some of the region's prettiest.

Orientation

Tourist Information: The **info point** in the station is for train info and tickets. The adjacent striped building, with a **national park shop** and info desk, is best for visitor information (both open daily 8:00-20:00, shorter hours off-season).

Arrival in Riomaggiore: The **train station** is separated from the town center by a bluff. To get to the center, take the pedestrian tunnel that parallels the rail

Jumping for joy in Riomaggiore

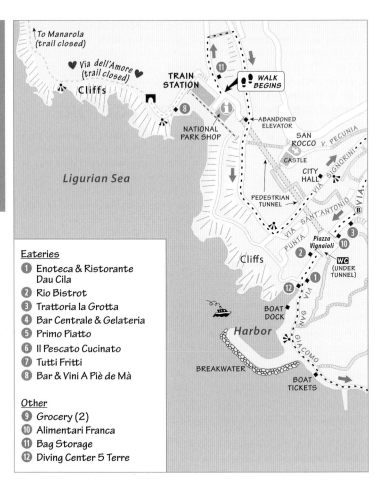

To Manarola
(trail closed)

♥ Via dell'Amore ♥
(trail closed)
Cliffs

TRAIN
STATION

WALK
BEGINS

ABANDONED
ELEVATOR

NATIONAL
PARK SHOP

SAN
ROCCO V. PECUNIA

CASTLE

CITY
HALL

VIA SIGNORINI

PEDESTRIAN
TUNNEL

Ligurian Sea

VIA SANT'ANTONIO

VIA

B

PUNTA

Piazza
Vignaioli

WC
(UNDER
TUNNEL)

Cliffs

BOAT
DOCK

Harbor

VIA SAN GIACOMO

BREAKWATER

BOAT
TICKETS

Eateries
① Enoteca & Ristorante
   Dau Cila
② Rio Bistrot
③ Trattoria la Grotta
④ Bar Centrale & Gelateria
⑤ Primo Piatto
⑥ Il Pescato Cucinato
⑦ Tutti Fritti
⑧ Bar & Vini A Piè de Mà

Other
⑨ Grocery (2)
⑩ Alimentari Franca
⑪ Bag Storage
⑫ Diving Center 5 Terre

tunnel. You'll exit at the bottom of Via Colombo. For a scenic route into town (for those not carrying luggage), take my "Riomaggiore Walk," later.

Drivers can park for the day at the two-story pay-and-display lot above town (€5/hour, €35/day). It is easier to park at La Spezia's train station and ride the train in.

Helpful Hints

Baggage Storage: You can check your bag at the casually run **deposito bagagli office**—it's behind the café/bar that's straight ahead as you exit the station (daily 9:00-12:00 & 14:00-19:00—confirm times, closed in winter).

Laundry: A self-service launderette is on the main street (daily in summer 8:00-20:00, shorter hours off-season, Via Colombo 107).

⊙ Riomaggiore Walk

This easy self-guided walk loops up and over, taking the long and scenic way from the station into town. You'll enjoy some fine views before strolling down the main street to the harbor.

• *Start at the train station. (If you arrive by boat, cross beneath the tracks and take a left, then hike through the tunnel along the tracks to reach the station.)*

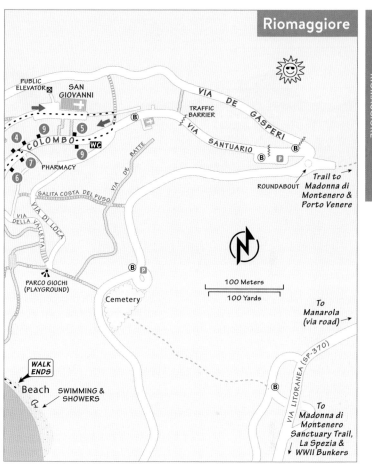

Riomaggiore

PUBLIC ELEVATOR
SAN GIOVANNI
VIA DE GASPERI
TRAFFIC BARRIER
VIA SANTUARIO
COLOMBO
WC
PHARMACY
VIA DE BATTE
SALITA COSTA DEL FUSO
VIA DELLA VALLETTA
VIA DI LOCA
ROUNDABOUT
Trail to Madonna di Montenero & Porto Venere
PARCO GIOCHI (PLAYGROUND)
Cemetery
100 Meters
100 Yards
To Manarola (via road)
WALK ENDS
Beach
SWIMMING & SHOWERS
VIA LITORANEA (SP·370)
To Madonna di Montenero Sanctuary Trail, La Spezia & WWII Bunkers

Climb to the Top of Town: Hike up the main street. Listen to the paved-over creek under your feet and at the first turn see the waterfall (and turtles in the cage). Farther along is a close-up look at dry-stone rockery work. Look down on the historic train line. A bit farther, you'll arrive at a fine **viewpoint,** with spectacular sea views.

• *When you're ready to move on, hook left around the bluff; rounding the bend, ignore the steps marked* marina seacoast *(which lead to the harbor) and continue another five minutes along the main (level) path toward the church. Along the way, consider a steep little side trip to the castle.*

Riomaggiore Castle: A steep stepped lane on the left leads to the castle (€2, daily 10:30-13:30). Taking this five-minute side trip, you'll find a humble art and heritage exhibit, the town's only well-preserved mural by Argentinian artist Silvio Benedetto, great sea views, and the tiny church of San Rocco (built for plague victims, and therefore outside of the town walls). More of Benedetto's murals are near the City Hall.

Town Views and Church of San Giovanni Battista (St. John the Baptist): Back down on the smooth and level lane, you'll go by the **City Hall** and several decaying **murals** (also by Silvio

Riomaggiore's harbor

Benedetto), celebrating the heroic grape-pickers and fishermen of the region.

Pause at the big **terrace** to enjoy the views of town and perhaps lots of local kids (the preschool is nearby). The major river of this region once ran through this valley, as implied by the name Riomaggiore (local dialect for "river" and "major"). As in the other Cinque Terre towns, the main street covers its *rio maggiore,* which carved the canyon now filled by the town's pastel high-rises.

The **church,** while rebuilt in 1870, was first established in 1340. It's dedicated to St. John the Baptist, the patron saint of Genoa, the maritime republic that once dominated the region.

• *Continue straight past the church and along the narrow lane leading down to the town's main street...*

Via Colombo: Heading down the hill on Via Colombo, you'll pass several handy fast-food joints. Farther along, the big covered terrace on the right belongs to the recommended **Bar Centrale,** a popular hangout day or night.

As you round the bend to the left, notice the old-timey pharmacy just above (on the right, with a good bakery under-neath). On your left, at #199, peek into the **Il Pescato Cucinato** shop, where Laura fries up her husband Edoardo's fresh catch; grab a paper cone of deep-fried seafood as a snack. Where the road bends sharply right, notice the bench on your left (just before La Zorza Café)—the hangout for the town's old-timers, who keep a running commentary on the steady flow of people. Straight ahead, you can already see where this street will dead-end. The last shop on the left, **Alimentari Franca** (at #251), is a well-stocked grocery where you can gather the makings for a perfect picnic out on the harbor.

Rick's Tip: *With a youthful spirit and lively evening bustle, Riomaggiore has an enjoyable* **night scene.** *Stroll the main drag, Via Colombo, to scope out fun spots to enjoy €6-8 cocktails.*

Where Via Colombo dead-ends, look right to see the tunnel leading back to the station. Look left to see two sets of stairs. Climb the "up" stairs to a parklike **square** built over the train tracks, which provides the children of the town a bit of level land on which to kick their soccer balls and to learn to ride bikes. The murals above, marking the town's middle school, celebrate the great-grandparents of these very children—the salt-of-the-earth locals who earned a humble living before the age of tourism.

• *Take the "down" stairs to the...*

Harbor: This most picturesque corner of Riomaggiore features a tight cluster of buildings huddling nervously around a tiny square and harbor. Because Riomaggiore lacks the naturally protected harbor of Vernazza, when bad weather is expected, fishermen pull their boats up to the safety of the little square. Sometimes the fishermen are busy beaching their boats even on a bright, sunny day—an indication that they know something you don't.

A couple of recommended restaurants—with high prices and memorable seating—look down over the action. Head past them and up the walkway along the left side of the harbor, and enjoy the **views** back at the town's colorful pastel buildings, with the craggy coastline just beyond. The best views are from up top, at the edge of the bluff. Below you, the breakwater curves out to sea. These rocks

are popular with sunbathers by day and romantics and photographers at sunset.

For a peek at Riomaggiore's **beach,** continue around the bluff on this trail toward Punta di Montenero, the cape that defines the southern end of the Cinque Terre. You'll pass the rugged boat landing and eventually run into Riomaggiore's rocky but still inviting beach *(spiaggia).* Ponder how Europeans manage to look relaxed when lounging on football-sized "pebbles."

Experiences
Hike

A scenic one-hour trail rises from Riomaggiore to the 14th-century **Madonna di Montenero sanctuary,** high above the town. Take the main road inland until you see signs at the roundabout at the top of town; or ride the shuttle bus 12 minutes from the town center to the sanctuary trail, then walk uphill another 20 minutes (great picnic spot up top).

Beach

Riomaggiore's tiny "beach" is rocky, but it's clean and peaceful. To find it, see the end of my self-guided walk, above. There's a shower here in the summer, and another

Sunbathers and kayakers flock to Riomaggiore.

by the boat landing—where many enjoy sunning on and jumping from the rocks.

Kayaks and Water Sports

Diving Center 5 Terre rents kayaks and snorkeling and scuba equipment; they also lead guided dives of the protected marine waters nearby (daily May-Sept 9:00-18:00, open only in good weather, likely weekends only in shoulder season, office down the stairs and under the tracks on Via San Giacomo, tel. 0187-920-011, www.5terrediving.it).

Eating

On the Harbor

$$$$ Enoteca & Ristorante Dau Cila (pronounced "dow CHEE-lah") is decked out like a black-and-white movie set in an old boat shed with extra tables outside on a rustic deck over dinghies. Try their antipasto specialty of several seafood appetizers (dinner only) and listen to the waves (cheaper lunch menu, daily 12:00-24:00, Via San Giacomo 65, tel. 0187-760-032).

$$$$ Rio Bistrot, small and intimate at the top of the harbor, tries to jazz up its Ligurian cuisine with international influences. You can order à la carte from the short but well-designed menu, or try their €39 tasting *menu* (cheaper lunch menu, daily 12:00-16:00 & 18:00-22:00, Via San Giacomo 46, tel. 0187-920-616).

On the Main Street, Via Colombo

$$ Trattoria la Grotta, right in the town center, has a passion for anchovies and mussels. You'll enjoy reliably good food surrounded by historical photos and wonderful stonework in a dramatic, dressy, cave-like setting (daily 12:00-14:30 & 17:30-22:30, closed Wed in winter, Via Colombo 247, tel. 0187-920-187).

$$ Bar Centrale is a casual, family-friendly place for hamburgers, salads, and pesto. They also serve breakfast, have a *gelateria* on site, and make great mojitos (daily 7:30-late, Via Colombo 144).

Light Meals: $ Primo Piatto, at the top of town, offers takeaway handmade pastas and sauces, cooked to order on the spot. It's cheap and delicious (Wed-Mon 10:30-19:30 or later, closed Tue, Via Colombo 72). For deep-fried seafood in a paper cone, **$ Il Pescato Cucinato** is where Edoardo fishes and his wife, Laura,

The catch of the day

Boats connect Cinque Terre towns.

Vernazza's train platform

fries (daily 11:20-20:30, near the bottom of Via Colombo at #199). A few doors away, **$ Tutti Fritti** serves only fried nibbles, including fish (daily 10:00-21:00, Via Colombo 161).

Picnics: Groceries and delis lining Via Colombo sell food to go for a picnic at the harbor or beach. **Co-op** grocery stores (several on the main drag) have the best prices. For a more appetizing selection, head to **Alimentari Franca** on the main street by the train-station tunnel (daily 8:00-20:00, Via Colombo 251).

Near the Train Station
$$ Bar & Vini A Piè de Mà, at the trailhead on the Manarola end of town, is good for a scenic light bite or quiet drink at night (daily 10:00-20:00, June-Sept until 24:00, closed Mon-Tue off-season, tel. 0187-921-037). Enjoy a meal on its dramatically situated terrace for an indelible Cinque Terre memory.

TRANSPORTATION

Arriving and Departing
By Train
The five towns of the Cinque Terre are on a milk-run line, with trains coming through about every 30 minutes; most trains connect to the Cinque Terre from La Spezia or Genoa. Big, fast trains usually speed right past the Cinque Terre, although a few IC trains connect Monterosso to Milan or Pisa.

Unless you're coming from another Cinque Terre town, you'll change trains at least once to reach Manarola, Corniglia, or Vernazza. From the south or east, you'll probably transfer at La Spezia's Centrale station. From the north, you'll transfer at Genoa's Piazza Principe station, Sestri Levante, Levanto, or Monterosso.

By Train After Parking Your Car
Given the narrow roads and parking headache, the only Cinque Terre town I'd drive to is Monterosso (and only if my hotel had parking). Otherwise, park your car in the nearest big city and take the train in—it's safer, cheaper, faster, and smarter. Parking is easy at the stations in Levanto or La Spezia.

TRAIN CONNECTIONS
Of the five Cinque Terre towns, Monterosso has the most direct train connections with towns outside the Cinque Terre.

From Monterosso by Train to: **Levanto** (3-4/hour, 4 minutes), **Sestri Levante** (hourly, 30 minutes, most trains to Genoa stop here), **Santa Margherita Ligure** (at least hourly, 45 minutes), **Genoa** (hourly, 1.5 hours; for destinations in France, you'll change trains here), **Milan** (8/day direct, otherwise hourly with change in Genoa, 3 hours), **Venice** (5/day, 6 hours, change in Milan), **La Spezia** (2-3/hour, 15-30 minutes), **Pisa** (hourly, 1-1.5 hours), **Rome** (hourly, 4.5 hours, change in La Spezia).

Florence

Florence is the birthplace of the Renaissance and the modern world. It's geographically small but culturally rich—containing more artistic masterpieces per square mile than anyplace else. In a single day, you can look Michelangelo's *David* in the eyes, fall under the seductive sway of Botticelli's *Birth of Venus,* and climb the modern world's first dome, which still dominates the skyline.

A cosmopolitan vibe courses through the city's narrow lanes. You'll encounter children licking gelato, students riding Vespas, supermodels wearing Gucci fashions, and artisans sipping Chianti—Florence has long been perfecting the art of civilized living.

FLORENCE IN 2 DAYS

Compact Florence is packed with sights, but crowds and long lines can ruin your day's agenda. To maximize your time, reserve ahead for the top two sights—Accademia (Michelangelo's *David*) and Uffizi Gallery (Renaissance paintings). Avoid both sights on Monday when they're closed, and on the first Sunday of the month from October through March, when they're free but impossibly crowded. Many other sights are either closed or have shorter hours Sundays and Mondays.

Day 1: See the Accademia (*David*) with a timed reservation. Afterward, visit the nearby Museum of San Marco (Fra Angelico's art, explore the Mercato Centrale (having lunch nearby), and drop by the Church of Santa Maria Novella (art by Masaccio). To avoid heat and crowds, take my Renaissance Walk in the morning or late afternoon.

On Any Evening: Linger over dinner. Take a stroll, gelato in hand. Or take a taxi or bus to Piazzale Michelangelo for spectacular city views, and walk back into town for dinner. You can sightsee late at some sights, attend a concert at a church, or drop by a wine bar.

Day 2: See the Bargello (best statues), then either the Duomo Museum (statues by Donatello and Michelangelo) or Galileo Science Museum (if art's not your thing). Then hit the street markets for some shopping and wandering. In the afternoon, see the Uffizi with a timed reservation. Then stroll to the river and cross the historic bridge, Ponte Vecchio, to the Oltrarno neighborhood for dinner.

With extra time: Fit in a day trip to Pisa (book ahead to climb the famous tower) or Siena (just 1.5 hours away by bus—and magic after dark).

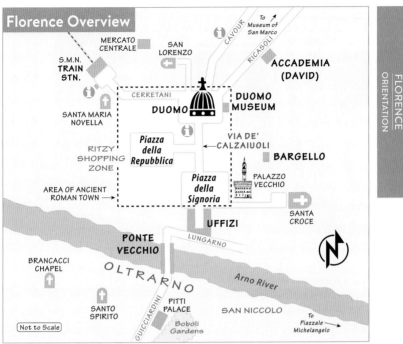

Florence Overview

MERCATO CENTRALE · SAN LORENZO · To Museum of San Marco · CAVOUR · RICASOLI · ACCADEMIA (DAVID) · S.M.N. TRAIN STN. · CERRETANI · DUOMO · DUOMO MUSEUM · SANTA MARIA NOVELLA · VIA DE' CALZAIUOLI · RITZY SHOPPING ZONE · Piazza della Repubblica · BARGELLO · AREA OF ANCIENT ROMAN TOWN → · Piazza della Signoria · PALAZZO VECCHIO · UFFIZI · SANTA CROCE · PONTE VECCHIO · LUNGARNO · BRANCACCI CHAPEL · OLTRARNO · Arno River · N · SANTO SPIRITO · PITTI PALACE · SAN NICCOLO · To Piazzale Michelangelo → · Boboli Gardens · GUICCIARDINI · Not to Scale

ORIENTATION

Florence (pop. 380,000) is small but intense. Prepare for scorching summer heat, crowded narrow lanes and sidewalks, slick pickpockets, few WCs, steep prices, and long lines. The best of the city lies on the north bank of the Arno River. The main historical sights cluster around the venerable dome of the cathedral (Duomo). Everything is within a 20-minute walk of the train station, cathedral, or Ponte Vecchio (Old Bridge). The less famous but more characteristic Oltrarno area (south bank) is just over the bridge.

Historic Core: The Duomo—with its iconic, towering dome—is the visual, geographical, and historical center of Florence. A 10-minute walk away is the Palazzo Vecchio (City Hall), with its skyscraping medieval spire. Connecting these two landmarks is the north-south pedestrian street called Via de' Calzaiuoli. This central axis—Duomo to the Palazzo Vecchio to

the Arno River—is the spine for Florentine sightseeing and the route of my self-guided Renaissance Walk. To the west of this axis is a glitzy shopping zone, and to the east is a characteristic web of narrow lanes.

Accademia/San Lorenzo (North of the Duomo): From the Duomo, Via Cavour runs north, bisecting the neighborhood. To the east lies the Accademia and the Museum of San Marco. The western part clusters around the Basilica of San Lorenzo, with its Medici Chapels. The area near San Lorenzo teems with tourists: There are the vendor stalls of San Lorenzo Market, the lively Mercato Centrale, and many hotels and trattorias.

Train Station/Santa Maria Novella (West of the Duomo): The area near the train station and Church of Santa Maria Novella has inexpensive hotels and characteristic eateries. Closer to the river (near Palazzo Strozzi) is a posh shopping zone.

Santa Croce (East of the Duomo): A 10-minute walk east from the Palazzo

FLORENCE AT A GLANCE

▲▲▲**Accademia** Michelangelo's *David* and powerful (unfinished) *Prisoners*. Reserve ahead. **Hours:** Tue-Sun 8:15-19:00, closed Mon; July-Sept open Tue and Thu 7:00-22:00. See page 184.

▲▲▲**Uffizi Gallery** Greatest collection of Italian paintings anywhere. Reserve well in advance. **Hours:** Tue-Sun 8:15-19:00, closed Mon; July-Sept Wed-Thu until 22:00. See page 186.

▲▲▲**Bargello** Underappreciated sculpture museum (Michelangelo, Donatello, Medici treasures). **Hours:** Daily 8:15-14:00 (until 17:00 for special exhibits); closed on second and fourth Sun and first, third, and fifth Mon of each month. See page 191.

▲▲▲**Duomo Museum** Freshly renovated cathedral museum with the finest in Florentine sculpture. **Hours:** Daily 9:00-19:00, closed first Tue of each month. See page 180.

▲▲▲**Pitti Palace** Several museums in lavish palace plus sprawling Boboli and Bardini Gardens. **Hours:** Palatine Gallery, Royal Apartments, Treasury, Museum of Costume and Fashion, and Gallery of Modern Art open Tue-Sun 8:15-19:00, closed Mon; Boboli and Bardini Gardens, and Porcelain Museum open daily June-Aug 8:15-19:30, April-May and Sept until 18:30, March and Oct until 17:30, Nov-Feb until 16:30, closed first and last Mon of each month. See page 192.

▲▲**Duomo** Gothic cathedral with colorful facade and the first dome built since ancient Roman times. **Hours:** Mon-Sat 10:00-16:30, Sun 13:30-16:45. See page 179.

▲▲**Museum of San Marco** Best collection anywhere of artwork by the early Renaissance master Fra Angelico. **Hours:** Tue-Fri 8:15-14:00, Sat-Sun until 17:00; also open until 14:00 on first, third, and fifth Mon of each month. See page 185.

▲▲**Medici Chapels** Tombs of Florence's great ruling family, designed and carved by Michelangelo. **Hours:** Tue-Sat 8:15-14:00; also open first, third, and fifth Sun and second and fourth Mon of each month. See page 185.

▲▲**Palazzo Vecchio** Fortified palace, once the home of the Medici family, wallpapered with history. **Hours:** Museum and excavations open daily 9:00-23:00 (Oct-March until 19:00), Thu until 14:00 year-round; shorter hours for tower. See page 189.

▲▲**Galileo Science Museum** Fascinating old clocks, telescopes, maps, and three of Galileo's fingers. **Hours:** Daily 9:30-18:00 except Tue until 13:00. See page 190.

▲▲**Santa Croce Church** Precious art, tombs of famous Florentines, and Brunelleschi's Pazzi Chapel in 14th-century church. **Hours:** Mon-Sat 9:30-17:00, Sun from 14:00. See page 191.

▲▲**Church of Santa Maria Novella** Thirteenth-century Dominican church with Masaccio's famous 3-D painting. **Hours:** Mon-Thu 9:00-19:00, Fri 11:00-19:00, Sat 9:00-17:30, Sun 13:00-17:30; Oct-March closes at 17:30. See page 192.

▲▲**Brancacci Chapel** Works of Masaccio, early Renaissance master who reinvented perspective. **Hours:** Wed-Mon 10:00-17:00 except Sun from 13:00, closed Tue. Reservations mandatory March-May. See page 193.

▲▲**San Miniato Church** Sumptuous Renaissance chapel and sacristy showing scenes of St. Benedict. **Hours:** Mon-Sat 9:30-13:00 & 15:00-19:30, until 19:00 off-season, Sun 8:15-19:30, closed sporadically for special occasions. See page 196.

▲**Climbing the Duomo's Dome** Grand view into the cathedral, close-up of dome architecture, and, after 463 steps, a glorious city vista; reservations required. **Hours:** Mon-Fri 8:30-19:00, Sat until 17:00, Sun 13:00-16:00. See page 179.

▲**Baptistery** Bronze doors fit to be the gates of paradise. **Hours:** Doors always viewable; interior open Mon-Sat 8:15-19:30 (closed 10:15-11:15), Sun until 13:30. See page 180.

▲**Piazza Santissima Annunziata** Lovely square epitomizing Renaissance harmony, with Brunelleschi's Hospital of the Innocents, considered the first Renaissance building. See page 184.

▲**Medici-Riccardi Palace** Lorenzo the Magnificent's home, with fine art, frescoed ceilings, and Gozzoli's lovely Chapel of the Magi. **Hours:** Thu-Tue 9:00-19:00, closed Wed. See page 186.

▲**Ponte Vecchio** Famous bridge lined with gold and silver shops. See page 177.

▲**Piazzale Michelangelo** Hilltop square with stunning view of Duomo and Florence, with San Miniato Church just uphill. See page 194.

Vecchio leads to the Church of Santa Croce. Along the way is the Bargello sculpture museum. This neighborhood is congested with tourists by day and students partying by night. But the area stretching north and west from Santa Croce is increasingly authentic and workaday, offering a glimpse of untouristy Florence.

Oltrarno (South of the River): Literally the "Other Side of the Arno River," this neighborhood reveals a Florence from a time before tourism. The Oltrarno starts just across Ponte Vecchio and stretches south to the giant Pitti Palace and surrounding gardens (Boboli and Bardini). To the west is the rough-but-bohemian Piazza di Santo Spirito (with its namesake church) and the lavishly frescoed Brancacci Chapel. To the east of Pitti, perched high on the hill, is Piazzale Michelangelo, with Florence's most popular viewpoint. Tucked between there and the river is the little San Niccolò neighborhood, with its lively bars and eateries.

Tourist Information

The city TI's main branch is across the square from the **train station** (Mon-Sat 9:00-19:00, Sun until 14:00; at the back corner of the Church of Santa Maria Novella at Piazza della Stazione 4; tel. 055-212-245, www.firenzeturismo.it). A smaller branch is centrally located **across from the Duomo,** at the west corner of Via de' Calzaiuoli (inside the Loggia, same hours as train station branch, tel. 055-288-496).

A less crowded and more helpful TI (covering both the city and the greater province of Florence) is a couple of blocks **north of the Duomo,** just past the Medici-Riccardi Palace (Mon-Fri 9:00-13:00, closed Sat-Sun, Via Cavour 1 red, tel. 055-290-832). There's also a TI booth at the **airport.**

A handy little ticket booth at the Orsanmichele Church often has reservations for the Uffizi and Accademia when other sources are sold out (Mon-Sat 9:00-16:15).

Helpful Hints

Sightseeing Tips: Everyone visiting Florence wants to see the same three or four sights. Consequently, these are mobbed with long lines. While, technically, you could wait in line to get into these places, it's flat-out stupid. Don't waste your time in line—get a reservation. The process for making reservations online is clearly explained under "Sights," later.

Among Florence's many sightseeing passes, one worth considering is the **Uffizi/Pitti Palace/Boboli Gardens combo-ticket** (called "PassePartout"), which is valid for three consecutive days and offers admission to these sights at a €12 savings (€38 March-Oct, €18 Nov-Feb). Note that with this ticket, you must start your visit at the Uffizi. You can purchase it in advance at www.uffizi.it; look for "Intero Cumulativo 3 giorni" in the ticket options.

The 72-hour **Firenze Card** sold by the TI gets you into nearly all the sights in town for €85. It requires you book a time to enter the Uffizi and Accademia. It's only a savings and worth buying if you'll be sightseeing like crazy for three days. And in very busy times as a last resort, you might find you can get a reservation with a Firenze Card for the Uffizi or Accademia when you otherwise can't get in.

Some state museums in Italy (including Florence's Uffizi Gallery, Accademia, and many others) are free to enter once or twice a month, usually on a Sunday. But **free days** are bad news—they attract crowds. Check sight websites in advance.

Theft Alert: Florence has hardworking gangs of thieves who hang out near the train station, the station's underpass (especially where the tunnel surfaces), around Mercato Centrale, and at major sights. American tourists are considered easy targets. Some thieves even dress like tourists to fool you. Any crowded bus likely holds at least one thief.

Visiting Churches: Modest dress is required in some churches, including the Duomo, Santa Maria Novella, Santa Croce, Santa Maria del Carmine/Brancacci Chapel, and the Medici Chapels. Be respectful of worshippers and the paintings; don't use a flash. Many churches, though not the biggies we mention, close from 12:00 or 12:30 until 15:00 or 16:00.

Addresses: Florence has a confusing system for street addresses, with "red" numbers for businesses and "black" numbers for residences. In print, addresses are indicated with "r" (as in Via Cavour 2r) or "n" (as in Via Cavour 25n). Red and black numbers are interspersed together on the same street, but their numbers bear no connection with each other.

WCs: Public restrooms are scarce. Use them when you can, in any café or museum you patronize. Pay public WCs are typically €1. Convenient locations include: at the Baptistery ticket office (near the Duomo); near the entrance to the Church of Santa Maria Novella; inside the train station (near track 5 and in the food court); just down the street from Piazza Santa Croce (at Borgo Santa Croce 29 red); on Piazza Santo Spirito; and up near Piazzale Michelangelo.

Laundry: The **Wash & Dry Lavara-pido** chain offers long hours and efficient self-service launderettes at several locations (generally daily 7:30-23:00). These locations are close to recommended hotels: Via del Sole 29 red and Via della Scala 52 red (this location is a Speed Queen, between train station and river), and Via Ghibellina 143 red (Palazzo Vecchio).

Rick's Tip: Carry a water bottle to refill at Florence's twist-the-handle **public fountains** *(around the corner from the "Piglet" at Mercato Nuovo, or in front of the Pitti Palace). Try the* fontanello *(dispenser of free cold water) on Piazza della Signoria, behind the statue of Neptune.*

Tours

Tour companies that offer a discount when you show this book are indicated in these listings with the abbreviation "RS%." In addition to the offerings mentioned here, some offer bus excursions to smaller towns in the Tuscan countryside (such as Siena, San Gimignano, Pisa, and into Chianti country for wine tasting).

WALKING (AND BIKING) TOURS

Artviva offers an intriguing variety of tours, including their popular overview tours (€33 "Original Florence" 3-hour town walk; €124 "Florence in One Glorious Day" combines town walk and tours of the Uffizi and Accademia, 6 hours total). They also have standalone Uffizi and Accademia tours, cooking classes, and more (RS%—10 percent discount, use the password "reader"). Their office is above Odeon Cinema near Piazza della

Avoid waiting in lines...   *...by making advance reservations.*

Florence

See Heart of Florence detail map

PIAZZA DEL CROCIFISSO

PORTA AL PRATO TRAIN STN.

To Airport & A-1 Autostrada (Firenze Nord exit)

V. FRATELLI ROSSELLI

V. FRATELLI ROSSELLI

VIA IL PRATO

VIA DELLA SCALA

SAN JACOPO DI RIPOLI

EPISCOPALE AMERICANA DI ST. JAMES

PALAZZO DEGLI AFFARI

CENACOLO DI FULIGNO

Piazza Adua

CASA DI RIPOSO D. BEATA

VIA LUIGI ALAMANNI

V. VALFONDA

SANTA MARIA NOVELLA TRAIN STATION

WC

BUS STN.

B #12

SANTA MARIA NOVELLA

Piazza della Stazione

Piazza dell'Unità Italiana

VIA NAZIONALE

VIA FAENZA

PALAZZO DEI CARTELLONI

V. PANZANI

TEATRO COMUNALE

CORSO ITALIA

LUNGARNO AMERIGO VESPUCCI

SAN LUCIA SUL PRATO

VIA DELLA SCALA

VIA PALAZZUOLO

PERFUMERY

Piazza di Santa Maria Novella

VIA DEI BANCHI

Arno River

PONTE AMERIGO VESPUCCI

L. AMERIGO

OGNISSANTI

Piazza d'Ognissanti

BORGO OGNISSANTI

VIA PORCELLANA

VIA DEL FOSSI

VIA DEL SOLE

B

RUCELLAI PALACE

VIA VIGNA NUOVA

V. DE' TORNABUONI

STROZZI PALACE

LUNGARNO SANTA ROSA

PORTA SAN FREDIANO

VIA PISANA

Piazza d. Verzaia

VIA SANT' ONOFRIO

LUNGARNO SODERINI

VIA DEL PARIONE

Piazza Goldoni

PONTE ALLA CARRAIA

PALAZZO CORSINI

L. CORSINI

SANTA TRINITÀ

VIA

BORGO ACCIAIUOLI

Cimitero Israelitico

VIA ALIARDI

Piazza de' Nerli

VIA CAMALDOLI

Piazza di Castello

BORGO SAN FREDIANO

Piazza Nazaro Sauro

L. GUICCIARDINI

VIA S. SPIRITO

PONTE SANTA TRINITÀ

Piazza de' Frescobaldi

CITY WALLS

Piazza T. Tasso

Piazza del Carmine

BRANCACCI CHAPEL

SANTA MARIA DEL CARMINE

VIA DELLA CHIESA

VIA DE' SERRAGLI

O L T R A R N O

VIA S. MARTINO

B. SAN JACOPO

SANTO SPIRITO

Pza d. Passera

Piazza di Santa Felicità

VIA DEL CAMPUCCIO

Giardino Torrigiani

VIA PETRARCA

Piazza di Santo Spirito

PAL. DE' COSIMO RIDOLFI

VIA MAGGIO

VIA D. S.

V. D. GUICCIARDINI

GROTTO

BACCHUS

Piazza di San Felice

Piazza de' Pitti

PITTI PALACE

VIA ROMANA

Giardino di Analena

3

GARDENS ENTRANCE

AMPHI-THEATER

Boboli Gardens

FONTANA D. NETTUNO

PORTA ROMANA

FONTANA DELL'OCEANO

CITY WALLS

Piazzale della Porta Romana

Hotels & Eateries outside the Center

1 Locanda de' Ciompi
2 Hotel Silla
3 Hotel Annalena
4 Ristorante Natalino
5 Caffè del Verone

Tour Companies

6 ArtViva Tours
7 Florencetown Tours

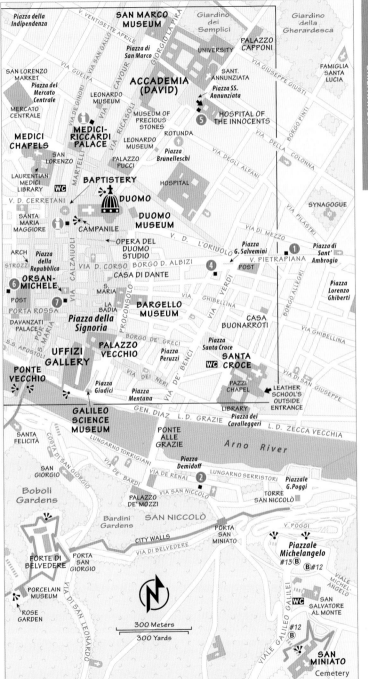

Piazza della
Indipendenza

V. VENTISETTE APRILE

SAN MARCO
MUSEUM

GIORGIO LA PIRA

Giardino
dei
Semplici

Giardino
della
Gherardesca

Piazza di
San Marco

UNIVERSITY

PALAZZO
CAPPONI

VIA GIUSEPPE GIUSTI

FAMIGLIA
SANTA
LUCIA

SAN LORENZO
MARKET

VIA GUELFA

VIA SAN GALLO

VIA CAVOUR

SANT.
ANNUNZIATA

Piazza SS.
Annunziata

BORGO PINTI

Piazza del
Mercato
Centrale

ACCADEMIA
(DAVID)

VIA DE' GINORI

VIA RICASOLI

MUSEUM OF
PRECIOUS
STONES

HOSPITAL OF
THE INNOCENTS

MERCATO
CENTRALE

LEONARDO
MUSEUM

ROTUNDA

VIA DELLA COLONNA

MEDICI
CHAPELS

MEDICI-
RICCARDI
PALACE

LEONARDO
MUSEUM

Piazza
Brunelleschi

VIA DEGLI ALFANI

SAN
LORENZO

MARTELLI

PALAZZO
PUCCI

SYNAGOGUE

LAURENTIAN
MEDICI
LIBRARY

WC

BAPTISTERY

HOSPITAL

VIA DI PILASTRI

V. D. CERRETANI

DUOMO

SANTA
MARIA
MAGGIORE

CAMPANILE

DUOMO
MUSEUM

VIA DI MEZZO

OPERA DEL
DUOMO
STUDIO

V. D. L'ORIUOLO

Piazza
G. Salvemini

Piazza di
Sant'
Ambrogio

ARCH

STROZZI

Piazza
della
Repubblica

VIA CALZAIUOLI

VIA D. CORSO

BORGO D. ALBIZI

V. PIETRAPIANA

ORSAN-
MICHELE

CASA DI DANTE

POST

BORGO ALLEGRI

POST

S.
MARIA

VIA

GHIBELLINA

VIA VERDI

Piazza
Lorenzo
Ghiberti

PORTA ROSSA

LA
BADIA

PROCONSOLO

BARGELLO
MUSEUM

CASA
BUONARROTI

VIA GHIBELLINA

DAVANZATI
PALACE

Piazza della
Signoria

BORGO DE' GRECI

Piazza
Santa Croce

S.S. APOSTOLI

UFFIZI
GALLERY

PALAZZO
VECCHIO

Piazza
Peruzzi

SANTA
CROCE

WC

VIA DI SAN GIUSEPPE

PONTE
VECCHIO

Piazza
Giudici

VIA DEI NERI

VIA DE' BENCI

PAZZI
CHAPEL

LEATHER
SCHOOL'S
OUTSIDE
ENTRANCE

Piazza
Mentana

GALILEO
SCIENCE
MUSEUM

GEN. DIAZ

L. D. GRAZIE

Piazza dei
Cavalleggeri

LIBRARY

SANTA
FELICITÀ

COSTA DI SAN GIORGIO

LUNGARNO TORRIGIANI

PONTE
ALLE
GRAZIE

Arno River

L. D. ZECCA VECCHIA

SAN
GIORGIO

VIA DE' BARDI

Piazza
Demidoff

LUNGARNO SERRISTORI

Piazzale
G. Poggi

Boboli
Gardens

PALAZZO
DE' MOZZI

VIA SAN NICCOLÒ

TORRE
SAN NICCOLÒ

Bardini
Gardens

SAN NICCOLÒ

PORTA
SAN
MINIATO

V. POGGI

FORTE DI
BELVEDERE

PORTA
SAN
GIORGIO

CITY WALLS

VIA DI BELVEDERE

Piazzale
Michelangelo

#13 B

B #12

VIA DI SAN LEONARDO

VIALE MICHEL. ANGELO

PORCELAIN
MUSEUM

WC

SAN
SALVATORE
AL MONTE

ROSE
GARDEN

N

300 Meters

300 Yards

VIALE GALILEO GALILEI

#12 B

SAN
MINIATO

Cemetery

Repubblica (Mon-Sat 8:00-18:00, Sun 8:30-13:30, Via de' Sassetti 1, second floor, tel. 055-264-5033, www.artviva.com).

Florencetown runs tours on foot or by bike. Their most popular offerings are "Walk and Talk Florence" (€29, 2.5 hours, daily at 10:00, basic stops including the Oltrarno) and "I Bike Florence" (€39; 2.5 hours on one-speed bike, 15-stop blitz of town's top sights, helmets optional; in bad weather it goes as a walking tour). Their office is at Via de Lamberti 1 (facing Orsanmichele Church). They also offer cooking classes and student rates for anyone with this book (RS%, tel. 055-281-103, www.florencetown.com).

For a more scholarly approach, **Florentia**'s tours are geared for travelers with longer-than-average attention spans and range from introductory city walks and museum visits to in-depth thematic walks (from €275, includes planning assistance by email, www.florentia.org, info@florentia.org), and Context Florence's tours are led by graduate students and professors (www.contexttravel.com, info@contexttravel.com).

Walks Inside Florence, led by two art historians—Paola Barubiani and Marzia Valbonesi—provide quality private tours and a discounted rate for Rick Steves readers (RS%, €190/group for 3-hour introductory walk, up to 6 people). Their "Florence in a Day" tour gives you the essentials in four hours (€260/group, up to 6 people, museum admissions extra—they make the reservations so there's no waiting in line; Paola's mobile 335-526-6496, www.walksinsideflorence.it, paola@walksinsideflorence.it).

LOCAL GUIDES

These guides offer a variety of private tours in and around Florence (generally €60-75/hour): **Alessandra Marchetti** (mobile 347-386-9839, www.tuscanydriverguide.com, alessandramarchettitours@gmail.com); **Paola Migliorini** (mobile 347-657-2611, www.florencetour.com, info@florencetour.com);

Elena Fulceri (mobile 347-942-2054, www.florencewithflair.com, info@florencewithflair.com); and **Vanessa Garau** (mobile 349-133-6894, garau.vanessa@gmail.com).

Rick's Tip: *Several tour companies (such as Florencetown or Artviva) offer* **regularly scheduled group tours** *that anyone can sign up for—usually the cheapest option for individual travelers. But families and small groups can* **book a private guide for a similar price,** *since rates are hourly for any size of group.*

RENAISSANCE WALK

This great and rich city is easily covered on foot. We'll start with the soaring church dome that stands as the proud symbol of the Renaissance spirit; just opposite, you'll find the Baptistery doors that opened the Renaissance. We'll then stroll down the city's pedestrian-only main street to the Palazzo Vecchio and the Arno River. Along the way, we'll pass elegant stores, lively eateries, and the parade of people that make up Florence today.

For more details on many of the stops on this walk, see the individual listings under "Sights," later.

Length of This Walk: The walk is less than a mile long. Allow two hours, including visits to the interiors of the Baptistery and Orsanmichele Church.

Tours: Download my free Renaissance Walk **audio tour.**

Background: The Renaissance—the "rebirth" of Greek and Roman culture that swept across Europe—started around 1400 and lasted about 150 years. In politics, the Renaissance meant democracy; in science, a renewed interest in exploring nature. The general mood was optimistic and "humanistic," with a confidence in the power of the individual.

Renaissance art was a return to the realism and balance of Greek and Roman

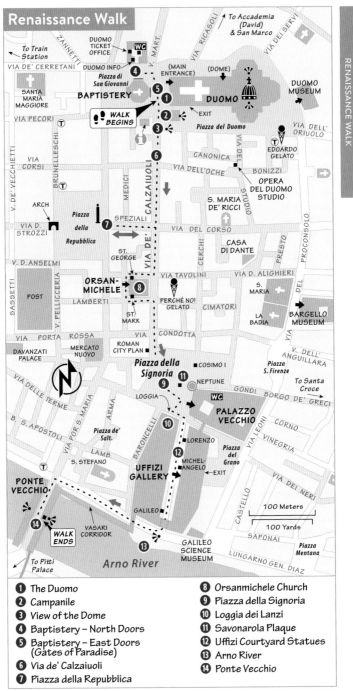

Renaissance Walk

❶ The Duomo
❷ Campanile
❸ View of the Dome
❹ Baptistery – North Doors
❺ Baptistery – East Doors (Gates of Paradise)
❻ Via de' Calzaiuoli
❼ Piazza della Repubblica
❽ Orsanmichele Church
❾ Piazza della Signoria
❿ Loggia dei Lanzi
⓫ Savonarola Plaque
⓬ Uffizi Courtyard Statues
⓭ Arno River
⓮ Ponte Vecchio

sculpture and architecture. Domes and round arches replaced Gothic spires and pointed arches. In painting and sculpture, Renaissance artists strove for realism. Merging art and science, they used mathematics, the laws of perspective, and direct observation of nature.

This was not an anti-Christian movement. Artists saw themselves as an extension of God's creative powers. The Church even supported the Renaissance and commissioned many of its greatest works. After 1,000 years of waiting, the embers of Europe's classical heritage burst into flames right here in Florence.

⦿ Self-Guided Walk

The Duomo—the cathedral with the distinctive red dome—is the center of Florence and the orientation point for this walk. Stroll around the piazza in front of the cathedral (the Duomo), and take in the sights. To the right of the Duomo rises its skyscraping bell tower (the Campanile). In front of the church is the Baptistery—an octagonal, black-and-white stone building that's bigger than many churches.

❶ The Duomo

Florence's massive cathedral is the city's geographical and spiritual heart. Its dome, visible from all over the city, inspired Florentines to do great things.

The church was begun in 1296 in the Gothic style. After generations of work, it was still unfinished. The facade was little more than bare brick, and it stood that way until it was completed in 1870 in the "Neo"-Gothic style. Its "retro" look captures the feel of the original medieval facade, with green, white, and pink marble sheets that cover the brick construction. This over-the-top facade is adored by many, while others call it "the cathedral in pajamas."

We won't go inside the church on this tour. It has a cavernous, bare interior with a few noteworthy sights. Entry is free, but there's often a long wait.

The Campanile

• *Now turn to the church's bell tower, to the right.*

❷ Campanile (Giotto's Tower)

The 270-foot bell tower was begun in the 1300s by the great painter Giotto. As a forerunner of the Renaissance genius, Giotto excelled in many artistic fields, just as Michelangelo would do two centuries later. In his day, Giotto was called the ugliest man to ever walk the streets of Florence, but he designed what many call the most beautiful bell tower in all of Europe.

You can climb the Campanile for great views. It doesn't require a reservation, just a Duomo combo-ticket.

• *Now take in the Duomo's star attraction: the dome. The best viewing spot is just to the right of the facade, from the corner of the pedestrian-only Via de' Calzaiuoli.*

❸ View of Brunelleschi's Dome

Though construction of the church had begun in 1296, by the 1400s there still was no suitable roof. City fathers intended to top it with a dome, but the technology to span the 140-foot-wide hole had yet to

The Renaissance and Brunelleschi's dome live on in Florence.

be invented. *Non c'è problema*. The brash Florentines knew that someday someone would come along who could handle the challenge. That man was Filippo Brunelleschi.

Brunelleschi used a dome within a dome. What you see is the outer shell, covered in terra-cotta tile. The inner dome is thicker and provides much of the structural support. The grand white skeletal ribs connect at the top, supporting each other in a way similar to a pointed arch. Hidden between them are interlocking bricks, laid in a herringbone pattern. Rather than being stacked horizontally, like traditional brickwork, the alternating vertical bricks act as "bookends." The dome grew upward like an igloo, supporting itself as it proceeded from the base. When the ribs reached the top, Brunelleschi arched them in and fixed them in place with the lantern at the top. His dome, built in only 14 years, was the largest since ancient Rome's Pantheon.

When completed in 1436, Brunelleschi's dome was the wonder of the age. It became the model for many domes to follow, from St. Peter's to the US Capitol.

You can climb the dome for Florence's best views, but it requires a reservation in advance.

• Next up, the Baptistery.

Baptistery and Ghiberti's Bronze Doors

Built in the 11th century, atop Roman foundations, this is Florence's oldest surviving building—a thousand years old. The spacious interior features a fine example of pre-Renaissance mosaic art (1200s-1300s) in the Byzantine style. But the Baptistery is best known for its doors. The most famous ones are the East Doors, which face the cathedral, but let's start with the North Doors—around to the right, where tourists go in—which may be even more important. (Note that the original doors are in the Duomo Museum and well worth seeing.)

Ghiberti's bronze Gates of Paradise

❹ **North Doors:** Some say that these doors actually started the Renaissance. It was the year 1401, and Florence was holding a competition to find the best artist to make some doors for the Baptistery entrance. All the greats entered the contest, including Donatello and Brunelleschi. The winner was relatively unknown 24-year-old Lorenzo Ghiberti. For the next 25 years, he worked on these North Doors.

• *Now return to the more famous doors facing the church.*

❺ **East Doors** (Gates of Paradise): Ghiberti's bronze panels for these doors added a whole new dimension to art—depth. Michelangelo said these doors were fit to be the "Gates of Paradise." Here we see how the Renaissance masters merged art and science. Realism was in, and Renaissance artists used math, illusion, and dissection to create it.

• *Head south, down the busy pedestrian-only street that runs from here toward the Arno River.*

❻ *Via de' Calzaiuoli*

Via de' Calzaiuoli (kahlts-ay-WOH-lee) was part of the ancient Roman grid plan that became Florence. Around the year 1400, as the Renaissance was blooming, this street connected the religious center (where we are now) with the political center (where we're heading), a five-minute walk away.

Since most vehicles were banned a few years back, this street has been transformed into a pleasant place to stroll, people-watch, window-shop, and wonder why American cities can't become more pedestrian-friendly.

• *Two blocks down from the Baptistery, turn right on Via degli Speziali toward the triumphal arch that marks...*

❼ Piazza della Repubblica

This large square sits on the site of the original Roman Forum. The lone column that still stands here once marked the intersection of the two main Roman roads (Via Corso and Via Roma). In the 1860s, the square got its magnificent arch, celebrating the unification of Italy. Venerable cafés and stores line the square. Gilli, on the northeast corner, is a favorite for its grand atmosphere and tasty sweets.

• *Return to the main street and continue walking toward the river. A block farther, at the intersection with Via Orsanmichele, is the...*

❽ Orsanmichele Church

Originally, this was an open loggia (covered porch) with a huge grain warehouse upstairs. The arches of the loggia were artfully filled in (14th century) to make walls, and the building gained a new purpose—

as a church. The 14 niches in the exterior walls feature remarkable-in-their-day statues paid for by the city's rising middle class of merchants and their 21 guilds.

Circle the church exterior counterclockwise to enjoy the statues. Start on the church's right side (along Via Orsanmichele). In the third niche is **Nanni di Banco's *Quattro Santi Coronati*** (c. 1415-1417). These four early Christians were sculptors martyred by the Roman emperor Diocletian because they refused to sculpt pagan gods. They seem to be contemplating the consequences of the fatal decision they're about to make.

Just to the right of Banco's saints is **Donatello's *St. George.*** He's alert, perched on the edge of his niche, scanning the horizon for dragons. He's anxious, but he's also self-assured. Comparing this Renaissance-style *St. George* to *Quattro Santi Coronati,* you can psychoanalyze the heady changes underway. This is humanism.

Continue counterclockwise around the church (bypassing the entrance), all the way to the opposite side. The first niche features **Donatello's *St. Mark*** (1411-1413). The evangelist cradles his gospel in his strong, veined hand and gazes out, resting his weight on the right leg while bending the left. Though subtle, St. Mark's twisting *contrapposto* pose was the first seen since antiquity. Eighty years after young Donatello carved this statue, a teenage Michelangelo Buonarroti stood here and marveled at it.

Donatello, St. George

Donatello, St. Mark

Piazza della Signoria

Upstairs is a free museum (open Mon and Sat only) displaying most of the originals of the statues you just saw outside.

• *Continue down the mall 50 more yards, to the huge and historic square...*

❾ *Piazza della Signoria*

What a view! This piazza—the main civic center of Florence—is dominated by the massive stone facade of the Palazzo Vecchio, with a tower that reaches for the sky. The square is dotted with statues. The stately Uffizi Gallery is nearby, and the marble greatness of old Florence litters the cobbles. Piazza della Signoria still vibrates with the echoes of the city's past—executions, riots, and great celebrations. There's even Roman history: Look for the **chart** showing the ancient city (in front of Chanel). Today, it's a tourist's world with pigeons, selfie sticks, horse buggies, and tired spouses. For a little pick-me-up, stop in at **$$$ Rivoire** café to enjoy its fine desserts, pudding-thick hot chocolate, and the best view seats in town.

Before you towers the **Palazzo Vecchio,** the palatial Town Hall of the Medici—a fortress designed to contain riches and survive the many riots that went with local politics. The windows are just beyond the reach of angry stones, and the tower was a handy lookout post. Justice was doled out sternly on this square. Until 1873, Michelangelo's **David** stood where you see the replica today.

Step through the front door into the Palazzo Vecchio's courtyard (free). This palace was Florence's symbol of civic power. You're surrounded by art for art's sake—a cherub frivolously marks the courtyard's center, and ornate stuccoes and frescoes decorate the walls and columns. Such luxury represented a big change 500 years ago.

• *Back outside, check out the arcade of three arches filled with statues.*

❿ *Loggia dei Lanzi*

The loggia, once a forum for public debate, was perfect for a city that prided itself on its democratic traditions. But later, when the Medici figured that good art was more desirable than free speech, it was turned into an outdoor sculpture gallery.

Two statues in the front deserve a closer look. At the right end of the loggia, ***The Rape of the Sabine Women*** (c. 1583)—with its pulse-quickening rhythm of muscles—

is from the restless Mannerist period. The sculptor, Giambologna, proved his mastery of the medium by sculpting three entangled bodies from one piece of marble. Benvenuto Cellini's **Perseus** (1545-1553), the loggia's most noteworthy piece, shows the Greek hero who decapitated the snake-headed Medusa.

• *Cross the square to Bartolomeo Ammanati's big* **fountain of Neptune.** *Near it, the guy on the horse is Cosimo I, the post-Renaissance Medici who commissioned the Uffizi. Find the round marble plaque on the ground 10 steps in front of the fountain.*

⓫ *Savonarola Plaque*

In the 1490s the Medici family was briefly thrown from power by an austere and charismatic monk named Savonarola, who made Florence a constitutional republic. He organized huge rallies lit by roaring bonfires here on the square where he preached. The devout brought their rich "vanities" (such as paintings, musical instruments, and playing cards) and threw them into the flames.

But not everyone wanted a return to the medieval past. Encouraged by the pope, the Florentines fought back and arrested Savonarola. For two days they tortured him. Finally, on the very spot where Savonarola's followers had built bonfires of vanities, the monk was burned, ending his theocracy. Soon after, the Medici returned to power and the Renaissance picked up where it left off.

• *Stay cool, we have 200 yards to go. Follow the gaze of the fake David into the courtyard of the two-tone horseshoe-shaped building, the Uffizi.*

⓬ *Uffizi Courtyard Statues*

The top floor of this building, known as the *uffizi* (offices) during Medici days, is filled with the greatest collection of Florentine painting anywhere. It's one of Europe's top art galleries. The courtyard is watched over by 19th-century statues of the great figures of the Renaissance: artists (Michelangelo, Giotto, Donatello, Leonardo), philosophers (Machiavelli), scientists (Galileo), poets (Dante and Petrarch), explorers (Vespucci), and the great patron of the Renaissance—Lorenzo "the Magnificent" de' Medici.

• *At the far end of the courtyard, pause at the* ⓭ *Arno River, with a magnificent view of the Ponte Vecchio, where we'll finish this walk.*

⓮ *Ponte Vecchio*

Since ancient times, a bridge has stood at this narrow spot in the Arno. When a flood washed away the old wooden bridge, this one was built in 1345, and is now called the Ponte Vecchio (Old Bridge).

In times past, the bridge's shops were inhabited by butchers and hide tanners—a natural fit, because they could empty their waste into the river below. In the 1500s, the Medici booted them out and installed gold- and silversmiths who

The Uffizi courtyard

Ponte Vecchio

still tempt visitors to this day. Fittingly, a famous goldsmith is honored with a fine bust at the central point of the bridge—the sculptor Benvenuto (*"Perseus"*) Cellini.

Look up to notice the windows running across the upper part of the buildings. This is the Vasari Corridor—a protected and elevated passageway, built by the Medici. It led from the Palazzo Vecchio through the Uffizi, across Ponte Vecchio, and up to the immense Pitti Palace, four blocks beyond the bridge.

Looking upstream and down, you have timeless views of the city. The neighborhood across the river, known as the Oltrarno, is more rustic and working-class.

The Ponte Vecchio is a very romantic spot, especially in the evening. Street musicians play and lovers hold hands. The city of Florence—born in Roman times, flourishing in the medieval age, and blossoming in the Renaissance—remains a vibrant cultural capital.

• *Several of the finest museums in Europe await your discovery—or perhaps it's time for a nice espresso or gelato. Enjoy.*

SIGHTS

Advance Reservations for Skipping Lines

To avoid long lines, make advance reservations for the Uffizi, Accademia, and climbing the Duomo's dome. Get reservations as soon as you know when you'll be in town. Though lines are less of a problem after 16:00, and from November through March, it's always crowded from April through October and on weekends. For peace of mind, I'd reserve a spot any time of year.

Uffizi and Accademia Tickets: Book your tickets in advance at the websites for these museums (see individual sight listings next)—available time-slots for full-price tickets are marked "Intero/Full." You'll receive an email with a voucher that you take to the ticket desk a few minutes before your visit to swap for an actual ticket.

If there's no availability at the official museum sites, you can try for-profit vendors such as Florence.net or Tickitaly. com, which may have time slots available, though you'll pay about €5 more per ticket.

Uffizi and Accademia tickets are also available by phone: From a US phone, dial 011-39-055-294-883, or from an Italian phone call 055-294-883 (€4/ticket reservation fee; booking office open Mon-Fri 8:30-18:30, Sat until 12:30, closed Sun).

Various tour companies—including those listed in this chapter—sell tours that include a reserved museum admission. If you're booking a private guide well in advance, they are often happy to obtain tickets and reservations for your tour with them.

Climbing the Duomo's Dome: For reservation information, see the next page.

Rick's Tip: You can **extend your sightseeing day** *into the night at a number of sights around Florence. The Uffizi, Accademia, and the Pitti Palace* **stay open into the early evening** *every day but Monday, and many other sights have evening hours (check individual sight listings). The stalls at the San Lorenzo Market (closed Mon in winter) and Mercato Nuovo stay open late for shoppers every night.*

The Duomo and Nearby

Florence's most distinctive monuments—the Duomo, Baptistery, and Campanile—are gathered around the pedestrian-only Piazza San Giovanni and Piazza del Duomo. The Duomo Museum, just behind the cathedral, is the most important of these sights—and it never has long lines. But you must plan ahead for the dome climb (only possible with an advance reservation).

Ticketing: While the Duomo is free to enter, several associated sights are covered by a single €18 **combo-ticket,** valid for 72 hours: the Baptistery, dome, Campanile, Duomo Museum, and Santa Reparata crypt (enter inside the Duomo).

A €13 audioguide covers all of the Duomo sights.

The only way to **climb the dome** is with a reservation. Buy the combo-ticket and make a reservation at www. museumflorence.com or in person at any Duomo ticket office. Time slots can fill up days in advance, so reserve well ahead. The main ticket office, with a staffed counter and self-service machines, faces the Baptistery entrance (at #7 on the square; it may be under renovation when you visit). There are also ticket counters and self-service machines in the Duomo Museum lobby.

Themed Tours: Three themed tours are organized by the Duomo (€33 each, includes combo-ticket, 1 hour, English only). These include a Duomo visit with access to the north terrace of the church (daily at 10:30); an opportunity to watch contemporary stonemasons at work in the same workshop where Michelangelo carved *David* (Mon, Wed, and Fri at 12:00); and an up-close look at the mosaics of the Baptistery (Mon, Wed, and Fri at 16:30). To book a spot, call 055-230-2885, email commerciale@operadelduomo. firenze.it, or stop by the main ticket office.

🎧 The Duomo, dome, Campanile, and Baptistery are also covered on my free Renaissance Walk **audio tour.**

▲▲DUOMO (CATTEDRALE DI SANTA MARIA DEL FIORE)

Florence's Gothic cathedral has the third-longest nave in Christendom. The church's noisy Neo-Gothic facade (from the 1870s) is covered with pink, green, and white Tuscan marble. The cathedral's claim to artistic fame is Brunelleschi's magnificent dome—the first Renaissance dome and the model for domes to follow. While viewing it from the outside is well worth ▲▲, the massive but empty-feeling interior is lucky to rate ▲—it doesn't justify the massive crowds that line up to get inside. Much of the great art is housed in the Duomo Museum behind the church.

Cost and Hours: Free; Mon-Sat 10:00-

16:30, Sun 13:30-16:45, opening times sometimes change due to religious functions, modest dress code enforced, tel. 055-230-2885, www.museumflorence.com.

Mass: The church is open to all for Mass: English Mass on Sun at 17:00 and old-school Latin Mass with Gregorian chants on Sun at 10:30.

▲CLIMBING THE DUOMO'S DOME

For a grand view into the cathedral from the base of the dome, a chance to see Brunelleschi's "dome-within-a-dome" construction, and a glorious Florence view from the top, climb 463 steps up the dome. The claustrophobic one-way route takes you up narrow, steep staircases and walkways to the top—but it's well worth the climb.

Cost: Covered by Duomo combo-ticket; must reserve dome-climb time—best to buy combo-ticket and reserve a time either

The Duomo with Brunelleschi's dome

at the ticket office (opposite the Baptistery, at #7, open daily 8:00-19:00) or online (www.museumflorence.com).

Hours: Mon-Fri 8:30-19:00, Sat until 17:00, Sun 13:00-16:00; enter from the north side of the church (get in line about 15 minutes before your reservation time). The dome is closed during rain.

Climbing the Dome: While waiting to enter at your reserved time, spend a few minutes studying the side-entrance door, called the Porta della Mandorla ("Almond Door"). Just above the delicately carved doorframe is a colorful Annunciation mosaic by Nanni di Banco, and above that, in a sculpted almond-shaped frame, the Madonna is borne up to heaven by angels. If you look up from here you'll see an empty pedestal atop the transept. Michelangelo's *David* was originally destined to adorn one of these.

The climb is long but there are small landings where you can pull over and take a breather. Halfway up, you'll stroll on the walkway high above the altar where you can get a close-up of Vasari's *Last Judgment* ceiling (especially the ghoulish lower portion, filled with scenes of eternal torment) and a vertigo-inducing view of the nave. After a few tight, winding staircases and a steep final climb, you'll pop out of the hatch on the crowded terrace with a grand city view. If possible, visit at sunset for a romantic experience.

▲CAMPANILE (GIOTTO'S TOWER)

The 270-foot bell tower has 50-some fewer steps than the Duomo's dome (but that's still 414 steps—no elevator); offers a faster, less-intense climb (with typically short lines); and has a view of that magnificent dome to boot. On the way up, there are several intermediate levels where you can catch your breath and enjoy ever-higher views. The stairs narrow as you go, creating a mosh-pit bottleneck near the very top—but the views are worth the hassle. While the viewpoints are enclosed by cage-like bars, the gaps are big enough to snap great photos.

Last Judgment *mosaic in the Baptistery*

Cost and Hours: Covered by Duomo combo-ticket; daily 8:15-19:30, last entry 40 minutes before closing.

▲BAPTISTERY

Michelangelo said the bronze doors of this octagonal building were fit to be the gates of paradise. Check out the gleaming copies of Lorenzo Ghiberti's bronze doors facing the Duomo (the originals are in the Duomo Museum). Making a breakthrough in perspective, Ghiberti used mathematical laws to create the illusion of receding distance on a basically flat surface.

The doors on the north side of the building (around to the right) were designed by Ghiberti when he was younger; he'd won the honor and opportunity by beating Brunelleschi in a competition (the rivals' original entries are in the Bargello).

Inside, sit and savor the medieval mosaic ceiling, where it's always Judgment Day and Jesus is giving the ultimate thumbs-up or thumbs-down.

Cost and Hours: Interior covered by Duomo combo-ticket; open Mon-Sat 8:15-19:30 (closed 10:15-11:15), Sun until 13:30. The (facsimile) bronze doors on the exterior are always viewable.

▲▲▲DUOMO MUSEUM (MUSEO DELL'OPERA DEL DUOMO)

The often-overlooked but superbly presented cathedral museum is filled with some of the best sculpture of the Renaissance, including a late pieta by Michelangelo and statues from the original Baptistery facade. Remarkably, it's almost never crowded. It also holds Brunelleschi's models for his dome, Donatello's emaciated *Mary Magdalene* and playful choir loft, and Ghiberti's original bronze Gates of Paradise panels (the ones on the Baptistery's doors today are copies).

Cost and Hours: Covered by Duomo combo-ticket; daily 9:00-19:00, closed first Tue of each month, last entry one hour before closing; one of the few museums in Florence always open Mon; behind the church at Via del Proconsolo 9, tel. 055-230-2885, www.museumflorence.com.

Visiting the Museum: Begin with the **model of the Duomo's facade** circa 1500, the era of Michelangelo (Room 4). Notice that only the lower third is faced with marble and statues; the rest was only bare brick. Church construction began in 1296, but after an initial burst of energy, petered out. The facade was meant to be a glorious showcase of great statues set into niches.

Now enter the **Hall of Paradise** (Sala del Paradiso, Room 6). On one wall, this room re-creates that lower third of the facade we saw on the model. The oppo-site wall re-creates the Baptistery facade. Both buildings were a showcase of the greatest art of Florence from roughly 1300 to 1600.

Facing the facade of the church, as they did in the Middle Ages, are the famous doors of the Baptistery. The oldest doors on the left are by Pisano (South Doors, c. 1330). The original competition doors on the right are the first ones done by Ghiberti (North Doors, 1403-1424). And in the center are the Gates of Paradise by Ghiberti (East Doors, 1425-1452).

These bronze "Gates of Paradise" revolutionized the way Renaissance people saw the world around them. They tell several Old Testament stories using perspective and realism as never before. Ghiberti poured his energy and creativity into these panels. That's him in the center of the doorframe, atop the second row of panels—the head on the left with the shiny male-pattern baldness.

Also on the ground floor are rooms dedicated to the museum's most famous statues. Donatello's ***Mary Magdalene*** (*Santa Maria Maddalena,* c. 1455), carved from white poplar and originally painted with realistic colors, is a Renaissance work of intense devotion (Room 8). The aging Michelangelo (1475-1564) designed his own tomb, with ***Pietà*** (1547-1555) as the centerpiece (Room 10). Three mourners tend the broken body of the crucified Christ. We see Mary, his mother (the shadowy figure on our right); Mary Magdalene (on the left); and Nicodemus, the converted Pharisee, whose face is that of Michelangelo himself.

Upstairs, the first floor displays original **statues and panels** from the bell tower's third story, where copies stand today, two marble **choir lofts** (*cantorie;* by Lucca della Robbia and Donatello) that once sat above the sacristy doors of the Duomo, and **Brunelleschi's model** of the dome. Don't miss the Terrazza Brunelleschiana on the third floor—an **outdoor terrace** with an up-close rooftop view of the Duomo.

Michelangelo, Pietà

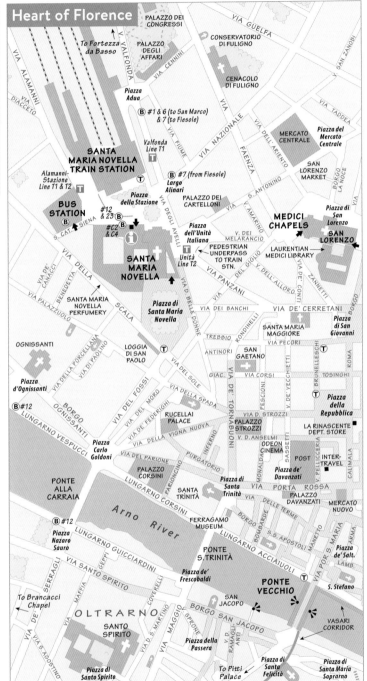

Heart of Florence

PALAZZO DEI CONGRESSI

VIA GUELFA

To Fortezza da Basso

PALAZZO DEGLI AFFARI

CONSERVATORIO DI FULIGNO

V. SAN ZANOBI

VIA VALFONDA

VIA CENNINI

CENACOLO DI FULIGNO

VIA TADDEA

Piazza Adua

VIA NAZIONALE

B #1 & 6 (to San Marco) & 7 (to Fiesole)

MERCATO CENTRALE

Piazza del Mercato Centrale

VIA ALAMANNI

VIA DIACCETO

Valfonda Line T1

SANTA MARIA NOVELLA TRAIN STATION

VIA FIUME

FAENZA

VIA DELL'ARIENTO

SAN LORENZO MARKET

BORGO LA NOCE

Alamanni-Stazione Line T1 & T2

B #7 (from Fiesole)

Largo Alinari

S. ANTONINO

MEDICI CHAPELS

Piazza di San Lorenzo

BUS STATION

Piazza della Stazione

PALAZZO DEI CARTELLONI

V. AMARINO

SAN LORENZO

B   #12 & 23

S. CAT. SIENA

#C2 & C4

B

Piazza dell'Unità Italiana

V. DEI MELARANCIO

LAURENTIAN MEDICI LIBRARY

VIA DE' ZANNETTI

VIA DE' CONTI

BORGO

VIA DE CANACCI

VIA DELLA SCALA

SANTA MARIA NOVELLA

PEDESTRIAN UNDERPASS TO TRAIN STN.

Unità Line T2

VIA DEL GIGLIO

V. DELL'ALLORO

VIA DE' BENEDETTA

VIA PANZANI

SANTA MARIA NOVELLA PERFUMERY

Piazza di Santa Maria Novella

VIA D. BELLE DONNE

VIA DEI BANCHI

VIA DE' CERRETANI

Piazza di San Giovanni

VIA PALAZZUOLO

TREBBIO

RONDINELLI

SANTA MARIA MAGGIORE

OGNISSANTI

VIA DELLA PORCELLANA

VIA DI PAOLINO

LOGGIA DI SAN PAOLO

ANTINORI

VIA PECORI

ROMA

Piazza d'Ognissanti

VIA DEL SOLE

SAN GAETANO

GIAC. V.

VIA CORSI

BRUNELLESCHI

TOSINGHI

Piazza della Repubblica

B #12

BORGO OGNISSANTI

VIA DELLA SPADA

DE' TORNABUONI

V. VECCHIETTI

T

LUNGARNO VESPUCCI

VIA DEL MORO

VIA DE FEDERIGHI

RUCELLAI PALACE

VIA D. STROZZI

PALAZZO STROZZI

V. D. ANSELMI

LA RINASCENTE DEPT. STORE

Piazza Carlo Goldoni

VIA DELLA VIGNA NUOVA

ODEON CINEMA

POST

INTER-TRAVEL

VIA DEL PARIONE

PURGATORIO

MONALDI

V. PELLICCERIA

CALIMALA

PONTE ALLA CARRAIA

PALAZZO CORSINI

LUNGARNO CORSINI

FARGINGTO

SANTA TRINITÀ

Piazza di Santa Trinità

Piazza de' Davanzati

VIA PORTA ROSSA

PALAZZO DAVANZATI

MERCATO NUOVO

Arno River

FERRAGAMO MUSEUM

BORGO S.S. APOSTOLI

DELLE TERME

BOMBARDE

VIA POR S. MARIA

MANETTO

ARMA

B #12

Piazza Nazaro Sauro

LUNGARNO GUICCIARDINI

VIA SANTO SPIRITO

VIA GEPPI

COVERELLI

SPRONE

LUNGARNO ACCIAIUOLI

PONTE S. TRINITÀ

Piazza de' Salt.

LAMB

To Brancacci Chapel

VIA DE' SERRAGLI

VIA MAFFIA

Piazza de' Frescobaldi

PONTE VECCHIO

S. Stefano

VASARI CORRIDOR

OLTRARNO

VIA S. AGOSTINO

SANTO SPIRITO

VIA D. S. MARTINO

VIA MAGGIO

SAN JACOPO

BORGO SAN JACOPO

V. D. RAMAGLI ANTI

Piazza di Santa Maria Soprarno

Piazza di Santo Spirito

Piazza della Passera

To Pitti Palace

Piazza di Santa Felicità

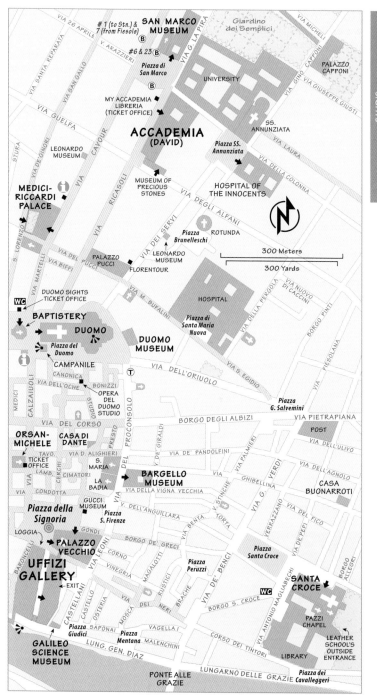

#1 (to Stn.) &
7 (from Fiesola)
#6 & 23 Ⓑ
Ⓑ
Ⓑ

SAN MARCO
MUSEUM

Giardino
dei Semplici

VIA 26 APRILE
V. ARAZZIERI
VIA SANTA REPARATA
VIA SAN GALLO
VIA G. LA PIRA
VIA GINO CAPPONI
VIA GIUSEPPE GIUSTI
VIA MICHELI

Piazza di
San Marco

UNIVERSITY

PALAZZO
CAPPONI

MY ACCADEMIA
LIBRERIA
(TICKET OFFICE)

VIA GUELFA
CAVOUR
RICASOLI

ACCADEMIA
(DAVID)

Piazza SS.
Annunziata

SS.
ANNUNZIATA

VIA LAURA
VIA DELLA COLONNA

STUFA
VIA DE' GINORI

LEONARDO
MUSEUM

MEDICI-
RICCARDI
PALACE

MUSEUM OF
PRECIOUS
STONES

VIA DEGLI ALFANI

HOSPITAL OF
THE INNOCENTS

Ⓝ

300 Meters

Piazza
Brunelleschi

ROTUNDA

VIA DEI SERVI

S. LORENZO
VIA MARTELLI
VIA DEL PUCCI
VIA DI BIFFI

PALAZZO
PUCCI

LEONARDO
MUSEUM

300 Yards

FLORENTOUR

VIA M. BUFALINI

HOSPITAL

WC
DUOMO SIGHTS
TICKET OFFICE

BAPTISTERY

DUOMO

Piazza del
Duomo

CAMPANILE

Piazza di
Santa Maria
Nuova

DUOMO
MUSEUM

VIA DELLA PERGOLA
VIA NUOVO
DI CACCINI
BORGO PINTI
VIA FIESOLANA

CANONICA

MEDICI
CALZAIUOLI
VIA DELL'OCHE

BONIZZI
STUDIO

OPERA
DEL
DUOMO
STUDIO

Ⓣ

VIA DELL'ORIUOLO
VIA S. EGIDIO

Piazza
G. Salvemini

VIA DEL CORSO

ORSAN-
MICHELE

CASA DI
DANTE

BORGO DEGLI ALBIZI

VIA PIETRAPIANA

POST

VIA DELL'ULIVO

TAVO.
TICKET
OFFICE
VIA
LAMB.

VIA
CERCHI
CONDOTTA

VIA D. ALIGHIERI

S.
MARIA
LA
BADIA

CIMATORI

VIA DEL PROCONSOLO
VIA DE' GIRALDI
PRESTO

VIA DE' PANDOLFINI

BARGELLO
MUSEUM

VIA DELLA VIGNA VECCHIA

VIA
GHIBELLINA
VIA G. VERDI
VIA PALMIERI
VIA DELL'AGNOLO

CASA
BUONARROTI

GUCCI
MUSEUM

Piazza
S. Firenze

V. DELL'ANGUILLARA

V. ISINCHE
TORTA
VIA DE' BENCI

VERAZZANO
VIA DEL FICO

Piazza della
Signoria

LOGGIA

PALAZZO
VECCHIO

GONDI
LEONI
CORNO

BORGO DE' GRECI

VIA BENTA

Piazza
Santa Croce

VIA DEPERI

BORGO ALLEGRI

UFFIZI
GALLERY

EXIT

BARONCELLI
CASTELLANI
CASTELLO
OSTERIA

VINEGRIA

MAGALOTTI
RUSTICI

DEI
NERI

Piazza
Peruzzi

VIA DE' BENCI

BRACHE

WC

SANTA
CROCE

BORGO S. CROCE

PAZZI
CHAPEL

Piazza
Giudici

SAPONAI
LUNG. GEN. DIAZ

Piazza
Mentana

VAGELLA I
MALENCHINI

CORSO DEI TINTORI

VIA ANTONIO MAGLIABECHI

LEATHER
SCHOOL'S
OUTSIDE
ENTRANCE

GALILEO
SCIENCE
MUSEUM

MOSCA

LIBRARY

PONTE ALLE
GRAZIE

LUNGARNO DELLE GRAZIE

Piazza dei
Cavalleggeri

North of the Duomo
▲▲▲ACCADEMIA (GALLERIA DELL'ACCADEMIA)

This museum houses Michelangelo's *David,* the consummate Renaissance statue of the buff, biblical shepherd boy ready to take on the giant. This six-ton, 17-foot-tall symbol of divine victory over evil represents a new century and a whole new Renaissance outlook. The Accademia also contains some of the master's other works, including his powerful (unfinished) *Prisoners* and *St. Matthew,* as well as a pietà (possibly by one of his disciples).

Cost and Hours: €12, additional €4 for recommended reservation, free and crowded on first Sun of the month Oct-March; Tue-Sun 8:15-19:00, closed Mon; July-Sept open Tue and Thu 7:00-22:00; audioguide-€6, Via Ricasoli 60, reservation tel. 055-294-883, www.galleriaaccademiafirenze.beniculturali.it.

Tours: ⋒ Download my free Accademia **audio tour.**

Visiting the Museum: In 1501, Michelangelo Buonarroti, a 26-year-old Florentine, was commissioned to carve a large-scale work for the Duomo. He was given a block of marble that other sculptors had rejected as too tall, shallow, and flawed to be of any value. But Michelangelo picked up his hammer and chisel, knocked a knot off what became *David*'s heart, and started to work.

The statue captures *David* as he's sizing up his enemy. He stands relaxed but

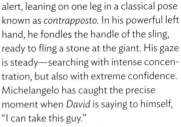

Michelangelo, David

alert, leaning on one leg in a classical pose known as *contrapposto.* In his powerful left hand, he fondles the handle of the sling, ready to fling a stone at the giant. His gaze is steady—searching with intense concentration, but also with extreme confidence. Michelangelo has caught the precise moment when *David* is saying to himself, "I can take this guy."

David is a symbol of Renaissance optimism. He's no brute. He's a civilized, thinking individual who can grapple with and overcome problems. He needs no armor, only his God-given physical strength and wits. Look at his right hand, with the raised veins and strong, relaxed fingers—many complained that it was too big and overdeveloped. But this is the hand of a man with the strength of God on his side. No mere boy could slay the giant. But David, powered by God, could... and did.

You'll also see some mildly interesting pre-Renaissance and Renaissance paintings, including a couple of Botticellis, the plaster model of Giambologna's *Rape of the Sabine Women,* and a musical instrument collection with an early piano.

▲PIAZZA SANTISSIMA ANNUNZIATA

The most Renaissance square in Florence is tucked just a block behind the Accademia. It's like an urban cloister (the image of the ideal city) from the 15th century, with three fine buildings—a convent church, a hospital, and an orphanage—ringing a fine equestrian statue of Ferdinand, a Medici grand duke of the then-independent state of Tuscany.

The 15th-century **Santissima Annunziata Church** is worth a peek. The welcoming cloister has early-16th-century frescoes by Andrea del Sarto, and the church's interior is slathered in Baroque—rare in Florence. Filippo Brunelleschi's **Hospital of the Innocents** (Ospedale degli Innocenti), built in the 1420s, is considered the first Renaissance building. Its graceful arches and columns, with each set of columns forming a square, embody the quintessence of Renaissance harmony and typified the new aesthetic of calm balance and symmetry. It's ornamented with terra-cotta medallions by Luca della Robbia—each showing a different way to wrap an infant (swaddled—meant to help babies grow straight, and practiced in Italy until about a century ago). With its mission to care for the least among society (parentless or unwanted children), this hospital was also an important symbol of the increasingly humanistic and humanitarian outlook of Renaissance Florence.

The **Museum of the Innocents** fills the hospital. A fine exhibit tells the story of these infants with artifacts that help you imagine what it was like living here. It also houses some fine art, including several iconic glazed terra-cotta medallions by the Della Robbia family (€7, daily 10:00-19:00, audioguide-€3, tel. 055-203-7301, www.museodeglinnocenti.it). **$$ Caffè del Verone,** on the museum's top terrace, offers a nice, peaceful break with rooftop views.

▲▲MUSEUM OF SAN MARCO (MUSEO DI SAN MARCO)

One block north of the Accademia, this 15th-century monastery houses the greatest collection anywhere of frescoes and paintings by the early Renaissance master Fra Angelico. Upstairs are 43 cells decorated by Fra Angelico and his assistants. Trained in the medieval religious style, he adopted Renaissance techniques to produce works that blended Christian symbols and Renaissance realism. Don't miss the cell of Savonarola, the charismatic monk who threw out the Medici and sponsored "bonfires of the vanities."

Cost and Hours: €8, Tue-Fri 8:15-14:00, Sat-Sun until 17:00; also open until 14:00 on first, third, and fifth Mon of each month; reservations possible but unnecessary, on Piazza San Marco, tel. 055-238-8608.

Tours: ∩ Download my free Museum of San Marco **audio tour.**

▲▲MEDICI CHAPELS (CAPPELLE MEDICEE)

The burial site of the ruling Medici family in the Basilica of San Lorenzo includes the dusky crypt; the big, domed Chapel of Princes; and the magnificent New Sacristy, featuring architecture, tombs, and statues almost entirely by Michelangelo. The Medici made their money in textiles and banking, and patronized a dream team of Renaissance artists that put Florence on the cultural map. Michelangelo, who spent his teen years living with the Medici, was commissioned to create the family's final tribute.

Cost and Hours: €9, free first Sun of the month Oct-March; Tue-Sat 8:15-14:00, last entry 45 minutes before closing; also open second and fourth Mon and first, third, and fifth Sun of each month; audioguide-€6, modest dress required, tel. 055-238-8602, www.bargellomusei.beniculturali.it.

▲MERCATO CENTRALE (CENTRAL MARKET)

Florence's giant iron-and-glass-covered central market is a wonderland of picturesque produce. While the San Lorenzo Market that fills the surrounding streets is only a step up from a flea market, Mercato Centrale retains its Florentine elegance.

Downstairs, you'll see parts of the cow (and bull) you'd never dream of eating (no, that's not a turkey neck), enjoy free samples, watch pasta being made, and have your pick of plenty of fun eater-

Michelangelo sculptures, Medici Chapels

Mercato Centrale hosts a popular food court.

ies sloshing out cheap and tasty pasta to locals (Mon-Fri 7:00-14:00, Sat until 17:00, closed Sun).

Upstairs, the meticulously restored glass roof and steel rafters soar over a modern and extremely touristy food court (daily 10:00-24:00). For eating ideas downstairs, upstairs, and around the market, see "Eating," later.

▲MEDICI-RICCARDI PALACE (PALAZZO MEDICI-RICCARDI)

Lorenzo the Magnificent's home is worth a look for its art. The tiny Chapel of the Magi contains colorful Renaissance gems such as *The Journey of the Magi* frescoes by Benozzo Gozzoli. The former library has a Baroque ceiling fresco by Luca Giordano, a prolific artist from Naples known as "Fast Luke" (*Luca fa presto*) for his speedy workmanship. While the Medici originally occupied this 1444 house, in the 1700s it became home to the Riccardi family, who added the Baroque flourishes.

Cost and Hours: €10, Thu-Tue 9:00-19:00, closed Wed, ticket entrance is off the central courtyard, enter from Via Cavour 1 or Via de' Ginori 1, tel. 055-276-8224, www.palazzomediciriccardi.it.

On and near Piazza della Signoria

▲▲▲UFFIZI GALLERY

This greatest collection of Italian paintings anywhere features works by Giotto, Leonardo, Raphael, Caravaggio, Titian, and Michelangelo, and a roomful of Botticellis, including the *Birth of Venus*. Start with Giotto's early stabs at Renaissance-style realism, then move on through the 3-D experimentation of the early 1400s to the real thing rendered by the likes of Botticelli and Leonardo. Finish off with Michelangelo and Raphael. Because only 600 visitors are allowed inside the building at any one time, there's generally a very long wait. The good news: no Vatican-style mob scenes inside. The museum is nowhere near as big as it is great.

Cost and Hours: €20 plus €4 for recommended reservation, cheaper in winter, usually free and crowded on first Sun of the month, covered by €38 Uffizi/Pitti Palace/Boboli Gardens combo-ticket;

Botticelli's Spring *at the Uffizi Gallery*

Tue-Sun 8:15-19:00, closed Mon, July-Sept Wed-Thu until 22:00 (except for two weeks in mid-Aug), last entry one hour before closing; reservation tel. 055-294-883, www.uffizi.it.

Reservations Necessary: To skip the notoriously long ticket-buying lines, book your Uffizi entrance in advance online or by calling the reservation number above. If you don't do that, try going at lunchtime or at the end of the day, 90 minutes before closing, and see the museum in a rush.

Getting In: If you arrive with a **reservation,** go first to the courtyard door #3 to pick up your ticket (labeled *Reservation Ticket Office*). There you exchange your email voucher/confirmation number for a ticket. Tickets are available for pickup 10 minutes before your appointed time. Then, with ticket in hand, walk briskly across the courtyard to door #1. Get in the queue for "individuals," not "groups."

To **buy a ticket on the spot,** line up with everyone else at door #2, marked *Main Entrance.*

Tours: A 1.5-hour **audioguide** costs €6 (€10/2 people; must leave ID). ∩ Download my free Uffizi Gallery **audio tour.**

Visiting the Museum: The Uffizi is U-shaped, running around an exterior courtyard. The highlights are up four long flights, on the top floor. The east wing contains Florentine paintings from medieval to Renaissance times. At the far end, you pass through a short hallway filled with ancient sculpture. The west wing has the Renaissance biggies—Leonardo, Michelangelo, and Raphael. Downstairs there are many more rooms of art, showing how the Florentine Renaissance morphed into Mannerism (Parmigianino), spread to Venice (Titian), and inspired the Baroque (Caravaggio).

Medieval (1200-1400): Three similar-looking Madonna and Bambinos—all painted within a few decades of each other, in about the year 1300—show the baby steps being made from the flat Byzantine style toward Renaissance realism (Room 2). **Giotto** creates a space and fills it. Like a set designer, he builds a three-dimensional "stage"—the canopied throne—then peoples it with real beings.

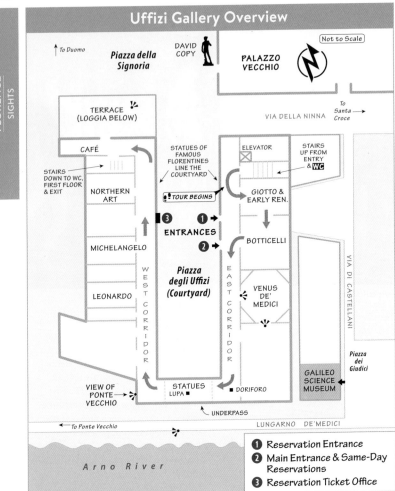

Uffizi Gallery Overview

Not to Scale

To Duomo

Piazza della Signoria

DAVID COPY

PALAZZO VECCHIO

VIA DELLA NINNA

To Santa Croce

TERRACE (LOGGIA BELOW)

CAFÉ

STAIRS DOWN TO WC, FIRST FLOOR & EXIT

NORTHERN ART

MICHELANGELO

LEONARDO

STATUES OF FAMOUS FLORENTINES LINE THE COURTYARD

TOUR BEGINS

ELEVATOR

STAIRS UP FROM ENTRY & WC

GIOTTO & EARLY REN.

❸ ❶ ENTRANCES ➤

❷ ➤

BOTTICELLI

WEST CORRIDOR

Piazza degli Uffizi (Courtyard)

EAST CORRIDOR

VENUS DE' MEDICI

VIA DI CASTELLANI

Piazza dei Giudici

VIEW OF PONTE VECCHIO

STATUES
LUPA ■

■ DORIFORO

GALILEO SCIENCE MUSEUM

UNDERPASS

To Ponte Vecchio

LUNGARNO DE'MEDICI

Arno River

❶ Reservation Entrance
❷ Main Entrance & Same-Day Reservations
❸ Reservation Ticket Office

The real triumph here is Mary herself—big and monumental, like a Roman statue. Beneath her robe, she has a real live body, with knees and breasts that stick out at us. This three-dimensionality was revolutionary, a taste of the Renaissance a century before it began.

Early Renaissance (mid-1400s): In the 1400s, painters worked out the problems of painting realistically, using mathematics to create the illusion of three-dimensionality. Paolo Uccello's colorful **Battle of San Romano** is not so much a piece of art as

an exercise in perspective (Room 8). The fallen horses and soldiers are experiments in "foreshortening"—creating the illusion of distance. We don't need the wispy halo over the head of Fra Filippo Lippi's **Madonna and Child with Two Angels** to tell us she's holy—she radiates sweetness and light from her divine face (Room 8). Lippi's radiant Madonnas are light years away from the generic Marys of the medieval era.

Piero della Francesca's portrait of husband and wife **Federico da Montefeltro** and Battista Sforza heralds the era of humanism and the new centrality of ordinary people in art.

The Renaissance (1450-1500): Florence in 1450 was in a Firenz-y of activity. There was a can-do spirit of optimism in the air, led by prosperous merchants and bankers and a strong middle class. Lorenzo de' Medici, head of the powerful Medici family, gathered Florence's best and brightest around him for evening wine and discussions of great ideas.

The Botticelli rooms (10-14) are filled with masterpieces and classical fleshiness (the famous **Birth of Venus** and **Spring**). Here is the Renaissance in its first bloom. This is a return to the pagan world of classical Greece, where things of the flesh are not sinful. Madonna is out, Venus is in.

Classical Sculpture: The foundation of the Renaissance was classical sculpture. Sculptors, painters, and poets turned for inspiration to ancient Greek and Roman works as the epitome of balance, 3-D perspective, human anatomy, and beauty.

In the Tribune Room, the highlight is the **Venus de' Medici,** a Roman copy of the lost original by the great Greek sculptor Praxiteles. Balanced, harmonious, and serene, the statue embodies the attributes of Greece's "Golden Age," when balance was admired in every aspect of life.

The **sculpture hall** has 2,000-year-old Roman copies of 2,500-year-old Greek originals... and the best view in Florence of the Arno River and Ponte Vecchio through the window, dreamy at sunset.

High Renaissance (1500-1550): A scientist, architect, engineer, musician, and painter, Leonardo da Vinci (1452-1519) was a true Renaissance Man. In his **Annunciation,** the angel Gabriel has walked up to Mary, and now kneels on one knee like an ambassador, saluting her (Room 35). Leonardo constructs a beautifully landscaped "stage" and puts his characters in it. He's taken a miraculous event—an angel appearing out of the blue—and presented it in a very human way.

Don't miss Michelangelo's **Holy Family** (a.k.a. *Doni Tondo,* Room 41), the only completed easel painting by the greatest sculptor in history. Florentine painters were sculptors with brushes; this shows it. Instead of a painting, it's more like three clusters of statues with some clothes painted on.

Nearby is Raphael's **Madonna of the Goldfinch,** with Mary and bambino brought down from heaven into the real world of trees, water, and sky.

More Art on the Lower Floor: On your way out, you'll pass a fine café, an open-air terrace, and the WC. You'll be led to an exit, if you're ready to go. But the first floor is worth a look. It features work from after the Renaissance: Mannerism (such as Parmigianino), Venetian (Titian), Baroque (Caravaggio), and finally Flemish and Dutch (Rubens and Rembrandt).

▲▲PALAZZO VECCHIO

This castle-like fortress with the 300-foot spire dominates Florence's main square. In Renaissance times, it was the Town Hall,

Palazzo Vecchio

where citizens pioneered the once-radical notion of self-rule. Its official name—Palazzo della Signoria—refers to the elected members of the city council. In 1540, the tyrant Cosimo I made the building his personal palace, redecorating the interior in lavish style. Today the building functions once again as the Town Hall.

Entry to the ground-floor Michelozzo courtyard is free. Paying customers can see Cosimo's (fairly) lavish royal apartments, decorated with (fairly) top-notch paintings and statues by Michelangelo and Donatello. The highlight is the 13,000-square-foot Grand Hall—lined with huge frescoes and interesting statues.

Cost and Hours: Michelozzo courtyard-free, museum-€16.50, tower climb-€12.50 (418 steps), museum plus tower-€21.50, excavations-€4, combo-ticket for all three-€23.50. Museum and excavations open daily 9:00-23:00, Oct-March until 19:00, except Thu until 14:00 year-round; tower keeps shorter hours (last entry one hour before closing) and closed in bad weather; last tickets for all sights sold one hour before closing; video-guide-€5, English tours available, Piazza della Signoria, tel. 055-276-8224, www.musefirenze.it.

▲▲GALILEO SCIENCE MUSEUM (MUSEO GALILEI)

When we think of the Florentine Renaissance, we think of visual arts: painting, mosaics, architecture, and sculpture. But when the visual arts declined in the 1600s (abused and co-opted by political powers), music and science flourished. Florence hosted many scientific breakthroughs, as you'll see in this fascinating collection of clocks, telescopes, maps, and ingenious gadgets. Trace the technical innovations as modern science emerges from 1000 to 1900. Some of the most talked about bottles in Florence are the ones here that contain Galileo's fingers. Exhibits include various tools for gauging the world, from a compass and thermometer to Galileo's telescopes. The museum is friendly, comfortably cool, never crowded, and just a block east of the Uffizi on the Arno River.

Cost and Hours: €10, daily 9:30-18:00 except Tue until 13:00, guided tours available, Piazza dei Giudici 1, tel. 055-265-311, www.museogalileo.it.

Celestial globe at Galileo Science Museum

Donatello's David *at the Bargello*

East of Piazza della Signoria

▲▲▲BARGELLO (MUSEO NAZIONALE DEL BARGELLO)

This underappreciated sculpture museum is in a former police station-turned-prison that looks like a mini Palazzo Vecchio. The Renaissance began with sculpture, and you can see the birth of this revolution of 3-D in the Bargello. It's a small, uncrowded museum and a pleasant break from the intensity of the rest of Florence. You'll see 150 years of great statues, spanning the history of Florence's heyday.

Highlights include Donatello's very influential, painfully beautiful *David* (the first male nude to be sculpted in a thousand years), multiple works by Michelangelo, and rooms of Medici treasures. Moody Donatello, who embraced realism with his lifelike statues, set the personal and artistic style for many Renaissance artists to follow. The best pieces are in the ground-floor room at the foot of the outdoor staircase (with fine works by Michelangelo, Cellini, and Giambologna) and in the "Donatello room" directly above (including his two different *David*s, plus Ghiberti and Brunelleschi's dueling competition entries for the Baptistery doors—and yet another *David* by Verrocchio).

Cost and Hours: €9, free on first Sun of the month Oct-March; daily 8:15-14:00—until 17:00 for special exhibits; closed on second and fourth Sun and first, third, and fifth Mon of each month, last entry 45 minutes before closing; reservations possible but unnecessary, audioguide-€6; Via del Proconsolo 4, tel. 055-238-8606, www.bargellomusei.beniculturali.it.

Tours: ⌗ Download my free Bargello **audio tour.**

▲▲SANTA CROCE CHURCH

This 14th-century Franciscan church, decorated with centuries of precious art, holds the tombs of great Florentines. The loud 19th-century Victorian Gothic facade faces a huge square ringed with tempting shops and littered with tired tourists. Escape into the church and admire its sheer height and spaciousness.

Cost and Hours: €8, Mon-Sat 9:30-17:00, Sun from 14:00, multimedia guide-€6, modest dress required, 10-minute walk east of the Palazzo Vecchio along Borgo de' Greci, tel. 055-246-6105, www.

Santa Croce Church, the final resting place of Michelangelo and Galileo.

santacroceopera.it. The **leather school,** at the back of the church, is free and sells church tickets—handy when the church has a long line (daily 10:00-18:00, closed Sun Nov-March, has own entry behind church plus an entry within the church, www.scuoladelcuoio.com).

Visiting the Church: On the left wall (as you face the altar) is the tomb of **Galileo Galilei** (1564-1642), the Pisan who lived his last years under house arrest near Florence. His crime? Defying the Church by saying that the earth revolved around the sun. His heretical remains were only allowed in the church long after his death.

Directly opposite (on the right wall) is the tomb of **Michelangelo Buonarroti** (1475-1564). Santa Croce was Michelangelo's childhood church, as he grew up a block west of here. Farther up the nave is the tomb of **Niccolò Machiavelli** (1469-1527), a champion of democratic Florence and author of *The Prince,* a how-to manual on hardball politics—which later Medici rulers found instructive.

The first chapel to the right of the main altar features the famous *Death of St. Francis* fresco by Giotto. With simple but eloquent gestures, Francis' brothers bid him a sad farewell. The Sacristy has Cimabue's impressive *Crucifixion* (before 1288), a survivor of the devastating flood of 1966. Beyond that is the leather school.

Exit the church nave between the Rossini and Machiavelli tombs to enter a delightful cloister. On the left is the small Brunelleschi-designed Pazzi Chapel, which captures the Renaissance in miniature.

Near the Train Station
▲▲CHURCH OF SANTA MARIA NOVELLA

This 13th-century Dominican church is rich in art. Along with crucifixes by Giotto and Brunelleschi, it contains the textbook example of the early Renaissance mastery of perspective: *The Trinity* by Masaccio. The exquisite chapels trace art in Florence from medieval times to early Baroque. The outside of the church features a dash of Romanesque (horizontal stripes), Gothic (pointed arches), Renaissance (geometric shapes), and Baroque (scrolls). Step in and look down the 330-foot nave for a 14th-century optical illusion.

Next to the church are the cloisters and the **museum,** located in the old Dominican convent of Santa Maria Novella. The museum's highlight is the breathtaking Spanish Chapel, with walls covered by a series of frescoes by Andrea di Bonaiuto.

Cost and Hours: Church and museum-€7.50; Mon-Thu 9:00-19:00, Fri 11:00-19:00, Sat 9:00-17:30, Sun 13:00-17:30, church closes Oct-March at 17:30, last entry 45 minutes before closing; multimedia guide-€3, modest dress required, main entrance on Piazza Santa Maria Novella, tel. 055-219-257, www.smn.it.

The Oltrarno (South of the Arno River)
▲▲▲PITTI PALACE

The imposing Pitti Palace, several blocks southwest of Ponte Vecchio, has many separate museums and two gardens. The main reason to visit is to see the Palatine Gallery, which houses a fine painting collection that picks up where the Uffizi leaves off, with the High Renaissance. Lovers of Raphael's Madonnas and Titian's portraits will find some of the world's

Pitti Palace

best of each. If it's a nice day, take a stroll in the Boboli Gardens, a rare and inviting patch of extensive green space within old Florence.

Cost and Hours: The €16 **Pitti Palace** ticket #1 covers the Palatine Gallery, Royal Apartments, Treasury of the Grand Dukes (silver museum), Museum of Costume and Fashion, and Gallery of Modern Art; open Tue-Sun 8:15-19:00, closed Mon, last entry one hour before closing. The €10 **Boboli Garden** ticket #2 covers the Boboli and Bardini Gardens as well as the Porcelain Museum located in the garden; open daily June-Aug 8:15-19:30, April-May and Sept until 18:30, March and Oct until 17:30, Nov-Feb until 16:30, closed first and last Mon of each month, last entry one hour before closing. The place is free on the first Sun of the month Oct-March. The €8 audioguide explains the sprawling palace. Tel. 055-238-8614, www.uffizi.it.

Visiting the Museum: In the **Palatine Gallery** you'll walk through one palatial room after another, with walls sagging with masterpieces by 16th- and 17th-century masters, including Titian and Rembrandt. The Pitti's Raphael collection is the second-biggest anywhere—the Vatican beats it by one. Use the information folders in each room to help find the featured paintings.

The collection is all on one floor. To see the highlights, walk straight down the spine through a dozen or so rooms. After the Palatine Gallery, the route flows naturally into the even more lavish rooms of the Royal Apartments. These 14 rooms (of which only a few are open at any one time) are where the Pitti's rulers lived in the 18th and 19th centuries. Each room features a different color and time period. Here, you get a real feel for the splendor of the dukes' world.

The rest of Pitti Palace is skippable, unless the various sights match your interests: the **Gallery of Modern Art** (second floor; Romantic, Neoclassical, and Impressionist works by 19th- and 20th-century

Tuscan painters), **Treasury of the Grand Dukes** (ground and mezzanine floors; Medici treasures from jeweled crucifixes to gilded ostrich eggs), **Museum of Costume and Fashion, Porcelain Museum,** and **Boboli and Bardini gardens** (behind the palace; enter from Pitti Palace courtyard—be prepared to climb uphill).

▲▲BRANCACCI CHAPEL

In the Brancacci Chapel, Masaccio created a world in paint that looks like the world we inhabit. For the first time in a thousand years, Man and Nature were frozen for inspection. Masaccio's painting techniques were copied by many Renaissance artists, and his people—sturdy, intelligent, and dignified, with expressions of understated astonishment—helped shape Renaissance men and women's own self-images.

Half of the chapel's frescoes are by Masaccio, and half by either Masolino or Filippino Lippi, who completed the chapel more than 50 years later. Although Masaccio is the star, the panels by his colleagues provide a good contrast in styles.

Masaccio, Expulsion from the Garden of Eden

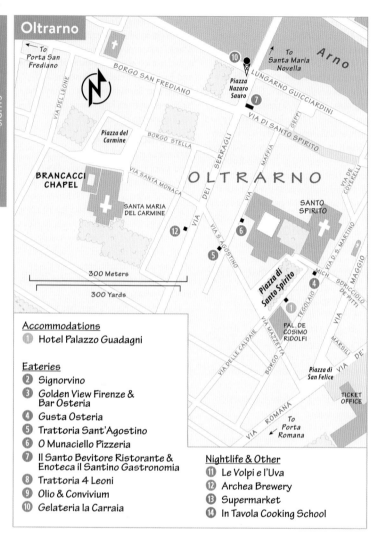

Oltrarno

Accommodations
1 Hotel Palazzo Guadagni

Eateries
2 Signorvino
3 Golden View Firenze & Bar Osteria
4 Gusta Osteria
5 Trattoria Sant'Agostino
6 O Munaciello Pizzeria
7 Il Santo Bevitore Ristorante & Enoteca il Santino Gastronomia
8 Trattoria 4 Leoni
9 Olio & Convivium
10 Gelateria la Carraia

Nightlife & Other
11 Le Volpi e l'Uva
12 Archea Brewery
13 Supermarket
14 In Tavola Cooking School

Cost and Hours: €10 Sat-Mon (obligatory combo-ticket with Fondazione Salvatore Romano, a skippable 14th-century refectory next to the Santo Spirito Church), €8 Wed-Fri, cash only; free and easy reservations mandatory March-May and advisable through the summer and fall; Wed-Mon 10:00-17:00 except Sun from 13:00, closed Tue, last entry 45 minutes before closing; videoguide-€3, knees and shoulders must be covered, in Church of Santa Maria del Carmine on Piazza del Carmine, reservations tel. 055-276-8224 or 055-276-8558 or email info@muse.comune.fi.it, http://musefirenze.it.

▲PIAZZALE MICHELANGELO

Overlooking the city from across the river (look for the huge bronze statue of *David*), this square has a superb view of Florence and the stunning dome of the Duomo. It's worth the 25-minute hike, taxi, or bus ride.

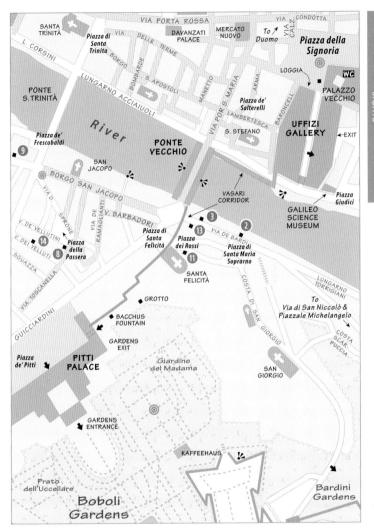

An inviting café (open seasonally) with great views is just below the overlook. The best photos are taken from the street immediately below the overlook. After dark, the square is packed with school kids licking ice cream and each other. About 200 yards beyond all the tour groups and teenagers is the stark, beautiful, crowd-free, Romanesque San Miniato Church (next listing). A WC is located just off the road, halfway between the two sights.

Getting There (and Back): While you can catch bus #12 (from near Piazza d'Ognissanti, can be a long ride) or a taxi up to the piazza, the walk up from the Oltrarno neighborhood of San Niccolò is popular—especially in the early evening—and not that challenging.

Start at the intersection of Via San Nic-colò and Via San Miniato, just below Porta San Miniato. Point yourself uphill, head through the old gate, and continue until

The view from Piazzale Michelangelo

San Miniato Church

you reach a broad, terraced hill-climb to the left. Up top, Piazzale Michelangelo will be to your left, and San Miniato Church to your right.

The hike down is quick and enjoyable (or take bus #13). You can retrace your steps, or you can turn this walk into a loop: From the parking lot, take the ramp leading down toward Ponte Vecchio (near the replica *David*). At the bottom of the ramp, cross the street and continue down the pathway. You'll cross one more street, then zigzag downhill toward the river. When you draw even with the big tower (Porta San Niccolò), turn left onto Via San Niccolò and make your way back to the passel of lively cafés and restaurants where you started (for recommendations, see page 210).

▲▲SAN MINIATO CHURCH

According to legend, the martyred St. Minias—this church's namesake—was beheaded on the banks of the Arno in AD 250. He picked up his head and walked here (this was before the #12 bus), where he died and was buried in what became the first Christian cemetery in Florence. In the 11th century, this church was built to house Minias' remains.

The church's green-and-white marble facade (12th century) is classic Florentine Romanesque, one of the oldest in town. Inside you'll find some wonderful 3-D paintings, a plush ceiling of glazed terra-cotta

panels by Luca della Robbia, and an exquisite Renaissance chapel (on the left side of the nave). The highlight for me is the brilliantly preserved art in the sacristy (upstairs to right of altar, in the room on right) showing scenes from the life of St. Benedict (circa 1350, by a follower of Giotto). Drop €2 into the electronic panel in the corner to light the room for five minutes. The evening vesper service with the monks chanting in Latin offers a meditative worship experience—a peaceful way to end your visit.

Cost and Hours: Free, Mon-Sat 9:30-13:00 & 15:00-19:30, until 19:00 off-season, Sun 8:15-19:30, closed sporadically for special occasions, tel. 055-234-2731, www.sanminiatoalmonte.it.

Getting There: It's about 200 yards above Piazzale Michelangelo. Follow the walking directions in the Piazzale Michelangelo listing earlier, or take bus #12 to the San Miniato al Monte stop (hop off and hike up the grand staircase); bus #13 takes you back down the hill.

EXPERIENCES

Shopping

Florence may be one of Europe's best shopping towns—it's been known for its sense of style since the Medici days. Smaller stores are generally open about 9:00-13:00 and 15:30-19:30, usually closed on Sunday, often closed on Monday (or

San Lorenzo Market

Florence is a popular place to buy leather.

at least Monday morning), and sometimes closed for a couple of weeks around August 15. Bigger stores have similar hours, without the afternoon break.

For authentic, locally produced wares, look for shops displaying the **Esercizi Storici Fiorentini** seal, with a picture of the Palazzo Vecchio's tower. At these city-endorsed "Historical Florentine Ventures," you may pay a premium, but quality is assured (for a list of shops, see www.esercizistoricifiorentini.it).

The open-air **San Lorenzo Market** stalls, between the Basilica of San Lorenzo and Mercato Centrale, are fun to browse and bargain (just hang onto your wallet—this is pickpocket central). You'll find many of the stalls in the narrow streets around Mercato Centrale (daily 9:00-19:00, closed Mon in winter).

Originally a silk-and-straw market, **Mercato Nuovo** still functions as a rustic yet touristy market (at the intersection of Via Calimala and Via Porta Rossa; daily 9:00-18:30). It's where you'll find *Il Porcellino* (a statue of a wild boar nicknamed "The Piglet"), which people rub and give

coins to ensure their return to Florence.

Other shopping areas, mostly upscale boutiques, can be found along Via dei Calzaiuoli, Via de' Tornabuoni, and the streets in between (particularly around Piazza della Repubblica).

Running parallel to the Arno through the heart of the Oltrarno, **Via di Santo Spirito** contains a number of old *palazzi* once owned by wealthy Florentine families such as the Machiavellis (#5) and the winemaking Frescobaldis (#11). Today, the ground floors of those buildings are filled with fine local shops, with some real artisans mixed in.

Nightlife

For me, nighttime is for eating a late meal, catching a concert, strolling through the old-town pedestrian zone and piazzas with a gelato, or hitting one of the many wine bars. Get the latest on nightlife and concerts in *The Florentine* monthly (updated biweekly online, www.theflorentine.net) or *Firenze Spettacolo* (www.firenzespettacolo.it; mostly in Italian, but there's an English section).

Ponte Vecchio after dark

Strolling After Dark: The historic center has a floodlit ambience that's ideal for strolling. The pedestrian zone around the Duomo and along Via de' Calzaiuoli, between the Uffizi and the Duomo, is lively with people. Piazza della Repubblica, lined with venerable 19th-century cafés, offers good people-watching. In the evening, it's a hub of activity, with opera singers, violinists, harpists, bizarre street performers, and a cover band that plays cheesy tunes for the seating area of one of the piazza's bars. Ponte Vecchio is a popular place to enjoy river views (and kiss), and often has a street musician after dark who encourages passersby to dance.

Live Music: Orsanmichele Church regularly holds concerts under its Gothic arches. Tickets are sold on the day of the concert from the door facing Via de' Calzaiuoli or, on Sunday, from the doorway opposite the church entrance. Orchestra della Toscana presents classical concerts from November to May in Teatro Verdi (€13-20, box office open Mon-Sat 10:00-13:00 & 16:00-19:00, closed Sun, near Bargello at Via Ghibellina 97, tel. 055-210-804, www.orchestradellatoscana.it). St. Mark's English Church offers concerts and opera several nights each week from February through October (full opera performance-€35, opera concerts-€25, Via Maggio 18, mobile 340-811-9192, www.concertoclassico.info).

Dinner Theater at Teatro del Sale is a quirky place for dinner and theater (Tue-Sat at 19:30). Sometimes the show is great for non-Italian speakers (live music, for example)—and sometimes it's not (call or check their website). You'll pay a €7 membership fee to "join" the association, plus €36 for the evening, including drinks (10 blocks behind the Duomo, northeast of Santa Croce at Via dei Macci 111 red, tel. 055-200-1492, www.teatrodelsale.com).

Drinks: An *enoteca* is fun for sampling regional wines and enjoying munchies, especially before dinnertime. **Le Volpi e l'Uva,** specializing in small, often organic wine producers, has a cozy interior and romantic seating on a quiet little piazza (daily 11:00-21:00, 65 yards south of Ponte Vecchio—walk through Piazza Santa Felicità to Piazza dei Rossi 1; see map on page

194 for location, tel. 055-239-8132, run by wine experts Riccardo, Ciro, and Emilio).

Caffè del Verone, a terrace bar on the top floor of the Hospital of the Innocents, keeps late hours in summer (some nights until 23:00) so you can enjoy a spritz while taking in rooftop views. They have jazz on some weekend nights—call for details (Piazza SS. Annunziata 13, for location see map on page 168, mobile 392-498-2559).

Italy is experiencing a craft beer fad, and Florence has several places where you can join in. Handy to many recommended hotels (and near Mercato Centrale) is **Mostodolce** (daily 11:00-24:00, Via Nazionale 114 red, for location see map on page 206, tel. 055-230-2928), or head across the river to **Archea Brewery,** a small pub that brews several of their own varieties, with a few other Italian-produced beers on tap (daily 18:00-24:00, Via de'Serragli 44 red, a 5-minute walk west of Piazza di Santo Spirito, for location see map on page 194, tel. 055-219-671, Carmine).

SLEEPING

Florence is notorious for its mosquitoes. If your hotel lacks air-conditioning, request a fan and don't open your windows, especially at night. Many hotels furnish a small plug-in bulb *(zanzariere)*—usually set in the ashtray—that helps keep the bloodsuckers at bay.

Around the Duomo
$$$$ Hotel Duomo's 24 rooms are modern and comfortable enough, but you're

paying for the location and the views—the Duomo looms like a monster outside the hotel's windows. If staying here, you may as well spring the extra €20 or so for a "classic" room with a view (RS%, air-con, historic elevator, Piazza del Duomo 1, fourth floor, tel. 055-219-922, www.hotelduomofirenze.it, info@hotelduomofirenze.it; Paolo, Gilvaneide, and Federico).

$$$ Residenza Giotto B&B offers a well-priced chance to stay on Florence's upscale shopping drag, Via Roma. Occupying the top floor of a 19th-century building, this place has six bright rooms (three with Duomo views) and a terrace with knockout views of the Duomo's tower. Reception is generally open Mon-Sat 9:00-17:00 and Sun 9:00-13:00; let them know your arrival time in advance (RS%, air-con, elevator, Via Roma 6, tel. 055-214-593, www.residenzagiotto.it, info@residenzagiotto.it, helpful Giorgio).

North of the Duomo
Near the Accademia
$$$$ Hotel dei Macchiaioli offers 15 fresh and spacious rooms on one high-ceilinged, noble floor in a restored palazzo owned for generations by a well-to-do Florentine family. You'll eat breakfast under original frescoed ceilings while enjoying modern comforts (RS%, air-con, Via Cavour 21, tel. 055-213-154, www.hoteldeimacchiaioli.com, info@hoteldeimacchiaioli.com, helpful Francesca and Paolo).

$$$$ Hotel Morandi alla Crocetta, a former convent, envelops you in a 16th-century cocoon. Located on a quiet street with 12 rooms, its period furnishings, squeaky clean parquet floors, and original frescoes take you back a few centuries and up a few social classes. A few rooms come with lovely patios (family rooms, air-con, elevator, pay parking, a block off Piazza Santissima Annunziata at Via Laura 50, tel. 055-234-4748, www.hotelmorandi.it, welcome@hotelmorandi.it, well-run by Maurizio, Rolando, and Cristiano).

$$$ Residenza dei Pucci rents 13 pleasant rooms (each one different) spread over three floors (with no elevator). The appealing decor, a mix of traditional fabrics and aristocratic furniture, makes this place feel upscale for the price range (RS%—use code "RICK," family rooms, air-con, reception open 9:00-20:00, shorter hours off-season—let them know if you'll arrive late, Via dei Pucci 9, tel. 055-281-886, www.residenza deipucci.com, info@residenzadeipucci.com, friendly Rossella and Marina).

Near the Medici Chapels

$$$$ Hotel Centrale is indeed central, just a short walk from the Duomo. The 35 spacious but overpriced rooms—with a tasteful mix of old and new decor—are over a businesslike conference center (RS%, air-con, elevator, Via dei Conti 3, check in at big front desk on ground floor, tel. 055-215-761, www.hotelcentralefirenze.it, info@hotelcentralefirenze.it, Roberto).

$$$$ Hotel Accademia has 18 quiet rooms on a pedestrianized street in a convenient location. The modern, sizeable rooms cluster around a sunny courtyard (RS%, air-con, no elevator, Via Faenza 7, tel. 055-290-993, www.hotelaccademia firenze.com, info@hotelaccademia firenze.com, Tea and Francesca).

East of the Duomo

$$$ Residenza il Villino has 10 charming rooms and a picturesque, peaceful little courtyard. The owner, Neri, has turned part of the breakfast room into a museum-like tribute to his grandfather, a pioneer of early Italian fashion. As it's in a "little villa" (as the name implies) set back from the street, this is a quiet refuge from the bustle of Florence (RS%, family rooms, air-con, parking available, just north of Via degli Alfani at Via della Pergola 53, tel. 055-200-1116, www.ilvillino.it, info@ilvillino.it, Giovanni).

$$ Locanda de' Ciompi, overlooking the inviting Piazza dei Ciompi in a lively neighborhood, is just right for travelers who want to feel like a part of the town. Alessio and daughter Lisa have five attractive rooms that are tidy, lovingly maintained, and a good value (RS%, cheaper room with private bath across the hall, includes breakfast at nearby bar, air-con, 8 blocks behind the Duomo at Via Pietrapiana 28 black—see map on page 168, tel. 055-263-8034, https://locandadeciompi.it, info@locandadeciompi.it).

$$ Hotel Dalí has 10 cheery, worn rooms in a nice location for a great price. Samanta and Marco, who run this guesthouse with a charming passion and idealism, are a delight to know (request one of the quiet and spacious rooms facing the courtyard when you book, cheaper rooms with shared bath available, nearby apartments sleep 2-6 people, no breakfast, fans but no air-con, elevator, free parking, 2 blocks behind the Duomo at Via dell'Oriuolo 17 on the second floor, tel. 055-234-0706, www.hoteldali.com, hoteldali@tin.it).

$$ Sanctuary Firenze, run by the Oblate Sisters of the Assumption, is an institutional 35-room hotel in a Renaissance building with a dreamy garden, great public spaces, appropriately simple rooms, and a quiet, prayerful ambience (family rooms, single beds only, air-con, elevator, 23:30 curfew, limited pay parking—request when you book, Borgo Pinti 15, tel. 055-248-0582, www.sanctuary bbfirenze.com, info@sanctuarybbfirenze.com). As there's no night porter, it's best to time your arrival and departure to occur during typical business hours.

South of the Duomo

Between the Duomo and Piazza della Signoria

$$$$ In Piazza della Signoria B&B, in a stellar location overlooking Piazza della Signoria, is peaceful, refined, and homey. The service is friendly and efficient. The nine rooms are beautifully decorated; the priciest ones have genuine views of the square. Guests enjoy socializing at the big, shared breakfast table (RS%, 2 family apartments, air-con, tiny elevator, Via dei Magazzini 2, tel. 055-239-9546, mobile 348-321-0565, www.inpiazzadellasignoria.com, info@inpiazzadellasignoria.com, Sonia and Alessandro).

$$$ Hotel Maxim Axial, run by the Maoli family since 1981, has 42 straight-forward rooms spread over three floors in a good location on the main pedestrian drag. Its painting-lined halls and cozy lounge have old Florentine charm. Budget travelers can choose an "economy" room on the fourth floor—which is a walk-up from the third floor (RS%—use code "RICK," family rooms, reception on third floor, air-con, elevator, Via de' Calzaiuoli 11, tel. 055-217-474, www.hotelmaximaxial.com, info@hotelmaximaxial.com, Chiara).

$$ B&B Il Bargello is a home away from home, run by friendly and helpful Canadian expat Gabriella. Hike up three long flights (no elevator) to reach six smart, relaxing rooms. Gabriella offers a cozy living room, a communal kitchen-ette, and an inviting rooftop terrace with close-up views of Florence's towers (RS%, fully equipped apartment across the hall sleeps up to six with one shared bathroom; air-con, 20 yards off Via Pro-consolo at Via de' Pandolfini 33 black, tel. 055-215-330, mobile 339-175-3110, www.firenze-bedandbreakfast.it, info@firenze-bedandbreakfast.it).

Near Ponte Vecchio

$$$$ Hotel Davanzati, bright and shiny with artistic touches, has 25 cheerful rooms with all the comforts. The place is a family affair, thoughtfully run by friendly Tom-maso and father Fabrizio, who offer drinks and snacks each evening at their candlelit happy hour, plus lots of other extras (RS%, family rooms, air-con, 20 steep steps to the elevator, handy room fridges, next to Piazza Davanzati at Via Porta Rossa 5—easy to miss so watch for low-profile sign above the door, tel. 055-286-666, www.hoteldavanzati.it, info@hoteldavanzati.it).

$$$$ Hotel Torre Guelfa has grand public spaces and is topped by a fun medieval tower with a panoramic rooftop terrace (72 stairs take you up—and back 720 years). Its 31 pricey rooms vary wildly in size and furnishings, but most come with the noise of the city center. Room 315, with a private terrace, is worth reserv-ing several months in advance (RS%, fam-ily rooms, air-con, elevator, a couple of blocks northwest of Ponte Vecchio, Borgo SS. Apostoli 8, tel. 055-239-6338, www.hoteltorreguelfa.com, info@hoteltorreguelfa.com, Niccolo).

$$$$ Relais Uffizi is a peaceful little gem, offering a friendly welcome and tight maze of 15 classy rooms tucked away down a tiny alley off Piazza della Signoria. The lounge has a huge window overlook-ing the action in the piazza—a unique view (RS%, family rooms, air-con, eleva-tor; official address is Chiasso del Buco 16—from the square, go down tiny Chi-asso de Baroncelli lane—right of the log-gia—and after 50 yards turn right through the arch and look for entrance on your right; tel. 055-267-6239, www.relaisuffizi.it, info@relaisuffizi.it, charming Alessan-dro and Elizabetta).

The Oltrarno

For locations, see the map on page 194.

$$$$ Hotel Palazzo Guadagni, perched high above Piazza Santo Spirito, is a romantic, Grand Tour retreat from modern Florence. The 15 refined rooms are spacious, with antique furnishings and frescoes. While the ample, chandeliered public spaces are pleasant, the highlight is the panoramic wraparound loggia/terrace with comfy, stay-awhile seating and lovely views (RS%, air-con, elevator, Piazza Santo Spirito 9, tel. 055-265-8376, www.palazzoguadagni.com, info@palazzoguadagni.com).

$$$ Hotel Silla is a classic three-star hotel with 36 cheery, spacious rooms. Across the river from Santa Croce Church, it has a breezy terrace and faces

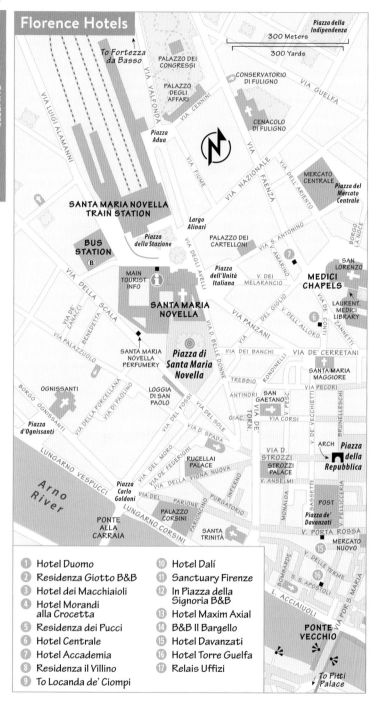

Florence Hotels

1. Hotel Duomo
2. Residenza Giotto B&B
3. Hotel dei Macchiaioli
4. Hotel Morandi alla Crocetta
5. Residenza dei Pucci
6. Hotel Centrale
7. Hotel Accademia
8. Residenza il Villino
9. To Locanda de' Ciompi
10. Hotel Dalí
11. Sanctuary Firenze
12. In Piazza della Signoria B&B
13. Hotel Maxim Axial
14. B&B Il Bargello
15. Hotel Davanzati
16. Hotel Torre Guelfa
17. Relais Uffizi

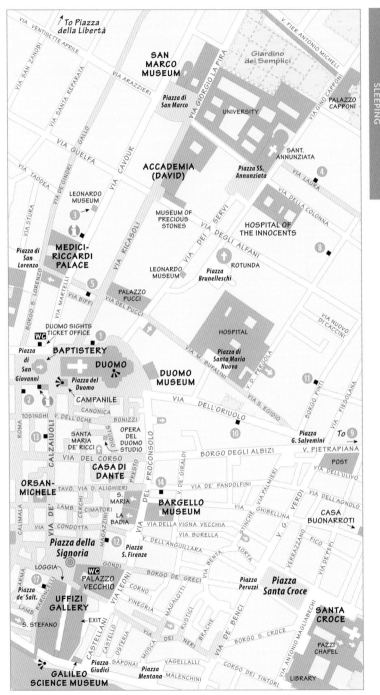

the river, overlooking a small park and near the San Niccolò neighborhood. There's free coffee and tea for guests in the late afternoon. The surroundings can be a bit noisy (RS%—use promo code "RICK," air-con, elevator, pricey self-service washing machine, pay parking, Via dei Renai 5, tel. 055-234-2888, www.hotelsilla. it, hotelsilla@hotelsilla.it; Laura, Chiara, Massimo, Ravin, and Stefano).

$$ Hotel Annalena, on the third floor of a faded palazzo, is a bit tatty but it's in a quiet location near the Pitti Palace. Many of its 20 tidy rooms (some with terraces) overlook a private park next door (family rooms, bar/lounge, air-con, no elevator, laundry service, pay parking, opposite the side entrance to the Boboli Gardens at Via Romana 34, tel. 055-222-402, www. annalenahotel.com, reception@anna lenahotel.com).

EATING

The old center of Florence is dominated by tourism. Locals still keep restaurants busy at lunch, but with the city's many Airbnb guests and city-center traffic restrictions, the hometown clientele retreats away from downtown in the evening. This makes it tough to find a "nontouristy" place for dinner. Still, you'll find plenty of fine options and good values even in the tourist zone. For the best experience and better-quality meals, hike to places further out and across the river in the Oltrarno.

Eating Tips: To save money and time, lunch at one of Florence's countless sandwich shops and stands, pizzerias, or self-service cafeterias. You can picnic your way through Mercato Centrale, near the Basilica of San Lorenzo. You'll also find good *supermercati* throughout the city. I like the classy Sapori & Dintorni markets (run by Conad), which have branches near the Duomo (Borgo San Lorenzo 15 red) and just over Ponte Vecchio in the Oltrarno (Via de Bardi 45). Carrefour Express is another handy gro-

cery chain (there's one around the corner from the Duomo Museum at Via dell'Ori-uolo 66).

Mercato Centrale and Nearby
In Mercato Centrale

Mercato Centrale (Central Market) is a fun-to-explore edible wonderland.

$ Ground Floor: The market zone, with lots of raw ingredients and a few humble food counters, is open only through lunchtime (Mon-Fri 7:00-14:00, Sat until 17:00, closed Sun). Buy a picnic of fresh mozzarella cheese, olives, fruit, and crunchy bread to munch on the steps of the nearby Basilica of San Lorenzo. The fancy deli, **Perini,** is famous for its quality products, enticing display, and generous samples. For a simple sit-down meal, head for the venerable **Nerbone in the Market.** Join the shoppers and workers who crowd up to the bar to grab their inexpensive plates, and then find a stool at the cramped shared tables nearby. Of the several cheap market diners, this feels the most authentic (lunch menu served Mon-Sat 12:00-14:00, cash only, on the side closest to the Basilica of San Lorenzo). Its less-famous sisters, nearby, have better seating and fewer crowds.

$$ Upstairs: The upper floor is a touristy, overcrowded and overpriced food court (daily 10:00-24:00) with counters selling pizza, pasta, fish, meat, *salumi, lampredotto,* wine, and so on.

Florentine and Tuscan Cuisine

In general, Tuscan cuisine is hearty, simple food: grilled meats, high-quality seasonal vegetables, fresh herbs, prized olive oil, and rustic bread. For more on Italian food, see the "Eating" section of the Practicalities chapter.

Antipasti (Appetizers)

Bruschetta: Toasted bread brushed with olive oil and rubbed with garlic, topped with chopped tomato, mushrooms, or whatever else sounds good

Crostini: Toasted bread rounds topped with meat or vegetable pastes. *Alla toscana* generally means with chicken liver pâté

Panzanella: Simple summer salad, made of day-old bread, chopped tomatoes, onion, and basil, tossed in a light vinaigrette

Pecorino cheese: Fresh (*fresco*) or aged (*stagionato*), from ewe's milk

Porcini mushrooms: Used as a topping for bruschetta; also served marinated or stewed

Salumi: Cold cuts, usually air- or salt-dried pork. Popular kinds include prosciutto, pancetta, *lardo* (cured pork lard), and *finocchiona* (fennel salami)

Tagliere: Selection of cold cuts and/or cheeses served on a wooden platter

Primo Piatto (First Course)

Carabaccia: Onion soup

Pappa al pomodoro: Thick stew of tomatoes, olive oil, and bread

Pappardelle al sugo di lepre: Rich wild hare sauce over long, broad noodles

Pici al ragù: Fat, spaghetti-like, hand-rolled pasta with a meat-tomato sauce

Ribollita: "Reboiled" soup, traditionally made with leftovers including white beans (*fagioli*), seasonal vegetables, and olive oil, with layers of day-old Tuscan bread

Zuppa alla volterrana: Volterra-style soup, similar to *ribollita* but with fresh bread

Secondo Piatto (Second Course)

Arrosto misto: Assortment of roasted meats, sometimes served on a skewer (*spiedino*)

Bistecca alla fiorentina: Thick T-bone steak, generally grilled very rare and lightly seasoned (often sold by weight—per *etto*, or 100 grams). The best—and most expensive—is from the white Chianina cattle you'll see grazing throughout Tuscany.

Cinghiale: Wild boar, served grilled; in soups, stews, and pasta; or made into many varieties of sausage and salami

Fegatelli: Liver meatballs

Game birds: Squab (*piccione*), pheasant (*fagiano*), and guinea hen (*faraona*) are popular.

Trippa alla fiorentina: Tripe and vegetables sautéed in tomato sauce, sometimes baked with parmesan. *Trippa* (and the similar *lampredotto*) are popular in sandwiches.

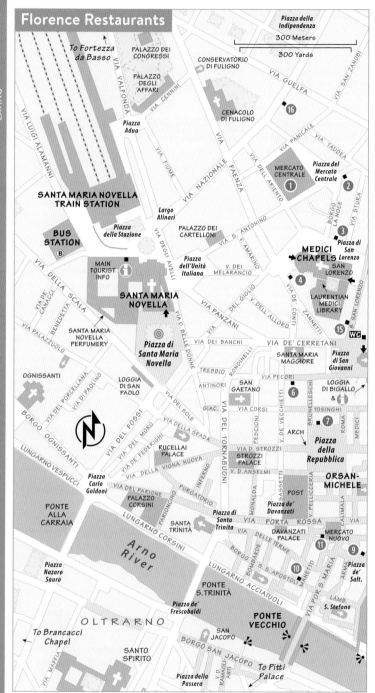

Florence Restaurants

300 Meters

300 Yards

To Fortezza da Basso

PALAZZO DEI CONGRESSI

PALAZZO DEGLI AFFARI

Piazza della Indipendenza

CONSERVATORIO DI FULIGNO

VIA GUELFA

VIA SAN ZANOBI

VIA VALFONDA

VIA CENNINI

VIA LUIGI ALAMANNI

Piazza Adua

VIA FIUME

CENACOLO DI FULIGNO

VIA DELL'ARIENTO

VIA PANICALE

VIA TADDEA

16

VIA NAZIONALE

VIA FAENZA

MERCATO CENTRALE

1

Piazza del Mercato Centrale

2

SANTA MARIA NOVELLA TRAIN STATION

Largo Alinari

PALAZZO DEI CARTELLONI

VIA S. ANTONINO

V. AMARINO

BORGO LA NOCE

VIA STURA

3

Piazza di San Lorenzo

BUS STATION B

Piazza della Stazione

VIA DEGLI AVELLI

Piazza dell'Unità Italiana

V. DEI MELARANCIO

MEDICI CHAPELS

SAN LORENZO

VIA DE' CANACCI

VIA DELLA SCALA

MAIN TOURIST INFO i

SANTA MARIA NOVELLA

DEL GIGLIO

V. DELL'ALLORO

VIA DE' CONTI

VIA DE' ZANNETTI

4

LAURENTIAN MEDICI LIBRARY

SAN LORENZO

15

WC

VIA BENEDETTA

VIA PALAZZUOLO

SANTA MARIA NOVELLA PERFUMERY

Piazza di Santa Maria Novella

VIA A BELLE DONNE

VIA PANZANI

VIA DEI BANCHI

VIA DE' CERRETANI

SANTA MARIA MAGGIORE

Piazza di San Giovanni

OGNISSANTI

VIA DEL PORCELLANA

VIA DI PAOLINO

LOGGIA DI SAN PAOLO

VIA DEL FOSSI

VIA DEL MORO

RONDINELLI

TREBBIO

ANTINORI

SAN GAETANO

VIA PECORI

VIA CORSI

6

BRUNELLESCHI

LOGGIA DI BIGALLO & i

BORGO OGNISSANTI

N

GIAC.

V. DE' VECCHIETTI

ARCH

TOSINGHI

7

ROMA

MEDICI

LUNGARNO VESPUCCI

VIA DELLA SPADA

VIA DE' FEDERIGHI

RUCELLAI PALACE

VIA DELLA VIGNA NUOVA

PESCIONI

VIA D. STROZZI

STROZZI PALACE

V. D. ANSELMI

Piazza della Repubblica

ORSAN-MICHELE

Piazza Carlo Goldoni

VIA DEL PARIONE

PALAZZO CORSINI

PARIONCINO

INFERNO

PURGATORIO

MONALDA

SASSETTI

POST

V. PELLICCERIA

PONTE ALLA CARRAIA

LUNGARNO CORSINI

SANTA TRINITÀ

Piazza di Santa Trinita

VIA PORTA ROSSA

Piazza de' Davanzati

DAVANZATI PALACE

CALIMALA

CALIMARA

MERCATO NUOVO

11

9

Piazza de' Salt.

Arno River

Piazza Nazaro Sauro

PONTE S.TRINITÀ

VIA

DELLE TERME

BORGO SS. APOSTOLI

LUNGARNO ACCIAIUOLI

MANETTO

10

VIA POR S. MARIA

ARM.

LAMB.

S. Stefano

To Brancacci Chapel

Piazza de' Frescobaldi

OLTRARNO

SAN JACOPO

BORGO SAN JACOPO

PONTE VECCHIO

To Pitti Palace

SANTO SPIRITO

VIA MAFFIA

V. D. RAMAGLI ANTI

Piazza della Passera

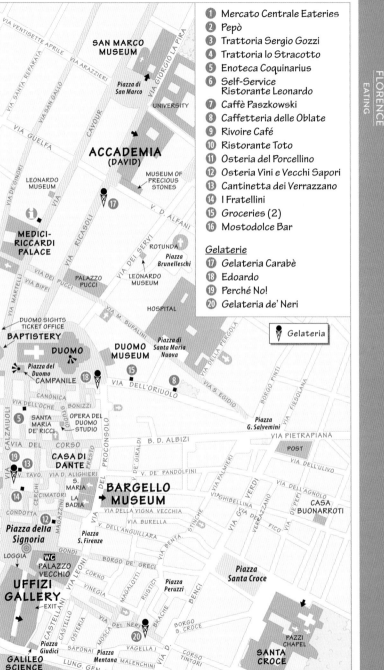

1. Mercato Centrale Eateries
2. Pepò
3. Trattoria Sergio Gozzi
4. Trattoria lo Stracotto
5. Enoteca Coquinarius
6. Self-Service Ristorante Leonardo
7. Caffè Paszkowski
8. Caffetteria delle Oblate
9. Rivoire Café
10. Ristorante Toto
11. Osteria del Porcellino
12. Osteria Vini e Vecchi Sapori
13. Cantinetta dei Verrazzano
14. I Fratellini
15. Groceries (2)
16. Mostodolce Bar

Gelaterie
17. Gelateria Carabè
18. Edoardo
19. Perché No!
20. Gelateria de' Neri

🍦 Gelateria

Near Mercato Centrale

$$ Pepò, a colorful and charmingly unpretentious space, is tucked just around the corner from the touristy glitz on Piazza del Mercato Centrale. The short menu offers simple but well-prepared Florentine classics such as *ribollita* and *pollo alla cacciatora*—chicken cacciatore (daily 12:00-14:30 & 19:00-22:30, Via Rosina 4 red, tel. 055-283-259).

$$ Trattoria Sergio Gozzi is your classic neighborhood lunch-only place, serving hearty, traditional Florentine fare to market-goers since 1915—long before the tourist crush of today. The handwritten menu is limited and changes daily, and the service can be hectic, but it remains a local favorite (Mon-Sat 12:00-15:00, closed Sun, reservations smart, Piazza di San Lorenzo 8, tel. 055-281-941).

$$ Trattoria lo Stracotto is an inviting eatery with a modern interior and good outdoor seating, where you'll enjoy good-value, standard Tuscan dishes in the shadow of the Medici Chapels (daily 12:00-15:00 & 18:00-22:30, Piazza di Madonna degli Aldobrandini 17, tel. 055-230-2062, Francesco and Tomasso).

Around the Duomo

$$ Enoteca Coquinarius feels as welcoming as someone's cool and spacious living room or library. It's an unstressful, hip place with a slow-food ethic and lots of tasty salads and pastas, and a nice selection of wines by the glass (daily 12:30-15:30 & 18:30-22:30, a few steps from the Duomo workshop at Via delle Oche 11 red, tel. 055-230-2153, Nicola and Luca).

$$ Ristorante Natalino is worth the short walk for a memorable dinner. It's a family-run fixture in its neighborhood with outdoor seating on a characteristic corner. The place is known for its homemade pasta, *bistecca alla fiorentina,* and classic Tuscan dishes (daily 12:00-14:30 & 18:30-22:30, Borgo degli Albizi 17 red, for location see map on page 168, tel. 055-289-404).

$ Self-Service Ristorante Leonardo is a quick, cheap, air-conditioned, and handy cafeteria just a block from the Duomo. While it's no-frills and stuck in the 1970s, the food is better than many table-service eateries in this part of town. Stefano and Luciano run the place with enthusiasm and free pitchers of tap water (lots of vegetables, daily 11:45-14:45 & 18:45-21:45, upstairs at Via Pecori 11, tel. 055-284-446).

$$ Caffè Paszkowski is a venerable place on Piazza della Repubblica. While famously expensive as a restaurant, it serves inexpensive, quick lunches. At the display case, order a salad or plate of pasta or cooked veggies (or half-and-half), pay the cashier, and find a seat upstairs. To get this deal, you'll need to sit where the staff designates (lunch served 12:00-15:00, Piazza della Repubblica 35 red—northwest corner, tel. 055-210-236).

$ Caffetteria delle Oblate is a laid-back budget eatery just a block from the Duomo located within a cultural center and library. You'll eat well-priced pastas with students in the top-floor cafeteria, either on an outdoor terrace or in the bright interior—with unobstructed views of the Duomo's dome (Mon 14:00-17:00, Tue-Sat 9:00-23:00, closed Sun, enter through the courtyard at Via dell'Oriuolo 26 and take the elevator to the top floor, tel. 055-263-9685).

Near Piazza della Signoria

$$$ Rivoire café is famous for its fancy desserts and thick hot chocolate (€7). A bowl of pasta or a salad—when enjoyed at the best view tables on the square—can be a worthwhile experience. Their delightful bar is perfectly affordable, and drinks often come with fine *aperitivo* munchies (daily 8:00-24:00, tel. 055-214-412).

$$ Ristorante Toto is a simple, fun, traditional eatery with a spacious dining hall serving classic Tuscan plates at decent prices. The focus is on steak and pizza (Thu-Tue 12:00-15:00 & 19:00-22:00,

Gelato

Italy's best ice cream is in Florence—many think they serve some of the world's best. But beware of scams at touristy joints on busy streets that turn a simple request for a cone into a €10 "tourist special" rip-off. To avoid this, survey the size options and specify what you want—for example, *un cono da tre euro* (a €3 cone). A rule of thumb: Stay away from places with heaping mounds of brightly (artificially) colored gelato. For more gelato tips, see the "Eating" section of the Practicalities chapter. The following places, which are a cut above the norm, are open long hours daily.

Near the Accademia: A Sicilian choice on a tourist thoroughfare, **Gelateria Carabè** is particularly famous for its pistachio and its luscious *granite*—Italian ices made with fresh fruit. A *cremolata* is a *granita* with a dollop of gelato (almond and pistachio work well together). If you'd like a real Sicilian cannoli, get it here (from the Accademia, it's a block toward the Duomo at Via Ricasoli 60 red—Simone clearly loves his work).

Near the Duomo: A favorite, **Edoardo** features organic ingredients and tasty handmade cones (facing the southwest corner of the Duomo at Piazza del Duomo 45 red).

Near Orsanmichele Church: This shop's name, **Perchè No!,** translates to "Why not!"—good advice when it comes to gelato. It feels touristy but serves one of the widest range of flavors around, and the quality's top notch (just off the busy main pedestrian drag, Via de' Calzaiuoli, at Via dei Tavolini 19).

Near the Church of Santa Croce: Florentines flock to **Gelateria de' Neri,** with an enticingly wide array of flavors (Via dei Neri 9 red).

Just Across the Carraia Bridge: On the Oltrarno side of the bridge, **Gelateria la Carraia** is a hit with locals (Piazza Nazario Sauro 25 red—see the map on page 194).

closed Wed, two blocks from the Ponte Vecchio at Borgo SS. Apostoli 6 red, tel. 055-212-096).

$$$ **Osteria del Porcellino** is a classic place deep in the center with a romantic ambience inside and quiet seating outside. Enzo—whose family has owned this restaurant since 1969—serves Tuscan classics. At dinner, he offers a complementary glass of bubbly when you sit down, and a vin santo with *contucci* after your meal (good €15 lunch special, daily 12:00-23:00, Via Val di Lamona 7 red, tel. 055-264-148).

$$ **Osteria Vini e Vecchi Sapori** is a colorful eatery—tight, tiny, and with attitude. They serve Tuscan food—like *pappardelle* with duck—from a fun, accessible menu of delicious pastas and *secondi* (Mon-Sat 12:30-14:30 & 19:30-22:30, closed Sun, reservations necessary—call ahead, Via dei Magazzini 3 red, tel. 055-293-045, run by Mario while wife Rosanna cooks and son Tommaso serves).

Sandwiches Near Piazza della Signoria

$$ **Cantinetta dei Verrazzano** is an elegant wine bar serving delightful sandwich plates. Their *selezione Verrazzano* is a plate of four little crostini featuring breads, cheeses, and meats from the Chianti region. The *tagliere di focacce,* a sampler of mini focaccia sandwiches, is also fun (daily 8:00-16:30, no reservations taken, off Via de' Calzaiuoli, at Via dei Tavolini 18 red, tel. 055-268-590).

$ **I Fratellini** is a hole-in-the-wall stand-up joint where the "little brothers" have served peasants more than 30 kinds of sandwiches and a fine selection of wine at great prices (see list on wall) since 1875. Join the local crowd to order, then sit on a nearby curb to eat, placing your glass on the wall rack before you leave. Be adventurous with the menu (order by number). It's worth ordering the most expensive wine they're selling by the glass (daily 9:00-19:30 or until the bread runs out, 20

yards in front of Orsanmichele Church on Via dei Cimatori, tel. 055-239-6096).

The Oltrarno

Dining in the Oltrarno, south of the Arno River, offers a more authentic experience. While it's just a few minutes' walk beyond Ponte Vecchio, this area sees fewer tourists. For locations, see the map on page 194.

Dining or Drinking with a Ponte Vecchio View

$$$ **Signorvino** is a bright and modern *enoteca* (wine shop) with a simple restaurant that has a rare terrace literally over the Arno River, with Ponte Vecchio views. Though it lacks historic charm with its stark-white IKEA vibe, it's a fun-loving place with no pretense and a passion for quality Italian ingredients. They serve regional dishes and plates of fine meats and cheeses to pair with a wonderful array of wines by the glass (food served 11:30-23:00, call to reserve, especially for terrace seating, Via dei Bardi 46 red, tel. 055-286-258, www.signorvino.com).

$$$ **Golden View Firenze** is two-in-one: a classy restaurant and the simpler **Bar Osteria,** both overlooking the Ponte Vecchio and Arno River. The white, minimalist interior is a dramatic contrast to atmospheric old Florence. Reservations for window tables are essential. Mixing their fine wine, river views, and live jazz makes for a wonderful evening (daily 12:00-24:00; jazz usually Mon, Fri, and Sat nights in the restaurant at 21:00; 50 yards east of Ponte Vecchio at Via dei Bardi 58, tel. 055-214-502, www.goldenviewopenbar.com, run by Paolo).

On or near Piazza di Santo Spirito

Piazza di Santo Spirito is a thriving neighborhood square, with a collection of fun eateries and bars. Several bars offer *aperitivo* buffets with their drinks during happy hour. Later in the evening, the area becomes a club scene.

Cooking Classes

The options listed below represent only a few of your many choices. As this is a fast-changing scene, it's worth doing some homework online and booking well ahead.

In Tavola is a dedicated cooking school in the heart of the Oltrarno. They feature trained, English-speaking Italian chefs who quickly demonstrate each step before setting you loose. You'll work in a functional kitchen, and then sit down to eat in the cozy wine cellar (classes range from €57-129/person, ideally book well ahead but you can try calling last-minute, between the Pitti Palace and Brancacci Chapel at Via dei Velluti 18 red, tel. 055-217-672, www.intavola.org, info@intavola.org, Fabrizio).

Both **Artviva** and **Florencetown** (see contact info under "Tours," earlier) offer cooking classes (Artviva: €59-73/person; Florencetown: from €79/person).

$$ Gusta Osteria, just around the corner from the piazza, serves big salads and predictable Tuscan fare at fun, cozy indoor seating or at outdoor tables (Tue-Sun 12:00-23:00, closed Mon, Via de' Michelozzi 13 red, tel. 055-285-033).

$$ Trattoria Sant'Agostino, a block away from the Piazza di Santo Spirito action, is charming and more relaxed with comfortable seating and a good place for traditional local cuisine (daily 12:00-23:00, Via Sant'Agostino 23 red, tel. 055-281-995).

$ O Munaciello Pizzeria, named after a ghost of Neapolitan folklore, is a kitschy, sprawling, family-friendly festival of happy eating. The menu is fun, there's a youthful energy, and the Naples-style pizza is a hit with locals (daily 12:30-15:00 & 19:00-24:00, Via Maffia 31 red, tel. 055-287-198).

Dining Well in the Oltrarno

Of the many good and colorful restaurants in the Oltrarno, these are my favorites. Reservations are a good idea in the evening.

$$$ Il Santo Bevitore Ristorante, lit like a Rembrandt painting and unusually spacious, serves creative, modern Tuscan cuisine at dressy tables. They're enthusiastic about matching quality local produce with the right wine (good wine list by the glass or bottle, daily 12:30-14:30 & 19:30-23:00, reservations smart, three tables on the sidewalk, can be noisy inside, Via di Santo Spirito 64 red, tel. 055-211-264, www.ilsantobevitore.com).

$$ Enoteca il Santino Gastronomia, Il Santo Bevitore's tiny wine bar next door, feels like the perfect after-work hangout for foodies who'd like a glass of wine and a light bite. Tight, cozy, and atmospheric, the place can be intimidating if you're shy. It has a prominent bar, where you can assemble an €8-12 *tagliere* of local cheeses and *salumi*. They also have a few affordable hot dishes (daily 12:30-23:00, Via di Santo Spirito 60 red, no reservations, tel. 055-230-2820).

$$$ Trattoria 4 Leoni creates the quintessential Oltrarno dinner scene and is understandably popular with tourists. The Tuscan-style food is made with an innovative twist and an appreciation

for vegetables. Their steak and *fiocchetti* pasta are big hits (daily 12:00-24:00, dinner reservations smart; midway between Ponte Vecchio and Piazza di Santo Spirito, on Piazza della Passera at Via de' Vellutini 1; tel. 055-218-562, www.4leoni.com).

$$$$ Olio & Convivium showcases their artful, slow-food cooking in three dressy and intimate rooms that are surrounded by fine *prosciutti,* cheeses, and wine shelves. It can seem a little formal, but well-dressed foodies will appreciate this place for its romantic, exclusive atmosphere. Their list of €14-25 *gastronomia* plates offers an array of taste treats and fine wines by the glass. They also have €35-49 tasting *menus* and stylish €22 lunches with wine (Tue-Sun 12:00-14:30 & 19:00-22:30, closed Mon, Via di Santo Spirito 4, tel. 055-265-8198, www.oliorestaurant.it, chef and owner Tommaso).

TRANSPORTATION

Getting Around Florence

I organize my sightseeing geographically and do it all on foot. You likely won't need public transit, except maybe to head up to Piazzale Michelangelo and San Miniato Church for the view.

By Bus

The city's full-size buses don't cover the old center well (the whole area around the Duomo is off-limits to motorized traffic). Pick up a map of transit routes at the ATAF windows (#8 and #9) at the train station; you'll also find routes online (www.ataf.net).

Buy bus tickets at tobacco shops (*tabacchi*), newsstands, or the ATAF ticket windows (€1.50/90 minutes). Be sure to validate your ticket in the machine on board (or risk a steep fine). Follow general bus etiquette: Board at front or rear doors, exit out the center.

Of the many bus lines, I find these to be of most value for seeing outlying sights: Bus **#12** goes from the train station,

over the Carraia bridge to Porta Romana, then up to San Miniato Church and Piazzale Michelangelo (3/hour). Bus **#13** makes the return trip down the hill.

Minibuses (many of them electric) wind through the tangled old center of town and up and down the river—just €1.50 gets you a 1.5-hour joyride. They run every 10 minutes from 7:00 to 21:00 (less frequent on Sun).

Bus **#C1** stops behind the Palazzo Vecchio and Piazza Santa Croce, then heads north, passing near San Marco and the Accademia before heading up to Piazza Libertà. On its southbound route, it also stops near the train station, the Basilica of San Lorenzo, and the Duomo.

Bus **#C2** twists through the congested old center from the train station, passing near Piazza della Repubblica and Piazza della Signoria to Piazza Beccaria.

Bus **#C3** goes up and down the Arno River, with stops near Piazza Santa Croce, Ponte Vecchio, the Carraia bridge to the Oltrarno (including the Pitti Palace), and beyond.

Bus **#C4** goes from near the Duomo to the train station, crosses the Carraia bridge, and cruises through the Oltrarno (passing the Pitti Palace) before heading into the San Niccolò neighborhood.

By Tram

The T1 and T2 tram lines are cheap, easy, and frequent. For travelers, they're generally useful only for service between the tram stops in town (near the train station) and either the airport (T2) or the big park-and-ride lots at Villa Costanza (T1) near the town of Scandicci (www.gestramvia.com).

By Taxi

The minimum cost for a taxi ride is €5 (€8.30 after 22:00, €7 on Sun); rides in the town center should be charged as tariff #1. Taxi fares and supplements (e.g., €2 extra to call a cab rather than hail one) are clearly explained on signs in each taxi.

Look for an official, regulated cab (white; marked with *Taxi/Comune di Firenze,* red fleur-de-lis, and one of the official phone numbers: 4390 or 4242). Before getting in a cab, ask for an approximate cost (*"Più o meno, quanto costa?"* pew oh MEH-noh, KWAHN-toh KOH-stah). If you can't get a straight answer or the price is outrageous, wait for the next one. It can be hard to find a cab on the street; to call one, dial 055-4390 or 055-4242 (or ask your waiter or hotelier to call for you).

Arriving and Departing
By Train
Florence's main train station is called **Santa Maria Novella** (*Firenze S.M.N.* on schedules and signs; Florence also has two suburban train stations: **Firenze Rifredi** and **Firenze Campo di Marte**).

Rick's Tip: Be on guard at train stations. Don't trust "porters" who want to help you find your train or carry your bags (they're not official), and **politely decline offers of help** *using the ticket machines by anyone other than uniformed staff.*

To orient yourself to Santa Maria Novella Station, stand with your back to the tracks. Look left to see the green cross of a 24-hour pharmacy (*farmacia*) and the exit to the taxi queue. **Baggage storage** (*deposito bagagli*) is also to the left, halfway down track 16 (long hours daily, passport required). **Fast-food outlets** and a **bank** are also along track 16. Directly ahead of you is the main hall (*salone biglietti*), where you can buy train and bus tickets. Pay WCs are to the right, near the head of track 5.

To reach the **TI,** walk away from the tracks and exit the station; it's straight across the square, 100 yards away, by the stone church.

Buying Tickets: For travel within Italy, it's quick and easy to buy tickets online; with the Trenitalia app, you can even purchase them minutes before the train departs. If you decide to buy tickets at the station, take advantage of the ticket (*biglietti*) machines that display schedules, issue tickets, and even make reservations for rail-pass holders. For most international tickets, you'll need to go to a Trenitalia ticket window (in the main hall).

For Trenitalia information, use window #18 or #19 (take a number). For Italo tickets and information, use window #10 or #11, or visit their main office, opposite track 5, near the exit. To buy ATAF city bus tickets, stop at windows #8-9 in the main hall—and ask for a transit map while you're there (TIs often do not have them).

Getting to the Duomo and City Center: The Duomo and town center are to your left (with your back to the tracks). Out the doorway to the left, you'll find city buses and the taxi stand. Taxis cost about €8 to the Duomo. To walk into town (10-15 minutes), exit the station straight ahead (with your back to the tracks) through the main hall and head straight across the square outside (toward the Church of Santa Maria Novella). On the far side of the square, keep left and head down the main Via dei Panzani, which leads directly to the Duomo.

TRAIN CONNECTIONS
For general information on train travel in Italy, see page 491.

From Florence by Train to: Pisa (2/hour, 45-75 minutes), Siena (direct trains hourly, 1.5 hours; bus is better because Siena's train station is far from the center), La Spezia (for the Cinque Terre, 5/day direct, 2.5 hours, otherwise nearly hourly with change in Pisa), Milan (hourly, 2 hours; Italo: 2/hour, 2 hours), Venice (hourly, 2-3 hours, may transfer in Bologna, often crowded—reserve ahead; Italo: 4/day, 2 hours, reservations required), Assisi (7/day direct, 2-3 hours), Orvieto (hourly, 2 hours, some with change in Campo di Marte or Rifredi Station), Rome (2-3/hour, 1.5 hours, most require seat reservations; Italo: 2/hour, 1.5 hours), Naples (at least hourly, 3 hours; Italo: hourly, 3 hours).

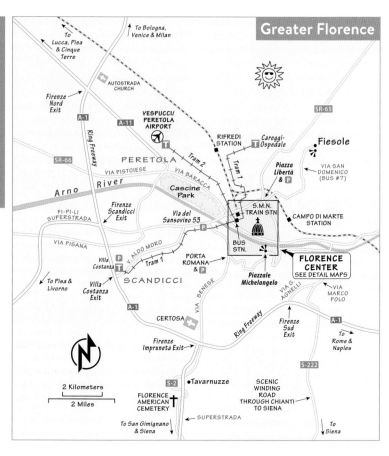

Greater Florence

By Bus

The BusItalia Station is 50 yards south-west of the train station, near the T1 tram stop. To get to the city center, exit the station through the main door, and turn left along the busy street. The train station is on your left, while downtown Florence is straight ahead and a bit to the right.

Schedules for regional trips are posted, and monitors show imminent departures. Bus service drops dramatically on Sunday. Generally it's best to buy tickets in the station, as you'll pay 30 percent more to buy tickets onboard. Bus info: Tel. 800-373-760 (Mon-Fri 9:00-15:00, closed Sat-Sun), www.fsbusitalia.it.

From Florence by Bus to: Siena (roughly 2/hour—fewer off-season, 1.5-hour *rapida/via superstrada* buses are fastest, avoid the slower *ordinaria* buses, in Siena get off at Piazza Gramsci or Via Tozzi, www.tiemmespa.it), **Montepulciano** (1-2/day, 2 hours, LFI bus, www.lfi.it; or train to Chiusi, then Tiemme/Siena Mobilità bus to Montepulciano, www.tiemmespa.it).

By Car

Don't even attempt driving into the city center. The autostrada has several exits for Florence. Get off at the Nord, Scandicci, Impruneta, or Sud exits and follow signs toward—but not into—the *Centro*. Park on the outskirts—see the next section—and take a bus, tram, or taxi in.

Florence has a traffic-reduction system that's complicated and confusing even to locals. Every car passing into the "limited traffic zone" (*Zona Traffico Limitato,* or *ZTL*) is photographed; those who haven't jumped through bureaucratic hoops to get a permit can expect a €100 ticket in the mail (and an "administrative" fee from the rental company). If you have a reservation at a hotel within the ZTL area— and it has parking—ask in advance if they can get you permission to enter town.

Parking in Florence: The city center is ringed with big, efficient parking lots (sign-posted with a big *P*). From these, you can ride into the center (via taxi, bus, or possibly tram). Check www.firenzeparcheggi.it for details on parking lots, availability, and prices. From the freeway, follow the signs to *Centro,* then *Stadio,* then *P.*

The huge park-and-ride lot called Villa Costanza, just outside the town of Scandicci (south of Florence), has its own dedicated freeway offramp (just north of Impruneta) and is the terminus for the T1 tram line that zips smart drivers downtown (€1.50, departing every five minutes). Just look for it as you approach Florence on the autostrada.

By Plane
Amerigo Vespucci Airport, also called Peretola Airport, is about five miles north-west of the city (code: FLR, tel. 055-306-1830, www.aeroporto.firenze.it).

On the ground floor, the **T2 tram** (to the left as you exit the arrivals hall) runs every five minutes from the airport to near the train station (Alamanni Stazione, across from the station) and Piazza dell'Unità (one stop beyond the station, slightly closer to downtown) in about 20 minutes (runs 5:00-24:00, €1.50, buy ticket from machine on platform, cash or credit card, validate onboard, good for 90 minutes and transferable to bus lines, www.gestramvia.com).

Shuttle buses (to the far right as you exit the arrivals hall) connect the airport with Florence's train and bus stations (2/hour until 22:00, 1/hour until 00:30, 30 minutes, runs 5:00-00:30, €6 one-way—buy ticket on board, €10 round-trip—buy ticket inside airport). If you're changing to a different intercity bus in Florence (for instance, one bound for Siena), stay on the bus through the first stop (at the train station); it will continue on to the bus station nearby.

Official **taxi** companies have fixed rates for the 20- to 30-minute ride between the airport and downtown: €22 during the day (6:00-22:00), €25.30 at night, and €24 on Sunday. Be sure to use an official taxi (white, marked with *Taxi/Comune di Firenze* and a red fleur-de-lis).

The airport's **rental-car** offices share one big parking lot that's a three-minute drive away (shuttle bus departs directly outside the arrivals door).

By Private Car
For small groups with more money than time, zipping to nearby towns by private car service can be a comfortable option. Consider **Transfer Chauffeur Service** (mobile 338-862-3129, www.transfercs.com, welcome@transfercs.com, Marco) or **Prestige Rent** (office at Via della Saggina 98, tel. 055-286-059, www.prestigerent.com, usa@prestigerent.com, Saverio).

BEST OF THE REST

Pisa

Centuries ago, Pisa was a major power—rivaling Venice and Genoa for control of the seas. City leaders erected an ensemble of Pisan Romanesque landmarks—the Duomo, Baptistery, and Tower—that float regally on the best lawn in Italy. Even as the church was being built in the late 11th century, Piazza del Duomo was nicknamed the Campo dei Miracoli, or Field of Miracles, for the grandness of the undertaking.

Day Plan

Pisa is a touristic quickie. Seeing the famous tipsy Tower (reservations required to climb it), wandering through the Duomo, and visiting the other sights around the Field of Miracles can be done in a half-day.

Extend your visit with a leisurely one-hour stroll from the train station to the Tower and Field of Miracles. The two main streets for tourists and shoppers are Via Santa Maria (running south from the Tower) and Corso Italia/Borgo Stretto (running north from the station).

Rick's Tip: **To ascend the Tower,** *it's smartest to* **book a time in advance** *online at OPAPisa.it. Otherwise, especially in summer,* **go straight to the ticket office** *upon arrival to snag an appointment—usually for a few hours later.*

Orientation

Pisa is framed on the north by the Field of Miracles (with the Leaning Tower) and on the south by Pisa Centrale train station. The Arno River flows east to west, bisecting the city. A thousand years ago the city was a fortified burg on the north side of the river between those two main streets.

Tourist Information: The main TI is located on the Field of Miracles, next to the Duomo's ticket office at the Museum of the Sinopias (daily 9:30-17:30, baggage storage available, Piazza Duomo 7, tel. 050-550-100, www.turismo.pisa.it). It sells bus tickets and offers videoguide walking tours of the main sights.

Local Guides: Dottore Vincenzo Riolo guides tours of the Field of Miracles and other Tuscan destinations (€150/3 hours, mobile 338-211-2939, www.pisatour.it, info@pisatour.it). **Martina Manfredi** happily guides visitors through the Field of Miracles and Pisa's other charms (€140/3 hours, mobile 328-898-2927, www.tuscany atheart.it, artemarty@libero.it).

Getting There

Pisa is an easy day trip from Florence, whether coming by **train** (frequent departures, 45-75 minutes) or **car** (excellent highways). Pisa's handy **Galileo Galilei Airport** is just two miles from the train station (www.pisa-airport.com).

Most trains arrive at Pisa Centrale station, about a mile south of the Tower and Field of Miracles (baggage check available). To get to the Field of Miracles, you can **walk** (30 minutes), take a **taxi** (taxi stand at station), or go by **bus** (which can be plagued by pickpockets).

Bus **LAM Rossa** (also marked L/R) stops in front of the station (to the right when you exit). Buy a €1.50 ticket from machines at the bus stop—or pay €2.50 on board. The bus lets you off at Piazza Manin, in front of the gate to the Field of Miracles (stop: Torre).

Drivers should try the **Parcheggio di Piazza dei Miracoli** lot, just west of the Tower (€2/hour, enter from Via Giovanni Battista Niccolini). Or leave your car at the big **Pietrasantina parking lot** (exit the autostrada at *Pisa Nord* and follow signs to *Pisa,* then *Bus Parking*). From there, you can walk to the Field of Miracles or hop on a LAM Rossa bus.

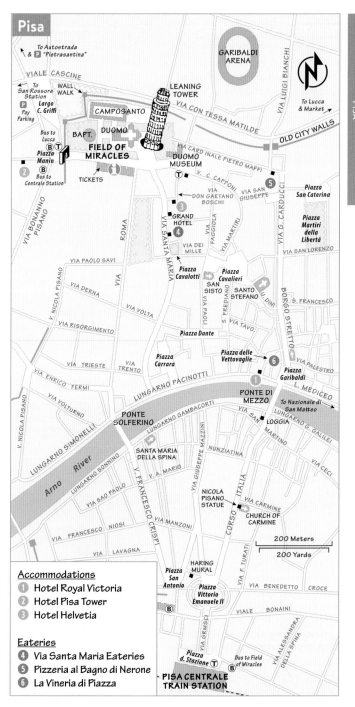

Pisa

To Autostrada
& P "Pietrasantina"

VIALE CASCINE

To
San Rossore
Station

WALL
WALK

P
Pay
Parking

Largo
C. Griffi

CAMPOSANTO

Bus to
Lucca

DUOMO

BAPT.

Piazza
Manin

FIELD OF
MIRACLES

Bus to
Centrale Station

TICKETS

VIA BONANNO PISANO

LEANING
TOWER

VIA CON TESSA MATILDE

GARIBALDI
ARENA

VIA LUIGI BIANCHI

To Lucca
& Market

OLD CITY WALLS

VIA CARDINALE PIETRO MAFFI

DUOMO
MUSEUM

V. C. CAPPONI

VIA DON GAETANO BOSCHI

VIA SAN GIUSEPPE

Piazza
San Caterina

VIA G. CARDUCCI

Piazza
Martiri
della
Libertà

ROMA

GRAND
HOTEL

VIA FAGGIOLA

VIA MARTIRI

VIA SAN LORENZO

VIA DEI MILLE

VIA SANTA MARIA

VIA PAOLO SAVI

Piazza
Cavalotti

Piazza
Cavalieri

VIA NICOLA PISANO

VIA DERNA

VIA PAOLI

SAN
SISTO

S. FREDIANO

SANTO
STEFANO

U. DINI

S. FRANCESCO

BORGO STRETTO

VIA VOLTA

V. NICOLA PISANO

VIA RISORGIMENTO

S. VIA TAVO

Piazza
Dante

VIA TRIESTE

VIA
TRENTO

Piazza
Carrara

Piazza delle
Vettovaglie

Piazza
Garibaldi

VIA PALESTRO

VIA ENRICO FERMI

LUNGARNO PACINOTTI

L. MEDICEO

VIA VOLTURNO

PONTE DI
MEZZO

To Nazionale di
San Matteo

LUNGARNO G. GALILEI

LUNGARNO SIMONELLI

PONTE
SOLFERINO

LUNGARNO GAMBACORTI

VIA SAN
MARTINO

LOGGIA

VIA GIUSEPPE MAZZINI

NUNZIATINA

VIA CECI

Arno   River

LUNGARNO SONNINO

SANTA MARIA
DELLA SPINA

V. A. MARIO

VIA SAO PAOLO

V. FRANCESCO CRISPI

NICOLA
PISANO
STATUE

CORSO ITALIA

VIA CARMINE

VIA MANZONI

CHURCH OF
CARMINE

200 Meters

VIA FRANCESCO NIOSI

200 Yards

VIA LAVAGNA

HARING
MURAL

Piazza
San
Antonio

Piazza
Vittorio
Emanuele II

VIA F. TURATI

VIA BENEDETTO

CROCE

B

VIALE   BONAINI

VIA GRAMSCI

VIA ALESSANDRA DELLA SPINA

Piazza
d. Stazione

Bus to Field
of Miracles

PISA CENTRALE
TRAIN STATION

Accommodations
1 Hotel Royal Victoria
2 Hotel Pisa Tower
3 Hotel Helvetia

Eateries
4 Via Santa Maria Eateries
5 Pizzeria al Bagno di Nerone
6 La Vineria di Piazza

Sights

Scattered across the Field of Miracles lawn are five grand buildings: the cathedral (or Duomo), its bell tower (the Leaning Tower), the Baptistery, the hospital (today's Museum of the Sinopias), and the Camposanto Cemetery. Each building, in a style called Pisan Romanesque, has a simple ground floor and rows of delicate columns and arches that form open-air arcades, giving the Campo a pleasant visual unity. Unlike traditional Romanesque, with its heavy fortress-like feel, Pisan Romanesque is light and elegant.

Traditionally, these buildings marked the main events of every Pisan's life: christened in the Baptistery, married in the Duomo, called to celebrate by the bells in the tower, healed in the hospital, and buried in the Camposanto Cemetery.

Rick's Tip: *Although the smooth green lawn of the Field of Miracles looks like the ideal picnic spot,* **lounging on it can result in a €25 fine.**

▲▲▲LEANING TOWER

A 15-foot lean from the vertical makes the Leaning Tower one of Europe's most recognizable images. You can see it for free—it's always viewable—or you can pay to climb to the top.

Cost and Hours: €18, kids under age 8 not allowed, 9:00-20:00, mid-June-Aug 8:30-22:00, Nov 9:00-19:00, Dec-Feb 10:00-17:00, March 9:00-18:00, ticket office opens 30 minutes early.

Getting In: Entry to the Tower is by a timed ticket good for a 30-minute visit. Every 15 minutes, 50 people can clamber up the 294 tilting steps to the top. Children ages 8-18 must be accompanied by an adult.

Reservations: Online bookings are accepted no earlier than 20 days and no later than one day in advance. Choose your entry time and buy your ticket at OPAPisa.it. Print out the voucher or save it on your phone, and bring it to the Tower 15 minutes before your entry time.

To reserve in person, go to either **ticket office:** behind the Tower on the left (in the yellow building) or (less crowded) at the Museum of the Sinopias.

Visiting the Tower: The Tower is nearly 200 feet tall and 55 feet wide, weighing 14,000 tons and currently leaning at a five-degree angle. Count the eight stories—a simple base, six stories of columns (forming arcades), and a belfry on top. The inner structural core is a hollow cylinder built of limestone bricks, faced with white marble. The thin columns of the open-air arcades make the heavy Tower seem light and graceful.

The Tower was built over two centuries by at least three different architects. The first stones were laid in 1173. Five years later, just as the base and the first arcade were finished, someone said, "Is it just me, or does that look crooked?" The heavy Tower—resting on a very shallow 13-foot foundation—was sinking on the south side into the marshy soil.

After the Tower's completion, several

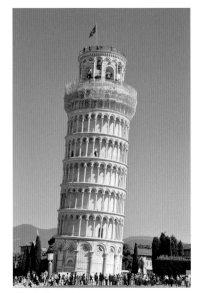
The Leaning Tower

attempts were made to stop its slow-motion fall, but it got so bad that in 1990 the Tower was closed for repairs to stabilize it. Engineers drilled 15-foot-deep holes in the ground on the north side and sucked out 60 tons of soil, allowing the Tower to straighten out its lean by about six inches. Still, art historians figure the Tower leans today as much as it did when Galileo reputedly conducted his gravity experiment here 400 years ago.

▲▲DUOMO (CATHEDRAL)

The Duomo is the centerpiece of the Field of Miracles' complex of religious buildings. Begun in 1063, it was financed by a galley-load of booty ransacked that year from the Muslim-held capital of Palermo, Sicily. The architect Buschetto created the frilly Pisan Romanesque style that set the tone for the Baptistery and Tower that followed. In the 1150s, the architect Rainaldo added the impressive main-entrance facade. The 15-foot-tall, octagonal pulpit, smothered in 400 figures intricately sculpted from creamy white Carrara marble, is the last, biggest, and most complex of the four pulpits created by the Pisano father-and-son team (c. 1311).

Cost and Hours: Free. If you have any combo-ticket you can walk right in; otherwise, pick up a voucher with an entry time (every 30 minutes) at either ticket office (daily 10:00-20:00, shorter hours off-season).

MORE SIGHTS ON THE FIELD OF MIRACLES

Pisa's **Baptistery** is Italy's biggest. It's interesting for its pulpit (by the elder Pisano) and interior ambience, and for its acoustics (demonstrated twice an hour). Notice that the Baptistery leans nearly six feet to the north (the Tower leans 15 feet to the south).

Until people started getting excited about the Leaning Tower around 1900, the big attraction in Pisa was its dreamy and exquisite cemetery, the **Camposanto.** Highlights are the building's cloistered interior courtyard, some ancient sarcophagi, and the large 14th-century fresco, *The Triumph of Death.* Housed in a 13th-century hospital, the **Museum of the Sinopias** features the original preliminary sketches (sinopias) for the Camposanto's frescoes.

Near the Tower is the entrance to the **Duomo Museum,** which displays treasures of the cathedral, paintings, silverware, and 12th- to 14th-century sculptures, as well as ancient Egyptian, Etruscan, and Roman artifacts. You'll see several large-scale wooden models of the Duomo, Baptistery, and Tower, as well as the Duomo's original 12th-century bronze doors of St. Ranieri.

Cost and Hours: €5 for one sight, €7 for two sights, €8 covers everything. All four sights are open daily April-Sept 8:00-20:00; shorter hours off-season.

Sleeping

If staying the night, consider the romantic **$$ Hotel Royal Victoria** (Lungarno Pacinotti 12, www.royalvictoria.it), the stately **$$ Hotel Pisa Tower** (Via Andrea Pisano 23, www.hotelpisatower.com), or the no-frills **$ Hotel Helvetia** (Via Don G. Boschi 31, www.pensionehelvetiapisa.com).

Eating

The Via Santa Maria strip is pedestrianized and lined with touristy eateries. From the Tower, walk past Grand Hotel Duomo to avoid the worst of the tourist traps and find a decent quick sandwich, pizza, or salad. **$$ Pizzeria al Bagno di Nerone** is a five-minute walk from the Tower (closed Tue, Largo Carlo Fedeli 26). For a real meal, try the area around the old Renaissance-style market, Piazza delle Vettovaglie. **$$ La Vineria di Piazza** is a quintessential little Tuscan trattoria (Piazza delle Vettovaglie 14).

The Hill Towns
of Central Italy

The sun-soaked hill towns of central Italy offer the quintessential Italian experience. Throughout Tuscany and Umbria, wispy cypress-lined driveways lead to fortified 16th-century farmhouses set in rolling fields, atmospheric *enoteche* serve famous wines alongside homemade pasta, and dusty old-timers warm the same bench day after day while soccer balls buzz around them like innocuous flies.

How in Dante's name does a traveler choose from Italy's hundreds of hill towns? I've listed my favorites. If you linger longer to explore, you're sure to find a favorite of your own. When sampling hill towns, spend the night if you can, as many towns can get mobbed by day-trippers. Hill towns are best enjoyed by adapting to the pace of the countryside. Slow down, and savor the delights this region offers.

THE HILL TOWNS IN 3 DAYS

Italy's best hill towns are Siena, Assisi, and Orvieto. They're each worth at least one full day and an overnight, and are accessible by train or bus.

Siena's main sight is the city itself. Its elegant Il Campo main square, marked by a tall tower, is a people magnet. The cathedral's eye-catching facade draws you inside. The Duomo Museum and Pinacoteca exhibit graceful art for the pleasure of art lovers. Enjoy a sleepy medieval evening on the main square. Although you could day-trip from Florence, it's worth staying over: Evenings are magical here.

Assisi's old town has a half-day of sightseeing and another half-day of wonder. The essential sight is the Basilica of St. Francis, dedicated to Assisi's hometown saint and decorated with dazzling frescoes by Giotto and Cimabue.

The town of **Orvieto,** conveniently close to Rome, can be seen in a few hours. It's famous for its cathedral and *Classico* wine (tastings, anyone?). A 45-minute bus ride away, the tiny, neighboring hill village of Civita is nearly huggable.

With extra time (and a car) you can visit the Tuscan wine towns of **Montepulciano** and **Montalcino.**

Getting Around the Hill Towns

While it's possible to visit the towns I recommend by public transportation, you can get around easier and quicker by car.

By Car: Exploring Italy's hill towns by car can be a great experience. Wait to pick up your car until the last sizable town you visit (or at the nearest airport to avoid big-city traffic), and carry a good, detailed road map in addition to a mapping app. Freeways are the fastest way to connect two points, but smaller roads, including

HILL TOWNS AT A GLANCE

▲▲▲**Siena** Italy's ultimate hill town, with its grand Il Campo square and striking striped cathedral. See page 224.

▲▲**Tuscan Wine Towns** The picturesque, wine-soaked villages of Italy's heartland: Montepulciano and Montalcino. See page 249.

▲▲**Assisi** St. Francis' hometown, perched on a hillside, with a divinely Giotto-decorated basilica. See page 260.

▲▲**Orvieto and Civita** More hill-town adventures, featuring Orvieto's classic views and ornate cathedral, plus the adorable pocket-sized village of Civita di Bagnoregio. See pages 284 and 300.

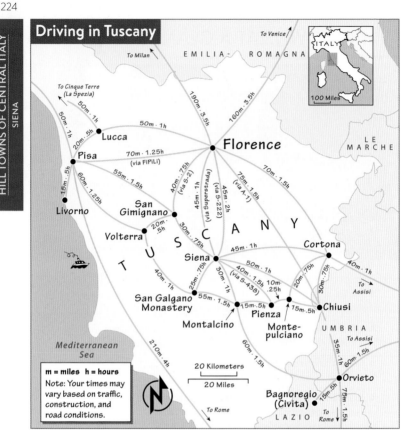

Driving in Tuscany

To Milan

To Venice

EMILIA- ROMAGNA

ITALY

100 Miles

To Cinque Terre
(La Spezia)

50m · 1h

50m · 1h

20m · .5h

Lucca

50m · 1h

190m · 3.5h

160m · 3.5h

Pisa

70m · 1.25h
(via FI·PI·LI)

Florence

LE
MARCHE

55m · 1.5h

40m · .75h
(via S-2)

45m · .75h (via superstrada)

45m · 2h (via A-1)

75m · 1.5h
(via A-1)

70m · 1.5h

1.5m · .5h

60m · 1.25h

Livorno

San
Gimignano

T U S C A N Y

Volterra

20m · .5h

30m · .75h

Cortona

Siena

45m · 1h

50m · 1h

40m · .75h

40m · 1h

To
Assisi

40m · 1h

25m · .75h

30m · 1h

40m · 1.5h
(via S-438)

10m · .25h

20m · .75h

30m · .75h

San Galgano
Monastery

55m · 1.5h

15m · .5h

Pienza

15m · .5h

Chiusi

Montalcino

Monte-
pulciano

UMBRIA

To Assisi

Mediterranean
Sea

m = miles h = hours
Note: Your times may
vary based on traffic,
construction, and
road conditions.

210m · 4h

60m · 1.5h

35m · 1h

60m · 1.5h

20 Kilometers

20 Miles

N

To Rome

Bagnoregio
(Civita)

L A Z I O

15m · .5h

75m · 1.5h

Orvieto

To
Rome

Scenic roads connect the hill towns.

the super-scenic S-222, connecting Florence and Siena, are more rewarding.

Some towns don't allow visitors to drive or park in the city center. Be alert for "ZTL" (*Zona Traffico Limitato*) signs, indicating no cars allowed. Leave your

car outside the walls and walk into town. Lots are usually free and plentiful outside city walls (and sometimes linked to the town center by elevators or escalators). For more driving and parking tips, see the Practicalities chapter.

By Public Transit: Public bus connections are slow, infrequent, and often require a transfer. Train stations are likely to be in the valley below the town center, connected by a local bus. Taxis can help connect the dots more efficiently.

SIENA

Siena's thriving historic center, with red-brick lanes cascading every which way, offers Italy's best medieval city experience. While Florence has the blockbuster

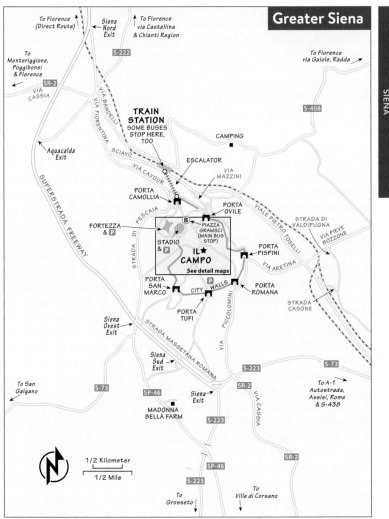

Greater Siena

To Florence (Direct Route)
Siena Nord Exit
To Florence via Castellina & Chianti Region
To Monteriggione, Poggibonsi & Florence
S-222
SR-2
VIA CASSIA
VIA BANDELLI
VIA FIORENTINA
TRAIN STATION SOME BUSES STOP HERE, TOO
CAMPING
To Florence via Gaiole, Radda
S-408
SCIAVO
VIA CAVOUR
Aquacalda Exit
ESCALATOR
VIA MAZZINI
SUPERSTRADA FREEWAY
PORTA CAMOLLIA
PORTA OVILE
STRADA DI PESCAIA
FORTEZZA & P
B
PIAZZA GRAMSCI (MAIN BUS STOP)
VIALE PIETRO TOSELLI
STRADA DI VALDIPUGNA
VIA PIEVE BOZZONE
STADIO & P
STRADA DI
IL CAMPO
See detail maps
PORTA PISPINI
PORTA SAN MARCO
CITY WALLS
P
PORTA ROMANA
VIA ARETINA
STRADA CASONE
PORTA TUFI
VIA PICCOLOMINI
Siena Ovest Exit
STRADA MASSETANA ROMANA
Siena Sud Exit
To San Galgano
S-73
SP-46
MADONNA BELLA FARM
Siena Exit
S-223
SR-2
VIA CASSIA
S-223
To A-1 Autostrada, Assisi, Rome & S-438
S-73
SR-2
SP-46
S-223
To Grosseto
To Ville di Corsano

N

1/2 Kilometer
1/2 Mile

museums, Siena has an easy-to-enjoy soul: Courtyards sport flower-decked wells, alleys dead-end at rooftop views, and today, even with all the tourists, a strong local spirit pervades.

Pedestrians rule in the old center of town, as the only drivers allowed are residents and cabbies. Nurse a drink on the main square. Wander narrow streets, tether an imaginary horse to the old metal rings, be stirred by colorful flags.

Orientation

Siena lounges atop a hill, stretching its three legs out from Il Campo. This pedestrianized main square is the historic meeting point of Siena's neighborhoods.

Just about everything you'll want to see is within a 10-minute walk of the square. Navigate by three major landmarks (Il Campo, Duomo, and Basilica of San Domenico), following the excellent system of street-corner signs. Sienese streets go in anything but a straight line, so it's easy to get lost—but equally easy to get found.

Siena itself is one big sight. Its individual attractions come in two clusters: Il Campo (Civic Museum and City Tower) and the cathedral (Baptistery and Duomo Museum, with its surprise viewpoint), plus the Pinacoteca for art lovers. Check off these sights, and then you're free to wander.

Tourist Information

The TI, just across from the cathedral, is next to worthless (daily 10:00-18:00; Piazza del Duomo 2, tel. 0577-280-551, www.terresiena.it).

Helpful Hints

Cooking Classes: At **Fonte Giusta Cooking School,** you'll prepare a meal (pasta, pizza, meats, dessert) under the instruction of a local chef—and then eat it. Lessons last two hours and cost €50-85, depending upon what you cook (Via Camollia 78, call info@trattoriafonte giusta.com for schedule and details, www.fontegiusta.it).

Laundry: Try **Lavanderia San Pietro** (daily 8:00-22:00, not far from the Duomo at Via San Pietro 70, and **Lavanderia Waterland** (daily 7:00-22:00, north of Il Campo near Porta San Francesco at Via dei Rossi 94).

Tours

LOCAL GUIDES

GSO Guides Co-op offers good tours covering Siena and all of Tuscany and Umbria (€158/half-day, €315/full day, RS%—10 percent discount, www.guide sienaeoltre.com). Among them, **Stefania Fabrizi** stands out (mobile 338-640-7796, stefaniafabriziguide@gmail.com). Other good guides include **Federica Olla** (€55/hour, minimum 2 hours, mobile 338-133-9525, www.ollaeventi.com) and **Anna Piperato** (€60/hour, minimum 2 hours, mobile 333-6829-336, www.sienaitaly-tours.com).

WALKING TOURS

The TI offers **walking tours** of the old town, including the Duomo (€20, pay guide directly, daily April-Oct at 11:00, 2 hours, depart from TI, Piazza del Duomo 2, tel. 0577-280-551).

Siena Info Point Walking Tour runs basic one-hour town walks, departing from their tiny office on Il Campo and ending at the Duomo (€15; daily at 11:15, 13:00, and 18:00; just show up, office open daily 9:30-19:30, mobile 331-742-2646, www.sienainfopoint.com, left of City Hall at Piazza del Campo 72).

Roberto Bechi and his guides offer private three-hour Siena walking tours (€180 for up to 8 people, admissions extra) or joinable group tours (€45/person, admissions extra, minimum 4 people; book online or call 320-147-6590, www.toursbyroberto.com). Roberto and his guides also lead off-the-beaten-path, full-day **minibus tours** of the countryside surrounding Siena (€100/person, see website for tour options, RS%—10 percent discount, entry fees extra).

◐ Siena City Walk

This short self-guided walk laces together Siena's most important sights. If you do the walk without entering the sights, it works great at night when the city is peaceful.

🎧 Download my free Siena City Walk audio tour.

• *Start in the center of the main square, Il Campo, standing just below the fountain.*

Il Campo

This square is the heart of Siena. First laid out in the 12th century, today Il Campo is the only town square I've seen where people stretch out as if at the beach. At the flat end of its clamshell shape is City Hall, where you can tour the Civic Museum and climb the City Tower. From there the square fans out as if to create an amphitheater. All eyes are on Il Campo twice each summer, when it

Siena's main square, Il Campo

hosts the famous Palio horse races (see page 241).

Originally, this area was just a field (*campo*) outside the city walls (which encircled the cathedral). In the 1200s, with the advent of the Sienese republic, the city expanded. Il Campo became its marketplace and the historic junction of Siena's various competing *contrade* (neighborhood districts). The square and its buildings are the color of the soil upon which they stand—a color known to artists and Crayola users as "burnt sienna."

City Hall (Palazzo Pubblico), with its looming tower, dominates the square. In medieval Siena, this was the center of the city, and the whole focus of Il Campo still flows down to it.

The **City Tower** (Torre del Mangia) was built around 1340. At 330 feet, it's one of Italy's tallest secular towers. Medieval Siena was a proud republic, and this tower stands like an exclamation point—an architectural declaration of independence from papacy and empire. The tower's Italian nickname, Torre del Mangia, comes from a hedonistic bell ringer who consumed his earnings like a glutton consumes food.

The open **chapel** at the base of the

tower was built as thanks to God for ending the Black Death of 1348 (after it killed more than a third of the population). These days, the chapel is where Palio contestants are blessed (and where EMTs stand by during the race).

• *Now turn around and take a closer look at the fountain in the top center of the square.*

Fountain of Joy (Fonte Gaia)

This fountain—a copy of an early 15th-century work by Jacopo della Quercia—marks the square's high point. The joy is all about how the Sienese republic blessed its people with water. Find Lady Justice with her scales and sword (right of center), overseeing the free distribution of water to all. The relief panel on the left shows God creating Adam by helping him to his feet. It's said that this reclining Adam (carved a century before Michelangelo's day) influenced Michelangelo when he painted his Sistine Chapel ceiling. The fountain's original statuary is exhibited at Santa Maria della Scala (see page 240).

• *Leave Il Campo uphill on the widest ramp (with your back to the tower, it's at 10 o'clock). After a few steps you reach Via di Città. Turn left and walk 100 yards uphill*

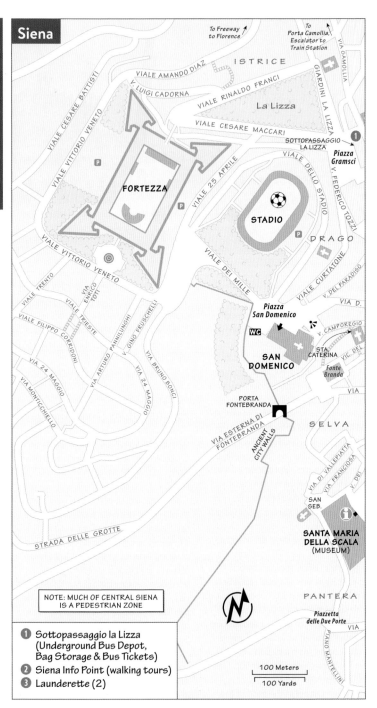

Siena

To Freeway
to Florence

To
Porta Camollia,
Escalator to
Train Station

ISTRICE

VIALE AMANDO DIAZ

V. LUIGI CADORNA

VIALE RINALDO FRANCI

La Lizza

GIARDINI LA LIZZA

VIA GAMOLLIA

VIALE CESARE MACCARI

SOTTOPASSAGGIO
LA LIZZA

VIALE CESARE BATTISTI

VIALE VITTORIO VENETO

Piazza
Gramsci

VIALE DELLO STADIO

V. FEDERICO TOZZI

P

FORTEZZA

VIALE 25 APRILE

STADIO

P

DRAGO

VIALE VITTORIO VENETO

VIALE DEI MILLE

VIALE CURTATONE

V. DEL PARADISO

VIA D.

VIALE TRENTO

VIA ENRICO TOTI

Piazza
San Domenico

V. CAMPOREGIO

VIALE TRIESTE

WC

VIALE FILIPPO CORRIDONI

VIA ARTURO PANNILUNGHI

V. GINO FRUSCHELLI

STA
CATERINA

VIC. DEL

VIA

VIA 24 MAGGIO

VIA BRUNO BONCI

SAN
DOMENICO

Fonte
Branda

VIA MONTICCHIELLO

VIA 24 MAGGIO

PORTA
FONTEBRANDA

SELVA

VIA ESTERNA DI
FONTEBRANDA

ANCIENT
CITY WALLS

VIA DI VALLEPIATTA

VIA FRANCIOSA

V. DEL

STRADA DELLE GROTTE

SAN
SEB.

SANTA MARIA
DELLA SCALA
(MUSEUM)

NOTE: MUCH OF CENTRAL SIENA
IS A PEDESTRIAN ZONE

PANTERA

Piazzetta
delle Due Porte

VIA

PIANO MANTELLINI

❶ Sottopassaggio la Lizza
(Underground Bus Depot,
Bag Storage & Bus Tickets)

❷ Siena Info Point (walking tours)

❸ Launderette (2)

100 Meters

100 Yards

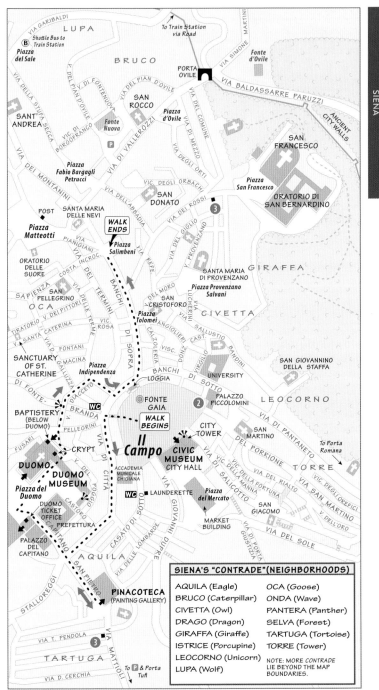

The Fountain of Joy on the Campo was the principal source of water in medieval Siena.

toward the imposing white palace with brick crenellations on top.

Halfway to the palace, at the first corner, notice small plaques on the first level of the building facades—these mark the boundary of a neighborhood, or **contrada.** You are stepping from the *contrada* of the Forest (Selva) into the *contrada* of the Eagle (Aquila). Notice also the once mighty and foreboding medieval **tower house.** Towers once soared all around town, but they're now truncated and no longer add to the skyline—look for their bases as you walk the city.

• *On the left, you reach the big curving facade of the...*

Chigi-Saracini Palace (Palazzo Chigi-Saracini)

This old fortified noble palace is today home to a prestigious music academy, the Accademia Musicale Chigiana. If open, step into the courtyard with its photogenic well (powerful medieval families enjoyed direct connections to the city aqueduct). The walls of the loggia are decorated with the busts of Chigi-Saracini patriarchs, and the vaults are painted in the Grotesque style popular

during the Renaissance. You can take a one-hour tour of the palace's library, art, and musical instruments (€7, Mon-Fri at 11:30 plus Thu-Fri at 16:00, closed Sun, call to request English tour, Via di Città 89, tel. 0577-22091, www.chigiana.it).

• *Walk uphill to the next major intersection...*

Quattro Cantoni

The intersection known as Quattro Cantoni (Four Corners) offers a delightful perch from which to study the city. The modern column (from 1996) with a Carrara marble she-wolf marks one of the three hills upon which the city is built. You are still in the Eagle district (see the fountain and the corner plaque)—but beware. Just one block up the street, a ready-to-pounce panther—from the rival neighboring district—awaits.

Only the very rich could afford stone residences. The fancy facades here hide their economical brick construction behind a stucco veneer. The stone tower on this corner had only one door—30 feet above street level and reached by ladder, which could be pulled up as necessary.

Take a little side trip, venturing up Via di San Pietro. Interesting stops include the window with Palio video clips playing (at #1), Simon and Paula's art shop with delightful Palio and *contrada* knickknacks (#5), a weaver's shop (#7), a *gelateria* (#10), an art gallery (#11), and four enticing little osterias. At the end of the block you'll reach the best art museum in town, the **Pinacoteca.**

• *Back at the Four Corners, head up Via del Capitano, passing another massive Chigi family palace (at #1). Up next, at the end of the street, is the...*

Piazza del Duomo and the Duomo

The pair of she-wolves atop columns flanking the cathedral's facade says it all: The church was built and paid for not by the pope but by the people and the republic of Siena.

This 13th-century Gothic cathedral, with its striped bell tower—Siena's ultimate tribute to the Virgin Mary—is heaped with statues, plastered with frescoes, and paved with art.

The current structure dates back to 1215, with the major decoration done during Siena's heyday (1250-1350). The lower story, by Giovanni Pisano (who worked from 1284 to 1297), features remnants of the fading Romanesque style (round arches over the doors), topped with the pointed arches of the new Gothic style that was seeping in from France. The upper half, in full-blown frilly Gothic, was designed and built a century later.

The six-story bell tower (c. 1315) looks even taller, thanks to an optical illusion: The white marble stripes get narrower toward the top, making the upper part seem farther away.

The interior is a Renaissance riot of striped columns, remarkably intricate inlaid-marble floors, a Michelangelo statue, evocative Bernini sculptures, and the amazing Piccolomini Library. (To enter, you'll need a ticket from the office in the corner near where you entered the piazza; for a self-guided tour of the interior, see page 236.)

Facing the cathedral is Santa Maria della Scala, a huge building that housed pilgrims and, until the 1990s, was used as a hospital. Its labyrinthine 12th-century cellars—carved from sandstone and finished with brick—go down several floors and, during medieval times, stored supplies for the hospital upstairs (for more on this sight, see page 240).

• *Walk along the right side of the church toward its rear end. This is part of what was once intended to be an extension of the Duomo.*

The Unfinished Church

Grand as Siena's cathedral is, it's actually the rump of a failed vision. After rival republic Florence began its grand cathedral (1296), proud Siena planned to build an even bigger one, the biggest in all Christendom.

To the right, find the unfinished wall with see-through windows (circa 1330). From here you can envision the audacity of this vision.

Picture it: Today's cathedral would have been just a transept. Worshippers would have entered the church through the unfinished wall. Some of the nave's green-and-white-striped columns were built, but the space between them is now partially filled in with brick. White stones in the pavement mark where a row of pillars would have been.

But this grand vision underestimated the complexity of constructing such a building without enough land. That, coupled with the devastating effects of the 1348 plague, killed the city's ability and will to finish the project. The Sienese canceled their plans and humbly faded into the background of Tuscan history.

• *Take note of the **Duomo Museum,** housing the church's art (see page 238). To continue our walk, exit the piazza through the doorway in the wall abutting the back end of the church. After a few steps, pause at the top of the marble stairs leading down.*

Supporting an Oversized Church

From here you can see how the church sticks out, high above the lower street level. Because there wasn't enough flat ground, builders propped up the over-hanging edge with the church's subterra-nean features—the Crypt and Baptistery. (Both are worth entering; see page 240.)

• *Descend the stairs, and below the Bap-tistery, jog right, then left, through a tunnel down Via di Diacceto. Just ahead, pause on the bridge (originally a drawbridge) to enjoy a beautiful view (to the left) of the towering brick Dominican church in the distance. Then continue straight up the lane until you reach the next big square.*

Piazza Indipendenza

This square celebrates the creation of a unified Italy (1860) with a 19th-century loggia sporting busts of the first two Ital-ian kings. Stacking history on history, the neo-Renaissance loggia is backed by a Gothic palace and an older medieval tower.

• *Head right downhill one block (on Via delle Terme), back to the grand Via di Città, and take a few steps to the left to see another, fancier loggia.*

Loggia della Mercanzia

This Gothic-Renaissance loggia was built about 1420 as a kind of headquarters for the union of merchants. Siena's nobility purchased the loggia, and eventually it became the clubhouse of the local elites. To this day, it's a private, ritzy, and notori-ously out-of-step-with-the-times men's club. The "Gli Uniti" above the door is a "let's stick together" declaration.

• *Next to the loggia, steep steps lead down to Il Campo, but we'll go left and uphill on Via Banchi di Sopra. Pause at the intersection of...*

Banchi di Sopra and Banchi di Sotto

These main drags are named "upper row of banks" and "lower row of banks." They were once lined with market tables (banchi), and vendors paid rent to the city for a table's position along the street. If the owner of a *banco* neglected to pay up, thugs came along and literally broke (*rotto*) his table. It is from this practice—*banco rotto,* broken table—that we get the English word "bankrupt."

In medieval times, these streets were part of the Via Francigena, the main thor-oughfare (busy with pilgrims, merchants, and crusaders) linking Rome with north-ern Europe. Today, strollers—out each evening for their *passeggiata*—fill Via Ban-chi di Sopra. Join the crowd, strolling past Siena's finest shops.

A block or so farther up the street, Piazza Tolomei faces the imposing Tolo-mei family palace (now an imposing bank). This is a center for the Owl *con-trada.* The column in the square, topped by the she-wolf, marks another of Siena's three hills.

• *Continue on Banchi di Sopra to Piazza Salimbeni; this gets my vote for Siena's finest stretch of palaces.*

Piazza Salimbeni

The next square, Piazza Salimbeni, is dominated by Monte dei Paschi, the head office of a bank founded in 1472. It's amaz-ing to think this bank has been in business on this square for more than 500 years. Originally Monte dei Paschi was a kind of community bank for common people. The statue in the center of the square honors Sallustio Antonio Bandini, a reformer who helped develop a system that let people secure firm title to their land.

Directly across from Piazza Salimbeni, the steep little lane called Costa dell'In-crociata leads straight (down and then up) to the Basilica of San Domenico (it's worth the hike; see page 241). Also nearby (behind the cute green newsstand) is the most elegant grocery store in town, Con-sorzio Agrario di Siena.

• *With this walk under your belt, you've got the lay of the land.*

Sights

Il Campo and Nearby

▲▲CITY HALL (PALAZZO PUBBLICO) AND CIVIC MUSEUM (MUSEO CIVICO)

Siena's fine Gothic City Hall is still the seat of city government. With its proud tower, this building symbolizes a republic independent from the pope and the Holy Roman Emperor. It also represents a rising secular society, one that appeared first in Tuscany in late medieval times, then spread throughout Europe as humanism took hold during the Renaissance. City Hall has a fine and manageable museum on its top floor, where you'll see the large assembly hall where democracy was forged, adorned with some of Siena's most historic frescoes.

Cost and Hours: Museum-€10, €14 combo-ticket with Santa Maria della Scala, €15 combo-ticket with City Tower, €20 combo-ticket includes City Tower and Santa Maria della Scala, ticket office is straight ahead as you enter City Hall courtyard; open daily 10:00-19:00, Nov-mid-March until 18:00, last entry 45 minutes before closing; videoguide-€5

in bookshop, tel. 0577-292-232, www.comune.siena.it.

Visiting the Museum: Start in the Sala del Risorgimento, with dramatic scenes of the 19th-century unification of Italy. Make your way to the chapel, where the city's governors and bureaucrats prayed, then enter the Sala del Mappamondo.

On one end of the room is the beautiful **Maestà** (*Enthroned Virgin,* 1315), by Siena's great Simone Martini (c. 1280-1344). Mary is surrounded by saints and angels, clearly echoing the *Maestà* of Simone's teacher, Duccio. This is a groundbreaking work. It's Siena's first fresco showing a Madonna not in a faraway, gold-leaf heaven, but under the blue sky of a real space that we inhabit. The saints are not a generic conga-line of Byzantine icons, but a milling crowd of 30 individuals with expressive faces.

On the opposite end of the room is the famous **Equestrian Portrait of Guidoriccio da Fogliano** (1330; traditionally attributed to Simone Martini), which depicts a mercenary commander surveys the scene of a six-month-long siege in which the Sienese

Siena's Civic Museum

Ambrogio Lorenzetti, Effects of Good and Bad Government

captured the fortified city of Montemassi (left). What looks like a castle (in the middle) is a siege fort the Sienese built just for that battle, flying their black-and-white flag and with the catapult that helped them win.

Next is the Sala della Pace, where the Council of Nine, who ruled Siena from 1287 to 1355, met. To remind them of their responsibility to rule wisely, they were surrounded by a fascinating fresco series showing the *Effects of Good and Bad Government,* by Ambrogio Lorenzetti (1337–1340).

Notice the better-preserved fresco (on the long wall to the right) depicting the beneficial effects of good government. Compare the whistle-while-you-work happiness against the crime, devastation, and societal mayhem of a community ruled by politicians with more typical values.

You can cap your visit by climbing the stairs to a grand view of the city and its surroundings.

▲CITY TOWER (TORRE DEL MANGIA)

The tower's nearly 400 steps get pretty skinny at the top, but the reward is one of Italy's best views. For more on the tower, see the Siena City Walk, earlier.

Cost and Hours: €10, also covered by combo-tickets with Civic Museum and Santa Maria della Scala, daily 10:00-19:00, mid-Oct-Feb until 16:00, last entry 45

minutes before closing, closed in rain, free and mandatory bag check.

Crowd Alert: Admission is limited to 50 people at a time. Wait at the bottom of the stairs for the green *Avanti* light. Try to avoid midday crowds (up to an hour wait at peak times).

▲PINACOTECA

If you're into medieval art, you'll likely find this quiet, uncrowded, colorful museum delightful. The museum (officially the Pinacoteca Nazionale di Siena) walks you through Siena's art chronologically, from the 12th through the 16th century, when a revolution in realism was percolating in Tuscany.

Cost and Hours: €4, Tue-Sat 8:15-19:15, Sun-Mon 9:00-13:00. From Il Campo, walk out Via di Città and go left on Via San Pietro to #29; tel. 0577-281-161, www. pinacotecanazionale.siena.it.

Visiting the Museum: In general, the collection lets you follow the evolution of painting styles from Byzantine to Gothic, then to International Gothic, and finally to Renaissance.

The core of the collection is on the second floor, in Rooms 1-19. Works by **Duccio di Buoninsegna** (who created the *Maestà* in the Duomo Museum) feature groundbreaking innovations that are subtle: less gold-leaf background, fewer gold creases in robes, translucent garments,

City Tower on Il Campo

bodies, twisting poses, and dramatic gestures, Beccafumi's works epitomize the Mannerist style of the High Renaissance.

Duomo and Related Sights

Siena's monumental cathedral complex encompasses the Duomo, Duomo Museum (and its panoramic terrace), Baptistery, and Crypt. While it's possible to enter the Duomo itself with an individual ticket, admission to the related sights is possible only with a combo-ticket, the **Opa Si Pass** (valid for 72 hours, includes Duomo admission). The price varies with the time of year: March-mid-Aug–€13, mid-Aug-Oct–€15, Nov-Feb–€8 (admission to the Duomo itself is free in winter). The **Porta del Cielo** (Heaven's Gate) Pass covers everything in the Opa Si Pass but adds an escorted visit up into the cathedral dome and onto the cathedral's rooftop (€20, available March-Dec).

Buying Passes and Tickets: Individual Duomo tickets and the Opa Si Pass can be bought online (www.operaduomo.siena.it) or from the on-site ticket office (facing the cathedral entry, the ticket office, with a fine bookstore, is behind you to the right). The Porta del Cielo pass is sold at the ticket office (not available online), but because of space limitations for the cathedral roof visit, it's smart to reserve in advance by phone (tel. 0577-286-300) or email (opa siena@operalaboratori.com).

▲▲▲DUOMO (DUOMO DI SIENA)

Siena's 13th-century cathedral and striped bell tower are one of the most illustrious examples of Romanesque-Gothic style in Italy. The cathedral's interior showcases the work of the greatest sculptors of successive eras—Pisano, Donatello, Michelangelo, and Bernini—and the Piccolomini Library features a series of 15th-century frescoes chronicling the adventures of Siena's philanderer-turned-pope, Aeneas Piccolomini.

Cost: €6; €9 mid-Aug-Oct and on Sundays when marble floors are on display,

inlaid-marble thrones, and a more human Mary and Jesus.

Works by Duccio's one-time assistant, **Simone Martini,** including his *St. Augustine of Siena,* show the saint's life in realistic Sienese streets, buildings, and landscapes. In each panel, the saint pops out at the oddest (difficult to draw) angles to save the day. (Simone Martini also did the *Maestà* and possibly the Guidoriccio frescoes in the Civic Museum.)

Also look for religious works by the hometown **Lorenzetti brothers** (Ambrogio is best known for the secular masterpiece, the *Effects of Good and Bad Government,* in the Civic Museum). Two famous small wooden panels, *Città sul Mare (City by the Sea)* and *Castello in Riva al Lago (Castle on the Lakeshore),* feature a strange, medieval-landscape Cubism. Notice the weird, melancholic light that captures the sense of the Dark Ages.

Several colorful rooms on the first floor are dedicated to **Domenico Beccafumi** (1486-1551), who designed many of the Duomo's inlaid pavement panels (including *Slaughter of the Innocents*). With strong includes cathedral and Piccolomini Library, covered by Duomo combo-ticket; admission to the Duomo is free Nov-Feb.

Hours: Mon-Sat 10:00-19:00, Sun 13:30-18:00, Nov-Feb closes daily at 17:30. Tel. 0577-286-300, www.operaduomo. siena.it.

Avoiding Lines: If there's a long line to get into the cathedral (or even to buy a ticket), use ticket office desk 1 or 2 to pay €1 extra for a reserved ticket that lets you use the short "fast entry" line at the church. Another good alternative is to purchase tickets online in advance.

Dress Code: Modest dress is required, but stylish paper ponchos are provided for the inappropriately clothed.

Cathedral Roof Visit: To make a 30-minute escorted (but not guided) visit to the dome's cupola and roof, buy the Porto del Cielo (Heaven's Gate) combo-ticket (reservation recommended; see "Buying Passes and Tickets," earlier; escorted visits go each half-hour, March-Dec Mon-Sat 10:30-19:00, Sun 13:30-17:30—but from 9:30 on some Sun).

● **Self-Guided Tour:** Grab a spot on a stone bench opposite the entry to take in this architectural festival of green, white, pink, and gold. The Duomo sits atop Siena's highest point, with one of the most extravagant facades in all of Europe. Like a medieval altarpiece, the facade is divided into sections, each frame filled with patriarchs and prophets, studded with roaring gargoyles, and topped with prickly pinnacles.

• *Step inside, putting yourself in the mindset of a pilgrim as you take in this trove of religious art.*

Nave: The heads of 171 popes—who reigned from the time of St. Peter to the 12th century—peer down from above, looking over the fine inlaid art on the floor. With a forest of striped columns, a coffered dome, a large stained-glass window at the far end (it's a copy—the original is viewable up close in the Duomo Museum), and an art gallery's worth of early Renaissance art, this is one busy interior. If you look closely at the popes, you'll see the same four faces repeated over and over.

Siena's Duomo is a classic of the Romanesque-Gothic style.

For almost two centuries (1373-1547), 40 artists paved the marble floor with scenes from the Old Testament, allegories, and intricate patterns. The series starts near the entrance with historical allegories; the larger, more elaborate scenes surrounding the altar are mostly stories from the Old Testament. Many of the floor panels are roped off and covered to prevent further wear and tear. But from mid-August through October, the cathedral uncovers them and holds Mass in another church. The second pavement panel from the entrance depicts Siena as a she-wolf. The proud city of Siena is the center of the Italian universe, orbited by such lesser lights as Roma, Florentia (Florence), and Pisa.

On the right wall hangs a dim **painting of St. Catherine** (fourth from entrance). Siena's homegrown saint had a vision in which she mystically married Christ.

• *On the opposite wall is a marble altarpiece decorated with statues.*

Piccolomini Altar: This was commissioned by the Sienese-born Pope Pius III (born Francesco Piccolomini) but was never used. The altar is most interesting for its statues: one by Michelangelo and three by his students. Michelangelo was originally contracted to do 15 statues, but another sculptor had started the marble blocks, and Michelangelo's heart was never in the project. He personally finished the figure of St. Paul (lower right, clearly more interesting than the bland, bored saints above him).

• *Now grab a seat under the dome. The dome sits on a 12-sided base, but its "coffered" ceiling is a painted illusion.*

Duccio's Stained-Glass Rose Window: At the far end of the church, high up above the altar, is the rose window. Dedicated to the Virgin Mary, it's a kaleidoscope of colors and intricate designs. This is a copy of the original window (c. 1287-1290, now housed in the Duomo Museum).

• *Closer to you is a stone podium sitting atop columns. This is...*

Pisano's Pulpit: The octagonal Carrara marble pulpit (1268) rests on the backs of lions, symbols of Christianity triumphant. Like the lions, the Church eats its catch (devouring paganism) and nurses its cubs. The seven relief panels tell the life of Christ in rich detail. The pulpit is the work of Nicola Pisano (c. 1220-1278), the "Giotto of sculpture," whose revival of classical forms (columns, sarcophagus-like relief panels) signaled the coming Renaissance. His son Giovanni (c. 1240-1319) carved many of the panels, mixing his dad's classicism and realism with the decorative detail and curvy lines of French Gothic.

• *A few steps to the left of the pulpit (in the left transept), find a panel in the floor, the...*

Slaughter of the Innocents Pavement Panel: Herod (left), sitting enthroned amid Renaissance arches, orders the massacre of all babies to prevent the coming of the promised Messiah. It's a chaotic scene of angry soldiers, grieving mothers, and dead babies, reminding locals that a republic ruled by a tyrant will always experience misery.

She-wolf pavement panel in the Duomo.

• *Nearby in the left transept is a small chapel with a well-known statue.*

Donatello's St. John the Baptist: The rugged saint in his famous rags stands in a quiet chapel. Donatello, the aging Florentine sculptor whose style was now considered passé in Florence, came here to build bronze doors for the church (similar to Ghiberti's in Florence). Donatello didn't complete the door project, but he did finish this bronze statue (1457).

• *Cross the church. Directly opposite find the Chigi Chapel (with its ironwork entrance), also known as the...*

Chapel of the *Madonna del Voto*: To understand why Bernini is considered the greatest Baroque sculptor, step into this sumptuous chapel (designed in the early 1660s for Fabio Chigi, a.k.a. Pope Alexander VII). Move up to the altar and look back at the **two Bernini statues** that frame the doorway: Mary Magdalene in a state of spiritual ecstasy and St. Jerome playing the crucifix like a violinist lost in heavenly music.

The painting over the altar is the ***Madonna del Voto,*** a Madonna and Child adorned with a real crown of gold and

Pisano's marble pulpit

jewels (painted by a Sienese master in the mid-13th century). This is the Mary to whom the Palio is dedicated, dear to the hearts of the Sienese.

• *Cross back to the other side of the church. Next to the Piccolomini Altar, look for the door to the...*

Piccolomini Library: Brilliantly frescoed, the library captures the exuberant, optimistic spirit of the 1400s, when humanism and the Renaissance were born. The never-restored frescoes look nearly as vivid now as the day they were finished 550 years ago. The painter Pinturicchio (c. 1454-1513) was hired to celebrate the life of one of Siena's hometown boys—a man many call "the first humanist," Aeneas Piccolomini (1405-1464), who became Pope Pius II. Each of the 10 scenes is framed with an arch, as if Pinturicchio were opening a window onto the spacious 3-D world we inhabit.

The library also contains intricately decorated, illuminated music scores and a statue (a Roman copy of a Greek original) of the Three Graces, who almost seem to dance to the beat. The oddly huge sheepskin sheets of music are from the days before individual hymnals—they had to be big so that many singers could read the music from a distance. Appreciate the fine painted decorations on the music—the gold-leaf highlights, the blue tones from expensive ultramarine (made from precious lapis lazuli), and the miniature figures. All of this exquisite detail was lovingly crafted by Benedictine monks for the glory of God.

▲▲DUOMO MUSEUM AND VIEWPOINT (MUSEO DELL'OPERA E PANORAMA)

Siena's most enjoyable museum, housing the cathedral's art, is located in the skeleton of the Duomo's grand but unfinished extension (to the right as you face the cathedral's main facade). Stand eye-to-eye with the saints and angels who once languished, unknown, in the church's upper reaches (where copies are found today).

Cost and Hours: Covered by Duomo combo-ticket, daily 10:00-19:00, Nov-Feb 10:30-17:30, videoguide-€4 (€6/2 people) but you'll do fine with just the commentary in this listing, tel. 0577-286-300, www.operaduomo.siena.it.

◐ **Self-Guided Tour:** Start on the ground floor, which houses the church's original statues, mainly from the facade and exterior. After descending a few steps, turn your back on the hall of statues and wrought-iron gate. You're now face-to-face with **Donatello's Madonna and Child** (c. 1458). In this round, carved relief, a slender and tender Mary gazes down at her chubby-cheeked baby. Her sad eyes say that she knows the eventual fate of her son.

At the opposite end of the room is **Duccio's Stained-Glass Rose Window** (c. 1287-1290). This splendid original window was installed for centuries above and behind the Duomo's altar. Now the church has a copy, and art lovers can enjoy a close-up look at this masterpiece. The rose window—20 feet across—is dedicated (like the church and the city itself) to the Virgin Mary.

The work is by Siena's most famous artist, Duccio di Buoninsegna (c. 1255-1319). Duccio combined elements from rigid Byzantine icons (Mary's almond-shaped bubble, called a *mandorla*, and the full-frontal saints that flank her) with a budding sense of 3-D realism (the throne turned at a three-quarter angle to simulate depth, with angels behind).

Upstairs awaits a private audience with **Duccio's Maestà** (*Enthroned Virgin*, 1311). The panels in this room were once part of the Duomo's main altarpiece. Grab a seat and study one of the great pieces of medieval art. Although the former altarpiece was disassembled (and the frame was lost), most of the pieces are displayed here, with the front side (*Maestà*, with Mary and saints) at one end of the room and the back side (26 Passion panels) at the other.

Duccio, Christ's Entry into Jerusalem, *from the* Maestà

The painting was revolutionary for the time in its sheer size and opulence, and in Duccio's budding realism, which broke standard conventions. Duccio, at the height of his powers, used every innovative arrow in his quiver. He replaced the standard gold-leaf background (symbolizing heaven) with a gold, intricately patterned curtain draped over the throne. Mary's blue robe opens to reveal her body, and the curve of her knee suggests real anatomy beneath the robe. Baby Jesus wears a delicately transparent garment. Their faces are modeled with light—a patchwork of bright flesh and shadowy valleys, as if lit from the left (a technique Duccio likely learned from his contemporary, Giotto, during a visit to Florence).

• *Our museum tour is done, but the finale of your visit—to the top of the unfinished Duomo facade—is yet to come. After cork-*

screwing up 140 narrow steps, you'll reach the...

Panorama del Facciatone: Standing on the wall from this high point in the city, you're rewarded with a stunning view of Siena...and an interesting perspective. Look toward the Duomo and remember this: To outdo Florence, Siena had planned to enlarge this cathedral by turning it into a transept and constructing an enormous nave. You're standing on top of what would have been the new entrance facade. Columns would have stood where you see the rows of white stones in the pavement below. Had the church been completed, you'd be looking straight down the nave toward the altar.

▲BAPTISTERY OF SAN GIOVANNI (BATTISTERO DI SAN GIOVANNI)

This richly adorned and quietly tucked-away cave of art is worth a look for its cool tranquility and exquisite art, including an ornately painted vaulted ceiling. The highlight is the baptismal font created in the 1420s by a host of early Renaissance all-stars from marble, bronze, and enamel. The overall design was by Jacopo ("Fountain of Joy") della Quercia. On the base, the first bronze panel you encounter was done by Lorenzo ("Gates of Paradise") Ghiberti. To the right, the tiny bronze statues of Lady Faith and (farther right) the Angel of Hope, were done by the great Donatello. Also on the right side, Donatello made the bronze panel depicting John the Baptist's severed head being brought in on a platter, set in a 3-D banquet hall of receding arches. With this font, we're witnessing the start of the Renaissance.

Cost and Hours: Covered by Duomo combo-ticket, daily 10:30-19:00, Nov-Feb until 17:30, located on the back end of the Duomo.

CRYPT (CRIPTA)

The site of a small 12th-century Romanesque church, the Duomo's crypt was filled in with dirt a century after its cre-ation to provide a foundation for the huge church that sits atop it today. Recently excavated, the several rediscovered rooms show off what are likely the oldest frescoes in town.

Cost and Hours: Covered by Duomo combo-ticket, daily 10:30-19:00, Nov-Feb until 17:30, located on the back end of the Duomo.

▲SANTA MARIA DELLA SCALA

This museum, opposite the Duomo, operated for centuries as a hospital, foundling home (orphanage), and pilgrim lodging. Many of those activities are visible in the 15th-century frescoes of its main hall, the Pellegrinaio. Today, the hospital and its cellars are filled with fascinating exhibits.

Cost and Hours: €9, €14 combo-ticket with Civic Museum, €20 combo-ticket includes Civic Museum and City Tower, also covered by Acropoli Pass; daily 10:00-19:00, Thu until 22:00; closes earlier mid-Oct-mid-March; on Piazza del Duomo, tel. 0577-534-571, www.santamariadellascala.com.

Visiting the Museum: It's easy to get lost in this gigantic complex, so stay focused on the main attractions—the fancily frescoed Pellegrinaio Hall (ground floor) and the Fountain of Joy statues (one floor down). Then explore the lower floors.

From the entrance, turn right to enter what was, until the 1970s, Siena's main hospital. Enter the first room on your right, the **Sacristy,** which displays some powerful relics preserved in golden and silver reliquaries. You may see a drop of Jesus' blood in a vial *(sangue di Christo)*, a nail from Jesus' cross *(sacro chiodo)*, a piece of the Virgin's robe *(beata Vergine)*, and lots of saints' bones. They're encased in reliquaries that befit the preciousness of these sacred bits and saintly pieces. Some of the oldest are Byzantine reliquaries made of gold, silver, and precious stones.

Continue down the hallway (browsing exhibits in side rooms) until you reach the sumptuously frescoed **Pellegrinaio Hall.** This was a reception hall for visiting pilgrims before being converted into a hospital room, lined with beds for the sick. The frescoes (mostly by Domenico di Bartolo, c. 1440) show medieval Siena's innovative healthcare and social welfare system in action.

Now head downstairs, following signs to *Fonte Gaia*. These are the original statues from the Fountain of Joy (Fonte Gaia), Siena's landmark fountain on Il Campo. Jacopo della Quercia's early 15th-century masterpiece began crumbling, so in the 19th century, it was dismantled and plaster casts were made. (These casts formed the replica that graces Il Campo today.) Here you'll see the badly eroded original statues and relief panels, paired alongside their casts (labeled "*calco*").

In the second basement, under the groin vaults of the **Archaeological Museum** (Museo Archeologico), you're alone with piles of ancient stuff, from Bronze Age axes to Roman pottery. The highlight is a group of Etruscan artifacts excavated from tombs dating from the seventh to second century before Christ—the Etruscan heyday. You'll see their coins, figurines, and terra-cotta funeral urns for ashes (often designed with a standard body but a personalized head). The sarcophagi show the deceased reclining atop the lid, a reminder of their lofty social status.

San Domenico Area
BASILICA OF SAN DOMENICO (BASILICA DI SAN DOMENICO)
This huge brick church is worth a quick look. Spacious and plain (except for the colorful flags of the city's 17 contrade), the Gothic interior fits the austere philosophy of the Dominicans and invites meditation on the thoughts and deeds of St. Catherine (1347-1380). Halfway up the nave on the right, find a copper bust of St. Catherine (for four centuries it contained her skull), a small case housing her thumb, and her little flagellation whip. In the chapel, surrounded by candles, you'll see Catherine's head (a clay mask around her skull with her actual teeth showing through) atop the altar.

Cost and Hours: Free, daily 7:00-18:30, shorter hours off-season, www.basilica cateriniana.com.

SANCTUARY OF ST. CATHERINE (SANTUARIO DI SANTA CATERINA)
Step into the cool and peaceful site of Catherine's home. Siena remembers its favorite hometown gal, a simple, unschooled but mystically devout soul who helped convince the pope to return to Rome from France, where the papacy had moved in 1309. Pilgrims have visited this place since 1464, and architects and artists have greatly embellished what was probably once a humble home (her family worked as wool dyers). You'll see paintings throughout showing scenes from Catherine's life.

Cost and Hours: Free, daily 9:00-18:00 but chapel closes 12:30-15:00, a few downhill blocks toward the center from San Domenico—follow signs to *Santuario di Santa Caterina*—at Costa di Sant'Antonio 6, tel. 0577-288-175.

Experiences
The Palio
Siena's 17 historic neighborhoods, or *contrade*—each with a parish church, well or fountain, and square—still play an active role in the life of the city. Each is represented by a mascot (porcupine, unicorn, wolf, etc.) and unique colors worn proudly by residents.

Contrada rivalries are most visible twice a year—on July 2 and August 16—during the city's world-famous horse race, the **Palio di Siena.** Ten of the 17 neighborhoods compete (chosen by rotation and lot), hurling themselves with medieval abandon into several days of trial races and traditional revelry. Jockeys—usually from out of town—are considered hired guns, no better than paid mercenaries. Bets are placed on which *contrada* will

Palio pageantry

win...and lose. Despite the shady behind-the-scenes dealing, on the big day the horses are taken into their *contrada's* church to be blessed. ("Go and return victorious," says the priest.) It's considered a sign of luck if a horse leaves droppings in the church.

On the evening of the race, Il Campo is stuffed to the brim with locals and tourists. Dirt is brought in and packed down to create the track's surface, while mattresses pad the walls of surrounding buildings. The most treacherous spots are the sharp corners, where many a rider has bitten the dust.

Ten snorting horses and their nervous riders line up near the pharmacy (on the west side of the square) to await the starting signal. Then they race like crazy while spectators wave the scarves of their neighborhoods.

When the winner crosses the line, 1/17th of Siena—the prevailing neighborhood—goes berserk. Winners receive a *palio* (banner), typically painted by a local artist and always featuring the Virgin Mary (the race is dedicated to her). But the true

prizes are proving that your *contrada* is *numero uno*.

While the actual Palio packs the city, you can more easily see the horse-race trials—called *prove*—on any of the three days before the main event (usually at 9:00 and after 19:00, bleacher seats may be available). Good sources for more information include IlPalio.org and ComitatoAmiciDelPalio.it.

Sleeping
Bigger Hotels near Il Campo

$$$$ **Pensione Palazzo Ravizza** is elegant, friendly, and well-run, with 40 rooms and an aristocratic feel—fitting for what was once a noble's residence (RS%, family rooms, rooms in back overlook countryside, air-con, elevator, free parking makes this a good value for drivers, Via Piano dei Mantellini 34, tel. 0577-280-462, www.palazzoravizza.it, bureau@palazzoravizza.it).

$$$ **Hotel Duomo** is dated but well-located, with 20 spacious but overpriced rooms—many with Duomo views—and a picnic-friendly roof terrace (family rooms, air-con, elevator with

some stairs, expensive pay parking; Via di Stalloreggi 38, tel. 0577-289-088, www. hotelduomo.it, booking@hotelduomo.it, Alessandro).

Simple Places near Il Campo

$$ Piccolo Hotel Etruria, with 20 simple rooms, is well-located, restful, and a fine value (RS%—use code "RSITA," family rooms, breakfast extra, air-con May-Oct only, elevator, at Via delle Donzelle 3, tel. 0577-288-088, www.hoteletruria.com, info@hoteletruria.com, friendly Leopoldo and Lucrezia). They also rent apartments nearby.

$ Albergo Tre Donzelle, run by the same family as Piccolo Hotel Etruria, has 20 homey rooms that may be the best value in the center (RS%—use code "RSITA," cheaper rooms with shared bath, family rooms, breakfast extra, fans, no elevator; with your back to the tower, head away from Il Campo toward 2 o'clock to Via delle Donzelle 5; tel. 0577-270-390, www.tredonzelle.com, info@tredonzelle. com, Leopoldo and Lucrezia).

$ Hotel Cannon d'Oro, a few blocks up Banchi di Sopra, is a bland, labyrinthine slumbermill renting 30 institutional, overpriced rooms (RS%, family rooms, fans, elevator with some stairs, Via dei Montanini 28, tel. 0577-44321, www.can nondoro.com, info@cannondoro.com; Maurizio, Tommaso, and Rodrigo).

B&Bs in the Old Center

$$ Antica Residenza Cicogna is a seven-room guesthouse with a homey elegance and an ideal location. Warmly run by the young and charming Elisa and her friend Ilaria, this is remarkably genteel for the price (air-con, no elevator, Via delle Terme 76, tel. 0577-285-613, mobile 347-007-2888, www.anticaresidenzacicogna.it, info@anticaresidenzacicogna.it).

$$ Palazzo Masi B&B, run by friendly Alizzardo and Daniela, has six pleasant, spacious, antique-furnished rooms with shared common areas on the second and third floors of a restored 13th-century building (RS%—use code "RICK," cheaper rooms with shared bath, no elevator; breakfast provided on Il Campo; from City Hall, walk 50 yards down Casato di Sotto to #29; mobile 349-600-9155, www. palazzomasi.com, info@palazzomasi. it). The place is sometimes unstaffed, so confirm your arrival time in advance.

$$ B&B Alle Due Porte is a charming little establishment renting three big rooms with sweet furniture under medieval beams. The shared breakfast room is delightful (air-con, Via di Stalloreggi 51, mobile 368-352-3530, www.sienatur.it, soldatini@interfree.it).

$$ Siena Gallery B&B, run by kind-hearted Elisabetta and Fabio, is tucked onto the fourth floor of a relatively modern building, offering four contemporary yet simple rooms (air-con, elevator, Via Banchi di Sopra 31, enter at Galleria Odeon—look for green pharmacy sign, mobile 334-3997-8694, www.sienagallery. it, info@sienagallery.it).

$$ I Terzi di Siena, run by the same family as Siena Gallery B&B, houses nine rooms in an 11th-century building. It's absent an elevator but full of humble charm and noteworthy views (air-con, cheaper rooms with shared bath, apartments available; Via dei Termini 13, mobile 339-6699-143, www.terzidisiena.it, info@terzidisiena.it).

$$ B&B Siena in Centro is a clearinghouse managing 15 rooms and 5 apartments. Their handy office functions as a reception area for picking up keys (RS%, some with air-con and others with fans, family rooms, reception open 9:00-13:30 & 15:00-22:00, Via di Stalloreggi 16, tel. 0577-48111, mobile 331-281-0136 or 347-465-9753, www.bbsienaincentro.com, info@bbsienaincentro.com, Gioia or Michela).

$ Le Camerine di Silvia, a romantic hideaway perched near a sweeping, grassy olive grove, rents five simple rooms in a converted 16th-century building (cash

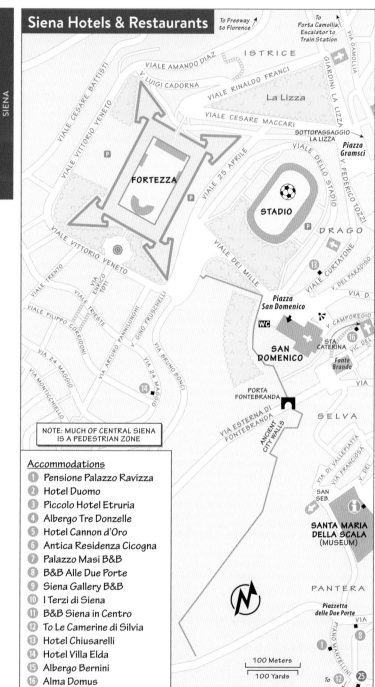

Siena Hotels & Restaurants

To Freeway to Florence

To Porta Camollia, Escalator to Train Station

ISTRICE

VIALE AMANDO DIAZ

V. LUIGI CADORNA

VIALE RINALDO FRANCI

La Lizza

VIALE CESARE BATTISTI

VIALE VITTORIO VENETO

VIALE CESARE MACCARI

GIARDINI LA LIZZA

VIA GAMOLLIA

SOTTOPASSAGGIO LA LIZZA

VIALE DELLO STADIO

Piazza Gramsci

FORTEZZA

VIALE 25 APRILE

VIA FEDERICO TOZZI

STADIO

DRAGO

VIALE VITTORIO VENETO

VIALE DEI MILLE

VIALE CURTATONE

V. DEL PARADISO

VIA D.

VIALE TRENTO

VIA ENRICO TOTI

VIALE TRIESTE

VIALE FILIPPO CORRIDONI

VIA GINO FRUSCHELLI

Piazza San Domenico

V. CAMPOREGIO

WC

VIC. DEL

VIA 24 MAGGIO

VIA ARTURO PANNILUNGHI

VIA BRUNO BONCI

VIA 24 MAGGIO

SAN DOMENICO

STA. CATERINA

VIA MONTICCHIELLO

Fonte Branda

VIA

PORTA FONTEBRANDA

SELVA

VIA ESTERNA DI FONTEBRANDA

ANCIENT CITY WALLS

VIA DI VALLEPIATTA

VIA FRANGIOSA

V. DEI

NOTE: MUCH OF CENTRAL SIENA IS A PEDESTRIAN ZONE

SAN SEB.

SANTA MARIA DELLA SCALA (MUSEUM)

Accommodations

1. Pensione Palazzo Ravizza
2. Hotel Duomo
3. Piccolo Hotel Etruria
4. Albergo Tre Donzelle
5. Hotel Cannon d'Oro
6. Antica Residenza Cicogna
7. Palazzo Masi B&B
8. B&B Alle Due Porte
9. Siena Gallery B&B
10. I Terzi di Siena
11. B&B Siena in Centro
12. To Le Camerine di Silvia
13. Hotel Chiusarelli
14. Hotel Villa Elda
15. Albergo Bernini
16. Alma Domus

PANTERA

Piazzetta delle Due Porte

VIA

PIANO MANTELLINI

100 Meters

100 Yards

To 12 25

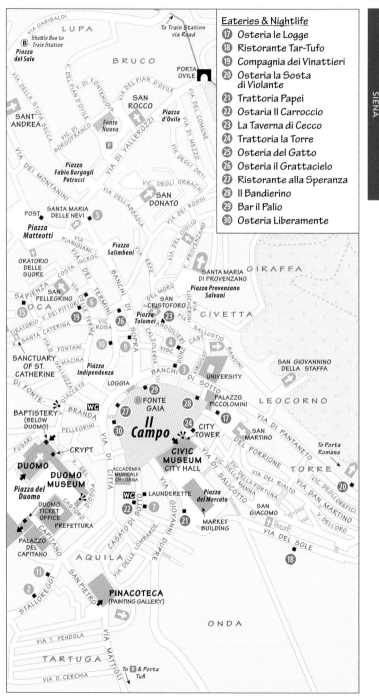

Eateries & Nightlife

17 Osteria le Logge
18 Ristorante Tar-Tufo
19 Compagnia dei Vinattieri
20 Osteria la Sosta di Violante
21 Trattoria Papei
22 Ostaria Il Carroccio
23 La Taverna di Cecco
24 Trattoria la Torre
25 Osteria del Gatto
26 Osteria il Grattacielo
27 Ristorante alla Speranza
28 Il Bandierino
29 Bar il Palio
30 Osteria Liberamente

only, view room on request, no breakfast, fans, free parking nearby, Via Ettore Bastianini 1, just below recommended Pensione Palazzo Ravizza, mobile 338-761-5052 or 339-123-7687, www.lecamerinedisilvia. com, info@lecamerinedisilvia.com, Conti family).

Near Basilica of San Domenico

$$$ Hotel Chiusarelli, with mix of 48 classic and modern rooms in a beautiful, frescoed Neoclassical villa, is just outside the medieval town center on a busy street—ask for a quieter room in back when you reserve (RS%, family rooms, air-con, limited free parking, across from San Domenico at Viale Curtatone 15, tel. 0577-280-562, www.chiusarelli.com, info@chiusarelli.com).

$$$ Hotel Villa Elda rents 11 bright and light rooms in a recently renovated villa. It's classy, stately, and run with a stylish charm (view rooms extra, air-con, no elevator, garden and view terrace, closed Nov-March, Viale Ventiquattro Maggio 10, tel. 0577-247-927, www.villaeldasiena. it, info@villaeldasiena.it).

$$ Albergo Bernini makes you part of a Sienese family in a modest, clean home with 10 traditional rooms. Giovanni, charming wife Daniela, and their daughters welcome you to their spectacular view terrace (cheaper rooms with shared bath, family rooms, breakfast extra, fans, on the main Il Campo-San Domenico drag at Via della Sapienza 15, tel. 0577-289-047, www.albergobernini.com, info@albergobernini.com).

$ Alma Domus is a church-run hotel and a great value, featuring 28 tidy, streamlined rooms with quaint balconies, some fantastic views (ask for a room *con vista*), stately public rooms, and a pleasant atmosphere (family rooms, air-con, elevator; from San Domenico, walk downhill toward the view with the church on your right, turn left down Via Camporegio, make a U-turn down the brick steps to Via Camporegio 37; tel. 0577-44177,

www.hotelalmadomus.it, info@hotel almadomus.it, Louis).

Eating

Sienese restaurants are a great value by Florentine and Venetian standards. Reservations are generally wise for dinner.

In the Old Town
FINE DINING

$$$$ Osteria le Logge caters to a fancy crowd and offers pricey Tuscan favorites with a gourmet twist, made with seasonal local ingredients (Mon-Sat 12:00-15:00 & 19:00-23:00, closed Sun, two blocks off Il Campo at Via del Porrione 33, tel. 0577-48013, www.osterialelogge.it, Mirko).

$$$$ Ristorante Tar-Tufo offers a spacious setting, a gourmet presentation, a twist of pretense, and contemporary and innovative Tuscan cuisine—much of it garnished with truffles (Thu-Tue 12:00-14:30 & 19:00-22:30, closed Wed, a 10-minute walk behind Il Campo at Via del Sole 6, tel. 0577-284-031, www.tartufo.com, chef Pino).

$$$ Compagnia dei Vinattieri, a good bet for wine lovers, serves Tuscan dishes with a creative touch. In this elegant space, you can enjoy a romantic meal under graceful brick arches (beef is big here, leave this book on the table for a complimentary *aperitivo* or *digestivo,* daily 12:30-15:00 & 19:30-23:00, Via delle Terme 79, tel. 0577-236-568, www.vinattieri.net).

$$ Osteria la Sosta di Violante, beyond the tourist zone, is the best fine-dining value of my listings. Diners with this book cap their meal with complimentary vin santo and *cantucci* (great indoor and outdoor seating, Mon-Sat 12:30-15:00 & 19:00-23:00, closed Sun, walk down Via Banchi di Sotto to Via Pantaneto 115, tel. 0577-43774).

TRADITIONAL AND RUSTIC PLACES

$$ Trattoria Papei is a sprawling place with a casual, rollicking family atmosphere and friendly servers dishing out generous portions of rib-stickin' Tuscan specialties and grilled meats (daily 12:00-15:00 & 19:00-22:30, on the market square behind City Hall at Piazza del Mercato 6, tel. 0577-280-894; Amedeo and Eduardo).

$$ Osteria il Carroccio, artsy and convivial, serves traditional "slow food" with innovative flair at affordable prices. To maintain their quality, they have only 35 seats and don't turn the tables—reserve ahead (€30 tasting *menu*—minimum two people, Thu-Tue 12:15-15:00 & 19:15-22:00, closed Wed, Casato di Sotto 32, tel. 0577-41165). They give complimentary vin santo and *cantucci* with this book.

$$ La Taverna di Cecco is a cozy, comfortable little eatery on a quiet back lane where grandma Olga cooks, and earnest Luca and Gianni serve. They offer a simple menu of traditional Sienese favorites along with hearty salads (daily 12:00-16:00 & 19:00-23:00, Via Cecco Angiolieri 19, tel. 0577-288-518).

$$ Trattoria la Torre is an unfussy family-run *casalinga* (home-cooking) place, popular for its homemade pasta. Its open kitchen and 10 tables are packed under one medieval brick arch (Fri-Wed 12:00-15:00 & 19:00-22:00, closed Thu, steps below Il Campo at Via di Salicotto 7, tel. 0577-287-548, Marco).

$ Osteria del Gatto is a classic neighborhood fixture thriving with townspeople and powered by a passion for good Sienese cuisine. Friendly Marco Coradeschi and his staff cook and serve daily specials with attitude (Mon-Sat 12:30-15:00 & 19:30-22:00, closed Sun, 10-minute walk from Il Campo at Via San Marco 8, look for *La Vecchia Osteria* sign, tel. 0577-287-133).

$ Osteria il Grattacielo is perfect for a cheap, hearty, memorable yet no-frills meal. Luca has no menu and just one solid house wine. You'll eat what he's cooking. Lunch is a mixed plate from the bar (be bold and point) or pasta (€10, includes wine). Dinner is three courses—antipasto bar, pasta, and a *secondi*—€15 for

Rick Steves readers; €3 extra adds a vin santo and cookies finale (daily 12:00-15:00 & 19:30-21:30, Via dei Pontani 8, mobile 331-742-2835).

On Il Campo

If you choose to dine on perhaps the finest town square in Italy, you'll pay a premium and eat mediocre food. And yet I highly recommend it. Surveying the scene during your sightseeing day and reserve a table at the place that suits you.

$$$ Ristorante alla Speranza has primo views and is a decent option for dining on the square (Piazza del Campo 32, tel. 0577-280-190, www.allasperanza.it).

$$$ Il Bandierino is another option for drinks or pizza, with an angled view of City Hall (no cover but a 20 percent service charge, Piazza del Campo 64, tel. 0577-275-894).

Rick's Tip: *Evenings are a wonderful time to be out and about in Siena.* **Join the passeggiata** *(peak strolling time is 19:00) along Via Banchi di Sopra with gelato in hand. You'll find bars all over town offering an* **aperitivo**—*a free buffet of food that's included with the purchase of a drink.*

$$$ Bar il Palio is the best bar on Il Campo for a before- or after-dinner drink: It has straightforward prices, no cover, and a fine view (Piazza del Campo 47, tel. 0577-282-055).

$$$ Osteria Liberamente, a dynamic little bar with a trendy vibe, is popular with young locals (Piazza del Campo 27, tel. 0577-274-733, Pino).

Transportation
Arriving and Departing

Siena has sparse train connections but is a handy hub for buses to the hill towns. For most, Florence is the gateway to Siena. The bus and train take about the same amount of time, but Siena's bus station is more convenient and central than its train station.

BY TRAIN

Siena's small train station is at the base of the hill, on the edge of town. It has a bar/tobacco shop, an intercity bus office (daily 9:00-12:15 & 14:30-18:30), and a newsstand (which sells city bus tickets). Stow bags at Piazza Gramsci where the city bus drops you—see "By Bus," later.

To reach central Siena, you can hop a city bus, ride a long series of escalators, or take a taxi (€8 to the center).

To reach either the bus or the escalators, head for the shopping mall across the square (far left corner as you leave station). The first of a series of **escalators** climbs through the mall up into the town. From the top of the escalators, it's a 20-minute walk to the town center.

To ride the **city bus,** head to the dreary, concrete, cave-like bus stop below the mall (catch the down elevator from inside the mall's first glass door on immediate right). All buses (big and small) go to Piazza Sale or Piazza Gramsci (within a block of each other). Buy your bus ticket from the train station newsstand, and before boarding, confirm that the bus is going to the center (ask *"Centro?"*).

To **return to the train station** from the city center, catch a small shuttle bus directly to the station from Piazza del Sale or take a big city bus from Piazza Gramsci. Look for *Ferrovia* or *Stazione* on schedules and marked on the bus, and confirm with the driver that the bus is going to the *stazione.*

From Siena by Train to: Florence (direct trains hourly, 1.5 hours), **Pisa** (2/hour, 1.5 hours, some change at Empoli), **Assisi** (10/day, about 4 hours, most involve 2 changes, bus is faster), **Rome** (1-2/hour, 3-4 hours, 1 change), **Orvieto** (12/day, 2.5 hours, change in Chiusi).

BY BUS

Most buses from Florence and other cities arrive in Siena at Piazza Gramsci (or the adjacent Via Tozzi), a few blocks north of the city center. (Some buses only go to the train station; others go first to the train station, then continue to Piazza Gramsci—to confirm, ask your driver, "pee-aht-sah GRAHM-shee?")

From Piazza Gramsci, it's an easy walk into the town center—just head in the opposite direction of the tree-filled park. Downstairs, beneath Piazza Gramsci, you'll find ticket offices, WCs, and a place to store baggage (at the Tiemme office, daily 7:00-19:00, carry-on-size luggage no more than 33 pounds, no overnight storage). If day-tripping, confirm your departure from timetables posted at the platform where you disembark or at the ticket counters downstairs. Late-afternoon buses back to Florence can fill up, so arrive 15 minutes early.

The main bus companies are **Tiemme/Siena Mobilità** (mostly regional destinations, tel. 0577-204-111, www.tiemmespa.it) and **Flixbus** (for long-distance connections, https://global.flixbus.com). You can buy tickets in the underground passageway (called Sottopassaggio la Lizza) beneath Piazza Gramsci—look for stairwells in front of NH Excelsior Hotel. You can also get bus tickets from a kiosk at the train station as well as on online.

Tiemme/Siena Mobilità Buses to: Florence (roughly 2/hour—fewer off-season, take the 1.5-hour *rapida/via superstrada* bus—*ordinaria* buses take longer), **Montepulciano** (6-7/day, none on Sun, 1.5 hours, from train station),

Montalcino (6/day Mon-Sat, 4/day Sun, 1.5 hours, from train station or Piazza del Sale), **Pisa's Galileo Galilei Airport** (3/day, 2 hours, one direct, two via Poggibonsi), **Rome's Fiumicino Airport** (3/day, 3.5 hours, from Piazza Gramsci).

Flixbus Buses to: Rome (13/day, 3 hours), **Naples** (6/day direct, 5.5 hours, one overnight bus that departs at 00:20), **Milan** (6-8/day direct, 5-7 hours), **Assisi** (3/day direct, 2 hours, departs from Siena train station.

BY CAR

Driving within Siena's city center is restricted to local cars and is policed by automatic cameras. Park in a big lot or garage and walk into town.

Coming from the autostrada, take the *Siena Ovest* exit and follow signs for *Centro,* then *Stadio* (stadium). The soccer-ball signs take you to the stadium lot (Parcheggio Stadio, pay when you leave) near Piazza Gramsci and the huge, bare-brick Basilica of San Domenico. The Fortezza lot is also nearby.

Another good option is the underground Santa Caterina garage (you'll see signs on the way to the stadium lot). From the garage, hike 150 yards uphill through a gate to an escalator on the right, which carries you up into the city. If you're staying in the south end of town, try the Il Campo lot, near Porta Tufi.

You can park for free in the lot west of the Fortezza; in white-striped spots south of the Fortezza; and overnight in most city lots (20:00-8:00).

TUSCAN WINE TOWNS

If your Tuscan dreams feature vibrant neon-green fields rolling to infinity, punctuated by snaking, cypress-lined driveways; humble but beautiful (and steep) hill towns; and world-class wines to make a connoisseur weep, set your sights on the heart of this region. Montepulciano and Montalcino are each a happy gauntlet of wine shops and art galleries. Montepulciano is the more all-around engaging town; it's the better choice for those without a car (though connections can be tricky). With its easy access to the vineyards, Montalcino makes sense for wine pilgrims.

Montepulciano

Curving its way along a ridge, Montepulciano (mohn-teh-puhl-CHAH-noh) delights visitors with *vino,* views,

Montepulciano has several classic wine cellars to explore.

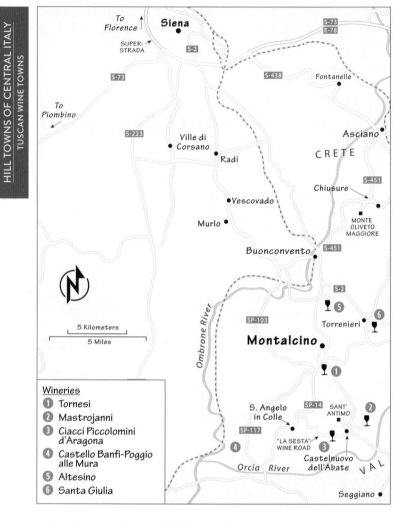

To Florence

Siena

SUPER-STRADA

S-2

To Piombino

S-73

S-73
E-78

S-438

Fontanelle

S-223

Ville di Corsano

Radi

Asciano

CRETE

Vescovado

Murlo

Chiusure

S-451

MONTE OLIVETO MAGGIORE

Buonconvento

S-451

S-2

5 Kilometers

5 Miles

Ombrone River

SP-103

Torrenieri

Montalcino

S. Angelo in Colle

SP-14

SANT' ANTIMO

SP-117

"LA SESTA" WINE ROAD

Orcia River

Castelnuovo dell'Abate

VAL

Seggiano

Wineries

1. Tornesi
2. Mastrojanni
3. Ciacci Piccolomini d'Aragona
4. Castello Banfi-Poggio alle Mura
5. Altesino
6. Santa Giulia

and—perhaps more than any other large town in this area—a sense of being a real, bustling community rather than just a tourist depot.

The city is a collage of architectural styles, but the elegant San Biagio Church, just outside the city walls at the base of the hill, is its best Renaissance building. Most visitors ignore the architecture and focus more on the city's other creative accomplishment, the tasty Vino Nobile di Montepulciano red wine.

Orientation

Commercial action in Montepulciano centers in the lower town, mostly along Via di Gracciano nel Corso (nicknamed "Corso"). This stretch begins at the town gate called Porta al Prato (near the TI, bus station, and some parking) and winds slowly up, up, up through town. The main square at the top of town is Piazza Grande, with a noble, Florentine feel.

Tourist Information: The helpful TI is just outside the lower Porta al Prato city

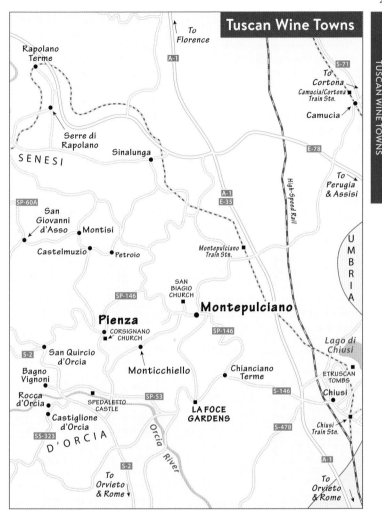

Tuscan Wine Towns

gate, in the small P1 parking lot (Mon-Sat 9:00-13:00 & 15:00-19:00, Sun 9:00-13:00, daily until 20:00 in July-Aug, sells bus and train tickets, Piazza Don Minzoni, tel. 0578-757-341, www.prolocomontepulciano.it).

The office on the main upper square that looks like a TI is actually the privately run Valdichiana Living agency. They provide wine-road maps, wine tours in the city, and minibus winery tours farther afield (Mon-Fri 10:00-13:30 & 14:30-18:00, shorter Sat hours, Sun 10:00-13:00, Piazza Grande 7, tel. 0578-717-484, www.valdichianaliving.it).

Shuttle Bus to the Top of Town: To avoid the hike up through town to Piazza Grande, hop on the orange shuttle bus. It departs about every 15 minutes from the parking lot near the bus station and from the lane leading to the Porta al Prato gate, just above the TI (€1.20, buy tickets at bars, tobacco shops, or the TI).

Laundry: An elegant self-service launderette is at the top of town at

Via del Paolino 2 (daily 8:00-22:00, tel. 0578-717-544).

Taxis: Call 330-732-723 for short trips within town (€10 for rides up or down hill); to reach other towns, call 348-733-5343.

Sights and Experiences
▲▲CONTUCCI CANTINA

Montepulciano's most popular attraction isn't made of stone—it's the famous wine, Vino Nobile. This robust red can be tasted in any of the cantinas lining Via Ricci and Via di Gracciano nel Corso, but the cantina in the basement of Palazzo Contucci is both historic and fun. Skip the palace's formal wine-tasting showroom facing the square, and instead head down the lane on the right to the actual cellars. After sipping a little wine, explore the palace basement with its 13th-century vaults. Originally part of the town's wall, these chambers have been filled since the 1500s with huge barrels of wine.

Cost and Hours: Free drop-in tasting, free cellar tour upon request, daily 10:00-18:30, shorter hours off-season, Piazza Grande 13, tel. 0578-757-006, www.contucci.it.

▲RAMAIO CESARE

Cesare the coppersmith is an institution in Montepulciano, carrying on his father's and grandfather's trade by hammering into existence an immense selection of copper objects in his cavernous workshop.

Though his English is limited, Cesare (CHEH-zah-ray) is happy to show you photos of his work—including the copper top of the Duomo in Siena. He has assembled a fine museum with items he and his relatives have made, as well as pieces from his personal collection.

Cost and Hours: Demonstration and museum are free, Cesare is generally in his workshop Mon-Sat 9:00-12:30 & 14:30-18:30, closed Sun, 50 yards steeply downhill from the Contucci Cantina at Via del Teatro 4, tel. 0578-758-753, www.rameria.com. Cesare's delightful shop is on the main drag, a block below, at Corso #64—look for *Rameria Mazzetti,* open long hours daily.

▲DE' RICCI CANTINE

The most impressive wine cellars in Montepulciano sit below the Palazzo Ricci, just a few steps off the main square (toward the Church of San Francesco). Enter through the unassuming door and find your way down, down, down a spiral staircase to the dramatic cellars, with gigantic barrels under even more gigantic vaults. Finally you wind up in the shop, where you're welcome to taste a few wines (with some local cheese). Don't miss their delightful dessert wine, vin santo.

Cost and Hours: First three tastings-free, two additional premium tastes-€5, affordable shipping, daily 10:30-18:30, enter Palazzo Ricci at Via Ricci 11—look for signs for *Cantine de' Ricci,* tel. 0578-757-166, www.cantinadericci.it, Enrico.

Montepulciano's resident coppersmith

Massive wine barrels at Contucci Cantina

Montepulciano

Accommodations

1. La Locanda di San Francesco & E Lucevan le Stelle Wine Bar
2. Mueblè il Riccio
3. Albergo Duomo
4. Vicolo dell'Oste B&B
5. Camere Bellavista

Eateries

6. Osteria dell'Acquacheta
7. Osteria del Conte
8. Le Pentolaccia
9. Ai Quattro Venti
10. Sgarbi Gelato Natura
11. To La Grotta

Other

12. Copper Shop
13. Copper Workshop
14. Contucci Cantina
15. Cantine de' Ricci
16. Cantina della Talosa
17. Launderette

Ⓑ Local Shuttle Bus

San Biagio Church

CANTINA DELLA TALOSA

This historic cellar, which goes down and down to an Etruscan tomb at the bottom, ages a well-respected wine. With a passion and love of their craft, Andrea and Cristian Pepi give enthusiastic tours and tastings. While you can drop by for a free sample, it's also possible to call ahead to book a complete tour and tasting (€20, including five wines to taste and light food).

Cost and Hours: Daily March-Oct 10:30-19:00, shorter hours off-season, a block off Piazza Grande at Via Talosa 8, tel. 0578-757-929, www.talosa.it.

▲SAN BIAGIO CHURCH (CHIESA DE SAN BIAGIO)

The church is just west of town, at the base of Montepulciano's hill, down a picturesque cypress-lined driveway. Often called the "Temple of San Biagio" because of its Greek-cross style, this church—designed by Antonio da Sangallo the Elder and built of locally quarried travertine—feels like Renaissance perfection.

Cost and Hours: €3.50, includes 20-minute audioguide, daily 10:00-18:00, longer hours in summer, shorter hours in winter.

Sleeping

$$$$ La Locanda di San Francesco is overpriced but luxurious, with four stylish view rooms over a classy wine bar on a quiet square at Montepulciano's summit (closed Nov-Easter, air-con, free parking nearby, Piazza San Francesco 5, tel. 0578-758-725, www.locandasanfrancesco.it, info@locandasanfrancesco.it, Luca).

$$ Mueblè il Riccio ("The Hedgehog") is medieval-elegant, with 10 modern and spotless rooms, an awesome roof terrace, and friendly owners (family rooms, breakfast extra, air-con, limited free parking—request when you reserve, a block below the main square at Via Talosa 21, tel. 0578-757-713, www.ilriccio.net, info@ilriccio.net, Gió and Ivana speak English).

$$ Albergo Duomo is big, modern, and nondescript, with 13 simple but dignified rooms (with small bathrooms) and a comfortable lounge downstairs. It's at the very top of town, with free private parking nearby (RS%—use code "Steves," family rooms, elevator, air-con in some rooms—extra charge, Via di San Donato 14, tel. 0578-757-473, www.albergoduomo.it, albergoduomo@libero.it, Simone).

$$ Vicolo dell'Oste B&B, just off the main drag halfway up through town, has five family-friendly modern rooms. Some are like tiny apartments (RS%, includes breakfast at nearby café, on Via dell'Oste 1—an alley leading right off the main drag just after Caffè Poliziano and opposite the *farmacia* at #47, tel. 0578-758-393, www.vicolodelloste.it, info@vicolodelloste.it, Luisa and Giuseppe).

$ Camere Bellavista has 10 tidy rooms. True to its name, the rooms have fine views—though some are better than others (cash only, no breakfast, lots of stairs with no elevator, reception not always staffed—call before arriving or ring bell, Via Ricci 25, mobile 347-823-2314, www.camerebellavista.it, info@camerebellavista.it, Gabriella and Alessio speak just enough English).

Eating

Unless otherwise noted, these places are all open for lunch (about 12:30-14:30) and again for dinner (about 19:30-22:00).

$$$ **Osteria dell'Acquacheta** is a carnivore's dream come true, beloved among locals for its beef steaks. Its long, narrow room is jammed with shared tables and tight, family-style seating, with an open fire in back. Typically, two people split a 1.6-kilo steak (that's 3.5 pounds; the smallest they'll cook is 1.2 kilos). They also serve hearty pastas and salads and a fine house wine (reservations required; seatings generally at 12:30, 14:30, 19:30, and 21:30 only; closed Tue and unpredictably on other days; Via del Teatro 22, tel. 0578-717-086, www.acquacheta.eu).

$$ **Osteria del Conte,** an attractive but humble family-run bistro, offers cooking like your Italian mom's (closed Mon, Via San Donato 19, tel. 0578-756-062).

$$ **Le Pentolaccia** is a small, family-run restaurant about two-thirds of the way up the main drag. With both indoor and outdoor seating, they make tasty traditional Tuscan dishes as well as daily fish specials (closed Thu, Corso 86, tel. 0578-757-582).

$$ **Ai Quattro Venti** is right on Piazza Grande, with a simple dining room and outdoor tables on the square. It offers reasonable portions of unfussy Tuscan food in an unpretentious setting (closed Thu, next to City Hall on Piazza Grande, tel. 0578-717-231, Chiara).

Wine Bar/Bistro: With a terrace on a tranquil square in front of the Church of San Francesco, $ **E Lucevan le Stelle,** part of La Locanda di San Francesco, is a fine place to nurse a glass of local wine (also pastas, salads, and soups; daily 12:00-24:00, closed Nov-Easter, Piazza San Francesco 5, tel. 0578-758-725, Luca).

Gelato: For the best gelato in town, look for **Sgarbi Gelato Natura,** near the bottom of the main drag. The gelato is ready around 13:00—and when it's gone, it's gone (daily 11:00-20:00, Corso 50; also runs Buon Gusto in Pienza).

Just Outside Montepulciano: Facing San Biagio Church (at the base of Montepulciano's hill), $$$ **La Grotta** has an excellent reputation for elevated Tuscan cuisine in a sophisticated, dressy setting. Reservations are recommended (Thu-Tue 12:30-14:15 & 19:30-22:00, closed Wed, Via di San Biagio 15, tel. 0578-757-479, www. lagrottamontepulciano.it).

Transportation
ARRIVING AND DEPARTING
By Car: Well-signed pay-and-display parking lots ring the city center (marked with blue lines). For quicker access to the main square up top, use one of the parking lots at the top end of town: Approaching Montepulciano, follow signs for *centro storico, duomo,* and *Piazza Grande,* and use the Fortezza or San Donato lots.

Avoid the "ZTL" no-traffic zone (signs marked with a red circle). If you're sleeping in town, your hotelier can give you a permit to park within the walls.

By Bus: Buses leave passengers at the bus station on Piazza Nenni, downhill from the Porta al Prato gate. From the station, cross the street and head inside the modern orange-brick structure burrowed into the hillside, where there's an elevator. Ride to level 1, walk straight down the corridor (following signs for *centro storico*), and ride a second elevator (to a different level 1 and the Poggiofanti Gardens); walk to the end of this park and hook left to find the Porta al Prato gate.

From Montepulciano by Bus to: **Florence** (1/day departs in the wee hours, 2/week additional departures a bit later in the morning, 2 hours, LFI bus, www.lfi.it; or take a bus to Chiusi to catch a train—see below), **Siena** (6-7/day, none on Sun, 1.5 hours, also possible to change here for Florence express bus), **Montalcino** (3-4/day, none Sun, change in Torrenieri, 1 hour; or consider a taxi—about €70, see contact info under "Helpful Hints," earlier). Check www.tiemmespa.it for schedules.

By Train: Trains are impractical here; the Montepulciano train station, five miles from town and connected by a 15-minute bus ride, has only milk-run trains (but could be useful for reaching Siena on a Sunday, when buses are scarce—get details at the TI).

Montalcino

On a hill overlooking vineyards and valleys, Montalcino is famous for its delicious and pricey Brunello di Montalcino red wines. It's a pleasant, low-impact town crawling with wine-loving tourists and a smattering of classy shops. Montalcino provides a handy springboard for exploring the surrounding wine region.

Orientation

Montalcino is surrounded by walls and dominated by its medieval fortress, the Fortezza (a.k.a. "La Rocca"). From here, roads lead down into the two main squares: Piazza Garibaldi and Piazza del Popolo.

Tourist Information: The helpful TI, just off Piazza Garibaldi in City Hall, sells bus tickets; can call ahead to book a visit at a countryside winery (small fee); and has information on taxis to nearby towns, abbeys, and monasteries (daily 10:00-13:00 & 14:00-17:50, tel. 0577-849-331, www.prolocomontalcino.com).

Wine Bars in Town

If you won't make it to the wineries outside Montalcino, simply visit a wine bar in town. This is a great strategy for Sundays, when many countryside wineries are closed.

Caffè Fiaschetteria Italiana, a classic café/wine bar, was founded by Ferruccio Biondi Santi, the creator of the famous Brunello wine. The wine library in the back of the café boasts many local choices. (Brunellos by the glass, light snacks and plates; daily 7:30-23:00, Piazza del Popolo 6, tel. 0577-849-043).

Enoteca di Piazza—part of a chain of wine shops with mechanical dispensers—is a fun way to efficiently taste a variety of wines in a forgettable setting. This is a good spot to assemble a box of wine from different local producers to ship home (daily 9:00-20:00, near Piazza del Popolo at Via Matteotti 43, tel. 0577-848-104, www.enotecadipiazza.com).

Enoteca la Fortezza di Montalcino offers a chance to taste top-end wines by the glass. While the prices are a bit higher than other *enoteche* in town, the medieval setting inside Montalcino's fort is popular with tourists (tastings start at €15 for 3

Montalcino's Piazza del Popolo

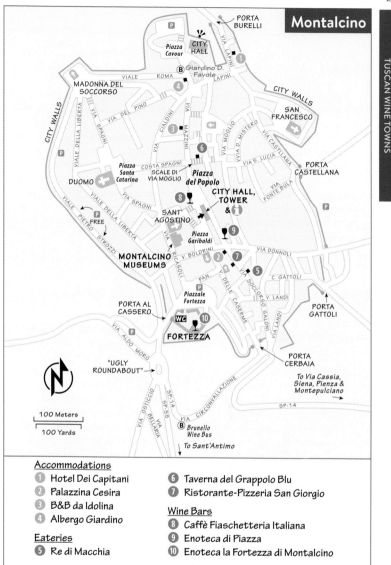

Montalcino

Map labels:
PORTA BURELLI, Piazza Cavour, CITY HALL, VIA LAPINI, Giardino D. Favole, B, VIALE ROMA, LAPINI, CITY WALLS, SAN FRANCESCO, MADONNA DEL SOCCORSO, VIA DEL PINO, VIA GIALDINI, VIA MAZZINI, VIA MOGLIO, VIA D. MISTERO, VIA CASTELLANA, PORTA CASTELLANA, CITY WALLS, VIALE DELLA LIBERTA, VIA SPAGNI, COSTA SPAGNI, SCALE DI VIA MOGLIO, VIA S. LUCIA, Piazza Santa Catarina, Piazza del Popolo, VIA FONTE BULA, DUOMO, Piazza Santa Catarina, VIA SPAGNI, CITY HALL, TOWER &, SANT' AGOSTINO, VIALE PIETRO STROZZI, FREE, VIALE DELLA LIBERTA, MONTALCINO MUSEUMS, Piazza Garibaldi, VIA RICASOLI, V. BOLDRINI, VIA DONNOLI, PAN., C. GATTOLI, VIA DELLE CASERME, V. SOCCORSO SALONI, V. LANDI, PORTA GATTOLI, Piazzale Fortezza, PORTA AL CASSERO, VIA ALDO MORO, WC, FORTEZZA, PORTA CERBAIA, "UGLY ROUNDABOUT", To Via Cassia, Siena, Pienza & Montepulciano, VIA OSTICCIO, SP-14, VIA BELARIA, SP-55, VIA CIRCONVALLAZIONE, VIA GIRCONVALLAZIONE, SP-14, 100 Meters, 100 Yards, B Brunello Wine Bus, To Sant'Antimo

Legend:

Accommodations
1 Hotel Dei Capitani
2 Palazzina Cesira
3 B&B da Idolina
4 Albergo Giardino

Eateries
5 Re di Macchia

6 Taverna del Grappolo Blu
7 Ristorante-Pizzeria San Giorgio

Wine Bars
8 Caffè Fiaschetteria Italiana
9 Enoteca di Piazza
10 Enoteca la Fortezza di Montalcino

wines and go up from there; daily 9:00–20:00, until 18:00 Nov-March, inside the Fortezza, tel. 0577-849-211).

Wineries near Montalcino

The countryside around Montalcino is littered with wineries, some of which offer tastings, and most require an advance reservation. The Montalcino TI can give you a list of regional wineries and will call ahead for you. Or check with the vintners' consortium (tel. 0577-848-246, www.consorziobrunellodimontalcino.it).

If you lack a car (or don't want to drive), you can take a tour on the **Brunello Wine**

Tuscan Wines

Montepulciano is known for its Vino Nobile, while Montalcino is famous for its Brunello. In each wine, the predominant grape is a clone of sangiovese, Tuscany's main red wine grape.

Vino Nobile di Montepulciano is a high-quality, dry ruby red. Aged two years (or three for a *riserva*), it pairs well with roasted meats, grilled portobello mushrooms, and local cheeses like pecorino. Several large wineries produce and age their Vino Nobile in the sprawling cellars beneath the town of Montepulciano. The oldest red wine in Tuscany, Vino Nobile has been produced since the late 1500s.

Brunello di Montalcino ranks among Italy's finest and most expensive wines. It's smooth, dry, and aged for a minimum of two years in wood casks, plus an additional four months in the bottle. *Riserva* wines are aged an additional year. Brunello is designed to cellar for 10 years or longer—but who can wait? It pairs well with the local cuisine, but the perfect match is the fine Chianina beef. You'll also see Rosso di Montalcino (a younger version of Brunello); this "poor man's Brunello" is very good, at half the price.

Bus, which laces together visits to four wineries, with a lunch break in the middle (€140; tours run March-Nov Tue and Thu only; departs at 10:00, returns at 19:00; www.winetravelsforyou.com).

TORNESI

This charmingly low-key, family-run winery is a short drive outside Montalcino, perched on a grand view terrace overlooking the famous Biondi Santi winery, where Brunello was invented (reserve ahead, closed Sun, mobile 349-093-2167, www.brunellotornesi.it). Leaving Montalcino, at the main roundabout, go uphill toward *Grosetto,* then watch for the brown *Benducce* sign on the left (just before the road bends right). Tornesi is a short drive down this gravel road, on the left.

MASTROJANNI

Perched high above the Romanesque Sant'Antimo Abbey, overlooking sprawling vineyards, this winery is big and glitzy (reserve ahead, Podere Loreto e San Pio, tel. 0577-835-681, www.mastrojanni.com). To reach it, head up into the town of Castelnuovo dell'Abate (just above Sant'Antimo Abbey), bear left at the Bassomondo restaurant, and continue up along the gravel road (enjoying vineyard and abbey views).

CIACCI PICCOLOMINI D'ARAGONA

This family-run vineyard has a classy tasting room/*enoteca* and an outdoor view terrace. If you're just dropping in, belly up to the wine bar for two or three free tastes. Or reserve ahead for a more formal tasting of top-quality wines, which includes a tour of the cellar (April-Oct Mon-Fri 9:00-19:00, Sat 10:30-18:30, closed Sun; down a back lane near Sant'Antimo Abbey—head toward Castelnuovo dell'Abate but go right before entering that town, following signs

Wine tasting near Montalcino

toward *Sant'Angelo in Colle,* tel. 0577-835-616, www.ciaccipiccolomini.com, visite@ciaccipiccolomini.com).

CASTELLO BANFI-POGGIO ALLE MURA
Despite its large size, this estate is charming, set in a castle located in a picturesque corner southwest of Sant'Antimo. It's a good option for Sundays, when other places are closed, or for a spontaneous drop-in tasting (daily 10:00-19:30, until 18:00 Nov-March, tours available on request, tel. 055-877-500, www.castello banfiilborgo.com, enoteca@banfi.it). You'll find Banfi about 20 minutes south of Montalcino; follow SP-14 to Borgo Santa Rita and cut back north, following signs to *Poggio alle Mura.*

ALTESINO
Elegant and stately, Altesino owns perhaps the most stunning location of all, just off the back road connecting Montalcino north to Buonconvento. You'll twist up on cypress-lined gravel lanes to this perch, which looks out over an expanse of vineyards with Montalcino hovering on the horizon (daily, reserve ahead, Loc. Altesino 54, tel. 0577-806-208, www.altesino.it, info@altesino.it). You'll find the turnoff for Altesino along the back road (SP-45) between Montalcino and Buonconvento.

SANTA GIULIA
This is a quintessential family-run winery, with an emphasis on quality (only 20,000 bottles a year). They also produce excellent olive oil, prosciutto, and salami. Less picturesque and much more rustic than the other wineries listed here, a tour at Santa Giulia is a Back Door experience (Loc. Santa Giulia 48, closed Sun, tel. 0577-834-270, www.santagiuliamontalcino.it, info@santagiuliamontalcino.it). From Torrenieri's main intersection, follow the brown *Via Francigena* signs. After crossing the train tracks and a bridge, watch on the left to follow signs for *Sasso di Sole,* then *Sta. Giulia;* you'll take gravel roads through farm fields to the winery.

Sleeping

$$$ Hotel Dei Capitani, at the end of town near the bus station, has plush public spaces, an inviting summertime pool, and a cliffside terrace offering plenty of reasons for lounging (RS%, air-con, elevator, limited free parking—first come, first served, Via Lapini 6, tel. 0577-847-227, www.deicapitani.it, info@deicapitani.it).

$$ Palazzina Cesira, right in the heart of the old town, is a gem, renting five spacious and tastefully decorated rooms in a fine 13th-century residence with a palatial lounge and a pleasant garden. (2-night minimum, air-con, free off-street parking, Via Soccorso Saloni 2, tel. 0577-846-055, www.montalcinoitaly.com, info@montalcinoitaly.com).

$ B&B da Idolina has four good rooms above a wine shop on the main street (includes basic breakfast in shared kitchen, check-in 15:00-19:00—call if arriving later, parking available, Via Mazzini 65, check in at the wine shop next door, tel. 0577-849-212, www.idolina1946.com, fulvia.soda@gmail.com, Fulvia).

$ Albergo Giardino, a great value, has nine big rooms done in a modern-minimalist style, no public spaces, and a convenient location near the bus stop (RS%, no breakfast, Piazza Cavour 4, tel. 0577-848-257, mobile 320-404-4655, www.albergoilgiardino.it, info@albergoilgiardino.it, Roberto and dad Mario).

Eating

$$$ Re di Macchia serves up big, hearty portions of Tuscan fare. Look for their seasonal menu and a fine Montalcino wine list (Fri-Wed 12:00-14:00 & 19:00-21:00, closed Thu, reservations strongly recommended, Via Soccorso Saloni 21, tel. 0577-846-116).

$$ Taverna del Grappolo Blu is serious about its wine, game, homemade pasta, and vegetarian options (reservations smart, daily 12:00-15:00 & 19:00-22:00, a few steps off Via Mazzini at Scale di Via Moglio 1, tel. 0577-847-150, www.grappoloblu.it, Luciano).

$$ Ristorante-Pizzeria San Giorgio is a homey trattoria/pizzeria with traditional decor and reasonable prices (daily 12:00-15:00 & 19:00-22:30, closed Tue off-season, Via Soccorso Saloni 10, tel. 0577-848-507, Mara).

Transportation

ARRIVING AND DEPARTING

The nearest train station is a 30-minute bus ride away, in Buonconvento.

By Car: For a short visit, drivers should head to the pay lot in Piazzale Fortezza (follow signs to *parking* and *Fortezza*). Or, if you don't mind a short climb, park for free below the fortress: At the roundabout with the ugly statue, take the small downhill lane into the big lower parking lot. If these lots are full, follow the town's western wall toward the Madonna del Soccorso church and a long pay lot.

By Bus: The bus stop is on Piazza Cavour, a little park about 300 yards from the town center. Check schedules at the TI, at the bus station, or online (www.tiemmespa.it).

From Montalcino by Bus to: Siena (6/day Mon-Sat, fewer Sun, 1.5 hours). En route, this bus goes through Torrenieri (change for **Montepulciano**, 3-4/day, none on Sun) and **Buonconvento** (where you can catch a train to **Florence**). Since the Montepulciano bus connection is sporadic, consider hiring a taxi (about €70 one-way).

ASSISI

Assisi is famous for its hometown boy, St. Francis, who made very, very good. While Francis the saint is interesting, Francesco Bernardone the man is even more so, and mementos of his days in Assisi are everywhere—where he was baptized, a shirt he wore, a hill he prayed on, and a church where a vision changed his life.

Around the year 1200, this simple friar from Assisi countered the decadence of Church government and society in general with a powerful message of nonmaterialism and a "slow down and smell God's roses" lifestyle. Like Jesus, Francis taught by example, living without worldly goods and aiming to love all creation. A huge monastic order grew out of his teachings, which were gradually embraced (some would say co-opted) by the Church. Christianity's most popular saint and its purest example of simplicity is now glorified in beautiful churches, along with his female counterpart, St. Clare.

Francis' message of love, simplicity, and sensitivity to the environment has a broad and timeless appeal. But every pilgrimage site inevitably gets commercialized: In summer, this Umbrian town bursts with Franciscan knickknacks. Look past the glow-in-the-dark rosaries and bobble-head friars. Even a block or two off the congested main drag, it's possible to find pockets of serenity that must have made Francis feel at peace.

Orientation

The city stretches across a ridge that rises from a flat plain. The Basilica of St. Francis sits at the low end of town; Piazza Matteotti (bus stop and parking lot) is at the high end; and the main square, Piazza del Comune, lies in between. The main drag (called Via San Francesco for most of its course) runs from Piazza del Comune to the basilica. Capping the hill above the town is the ruined castle, the Rocca Maggiore, and rising above that is Mount Subasio. Walking uphill from the basilica to Piazza Matteotti takes 30 minutes, while the downhill journey takes about 15 minutes.

Some Francis sights lie outside the city walls, in the flat area beneath the ridge (the modern part of town, called Santa Maria degli Angeli) and in the hills above.

Tourist Information

The TI is in the center of the old town on Piazza del Comune (daily 9:00-19:00, tel. 075-813-8680, www.visit-assisi.it). From April to October, there's also a branch (with shorter hours) down in the valley, across the street from the big piazza in front of the Basilica of Santa Maria degli Angeli.

Rick's Tip: *Tacky knickknacks line the streets leading to the Basilica of St. Francis. For better shops (with* **local handicrafts***), head to Via San Rufino and Corso Mazzini, both just off Piazza del Comune.*

Helpful Hints

Laundry: 3 Elle Blu' Lavanderia can do same-day laundry for you at a reasonable price (Mon-Fri 9:00-18:00, Sat until 13:00, closed Sun, Via Borgo Aretino 6a, tel. 075-816-084).

Local Guides: Giuseppe Karabotis is a good licensed guide (€130/3 hours, €260/6 hours, mobile 328-867-0567, iokarabot@libero.it). **Daniela Moretti** knows Assisi and all of Umbria (€120/ half-day, €240/day, mobile 335-829-9984, www.danyguide.com).

○ Assisi Walk

This self-guided walk, worth ▲▲, covers the town from top to bottom, starting near Piazza Matteotti. To trace the route, see the map on page 262.

🎧 Download my free Assisi Town Walk **audio tour.**

• *Start 50 yards beyond Piazza Matteotti (down the small lane between two stone houses, away from city center—see map).*

❶ *Roman Amphitheater (Anfiteatro Romano)*

A lane named Via Anfiteatro Romano skirts the cozy neighborhood built around the site of a long-gone Roman amphitheater—a reminder that Assisi was once an important Roman town. While the amphitheater dates from the first century AD, the buildings filling it today were built in the 13th and 14th centuries. The Roman stones have long been absorbed into the medieval architecture.

Circle to the right along the curved lane that marks the amphitheater's footprint. Imagine how colorful the town laundry basin (on the right) must have been in previous generations, when the women of Assisi gathered here to do their wash. Just beyond, above another small rectangular basin, are the coats of arms of Assisi's leading families. A few steps farther, leave the amphitheater, hiking up the stairs on the right to the top of the hill, for an overhead view of the ancient oval. It was Roman tradition to locate the amphitheater outside of town, which this used to be. Notice the town's carefully maintained complexion: When redoing a roof, locals will mix old and new tiles.

• *Continue on, enjoying the grand view of the fortress in the distance. Take the gravel lane that branches off to the right, leading down to a city gate (on the right). Step through the gate for an...*

Assisi

Medieval Assisi's builders preserved the outline of the Roman amphitheater

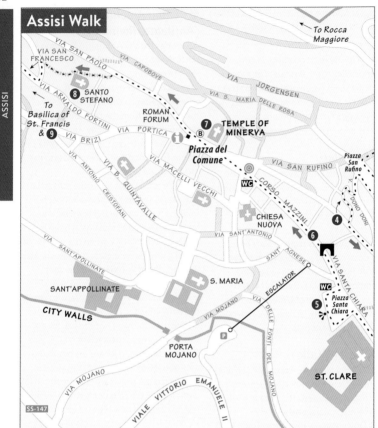

Assisi Walk

❷ *Umbrian View*

Outside Assisi's Porta Perlici stretches
a commanding view. Enjoy the various
shades of green: silver green on the valley
floor (olives), emerald green (grapevines),
and deep green on the hillsides (ever-
green oak trees). The valleys are dotted
by small family farms, many of which rent
rooms as *agriturismi*. Also notice Rocca
Maggiore ("big fortress"), which provided
townsfolk a refuge in times of attack. In
the opposite direction, Rocca Minore
("little fortress") gives the town's young
lovers a little privacy. A quarry under the
Rocca Maggiore was a handy source for
Assisi's characteristic pink limestone.
• *Go back through the gate and follow Via
Porta Perlici—it's immediately on your*

*right—downhill into town (toward Hotel
la Rocca). Fifty yards down, to the left of
the arched gate, find the wall containing an
aqueduct that dates from Roman times.
It still brings water from a mountain spring
into the city (push the brass tap for a taste).
After another 50 yards, turn left through a
medieval town gate (with Hotel la Rocca on
your right). Just after the hotel, you'll pass
a second gate dating from Roman times.
Follow Via Porta Perlici a few atmospheric
blocks downhill until you hit a fine square
facing a big church.*

❸ *Cathedral of San Rufino
(Cattedrale San Rufino)*

Trick question: Who's Assisi's patron

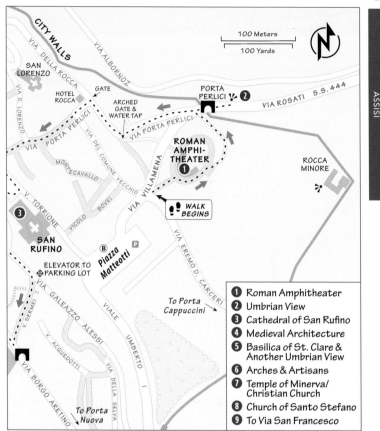

CITY WALLS
VIA DELLA ROCCA
VIA ALBORNOZ
SAN LORENZO
VIA S. LORENZO
HOTEL ROCCA
GATE
ARCHED GATE & WATER TAP
PORTA PERLICI
VIA ROSATI S.S. 444
100 Meters
100 Yards
VIA PORTA PERLICI
VIA PORTA PERLICI
VIA DEL COMUNE VECCHIO
MONTE CAVALLO
VICOLO BOVEI
VIA VILLAMENA
ROMAN AMPHI-THEATER ❶
ROCCA MINORE
V. TORRIONE
VICOLO BOVEI
WALK BEGINS
❸ SAN RUFINO
VIA EREMO D. CARCERI
ⓑ Piazza Matteotti Ⓟ
ELEVATOR TO PARKING LOT
To Porta Cappuccini
V. SERMEI
VIA GALEAZZO ALESSI
V. ACQUEDOTTI
VIALE UMBERTO
VIA DELLA SELVA
VIA BORGO ARETINO
To Porta Nuova

❶ Roman Amphitheater
❷ Umbrian View
❸ Cathedral of San Rufino
❹ Medieval Architecture
❺ Basilica of St. Clare & Another Umbrian View
❻ Arches & Artisans
❼ Temple of Minerva/ Christian Church
❽ Church of Santo Stefano
❾ To Via San Francesco

saint? While Francis is one of Italy's patron saints, Rufino (the town's first bishop, martyred and buried here in the third century) is Assisi's. This cathedral (seat of the local bishop)—worth ▲▲— is 11th-century Romanesque with a Neo-classical interior, and dedicated to Rufino. Although it has one of the best and purest Romanesque facades in all of Umbria, the big triangular top (just a decorative wall) was added in Gothic times.

Cost and Hours: Cathedral—free, daily 7:00-19:00, Nov-mid-March closed Mon-Fri 12:30-14:30, tel. 075-812-283; museum—€3.50, Thu-Tue 10:00-13:00 & 15:00-18:00, closed Wed, shorter hours off-season and Sun, www.assisimuseo diocesano.it.

Visiting the Church: Before going in, study the facade—a jungle of beasts emphasizing how the church was a refuge and sanctuary in a scary world. Notice the lions at the base of the facade, flanking each door. One is eating a Christian martyr, reminding worshippers of the courage of early Christians.

Enter the church. While the front of the church is an unremarkable mix of 17th- and 18th-century Baroque and Neoclassical, the rear (near where you enter) has several points of interest. Notice the two fine statues at the bases of the first pillars: *St. Francis* and *St. Clare* (by Giovanni Dupré, 1888).

In the church's back-right corner is an old baptismal font (surrounded by a

St. Francis of Assisi (1181-1226)

In 1202, young Francesco Bernardone donned armor and rode out to battle the Perugians (residents of Umbria's capital city). After being captured and imprisoned for a year, Francis returned a changed man. He avoided friends and his father's lucrative business and spent more and more time outside the city walls fasting, praying, and searching for something.

In 1206, a vision changed his life, culminating in a dramatic confrontation. He stripped naked before the town leaders, threw his clothes at his father—turning his back on the comfortable material life—and declared his loyalty to God alone.

Francis became a cult figure, attracting huge crowds who'd never seen anything like him. He preached sermons outdoors, in the local language (not Church Latin), making God accessible to all. Francis' new order of monks was also extremely unmaterialistic, extolling poverty and simplicity. Despite their radicalism, the order eventually gained the pope's approval and spread through the world. Francis, who died in Assisi at the age of 44, left a legacy of humanism, equality, and love of nature that would eventually flower in the Renaissance.

semicircular black iron grate). In about 1181, a baby boy was baptized in this font. His parents were upwardly mobile Francophiles who called him Francesco ("Frenchy"). In 1194, a nobleman baptized his daughter Clare here. Eighteen years later, their paths crossed in this same church, when Clare attended a class and became mesmerized by the teacher—

Cathedral of San Rufino

Francis. Traditionally, the children of Assisi are still baptized here.

In the nave, the striking glass panels in the floor reveal foundations preserved from the ninth-century church that once stood here. You're walking on history. After a 1997 earthquake, structural inspectors checked the church from ceiling to floor. When they looked under the paving stones, they discovered graves (it was common practice to bury people in churches). Underneath that level, they found Roman foundations and some animal bones (suggesting the possibility of animal sacrifice). There might have been a Roman temple here; churches were often built upon temple ruins.

Diocesan Museum: Underneath the church, incorporated into the Roman ruins and columns, are the foundations of an earlier Church of San Rufino, now the crypt and a fine little museum.

• *Leaving the church, walk to the end of the square and take a sharp left (at the pizza-by-the-slice joint, on Via Dono Doni). After 20 yards, take a right and go all the way down the stairway to see some...*

❹ Medieval Architecture

At the bottom of the stairs, notice the pink limestone pavement, part of the surviving medieval town. The arches built over doorways indicate that the buildings date from the 12th through the 14th century, when Assisi was booming, thriving on the north-south trade between northern Europe and Rome. The vaults you see that turn lanes into tunnels are reminders of medieval urban expansion—creating more living space (mostly 15th century). While the population grew, people wanted to live within the town's protective walls.

• *From the bottom of the stairs, head to the left and continue downhill. When you arrive at a street, turn left, going slightly uphill for a long block, then take the low road (right) at the Y, and head down Via Sermei. Continue down to the big church. Walk right, under the three massive buttresses, to Piazza Santa Chiara and the front of the church.*

❺ Basilica of St. Clare (Basilica di Santa Chiara)

Dedicated to the founder of the Order of the Poor Clares, this Umbrian Gothic church—worth ▲▲—is simple, in keeping with a life dedicated to contemplation. At age 18, Clare (1194-1253) became a nun after listening to Francis' teaching. She spent the rest of her days following a regimen of prayer, meditation, and simple manual labor. In her lifetime, the order was located in the humble Church of San Damiano, in the valley below, but after Clare's death, they needed a bigger building. The church was built in 1265, and the huge buttresses were added in the next century.

Cost and Hours: Free, daily 6:30-12:00 & 14:00-19:00, until 18:00 in winter, crypt opens Mon-Fri at 9:00, tel. 075-812-282.

Visiting the Basilica: The interior's fine frescoes were whitewashed in Baroque times. The battered remains of one on the left show how the fresco surface was hacked up so whitewash would stick. Imagine all the pristine frescoes hiding behind the whitewash (here and all over Europe).

On the right is the door to the Chapel of the Crucifix of San Damiano, with the simple wooden crucifix that changed Francis' life. In 1206, an emaciated, soul-searching, stark-raving Francis knelt before this crucifix of a living Christ (then located in the Church of San Damiano) and asked for guidance. According to legend, the crucifix spoke: "Go and rebuild my Church, which you can see has fallen into ruin." Francis followed the call.

Stairs lead from the nave down to the tomb of St. Clare. Her tomb—discovered in about 1850—is at the far right end of the neo-Gothic crypt (the image is fiberglass; her actual bones lie underneath). As you circulate with the crowd of pilgrims, notice the paintings on the walls depicting spiritual lessons from Clare's life and death. At the opposite end of the crypt are important relics: the saint's robes, hair (in a silver box), and an enormous tunic she made—along with relics of St. Francis (including a bloodstained stocking he wore after receiving the stigmata). The attached cloistered community of the Poor Clares has flourished for 700 years.

• *Leave the church and head for the viewpoint at the edge of the square for...*

Another Umbrian View: On the left is the convent of St. Clare (global headquarters of all the Poor Clares). Below you lies the olive grove of the Poor Clares, which has been there since the 13th century. In the distance is a grand Umbrian view. Across the valley to the far right (and over the Tiber River), the rival town Perugia sits on its own hill.

The lower town, called Santa Maria degli Angeli, grew up with the coming of the railway in the 19th century. In the haze, the church with the grayish-blue dome is the Basilica of Santa Maria degli Angeli (described later), the cradle of the Franciscan order.

• *From the church square, step out into Via Santa Chiara.*

❻ Arches and Artisans

Look left and right to find three old town gates, which illustrate how the city has grown (in concentric circles) since antiquity. First, look to the left, uphill on Via Santa Chiara, the high road. This first arch marks the site of the original Roman wall. In Roman days, this was the extent of Assisi. Now look right, beyond the church. This old gate over the road dates from 1265, as the town expanded during the boom years and the city wall was pushed outward. Farther on, you can just make out the crenellations of the third gate: Porta Nuova, built in 1316.

Walk uphill along Via Santa Chiara (which becomes Corso Mazzini) to the city's main square. As you pass under the arch you enter the city that Francis knew. The street is lined with interesting shops selling traditional embroidery, religious souvenirs, and gifty edibles. The shops on Corso Mazzini, on the stretch between the gate and Piazza del Comune, show off many local crafts.

You're walking up what was, in ancient times, the main drag into town. Ahead of you, the six fluted Corinthian columns of the Temple of Minerva marked the forum (today's Piazza del Comune). Within a few hundred yards of this square, on either side, were the medieval walls. Imagine the commotion of 5,000 people confined within these walls. No wonder St. Francis needed an escape for some peace and quiet.

• *Now, head over to the temple on the square.*

❼ Temple of Minerva and a Christian Church

The Romans went to great lengths to make this first-century BC Temple of Minerva a centerpiece of their city. Notice the columns that cut into the stairway. It was a tight fit here on the hilltop. The Church of Santa Maria sopra ("over") Minerva was added in the 9th century.

Pop inside the temple/church (free, daily 7:15-19:30, in winter closes at sunset and midday). Today's interior is 17th-century Baroque. Walk to the front. Flanking the altar to the back are the original Roman temple floor stones. You can even see the drains for the bloody sacrifices that took place here. Behind the statues of Peter and Paul, the original Roman embankment peeks through.

• *Across the square next to #11, step into the 16th-century frescoed vaults of the...*

Loggia of the Palazzo del Comune: Notice the Italian flair for fine design. Even this little loggia features decorative art (in the Grotesque style—named for the fanciful paintings of bizarre creatures found at Nero's Golden House in Rome). This scene was indisputably painted after 1492. How do we know? Because it features turkeys—first seen in Europe after Columbus returned from the Americas with his ship full of exotic souvenirs.

• *From the main square, hike left past the temple up the high road, Via San Paolo. After 150 yards (across from #24), a sign on the left directs you down a stepped lane to the...*

Basilica of St. Clare

Porta Nuova Gate

Temple of Minerva

Church of Santo Stefano

❽ Church of Santo Stefano (Chiesa di Santo Stefano)

Surrounded by cypress, fig, and walnut trees, this church—which was outside the town walls in the days of St. Francis—is a delightful bit of offbeat Assisi (free, daily 8:30-20:00, shorter hours off-season). Legend has it that Santo Stefano's bells miraculously rang on October 3, 1226, the day St. Francis died. Step inside. This is the typical rural Italian Romanesque church—no architect, just built by simple stonemasons who put together the most basic design. Hundreds of years later, it still stands.

• *The lane zigzags down to Via San Francesco. When you reach the narrow lane, go left (downhill). Then, emerging at the wider street, turn right and walk under the arch toward the Basilica of St. Francis.*

❾ Via San Francesco

This main drag leads from the town to the basilica holding the body of St. Francis. He was made a saint in 1228—the same year that the basilica's foundations were laid—and his body was moved here by 1230. Assisi was a big-time pilgrimage center, and this street was its booming hub. The arch marks the end of what was Assisi in St. Francis' day.

About 30 yards farther down (on the left), find the **fountain** where medieval pilgrims may have cooled themselves. The hospice next door was built in 1237 to house pilgrims. Notice the three surviving faces of its fresco: Jesus, Francis, and Clare.

Farther down on the left, across from #12A, is the **Oratorio dei Pellegrini,** dating from the 1450s. A brotherhood ran a hostel here for travelers passing through to pay homage to St. Francis. The chapel offers a richly frescoed 14th-century space designed to inspire pilgrims—perfect for any traveler to pause and contemplate the saint's message.

• *Continuing on, you'll reach Assisi's main sight, the Basilica of St. Francis. For the start of my self-guided tour, walk downhill to the basilica's lower courtyard.*

A friendly friar on Via San Francesco

Sights
In the Old Town
▲▲▲ BASILICA OF ST. FRANCIS

The Basilica of St. Francis (Basilica di San Francesco) is one of the artistic and religious highlights of Europe. It stands where, in 1226, St. Francis was buried. The basilica is frescoed from top to bottom with scenes by the leading artists of the day: Cimabue, Giotto, Simone Martini, and Pietro Lorenzetti. A 13th-century historian wrote, "No more exquisite monument to the Lord has been built."

The church has three parts: the upper basilica, the lower basilica, and the saint's tomb (below the lower basilica). We'll tour the complex from the bottom up. To get oriented, head down the ramp next to the grassy lawn and stand in the big plaza that stretches in front of the lower entrance. While empty today, centuries ago this main piazza was cluttered with pilgrim services and the medieval equivalent of souvenir shops. The information office is under the arcade (on the right as you face the church) and WCs are just behind that.

Cost and Hours: The complex is free to enter, with different hours for various parts. The **lower basilica** and **tomb** are open to tourists daily 6:00-17:30, Nov-March until 16:30—but in practice, the space remains open for worship (and discreet sightseers) more than an hour later. Within the lower basilica, the **reliquary chapel** opens at 9:00 but is often closed Sat-Sun (and occasionally at other times for religious services). The **upper basilica** is open daily 8:30-18:50, Nov-March until 18:00.

Dress Code: Modest dress is required to enter the church—no above-the-knee skirts or shorts and no sleeveless tops for men, women, or children.

Information: Tel. 075-819-0170, www.sanfrancescoassisi.org. The handy information office is in the arcade of the lower courtyard (Mon-Sat 9:00-18:00, closed Sun, shorter hours off-season).

Tours: Videoguides loaded with a one-hour tour are available at the information office (€6, €10/2 people).

🎧 Download my free Basilica of St. Francis **audio tour.**

Bookstore: The church bookshop is in the inner courtyard behind the upper and lower basilica.

Church Services: Consider joining the Franciscan brothers for Mass in *Italiano* (Mon-Sat at 7:15, 11:00, and 18:00—or 17:00 off-season; Sun at 7:30, 9:00, 10:30, 12:00, 17:00, and 18:30), or experience a Mass sung by the basilica choir many Sundays at 10:30. On Sundays in summer (Easter-Oct), there's an English Mass in the upper basilica at 9:00. Additional English and sung Masses don't follow a set schedule. Call the basilica to find out when English-speaking pilgrimage groups or choirs have reserved Masses, and attend with them (tel. 075-819-0170).

⊙ **Self-Guided Tour:** Enter through the grand doorway of the lower basilica. Just inside, decorating the top of the first arch, look up and see St. Francis, who greets you with a Latin inscription. Sounding a bit like John Wayne, he says the equivalent of, "Slow down and be joyful, pilgrim. You've reached the Hill of Paradise. And, if you're observant and thoughtful, this church will knock your spiritual socks off."

• *Start with the tomb. To get there, turn left into the nave. Midway down, follow the signs and go right, to the tomb downstairs.*

The Tomb: The saint's remains are above the altar in the stone box with the iron ties. In medieval times, pilgrims came to Assisi because St. Francis was buried here. Holy relics were the "ruby slippers" of medieval Europe. Relics gave you power—they answered your prayers and won your wars—and ultimately helped you get back to your eternal Kansas. Assisi made no bones about promoting the saint's relics but hid his tomb for obvious reasons of security. His body was buried secretly while the basilica was under construction, and over the next 600 years, the

Basilica of St. Francis and entrance to the lower basilica

exact location was forgotten. When the tomb was to be opened to the public in 1818, it took more than a month to find his actual remains.

The candles you see are the only real candles in the church (others are electric). Pilgrims pay a coin, pick up a candle, and place it in the small box on the side. The friars will light it later.

• *Climb back up to the lower nave.*

Lower Basilica: Appropriately Franciscan—subdued and Romanesque—this nave is frescoed with parallel scenes from the lives of Christ (right) and Francis (left), connected by a ceiling of stars. The Passion of Christ and the Compassion of Francis lead to the altar built over Francis' tomb. After the church was built and decorated, side chapels were erected to provide mausoleums for the rich families that patronized the work of the order. Unfortunately, in the process, huge arches were cut out of some frescoed scenes, but others survive.

In the fresco directly above the entry to the tomb, Christ is being taken down from the cross (just the bottom half of his body can be seen, on the left), and it looks like the story is over. Defeat. But in the opposite fresco (above the tomb's exit), we see Francis preaching to the birds, reminding the faithful that the message of the Gospel survives.

These stories directed the attention of the medieval pilgrim to the altar, where he could meet God through the sacraments. The church was thought of as a community of believers sailing toward God. The prayers coming out of the nave (*navis,* or ship) fill the triangular sections of the ceiling—called *vele,* or sails—with spiritual wind. With a priest for a navigator and the altar for a helm, faith propels the ship.

Walk around the altar, stand behind it (toes to the bottom step, facing the entrance), and look up. The three scenes above you represent the creed of the Franciscans: Directly above the tomb of St. Francis, to the right, **Obedience** (Francis appears twice, wearing a rope harness and kneeling in front of Lady Obedience);

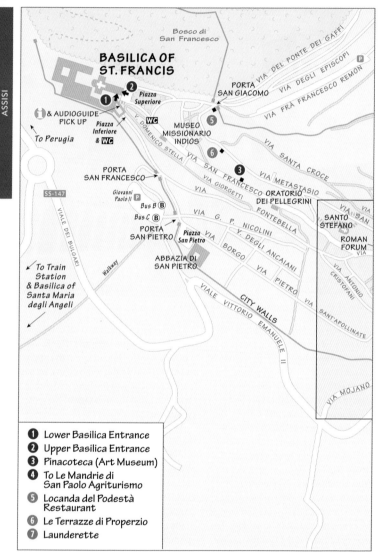

**BASILICA OF
ST. FRANCIS**

Bosco di
San Francesco

Piazza
Superiore

& AUDIOGUIDE
PICK UP

Piazza
Inferiore
& **WC**

To Perugia

PORTA
SAN FRANCESCO

Giovanni
Paolo II

Bus B **B**

Bus C **B**

PORTA
SAN PIETRO

Piazza
San Pietro

ABBAZIA DI
SAN PIETRO

To Train
Station
& Basilica of
Santa Maria
degli Angeli

Walkway

VIALE DEI BULGARI

SS-147

PORTA
SAN GIACOMO

VIA DEL PONTE DEI GAFFI

VIA DEGLI EPISCOPI

VIA FRA FRANCESCO REMON

WC

MUSEO
MISSIONARIO
INDIOS

V. DOMENICO STELLA

VIA SAN FRANCESCO

VIA GIORGETTI

VIA

VIA SANTA CROCE

VIA METASTASIO

ORATORIO
DEI PELLEGRINI

FONTEBELLA

VIA G. P. NICOLINI

V. DEGLI ANCAIANI

BORGO

VIA

VIA PIETRO

VIALE VITTORIO EMANUELE II

CITY WALLS

VIA SAN

SANTO
STEFANO

ROMAN
FORUM

VIA

VIA ANTONIO
CRISTOFANI

SANT APOLLINATE

VIA MOJANO

1 Lower Basilica Entrance
2 Upper Basilica Entrance
3 Pinacoteca (Art Museum)
4 To Le Mandrie di
San Paolo Agriturismo
5 Locanda del Podestà
Restaurant
6 Le Terrazze di Properzio
7 Launderette

to the left, **Chastity** (in her tower of purity held up by two angels); and straight ahead, **Poverty.**

St. Francis called money the "devil's dung." The jeweled belt of a rich person was all about material wealth. A bag of coins hung from it, as did a weapon to protect that wealth. The simple rope Franciscan monks use to tie their tunics

has three knots that symbolize—and serve as constant reminders of—their vows of obedience, chastity, and poverty.

Now turn around and put your heels to the altar and—bending back like a drum major—look up for a peek at the reward for a life of obedience, chastity, and poverty: **Francis on a heavenly throne** in a rich, golden robe. He traded a life of

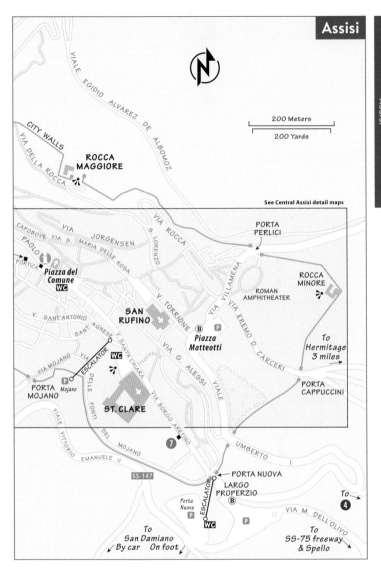

Map labels:

VIALE EGIDIO ALVAREZ DE ALBORNOZ

N

200 Meters
200 Yards

CITY WALLS

VIA DELLA ROCCA

ROCCA MAGGIORE

See Central Assisi detail maps

CAPOBOVE VIA S. MARIA DELLE ROSA

VIA JORGENSEN

S. LORENZO

VIA ROCCA

PORTA PERLICI

PAOLO

PORTICA

Piazza del Comune

WC

V. SANT'ANTONIO

SAN RUFINO

V. TORRIONE

VIA VILLAMENA

ROMAN AMPHITHEATER

ROCCA MINORE

VIA EREMO D. CARCERI

SANT'AGNESE

SANTA CHIARA

B   P

Piazza Matteotti

V. MOJANO

VIA MOJANO

ESCALATOR

WC

VIA DELLE FONTI

VIA G. ALESSI

VIALE

To Hermitage 3 miles

PORTA MOJANO

P   Mojano

ST. CLARE

VIA BORGO ARETINO

PORTA CAPPUCCINI

VIALE VITTORIO EMANUELE II

DEL MOJANO

7

UMBERTO   I

SS-147

ESCALATOR

PORTA NUOVA

LARGO PROPERZIO

B

To   4

Porta Nuova   P

WC   P

VIA M. DELL'OLIVO

To San Damiano
By car   On foot

To SS-75 freeway & Spello

---

earthly simplicity for glory in heaven.

• *Turn to the right and march to the corner, where steps lead down into the...*

Reliquary Chapel: This chapel is filled with fascinating relics. Step in and circle the room clockwise. You'll see the silver chalice and plate that Francis used for the bread and wine of the Eucharist (in a small, dark, windowed case set into

the wall, marked *Calice e Patena*); the tunic and slippers that Francis donned during his last days; a prayer (in a fancy silver stand) that St. Francis wrote; a papal document (1223) legitimizing the Franciscan order; and the tunic that was lovingly patched and stitched by followers of the five-foot, four-inch-tall St. Francis.

• *Return up the stairs, stepping into the...*

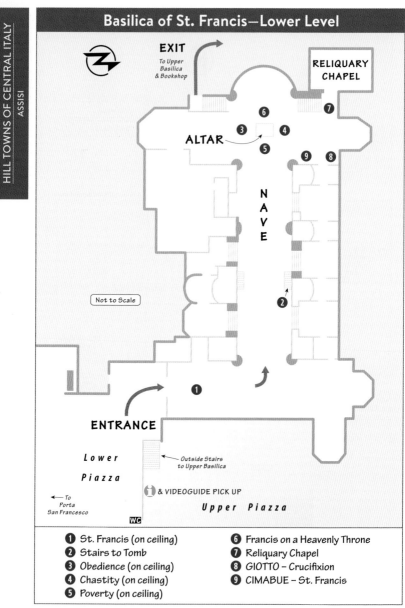

Basilica of St. Francis—Lower Level

EXIT
To Upper
Basilica
& Bookshop

RELIQUARY
CHAPEL

ALTAR

NAVE

Not to Scale

ENTRANCE

Lower

Piazza

← To
Porta
San Francesco

Outside Stairs
to Upper Basilica

& VIDEOGUIDE PICK UP

Upper Piazza

WC

1 St. Francis (on ceiling)
2 Stairs to Tomb
3 Obedience (on ceiling)
4 Chastity (on ceiling)
5 Poverty (on ceiling)

6 Francis on a Heavenly Throne
7 Reliquary Chapel
8 GIOTTO – Crucifixion
9 CIMABUE – St. Francis

Lower Basilica's Transept: The decoration of this church brought together the greatest Sienese (Lorenzetti and Simone Martini) and Florentine (Cimabue and Giotto) artists of the day.

Look around at the painted scenes. In 1300, this was radical art—believable homespun scenes, landscapes, trees, real people. Directly opposite the reliquary chapel, study **Giotto's painting of the**

Giotto, Crucifixion

Crucifixion, with the eight sparrow-like angels. For the first time, holy people are expressing emotion: One angel turns her head sadly at the sight of Jesus, and another scratches her hands down her cheeks, drawing blood. Mary (lower left), previously in control, has fainted in despair. The Franciscans, with their goal of bringing God to the people, found a natural partner in Europe's first naturalist (and therefore modern) painter, Giotto.

To grasp Giotto's artistic leap, compare his work with the painting to the right, by Cimabue. It's Gothic, without the 3-D architecture, natural backdrop, and slice-of-life reality of Giotto's work. **Cimabue's St. Francis** (far right) shows the saint with the stigmata—Christ's marks of the Crucifixion. Contemporaries described Francis as being short, with a graceful build, dark hair, and sparse beard. (This is considered the most accurate portrait of Francis—done according to the description of one who knew him.)

To the left, at eye level under the sparrow-like angels, are paintings of **saints** and their exquisite halos (by Simone Martini or his school). To the right of the door at the same level, see five of Francis' closest **followers**—clearly just simple folk.

• *Now, cross the transept to the other side of the altar and find the staircase going up. Immediately above the stairs is* **Lorenzetti's Francis Receiving the Stigmata.** *Make your way up the stairs to the...*

Courtyard: The courtyard overlooks the 15th-century cloister, the heart of this monastic complex. Pope Sixtus IV (of Sistine Chapel fame) had it built as a secure retreat for himself. Balanced and peaceful by design, the courtyard also functioned as a cistern to collect rainwater, supplying enough for 200 monks.

• *From the courtyard, climb the stairs (next to the bookshop) to the...*

Upper Basilica: Built later than its counterpart below, the brighter upper basilica is considered the first Gothic

Basilica of St. Francis, upper level

church in Italy (started in 1228). You've followed the intended pilgrims' route, entering the lower church and finishing here. Notice how the pulpit (embedded in the corner pillar) can be seen and heard from every spot in the packed church. The spirit of the order was to fill the church and preach.

The windows here are treasures from the 13th and 14th centuries. Those behind the altar are among the oldest and most precious in Italy. Imagine illiterate medieval peasants entranced by these windows, so full of meaning that they were nicknamed "Bibles of the Poor."

But for art lovers, the basilica's draw is that Giotto and his assistants practically wallpapered it circa 1297-1300. Or perhaps the job was subcontracted to other artists—scholars debate it. Whatever the case, the anatomy, architectural depth, and drama of these **frescoes** helped to kick off the Renaissance. The gallery of frescoes shows 28 scenes from the life of St. Francis. The events are a mix of documented history and folk legend.

• *Take a walk through Francis' life, via these glorious illustrations. As you face the altar in the front of the church, begin with the first fresco on the right. From here, you'll work clockwise (moving to the right) along the north wall. Follow along with the help of the numbered map key. The subtitles in the faded black strip below the frescoes describe each scene in clear Latin—and affirm my interpretation.*

❶ **A common man spreads his cape before Francis** in front of the Temple of Minerva on Piazza del Comune. Medieval pilgrims understood the deeper meaning of this scene: The "eye" of God (symbolized by the rose window in the Temple of Minerva) looks over the young Francis, a dandy "imprisoned" in his own selfishness (the Temple—with barred windows—was once a prison).

❷ **Francis offers his cape to a needy stranger.** Francis was always generous of spirit. He became more so after being captured in battle and held for a year as a prisoner of war.

❸ **Francis is visited by the Lord in a dream.** Unsure of his calling, Francis rode off to the Crusades. One night, he dreams of a palace filled with armor marked with crosses. Christ tells him to leave the army—to go home to wait for a nonmilitary assignment in a new kind of knighthood.

Basilica of St. Francis—Upper Level

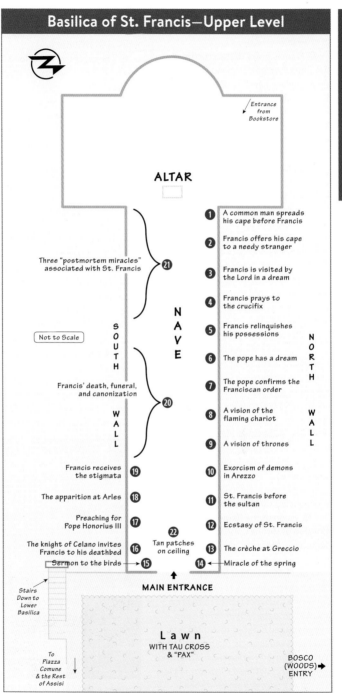

Entrance from Bookstore

ALTAR

N A V E

S O U T H

Not to Scale

W A L L

N O R T H

W A L L

Three "postmortem miracles" associated with St. Francis — **21**

Francis' death, funeral, and canonization — **20**

Francis receives the stigmata — **19**

The apparition at Arles — **18**

Preaching for Pope Honorius III — **17**

The knight of Celano invites Francis to his deathbed — **16**

Sermon to the birds → **15**

22 — Tan patches on ceiling

1 A common man spreads his cape before Francis

2 Francis offers his cape to a needy stranger

3 Francis is visited by the Lord in a dream

4 Francis prays to the crucifix

5 Francis relinquishes his possessions

6 The pope has a dream

7 The pope confirms the Franciscan order

8 A vision of the flaming chariot

9 A vision of thrones

10 Exorcism of demons in Arezzo

11 St. Francis before the sultan

12 Ecstasy of St. Francis

13 The crèche at Greccio

14 ← Miracle of the spring

MAIN ENTRANCE

Stairs Down to Lower Basilica

L a w n
WITH TAU CROSS & "PAX"

To Piazza Comune & the Rest of Assisi

BOSCO (WOODS) ENTRY →

He returned to Assisi and, though reviled as a coward, would end up fighting for spiritual wealth.

❹ Francis prays to the crucifix in the Church of San Damiano. The crucifix speaks, telling him: "Go and rebuild my Church, which you can see has fallen into ruin." Francis hurried home and sold his father's cloth to pay for God's work. His furious father dragged him before the bishop.

❺ Francis relinquishes his possessions. In front of the bishop and the whole town, Francis strips naked and gives his dad his clothes, credit cards, and a time-share on Capri. Francis raises his hand and says, "Until now, I called you father. From now on, my only father is my Father in Heaven." Notice the disbelief and concern on the bishop's advisors' faces; subtle expressions like these wouldn't have made it into other medieval frescoes of the day.

❻ The pope has a dream. Francis headed to Rome, seeking the pope's blessing on his fledgling movement. Initially rebuffing Francis, the pope then dreams of a simple, barefooted man propping up his teetering Church, and then...

❼ The pope confirms the Franciscan order, handing Francis and his gang the 1223 document now displayed in the reliquary chapel.

Francis' life was peppered with visions and miracles, shown in three panels in a row: **❽ vision of the flaming chariot, ❾ vision of thrones,** and **❿ exorcism of demons in Arezzo.**

• *Next see...*

⓫ St. Francis before the sultan. Francis' wandering ministry took him to Egypt during the Crusades (1219). He walked unarmed into the Muslim army camp. They captured him, but the sultan was impressed with Francis' manner and let him go, reportedly whispering, "I'd convert to your faith, but they'd kill us both." Here the sultan gestures from his throne.

⓬ Ecstasy of St. Francis. This oft-painted scene shows the mystic communing with Christ.

⓭ The crèche at Greccio. A creative teacher, Francis invents the tradition of manger scenes.

• *Around the corner, see the...*

⓮ Miracle of the spring. Shown here getting water out of a rock to quench a stranger's thirst, Francis felt closest to God when in the hills around Assisi, seeing the Creator in the creation.

• *Cross over to the far side of the entrance door.*

⓯ Sermon to the birds. In his best-known miracle, Francis is surrounded by birds as they listen to him teach. This image of well-fed birds is designed to remind pilgrims that, like the birds, God gave us life, plenty of food, feathers, wings, and a world to fly around in. Francis, patron saint of the environment and animals, taught his followers to see God in nature and to count their blessings.

• *Continue to the south wall for the rest of the panels.*

Despite the hierarchical society of his day, Francis was welcomed by all classes, shown in these three panels: **⓰ the knight of Celano invites Francis to his death-**

Giotto, St. Francis' Sermon to the Birds

bed; **🅐 preaching for Pope Honorius III,** who listens intently; and **🅑 the apparition at Arles,** which illustrates how Francis could be in two places at once (something only Jesus and saints can pull off). The proponents of Francis, who believed he was destined for sainthood, show him performing the necessary miracles.

🅒 Francis receives the stigmata. It's September 17, 1224, and Francis is fasting and praying on nearby Mount Alverna when a six-winged angel (called a seraph) appears with holy laser-like powers to burn in the marks of the Crucifixion, the stigmata. For the strength of his faith, Francis is given the marks of his master, the "battle scars of love." These five wounds suffered by Christ (nails in palms and feet, lance in side) marked Francis' body for the rest of his life.

The next panels deal with **🅓 Francis' death, funeral, and canonization.** The last panels show **🅔 miracles** associated with the saint after his death, proving that he's in heaven and bolstering his eligibility for sainthood.

Before leaving through the front entrance, look up at the ceiling and the walls near the rose window to see **🅕 large tan patches.** In 1997, a 5.5-magnitude quake hit Assisi, shattering the upper basilica's frescoes into 300,000 fragments. An aftershock then shook the ceiling frescoes down, killing two monks and two art scholars who were standing here. Later, the fragments were meticulously picked up and pieced back together.

▲ROMAN FORUM (FORO ROMANO)

For a look at Assisi's Roman roots, check out the Roman Forum from the town of "Asisum"—beneath today's Piazza del Comune. You'll enter through a nondescript doorway (just a few steps off the main square) into a room filled with carved stone capitals, tombstones, sarcophagi, and sculpture fragments. From there, you'll follow tunnels back under the square itself, seeing various land-

marks that once lined the streets of Asisum: a tribunal for speeches, a fountain, columns, the original Roman road, and much more, all displayed in situ. A helpful five-minute video (subtitled in English) helps resurrect the rubble.

Cost and Hours: €5, daily 10:00-18:00, June-Sept until 19:00, enter at Via Portica 2, tel. 075-815-5077.

▲ROCCA MAGGIORE

The "big fortress" offers a few restored medieval rooms, a good look at a 14th-century fortification, and a fine view of Assisi and the Umbrian countryside. If you're pinching your euros, skip it—the view is just as good from outside the castle.

Cost and Hours: €6, €9 combo-ticket includes Forum and Pinacoteca, daily June-Aug 9:00-20:00, Sept from 10:00, April-May and Oct 10:00-18:30, shorter hours off-season, last entry 45 minutes before closing, Via della Rocca, tel. 075-815-5077.

On the Outskirts

▲▲▲BASILICA OF SANTA MARIA DEGLI ANGELI (BASILICA OF ST. MARY OF THE ANGELS)

This huge basilica towers above the buildings of Assisi's lower town, Santa Maria degli Angeli. It marks the spot where Francis lived, worked, and died. It's a grandiose church built around a humble chapel—reflecting the monumental impact of this simple saint on his town and the world.

Cost and Hours: Free, Mon-Sat 6:15-12:40 & 14:30-19:30, Sun from 6:45, tel. 075-805-11.

Dress Code: Modest dress is required (no shorts or tank tops).

Visitor Services: A little TI is across the street from the souvenir stands, under the arches (generally Tue-Sun 10:00-12:30 & 15:30-18:00, closed Mon, tel. 075-804-4554). As you face the church, there are big pay WCs behind the bushes on your right.

Getting There: It's most practical to visit this sight on the way into or out of

Basilica of Santa Maria degli Angeli

town. From Assisi's train station, it's a five-minute walk (exit station left, after 50 yards take the underground pedestrian walkway—*sottopassaggio*—on your left, then walk straight ahead, passing several handy eateries). There's ample well-marked parking next to the train station, and some free (time-limited) spaces tucked behind the basilica.

From the old town, you can reach the basilica on the same Busitalia (line #C) that runs down to the train station (2/hour, stay on one more stop to reach the basilica; confirm with driver). Leaving the church, the stop is on your right, by the side of the building.

Visiting the Basilica: This grand church was built in the 16th century around the tiny but historic **Porziuncola Chapel** (now directly under the dome) after the chapel became too small to accommodate the many pilgrims wanting to pay homage to St. Francis. Some local monks had given Francis this *porziuncola,* or "small portion," after his conversion—a

little land with a fixer-upper chapel. Francis lived here after he founded the Franciscan order, and this was where he consecrated St. Clare as a Bride of Christ. What would humble Francis think of the huge church—Christianity's 10th largest—built over his tiny chapel?

Behind the Porziuncola Chapel on the right, find the **Cappella del Transito,** which marks the site of Francis' death on October 3, 1226. Only 44 years old, Francis died as he'd lived—simply, in a small hut located here.

From the right transept, follow *Roseto* signs to the **rose garden.** Francis, fighting a temptation that he never named, once threw himself onto the roses. As the story goes, the thorns immediately dropped off. Thornless roses have grown here ever since.

Exiting the passage, turn right to find the **Rose Chapel** (Cappella delle Rose), built over the place where Francis lived.

Porziuncola Museum: Continuing on, you'll pass this small museum featuring early depictions of St. Francis by 13th-century artists, a model of Assisi during Francis' lifetime, and religious art and objects from the basilica (€3, ask for English brochure, Thu-Tue 9:00-13:00 & 14:30-17:00, closed Wed, tel. 075-805-1419, www.porziuncola.org).

CHURCH OF SAN DAMIANO (CHIESA DI SAN DAMIANO)

Located on the slope steeply below the Basilica of St. Clare, this modest church and convent was where Francis received his call and where Clare spent her days as mother superior of the Poor Clares. Drivers can zip right there (watch for the turnoff on the road up to Piazza Matteotti), while walkers descend pleasantly from Assisi for 15 minutes through an olive grove.

Cost and Hours: Free, daily, convent open 10:00-12:00 & 14:00-18:00, until 16:30 in winter, church opens at 6:15; start walking from the Porta Nuova parking lot at the south end of Assisi and follow the signs; tel. 075-812-273, www.assisiofm.it.

▲HERMITAGE (EREMO DELLE CARCERI)

If you want to follow further in St. Francis' footsteps, take a trip up the rugged slopes of nearby Mount Subasio to the humble, peaceful hermitage where Francis and his followers retreated for solitude. Today the spot is marked by a 14th-century friary that's still occupied by Franciscan monks. You'll twist through the head-thumping doorframes and steep stairways of the medieval structure, the highlight of which is the tiny, dank cave where Francis would retire for private prayer. Emerging at the far side, near a stone bridge, you'll see a tree (held together with braces). This is said to be where Francis preached to the birds.

Cost and Hours: Free, daily 8:30-19:00, until 18:00 in winter, tel. 075-812-301.

Getting There: Drive, take a taxi, or hike—there is no public transportation. Drivers can follow signs out of Assisi toward Mount Subasio, then park on the switchback just above the entrance. For hikers starting from Assisi's Porta Cappuc-cino gate, it's a stiff 3-mile, 1.5-hour hike with an elevation gain of about 1,000 feet.

Sleeping
Hotels and Rooms

$$ Hotel Umbra, a peaceful villa in the middle of town, has 24 spacious, antique-furnished rooms with great view terraces. It's a bit old-fashioned, but well-run, well-maintained, friendly, and beautifully located (RS%, family rooms, air-con, elevator, garden, and view sun terrace, most rooms have views, closed Dec-March, just off Piazza del Comune under the arch at Via degli Archi 6, tel. 075-812-240, www.hotelumbra.it, info@hotel umbra.it, Laudenzi family).

$$ Hotel Ideale, on a ridge overlooking the valley, offers 13 bright and airy rooms (all with views and balconies), a tranquil garden setting, and free (but tight) private parking. As it's just off the main road into town, it's a handy pick for timid drivers (RS%, two apartments with kitchens available, air-con, Piazza Matteotti 1, tel. 075-813-570, www.hotelideale.it, info@ hotelideale.it, sisters Lara and Ilaria).

$ Hotel Belvedere, along the road into town from Porta Nuova, has 12 dated rooms—eight with sweeping views (breakfast extra, elevator, large communal view terrace, 2 blocks past Basilica of St. Clare at Via Borgo Aretino 13, tel. 075-812-460, www.assisihotelbelvedere.com, hotelbelvedereassisi@yahoo.it, thoughtful Enrico speaks fluent New Jerseyan).

$ Hotel Pallotta offers seven tight rooms and a beautiful top-floor lounge with rooftop views. The conscientious hosts provide guests with loads of extra niceties including a loaner Assisi guide-book, 24-hour laundry service, and free hot drinks and cake at teatime (RS%, a steep block up from Piazza del Comune at Via San Rufino 6, mobile 338-740-7574, www.pallottaassisi.it, pallotta@pallotta assisi.it; Stefano and Jenni).

$ Hotels on Via Porta Perlici: This steep and characteristic lane, stretching

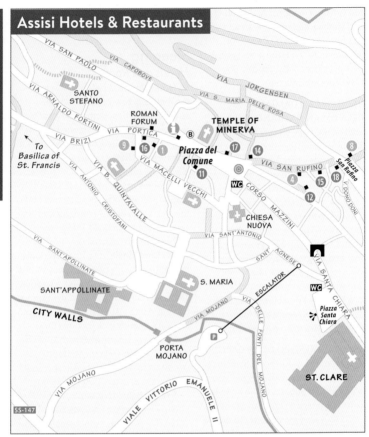

Assisi Hotels & Restaurants

uphill from the Church of San Rufino, is home to three inexpensive and straightforward hotels with the same owners (Carlo and Christian), nicely located at the top of town (all have air-con, elevators, and pay parking nearby). In order from the bottom to the top, there's **Hotel San Rufino** (11 rooms, breakfast extra, at #7a; tel. 075-812-803, www.hotel sanrufino.it, info@hotelsanrufino.it); **Hotel il Duomo** (14 modern rooms with somewhat less character, a bit pricier but breakfast is included, at #13, tel. 075-812-742, www.hotelilduomo.it); and **Hotel la Rocca** (at the peaceful top end of town, 32 rooms in a medieval shell, breakfast extra, sunny rooftop terrace, decent

restaurant upstairs, at #27, tel. 075-812-284, www.hotelarocca.it, info@hotela rocca.it).

$ Camere Carli has six spacious rooms with bizarre floor plans in a solid, minimalist place above an art gallery. The loft rooms are a great value for families (RS%, no breakfast, family rooms, lots of stairs and no elevator, free parking 150 yards away, just off Piazza San Rufino at Via Porta Perlici 1, tel. 075-812-490, mobile 339-531-1366, www. camerecarli.it, carliarte@live.it, pleasant Franco runs the pottery shop below and speaks limited English).

¢ Camere Annalisa Martini is a cheery home amid vines and roses in the town's medieval core. This is a good budget

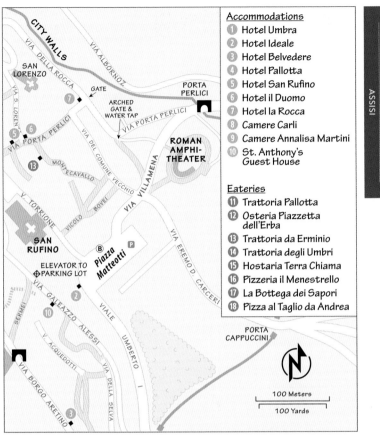

Accommodations
1. Hotel Umbra
2. Hotel Ideale
3. Hotel Belvedere
4. Hotel Pallotta
5. Hotel San Rufino
6. Hotel il Duomo
7. Hotel la Rocca
8. Camere Carli
9. Camere Annalisa Martini
10. St. Anthony's Guest House

Eateries
11. Trattoria Pallotta
12. Osteria Piazzetta dell'Erba
13. Trattoria da Erminio
14. Trattoria degli Umbri
15. Hostaria Terra Chiama
16. Pizzeria il Menestrello
17. La Bottega dei Sapori
18. Pizza al Taglio da Andrea

choice with six homey rooms with cheerful peeling wallpaper and flea market furniture (cash only, 3 rooms share 2 bathrooms, laundry service, no breakfast; one block from Piazza del Comune—go downhill toward the Basilica of St. Francis, turn left on Via San Gregorio to #6; tel. 075-813-536, cameremartini@libero.it). Mamma Rosignoli doesn't speak English, but Annalisa does.

Sweet Dreams in a Convent
$ St. Anthony's Guest House is where the Franciscan Sisters of the Atonement offer a very warm and tranquil welcome just above the Basilica of St. Clare. They have 35 beds in 19 sparkling-clean rooms, some with great views—request when you reserve (family rooms available, 2-night minimum, elevator, no air-con but fans, 23:00 curfew, closed mid-Nov-Feb, library, parking by donation; from the parking cashier in Piazza Matteotti, take the stairs down to the "tunnel romano," walk around the little park, then continue down on the elevator—it's just to the left at Via Galeazzo Alessi 10; tel. 075-812-542, atoneassisi@tiscali.it).

Agriturismo near Assisi
$$ Le Mandrie di San Paolo ("The Herd of St. Paul") is a meticulously restored 1,000-year-old stone house renting 13 rustic but comfortable rooms on a hill-

side high above the valley. They have an olive grove, lots of animals, a beautiful swimming pool, a sauna, a fine restaurant, and spectacular views over Assisi and the valleys of Umbria (apartments and family rooms, mobile 349-821-7867, tel. 075-806-4070, www.agriturismomandrie sanpaolo.it, mandrie10@gmail.com).

Eating
In the Town Center
$$$ Trattoria Pallotta is a local favorite with white tablecloths and a living-room ambience. It's run by a friendly and hard-working family—with Margarita in charge of the kitchen—and offers delicious, well-presented regional specialties, such as *piccione* (squab, a.k.a. pigeon) and *coniglio* (rabbit). Reservations are smart (Wed-Mon 12:00-14:30 & 19:00-21:30, closed Tue, a few steps off Piazza del Comune across from temple/church at Vicolo della Volta Pinta 2, tel. 075-815-5273, www.pallottaassisi.it).

$$$ Osteria Piazzetta dell'Erba is an inviting, trendy, youthful-feeling restaurant under medieval vaulted ceilings. Dishes are beautifully presented and inspired by local cuisine (Tue-Sun 12:30-14:30 & 19:30-22:30, closed Mon, seating indoors and on a peaceful square, reservations smart, just off the main piazza toward the Cathedral of San Rufino at Via S. Gabriele dell'Addolorata 15a, tel. 075-815-352, www.osterialapiazzetta.it, chef Matteo).

$$ Trattoria da Erminio has peaceful tables on a tiny square and indoor seating under a big, medieval (but air-conditioned) brick vault. Run by Federico and his family for three generations, it specializes in local meat cooked on an open-fire grill (Fri-Wed 12:00-14:30 & 19:00-21:00, closed Thu; from Piazza San Rufino, go a block up Via Porta Perlici and turn right to Via Montecavallo 19a; tel. 075-812-506).

$$ Trattoria degli Umbri has a few nice tables just above the fountain over-looking Assisi's main square (the main reason to come here). They serve delight-ful Umbrian dishes and quality wines by the glass (Fri-Wed 12:00-15:00 & 19:00-22:00, closed Thu, Piazza del Comune 40, tel. 075-812-455).

$$ Hostaria Terra Chiama is a bright, modern little place run by Diego and his family, who serve traditional Umbrian dishes with seasonal specials (daily, lunch from 12:30, dinner from 19:00, Via San Rufino 16, tel. 075-819-9051).

$ Pizzeria il Menestrello serves huge, inexpensive Umbrian-style pizzas (wood-fired, thin, and crisp) in an elegant medi-eval vaulted setting that makes your beer and pizza feel like something King Arthur would eat for dinner (daily 12:00-14:30 & 19:00-22:30, Via San Gregorio 1a, tel. 075-812-746).

Picnic on the Main Square
La Bottega dei Sapori is handy for assembling a picnic of Umbrian treats: good *porchetta* sandwiches and specialty items, including truffle paste and olive oil. Sandwich chef Saverio also makes a nice *taglieri misti* (meat and cheese plate). It can get pricey here—be sure you're clear on the cost when you order (daily 9:30-21:00, shorter hours off-season, Piazza del Comune 34, tel. 075-812-294, Fabrizio).

Pizza al Taglio da Andrea, facing the Church of San Rufino on Piazza San Rufino, has perhaps the best pizza-by-the-slice in town. Locals also like their *torta al testo,* the Umbrian flatbread sandwich (daily 8:00-21:30, Via San Rufino 26, tel. 075-815-325).

Above the Basilica of St. Francis
For locations, see the "Assisi" map, earlier.

$$ Locanda del Podestà, tucked inside a medieval gate just above the basilica, is a cozy spot with a traditional menu of tasty grilled Umbrian sausages, *gnocchi della locanda* (with gorgonzola and truf-fles), and tasty *scottadito* ("scorch your fingers") lamb chops (Thu-Tue 12:00-

14:30 & 19:00-21:30, closed Wed and Feb, 5-minute walk uphill along Via Cardinale Merry del Val from basilica, Via San Giacomo 6C—see map on page 271, tel. 075-816-553).

$$$ Le Terrazze di Properzio, just up the street from Podestà, is the place to go to dine outside with a big view on a lovely terrace. The traditional menu includes seasonal specials (daily 12:00-14:30 & 19:00-21:30, terrace closed in bad weather, Via Metastasio 9, tel. 075-816-868).

Transportation
Getting Around Assisi

Within the old town, minibuses #A and #B run every 20-40 minutes, linking the lower end (near the Basilica of St. Francis) with the middle (Piazza del Comune) and the top (Piazza Matteotti). Hop on a bus marked *Piazza Matteotti* if you're exhausted after your Basilica of St. Francis visit and need a sweat-free five-minute return to the top of the old town (catch the bus below the basilica, just outside the Porta San Francesco).

You can buy a bus ticket (good on any city bus) at a newsstand or tobacco shop for €1.30, or get a ticket from the driver for €2 (exact change only). After you've stamped your ticket on board, it's valid for 90 minutes.

Arriving and Departing
BY TRAIN

The train station is about two miles below Assisi, in the modern town of Santa Maria degli Angeli. There is no official baggage storage, but the bar on the main floor will hold bags for a small charge.

Gray-and-blue Busitalia city **buses** (line #C) connect the station with the hilltop old town (2/hour, daily 5:30-23:00, schedule posted at stop outside station, 15-minute ride; buy tickets at the newsstand inside the train station for €1.30, or on board the bus for €2—exact change only, validate ticket at yellow box as you board).

The bus makes three stops on the way into town: **Piazza Unità d'Italia** (near Porta San Pietro, below the Basilica of St. Francis), **Largo Properzio** (just outside Porta Nuova), and finally up top at **Piazza Matteotti.** The middle stop, Largo Properzio, is best for hotels in the center—just walk through the gateway and take the straight, mostly level street (past the Basilica of St. Clare) about 10 minutes to the main square.

Taxis from the train station to the old town cost about €15.

From Assisi by Train to: Rome (6/day direct, 2 hours), **Florence** (7/day direct, 2-3 hours), **Orvieto** (roughly hourly, 2-3 hours with transfer), **Siena** (10/day, about 4 hours, most involve 2 changes; bus is faster).

BY BUS

Most intercity buses arrive at the base of the old town, near the Basilica of St. Francis, although buses from Siena generally arrive at the stop next to the Basilica of Santa Maria degli Angeli, near the train station.

From Assisi by Bus to: FlixBus runs buses to **Siena** (2 hours, better than the long train ride, https://global.flixbus.com), departing from Santa Maria degli Angeli, below Assisi, or from Piazza Unità d'Italia, below the Basilica of St. Francis.

BY CAR

Drivers coming in for the day can follow the signs to several handy parking lots (*parcheggi*). Piazza Matteotti's wonderful underground parking garage is at the top of the town; another big lot, Parcheggio Giovanni Paolo II, is at the bottom end of town, 200 yards below the Basilica of St. Francis. At Parcheggio Porta Nuova, at the south end of town, an escalator delivers you to Porta Nuova near St. Clare's. For day-trippers, the best plan is to park at Piazza Matteotti, follow my self-guided town walk, tour the Basilica of St. Francis, and then either catch a bus back to Piazza Matteotti or simply wander back up through town to your car.

BY PLANE

Perugia/Assisi Airport is about 10 miles from Assisi (code: PEG, www.airport. umbria.it). Bus service between Assisi and the airport is so sporadic (www.umbria mobilita.it) that most travelers wind up taking a taxi (about €30).

ORVIETO

Just off the freeway and the main train line, Umbria's grand hill town entices those zipping between Florence and Rome. Orvieto sits majestically on its throne a thousand feet above the valley floor. The city's winding lanes are a delight to explore. With its stony cityscape, atmospheric covered alleys, and well-tended flowerpots, Orvieto is a photographer's dream.

Orvieto has three claims to fame: its cathedral (slathered in colorful art by Renaissance big shots), Classico wine, and ceramics. Drinking a shot of the local white wine in a ceramic cup as you gaze up at the cathedral lets you experience Orvieto's three C's all at once. A visit here comes with a wonderful bonus: close proximity to the unforgettable Civita di Bagnoregio (see page 300).

Orientation

Orvieto has two distinct parts: the old-town hilltop and the dreary modern town below (called Orvieto Scalo). Whether

Orvieto's Duomo towers above the rooftops.

Orvieto's outdoor market on Piazza del Popolo

coming by train or car, you first arrive in the nondescript lower part of town. From there you can drive or take the funicular to the medieval upper town, an atmospheric labyrinth of streets and squares where all the sightseeing action is.

Tourist Information

The well-organized TI is on the cathedral square at Piazza del Duomo 24 (Mon-Thu 8:15-13:50 & 16:00-19:00, Fri-Sun 9:00-19:00, tel. 0763-341-772, www.liveorvieto.com). The ticket office next door sells combo-tickets and books reservations for Orvieto Underground Tours (tel. 0763-340-688).

Combo-Tickets: Orvieto's sights are covered by a constantly changing array of combo-tickets.

The €20 **Carta Unica** combo-ticket covers virtually every sight recommended here (including the underground tours) and one round-trip on the bus and funicular—buy it on arrival at the lower funicular station (also available at the bar inside the train station). It's also sold at the ticket office next to the TI on Piazza del Duomo and at most covered sights.

For a quicker, more targeted visit, consider the €10 **La Piazza dei Musei** combo-ticket, which covers the cathedral, MoDo City Museum, Etruscan Museum, and National Archaeological Museum (sold at covered sights).

Helpful Hints

Bag Check: The bright and helpful **Info Point** just below and behind the train station offers pay WCs and have a secure bag check—the only one in town (daily 9:00-18:00).

*Rick's Tip: The city's biggest event is **Corpus Domini** (June 16 in 2022, June 8 in 2023), a medieval procession and festival that features flag tossing, concerts, and a giant chess game with costumed people as pieces.*

Laundry: The central **Lavagettone** self-service launderette is handy (daily 7:00-22:00, Via Garibaldi 30, www.lavagettone.it).

Orvieto

Accommodations
1. Grand Hotel Italia
2. Hotel Virgilio
3. Hotel Duomo
4. Hotel Corso
5. La Magnolia B&B
6. B&B Michelangeli
7. Affitacamere Valentina
8. Hotel Posta
9. Villa Mercede
10. Istituto S.S. Salvatore

Eateries
11. Trattoria la Palomba
12. L'Antica Trattoria dell'Orso
13. Trattoria la Pergola
14. Trattoria del Moro Aronne
15. Trattoria la Grotta
16. Trattoria da Carlo

Tours

LOCAL GUIDES

Guided walks of about 1.5 hours are the specialty of David Tordi and his colleagues (€12, 3/week, April-Oct only, schedule at www.teseotur.com/en/shared-tours; buy ticket from guide, meet at Underground Orvieto ticket office at Piazza Duomo 23).

They also offer cathedral tours. Another good choice is **Manuela del Turco** (€130/2.5-hour tour, mobile 333-221-9879, manueladel@virgilio.it).

TAXI EXCURSIONS TO CIVITA

For excursions to Civita, **Giuliotaxi,** run by English-speaking Giulio and his sister,

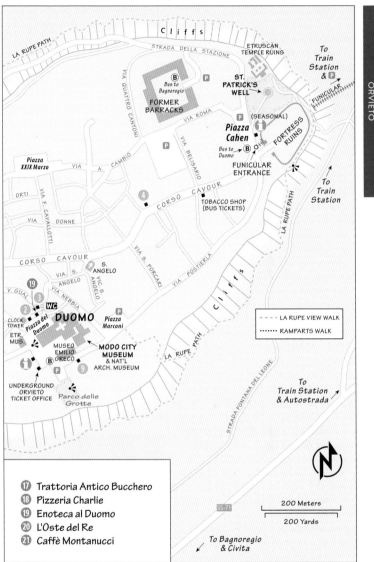

LA RUPE VIEW WALK

RAMPARTS WALK

17 Trattoria Antico Bucchero
18 Pizzeria Charlie
19 Enoteca al Duomo
20 L'Oste del Re
21 Caffè Montanucci

200 Meters

200 Yards

To Bagnoregio
& Civita

Maria Serena, offers two options from Orvieto for Rick Steves readers: to and from Civita with a one-hour wait (€100/car for up to 4 people, €130/minibus for up to 8), or a two-hour visit to Civita and Lake Bolsena (5 hours total, €160/car, €200/minibus, mobile 349-690-6547, giuliotaxi@libero.it). **Taxis** hang around the Orvieto train station ready to negotiate a little excursion to Civita, likely for a better price than Giuliotaxi.

Orvieto Walk

This quickie L-shaped self-guided walk takes you from the Duomo through Orvieto's historic center to the ramparts above the original Etruscan part of town, with vast Umbrian views. Each evening, this route is the scene of the local *passeggiata.*

Piazza del Duomo: Start at the cathedral and admire its attention-grabbing facade. As you face the cathedral, the papal palace (now hosting various museums) is to your right, and the TI and shuttle bus to the funicular are over your right shoulder. A nice gelato shop is around the church to the left.

• *Head left a few steps to the...*

Clock Tower and **Via del Duomo:** Also known as the Maurizio Tower, this was built in the 14th century and equipped with an early mechanized clock, originally used to keep track of workers' time while building the cathedral.

The tower marks the start of Via del Duomo, lined with shops selling ceramics. The tradition of fine ceramics in Orvieto goes way back—the clay from the banks of the nearby Tiber is ideal for pottery. During the Renaissance, the town's pottery was brightly painted and highly prized.

• *Stroll down Via del Duomo.*

At the second left, The Wizard of Oz (Il Mago di Oz) shop awaits a few steps down Via dei Magoni (at #3). This shop is a wondrous toy land created by eccentric Giuseppe Rosella. Have Giuseppe push a few buttons, and you're far from Kansas.

Back on Via del Duomo, about 30 yards before the next tower is Emilio's meat-and-cheese shop (on the right, at #11). Pop in for a fragrant reminder that wild boar is an Umbrian specialty—and they love their other meats and cheeses, too.

• *Follow Via del Duomo to Orvieto's main intersection, where it meets Corso Cavour. Here you'll find the tall, stark, 11th-century...*

Tower of the Moor (Torre del Moro): Eighty such towers, each the pride and security of a powerful noble family, once decorated the town's skyline. Today only a few survive. This tower marks the center of town, serves as a handy orientation tool, and is decorated by the coats of arms

of past governors. An elevator leaves you with 173 steps still to go to earn a commanding view (€2.80, daily March-Oct 10:00-19:00, May-Aug until 20:00, shorter hours off-season).

This crossroads divides the town into four quarters (notice the *Quartiere* signs on the corners). In the past, residents of the four districts competed in a lively equestrian competition, parading all over town during the annual Corpus Domini celebration. Historically, the four streets led from here to four landmarks: Piazza del Popolo with its market and fine palazzo, St. Patrick's Well, the Duomo, and the City Hall.

• *Side-trip a block farther ahead, behind the tower, for a look at the striking...*

Palazzo del Popolo: This is a textbook example of a fortified medieval public palace: a fortress designed to house the city's leadership and military (built atop an Etruscan temple), with a market at its base, fancy meeting rooms upstairs, and aristocratic living quarters on the top level. A lively market still bustles here Thursday and Saturday mornings, selling food, clothes, and household goods.

• *Return to the tower, turn right, and head down Corso Cavour past classic storefronts to...*

Via dei Magoni

Piazza della Repubblica and the **Church of Sant'Andrea:** The original vision—though it never came to fruition—was for the City Hall to have five arches flanking the central arch (marked by the flags today). The Church of Sant'Andrea (left of City Hall) sits atop the Etruscan forum that was likely the birthplace of Orvieto, centuries before Christ. Inside is an interesting architectural progression: 11th-century Romanesque (with few frescoes surviving), Gothic (the pointy vaults over the altar), and a Renaissance barrel vault in the apse (behind the altar)—all dimly lit by alabaster windows.

On this spot, visitors can track a layer cake of history: Under the Christian church lie the remains of the Etruscan city, destroyed by the Romans. The ruins, currently accessible only with a tour, give you a sense of the history stacked beneath your feet throughout Orvieto (€5/person, call archaeologist Francesco Pacelli to book, mobile 328-191-1316).

• *From Piazza della Repubblica, continue straight downhill on Via Filippeschi—passing a public WC on the left—for 100 yards until you reach a fork. (Check out the friendly, traditional Galleria del Pane **bakery** on the right.) Walk downhill along Via della Cava about 70 yards to a restaurant with a green sign (at #26, on the right) to find the...*

Well of the Quarry (Pozzo della Cava): While renovating their trattoria here in the oldest part of town, an Orvieto family discovered a vast underground network of Etruscan-era caves, wells, and tunnels. The excavation started in 1984 and continues to this day. A visit to the well makes for a fun subterranean wander (see more details in "Underground Orvieto," later).

• *Climb back up to the fork (with the bakery) and do a sharp U-turn left up Via Malabranca. After about 70 yards, at #22, you'll reach...*

Palazzo Filippeschi and Viewpoint: The friendly, noble Filippeschi family sometimes leaves their big green door open so visitors can peek into their classic medieval courtyard, with black travertine columns scavenged from nearby ancient Roman villas. Enjoy a moment of exquisite medieval tranquility.

Immediately across from the palazzo, belly up to the viewpoint overlooking a commotion of faded red-tile roofs. This tradition goes back to Etruscan times, when such tiles were molded on a seated tile-maker's thigh—wide to narrow. They nest so that water flows without leaking—handy for both rooftops and plumbing.

• *Continue on, downhill now, as the street crests.*

Soon you'll reach a square with the Church of Sant'Agostino, with some frescoes depicting the life of St. Augustine (covered by your MoDo City Museum ticket). At the far end of the square, to the right, little Via Volsinia leads to the Church of San Giovenale—the oldest in town, with 11th-century frescoes.

• *Here you'll pop out at a commanding...*

Rampart View: You're at the end of Orvieto. The fertility of the land (with its olives, vines, and fruit orchards) is clear. The manicured little forest of cypress trees straight ahead marks the Orvieto cemetery. In the distance to the right is Mount Cetona, guarding the south end of Tuscany.

Go 50 yards along the rampart to the left for the best view of the natural fortification that made this town the choice of Etruscans before the rise of ancient Rome, of stability-starved peasants after the fall of Rome, and of several popes in the high Middle Ages. From this perch you can understand why the city was never taken by force.

Sights

Duomo and Nearby

▲▲▲ORVIETO DUOMO (DUOMO DI ORVIETO)

Orvieto's cathedral has Italy's liveliest facade. This colorful, prickly Gothic facade, divided by four pillars, has been compared to a medieval altarpiece. The optical-illusion interior features some

Orvieto's Duomo

fine art, including Luca Signorelli's lavishly frescoed Chapel of San Brizio.

Cost and Hours: €4, €5 combo-ticket with MoDo City Museum; buy ticket in building to the right as you face the facade (also covered by various combo-tickets described under "Tourist Information," earlier); April-Sept Mon-Sat 9:30-19:00, Sun 13:00-17:30; closes one hour earlier March and Oct; shorter hours Nov-Feb; sometimes closes for religious services, www.opsm.it.

◗ **Self-Guided Tour:** After buying your ticket, return to the front of the church. Begin by viewing the…

Exterior Facade: Study this gleaming mass of mosaics, stained glass, and sculpture (c. 1300, by Lorenzo Maitani and others). Note how it's literally just a facade, ornamenting an otherwise very plain, mostly Romanesque exterior.

At the base of the cathedral, the four broad **marble pillars** carved with biblical scenes tell the history of the world in four acts, from left to right. The relief on the far left shows the ❶ **Creation** (see God creating Eve from Adam's rib, Cain clubbing Abel, the snake tempting Eve, and a dramatic expulsion). Next is the ❷ **Tree of Jesse** (Jesus' family tree—with Jesus on top, and Mary just below, flanked by Old Testament stories). Look up at the roaring lion of St. Mark and the grand facade filling your view—awe-inspiring as intended. In the third panel, with scenes from the ❸ **New Testament,** look for the unique manger scene and other events from the life of Christ. On the far right is the ❹ **Last Judgment;** see Christ judging on top, with a commotion of sarcophagi popping open and all hell breaking loose at the bottom. Each pillar is topped with a bronze symbol of one of the Evangelists (left to right): angel (Matthew), lion (Mark), eagle (John), and ox (Luke).

Stand back and survey the facade, looking for the central theme— the ascension of Mary. In the mosaic below the rose window, Mary is transported to heaven. In the uppermost mosaic, Mary is crowned.

• *Ticket in hand, step inside.*

Nave: The nave feels spacious and less cluttered than most Italian churches, even with statues of the apostles positioned at each column. Those statues have only recently returned to the cathedral: In 1897, the people decided they wanted to "un-Baroque" their church, and they moved the apostles out (for 122 years, they sat in another church in town). From the back of the nave you can appreciate the fine stained glass above the altar—it's original from the 14th century and some of the oldest in Italy.

The interior is warmly lit by **alabaster windows,** highlighting the black-and-white striped stonework. Why such a big and impressive church in such a little town? First of all, it's not as big as it looks. By lining the nave with striped columns and opening up the side aisles with arcaded chapels, the architect made the space seem longer and bigger than it is. Still, it's a big and rich cathedral—the seat of a bishop.

The cathedral's historic importance and wealth is thanks to a miracle that

Orvieto's Duomo

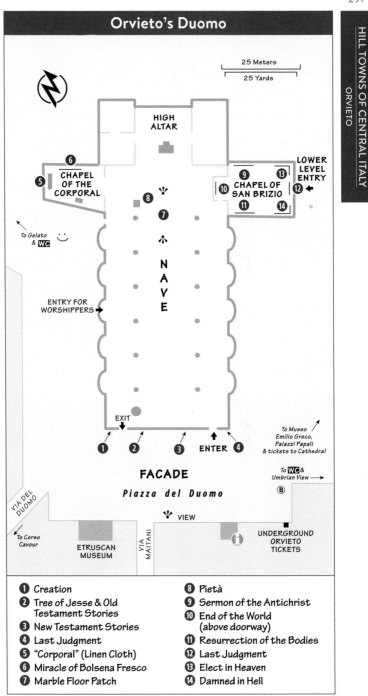

25 Meters
25 Yards

HIGH ALTAR

CHAPEL OF THE CORPORAL

CHAPEL OF SAN BRIZIO

LOWER LEVEL ENTRY

To Gelato & WC

ENTRY FOR WORSHIPPERS

NAVE

EXIT

ENTER

To Museo Emilio Greco, Palazzi Papali & tickets to Cathedral

FACADE

Piazza del Duomo

VIEW

VIA DEL DUOMO

To Corso Cavour

ETRUSCAN MUSEUM

VIA MAITANI

To WC & Umbrian View →

UNDERGROUND ORVIETO TICKETS

1 Creation
2 Tree of Jesse & Old Testament Stories
3 New Testament Stories
4 Last Judgment
5 "Corporal" (Linen Cloth)
6 Miracle of Bolsena Fresco
7 Marble Floor Patch
8 Pietà
9 Sermon of the Antichrist
10 End of the World (above doorway)
11 Resurrection of the Bodies
12 Last Judgment
13 Elect in Heaven
14 Damned in Hell

happened nearby in 1263. According to the story, a skeptical priest named Peter of Prague passed through the town of Bolsena (12 miles from Orvieto) while on a pilgrimage to Rome. He had doubts that the bread used in communion could really be transformed into the body of Christ. But during Mass, as he held the host aloft and blessed it, the bread began to bleed, running down his arms and dripping onto a linen cloth (a "corporal") on the altar. That miraculously bloodstained cloth is now kept here, in the Chapel of the Corporal.

• *We'll tour the church's interior. First, find the chapel in the north transept, left of the altar.*

Chapel of the Corporal: The ❺ **bloody cloth** from the miracle is displayed in the turquoise frame atop the chapel's altar. It was brought from Bolsena to Orvieto, where Pope Urban IV happened to be visiting. The amazed pope proclaimed a new holiday, Corpus Domini (Body of Christ), and the Orvieto cathedral was built (begun in 1290) to display the miraculous relic. The ❻ **miracle of Bolsena** (here set in 13th-century Orvieto) is depicted on the chapel's right wall.

• *Now walk to the middle front of the church, where (just before the two steps) you'll see a decorative area in the floor the size of a Turkish carpet.*

❼ **Marble Floor Patch:** This patch in the marble floor marks where the altar stood before the Counter-Reformation. It's a reminder that as the Roman Catholic Church countered the Reformation, it made reforms of its own. For instance, altars were moved back so that the congregation could sit closer to the spectacular frescoes and stained glass.

Enjoy the richness that surrounds you. Over the altar, the brilliant stained glass is the painstakingly restored 14th-century original. The fine organ, high on the left, has more than 5,000 pipes. Look high up in the right transept at the alabaster rose window.

• *A few steps to your left as you face the altar, near the first pillar, is a beautiful, white marble statue.*

❽ *Pietà:* The marble statue of Mary holding Jesus' just-crucified body was carved in 1579 by local artist Ippolito Scalza. Clearly inspired by Michelangelo's *Pietà,* this exceptional work, with four figures, was

Duomo interior looking toward the high altar

sculpted from one piece of marble.

• *Now face the main altar. To the right is Orvieto's one must-see artistic sight, the...*

Chapel of San Brizio: This chapel features Luca Signorelli's brilliantly lit frescoes of the *Day of Judgment* and *Life after Death* (painted 1499-1504). Although the frescoes refer to themes of resurrection and salvation, they also reflect the turbulent political and religious atmosphere of late 15th-century Italy.

The chapel is decorated in one big and cohesive story. Start with the panel on your left as you enter: In the ❾ **Sermon of the Antichrist** (left wall), a crowd gathers around a man preaching from a pedestal. It's the Antichrist, who comes posing as Jesus to mislead the faithful. This befuddled Antichrist forgets his lines midspeech, but the Devil is on hand to whisper what to say next. His words sow wickedness through the world, including executions (upper right). The worried woman in red and light blue (foreground, left of pedestal) gets money from a man for something she's not proud of. Many of the faces in the crowd are probably actual portraits.

Most likely, the Antichrist himself is a veiled reference to Savonarola (1452-1498), the charismatic Florentine monk who defied the pope, drove the Medici family from power, and riled the populace with apocalyptic sermons. Many Italians—including the painter Signorelli—viewed Savonarola as a tyrant and heretic, the Antichrist who was ushering in the Last Days.

In the bottom left is a self-portrait of the artist, **Luca Signorelli** (c. 1450-1523), well dressed in black with long golden hair. Signorelli, from nearby Cortona, was at the peak of his powers, and this chapel was his masterpiece. He looks out proudly as if to say, "I did all this in just a few years, on time and on budget," confirming his reputation as a speedy, businesslike painter. Next to him (also in black) is the artist Fra Angelico, who started the chapel decoration five decades earlier but completed only the Last Judgment over the window and the angels around it.

Around the arch opposite the windows are signs of the ❿ **end of the world:** eclipse, tsunami, falling stars, earthquakes,

Signorelli's Resurrection of the Bodies *in the Chapel of San Brizio*

violence in the streets, and a laser-wielding gray angel.

On the right wall (opposite the Antichrist) is the ⓫ **Resurrection of the Bodies.** Trumpeting angels blow a wake-up call, and the dead climb dreamily out of the earth to be clothed with new bodies, some of the randy skeletons finding time for flirting. On the same wall (below the action, at eye level) is a gripping pietà, also by Signorelli. The small black-and-white Deposition scene (behind Jesus' leg) seems inspired by ancient Greek scenes of a pre-Christian hero's death. In the confident spirit of the Renaissance, the artist incorporates a pagan scene to support a Christian story.

The altar wall (with the windows) features the ⓬ **Last Judgment.** To the left of the altar (and continuing around the corner, filling half the left wall) are the ⓭ **Elect in Heaven.** They spend eternity posing like bodybuilders while listening to celestial Muzak. To the right (and continuing around the corner on the right wall) are the ⓮ **Damned in Hell,** in the scariest mosh pit ever. Signorelli's ability to tell a story through human actions and gestures, rather than symbols, inspired his younger contemporary, Michelangelo.

In this chapel, Christian theology sits physically and figuratively upon a foundation of Classical logic. Below everything are Greek and Latin philosophers, plus Dante, struggling to reconcile Classical truth with Church doctrine. You can see the intellectual challenge on their faces as they ponder the puzzle of theology that survives the test of reason.

▲▲MODO CITY MUSEUM (MUSEO DELL'OPERA DEL DUOMO)

This museum is an ensemble of three different sights: the Emilio Greco collection (in Palazzo Soliano, next to the cathedral); the Cathedral Art Collections, immediately behind the cathedral (enter through the lower level of the right transept); and, at the far end of town, the Church of Sant'Agostino.

Cost and Hours: €4 MoDo ticket covers all MoDo sights, €5 combo-ticket includes the Duomo; also covered by La Piazza dei Musei and Carta Unica combo-tickets; April-Sept daily 9:30-19:00; March and Oct daily 10:00-18:00; Nov-Feb until 17:00 and closed Mon; Piazza Duomo, tel. 0763-343-592, www.opsm.it.

Visiting the MoDo City Museum Branches: You'll buy your ticket for the MoDo (and for the cathedral) inside Palazzo Soliano. It's the building marked *MUSEO,* to the right as you face the cathedral (this building also houses the Museo Emilio Greco).

Museo Emilio Greco: This fresh little collection shows off the work of Emilio Greco (1913-1995), a Sicilian artist who designed the modern doors of Orvieto's cathedral.

Cathedral Art Collections: Behind the Duomo, a complex of medieval palaces called the Palazzi Papali (Papal Palaces) shows off the city's best devotional art. This is the main attraction of the MoDo City Museum and well worth a visit.

The highlight is just inside the upstairs entrance: a marble Mary and Child who sit beneath a bronze canopy, attended by exquisite angels. This proto-Renaissance ensemble, dating from around 1300, once filled the niche in the center of the cathedral's facade (where a replica sits today). In several art-filled rooms on this floor you'll find, among other treasures, an exquisite *Madonna and Child* from 1322 by the Sienese great Simone Martini; saintly wooden statues and fine inlaid woodwork from the original Duomo choir; and Luca Signorelli's *Mary Magdalene* (1504).

Church of Sant'Agostino: At the west end of town, this church is skippable for most visitors, but those taking my "Orvieto Walk" can drop in with their MoDo ticket.

▲ETRUSCAN MUSEUM (MUSEO CLAUDIO FAINA E MUSEO CIVICO)

This 19th-century, Neoclassical nobleman's palace stands on the main square facing the cathedral. Its elegantly frescoed rooms hold an impressive Etruscan collection. The ground floor features the Museo Civico, with fragments of Etruscan sculpture. On the first floor is the Collezione Conti Faina, with Etruscan jewelry and an extensive array of Roman coins. The top floor features Etruscan and proto-Etruscan vases and bronzes from the ninth century BC, lots of votives found buried in nearby tombs, and fine views of the Duomo.

Cost and Hours: €4.50, also covered by La Piazza dei Musei and Carta Unica combo-tickets; April-Sept daily 9:30-18:00, Oct-March Tue-Sun 10:00-17:00, closed Mon Nov-Feb; tel. 0763-341-511, www.museofaina.it.

Underground Orvieto

These sights—showing off the remarkable bounty of history beneath your feet—are scattered around the old center.

▲▲▲ST. PATRICK'S WELL (POZZO DI SAN PATRIZIO)

Modern engineers are impressed by this deep well—175 feet deep and 45 feet wide—designed in the 16th century with a double-helix pattern. The two spiral stairways allow an efficient one-way traffic flow: intriguing now, but critical then. Imagine if donkeys and people, balancing jugs of water, had to go up and down the same stairway. At the bottom is a bridge that people could walk on to scoop up water. Touring the well requires hiking 248 (awkwardly spaced) steps down, then back up (allow 20-30 minutes round-trip).

The well was built because a pope got nervous. After Rome was sacked in 1527 by renegade troops of the Holy Roman Empire, the pope fled to Orvieto. He feared that even this little town (with no water source on top) would be besieged. He commissioned a well, which was started in 1527 and finished 10 years later. It was a huge project. Even today, when a local is faced with a difficult task, people say, "It's like digging St. Patrick's Well." (As it turns out, the town was never besieged.)

Cost and Hours: €5, interesting €2 audioguide, daily May-Aug 9:00-20:00, shorter hours off-season, ticket office immediately to your right as you exit the funicular, you'll walk a few minutes down the path to enter the well, Viale Sangallo, tel. 0763-343-768.

▲WELL OF THE QUARRY (POZZO DELLA CAVA)

A five-minute walk west of Piazza della Repubblica, this complex of Etruscan-era caves, wells, and tunnels leads down to a fat, cylindrical, beautifully carved 2,500-year-old well. Go ahead, spit (or drop a coin 100 feet down—coins are collected for a local charity). Your visit is capped with a review of local pottery-making.

Cost and Hours: €4, RS%—€2.50 with this book, Tue-Sun 9:00-20:00, closed Mon, enter through restaurant at Via della Cava 26, tel. 0763-342-373, www.pozzo dellacava.it.

ORVIETO UNDERGROUND TOURS (PARCO DELLE GROTTE)

Guides weave archaeological history into a good look at about 100 yards of Etruscan and medieval caves. You'll see the remains of an old olive press, an impressive 130-foot-deep Etruscan well shaft, a primitive cement quarry, and an extensive dovecote (pigeon coop) where the birds were reared for roasting (pigeon dishes are still featured on many Orvieto menus; look for—or avoid—*piccione*).

Cost and Hours: €7; one-hour English tours depart daily at 11:15, 12:30, 16:15, and 17:30; book in advance and confirm schedule for English guide, book tour and depart from ticket office facing the cathedral at Piazza Duomo 23, tel. 0763-340-688, www.orvietounderground.it.

Experiences
Hike Around the City on the Rupe

Orvieto's Rupe is a three-mile path (worth ▲) that completely circles the base of the cliff upon which the town sits.

With the help of the TI's *Anello della Rupe* map, you'll see there are five access points that take you down, down, down to the trail that hugs the cliff. The easy-to-follow path is wide and partially paved, though it has some steep, gravelly descents—wear good shoes and be prepared for a climb. I'd leave Orvieto at Piazza Marconi and walk left (counterclockwise) three-quarters of the way around the town (there's a fine view down onto the Etruscan Necropolis midway), and ride the escalator and elevator back up to the town from the big Campo della Fiera parking lot.

Romantic Rampart Stroll

Several fine little walks, worth ▲, wind around the edges of Orvieto's dramatic hilltop setting. My favorite is along the ramparts at the far west end of town—go after dark, when it's lamp-lit and romantic. Start at the Church of San Giovenale (near the end of my self-guided Orvieto Walk). With your back to the church, head left along the ramparts, with cypress-dotted Umbria to your right. Follow the brick pathway to the Church of San Giovanni, where you can reenter the old-town center.

Wine Tasting

Orvieto Classico wine is justly famous, and several inviting wineries sit just outside town on the scenic road (SP-12) between Orvieto and Civita (follow signs toward Canale and Bagnoregio).

For a tour of a historic winery with Etruscan cellars, make an appointment to visit **Tenuta Le Velette,** where English-speaking Corrado, Cecilia (cheh-CHEEL-yah), and Teresa Bottai offer a warm welcome and some of the best wines in the region (€8-25 for tour and tasting, price depends on wines, number of people, and food requested; Mon-Fri 8:30-12:00 & 14:00-17:00, Sat 8:30-12:00, closed Sun; must call ahead—no drop-ins; from Orvieto, look for their sign after completing a set of switchback turns on

SP-12; tel. 0763-29090, mobile 348-300-2002, www.levelette.it).

Custodi is another respected family-ly-run winery that produces Orvieto Classico, grappa, and olive oil on a modern 140-acre estate. Helpful Chiara and Laura Custodi speak English. Reserve ahead for a tour of their cantina, an explanation of the winemaking process, and a tasting (€13/person for wines only, €23/person with light lunch, daily 8:30-12:30 & 15:30-18:30 except closed Sun afternoon, Viale Venere S.N.C. Loc. Canale, just before the town of Canale; tel. 0763-29053, mobile 338-316-0405, www.cantinacustodi.com).

To the North: In the rolling hills just north of Orvieto, **Neri** rests amid postcard-pretty estate grounds, with an ancient manor house and grand views of Orvieto and the countryside. Their wines are simple and traditional (tour and tastings from €10, reservations preferred, daily 9:30-17:00; at Località Bardano 28—head north from Orvieto following signs to *Sferracavallo* and *Bardano;* tel. 0763-316-196, mobile 393-331-3844, www.neri-vini.it, visite@neri-vini.it, Enrico).

Sleeping

$$$ Grand Hotel Italia brings predictable modern amenities to this small town. The 46 overpriced rooms are well located in the heart of Orvieto, a block off the main drag and near the market square (RS%, air-con, elevator, off-site pay parking—reserve ahead, Via di Piazza del Popolo 13, tel. 0763-342-065, www.grandhotelitalia.it, hotelita@libero.it).

$$$ Hotel Virgilio is small, cheery, modern, and a bit pricey, renting 13 rooms facing the side of the cathedral (air-con, elevator, Piazza Duomo 5, tel. 0763-394-937, www.orvietohotelvirgilio.com, booking@orvietohotelvirgilio.com).

$$ Hotel Duomo is centrally located and modern, with splashy art in 17 rooms and a friendly welcome. It's tucked a few steps off the cathedral square (RS%, family rooms, air-con, elevator, private pay parking, sunny terrace, a block from the Duomo at Vicolo di Maurizio 7, tel. 0763-341-887, www.orvietohotelduomo. com, orvietohotelduomo@gmail.com; Gianni and Maura Massaccesi don't speak English, daughter Elisa and son-in-law Diego do). They also run a three-room B&B 50 yards from the hotel.

$$ Hotel Corso is friendly, with 18 frilly and flowery rooms—a few with balconies and views. Their sunlit little terrace is enjoyable, but the location—halfway between the center of town and the funicular—is less convenient than others (RS%, family rooms, ask for quieter room off street, air-con, elevator, reserved pay parking, Corso Cavour 339, tel. 0763-342-020, www.hotelcorso.net, info@hotel corso.net, Carla).

$ La Magnolia B&B has lots of fancy terra-cotta tiles, a couple of rooms with frescoed ceilings, terraces, and other welcoming touches. Its seven unique rooms—some of them mini-apartments with kitchens—are cheerfully decorated and on the town's main drag. The three units facing the busy street are air-conditioned and have double-paned windows (RS%, family rooms, no elevator, washing machine, Via del Duomo 29, tel. 0763-342-808, mobile 349-462-0733, www. bblamagnolia.it, info@bblamagnolia.it, Serena).

$ B&B Michelangeli offers two comfortable and well-appointed apartments hiding along a residential lane a few blocks from the tourist scene. It's run by eager-to-please Francesca, who speaks limited English but provides homey touches and free tea, coffee, and breakfast supplies (family rooms, fully equipped kitchen, washing machine, private pay parking, Via dei Saracinelli 20—ring bell labeled *M. Michelangeli*, tel. 0763-393-862, mobile 347-089-0349, www.bbmichelangeli.com).

$ Affittacamere Valentina rents six clean, airy, well-appointed rooms, all with big beds and antique furniture. It's in the heart of Orvieto, on a quiet street behind the palace on Piazza del Popolo (RS%, no breakfast, family rooms, air-con, pay parking, Via Vivaria 7, tel. 0763-341-607, mobile 393-970-5868, www.bandbvalen tina.com, camerevalentina@gmail.com). Welcoming Valentina also rents four apartments in the center.

$ Hotel Posta is a centrally located, long-ago-elegant palazzo renting 20 quirky, clean, cheap rooms with dark wood floors and vintage furniture (breakfast extra, elevator, Via Luca Signorelli 18, tel. 0763-341-909, www.hotelposta orvieto.it, hotelposta@orvietohotels.it, Alessia).

$ Villa Mercede, a good value and excellent location, is owned by a religious institution and offers 26 cheap, simple, mostly twin-bedded rooms, each with a big modern bathroom and many with glorious Umbrian views (elevator, free parking, a half-block from Duomo at Via Soliana 2, reception upstairs, tel. 0763-341-766, www.villamercede.it, info@villa mercede.it).

$ Istituto SS. Salvatore rents nine spotless twin rooms and five singles in their convent, which comes with a peaceful terrace and garden, great views, and a 24:00 curfew. Though the nuns don't speak English, they have mastered Google Translate, and will happily use it to answer your questions (cash only, no breakfast, elevator, Wi-Fi in common areas only, free parking, just off Piazza del Popolo at Via del Popolo 1, tel. 0763-342-910, istituto sansalvatore@tiscali.it).

Eating
Trattorias in the Center

$$$ Trattoria la Palomba features excellent game and truffle specialties in a wood-paneled dining room. Truffles are shaved right at your table—try the *umbricelli al tartufo*—homemade pasta with truffles (Thu-Tue 12:30-14:15 & 19:30-22:00, closed Wed and July, reservations smart, off Piazza della Repubblica at Via Cipriano Manente 16, tel. 0763-343-395).

$$$ L'Antica Trattoria dell'Orso offers well-prepared Umbrian cuisine paired with fine wines in a homey, bohemian-chic, peaceful atmosphere. Owner Stefano and chef Hania offer a good deal for my readers: €30 for two people—my vote for the best dining value in town (Wed-Mon 12:00-14:30 & 19:30-22:00, closed Tue and Feb, just off Piazza della Repubblica at Via della Misericordia 18, tel. 0763-341-642).

$$$ Trattoria la Pergola, run by chef Enrico and family, with a serious kitchen in back next to a covered patio, offers a small, accessible menu of seasonal Umbrian specialties (reservations smart, air-con, Thu-Tue 12:15-15:00 & 19:15-22:00, closed Wed, Via dei Magoni 9, tel. 0763-343-065).

$$ Trattoria del Moro Aronne is a long-established family bistro run by Cristian and his mother, Rolanda, who lovingly prepare homemade pasta and market-fresh Umbrian specialties. Consider their *nidi*—folds of fresh pasta enveloping warm, gooey pecorino cheese sweetened with honey. While not particularly atmospheric, this place is an excellent value (Wed-Mon 12:30-14:30 & 19:30-22:00, closed Tue, Via San Leonardo 7, tel. 0763-342-763).

$$ Trattoria la Grotta prides itself on serving only the freshest food and finest wine. The ambience is quiet, with courteous service. They've been at it for more than 50 years, and promise diners a free coffee, grappa, *limoncello,* or vin santo with this book (Wed-Mon opens at 12:00 for lunch and at 19:00 for dinner, closed Tue, Via Luca Signorelli 5, tel. 0763-341-348).

$$ Trattoria da Carlo, hiding on its own little *piazzetta* between Via Corso Cavour and Piazza del Popolo, is a cozy spot. Animated and opinionated Carlo likes big flavors and putting a modern twist on traditional dishes (daily 12:00-15:00 & 19:00-24:00, often closed Sun dinner, Vicolo del Popolo 1, tel. 0763-343-916).

$$ Trattoria Antico Bucchero, elegant under a big, white vault, makes for a nice memory with its delicious food—especially game and wild boar (daily 12:00-15:00 & 19:00-23:00 except closed Wed Nov-March, seating indoors and on a peaceful square in summer, air-con, a half-block south of Corso Cavour, between Torre del Moro and Piazza della Repubblica at Via de Cartari 4, tel. 0763-341-725; Piero and Silvana, plus sons Fabio and Pericle).

$$ Pizzeria Charlie is a local favorite. Its noisy dining room and stony courtyard are reminiscent of a beer hall, and popular with families and students for casual dinners of wood-fired gourmet pizzas. In a quiet courtyard guarded by a medieval tower, it's a block southwest of Piazza della Repubblica (Wed-Mon 19:00-23:00, closed Tue, Via Loggia dei Mercanti 14, tel. 0763-344-766).

$$$ Enoteca al Duomo is to the left of the Duomo and has pleasant outdoor seating with a cathedral view. They serve wines by the glass and a vast selection of Italian wines by the bottle, and a full menu of local dishes in a contemporary wine-bar atmosphere (daily 10:00-22:00, closed Feb, Piazza del Duomo 13, tel. 0763-344-607).

Fast and Cheap Eats

$ L'Oste del Re is a simple osteria on Corso Cavour, where Maria Grazia and Claudio offer pasta, bruschetta, enticing meat-and-cheese plates, and hearty, made-to-order sandwiches to eat in or take out (daily 11:00-15:30 & 19:00-22:00—but usually closed for dinner Nov-May, Corso Cavour 58, tel. 0763-343-846).

$ Caffè Montanucci, the dominant hangout on the main street—for good reason—lays out an appetizing display of pastas and main courses behind the counter. Choose one (or two—called a *bis*), find a seat in the modern interior or sunny courtyard, and they'll bring it out on a tray. They also have good *caffè*, simple sandwiches, and tasty sweets all day (daily 7:00-24:00, meals for lunch only—though they may be open for dinner in summer, Corso Cavour 21, tel. 0763-341-261).

Transportation
Arriving and Departing
BY TRAIN

The train station is at the foot of the hill the old town sits on. There's a convenient baggage-check service below and behind the station at the bus parking lot (see "Helpful Hints," earlier).

The easiest way to the top of town is by **funicular** (runs about every 10 minutes Mon-Sat 7:15-20:30, less frequent Sun from 8:00). Exiting the train station, it's across the square to the left (look for *Funicolare* sign). Tickets (€1.30) include both the funicular and the connecting bus to Piazza del Duomo. If you plan to get a Carta Unica combo-ticket (described earlier), buy it at the lower funicular station and use it to cover the funicular ride.

The funicular brings you up to Piazza Cahen, at the east end of the upper town, where a small **shuttle bus** waits to take you to Piazza del Duomo (runs roughly every 10-15 minutes, timed to arriving funiculars). Or you can just walk to the cathedral (head uphill on Corso Cavour;

after about 10 minutes, take a left at the clock tower onto Via del Duomo).

If you arrive outside the funicular's operating hours, you can reach the upper part of town by **taxi** (an exorbitant €15) or **bus** to Piazza della Repubblica (roughly 2/hour until midnight; buy €1.30 ticket at bar inside station).

From Orvieto by Train to: Rome (every 1-2 hours, 1-1.5 hours), **Florence** (6/day, 2.5 hours), **Siena** (12/day, 2.5 hours, change in Chiusi), **Assisi** (roughly hourly, 2-3 hours, 1 or 2 transfers), **Milan** (2/day direct, 5.5 hours).

Rick's Tip: *If you're thinking of driving to Rome,* **stash your car in Orvieto** *instead. You can easily park the car, safe and free, in the big lot below the Orvieto train station (for up to a week or more), and* **zip effortlessly into Rome by train** *(1-1.5 hours).*

BY CAR

The upper town of Orvieto is a maze of narrow lanes, several of which are marked with red "ZTL" circles (if you drive there, you could get an expensive ticket). Consider using one of two parking lots outside the old center. The free option is the big lot **below the train station** (turn right immediately after the autostrada underpass and follow *Tour Bus Parking* signs). From the parking lot, walk through the station and ride the funicular up the hill (see earlier). The other stress-free option is the pay **Campo della Fiera** garage, which is tucked behind Orvieto's hill (as you approach town, follow signs with a *P*, a little bullseye, and elevator and escalator icons—you'll curl around the left side of Orvieto's ridge, then switchback up to the lot).

Those comfortable driving in Italian cities (and careful to avoid ZTL zones) can enter Orvieto's old center by driving up Via Postierla and Via Roma, then take your pick of short-term, pay-and-display parking areas.

NEAR ORVIETO

Civita di Bagnoregio

Perched on a pinnacle in a grand canyon, just 30 minutes by car from Orvieto, the 2,500-year-old, traffic-free village of Civita di Bagnoregio is Italy's ultimate hill town. Civita's only connection to the world is a long pedestrian bridge to the neighboring town of Bagnoregio (ban-yoh-REH-joh). In the last decade, the old, self-sufficient Civita (chee-VEE-tah) died, as the last of its lifelong residents passed on. But Civita remains an amazing place to visit.

Despite being a "dead city," Civita can be very crowded with tourists—especially on the weekends and at lunchtime. The best way to enjoy Civita is early or late in the day, when you have the village to yourself.

Getting There

To reach Civita from Orvieto, you'll first head for the adjacent town of Bagnoregio. From there, it's a 30-minute walk or 5-minute drive to the base of Civita's pedestrian bridge, followed by a steep 10-minute hike up to the town's main square.

By Bus to Bagnoregio: Cotral buses connect Orvieto and Bagnoregio (about 10/day Mon-Sat only—no buses Sun or holidays, 45 minutes, €2.20 one-way if purchased in advance, €7 one-way from driver). For information, call 06-7205-7205 or 800-174-471 (press 7 for English), or see www.cotralspa.it (click "Orari," then fill in "Bagnoregio" and "Orvieto" in the trip planner—Italian only).

In Orvieto's upper town, buy your ticket at the tobacco shop at Corso Cavour 306, a block up from the funicular (daily 7:00-13:00 & 16:00-20:00. If you'll be returning to Orvieto by bus, buy two tickets now (they're harder to get in Bagnoregio).

Buses depart from a courtyard within the former military barracks, a short walk from the upper funicular station at the east end of Orvieto. It's tricky to find: With your back to the funicular, walk to the right, bear left (uphill) with the street, then go under

Civita di Bagnoregio

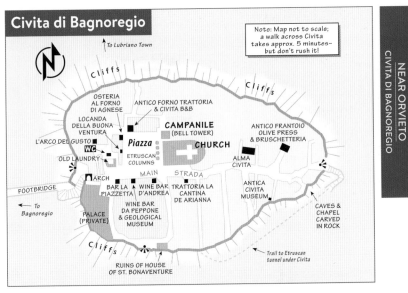

Civita di Bagnoregio

Note: Map not to scale;
a walk across Civita
takes approx. 5 minutes—
but don't rush it!

To Lubriano Town

N

Cliffs

Cliffs

OSTERIA
AL FORNO
DI AGNESE

ANTICO FORNO TRATTORIA
& CIVITA B&B

LOCANDA
DELLA BUONA
VENTURA

CAMPANILE
(BELL TOWER)

ANTICO FRANTOIO
OLIVE PRESS
& BRUSCHETTERIA

L'ARCO DEL GUSTO

Piazza

CHURCH

WC

ETRUSCAN
COLUMNS

OLD LAUNDRY

ALMA
CIVITA

ARCH

MAIN   STRADA

FOOTBRIDGE

BAR LA
PIAZZETTA

WINE BAR
D'ANDREA

TRATTORIA LA
CANTINA
DE ARIANNA

ANTICA
CIVITA
MUSEUM

To
Bagnoregio

WINE BAR
DA PEPPONE
& GEOLOGICAL
MUSEUM

PALACE
(PRIVATE)

CAVES &
CHAPEL
CARVED
IN ROCK

Cliffs

Trail to Etruscan
tunnel under Civita

RUINS OF HOUSE
OF ST. BONAVENTURE

the arch on the right marked *Caserma Piave*. Angle left through the parking lot to find the blue Cotral bus, under and behind the tall trees. (Note: Lots of buses marked *Umbria Mobilità* stop in front of the funicular, but Civita is served by a different bus company, Cotral.)

Buses departing the barracks stop five minutes later at Orvieto's train station—to catch the bus there, wait to the left of the funicular station (as you're facing it); schedule and tickets are available in the tobacco shop/bar in the train station.

Getting from Bagnoregio Bus Stop to Civita: You'll arrive in Bagnoregio at Piazzale Battaglini. To get to Civita's bridge, it's a 20- to 30-minute, mostly downhill **walk** through the middle of Bagnoregio (see map on page 303).

A **shuttle** runs to and from Civita from near the Piazzale Battaglini bus stop—look for white minibuses labeled *EPF Tours* (usually 1-2/hour, 5 minutes, 7:30-18:15 but few buses 13:15-15:00 or on Sun Oct-March, €1 round-trip, pay driver).

By Taxi or Shared Taxi to Civita: If you can share the cost with other travelers, a 30-minute taxi ride from Orvieto to Civita

is a reasonable value (basic rate: €50 one-way, €80 round-trip with an hour wait). Giuliotaxi can take groups by car or minibus (see "Taxi Excursions to Civita" on page 286).

By Car to Bagnoregio and Civita: Driving from Orvieto to Civita takes about 30 minutes. From the Orvieto exit off the autostrada, the shortest way to Civita is to turn left (below Orvieto), and then follow the signs to *Lubriano* and *Bagnoregio*.

A more winding and scenic route takes a few minutes longer: From the Orvieto exit on the autostrada, go right (toward *Orvieto*), then at the first big roundabout, follow signs to *Bolsena* (passing under hill-capping Orvieto on your right). Take the first left (direction: Bagnoregio), winding up past great Orvieto views and the recommended Tenuta Le Velette and Custodi wineries (reservations required).

Rick's Tip: *For a* **breathtaking view of Civita** *from the Lubriano/Bagnoregio road, follow signs to Lubriano. As the road curves sharply right as you enter town, pull into the little square by the yellow church (on the left).*

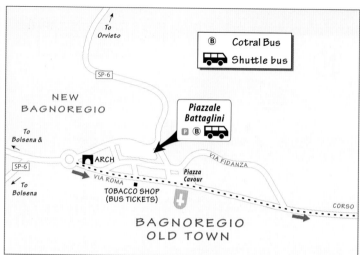

Once in Bagnoregio, drive right up the main street (follow yellow *Civita* signs). You'll begin to see pay-and-display parking lots and blue-painted lines along the side of the road (all charge €2/hour). The closest you can get is the lot at the end of the tree-lined stretch of road, right in front of the belvedere.

Orientation

Whether arriving at the Civita **footbridge** by foot, shuttle bus, or car, first head out to the belvedere at the very end of Bagnoregio for a superb viewpoint (through the little garden). From there, backtrack a few steps (the staircase next to the viewpoint is a dead end) and take the stairs down to the road leading to the bridge. Civita charges a €5 **admission fee** to enter the old town (waived for overnight guests). The revenue helps with its extensive maintenance expenses. Buy your ticket from the brown kiosk, just before the bridge, on the left, and then hike up the narrow bridge.

❸ Civita Walk

Civita was once connected to Bagnoregio, before the saddle between the separate towns eroded away. Photographs around

town show the old donkey path—the original bridge. It was bombed in World War II and replaced in 1966 with the footbridge that you're climbing today.

• *Entering the town, you'll pass through* **Porta Santa Maria,** *a 12th-century Romanesque arch. This stone passageway was cut by the Etruscans 2,500 years ago, when this town was a stop on an ancient trading route. Inside the archway, you enter a garden of stones. Stand in the little square—the town's antechamber—facing the Bar La Piazzetta. Over your right shoulder are the remains of a...*

Renaissance Palace: The wooden door and windows (above the door) lead only to thin air. They were part of the facade of one of five palaces that once graced Civita. Much of the palace fell into the valley, riding a chunk of the ever-eroding rock pinnacle. Today, the door leads to a remaining section of the palace—complete with Civita's first hot tub. It was once owned by the "Marchesa," a countess who married into Italy's biggest industrialist family.

• *A few steps uphill, farther into town (on your left, beyond the Bottega souvenir store), notice the two shed-like buildings.*

Old WC and Laundry (Vecchio Lavatoio): In the nearer building (covered

Bagnoregio & Civita Area

400 Meters

400 Yards

CIVITA DI BAGNOREGIO

CIVITA TICKET OFFICE

FOOTBRIDGE

BELVEDERE

MAZZINI

STREET PARKING

PARKING (BIGGEST)

STAIRS

DEAD-END STAIRS

with ivy), you'll see the town's old laundry, which dates from just after World War II, when water was finally piped into the town. Until a few years ago, this was a lively village gossip center. Now, locals park their mopeds here. Behind that a stone shed houses a poorly marked and less-than-pristine WC.

• *The main square is just a few steps farther along, but we'll take the scenic circular route to get there, detouring around to the right. Walk past the ruined palace and belly up to the...*

Canyon Viewpoint: Lean over the banister and listen to the sounds of the birds and the bees. Survey old family farms, noticing how evenly they're spaced. Historically, each one owned just enough land to stay in business. Turn left along the belvedere and walk a few steps to the site of the long-gone home of Civita's one famous son, St. Bonaventure, known as the "second founder of the Franciscans" (see the small plaque on the wall).

• *From here, a lane leads past delightful old homes and gardens, and then to...*

Civita's Main Square: The town church faces Civita's main piazza. Grab a stone seat along the biggest building fronting the square (or a drink at Pep-

pone's bar) and observe the scene. They say that in a big city you can see a lot, but in a small town like this you can feel a lot. When I first discovered Civita back in the 1970s and 1980s, the town's old folks would gather here every night. While Civita is humble today, imagine the town's former wealth, when mansions of the leading families faced this square, along with the former City Hall (opposite the church, to your left).

Here in the town square, you'll find **Bar Da Peppone** (open daily, local wines and microbrews, inviting fire in the winter) and two restaurants. There are wild donkey races on the first Sunday of June and the second Sunday of September.

Renaissance Palace facade in Civita

At Christmastime, a living Nativity scene is enacted in this square, and if you're visiting at the end of July or beginning of August, you could catch a play here. The pillars that stand like giants' bar stools are ancient Etruscan. The church marks the spot where an Etruscan temple, and then a Roman temple, once stood.

The humble **Geological Museum,** next to Peppone's, tells the story of how erosion is constantly shaping the surrounding "Badlands" valley, how landslides have shaped (and continue to threaten) Civita, and how the town plans to stabilize things (€3, June-Aug Tue-Sun 9:30-13:30 & 14:00-18:30, closed Mon, shorter hours and closed Mon-Thu off-season, www. museogeologicoedellefrane.it).

• *Now step inside…*

Civita's Church: A cathedral until 1699, the church houses records of about 60 bishops that date back to the seventh century (church open daily 10:00-13:00 & 15:00-17:00, often closed Feb). Inside you'll see Romanesque columns and arches with faint Renaissance frescoes peeking through Baroque-era whitewash. The central altar is built upon the relics of the Roman martyr St. Victoria, who once was the patron saint of the town. St. Marlonbrando served as a bishop here in the ninth century; an altar dedicated to him is on the right. The fine crucifix over this altar, carved out of pear wood in the 15th century, is from the school of Donatello. It's remarkably expressive and greatly venerated by locals.

On the left side, midway up the nave above an altar, is an intimate fresco known as *Madonna of the Earthquake,* given this name because—in the great shake of 1695—the whitewash fell off and revealed this tender fresco of Mary and her child.

• *From the square, you can follow the main street to the end of town.*

Main Street: Along the way, you'll pass a couple of little eateries, olive presses, gardens, a rustic town museum, and valley views. The rock below Civita is honeycombed with ancient tunnels, caverns (housing olive presses), cellars (for keeping wine at a constant temperature all year), and cisterns (for collecting rainwater, since there was no well in town). Many date from Etruscan times. If you choose to eat (or just grab a bruschetta snack), be sure to take advantage of the opportunity to poke around—every place has a historic cellar.

Civita's main square and church

• *Across the street from the recommended Antico Frantoio Bruschetteria and down a tiny lane, find...*

Antica Civita: This is the closest thing the town has to a history museum. The humble collection is the brainchild of Felice, an old farmer who has hung black-and-white photos, farm tools, olive presses, and local artifacts in a series of old caves. Climb down to the "warm blood machine" (another donkey-powered grinding wheel) and a viewpoint. You'll see rooms where a mill worker lived until the 1930s. Felice wants to give visitors a feeling for life in Civita when its traditional economy was strong (€1, daily 10:00-19:00, until 17:00 in winter, some English explanations, tel. 320-110-4279).

• *Another few steps along the main street take you to...*

The End of Civita: Here the road is literally cut out of the stone, with a dramatic view of the Badlands. To savor the scene, consider popping into the cute "Garden of Poets" (immediately on the left just outside town; donation requested, or you can purchase something at their little local-products shop). Then, look back up at the end of town and ponder the precarious future of Civita. There's a certain stillness here, far from the modern world and high above the valley.

Continue along the path a few steps toward the valley below, and you come to some shallow caves used as stables until a few years ago. The third cave, cut deeper into the rock, with a barred door, is the **Chapel of the Incarcerated** (Cappella del Carcere). In Etruscan times, the chapel—with a painted tile depicting the Madonna and child—may have been a tomb, and in medieval times, it was used as a jail.

An Etruscan tunnel just beyond the Chapel of the Incarcerated cuts completely through the hill (closed to the public). Tall enough for a woman with a jug on her head to pass through, it may have served as a shortcut to the river below. It was widened in the 1930s so that farmers could get between their scattered fields more easily. Later, it served as a refuge during WWII bombing raids.

• *Hike back into town, taking some time to explore the peaceful back lanes before returning to the modern world.*

Sleeping and Eating

Off-season, when Civita is deadly quiet—and cold—I'd side-trip in from Orvieto rather than spend the night. If you do sleep here, consider **$$ Alma Civita,** in a classic old stone house; they also have a recommended restaurant (www.alma-civita.com). **$$ Locanda della Buona Ventura** rents four overpriced rooms decorated in medieval rustic-chic (www.locandabuonaventura.com). **$ Civita B&B** has three little rooms (RS%, www.civitadibagnoregio.it).

$$ Osteria Al Forno di Agnese is a delightful spot for simple yet delicious meals (daily for lunch, June-Sept also dinner). **$$ Trattoria Antico Forno** serves up rustic dishes and homemade pasta (daily for lunch and sometimes dinner). **$$ Trattoria La Cantina de Arianna** is a family affair, with a busy open fire specializing in grilled meat and wonderful bruschetta (daily for lunch, Sat also dinner). **$ Antico Frantoio Bruschetteria** is a super-atmospheric spot for delicious bruschetta toasted over hot coals (daily until 18:00—sometimes later in summer). If you're looking for just a sandwich, try **$ L'Arco del Gusto** (daily).

Rome

Rome is magnificent and brutal at the same time. It's a showcase of Western civilization, with truly ancient sights and a modern vibrance. But with the wrong attitude, you'll be frustrated by the kind of chaos that only an Italian can understand. On my last visit, a cabbie struggling with the traffic said, *"Roma chaos."* I responded, *"Bella chaos."* He agreed.

Over 2,000 years ago the word "Rome" meant civilization itself. Today, Rome is Italy's political capital, the capital of Catholicism, and an open-air museum of its ancient empire, littered with evocative remains. As you peel through its fascinating and jumbled layers, you'll find Rome's buildings, cats, laundry, traffic, and 2.8 million people endlessly entertaining.

Despite Rome's rough edges, you'll fall in love with it...if you choose a comfortable hotel for a refuge, pace yourself, organize your sightseeing, and take sensible precautions to protect your valuables. Soon you'll be the one at the Trevi Fountain throwing in a coin to ensure your return.

ROME IN 3 DAYS

Rome wasn't built in a day, and you can't hope to see it all in three. Pace yourself; never regret a siesta. If you miss something, add it to your list of excuses to return.

Day 1: The Colosseum is the best place to begin your tour of ancient Rome (book an entry time in advance). Continue to the Arch of Constantine, the Roman Forum, then over Capitoline Hill (visiting the Capitoline Museums), and on to the Pantheon. Have dinner on the atmospheric Campo de' Fiori. Then take this book's Heart of Rome Walk to the Trevi Fountain and Spanish Steps.

Day 2: Tour the Vatican Museums, featuring the divine Sistine Chapel (closed Sun, except first Sun of month; reserve a museum entry time in advance), then see St. Peter's Basilica and climb its dome. With any remaining stamina, choose among these sights (or save for tomorrow afternoon): the National Museum of Rome (ancient sculpture), St. Peter-in-Chains (Michelangelo's *Moses*), and Castel Sant'Angelo (castle-museum).

Day 3: See the Borghese Gallery (reservations required, closed Mon; stroll through the park afterwards). Zip up to the top of the nearby Victor Emmanuel Monument for a grand view of the Eternal City.

Evening options: Do as the Romans do—join the Dolce Vita Stroll along the Via del Corso. Explore the Monti neighborhood; linger over dinner, or stop by an enoteca (wine bar) for a drink. Enjoy a classical concert or jazz. Or take in a sound-and-light show at the Imperial Forums.

With extra time: Take a day trip to the hill town of Orvieto or visit Naples and Pompeii in a blitz day trip: Take the early Rome-Naples express train, connect by

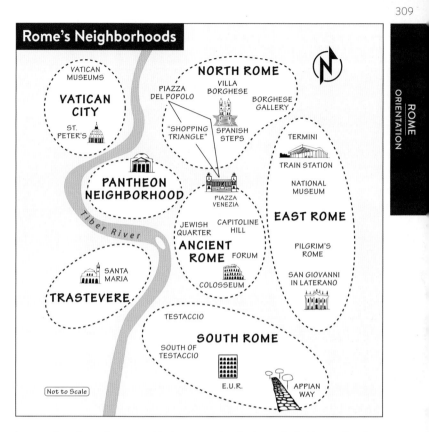

Rome's Neighborhoods

VATICAN MUSEUMS

VATICAN CITY

ST. PETER'S

NORTH ROME

PIAZZA DEL POPOLO

VILLA BORGHESE

BORGHESE GALLERY

"SHOPPING TRIANGLE"

SPANISH STEPS

TERMINI

TRAIN STATION

NATIONAL MUSEUM

PANTHEON NEIGHBORHOOD

PIAZZA VENEZIA

EAST ROME

JEWISH QUARTER

CAPITOLINE HILL

ANCIENT ROME FORUM

PILGRIM'S ROME

SAN GIOVANNI IN LATERANO

COLOSSEUM

Tiber River

SANTA MARIA

TRASTEVERE

TESTACCIO

SOUTH ROME

SOUTH OF TESTACCIO

E.U.R.

APPIAN WAY

Not to Scale

---

bus or train to Pompeii, return to Naples for its archaeological museum, and you'll be back in Rome around bedtime (but avoid this trip on Tue, when Naples' archaeological museum is closed). See those chapters for details.

Rick's Tip: *The* **siesta is the key to survival** *in summertime Rome. Lie down and contemplate the extraordinary power of gravity in the Eternal City. Drink lots of cold, refreshing water from Rome's many drinking fountains.*

ORIENTATION

Sprawling Rome actually feels manageable once you get to know it. The old core, with most of the tourist sights, sits inside a diamond formed by Termini train station (in the east), the Vatican (west), Villa Borghese Gardens (north), and the Colosseum (south). The Tiber River snakes through the diamond from north to south. At the center of the diamond is Piazza Venezia, a busy square and traffic hub. Think of Rome as a collection of neighborhoods, huddling around major landmarks.

Ancient Rome: In ancient times, this was home to the grandest buildings of a city of a million people. Today, the best of the classical sights stand in a line from the Colosseum to the ruined Roman Forum over Capitoline Hill to the Pantheon. Just north of this area, between Via Nazionale and Via Cavour, is the trendy Monti district.

Pantheon Neighborhood: The Pantheon anchors the neighborhood I like to call the "Heart of Rome," which includes

ROME AT A GLANCE

▲▲▲**Colosseum** Huge stadium where gladiators fought. **Hours:** Daily 9:00 until one hour before sunset: April-Aug until 19:15, Sept until 19:00, Oct until 18:30, off-season closes as early as 16:30. See page 326.

▲▲▲**Roman Forum** Ancient Rome's main square, with ruins and grand arches. **Hours:** Same as Colosseum. See page 331.

▲▲▲**Capitoline Museums** Ancient statues, mosaics, and expansive view of Forum. **Hours:** Daily 9:30-19:30. See page 339.

▲▲▲**Pantheon** The defining domed temple. **Hours:** Daily 9:00-19:00, closed for Mass Sat at 17:00 and Sun at 10:30. See page 343.

▲▲▲**St. Peter's Basilica** Most impressive church on earth, with Michelangelo's *Pietà* and dome. **Hours:** Church—daily April-Sept 7:00-19:00, Oct-March 7:00-18:30, often closed Wed mornings; dome—daily April-Sept 7:30-19:00, Oct-March 7:30-18:00. See page 346.

▲▲▲**Vatican Museums** Four miles of the finest art of Western civilization, culminating in Michelangelo's glorious Sistine Chapel. **Hours:** Mon-Sat 9:00-18:00. Closed on religious holidays and Sun, except last Sun of the month (open 9:00-14:00). Open Fri nights mid-April-Oct by online reservation only. See page 352.

▲▲▲**Borghese Gallery** Bernini sculptures and paintings by Caravaggio, Raphael, and Titian in a Baroque palazzo. Reservations mandatory. **Hours:** Tue-Sun 9:00-19:00, Thu until 21:00, closed Mon. See page 359.

▲▲▲**National Museum of Rome** Greatest collection of Roman sculpture anywhere. **Hours:** Tue-Sun 9:00-19:45, closed Mon. See page 362.

▲▲▲**Heart of Rome Walk** A stroll lacing the narrow lanes, intimate piazzas, fanciful fountains, and lively scenes of Rome's most colorful neighborhood. **Hours:** Anytime, but best in evening. See page 318.

▲▲**Palatine Hill** Ruins of emperors' palaces, Circus Maximus view, and museum. **Hours:** Same as Colosseum. See page 338.

▲▲**Trajan's Column, Market, and Forum** Tall column with narrative relief, forum ruins, and museum with entry to Trajan's Market. **Hours:** Forum and column always viewable; museum open daily 9:30-19:30. See page 342.

▲▲**Museo dell'Ara Pacis** Shrine marking the beginning of Rome's Golden Age. **Hours:** Daily 9:30-19:30. See page 362.

▲▲**Dolce Vita Stroll** Evening *passeggiata* where Romans strut their stuff. **Hours:** Roughly Mon-Sat 17:00-19:00 and Sun afternoons. See page 316.

▲**Arch of Constantine** Honors the emperor who legalized Christianity. **Hours:** Always viewable. See page 330.

▲**St. Peter-in-Chains** Church with Michelangelo's *Moses*. **Hours:** Daily 8:00-12:30 & 15:00-19:00, Oct-March until 18:00. See page 342.

▲**Piazza del Campidoglio** Square atop Capitoline Hill, designed by Michelangelo, with a museum, grand stairway, and Forum overlooks. See page 339.

▲**Victor Emmanuel Monument** Gigantic edifice celebrating Italian unity, with Rome from the Sky elevator ride up to 360-degree city view. **Hours:** Monument open daily 9:30-18:45 (shorter in winter), elevator until 19:00. See page 341.

▲**Trevi Fountain** Baroque hot spot into which tourists throw coins to ensure a return trip to Rome. **Hours:** Always flowing. See page 345.

▲**Castel Sant'Angelo** Hadrian's Tomb turned castle, prison, papal refuge, now museum. **Hours:** Daily 9:00-19:30. See page 359.

▲**Baths of Diocletian/Basilica S. Maria degli Angeli** Once ancient Rome's immense public baths, now a Michelangelo church. **Hours:** Daily 7:30-18:30, closes later May-Sept and Sun year-round. See page 364.

the atmospheric squares of Campo de' Fiori and Piazza Navona, the dramatic Trevi Fountain, and several historic churches.

Vatican City: Located west of the Tiber River, this is a compact world of its own, with two great, massive sights: St. Peter's Basilica and the Vatican Museums.

North Rome: This modern, classy area hosts the people-friendly Spanish Steps, an elegant grid of trendy shopping streets (between the main drag—Via del Corso—and the Spanish Steps), and the Borghese Gallery set within the fun-on-a-sunny-day Villa Borghese Gardens.

East Rome: This neighborhood around Termini Station boasts the stunning National Museum of Rome and includes Piazza della Repubblica, many recommended hotels, and convenient public-transportation connections.

Tourist Information

Rome has about a dozen small city-run tourist information offices scattered around town. The largest TIs are at Fiumicino Airport (Terminal 3, daily 8:00-21:00) and Termini train station (daily 8:00-18:45, exit by track 24 and walk 100 yards down along Via Giovanni Giolitti). Little kiosks (most open daily 9:30-19:00; can close seasonally) are between the Trevi Fountain and Pantheon (at the corner of Via del Corso and Via Minghetti), and in Trastevere (at Piazza Sidney Sonnino).

The TI's website is www.turismoroma.it,

but a better site for practical information is www.060608.it. That's also the number for Rome's **call center**—the best source of up-to-date tourist information, with English speakers on staff (answered daily 9:00-19:00, tel. 06-0608, press 2 for English).

Helpful Hints

Sightseeing Tips: Despite the crowds in Rome, you'll only find lines a problem at **St. Peter's Basilica** (go early or late to minimize), **Vatican Museums** (avoid by booking in advance online), and the **Colosseum** and **Roman Forum** (book online and go early morning or late afternoon). The **Borghese Gallery** requires a ticket with timed entry purchased in advance.

The **Roma Pass** is only worthwhile if you want a public transit pass (covers 2 or 3 days of transit, entry to 1 or 2 sights, and discounts at others—but you'll still need reservations at the Colosseum and Borghese Gallery).

Theft Alert: While violent crime is rare in the city center, petty theft is rampant. Always use your money belt. If you carry a backpack, never leave it unattended and try to keep it attached to your body in some way (even when you're seated for a meal).

Be particularly on guard in crowds, especially when boarding and leaving buses and subways. Thieves are particularly thick on the Metro and the crowded, made-for-tourists buses #40 and #64.

To report lost or stolen items, file a

Spiral staircase at the Vatican Museums

Backstreet Rome

police report (at Termini Station, with *polizia* at track 11 or with Carabinieri at track 20; offices are also at Piazza Venezia and at the corner of Via Nazionale and Via Genova).

Pedestrian Safety: Your main safety concern in Rome is crossing streets without incident. Use caution. Some streets have pedestrian-crossing signals (red means stop—or jaywalk carefully; green means go...also carefully; and yellow means go...extremely carefully, as cars may be whipping around the corner). But just as often, multilane streets have crosswalks with no signals at all.

Follow locals like a shadow when you cross a street. When you do cross alone, find a gap in the traffic and walk with confidence while making eye contact with approaching drivers—they won't hit you if they can tell where you intend to go.

Laundry: Coin launderettes are common in Rome. Your hotelier can direct you to the closest one. The **Wash & Dry Lavarapido** chain has a branch near Piazza Barberini (Mon-Sat 9:00-21:00, closed Sun, Via degli Avignonesi 17—see map on page 372, tel. 06-4201-3158).

Rick's Tip: Can't get reservations to the main sights (or just can't stand crowds)? *Rome has many magnificent attractions without the hordes. Try the Palatine Hill, National Museum of Rome, Museo dell'Ara Pacis, or Capitoline Museums. Even in peak season, you'll often be all alone with the wonders of ancient world, wondering, "Where is everyone?"*

Tours
LOCAL GUIDES
I've worked with and enjoyed each of these licensed independent local guides. Prices (roughly €60/hour) flex with the day, season, and demand: **Carla Zaia** (carlaromeguide@gmail.com); **Cristina Giannicchi** (mobile 338-111-4573, www.crisromanguide.com); **Sara Magister**

(a.magister@iol.it); **Giovanna Terzulli** (gioterzulli@gmail.com); **Alessandra Mazzoccoli** (www.romeandabout.com); and **Massimiliano Canneto** (massicanneto@gmail.com). **Francesca Caruso,** who works almost full-time with my tours when in Rome, has contributed generously to this book (www.francescacaruso.com)—if she's busy, she'll recommend one of her colleagues.

WALKING TOURS
Three-hour guided walks generally cost €25-30 per person. These companies are each well-established, creative, and competitive. Each offers a 10 percent discount with most online bookings for Rick Steves travelers: **Walks of Italy** (RS%—enter "RICKWALKSROME," US tel. 888/683-8670, tel. 06-9480-4888, www.walksofitaly.com), **Europe Odyssey** (RS%, tel. 06-8854-2416, www.europeodyssey.com), **Through Eternity** (RS%—look for "Group Tours Rome" and enter "RICKSTEVES," tel. 06-700-9336, www.througheternity.com), and **The Roman Guy** (RS%—enter "rick steves," theromanguy.com, Sean Finelli).

HOP-ON, HOP-OFF BUS TOURS
Several different agencies run hop-on, hop-off, double-decker bus tours around Rome. These tours make the same 90-minute, eight-stop loop through the traffic-congested town center with about four pickups at each stop per hour. You can join one (and pay as you board; usually around €20) at any stop; Termini Station and Piazza Venezia are handy hubs.

CAR AND DRIVER SERVICE
Autoservizi Monti Concezio, run by gentle, capable, and English-speaking Ezio (pronounced Etz-io), offers private cars or minibuses with driver/guides (car-€40/hour, minibus-€45/hour, 3-hour minimum for city sightseeing, transfers between cities are more expensive, mobile 335-636-5907 or 349-674-5643, info@tourservice-monti.it).

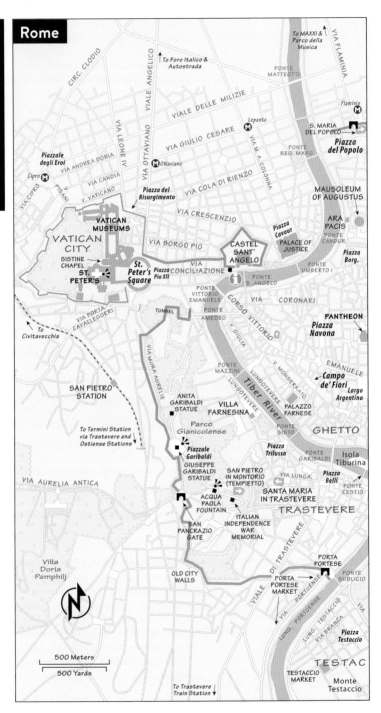

Rome

To MAXXI &
Parco della
Musica

CIRC. CLODIO

VIALE ANGELICO

VIA FLAMINIA

PONTE
MATTEOTTI

→ To Foro Italico &
Autostrada

VIALE DELLE MILIZIE

Flaminio Ⓜ

Lepanto Ⓜ

S. MARIA
DEL POPOLO →

*Piazza
del Popolo*

VIA GIULIO CESARE

VIA OTTAVIANO

VIA LEONE IV

VIA M.A. COLONNA

PONTE
REG. MARG.

*Piazzale
degli Eroi*

VIA ANDREA DORIA

Ottaviano Ⓜ

VIA COLA DI RIENZO

MAUSOLEUM
OF AUGUSTUS

Cipro Ⓜ

V. PISANI

VIA CIPRO

VIA CANDIA

V. VATICANO

*Piazza del
Risorgimento*

VIA CRESCENZIO

ARA
PACIS

*Piazza
Cavour*

PONTE
CAVOUR

**VATICAN
MUSEUMS**

VIA BORGO PIO

**CASTEL
SANT'
ANGELO**

PALACE OF
JUSTICE

*Piazza
Borg.*

**VATICAN
CITY**

VIA
CONCILIAZIONE

*Piazza
Pio XII*

PONTE
UMBERTO I

**SISTINE
CHAPEL
ST.
PETER'S**

St.
Peter's
Square

PONTE
S. ANGELO

ⓘ

PONTE
VITTORIO
EMANUELE

CORSO VITTORIO

VIA CORONARI

VIA PORTA
CAVALLEGGERI

PONTE
AMEDEO

V. GIULIA

VIA

PANTHEON

← To
Civitavecchia

TUNNEL

*Piazza
Navona*

VIA MURA AURELIE

EMANUELE

PONTE
MAZZINI

V. MONSERRATO

LUNGOTEVERE

Tiber River

*Campo
de' Fiori*

*Largo
Argentina*

**SAN PIETRO
STATION**

ANITA
GARIBALDI
STATUE

**VILLA
FARNESINA**

LUNGOTEVERE

PALAZZO
FARNESE

*Parco
Gianicolense*

PONTE
SISTO

GHETTO

To Termini Station
via Trastevere and
Ostiense Stations ↓

*Piazzale
Garibaldi*

*Piazza
Trilussa*

PONTE
GARIBALDI

**Isola
Tiburina**

GIUSEPPE
GARIBALDI
STATUE

SAN PIETRO
IN MONTORIO
(TEMPIETTO)

VIA LUNGA

*Piazza
Belli*

PONTE
CESTIO

VIA AURELIA ANTICA

**SANTA MARIA
IN TRASTEVERE**

ACQUA
PAOLA
FOUNTAIN

TRASTEVERE

ITALIAN
INDEPENDENCE
WAR
MEMORIAL

SAN
PANCRAZIO
GATE

**Villa
Doria
Pamphilj**

VIALE DI TRASTEVERE

**PORTA
PORTESE**

OLD CITY
WALLS

PORTA
PORTESE
MARKET →

PONTE
SUBLICIO

VIA

VIA PORTUENSE

LUNG. PORTUENSE

VIA TESTACCIO

VIA BRANCA

*Piazza
Testaccio*

N

500 Meters

500 Yards

TESTAC

TESTACCIO
MARKET

Monte
Testaccio

↓ To Trastevere
Train Station

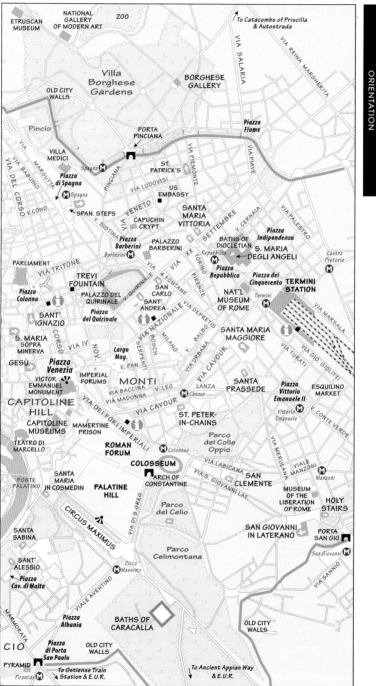

WALKS IN ROME

Take a refreshing early evening walk (Dolce Vita Stroll) and enjoy the thriving local scene, best at night (Heart of Rome Walk).

⊙ Dolce Vita Stroll

All over the Mediterranean world, people are out strolling in the early evening in a ritual known in Italy as the *passeggiata,* worth ▲▲ (see the sidebar on page 365). Rome's *passeggiata* is both elegant (with chic people enjoying fancy window shopping in the grid of streets around the Spanish Steps) and a little crude (with young people on the prowl). The major sights along this walk are covered later in this chapter.

Romans' favorite place for a chic evening stroll is along **Via del Corso.** Join in as you walk from Piazza del Popolo (Metro: Flaminio) down a wonderfully traffic-free section of Via del Corso, and up Via Condotti to the Spanish Steps. Historians can continue to Capitoline Hill. Although busy at any hour, this area really attracts crowds from around 17:00 to 19:00 each evening (Fri and Sat are best), except on Sunday, when it occurs earlier in the afternoon. Leave before 18:00 if you plan to visit the Ara Pacis (Altar of Peace), which closes at 19:30. If you get hungry during your stroll, see page 380 for listings of neighborhood wine bars and restaurants.

To reach **Piazza del Popolo,** take Metro line A to Flaminio and walk south to the square. Delightfully car-free, Piazza del Popolo is marked by an obelisk that was brought to Rome by Augustus after he conquered Egypt. (It used to stand in the Circus Maximus.)

If starting your stroll early enough, the Baroque church of **Santa Maria del Popolo** is worth popping into (next to gate in old wall on north side of square). Inside, look for Raphael's Chigi Chapel (second on left as you face the main altar) and two paintings by Caravaggio (in the Cerasi Chapel, left of altar).

From Piazza del Popolo, stroll down **Via del Corso.** While many Italians shop online or at the mall these days, and the elegance of this street has been replaced by international chains targeting local teens, this remains a fine place to feel the pulse of Rome at twilight.

Historians can side-trip right down Via Pontefici past the fascist architecture to see the massive, round-brick **Mausoleum of Augustus,** topped with overgrown

Twin Baroque churches on bustling Piazza del Popolo

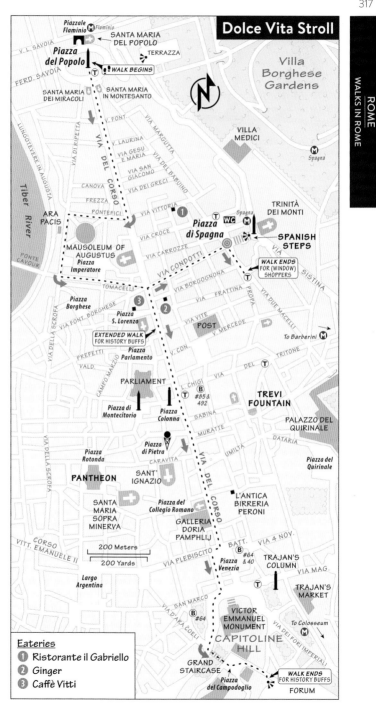

Dolce Vita Stroll

Piazzale Flaminio — M Flaminio

SANTA MARIA DEL POPOLO

Piazza del Popolo

TERRAZZA

WALK BEGINS

V.L. SAVOIA

FERD. SAVOIA

SANTA MARIA DEI MIRACOLI

SANTA MARIA IN MONTESANTO

Villa Borghese Gardens

V. FONT.

V. LAURINA

VIA GESU E. MARIA

VIA SAN GIACOMO

VIA DEI GRECI

CANOVA

FREZZA

PONTEFICI

VILLA MEDICI

M Spagna

VIA VITTORIA

VIA CROCE

VIA CARROZZE

Piazza di Spagna

WC

T Spagna M

TRINITÀ DEI MONTI

SPANISH STEPS

VIA DI RIPETTA

VIA DEL CORSO

VIA DEL BABUINO

VIA MARGUTTA

Tiber River

LUNGOTEVERE IN AUGUSTA

ARA PACIS

MAUSOLEUM OF AUGUSTUS

Piazza Imperatore

PONTE CAVOUR

TOMACELLI

VIA CONDOTTI

VIA BORGOGNONA

VIA FRATTINA

PROPA.

VIA DUE MACELLI

SISTINA

WALK ENDS FOR (WINDOW) SHOPPERS

T

Piazza Borghese

VIA FONT. BORGHESE

Piazza S. Lorenzo

EXTENDED WALK FOR HISTORY BUFFS

Piazza Parlamento

VIA DELLA SCROFA

PREFETTI

VALD.

CAMPO MARZIO

VIA VITE

POST

V. MERCEDE

V. CON.

VIA DEL

T

To Barberini M

TRITONE

PARLIAMENT

Piazza di Montecitorio

Piazza Colonna

L. CHIGI

T

B #85 & 492

SABINA

MURATTE

TREVI FOUNTAIN

PALAZZO DEL QUIRINALE

DATARIA

UMILTA

Piazza del Quirinale

Piazza Rotonda

Piazza di Pietra

CARAVITA

VIA DELLA SCROFA

PANTHEON

SANT' IGNAZIO

SANTA MARIA SOPRA MINERVA

Piazza del Collegio Romano

GALLERIA DORIA PAMPHLIJ

L'ANTICA BIRRERIA PERONI

VIA DEL CORSO

200 Meters

200 Yards

CORSO VITT. EMANUELE II

VIA PLEBISCITO

BATT.

Piazza Venezia

B #64 & 40

VIA 4 NOV.

TRAJAN'S COLUMN

VIA MAG.

TRAJAN'S MARKET

T

Largo Argentina

SAN MARCO

VIA D'ARA COELI

B #64

VICTOR EMMANUEL MONUMENT

CAPITOLINE HILL

VIA DEI FORI IMPERIALI

To Colosseum M

GRAND STAIRCASE

Piazza del Campodoglio

WALK ENDS FOR HISTORY BUFFS

FORUM

<u>Eateries</u>

1 Ristorante il Gabriello

2 Ginger

3 Caffè Vitti

Spanish Steps

has been straight since Roman times, and walk a half-mile down to the **Victor Emmanuel Monument.** Climb Michelangelo's stairway to his glorious (especially when floodlit) square atop Capitoline Hill. Stand on the balcony (just past the mayor's palace on the right), which overlooks the Forum. As the horizon reddens and cats prowl the unclaimed rubble of ancient Rome, it's one of the finest views in the city.

◑ Heart of Rome Walk

Rome's most colorful neighborhood features narrow lanes, intimate piazzas, fanciful fountains, and some of Europe's best people-watching. During the day, this walk—worth ▲▲▲—shows off the colorful Campo de' Fiori market and trendy fashion boutiques as it meanders past major monuments such as the Pantheon and the Spanish Steps.

But the sunset brings unexpected magic. A stroll in the cool of the evening is made memorable by the romance of the Eternal City at its best. Sit so close to a bubbling fountain that traffic noise evaporates. Jostle with kids to see the gelato flavors. Watch lovers straddling more than the bench. Jaywalk past *polizia* in bullet-proof vests. And marvel at the ramshackle elegance that softens this brutal city for those who were born here and can't imagine living anywhere else. These are the flavors of Rome, best enjoyed after dark.

Allow one to three hours for this mile-long walk, depending on whether you linger and tour the Pantheon. The walk is equally pleasant in reverse order. You could ride the Metro to the Spanish Steps and finish at Campo de' Fiori, near many recommended restaurants.

🎧 Download my free Heart of Rome **audio tour,** which complements this walk.
• *Start in one of Rome's most colorful spots,* ***Campo de' Fiori.*** *It's a few blocks west of Largo Argentina, a major transportation hub.*

cypress trees. This long-neglected sight, honoring Rome's first emperor, is slated for restoration and redevelopment. Beyond it, next to the river, is the **Ara Pacis** (Altar of Peace)**,** consecrated by Augustus in 9 BC and today enclosed within a protective glass-walled museum worth ▲▲ (€10.50, or look in through huge windows for free, daily 9:30-19:30). From the mausoleum, walk down Via Tomacelli to return to Via del Corso and the 21st century.

From Via del Corso, window shoppers should take a left down **Via Condotti** to join the parade to the **Spanish Steps,** passing big-name boutiques. The streets that parallel Via Condotti to the south (Borgognona and Frattina) are also elegant and filled with high-end shops. A few streets to the north hides the narrow Via Margutta. This is where Gregory Peck's *Roman Holiday* character lived (at #51); today it has a leafy tranquility and is filled with pricey artisan and antique shops.

History Buffs: Another option is to ignore Via Condotti and forget the Spanish Steps. Stay on Via del Corso, which

❶ *Campo de' Fiori*

In the morning, this bohemian piazza hosts a fruit-and-vegetable market. In the evening, the cafés and restaurants that line the square predominate. On weekend nights, beer-drinking kids (mostly American students) pack the medieval square, transforming it into a vast Roman street party.

In ancient times, it was a pleasant meadow—literally a *campo de' fiori,* or "field of flowers." Then the Romans built a massive entertainment complex, the Theater of Pompey, right next to it. The complex covered several city blocks, stretching from here to Largo Argentina (and including the spot where Julius Caesar was stabbed to death).

Lording over the center of the square is the statue of **Giordano Bruno,** an intellectual who was burned on this spot in 1600. The pedestal shows scenes from Bruno's trial and execution, and an inscription translates, "And the flames rose up." The statue, facing a Vatican administration building, was erected in 1889, a time when the new state of Italy and the Vatican were feuding. Vatican officials protested the heretic in their

midst, but they were overruled by angry neighborhood locals. This district is still known for its free spirit and antiauthoritarian demonstrations.

The square is surrounded by fun eateries and is great for people-watching. Bruno faces the bustling **Forno** (in the left corner of the square), where takeout *pizza bianca* is sold hot from the oven.
• *If Bruno did a hop, step, and jump forward, then turned left, in a block he'd reach...*

❷ *Piazza Farnese*

While the higgledy-piggledy Campo de' Fiori feels free and easy, the 16th-century Renaissance Piazza Farnese, named for the family whose palace dominates it, seems to stress order. The Farnese family hired Michelangelo to help design their palace. He created the jutting roofline (the cornice), and made the window in the very center a little wider than the others. This gave the whole facade a pleasant symmetry. The palazzo now houses the French embassy. The twin fountains decorating the square date from the third century and were made with repurposed stone tubs from the ancient Baths of Caracalla. These

Campo de' Fiori and statue of Giordano Bruno

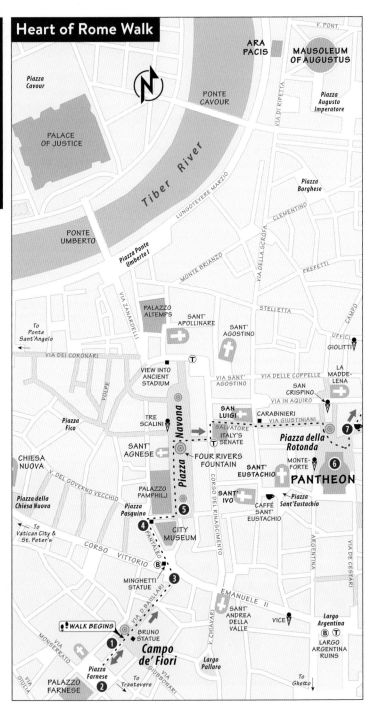

Heart of Rome Walk

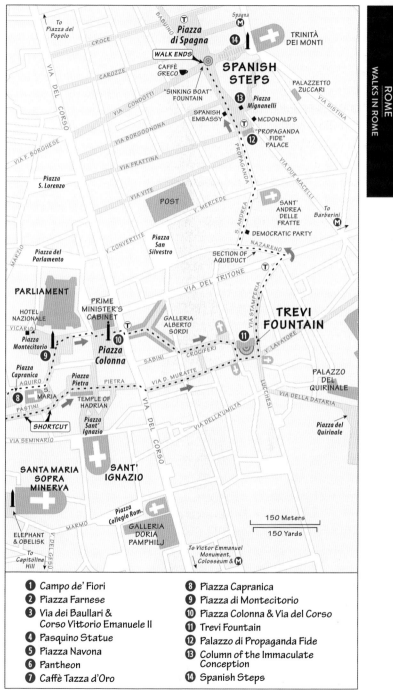

1. Campo de' Fiori
2. Piazza Farnese
3. Via dei Baullari &
   Corso Vittorio Emanuele II
4. Pasquino Statue
5. Piazza Navona
6. Pantheon
7. Caffè Tazza d'Oro
8. Piazza Capranica
9. Piazza di Montecitorio
10. Piazza Colonna & Via del Corso
11. Trevi Fountain
12. Palazzo di Propaganda Fide
13. Column of the Immaculate
    Conception
14. Spanish Steps

particular fountains are fed by an ancient aqueduct, the Acqua Vergine, the same source that feeds the Trevi Fountain.

• *Walk back to Campo de' Fiori, cross the square, and continue a couple of blocks down...*

❸ Via dei Baullari to Corso Vittorio Emanuele II

As you slalom through the crowds, notice the crush of cheap cafés, bars, and restaurants—the center of medieval Rome is morphing into a playground for tourists, students, and locals visiting from the suburbs. High rents are driving families out and changing the character of this district.

After a couple of blocks, you reach the busy boulevard, Corso Vittorio Emanuele II. In Rome, any road big enough to have city buses like this is post-unification: constructed after 1870. Look left and right down the street—the facades are mostly 19th-century neo-Renaissance, built after this main thoroughfare sliced through the city. Traffic in much of central Rome is limited to city buses, taxis, motorbikes, "dark cars" (limos and town cars of VIPs), delivery vans, residents, and disabled people with permits (a.k.a. friends of politi-

cians). This is one of the increasingly rare streets where any vehicle is welcome.

• *Cross Corso Vittorio Emanuele II, and enter a square with a statue of Marco Minghetti, an early Italian prime minister. Angle left at the statue, walking along the left side of the skippable City Museum of Rome, down Via di San Pantaleo. A block down, at the corner, you'll find a beat-up old statue.*

❹ Pasquino

Pasquino—a third-century-BC statue that was discovered near here—is one of Rome's "talking statues." For 500 years, this statue has served as a kind of community billboard, allowing people to complain anonymously when it might be dangerous to speak up. To this day, you'll see old Pasquino strewn with political posters, strike announcements, and grumbling graffiti. The statue looks worn down by centuries of bitching.

• *Facing Pasquino, veer to the left and head up Via di Pasquino to...*

❺ Piazza Navona

This long, oblong square is dotted with fountains, busy with outdoor cafés, lined with palazzos and churches, and thronged

Piazza Navona with Bernini's Four Rivers fountain

with happy visitors. By its shape you might guess that this square started out as a racetrack, part of the training grounds built here by Emperor Domitian around AD 80. That was the same year the Colosseum opened: Rome was at its peak.

But much of what we see today came in the 1600s, when the whole place got a major renovation. At the time, the popes were trying to put some big scandals behind them, and beautification projects like this were a peace offering to the public.

Three Baroque fountains decorate the piazza. The first fountain, at the southern end, features a Moor wrestling with a dolphin. In 17th-century Rome, Moors (North Africans) represented all that was exotic and mysterious. In the fountain at the northern end, Neptune slays a giant octopus.

The most famous fountain, though, is in the center: the **Four Rivers Fountain** by Gian Lorenzo Bernini, the man who in the mid-1600s remade Rome in the Baroque style. It's topped with an Egyptian-style obelisk—another of the themes we'll see along this walk. Obelisks were popular with Roman emperors because Egyptian society saw its rulers as divine—an idea Roman rulers liked to promote. Get close to admire Bernini's four enormous statues at the base. As the water of the world gushes everywhere, these four burly river gods represent the four quarters of the world.

Piazza Navona is Rome's most interesting night scene, with street music, artists, fire-eaters, local Casanovas, ice cream, and outdoor cafés that are worthy of a splurge if you've got time to sit and enjoy Italy's human river.

• Leave Piazza Navona directly across from **Tre Scalini** (famous for its tartufo, a rich, chocolate gelato concoction), and go east down Corsia Agonale, past rose peddlers and palm readers. Ahead of you (across the busy street) stands the stately Palazzo Madama, where the **Italian Senate** meets. (Hence, security is high.) Jog left around this building, and follow the brown Pantheon sign straight down Via del Salvatore.

After a block, you'll pass (on your left) the **Church of San Luigi dei Francesi,** with its très French decor and precious Caravaggio paintings. If it's open, pop in. Otherwise, continue along, following the crowd to...

Pantheon

❻ The Pantheon

Perhaps the most magnificent building surviving from ancient Rome is this temple to the "pantheon" (literally, all the gods). The 40-foot, single-piece granite columns of the Pantheon's entrance show the scale the ancient Romans built on. The columns support a triangular Greek-style roof with an inscription that proclaims, "M. Agrippa built this." In fact, the present structure was built (*fecit*) by Emperor Hadrian (AD 120), who gave credit to the builder of an earlier temple. This impressive entranceway gives no clue that the greatest wonder of the building is inside—a domed room that inspired later domes, including Michelangelo's St. Peter's and Brunelleschi's Duomo in Florence.

If the Pantheon is open, pop in and take a look around (for details on the interior, see page 344). If the Pantheon is closed, just stand for a while under the portico, which is romantically floodlit and moonlit at night.

• *With your back to the Pantheon, veer to the right, uphill toward the yellow sign on Via Orfani that reads Casa del Caffè— you've reached the...*

❼ Caffè Tazza d'Oro

This is one of Rome's top coffee shops, dating back to the days when this area was licensed to roast coffee beans. Locals come here for a shot of espresso or, when it's hot, a refreshing *granita di caffè con panna* (coffee and crushed ice with whipped cream).

• *From here, our walk continues past some interesting landmarks to the Trevi Fountain. Bear left at the coffee shop and continue up Via degli Orfani to the next square...*

❽ Piazza Capranica

This square is home to the big, plain Florentine-Renaissance-style Palazzo Capranica (directly opposite as you enter the square). Its stubby tower was once much taller, but when a stronger government arrived, the nobles were all ordered to shorten their towers. Like so many of Rome's churches, the church on the square—Santa Maria in Aquiro—is older than its Baroque-era facade. Notice the circular little shrine on the street corner.

• *Leave the piazza to the right of the palace, heading down Via in Aquiro. The street jogs to the left and into a square called...*

❾ Piazza di Montecitorio

This square is marked by an **Egyptian obelisk** from the sixth century BC. Emperor Augustus brought it to Rome as a trophy proclaiming his victory over Mark Antony and Cleopatra. In Augustus' day, the obelisk acted as a sundial and calendar, and it still functions as a sundial today. Follow the zodiac markings in the pavement to the square's other big sight— the **Italian Parliament.**

• *One block to your right is Piazza Colonna, where we're heading next—unless you like gelato. A one-block detour to the left (past Hotel Nazionale) brings you to a famous Roman gelateria, Giolitti.*

❿ Piazza Colonna and Via del Corso

The square features a massive **column** that has stood here since the second century AD. The column's shaft is 12 feet across, almost 100 feet tall, and stands on a 30-foot base, which rests on a platform. It's 28 cylindrical blocks stacked atop each other like a pile of 10-ton checkers. A carved frieze winds from the bottom to the top, telling the story of Emperor Marcus Aurelius heroically battling barbarians about AD 170.

Beyond Piazza Colonna runs noisy **Via del Corso,** Rome's main north-south boulevard. In ancient times, this was the Via Flaminia, the highway that stretched from the Roman Forum to the Adriatic coast. The street was renamed "corso" for a famous medieval horse race that took place here during the crazy Carnevale season leading up to Lent. Every evening, the pedestrian-only stretch of the Corso is packed with people on parade, taking to the streets for their *passeggiata*.

Before crossing the street, look left (to the obelisk marking Piazza del Popolo—the ancient north gate of the city) and right (to the Victor Emmanuel Monument).

• *Cross Via del Corso to enter a big palatial building with columns, the* **Galleria Alberto Sordi** *shopping mall. To the left are convenient WCs.*

Go to the right and exit out the back. (If you're here after 21:00, when the mall is closed, circle around the right side of the Galleria on Via dei Sabini.) At any time, be on guard for pickpockets, who thrive in the nearby Trevi Fountain crowds. Once out the back, the tourist kitsch builds as you head up Via de Crociferi to the roar of the water, lights, and people at the...

⓫ *Trevi Fountain*

The Trevi Fountain is the ultimate showcase for Rome's love affair with water. Architect Nicola Salvi conceived this liquid Baroque avalanche in 1762, cleverly incorporating the palace behind the fountain as a theatrical backdrop. Centerstage is the enormous figure known simply as the "Ocean." The statue stands in his shell-shaped chariot, surfing through his wet dream. Water gushes from 24 spouts and tumbles over 30 different kinds of plants. Winged horses represent cresting waves. They're led by Tritons who blow on their conch shells. *Drammatico!*

The square that faces the fountain has a lively atmosphere. The magic is enhanced by the fact that no streets directly approach it. You can hear the excitement as you draw near, and then—*bam!*—you're there. Enjoy the scene. Romantics toss a coin over their shoulder into the fountain. Legend says it will assure your return to Rome. Every year I go through this tourist ritual...and so far it's working.

• *Facing the Trevi Fountain, walk along its right side up Via della Stamperia. Cross busy*

Via del Tritone. Angle left as you continue about 30 yards up Via del Nazareno to #9, where you'll pass a fence on the left, with an exposed bit of that ancient Acqua Vergine aqueduct. At the T-intersection ahead, turn right on Via Sant'Andrea delle Fratte. The street becomes Via di Propaganda. You'll pass alongside the...

⓬ *Palazzo di Propaganda Fide*

At #1, on the right, the white-and-yellow entrance marks the palace from which the Catholic Church "propagated," or spread, its message to the world. Back in the 1600s, this "Propaganda Palace" was the headquarters of the Catholic Church's P.R. department—a priority after the Reformation. The building was designed by that dynamic Baroque duo, Bernini and Borromini (with his concave lines). It flies the yellow-and-white flag signifying that it is still owned by the Vatican.

• *The street opens up into a long piazza. You're approaching the Spanish Steps. But first, pause at the...*

Trevi Fountain

⑬ *Column of the Immaculate Conception*

Atop a tall column stands a bronze statue of Mary. She wears a diadem of stars for a halo, and stands on a crescent moon atop a globe of the earth, which is crushing a satanic serpent. To Mary's immediate left stands the Spanish embassy to the Vatican. Rome has double the embassies of a normal capital because here countries need two: one to Italy and one to the Vatican. And because of this 300-year-old embassy, the square and its famous steps are called "Spanish."

• *Just 100 yards past Mary, you reach the climax of our walk, the...*

⑭ *Spanish Steps*

The wide, curving staircase is one of Rome's iconic sights. Its 138 steps lead sharply up from Piazza di Spagna. Partway up, the steps fan out around a central terrace, forming a butterfly shape. The design culminates at the top in an obelisk framed between two Baroque church towers.

For decades the steps were a favorite Roman hangout, but recently the city banned anyone from sitting on them. You can walk up and down the steps, but if you sit, you'll face a €250 fine.

At the foot of the steps is the aptly named Sinking Boat Fountain. It was built by Gian Lorenzo Bernini's father, Pietro. Because the water pressure here is low, the water can't shoot high in the air. So Bernini designed the fountain to be low key—a sinking boat filled with water.

The piazza is a thriving scene both day and night. It features many of the themes we've enjoyed on this walk—fountains, obelisks, public spaces, statues, and gelato. Most of all, it's a glimpse at today's Rome—a city where friends and families live much the same kind of life as their ancient cousins.

• *Our walk is finished. To reach the top of the steps sweat-free, take the free elevator just inside the Spagna Metro stop (to the left, as you face the steps; elevator closes at 23:30).*

SIGHTS

I've clustered Rome's sights into walkable neighborhoods. When you see a 🎧 in a listing, it means the sight is also covered in a free audio tour (via my Rick Steves Audio Europe app—see page 28). Rome's good city-run information website, www.060608.it, lists current opening hours.

State museums in Italy are free to enter once or twice a month, usually on a Sunday. Free days are actually bad news—they attract crowds. In peak season, check state museum websites in advance and make a point to avoid their free days. For Rome, that means the Colosseum, Roman Forum, Palatine Hill, Borghese Gallery, National Museum of Rome, and Castel Sant'Angelo.

Ancient Rome

The core of ancient Rome, where the grandest monuments were built, is between the Colosseum and Capitoline Hill. I've listed these sights generally from south to north, starting with the biggies—the Colosseum and Forum—and continuing up to Capitoline Hill and Piazza Venezia. As a pleasant conclusion to your busy day, walk back south along the broad, parklike main drag—Via dei Fori Imperiali.

Ancient Core

▲▲▲COLOSSEUM (COLOSSEO)

This 2,000-year-old building is the classic example of Roman engineering. Used as a venue for entertaining the masses, this colossal, functional stadium is one of Europe's most recognizable landmarks. Whether you're playing gladiator or simply marveling at the remarkable ancient design and construction, the Colosseum gets a unanimous thumbs-up.

Cost: €18 combo-ticket covers the Colosseum and the Roman Forum/Palatine Hill and is valid 24 hours. Buy it online well in advance to get a timed-entry

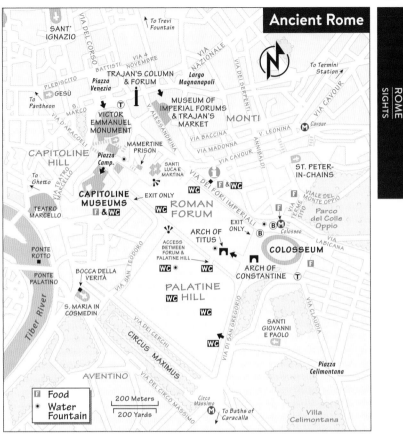

Map labels:
SANT' IGNAZIO · To Trevi Fountain · VIA DEL CORSO · VIA 4 NOVEMBRE · BATTISTI · VIA NAZIONALE · VIA DEI SERPENTI · To Termini Station · PLEBISCITO · TRAJAN'S COLUMN & FORUM · Piazza Venezia · Largo Magnanapoli · GESÙ · To Pantheon · S. MARCO · VICTOR EMMANUEL MONUMENT · MUSEUM OF IMPERIAL FORUMS & TRAJAN'S MARKET · MONTI · VIA BACCINA · V. LEONINA · Cavour · VIA CAVOUR · VIA D'ARACOELI · MAMERTINE PRISON · VIA MADONNA · VIA CAVOUR · ANNIBALDI · CAPITOLINE HILL · Piazza Camp. · SANTI LUCA E MARTINA · ST. PETER-IN-CHAINS · To Ghetto · VIA TEATRO MARCELLO · CAPITOLINE MUSEUMS · EXIT ONLY · ROMAN FORUM · VIA DEI FORI IMPERIALI · VIALE DEL MONTE OPPIO · VIA TERME TITO · Parco del Colle Oppio · TEATRO MARCELLO · Colosseo · VIA LABICANA · ARCH OF TITUS · EXIT ONLY · COLOSSEUM · PONTE ROTTO · ACCESS BETWEEN FORUM & PALATINE HILL · ARCH OF CONSTANTINE · PONTE PALATINO · BOCCA DELLA VERITÀ · VIA SAN TEODORO · PALATINE HILL · S. MARIA IN COSMEDIN · Tiber River · VIA DEI CERCHI · SANTI GIOVANNI E PAOLO · VIA DI SAN GREGORIO · VIA CLAUDIA · CIRCUS MAXIMUS · Piazza Celimontana · AVENTINO · VIA DEL CIRCO MASSIMO · Circo Massimo · To Baths of Caracalla · Villa Celimontana

Food · Water Fountain · 200 Meters · 200 Yards

reservation for the Colosseum. Do not show up without a reserved entry. A Full Experience ticket costs €24, is valid for two consecutive days, and covers the Colosseum, Palatine Hill/Roman Forum, and all the minor sights at these archaeological areas. Kids 17 and under are free (must present proof of age).

Hours: Daily from 9:00 until one hour before sunset: April-Aug until 19:15, Sept until 19:00, Oct until 18:30, Nov-Feb until 16:30, March until 17:30; last entry one hour before closing.

Information: www.parcocolosseo.it; tickets: www.coopculture.it; call center: +39 06 3996 7700 (English spoken, daily 10:00-15:00).

Mandatory Advance Ticketing: As of this writing, there are no on-site ticket sales at the Colosseum, Forum, or Palatine Hill. Tickets must be reserved in advance, and for the Colosseum, you must book a specific entrance time (even for those with free tickets, such as kids 17 and under). Book online at www. coopculture.it (select English, then search for "Colosseum" and choose your ticket type; you'll be emailed a ticket/QR code to use at entry).

Get an early-morning or late-afternoon time slot to avoid the midday crush. Generally, crowds are thinner in the afternoon (especially after 16:00 in summer); this is also true at the Forum.

Colosseum

Colosseum interior

If the time slot you want is sold out, you may find availability by paying extra for an audioguide or a guided tour. If you show up without a reservation, you can try booking a same-day ticket on the spot on your phone, or, as a last resort, join one of the tours sold by hawkers outside the gate, then ditch it once you get inside.

Getting There: The Colosseo Metro stop on line B is just across the street from the monument. Buses #51, #75, #85, #87, and #118 stop along Via dei Fori Imperiali near the Colosseum entrance (buses don't run on this street on Sun but still stop nearby), one of the Forum/Palatine Hill entrances, and Piazza Venezia. Tram #3 stops behind the Colosseum.

Getting In: The single entry point has two lines: one for those with reservations and another for the sorry lot without reservations.

Tours: A fact-filled **audioguide** is available just past the turnstiles (€5.50/1 hour). A handheld **videoguide** senses where you are in the site and plays related clips (€6/50 minutes) but can be hard to see in bright sunlight.

🎧 Download my free Colosseum **audio tour.**

Official **guided tours** in English depart roughly hourly between 9:45 and 15:00 (€5 plus Colosseum ticket, 45-60 minutes, purchase inside Colosseum near ticket booth marked *Visite didattiche*).

Private guides stand outside the Colosseum looking for business (€25-30/2-hour tour of the Colosseum, Forum, and Palatine Hill; includes admission). Make sure that your tour will start right away and that the ticket you receive covers all three sights: the Colosseum, Forum, and Palatine Hill.

Visitor Services: A WC (often crowded) is inside the Colosseum, and there are also water fountains.

Background: Built when the Roman Empire was at its peak in AD 80, the Colosseum represents Rome at its grandest. The Flavian Amphitheater (the Colosseum's real name) was an arena for gladiator contests and public spectacles. When killing became a spectator sport, the Romans wanted to share the fun with as many people as possible, so they stuck two semicircular theaters together to create a freestanding amphitheater. With four oversized stories, it's 160 feet high, nearly a third of a mile around, and makes an oval-shaped footprint that covers six acres. The stadium could accommodate 50,000 roaring fans (that's 100,000 thumbs). As Romans arrived for the games, they'd be greeted outside by a huge bronze statue of the emperor Nero—100 feet tall, gleaming in the sunlight—standing where the cypress trees stand today, between the Colosseum and the Metro stop.

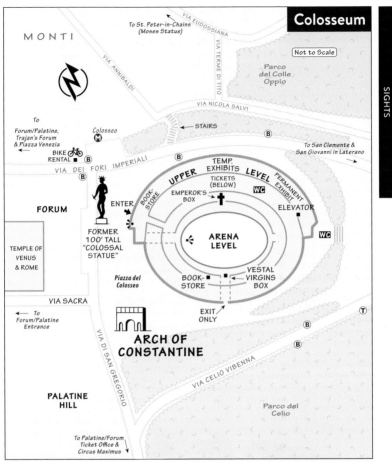

Colosseum

Not to Scale

MONTI

To St. Peter-in-Chains
(Moses Statue)

VIA EUDOSSIANA

VIA ANNIBALDI

VIA TERME DI TITO

Parco
del Colle
Oppio

VIA NICOLA SALVI

To
Forum/Palatine,
Trajan's Forum
& Piazza Venezia

Colosseo
Ⓜ

STAIRS

Ⓑ

To San Clemente &
San Giovanni in Laterano

BIKE
RENTAL ■ Ⓑ

VIA DEI FORI IMPERIALI

Ⓑ

Ⓑ

TEMP.
EXHIBITS

UPPER

LEVEL

PERMANENT
EXHIBIT

TICKETS
(BELOW)

WC

EMPEROR'S
BOX

ENTER

BOOK-
STORE

FORUM

ELEVATOR

FORMER
100' TALL
"COLOSSAL
STATUE"

ARENA
LEVEL

WC

TEMPLE OF
VENUS
& ROME

Piazza del
Colosseo

BOOK-
STORE

VESTAL
VIRGINS
BOX

VIA SACRA

EXIT
ONLY

Ⓣ

← To
Forum/Palatine
Entrance

Ⓑ

ARCH OF
CONSTANTINE

VIA DI SAN GREGORIO

Ⓑ

VIA CELIO VIBENNA

PALATINE
HILL

Parco del
Celio

To Palatine/Forum
Ticket Office &
Circus Maximus ↓

Visiting the Colosseum: After the turnstiles, walk directly to the arena and view it from ground level—near the Christian cross (see the "Colosseum" map in your book). Then, climb the stairs to the permanent exhibit on the upper level. Tour the exhibit. Then step out to view the arena from that upper level. Circle the arena clockwise three-quarters of the way around. From there, enjoy a viewpoint overlooking the Arch of Constantine and Roman Forum, check out the fine bookstore, then take the stairs down to ground level and head for the exit.

The games took place in the oval-shaped **arena,** 280 feet long by 165 feet

wide. When you look down into the arena, you're seeing the underground passages beneath the playing surface (which can be visited only on a private tour). The arena was originally covered with a wooden floor, then sprinkled with sand (*arena* in Latin). The bit of reconstructed floor gives you an accurate sense of the original arena level and the subterranean warren where animals and prisoners were held. Around you are the big brick masses that supported the tiers of seats.

The **games** pitted men against men, men against beasts, and beasts against beasts. First came the animals, things like watching dogs bloody themselves attacking porcupines. At lunchtime came Act Two. This was when criminals and POWs were executed, often in creative ways. Finally, in the afternoon, came the main event: the gladiators. Trumpets would blare, drums would pound, and the gladiators would enter the arena from the west end, parade around to the music, and pause at the south side. There, they'd acknowledge the Vestal Virgins sitting in their special box seats on the 50-yard line. After a nod to the Virgins, the gladiators continued on to the emperor's box. There, they'd raise their weapons, salute, and shout *"Ave, Caesar!"*—"Hail Caesar! We who are about to die salute you!" (Though some scholars doubt they actually said that.)

The Colosseum spectacles were a way to bring home the environments, animals, and people of Rome's conquered lands, parade them before the public, and make them real. Imagine never having seen an actual lion, and suddenly one jumps out to chase a prisoner in the arena.

Don't miss the upper-level **permanent exhibit,** with lots of ancient artifacts and fascinating reconstruction models (all well-described in English); it helps bring to life both the ancient and medieval scene. It features intimate details, including pullies, pastimes, and seating hierarchy, and gives a close-up look at architectural details. Stairs are at the east and west sides, with an elevator at the east end (accessible only to those who really need it). The upper deck also offers more colossal views of the arena, plus a bookstore and temporary exhibits.

▲ARCH OF CONSTANTINE

This well-preserved arch, which stands between the Colosseum and the Forum, commemorates a military coup and, more important, the acceptance of Christianity by the Roman Empire. When the ambitious Emperor Constantine (who had a vision that he'd win under the sign of the cross) defeated his rival Maxentius in AD 312, Constantine became sole emperor of the Roman Empire and legalized Christianity. The arch is free to see—always open and viewable.

Roman Forum and Palatine Hill

The Forum and Palatine Hill are organized as a single sight with one admission. You'll need to see both sights in a single visit.

Arch of Constantine

Roman Forum looking east, down Via Sacra

Cost and Hours: €18 for basic ticket, which includes the Colosseum and Palatine Hill (valid 24 hours); the €24 Full Experience ticket also covers all three sights (valid 48 hours; includes a few lesser sights as well). Tickets must be booked in advance at www.coopculture.it (no on-site sales). Same hours as the Colosseum.

Information: www.parcocolosseo.it; tickets: www.coopculture.it; call center: +39 06 3996 7700 (English spoken, daily 10:00-15:00).

▲▲▲ROMAN FORUM (FORO ROMANO)

This is ancient Rome's birthplace and civic center, and the common ground between Rome's famous seven hills. As just about anything important that happened in ancient Rome happened here, it's arguably the most important piece of real estate in Western civilization. While only a few fragments of that glorious past remain, history seekers find plenty to ignite their imaginations amid the half-broken columns and arches.

Avoiding Crowds: Generally, crowds are smaller in the afternoon, especially after 16:00 in summer.

Getting There: The closest Metro stop is Colosseo. Buses #51, #75, #85, #87, and #118 stop along Via dei Fori Imperiali near the Colosseum, the Forum, and Piazza Venezia (buses don't run on this street on Sun but still stop nearby).

Getting In: There are three main entrances to the Forum/Palatine Hill sight: 1) from the Colosseum (the most crowded entry)—nearest the Arch of Titus, where this guided walk starts; 2) from Via dei Fori Imperiali; and 3) from Via di San Gregorio—at south end of Palatine Hill, which is least crowded. With a Full Experience ticket, you can also enter near Trajan's Column.

Tours: An unexciting yet informative **audioguide** helps decipher the rubble (€5/2 hours, €7 version includes Palatine Hill and lasts 3 hours, must leave ID). You must return it to where you rented it.

∩ Download my free Roman Forum **audio tour.**

Visitor Services: A free information center, located across from the Via dei Fori Imperiali entrance, has a bookshop, small café, food stand, and WCs (daily 9:30-19:00).

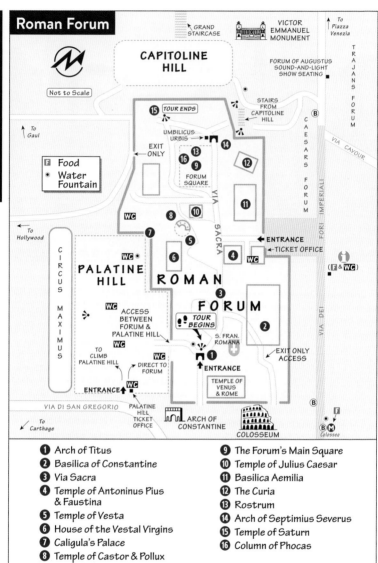

Roman Forum

- ❶ Arch of Titus
- ❷ Basilica of Constantine
- ❸ Via Sacra
- ❹ Temple of Antoninus Pius & Faustina
- ❺ Temple of Vesta
- ❻ House of the Vestal Virgins
- ❼ Caligula's Palace
- ❽ Temple of Castor & Pollux
- ❾ The Forum's Main Square
- ❿ Temple of Julius Caesar
- ⓫ Basilica Aemilia
- ⓬ The Curia
- ⓭ Rostrum
- ⓮ Arch of Septimius Severus
- ⓯ Temple of Saturn
- ⓰ Column of Phocas

⊙ SELF-GUIDED TOUR

As you begin this Forum tour, see things with "period eyes." We imagine the structures in ancient Rome as mostly white, but ornate buildings and monuments like the Arch of Titus were originally more colorful. Through the ages, builders scavenged stone from the Forum, and the

finest stone—the colored marble—was cannibalized first. If any was left, it was generally the white stone. Statues that filled the niches were vividly painted, but the organic paint rotted away as statues lay buried for centuries. Lettering was inset bronze and eyes were inset ivory. Even seemingly intact structures, like the

Arch of Titus, have been reassembled. Notice the columns are half smooth and half fluted. The fluted halves are original; the smooth parts are reconstructions.

• *Start at the Arch of Titus, which rises above the rubble on the Colosseum end of the Forum.*

❶ **Arch of Titus** (Arco di Tito): The Arch of Titus commemorated the Roman victory over the province of Judaea (Israel) in AD 70. The Romans had a reputation as benevolent conquerors who tolerated local customs and rulers. All they required was allegiance to the empire, shown by worshipping the emperor as a god. No problem for most conquered people, who already had a half-dozen gods on their prayer lists anyway. But Israelites believed in only one god, and it wasn't the emperor. Israel revolted. After a short but bitter war, the Romans defeated the rebels, took Jerusalem, destroyed their temple (leaving only a fragment of one wall's foundation—today's revered "Wailing Wall"), and brought home 50,000 Jewish slaves...who were forced to build this arch (and the Colosseum).

• *Walk down Via Sacra into the Forum. Imagine Roman sandals on these original basalt stones—perhaps the oldest street you'll ever walk. Many of the stones under your feet were walked on by Caesar Augustus 2,000 years ago. After about 50 yards, turn right and follow a path uphill to the three huge arches of the...*

❷ **Basilica of Constantine** (Basilica Maxentius): Yes, these are big arches. But they represent only one-third of the original Basilica of Constantine, a mammoth hall of justice. The arches were matched by a similar set along the Via Sacra side (only a few squat brick piers remain). Between them ran the central hall, which was spanned by a roof 130 feet high— about 55 feet higher than the side arches you see. (The stub of brick you see sticking up began an arch that once spanned the central hall.) The hall itself was as long as a football field, lavishly furnished (with colorful inlaid marble, a gilded bronze ceiling, and statues), and filled with strolling Romans. At the far (west) end was an enormous marble statue of Emperor Constantine on a throne. (Pieces of this statue, including a hand the size of a man, are on display in Rome's Capitoline Museums.)

This "basilica" was not a church but a Roman hall of justice. In a society that was as legal-minded as America is today, you needed a lot of lawyers—and a big place to put them. Citizens came here to work out matters like inheritances and building permits, or to sue somebody.

• *Now backtrack downhill and stroll deeper into the Forum, turning right along the...*

❸ **Via Sacra:** Stroll through the trees, down this main drag of the ancient city. Imagine being an out-of-town visitor during Rome's heyday—maybe from Gaul (modern France) or Londinium (modern London). You know a little Latin, but nothing would have prepared you for the bustle of Rome—a city of a million people—by far the biggest city in Europe. This street would be swarming with tribunes, slaves, and courtesans. Chariots whizzed by. Wooden stalls lined the roads, where merchants peddled their goods.

On your right, you'll pass a building with a green door still swinging on its fourth-century hinges—the original bronze door to a temple that survived because it became a church shortly after the fall of Rome. This ancient temple is still in use, sometimes hosting modern exhibits. No wonder they call Rome the Eternal City.

• *Just past the ancient temple, 10 huge columns stand in front of a much newer-looking church. This colonnade was part of the...*

❹ **Temple of Antoninus Pius and Faustina:** The Senate built this temple to honor Emperor Antoninus Pius (AD 138-161) and his deified wife, Faustina. The 50-foot-tall Corinthian (leafy) columns must have been awe-inspiring to out-of-towners who grew up in thatched huts.

Rome: Republic and Empire (500 B.C.–A.D. 500)

Ancient Rome lasted for a thousand years, from about 500 BC to AD 500. During that time, Rome expanded from a small tribe of barbarians to a vast empire, and then dwindled slowly to city size again. For the first 500 years, when Rome's armies made her ruler of the Italian peninsula and beyond, Rome was a republic governed by elected senators. Over the next 500 years, a time of world conquest and eventual decline, Rome was an empire ruled by a military-backed dictator.

Julius Caesar bridged the gap between republic and empire. This ambitious general and politician, popular with the people because of his military victories and charisma, suspended the Roman constitution and assumed dictatorial powers in about 50 BC. A few years later, he was assassinated by a conspiracy of senators. His adopted son, Augustus, succeeded him, and soon "Caesar" was not just a name but a title.

Emperor Augustus ushered in the Pax Romana, or Roman peace (AD 1-200), a time when Rome reached her peak and controlled an empire that stretched even beyond Eurail—from England to Egypt, Turkey to Morocco.

Although the temple has been inhabited by a church, you can still see the basic layout—a staircase led to a shaded porch (the columns), which admitted you to the main building (now a church), where the statue of the god sat.

Picture these columns supporting brightly painted statues in a triangular pediment, and the whole building capped with a gleaming bronze roof. The stately gray rubble of today's Forum is a faded black-and-white photograph of a 3-D Technicolor era.

• *With your back to the colonnade, walk straight ahead—jogging a bit to the right to stay on the path. The dirt path leads to two sights associated with Rome's Vestal Virgins. Head for the three short columns, all that's left of the...*

❺ **Temple of Vesta:** This is perhaps Rome's most sacred spot. Although we think of the Romans as decadent, in fact they prided themselves on their family values. People venerated their parents, grandparents, and ancestors, even keeping small statues of them in sacred shrines in their homes. This temple represented those family values on a large scale; its fire symbolized the "hearth" of the extended family that was Rome. As long as the sacred flame burned, Rome would stand. The flame was tended by six priestesses known as the Vestal Virgins.

• *Backtrack a few steps up the path, behind the Temple of Vesta. You'll find a few stairs that lead up to a big, enclosed field with two rectangular brick pools (just below the hill). This was the courtyard of the...*

❻ **House of the Vestal Virgins:** The Vestal Virgins lived in a two-story building surrounding a long central courtyard with two pools at one end. Rows of statues depicting leading Vestal Virgins flanked

Temple of Antoninus Pius and Faustina

the courtyard. This place was the model—both architecturally and sexually—for medieval convents and monasteries.

Chosen from noble families before they reached the age of 10, the six Vestal Virgins each served a 30-year term. Honored and revered by the Romans, the Vestals even had their own box seats opposite the emperor in the Colosseum. The statues that line the courtyard honor dutiful Vestals.

As the name implies, a Vestal took a vow of chastity. If she served her term faithfully—abstaining for 30 years—she was given a huge dowry and allowed to marry. But if they found any Virgin who wasn't, she was strapped to a funeral car, paraded through the streets of the Forum, taken to a crypt, given a loaf of bread and a lamp...and buried alive. Many Vestals suffered the latter fate.

• *Looming just beyond this field is Palatine Hill—the corner of which may have been...*

❼ Caligula's Palace (Palace of Tiberius): Emperor Caligula (ruled AD 37-41) had a huge palace on Palatine Hill overlooking the Forum. It actually sprawled down the hill into the Forum (some supporting arches remain in the hillside). Caligula was not a nice person. He tortured enemies, stole senators' wives, and parked his chariot in handicap spaces. Each of Rome's luxury-loving emperors added to the glory of the Forum, trying to make his mark on history.

• *Continue downhill, passing the three short columns of the Temple of Vesta, where you'll get a view of three very tall columns just beyond.*

❽ Temple of Castor and Pollux: These three columns are all that remain of a once-prestigious temple—one of the city's oldest, built in the fifth century BC. It commemorated the Roman victory over the Tarquin, the notorious Etruscan king. After the battle, the legendary twin brothers Castor and Pollux watered their horses here, at the Sacred Spring of Juturna (which has been excavated nearby). As a

symbol of Rome's self-governing republic, the temple was often used as a meeting place of senators, and its front steps served as a podium for free speech.

• *The path spills into a flat, open area that stretches before you. This was the center of the ancient Forum.*

❾ The Forum's Main Square: The original Forum, or main square, was this flat patch about the size of a football field, stretching to the foot of Capitoline Hill. Surrounding it were temples, law courts, government buildings, and triumphal arches.

Rome was born right here. According to legend, twin brothers Romulus (Rome) and Remus were orphaned in infancy and raised by a she-wolf on top of Palatine Hill. Growing up, they found it hard to get dates. So they and their cohorts attacked the nearby Sabine tribe and kidnapped their women. After they made peace, this marshy valley became the meeting place and then the trading center for the scattered tribes on the surrounding hillsides.

Temple of Castor and Pollux

Ancient Rome's population exceeded one million, more than any city until London and Paris in the 19th century. All those Roman masses lived in tiny apartments as we would live in tents at a campsite, basically just to sleep. The public space—their Forum, today's piazza—is where they did their living. Consider how, to this day, the piazza is still such an important part of any Italian town.

The Forum is now rubble, but imagine it in its prime: blindingly brilliant marble buildings with 40-foot-high columns and shining metal roofs; rows of statues painted in realistic colors; processional chariots rattling down Via Sacra. Mentally replace tourists in T-shirts with tribunes in togas. Imagine the buildings towering and the people buzzing around you while an orator gives a rabble-rousing speech from the Rostrum. If things still look like just a pile of rocks, at least tell yourself, "But Julius Caesar once leaned against these rocks."

• And speaking of Julius Caesar, at the near end of the main square (the end closest to the Colosseum) find the foundations of a temple now sheltered by a peaked wood-and-metal roof.

⓾ Temple of Julius Caesar (Tempio del Divo Giulio, or Ara di Cesare): On March 15, in 44 BC, Julius Caesar (100-44 BC) was stabbed 23 times by political conspirators. After his assassination, Caesar's body was cremated on this spot (under the metal roof). Afterward, this temple was built to honor him. Peek behind the wall into the small apse area, where a mound of dirt usually has fresh flowers—given to remember the man who, more than any other, personified the greatness of Rome.

Although he was popular with the masses, not everyone liked Caesar's urban design or his politics. When he assumed dictatorial powers, he was ambushed and stabbed to death by a conspiracy of senators, including his adopted son, Brutus ("Et tu, Brute?").

The funeral was held here, facing the main square. The citizens gathered, and speeches were made. Mark Antony stood up to say (in Shakespeare's words), "Friends, Romans, countrymen, lend me your ears. I come to bury Caesar, not to praise him." When Caesar's body was burned, his adoring fans threw anything at hand on the fire, requiring the fire department to come put it out. Later, Emperor Augustus dedicated this temple in his name, making Caesar the first Roman to become a god.

• Continue past the Temple of Julius Caesar, to the open area between the columns of the Temple of Antoninus Pius and Faustina (which we passed earlier) and the boxy brick building (the Curia). You can view the ruins of the Basilica Aemilia from a ramp next to the Temple of Antoninus Pius and Faustina, or (if the path is open) walk among them.

⓫ Basilica Aemilia: Notice the layout. This was a long, rectangular building. The stubby columns all in a row form one long, central hall flanked by two side aisles. Medieval Christians required a larger meeting hall for their worship services than Roman temples provided, so they used the spacious Roman basilica as the model for their churches. Cathedrals from France to Spain to England, from Romanesque to Gothic to Renaissance, all have the same basic floor plan as a Roman basilica.

• Now head for the big, well-preserved brick building with the triangular roof—the Curia. It's just to the right of the big triumphal arch at the foot of Capitoline Hill. While often closed, the building is impressive even from outside.

⓬ The Curia (Senate House): The Curia was the most important political building in the Forum. Since the birth of the republic, this was the site of Rome's official center of government. Three hundred senators, elected by the citizens of Rome, donned their togas, tucked their scrolls under their arms, and climbed the steps into this great hall. Inside, they gave speeches, debated policy, and created the laws of the land. They sat with their backs to the walls, surrounding the big hall on three sides, in three rows of seats. At the far end sat the Senate president—and later, the emperor—on his podium. The vast room still echoes with stirring speeches and passionate debates.

The present Curia building dates from AD 283, when it replaced an earlier Senate building. It's so well-preserved because it was used as a church since early Christian times. In the 1930s, it was restored as a historic site.

• *Go back down the Senate steps and find the 10-foot-high wall just to the left of the big arch, marked...*

⑬ Rostrum: Nowhere was Roman freedom of speech more apparent than at this "Speaker's Corner." The Rostrum was a raised platform, 10 feet high and 80 feet long, decorated with statues, columns, and the prows of ships.

On a stage like this, Rome's orators, great and small, tried to draw a crowd and sway public opinion. Picture the backdrop these speakers would have had—a mountain of marble buildings piling up on Capitoline Hill. Mark Antony rose to offer Caesar the laurel-leaf crown of kingship, which Caesar publicly (and hypocritically) refused—while privately becoming a dictator. Men such as Cicero—a contemporary of Julius Caesar—railed against the corruption and decadence that came with the city's newfound wealth. (Cicero paid

the price: he was executed, and his head and hands were nailed to the Rostrum.)

In later years, when emperors ruled, it took real daring to speak out against the powers that be. Rome's democratic spirit was increasingly squelched. Eventually, the emperor and the army—not the Senate and the citizens—held ultimate power, and Rome's vast empire began to rot from within.

• *In front of the Rostrum are **trees** bearing fruits that were sacred to the ancient Romans: olives (provided food, oil for light, and preservatives), figs (tasty), and wine grapes (made a popular export product). Now turn your attention to the big arch to the right of the Rostrum, the...*

⑭ Arch of Septimius Severus: In imperial times, the Rostrum's voices of democracy would have been dwarfed by images of the empire, such as the huge six-story-high Arch of Septimius Severus (AD 203). The reliefs commemorate the African-born emperor's battles in Mesopotamia. Near ground level, see soldiers marching captured barbarians back to Rome for the victory parade.

• *As we near the end of Rome's history, we're also nearing the end of our tour. Our next stop is the Temple of Saturn. You can see it from here—it's the eight big columns just up the slope of Capitol Hill. Or you could make your way to it for a closer look.*

⑮ Temple of Saturn: These columns framed the entrance to the Forum's oldest

Arch of Septimius Severus

Temple of Saturn

temple (497 BC). Inside was a humble, very old wooden statue of the god Saturn. The statue's claim to fame was its pedestal, which held the gold bars, coins, and jewels of Rome's state treasury, the booty collected by conquering generals.

Even older than the Temple of Saturn is the **Umbilicus Urbis,** which stands nearby (next to the Arch of Septimius Severus). A humble brick ruin marks this historic "Navel of the City." The spot was considered the center of the cosmos, and all distances in the empire were measured from here.

• *Now turn your attention from the Temple of Saturn, one of the Forum's first buildings, to one of its last monuments. Find a lone, tall column standing in the Forum in front of the Rostrum. It's fluted and topped with a leafy Corinthian capital. This is the...*

🖲 **Column of Phocas:** This is the Forum's last monument (AD 608), a gift from the powerful Byzantine Empire to a fallen empire—Rome. Given to commemorate the pagan Pantheon's becoming a Christian church, it was a symbolic last nail in ancient Rome's coffin. After Rome's 1,000-year reign, the city was looted by vandals, the population of a million-plus shrank to about 10,000, and the once-grand city center—the Forum—was abandoned, slowly covered up by centuries of silt and dirt. In the 1700s, an English historian named Edward Gibbon overlooked this spot from Capitoline Hill. Hearing Christian monks singing at these pagan ruins, he looked out at the few columns poking up from the ground, pondered the decline and fall of the Roman Empire, and thought, "Hmm, that's a catchy title..."

• *Your tour is over. If you want to see Palatine Hill, don't leave the Forum complex; you won't be allowed back in without a new ticket. Instead, return to the Arch of Titus.*

If you'd rather exit the Forum, be aware that the exact ways in and out change from year to year. Refer to your map for possible exit locations. If heading for Capitoline Hill, your best escape is likely on the west side (behind #16 on the map in this chapter).

▲▲PALATINE HILL (MONTE PALATINO)

While nearly empty of tourists, Palatine Hill is jam-packed with history—"the huts of Romulus," the huge Imperial Palace, a view of the Circus Maximus—but only the barest skeleton of rubble is left to tell the story.

We get our word "palace" from this hill, where the emperors chose to live. It was once so filled with palaces that later emperors had to build out. (Looking up at it from the Forum, you see the substructure that supported these long-gone palaces.) The Palatine Museum contains statues and frescoes that help you imagine the luxury of the imperial Palatine. From the pleasant garden, you'll get an overview of the Forum. On the far side, unless excavations are blocking the viewpoint, look down into an emperor's private stadium and then beyond at the grassy Circus Maximus, once a chariot course. Imagine the cheers, jeers, and furious betting.

While many tourists consider Palatine Hill just extra credit after the Forum, it offers insight into the greatness of Rome that's well worth the effort. (And, if you're visiting the Colosseum or Forum, you've got a ticket whether you like it or not.)

Cost and Hours: Covered by same tickets and open same hours as Roman Forum, listed earlier.

Getting There: The nearest Metro stop is Colosseo. Buses #51, #75, #85, #87, and #118 stop along Via dei Fori Imperiali near the Colosseum, the Forum, and Piazza Venezia (buses don't run on this street on Sun but still stop nearby).

Getting In: There are three entrances to the combined Palatine/Forum sight; see the map on page 332. The easiest is the entrance on Via di San Gregorio, 150 yards from the Colosseum. Upon entering, follow the path to the left as it winds to the top. Alternatively, if you sightsee the Forum first, to get to Palatine Hill you must walk up from the Arch of Titus.

Capitoline Hill

Of Rome's famous seven hills, this is the smallest, tallest, and most famous—home of the ancient Temple of Jupiter and the center of city government for 2,500 years. There are several ways to get to the top of Capitoline Hill. If you're coming from the north (from Piazza Venezia), take Michelangelo's impressive stairway to the right of the big, white Victor Emmanuel Monument. Coming from the southeast (the Roman Forum), take the steep staircase near the Arch of Septimius Severus. From near Trajan's Forum along Via dei Fori Imperiali, take the winding road. All three converge at the top, in the square called Campidoglio (kahm-pee-DOHL-yoh).

▲PIAZZA DEL CAMPIDOGLIO

This square atop the hill, once the religious and political center of ancient Rome, is still the home of the city's government. In the 1530s, the pope called on Michelangelo to reestablish this square as a grand center. Michelangelo placed the ancient equestrian statue of Marcus Aurelius as its focal point—very effective. (The original statue is now in the adjacent museum.) The twin buildings on either side are the Capitoline Museums. Behind the replica of the statue is the mayoral palace (Palazzo Senatorio).

Michelangelo intended that people approach the square from his grand stairway off Piazza Venezia. From the top of the stairway, you see the new Renaissance face of Rome, with its back to the Forum. Michelangelo gave the buildings the "giant order"—huge pilasters make the existing two-story buildings feel one-storied and more harmonious with the new square. Notice how the statues atop these buildings welcome you and then draw you in.

▲▲▲CAPITOLINE MUSEUMS

Some of ancient Rome's most famous statues and art are housed in the two palaces (Palazzo dei Conservatori and Palazzo Nuovo) that flank the equestrian statue in the Campidoglio. They're connected by an underground passage that leads to the Tabularium, an ancient building with a panoramic overlook of the Forum.

Cost and Hours: €15, daily 9:30-19:30, last entry one hour before closing, video-guide-€6, good children's audioguide-€4, tel. 06-0608, www.museicapitolini.org.

Visiting the Museum: You'll enter at

Piazza del Campidoglio and statue of Marcus Aurelius

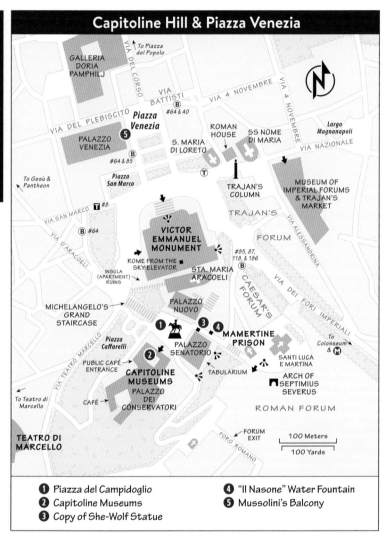

Capitoline Hill & Piazza Venezia

GALLERIA
DORIA
PAMPHILJ

To Piazza
del Popolo

VIA DEL CORSO

VIA
BATTISTI
B
#64 & 40

VIA 4 NOVEMBRE

VIA 4 NOVEMBRE

VIA DEL PLEBISCITO

**Piazza
Venezia**

ROMAN
HOUSE

SS NOME
DI MARIA

Largo
Magnanapoli

PALAZZO
VENEZIA 5

S. MARIA
DI LORETO

VIA NAZIONALE

B
#64 & 85

T

To Gesù &
Pantheon

**Piazza
San Marco**

TRAJAN'S
COLUMN

MUSEUM OF
IMPERIAL FORUMS
& TRAJAN'S
MARKET

VIA SAN MARCO
T #8

TRAJAN'S

B #64

**VICTOR
EMMANUEL
MONUMENT**

FORUM

VIA ALESSANDRINA

VIA D'ARACOELI

ROME FROM THE
SKY ELEVATOR

#85, 87,
118, & 186
B

STA. MARIA
ARACOELI

INSULA
(APARTMENT)
RUINS

CAESAR'S
FORUM

VIA DEI FORI IMPERIALI

MICHELANGELO'S
GRAND
STAIRCASE

PALAZZO
NUOVO

**Piazza
Caffarelli**

1
3 4

**MAMERTINE
PRISON**

To
Colosseum
& M

PUBLIC CAFÉ
ENTRANCE

2

PALAZZO
SENATORIO

VIA TEATRO MARCELLO

SANTI LUCA
E MARTINA

**CAPITOLINE
MUSEUMS**

TABULARIUM

ARCH OF
SEPTIMIUS
SEVERUS

To Teatro di
Marcello

CAFÉ

PALAZZO
DEI
CONSERVATORI

ROMAN FORUM

**TEATRO DI
MARCELLO**

FORUM
EXIT

FORO ROMANO

100 Meters

100 Yards

❶ Piazza del Campidoglio
❷ Capitoline Museums
❸ Copy of She-Wolf Statue

❹ "Il Nasone" Water Fountain
❺ Mussolini's Balcony

the **Palazzo dei Conservatori** (on your right as you face the equestrian statue), cross underneath the square (beneath the Palazzo Senatorio, the mayoral palace, not open to public), and exit from the Palazzo Nuovo (on your left). This enjoyable museum complex claims to be the world's oldest, founded in 1471 when a pope gave ancient statues to the citizens of Rome. Many of the museum's statues have become instantly recognizable

cultural icons, including the 13th-century *Capitoline She-Wolf* (the little statues of Romulus and Remus were added in the Renaissance). Don't miss the *Boy Extracting a Thorn* and the enchanting *Commodus as Hercules.* Behind Commodus is a statue of his dad, Marcus Aurelius, on a horse. The only surviving equestrian statue of a Roman emperor, this was the original centerpiece of the square (where a copy stands today). Christians in the

Dark Ages thought that the statue's hand was raised in blessing, which probably led to their misidentifying him as Constantine, the first Christian emperor. While most pagan statues were destroyed by Christians, "Constantine" was spared.

The museum's second-floor café, **Caffè Capitolino,** has a splendid patio offering city views. It's lovely at sunset (public entrance for those without a museum ticket off Piazzale Caffarelli and through door #4).

The **Tabularium,** built in the first century BC, once held the archives of ancient Rome. (The word Tabularium comes from "tablet," on which Romans wrote their laws.) You won't see any tablets, but you will see a stunning head-on view of the Forum from the windows.

The **Palazzo Nuovo** houses mostly portrait busts of forgotten emperors. But it also has two must-see statues: the *Dying Gaul* and the *Capitoline Venus* (both on the first floor up).

Piazza Venezia and Nearby

This vast square, dominated by the big, white Victor Emmanuel Monument, is a major transportation hub and the focal point of modern Rome. With your back to the monument, circle around the left side to reach two staircases leading up Capitoline Hill. One is Michelangelo's grand staircase up to the Campidoglio. The steeper of the two leads to **Santa Maria in Aracoeli,** a good example of the earliest style of Christian church. The contrast between this climb-on-your-knees ramp to God's house and Michelangelo's elegant stairs illustrates the changes Renaissance humanism brought civilization.

▲VICTOR EMMANUEL MONUMENT

This oversized monument to Italy's first king, built to celebrate the 50th anniversary of the country's unification in 1861, was part of Italy's push to overcome the new country's strong regionalism and create a national identity. Today, the monu-

Victor Emmanuel Monument

ment houses museums and a €10 elevator to an excellent view.

The scale of the monument is over the top: 200 feet high, 500 feet wide. The 43-foot-tall statue of the king on his high horse is one of the biggest equestrian statues in the world. The king's moustache forms an arc five feet long, and a person could sit within the horse's hoof. At the base of this statue, Italy's Tomb of the Unknown Soldier (flanked by Italian flags and armed guards) is watched over by the goddess Roma (with the gold mosaic background).

With its gleaming white sheen (from a recent scrubbing) and enormous scale, the monument provides a vivid sense of what Ancient Rome looked like at its peak—imagine the Forum filled with shiny, grandiose buildings like this one.

Cost and Hours: Monument—free, daily 9:30-18:45, a few WCs scattered throughout; Rome from the Sky elevator—€10, daily until 19:00; ticket office closes 15 minutes earlier, tel. 06-0608; follow *ascensori panoramici* signs inside the Victor Emmanuel Monument (no elevator access from street level).

THE IMPERIAL FORUMS

Though the original Roman Forum is the main attraction for today's tourists, there are several more ancient forums nearby, known collectively as "The Imperial Forums." The forums stretch in a line along Via dei Fori Imperiali, from Piazza Venezia to the Colosseum. The ruins are out in the open, never crowded, and free to look down on from street level at any time, any day. (With some Forum tickets, you can access the Forum of Julius Caesar and the Forum of Trajan via a pathway that passes beneath Via dei Fori Imperiali.) If you'll be here in the evening, consider taking in a sound-and-light show (see page 366).

Trajan's Column: The world's grandest column from antiquity (rated ▲▲) anchors the first of the forums we'll see—Trajan's Forum. The 140-foot column is decorated with a spiral relief of 2,500 figures trumpeting the emperor's exploits. It has stood for centuries as a symbol of a truly cosmopolitan civilization. At one point, the ashes of Trajan and his wife were held in the base, and the sun glinted off a polished bronze statue of Trajan at the top. Since the 1500s, St. Peter has been on top.

Trajan's Forum: The dozen-plus gray columns mark one of the grandest structures in Trajan's Forum, the Basilica Ulpia, the largest law court of its day. Nearby stood two libraries that contained the world's knowledge in Greek and Latin. To build his forum, Trajan cut away a ridge

Trajan's Column

that once connected the Quirinal and Capitoline hills, creating this valley. This was the largest forum ever, and its opulence astounded even jaded Romans. But for every grand monument here, there was untold hardship and suffering in the Barbarian world.

Trajan's Market: This structure was part shopping mall, part warehouse, and part administration building and/or government offices. Shoppers could browse through goods from every corner of Rome's vast empire—exotic fruits from Africa, spices from Asia, and fish-and-chips from Londinium. Above the semicircle, the upper floors of the complex housed bureaucrats in charge of a crucial element of city life: doling out free grain to unemployed citizens, who lived off the wealth plundered from distant lands.

To walk around the market complex and see some excavated statues, you can visit the **Museum of the Imperial Forums,** which features discoveries from the forums built by the different emperors. It's well-displayed and helps put all these ruins in context (€14, daily 9:30-19:30, last entry one hour before closing).

The Forums of Augustus and Nerva: The statue captures **Emperor Augustus** in his famous hailing-a-cab pose (a copy of the original, which you can see at the Vatican Museums). This is his "commander talking to his people" pose. Behind him was the Forum of Augustus. It separated fancy "downtown Rome" from the workaday world beyond.

Farther along is a statue of **Emperor Nerva,** trying but failing to have the commanding presence of Augustus. Walk behind him for a closer look at his forum.

▲ST. PETER-IN-CHAINS CHURCH (SAN PIETRO IN VINCOLI)

A church was first built on this spot in the fifth century, to house the chains that once restrained St. Peter. Today's church, restored in the 15th century, is famous for its Michelangelo statue of Moses,

Michelangelo's Moses *dominates the tomb of Pope Julius II.*

intended for the (unfinished) tomb of Pope Julius II. Check out the chains under the high altar, then focus on mighty Moses. (Note this isn't the famous St. Peter's—that's in Vatican City.)

Pope Julius II commissioned Michelangelo to build a massive tomb, with 48 huge statues, topped with a grand statue of this egomaniacal pope. The pope had planned to have his tomb placed in the center of St. Peter's Basilica. When Julius died, the work had barely begun, and no one had the money or necessary commitment to Julius to finish the project.

In 1542, some of the remnants of the tomb project were brought to St. Peter-in-Chains and pieced together by Michelangelo's assistants. Some of the best statues ended up elsewhere, such as the *Prisoners* in Florence and the *Slaves* in the Louvre. *Moses* and the Louvre's *Slaves* are the only statues Michelangelo personally completed for the project. Flanking *Moses* are the Old Testament sister-wives of Jacob, Leah (to our right) and Rachel, both begun by Michelangelo but probably finished by pupils.

Cost and Hours: Free, daily 8:00-12:30 & 15:00-19:00, Oct-March until 18:00,

modest dress required; the church is a 10-minute uphill walk from the Colosseum, or a shorter, simpler walk (but with more steps) from the Cavour Metro stop; tel. 06-9784-4950.

Pantheon Neighborhood

Besides being home to ancient sites and historic churches, the area around the Pantheon is another part of Rome with an urban village feel. Wander narrow streets, sample the many shops and eateries, and gather with the locals in squares marked by bubbling fountains.

▲▲▲PANTHEON

For the greatest look at the splendor of Rome, antiquity's best-preserved interior is a must. Built two millennia ago, this influential domed temple served as the model for Michelangelo's dome of St. Peter's and many others.

Cost and Hours: Free, daily 9:00-19:00, tel. 06-6830-0230, www.pantheon roma.com.

On busy weekends and holidays, free advance reservations may be required. Check online to confirm (https://pantheon.cultura.gov.it/en).

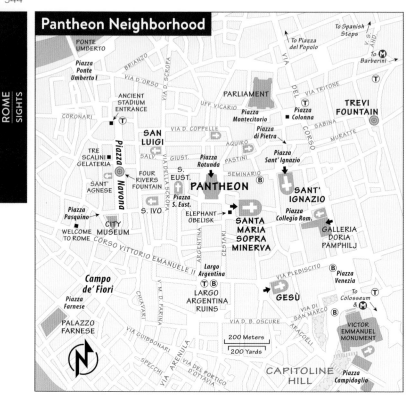

Pantheon Neighborhood

To Spanish Steps
To Piazza del Popolo
To Barberini

PONTE UMBERTO
Piazza Ponte Umberto I
BRIANZO
VIA D. ORSO
VIA D. SCROFA
CORONARI
ANCIENT STADIUM ENTRANCE
PARLIAMENT
UFF. VICARIO
Piazza Montecitorio
Piazza Colonna
VIA DEL CORSO
VIA TRITONE
TREVI FOUNTAIN
SABINA
MURATTE
SAN LUIGI
VIA D. COPPELLE
AQUIRO
Piazza di Pietra
Piazza Sant' Ignazio
TRE SCALINI GELATERIA
SALV.
GIUST.
VIA DELLA SCROFA
Piazza Rotunda
PASTINI
SANT' AGNESE
FOUR RIVERS FOUNTAIN
S. EUST.
PANTHEON
SEMINARIO
SANT' IGNAZIO
Piazza Navona
S. IVO
Piazza S. Eust.
Piazza Pasquino
ELEPHANT OBELISK
SANTA MARIA SOPRA MINERVA
Piazza Collegio Rom.
GALLERIA DORIA PAMPHILJ
CITY MUSEUM
WELCOME TO ROME
CORSO VITTORIO EMANUELE II
ARGENTINA
CESTARI
Largo Argentina
LARGO ARGENTINA RUINS
VIA PLEBISCITO
Piazza Venezia
Campo de' Fiori
V. M. D. FARINA
CHIAVARI
GESÙ
VIA DI SAN MARCO
To Colosseum & M
Piazza Farnese
VIA D. B. OSCURE
ARACOELI
VICTOR EMMANUEL MONUMENT
PALAZZO FARNESE
VIA GIUBBONARI
SPECCHI
VIA ARENULA
VIA DEL PORTICO D'OTTAVIA
200 Meters
200 Yards
CAPITOLINE HILL
Piazza Campidoglio

Dress Code: No visitors with skimpy shorts or bare shoulders allowed inside the Pantheon.

Tours: The Pantheon has a €6, 30-minute **audioguide** (€10/2 people). ∩ Download my free Pantheon **audio tour.**

Visiting the Pantheon: The Pantheon was a Roman temple dedicated to all (*pan*) of the gods (*theos*). The original temple was built in 27 BC by Emperor Augustus' son-in-law, Marcus Agrippa. In fact, the inscription below the triangular **pediment** proclaims (in Latin), "Marcus Agrippa, son of Lucio, three times consul made this." But after a couple of fires, the structure we see today was completely rebuilt by Emperor Hadrian around AD 120. After the fall of Rome, the Pantheon became a Christian church (from "all the gods" to "all the martyrs"), which saved it from architectural cannibalism.

The dome is what makes this building unique—and perhaps the most influential architectural design in art history. The Pantheon's dome was the model for the Florence cathedral dome, which launched the Renaissance, and for Michelangelo's dome of St. Peter's, which capped it all off. Even the US Capitol in Washington, DC, was inspired by this dome.

Wander into the **portico** with its forest of 16 enormous **columns.** They're 40 feet tall and 15 feet around, made of red-and-gray granite. Whereas many ancient columns are a stack of cylindrical drums, these columns are each a single piece of stone.

The magnificent, soaring **dome,** the largest made until the Renaissance, is set on a circular base. The mathematical perfection of this dome-on-a-base design is a testament to Roman engineering; it's as high as it is wide—142 feet. To picture

The Pantheon's dome and oculus

it, imagine a basketball wedged inside a wastebasket so that it just touches bottom. The dome is made from concrete, a Roman invention. It gets lighter and thinner as it reaches the top. The base of the dome is 23 feet thick and made from heavy concrete mixed with travertine, while near the top, it's less than five feet thick and made with a lighter volcanic rock (pumice) mixed in.

At the top, the **oculus** is the building's only light source. It's completely open and almost 30 feet across. The 1,800-year-old **floor**—with 80 percent of its original stones surviving—has holes in it and slants toward the edges to let rainwater drain. Although some of the floor's marble has been replaced, the design—alternating circles and squares—is original.

The Pantheon's interior holds the tombs of important people from more recent centuries. The artist **Raphael** (1483-1520) lies in a stone coffin to the left of the main altar. Facing each other across the rotunda are the tombs of modern Italy's first two kings: **Victor Emmanuel II** and **Umberto I.**

▲TREVI FOUNTAIN

The bubbly Baroque fountain, worth ▲▲ by night, is a minor sight to art scholars... but a major nighttime gathering spot for teens on the make and tourists tossing coins. Those coins are collected daily to feed Rome's poor. For more on the fountain, see page 325.

Vatican City

Vatican City, the world's smallest country, contains St. Peter's Basilica (with Michelangelo's exquisite *Pietà*) and the Vatican Museums (with Michelangelo's Sistine Chapel). A helpful **TI** is just to the left of St. Peter's Basilica as you're facing it (Mon-Sat 8:30-18:15, closed Sun, tel. 06-6988-2019, www.vaticanstate.va). The entrances to St. Peter's and the Vatican Museums are a 15-minute walk apart (follow the outside of the Vatican wall, which links the two sights). The nearest Metro stop—Ottaviano—still involves a 10-minute walk to either sight. For a map of the entire district and nearby sights, see page 354.

Dress Code: Modest dress is technically required of men, women, and children

St. Peter's Square and Basilica

throughout Vatican City, even outdoors. The policy is strictly enforced in the Sistine Chapel and at St. Peter's Basilica but is more relaxed elsewhere (though always at the discretion of guards). To avoid problems, cover your shoulders; bring a light jacket or cover-up if you're wearing a tank top. Wear long pants or capris instead of shorts. Skirts or dresses should extend below your knee.

▲▲▲ST. PETER'S BASILICA

There is no doubt: This is the richest and grandest church on earth. To call it vast is like calling Einstein smart. Plaques on the floor show you where other, smaller churches would end if they were placed inside. The ornamental cherubs would dwarf a large man. Birds roost inside, and thousands of people wander about, heads craned heavenward, hardly noticing each other. Don't miss Michelangelo's *Pietà* (behind bulletproof glass) to the right of the entrance. Bernini's altar work and twisting, towering canopy are brilliant.

Cost and Hours: Free, daily April-Sept 7:00-19:00, Oct-March 7:00-18:30. The church closes on Wednesday mornings during papal audiences (until roughly 13:00). Masses occur daily throughout the day. The view from the dome is worth the climb (€10 for elevator to roof, then take stairs; €8 to climb stairs all the way, cash only, allow an hour to go up and down, daily April-Sept 7:30-19:00, Oct-March 7:30-18:00, last entry one hour before closing if you take the stairs the whole way). Tel. 06-6988-2019, www.vaticanstate.va.

Avoiding Lines: There's often a bottleneck at the security check. The checkpoint is typically on the north side of the square, but is sometimes closer to the church or tucked under the south colonnade.

Visit before 10:00 to avoid the worst crowds. Crowds are also thinner after 16:00—just as sunbeams begin working their magic on the altar. But after 16:00, the crypt is closed, and the altar area is often roped off.

Getting There: Take the Metro to Ottaviano, then walk 10 minutes south on Via Ottaviano. The #40 express bus drops off at Piazza Pio, next to Castel Sant'Angelo—a 10-minute walk from St. Peter's. The more crowded bus #64, beloved by pickpockets, stops just outside St. Peter's

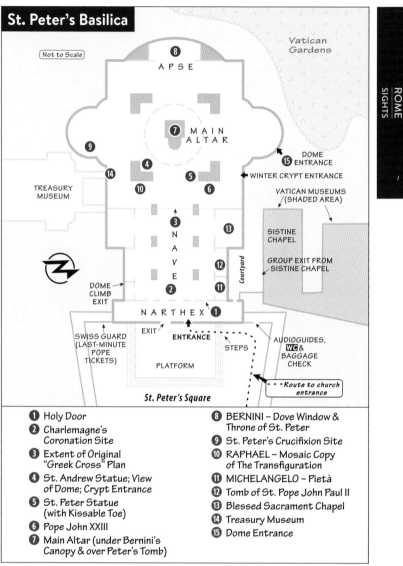

St. Peter's Basilica

Not to Scale

Vatican Gardens

APSE

MAIN ALTAR

DOME ENTRANCE

WINTER CRYPT ENTRANCE

VATICAN MUSEUMS (SHADED AREA)

TREASURY MUSEUM

SISTINE CHAPEL

GROUP EXIT FROM SISTINE CHAPEL

NAVE

Courtyard

DOME CLIMB EXIT

NARTHEX

EXIT ENTRANCE

SWISS GUARD (LAST-MINUTE POPE TICKETS)

STEPS

AUDIOGUIDES, WC & BAGGAGE CHECK

PLATFORM

Route to church entrance

St. Peter's Square

- ❶ Holy Door
- ❷ Charlemagne's Coronation Site
- ❸ Extent of Original "Greek Cross" Plan
- ❹ St. Andrew Statue; View of Dome; Crypt Entrance
- ❺ St. Peter Statue (with Kissable Toe)
- ❻ Pope John XXIII
- ❼ Main Altar (under Bernini's Canopy & over Peter's Tomb)
- ❽ BERNINI – Dove Window & Throne of St. Peter
- ❾ St. Peter's Crucifixion Site
- ❿ RAPHAEL – Mosaic Copy of The Transfiguration
- ⓫ MICHELANGELO – Pietà
- ⓬ Tomb of St. Pope John Paul II
- ⓭ Blessed Sacrament Chapel
- ⓮ Treasury Museum
- ⓯ Dome Entrance

Square to the south. A taxi from Termini train station costs about €15.

Church Services: Mass, generally in Italian, is said varyingly in the south (left) transept, the Blessed Sacrament Chapel (on right side of nave), or at the main altar. Confirm times on the signboard as you enter. Typical schedule: Mon-Sat at 8:30, 9:00, 10:00, 11:00, 12:00, and at 17:00 (in Latin, at the main altar); Sun and holidays at 9:00, 10:30 (in Latin), 11:30, 12:15, 13:00, 16:00, 16:45 (vespers), and 17:30.

Tours: Audioguides can be rented near the baggage check (€5 plus ID, for church only, daily 8:30-17:00). ∩ Download my free St. Peter's Basilica **audio tour.**

Dome Climb: You can take an elevator or climb 231 stairs to the roof, then climb another 323 steps to the top of the dome. The entry to the elevator is just outside the north side of the basilica—look for signs to the *cupola.* If you're climbing the dome without your travel partner, confirm where you'll exit before you split up. For more on the dome, see the end of my self-guided tour.

Baggage Check: The free bag check (mandatory for bags larger than a purse or daypack) is inside security, but outside the basilica (to the right as you face the entrance). Pocketknives are not allowed inside the basilica.

Visitor Services: You'll find **WCs** on both sides of St. Peter's Square (by the TI and just outside security), near the baggage check down the steps by the church entrance, and on the roof.

◐ SELF-GUIDED TOUR

To sample the basilica's highlights, follow these points:

❶ The **narthex** (portico) is itself bigger than most churches. Its huge white columns date from the first church (fourth century). Five famous bronze doors lead into the church. Made from the melted-down bronze of the original door of Old St. Peter's, the central door was the first Renaissance work in Rome (c. 1450). It's only opened on special occasions.

The far-right entrance is the **Holy Door,** opened only during Holy Years (and special "Jubilee" years designated by the pope). On Christmas Eve every 25 years, the pope knocks three times with a silver hammer and the door opens, welcoming pilgrims to pass through.

Looking down the nave, we get a sense of the splendor of ancient Rome that was carried on by the Catholic Church. The floor plan, with a central aisle (nave) flanked by two side aisles, is based on that of ancient Roman basilicas—large halls built to accommodate business and legal meetings. In fact, many of the stones used to build St. Peter's were scavenged from the ruined law courts of ancient Rome.

❷ On the floor near the central doorway is a round slab of porphyry stone in the maroon color of ancient Roman officialdom. This is the spot where, on Christmas night in AD 800, the king of the Franks **Charlemagne was crowned** Holy Roman Emperor. Look down the main hall—this church is huge. Stand at the very back of the nave and survey the heavenly expanse. It's a riot of marble, gold, stucco, mosaics, columns of stone, and pillars of light. As the symbol of global Catholicism, this church is appropriately big. Size before beauty: The golden window at the far end is two football fields away. The dove in the golden window has the wingspan of a 747 (OK, maybe not quite, but it *is* big). The church covers six acres. The babies at the base of the pillars along the main hall (the nave) are adult-size. The lettering in the gold band along the top of the pillars is seven feet high. Really. The church has a capacity of 60,000 standing worshippers (or 1,200 tour groups).

• *Now, walk straight up the center of the nave toward the altar.*

❸ Michelangelo was 71 when the pope persuaded him to take over the church project and cap it with a dome. He agreed, intending to put the dome over Donato Bramante's original **Greek-cross floor plan.** But the Church, struggling against Protestants and its own corruption, opted for a plan designed to impress the world with its grandeur—the Latin cross of the Crucifixion, with its nave extended to accommodate the grand religious spectacles of the Baroque period.

❹ Park yourself in front of the **statue of St. Andrew** to the left of the altar, the guy holding an X-shaped cross. (Note that the **entrance to the crypt** is usually here; in winter it's by the dome entrance.) Like Andrew, gaze up into the dome, and also like him, gasp.

The **dome** soars higher than a football field on end, 448 feet from the floor of

The nave of St. Peter's Basilica is two football fields long.

the cathedral to the top of the lantern. It glows with light from its windows, the blue-and-gold mosaics creating a cool, solemn atmosphere. In this majestic vision of heaven (not painted by Michelangelo), we see (above the windows) Jesus, Mary, and a ring of saints, rings of more angels above them, and, way up in the ozone, God the Father (a blur of blue and red, unless you have binoculars).

❺ Back in the nave sits a bronze **statue of St. Peter** under a canopy. This is one of a handful of pieces of art that were in the earlier church. In one hand he holds keys, the symbol of the authority given him by Christ, while with the other hand he blesses us. His big right toe has been worn smooth by the lips of pilgrims and foot fetishists. Stand in line and kiss it, or, to avoid foot-and-mouth disease, touch your hand to your lips, then rub the toe. This is simply an act of reverence with no legend attached, though you can make one up if you like.

• *Circle to the right around the statue of Peter to find the lighted glass niche.*

❻ The red-robed body is **Pope John XXIII,** whose papacy lasted from 1958 to 1963. Nicknamed "the good pope,"

he is best known for initiating the landmark Vatican II Council (1962-1965) that instituted major reforms, bringing the Church into the modern age. In 2000, Church authorities checked his body, and it was surprisingly fresh. So they moved it upstairs, put it behind glass, and now old Catholics who remember him fondly enjoy another stop on their St. Peter's visit. Pope John was canonized in 2014.

❼ Sitting over St. Peter's tomb, the **main altar** (the white marble slab with cross and candlesticks) beneath the dome and canopy is used only when the pope himself says Mass. He sometimes conducts the Sunday morning service when he's in town, a sight worth seeing.

The tiny altar would be lost in this enormous church if it weren't for Gian Lorenzo Bernini's seven-story bronze canopy (God's "four-poster bed"), which "extends" the altar upward and reduces the perceived distance between floor and ceiling. The corkscrew columns echo the marble ones that surrounded the altar/tomb in Old St. Peter's. Some of the bronze used here was taken and melted down from the ancient Pantheon.

Michelangelo, Pietà

❽ Bernini (1598-1680), the Michelangelo of the Baroque era, is the man most responsible for the interior decoration of the church.

His **dove window** shines above the smaller front altar used for everyday services. The Holy Spirit, in the form of a six-foot-high dove, pours sunlight onto the faithful through the alabaster windows, turning into artificial rays of gold and reflecting off swirling gold clouds, angels, and winged babies. During a service, real sunlight passes through real clouds of incense, mingling with Bernini's sculpture. Beneath the dove is the centerpiece of this structure, the so-called **Throne of St. Peter,** an oak chair built in medieval times for a king. Subsequently, it was encrusted with tradition and encased in bronze by Bernini as a symbol of papal authority. In the apse, Mass is said daily for pilgrims, tourists, and Roman citizens alike.

• *To the left of the main altar is the* **south transept.** *It may be roped off for worship, but anyone can step past the guard if you say you're there "for prayer." At the far end, left side, find the dark "painting" of St. Peter crucified upside down.*

❾ This marks the exact spot (according to tradition) of **Peter's crucifixion.** Peter had come to the world's greatest city to preach Jesus' message of love to the pagan, often hostile Romans. During the reign of Emperor Nero, he was arrested and brought to Nero's Circus so all of Rome could witness his execution. When the authorities told Peter he was to be crucified just like his Lord, Peter said, essentially, "I'm not worthy" and insisted they nail him on the cross upside down.

❿ Around the corner on the right (heading back toward the central nave), pause at the mosaic copy of Raphael's epic painting of **The Transfiguration.** The original is now beautifully displayed in the Pinacoteca of the Vatican Museums. This and all the other "paintings" in the church are actually mosaic copies made from thousands of colored chips the size of your little fingernail.

• *Back near the entrance of the church, in the far corner behind bulletproof glass, is the sculpture everyone has come to see, the Pietà.*

⓫ Michelangelo was 24 years old when he completed this **pietà**—a representation of Mary with the body of Christ taken from the cross. It was his first major commission, done for Holy Year 1500.

Michelangelo, with his total mastery of the real world, captures the sadness of the moment. Mary cradles her crucified son in her lap. Christ's lifeless right arm drooping down lets us know how heavy this corpse is. Mary looks at her dead son with sad tenderness. Her left hand turns upward, asking, "How could they do this to you?"

• *In the chapel to the left is the Tomb of Pope John Paul II.*

⑫ John Paul II (1920-2005) was one of the most beloved popes of recent times. During his papacy (1978-2005), he was the highly visible face of the Catholic Church as it labored to stay relevant in an increasingly secular world. The first non-Italian pope in four centuries, he oversaw the fall of communism in his native Poland. He survived an assassination attempt, and he publicly endured his slow decline from Parkinson's disease with great stoicism. He was sainted in April 2014, just nine years after his death.

⑬ You're welcome to step through the metalwork gates into the **Blessed Sacrament Chapel** (Capella di Santissimo Sacramento), an oasis of peace reserved for prayer and meditation (on right side of church, about midway to the altar). Mass is sometimes said here.

⑭ The **Treasury Museum** (Museo-Tesoro), on the left side of the nave near the altar, contains the room-size tomb of Sixtus IV by Antonio Pollaiuolo, a big pair of Roman pincers used to torture Christians, an original corkscrew column from Old St. Peter's, and assorted jewels, papal robes, and golden reliquaries—a marked contrast to the poverty of early Christians.

The foundations of Old St. Peter's, the **Crypt** (Grotte/Tombe), contains tombs of popes and memorial chapels. In summer, the crypt entrance is usually beside the statue of St. Andrew, to the left of the main altar (near #4 on the map); in winter, it's by the dome entrance. Stairs

The view from atop St. Peter's

lead you down to the floor level of the previous church, where you'll pass the sepulcher of Peter. This lighted niche with an icon is not Peter's actual tomb, but part of a shrine that stands atop Peter's tomb. Continue your one-way visit until it spills you out, usually near the checkroom.

⑮ For one of the best views of Rome, go up to the **dome.** The entrance is along the right (north) side of the church, but the line begins to form out front, at the church's right door (as you face the church). Look for *cupola* signs.

There are two levels: the rooftop of the church and the very top of the dome. Climb or take an elevator to the first level, on the church roof just above the facade. From the roof, you can also go inside the gallery ringing the interior of the dome and look down inside the church. To go all the way up to the top of the dome, you'll take a staircase that actually winds between the outer shell and the inner one. It's a sweaty, crowded, claustrophobic 15-minute, 323-step climb, but worth it. The view from the summit is great, the fresh air even better.

Vatican City

The tiny independent country of Vatican City is contained entirely within Rome. The Vatican has its own postal system, armed guards, beautiful gardens, helipad, mini train station, and radio station (KPOP). It also has two huge sights: St. Peter's Basilica and the Vatican Museums. Politically powerful, the Vatican is the religious capital of 1.2 billion Roman Catholics. If you're not a Catholic, become one for your visit.

The pope is both the religious and secular leader of Vatican City. For centuries, the Vatican was the capital of the Papal States, and locals referred to the pontiff as "King Pope." Because of the Vatican's territorial ambitions, it didn't always have good relations with Italy. Even though modern Italy was created in 1870, the Holy See didn't recognize it as a country until 1929.

Preparing for papal pageantry

Vatican Gardens: To walk through the manicured Vatican Gardens (with views over Rome and a good look at St. Peter's dome), book a guided tour several days in advance at www.museivaticani.va (€33, 2 hours, daily except Wed and Sun, includes entry to Vatican Museums; tours usually start at 9:30 or 11:00 at Vatican

▲▲▲VATICAN MUSEUMS (MUSEI VATICANI)

The four miles of displays in this immense museum complex—from ancient statues to Christian frescoes to modern paintings—culminate in the Raphael Rooms and Michelangelo's glorious Sistine Chapel. This is one of Europe's top three and four houses of art. It can be exhausting, so plan your visit carefully, focusing on a few themes. Allow two hours for a quick visit, three or four hours to really enjoy it.

Cost and Hours: €17, €4 online reservation fee, Mon-Sat 9:00-18:00, last entry at 16:00 (though the official closing time is 18:00, the staff starts ushering you out at 17:30), closed on religious holidays and Sun except last Sun of the month (when it's free, more crowded, and open 9:00-14:00, last entry at 12:30); open Fri nights mid-April-Oct 19:00-23:00 (last entry at 21:30) by online reservation only—check the website. Hours are subject to frequent change and holidays; look online for current times.

Closed Days: The museum is closed on many holidays (mainly religious ones). Always check the current hours and calendar on the museum website. Individual rooms may close at odd hours, especially in the afternoon. The rooms described here are usually open.

Information: Tel. 06-6988-4676, www.museivaticani.va.

Reservations: You're crazy to come without a reservation: The Vatican Muse-

Museums tour desk). A 45-minute open-bus tour through the gardens is offered in good weather (€37, includes audioguide and entry to Vatican Museums).

General Audience Tickets: For the Wednesday audience at 10:00, a (free) ticket gets you closer to the papal action. Reserve tickets (available a month or two in advance) by sending a request by mail or fax (access the form at www. vatican.va—select "Prefecture of the Papal Household"). You'll then pick up the tickets at St. Peter's Square before the audience (available Tue 15:00-19:00 and Wed 7:00-9:00; usually under Bernini's colonnade, to the right when facing the church).

Starting the Monday before the audience, Swiss Guards hand out tickets from their station near the basilica exit (see the "Vatican Museums Overview" map). Don't go through security—just march up, ask nicely, and say *"danke."* While this is perhaps easiest, I'd reserve in advance to guarantee a ticket.

General Audience Tips: On Wednesday morning, you'll need to be dressed modestly (shoulders covered, no short shorts or tank tops—long pants or knee-length skirts are safest) and clear security (no big bags). To get a seat (much less a good one), it's smart to be there a couple of hours early—there are far fewer seats than ticketholders. If you just want to see the pope, get a good photo, and don't mind standing, you can show up later (though still at least 30 minutes early) and take your place in the standing-room section in the back half of the square. The service gets underway around 9:30. Shortly thereafter, the Popemobile appears, winding through the adoring crowd (the best places—seated or standing—are near the cloth-covered wooden fences that line the Popemobile route). Around 10:00, the Pope's multilingual message begins and lasts for about an hour (you can leave at any time).

ums can be extremely crowded, with waits of up to two hours just to buy tickets. Bypass these long lines by reserving an entry time online for €21 (€17 ticket plus €4 booking fee). For sights covered by my self-guided tour, select the ticket called "Vatican Museums and Sistine Chapel." Print the emailed voucher to present at the museum (see "Getting In," later). You can also receive your reservation on your mobile phone.

When to Go: The museum is generally crowded, with shoulder-to-shoulder sightseeing through much of it. The best time to visit is a weekday after 14:00—the later the better. Another good time is during the papal audience on Wednesday morning, when many tourists are at St. Peter's Square (the drawback is that St. Peter's Basilica is closed until roughly 13:00).

The worst days are Saturdays, the last Sunday of the month (when the museum is free), Mondays, rainy days, and any day before or after a holiday closure.

More Line-Beating Tips: Booking a **guided tour** (described later, under "Tours") gets you right in—just show the guard your voucher. You can often buy **same-day timed-entry reservations** without a ticket-buying line at the Vatican TI in St. Peter's Square (to the left as you face the basilica). **Hawkers** peddling skip-the-line access swarm the Vatican area, offering guided tours—but the museum staff advises against accepting their offers

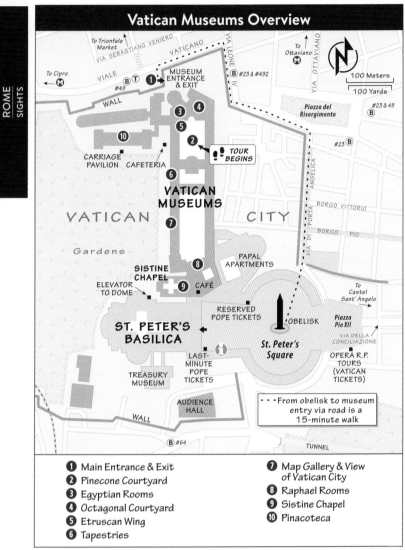

Vatican Museums Overview

To Trionfale Market
VIA SEBASTIANO VENIERO
VATICANO
VIA LEONE IV
To Ottaviano
VIA OTTAVIANO
N
100 Meters
100 Yards
To Cipro
VIALE
WALL
#49
B T ❶ MUSEUM ENTRANCE & EXIT
B #23 & #492
Piazza del Risorgimento
#23 & 49 B
❸
❹
Piazza del Risorgimento
#23 B
❺
❷ TOUR BEGINS
⓾
CARRIAGE PAVILION   CAFETERIA
❻
VATICAN MUSEUMS
VATICAN   CITY
BORGO VITTORIO
❼
BORGO PIO
VIA DI PORTA ANGELICA
Gardens
❽ PAPAL APARTMENTS
SISTINE CHAPEL
ELEVATOR TO DOME
❾ CAFÉ
To Castel Sant' Angelo
RESERVED POPE TICKETS
OBELISK
Piazza Pio XII
ST. PETER'S BASILICA
St. Peter's Square
VIA DELLA CONCILIAZIONE
LAST-MINUTE POPE TICKETS
OPERA R.P. TOURS (VATICAN TICKETS)
TREASURY MUSEUM
AUDIENCE HALL
- - - From obelisk to museum entry via road is a 15-minute walk
WALL
B #64
TUNNEL

❶ Main Entrance & Exit
❷ Pinecone Courtyard
❸ Egyptian Rooms
❹ Octagonal Courtyard
❺ Etruscan Wing
❻ Tapestries
❼ Map Gallery & View of Vatican City
❽ Raphael Rooms
❾ Sistine Chapel
⓾ Pinacoteca

(while legitimate, the tour caliber is often low—use them only as a last resort).

Getting There: The Ottaviano Metro stop is a 10-minute walk from the entrance. Bus #49 from Piazza Cavour/Castel Sant'Angelo stops right at the entrance. Bus #23 from Trastevere stops on Via Leone IV, just downhill from the entrance. Bus #492 heads from the city center and stops on Via Leone IV. Bus #64 stops on the other side of St. Peter's Square, a 15- to 20-minute walk (facing the church from the obelisk, take a right through the colonnade and follow the Vatican Wall). Or take a taxi from the city center—they are reasonable.

Getting In: Approaching the exterior entrance (the big white door), you'll see three lines: individuals without reservations (far left), individuals with reservations (usually shorter and faster), and groups (on the right).

With a reservation, show your voucher to the guard and enter via the reserved ticket-holder line. Inside, after the security check, go to any window on the left to show your voucher and pick up your ticket, then go up the steps and enter the museum. (Or, you can skip the ticket-window line by going upstairs and processing your voucher on a machine.)

Without a reservation, enter via the far left line. Once you clear security, go upstairs to buy your ticket.

Tours: An €8 **audioguide** is available at the top of the spiral ramp/escalator and can be prepaid when you book tickets online. No ID is required to rent an audioguide. Confirm the drop-off location when renting.

🎧 Download my free Vatican Museums and Sistine Chapel **audio tours.**

The Vatican offers **guided tours** in English that are easy to book on their website (€33, includes admission). Present your confirmation voucher to a guard to the right of the entrance; then, once inside, go to the Guided Tours desk (in the lobby, up a few stairs).

Visitor Services: The museum's "checkroom" (to the right after security) takes only bigger bags, not day bags.

WCs are mainly at the entrance/exit, plus a few scattered within the collection.

⊘ SELF-GUIDED TOUR

Our tour starts in the large open-air **"Pinecone Courtyard."** This vast space sums up the Vatican's vast collection: Pinecone—ancient, a 2,000 year-old offering to Isis. Bronze sphere—modern, created in 1990. And the courtyard around it—Renaissance, designed by Bramante.

We'll begin our museum visit as civilization did, in **Egypt and Mesopotamia.** Backtrack inside and up the stairs to the right to find linen-wrapped mummies, stiff statues, and early writing on clay tablets.

Laocoön, *in the Octagonal courtyard*

After a stop at a view balcony, make your way to the **Octagonal Courtyard**, decorated with some of the best Greek and Roman statues in captivity. The *Apollo Belvedere* is a Roman copy (4th century BC) of a Hellenistic original that followed the style of the great Greek sculptor Praxiteles. It fully captures the beauty of the human form. The anatomy is perfect, his pose is natural. Instead of standing at attention, face-forward with his arms at his sides (Egyptian-style), Apollo is on the move, coming to rest with his weight on one leg.

Laocoön was sculpted some four centuries after the Golden Age (5th-4th century BC), after the scales of "balance" had been tipped. Whereas *Apollo* is a balance between stillness and motion, this is unbridled motion. *Apollo* is serene, graceful, and godlike, while *Laocoön* is powerful, emotional, and gritty. The figures (carved from four blocks of marble pieced together seamlessly) are powerful, not light and graceful. The poses are as twisted as possible, accentuating every rippling muscle and bulging vein.

The centerpiece of the next hall is the *Belvedere Torso* (just a 2,000-year-old torso, but one that had a great impact on the art of Michelangelo). Finishing off the classical statuary are two fine fourth-century porphyry sarcophagi. These royal purple tombs were made (though not used) for the Roman emperor Constantine's mother (Helena, on left) and daughter (Constanza, on right).

Raphael, School of Athens

Overachievers may first choose to pop into the **Etruscan Wing**—labeled *Museo Gregoriano Etrusco.* Otherwise, after long halls of **tapestries, old maps,** broken penises, and fig leaves, you'll come to what most people are looking for: the Raphael Rooms and Michelangelo's Sistine Chapel.

Raphael Rooms: The highlight of the Raphael Rooms, frescoed by Raphael and his assistants, is the restored *School of Athens.* It is remarkable for its blatant pre-Christian classical orientation, especially considering it originally wallpapered the apartments of Pope Julius II. Raphael honors the great pre-Christian thinkers— Aristotle, Plato, and company—who are portrayed as the leading artists of Raphael's day. There's Leonardo da Vinci, whom Raphael worshipped, in the role of Plato. Michelangelo broods in the foreground, added later. When Raphael snuck a peek at the Sistine Chapel, he decided that his arch-competitor was so good that he had to put their personal differences aside and include him in this tribute to the artists

of his generation. Today's St. Peter's was under construction as Raphael was working. In the *School of Athens,* he gives us a sneak preview of the unfinished church.

Sistine Chapel: Next is the brilliantly restored Sistine Chapel. This is the pope's personal chapel and also the place where, upon the death of the ruling pope, a new pope is elected.

The Sistine Chapel is famous for Michelangelo's pictorial culmination of the Renaissance, showing the story of creation, with a powerful God weaving in and out of each scene through that busy first week. This is an optimistic and positive expression of the High Renaissance and a stirring example of the artistic and theological maturity of the 33-year-old Michelangelo, who spent four years on this work.

The ceiling shows the history of the world before the birth of Jesus. We see God creating the world, creating man and woman, destroying the earth by flood, and so on. God himself, in his purple robe, actually appears in the first five scenes. Along the sides (where the ceiling starts

Sistine Chapel, packed with travelers marveling at Michelangelo's frescoes.

to curve), we see the Old Testament prophets and pagan Greek prophetesses who foretold the coming of Christ. Dividing these scenes and figures are fake niches (a painted 3-D illusion) decorated with nude statue-like figures with symbolic meaning.

In the central panel of the *Creation of Adam,* God and man take center stage in this Renaissance version of creation. Adam, newly formed in the image of God, lounges dreamily in perfect naked innocence. God, with his entourage, swoops in with a swirl of activity (which—with a little imagination—looks like a cross-section of a human brain...quite a strong humanist statement). Their reaching hands are the center of this work. Adam's is limp and passive; God's is strong and forceful, his finger twitching upward with energy. Here is the very moment of creation, as God passes the spark of life to man, the crowning work of his creation.

This is the spirit of the Renaissance. God is not a terrifying giant reaching down to puny and helpless man from way on high. Here they are on an equal plane, divided only by the diagonal bit of sky. God's billowing robe and the patch of green upon which Adam is lying balance each other. They are like two pieces of a jigsaw puzzle, or two long-separated continents, or like the yin and yang symbols finally coming together—uniting, complementing each other, creating wholeness. God and man work together in the divine process of Creation.

When the ceiling was finished and revealed to the public, it simply blew 'em away. It both caps the Renaissance and turns it in a new direction. In perfect Renaissance spirit, it mixes Old Testament prophets with classical figures. But the style is more dramatic, shocking, and emotional than the balanced Renaissance works before it. This is a very personal work—the Gospel according to Michelangelo—but its themes and subject matter are universal. Many art scholars contend that the Sistine ceiling is the single greatest work of art by any one human being.

Later, as part of the Counter-Reformation, a much older Michelangelo was commissioned to paint the *Last Judgment* (behind the altar). It's Judgment Day, and Christ—the powerful figure in the center, raising his arm to spank the wicked—has come to find out who's naughty and who's nice. Beneath him, a band of angels blows its trumpets Dizzy Gillespie-style, giving a wake-up call to the sleeping dead. The dead at lower left leave their graves and prepare to be judged. The righteous, on Christ's right hand (the left side of the picture), are carried up to the glories of heaven. The wicked on the other side are hurled down to hell, where demons wait to torture them. Charon, from the underworld of Greek mythology, waits below to ferry the souls of the damned to hell.

When *The Last Judgment* was unveiled to the public in 1541, it caused a sensation. The pope is said to have dropped to his knees and cried, "Lord, charge me not with my sins when thou shalt come on the Day of Judgment."

The dramatic painting changed the course of art. The complex composition, with more than 300 figures swirling around the figure of Christ, went far beyond traditional Renaissance balance. The twisted figures shown from every imaginable angle challenged other painters to try and top this master of 3-D illusion. And the sheer terror and drama of the scene was a striking contrast to the placid optimism of, say, Raphael's *School of Athens.* Michelangelo had Baroque-en all the rules of the Renaissance, signaling a new era of art.

On the long march back to the exit, you'll find the **Pinacoteca** (paintings by Raphael, Leonardo, Caravaggio, and others), a cafeteria (long lines, uninspired food), the underrated early Christian art section, and the exit via the souvenir shop.

Castel Sant'Angelo, Hadrian's mausoleum

▲CASTEL SANT'ANGELO

Built in ancient times as a tomb for the emperor Hadrian, used through the Middle Ages as a castle, prison, and place of last refuge for popes under attack, and today a museum, this giant pile of ancient bricks is packed with history. The structure itself is striking, the opulent papal rooms are dramatic (and cool inside during the summer), and the views up top are some of the best in Rome.

Cost and Hours: €15, more with special exhibits, daily 9:00-19:30, last entry one hour before closing, near Vatican City, 10-minute walk from St. Peter's Square at Lungotevere Castello 50, Metro: Lepanto or bus #40 or #64, café, tel. 06-681-9111, www.castelsantangelo.beniculturali.it.

Visiting the Castle: Ancient Rome allowed no tombs within its walls, so Emperor Hadrian grabbed the most commanding position across the river and built this towering tomb. In the year 590, the archangel Michael appeared above the mausoleum to signal the end of a plague. The tomb became a fortified palace, renamed for the "holy angel." Castel Sant'Angelo spent the Dark Ages as a fortress and prison, but was connected to the Vatican via an elevated corridor in the 13th century (since Rome was repeatedly plundered by invaders, Castel Sant'Angelo was a handy place of last refuge for popes). In anticipation of long sieges, rooms were decorated with papal splendor.

A one-way route circulates visitors through the medieval and then the ancient parts of the monument. After the ticket booth, head upstairs to the rampart with its four bastions (named for the evangelists: Matthew, Mark, Luke, and John). Then climb a ramp and cross a bridge that traverses the sacred chamber in the center. Next, you reach a sunny courtyard with a 16th-century statue of St. Michael. Climbing to another rampart, you then pass the little 19th-century military museum and later enter medieval rooms built for the pope. The papal library was painted by followers of Raphael. Eventually you reach the rooftop terrace with the statue of the Archangel Michael sheathing his sword—and one of the best views anywhere of Rome and St. Peter's Basilica.

North Rome

▲VILLA BORGHESE GARDENS

Rome's somewhat scruffy three-square-mile "Central Park" is great for its quiet shaded paths and for people-watching plenty of modern-day Romeos and Juliets. The best entrance is at the head of Via Veneto (Metro: Barberini, then 10-minute walk—or catch a cab). You can also enter the gardens from the top of the Spanish Steps.

▲▲▲BORGHESE GALLERY (GALLERIA BORGHESE)

This plush museum, filling a cardinal's mansion in the park, offers one of Europe's most sumptuous art experiences. You'll enjoy a collection of world-class Baroque sculpture, including Bernini's *David* and his excited statue of Apollo chasing Daphne, as well as paintings by Caravaggio, Raphael, Titian, and Rubens. The museum's mandatory reservation system keeps crowds to a manageable size.

Cost and Hours: €15, covered by Roma Pass; Tue-Sun 9:00-19:00, Thu until 21:00, closed Mon; free and very crowded once or twice a month when no reservations are taken, usually on a Sun. Check in

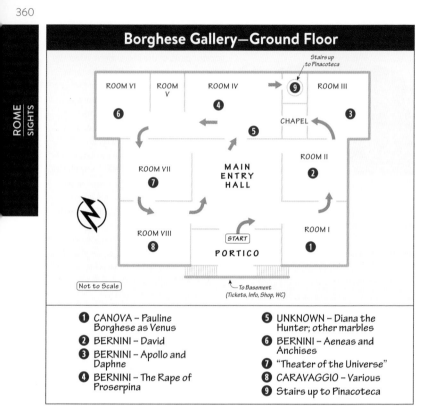

Borghese Gallery—Ground Floor

- **①** CANOVA – Pauline Borghese as Venus
- **②** BERNINI – David
- **③** BERNINI – Apollo and Daphne
- **④** BERNINI – The Rape of Proserpina
- **⑤** UNKNOWN – Diana the Hunter; other marbles
- **⑥** BERNINI – Aeneas and Anchises
- **⑦** "Theater of the Universe"
- **⑧** CARAVAGGIO – Various
- **⑨** Stairs up to Pinacoteca

advance and avoid going on a free day. The 1.5-hour audioguide is excellent.

Information: Tel. 06-32810, www.galleria borghese.it.

Advance Reservations Required: Reservations are mandatory. Entry times are 9:00, 11:00, 13:00, 15:00, and 17:00 plus 19:00 on Thu. You'll get exactly two hours for your visit. The sooner you reserve, the better. It's easiest to book online at www.tosc.it (€2/person booking fee; choose to pick up tickets at venue). You can also reserve over the telephone (€2/person booking fee, tel. 06-32810, press 2 for English, phones answered Mon-Fri 9:00-18:00, Sat 9:00-13:00, closed Sat in Aug and Sun year-round). Arrive 30 minutes before your appointed time to pick up your ticket (remember to bring your reservation confirmation). Don't cut it close—arriving late can

mean forfeiting your reservation.

Getting There: The museum, at Piazzale del Museo Borghese 5, is set idyllically but inconveniently in the vast Villa Borghese Gardens. A taxi drops you 100 yards from the museum. Your destination is the Galleria Borghese, near Via Pinciana. Don't tell the cabbie "Villa Borghese," which is the park, not the museum. To go by public transit, take bus #910 from Termini train station to the Puccini stop, walk to the park, turn left, and use the first park entrance (but note that #910 runs back to Termini by a different, less convenient route). You can also go by foot (20 minutes) from the Barberini Metro stop: Walk 10 minutes up Via Veneto, enter the park, and turn right, following signs another 10 minutes to the Borghese Gallery.

Tours: Guided English tours are offered every day at 9:00 and 11:00 (€6.50;

reserve online or by phone). Or consider the museum's excellent 1.5-hour audioguide (€5).

Baggage Check: Baggage check is free, mandatory, and strictly enforced. Even small purses must be checked.

Visiting the Museum: Two hours is all you get...and you'll want every minute. Budget most of your time for the more interesting ground floor, but set aside 30 minutes for the paintings of the Pinacoteca upstairs (highlights are marked by the audioguide icons).

The essence of the collection is the connection of the Renaissance with the classical world. As you enter, notice the second-century Roman reliefs with Michelangelo-designed panels above either end of the portico. The villa was built in the early 17th century by the great art collector Cardinal Scipione Borghese, who wanted to prove that the glories of ancient Rome were matched by the Renaissance.

Each room seems to feature a Baroque masterpiece. In Room I is *Pauline Borghese as Venus,* for which Napoleon's sister went the full monty for the sculptor Canova, scandalizing Europe. ("How could you have done such a thing?!" she was asked. She replied, "The room wasn't cold.") With the famous nose of her conqueror brother, she strikes the pose of Venus as conqueror of men's hearts. Her relaxed afterglow and slight smirk say she's already had her man. The light dent she puts in the mattress makes this goddess human.

In Room II, Gian Lorenzo Bernini's *David* twists around to put a big rock in his sling. He purses his lips, knits his brow, and winds his body like a spring as his eyes lock onto the target: Goliath, who's somewhere behind us, putting us right in the line of fire. Compared with Michelangelo's *David,* this is unvarnished realism—an unbalanced pose, bulging veins, unflattering face, and armpit hair. Michelangelo's *David* thinks, whereas Bernini's acts.

Bernini slays the pretty-boy *David*s of the Renaissance and prepares to invent Baroque.

The best one of all is in Room III: Bernini's *Apollo and Daphne.* It's the perfect Baroque subject—capturing a thrilling, action-filled moment. In the mythological story, Apollo—made stupid by Cupid's arrow of love—chases after Daphne, who has been turned off by the "arrow of disgust." Just as he's about to catch her, she calls to her father to save her. Magically, her fingers begin to sprout leaves, her toes become roots, her skin turns to bark, and she transforms into a tree. Frustrated Apollo will end up with a handful of leaves. Walk slowly around the statue. It's more air than stone.

In Room IV, admire Bernini's *The Rape of Proserpina,* proof that even at the age of 24 the sculptor was the master of marble. **Diana the Hunter** is a rare Greek original, with every limb and finger intact.

Bernini, Apollo and Daphne

Ara Pacis — Augustus' Altar of Peace

Room VII is called the "**Theater of the Universe**," with decor that sums up the eclectic nature of the villa. And in Room VIII is a fabulous collection of paintings by **Caravaggio,** who brought Christian saints down to earth with gritty realism.

Upstairs, in the **Pinacoteca** (Painting Gallery), are busts and paintings by Bernini, as well as paintings by Raphael, Titian, Correggio, and Domenichino.

▲▲MUSEO DELL'ARA PACIS (MUSEUM OF THE ALTAR OF PEACE)

On January 30, 9 BC, soon-to-be-emperor Augustus led a procession of priests up the steps and into this newly built "Altar of Peace." They sacrificed an animal on the altar and poured an offering of wine, thanking the gods for helping Augustus pacify barbarians abroad and rivals at home. This marked the dawn of the Pax Romana (c. AD 1-200), a Golden Age of good living, stability, dominance, and peace (*pax*). The Ara Pacis (AH-rah PAH-chees) hosted annual sacrifices by the emperor until the area was flooded by the Tiber River. For an idea of how high the water could get, find the measure (*idrometro*) scaling the right side of the church closest to the entrance. Buried under silt, it was abandoned and forgotten until the 16th century, when various parts were discovered and excavated. Mussolini gathered the altar's scattered parts and reconstructed them in a building here in 1938. Today, the Altar of Peace stands in a pavilion designed by American architect Richard Meier (opened 2006).

Cost and Hours: €10.50, more with special exhibits, tightwads can look in through huge windows for free, daily 9:30-19:30, last entry one hour before closing; videoguide-€6; a long block west of Via del Corso on Via di Ara Pacis, on the east bank of the Tiber near Ponte Cavour, Metro: Spagna plus a 10-minute walk down Via dei Condotti; tel. 06-0608, www.arapacis.it.

East Rome

▲▲▲NATIONAL MUSEUM OF ROME (MUSEO NAZIONALE ROMANO PALAZZO MASSIMO ALLE TERME)

The National Museum's main branch, at Palazzo Massimo, houses the greatest collection of ancient Roman art anywhere. Think of this museum as a walk back in time. As you gaze at the same statues that the Romans swooned over, the history of Rome comes alive—from Julius Caesar's murder to Caligula's incest to Vespasian's Colosseum to the coming of Christianity.

The Discus Thrower *in the National Museum of Rome*

Cost and Hours: €10, €12 combo-ticket covers three other branches—all skippable; free and crowded once or twice a month usually on a Sun—check in advance and avoid visiting on any free days; open Tue-Sun 9:00-19:45, closed Mon, last entry one hour before closing; audioguide—€5, about 100 yards from Termini station at Largo di Villa Peretti 2, Metro: Repubblica or Termini, tel. 06-3996-7700, www.museonazionaleromano.beniculturali.it.

Visiting the Museum: The ground-floor sculptures follow Rome's history as the city changes from a republic to a dictatorial empire. The first-floor exhibits take Rome from its peak through its slow decline. The second floor houses rare frescoes and fine mosaics, and the basement presents coins and everyday objects. Take advantage of the thoughtfully written information panels throughout.

On the first floor, along with statues and busts showing such emperors as Trajan and Hadrian, you'll see the best-preserved Roman copy of the Greek *Discus Thrower*. Statues of athletes like this commonly stood in the baths, where Romans cultivated healthy bodies, minds, and social skills, hoping to lead well-rounded lives. Other statues on this floor originally stood in the pleasure gardens of the Roman rich—surrounded by greenery with the splashing sound of fountains, all painted in bright, lifelike colors. Though created by Romans, the themes are mostly Greek, with godlike humans and human-looking gods.

The second floor contains frescoes and mosaics that once decorated the walls and floors of Roman villas. They're remarkably realistic and unstuffy, featuring everyday people, animals, flowery patterns, and geometrical designs. The Villa Farnesina frescoes—in black, red, yellow, and blue—are mostly architectural designs, with fake columns, friezes, and garlands. The Villa di Livia frescoes, owned by the wily wife of Augustus, immerse you in a leafy green garden full of birds and fruit trees, symbolizing the gods.

Finally, descend into the basement to see fine gold jewelry, a mummified body, and vault doors leading into the best coin collection in Europe, with fancy magnifying glasses maneuvering you through cases of coins from ancient Rome to modern times.

Baths of Diocletian

▲BATHS OF DIOCLETIAN/CHURCH OF SANTA MARIA DEGLI ANGELI (TERME DI DIOCLEZIANO/BASILICA STA. MARIA DEGLI ANGELI)

Of all the marvelous structures built by the Romans, their public baths were arguably the grandest, and the Baths of Diocletian were the granddaddy of them all. Built by Emperor Diocletian around AD 300 and sprawling over 30 acres—roughly five times the size of the Colosseum—these baths could cleanse 3,000 Romans at once. They functioned until AD 537, when barbarians attacked and the city's aqueducts fell into disuse, plunging Rome into a thousand years of poverty, darkness, and BO. Today, tourists can visit one grand section of the baths, the former main hall. This impressive remnant of the ancient complex was later transformed (with help from Michelangelo) into the Church of Santa Maria degli Angeli.

Cost and Hours: Free, daily 7:30-18:30, closes slightly later May-Sept and Sun year-round, entrance on Piazza della Repubblica (Metro: Repubblica), www.santamariadegliangeliroma.it.

EXPERIENCES

Shopping

Rome is a wonderful city to shop in. Even if you're not aiming to buy anything, exploring popular shopping areas provides a break from stressful, clogged tourist sights and an excuse to lose yourself on a charming street. Sometimes window-shopping, rather than museum-going, is the best way to connect with the contemporary life of a city. And that's certainly true in Rome.

Department Stores

The shopping complex under Termini train station is a convenient place to peruse clothes, bags, shoes, and perfume at several major Italian chain stores (most open daily 8:00-22:00). A good upscale department store is **La Rinascente** (Via del Tritone 61). Besides deluxe brands, it has a fine design section with great and often affordable ideas for gifts, a magnificent rooftop terrace for a romantic *aperitivo*, good restaurants, free bathrooms, and a section of an ancient aqueduct in the basement. The **Galleria Alberto Sordi** is an elegant 19th-century "mall" (across from Piazza Colonna, described earlier in my "Heart of Rome Walk"). **UPIM** is a popular midrange department store (many branches, including inside Termini train station, Via Nazionale 111, and Piazza Santa Maria Maggiore).

Affordable Shopping

The shopping area all along **Via del Corso** features moderately priced goods, with prices increasing as you head toward Piazza di Spagna (by the Spanish Steps). **Via Nazionale** also features a range of reasonably priced shops, especially for clothes and shoes. Near the bottom of Via Nazionale, in the **Monti** neighborhood near the Roman Forum, Via del Boschetto and Via dei Serpenti are more unique, with a mix of clothing shops and designer bric-a-brac. **Via Cola di Rienzo,** near the Vatican, is good for midrange clothes.

The Passeggiata

Throughout Italy, early evening is time to stroll. While elsewhere in Italy this is called the *passeggiata,* in Rome it's a cruder, big-city version called the *struscio* (meaning "to rub").

Many of Italy's youth live with their parents even into their 30s. They spend a lot of time being trendy and hanging out. Like American kids once gathered at the mall, working-class suburban youth *(coatto)* converge on the old center, as there's little to keep them occupied in Rome's dreary outskirts (which lack public spaces). The hot *vroom-vroom* motor scooter is their symbol; haircuts and fashion are follow-the-leader.

In a more genteel small town, the *passeggiata* comes with sweet whispers of *"bella"* and *"bello"* ("pretty" and "handsome"). In Rome, the admiration is a little cruder and oriented toward consumption—they say *"buona"* and *"buono"*—roughly meaning "tasty."

You can be a spectator, sipping a drink at a sidewalk table, but it's more fun to stroll along with everyone else.

Boutique Shopping

The triangular-shaped area between the Spanish Steps, Piazza Venezia, and Piazza del Popolo (along Via del Corso) contains Rome's highest concentration of upscale boutiques and fashion stores. For top fashion, stroll the streets around the Spanish Steps, including **Via Condotti, Via Borgognona** (for the big-name shops), and **Via del Babuino** (more big names and a few galleries). For antiques and vintage items, wander **Via dei Coronari** (between Piazza Navona and the bend in the river), **Via Giulia** (between Campo de' Fiori and the river), **Via dei Banchi Vecchi** (parallel to Via Giulia), and the super-chic **Via Margutta,** with art galleries, too (hidden parallel to Via del Babuino and running from the Spanish Steps to Piazza del Popolo). For dozens of stores selling affordable apparel aimed mainly at a younger crowd, try **Via Giubbonari** near Campo de' Fiori.

Flea Markets

For antiques and fleas, the granddaddy of markets is the **Porta Portese** *mercato delle pulci* (flea market). While the shopping gets old (and the vendor food shouldn't be consumed), the people-watching is endlessly entertaining (6:30-13:00 Sun only, on Via Portuense and Via Ippolito Nievo; to get to the market, catch bus #75 from Termini train station or tram #8 from Piazza Venezia, get off on Viale di Trastevere, and walk toward the river—and the noise).

Nightlife

For most visitors, the best after-dark activity is simply to grab a gelato and join in the *passeggiata,* the evening stroll through the medieval lanes that connect Rome's romantic, floodlit squares and fountains. Head for Piazza Navona, the

Pantheon, Campo de' Fiori, Trevi Fountain, the Spanish Steps, Via del Corso, or the Monti area. For recommended bars and eateries in these neighborhoods, see "Eating," later).

Sound-and-Light Shows

The Imperial Forums area hosts two atmospheric and inspirational sound-and-light shows that give you a chance to fantasize about the world of the Caesars (€15, both for €25, nightly mid-April–mid-Nov—bring your warmest coat, tickets sold online and at the gate, shows can sell out on busy weekends, tel. 06-0608, www.viaggioneifori.it).

The **Caesar's Forum Stroll,** starting at Trajan's Column, leads you to eight stops along a wooden sidewalk of a few hundred yards, while an hour's narration tells the dramatic story of Julius Caesar. In the **Forum of Augustus Show,** from your perch on wooden bleachers overlooking the remains of a vast forum, you'll learn the story of Augustus.

Contemporary Music

Music lovers will seek out the mega-music complex of the Rome **Auditorium** (Auditorium Parco della Musica), hosting concerts by Italian and international artists (€20-60 tickets, check availability in advance—concerts often sell out, Viale Pietro de Coubertin 30, take Metro to Flaminio and then catch tram #2 to Apollodoro, from there it's a 5-minute walk east, just beyond the elevated road, tram/metro runs until 23:30, box office tel. 02-6006-0900, www.auditorium.com).

Classical Music and Opera

The **Teatro dell'Opera** has an active schedule of opera and classical concerts. In the summer, the productions move to the Baths of Caracalla, south of the Colosseum, where ancient ruins make an evocative backdrop (tickets from €25, online reservations encouraged, box office takes phone reservations begin-ning five days prior at tel. 06-4816-0255; Via Firenze 72, a block off Via Nazionale, Metro: Repubblica; www.operaroma.it).

Opera da Camera di Roma is a cute, tourist-oriented, greatest-hits-of-opera performance in the Palazzo Albertoni Spinola. Enjoy some of the most beloved works of Verdi, Rossini, Puccini, Bellini, and Vivaldi in an intimate space—much as the Italian nobility would have heard them in private concerts. There's no reason to pay for more than the cheapest seats. Book direct: Buy the cheapest tickets and request the Rick Steves upgrade (RS%, performances Tue-Sun at 19:30, none on Mon, near the Jewish quarter at Piazza Capizucchi 6; call for ticket info, mobile 320-530-7112).

Tourist-oriented musical events take place at the Episcopal **Church of St. Paul's Within the Walls.** The music ranges from orchestral concerts (usually Tue and Fri at 20:30) to full operatic performances (usually Sat at 20:30). Some Sunday evenings at 18:30, the church hosts hour-long candlelit "Luminaria" concerts. Check the church website (under "Music") to see what's on (€10-30, same-day tickets usually available, arrive 30-45 minutes early for best seat, Via Napoli 58 at corner of Via Nazionale, Metro: Repubblica, tel. 06-482-6296, www.stpaulsrome.it).

Jazz

Rome has a small but vibrant jazz scene. **Alexanderplatz** is the venerable club in town, with performances most evenings (Sun-Thu concerts at 21:45, Fri-Sat at 22:30, closed in summer, Via Ostia 9, Metro: Ottaviano, tel. 06-3972-1867, alexanderplatzjazzclub.com).

Il Pentagrappolo is an *enoteca* that hosts live music (usually jazz) many Friday and Saturday evenings starting at 22:00 from September to June—check under "Eventi musicali" on their website to confirm (best to reserve on weekends, three blocks east of the Colosseum at Via

Celimontana 21, www.ilpentagrappolo. com, tel. 06-709-6301).

TramJazz, a creative venture by the public transit company, combines dinner, music, and a journey through the city in a vintage cable car for a mostly local crowd (€65, daily at 21:00, 3 hours, leaves from Piazza di Porta Maggiore—reached by tram #5 or #14 from Termini Station, book at least a week in advance, www. tramjazz.com).

SLEEPING

Choosing the right neighborhood in Rome is as important as choosing the right hotel. All of my recommended accommodations are in safe areas convenient to sightseeing.

Near Ancient Rome

This area is central, so you'll find these hotels are a short walk from the Colosseum and Roman Forum, as well as restaurants and shopping in the Monti district (see the next page).

$$$$ Hotel Lancelot is a 60-room hotel with an elegant feel at a fair price. Located in a pleasant, low-key residential neighborhood, it's quiet and safe, with a shady courtyard, restaurant, bar, and tiny communal sixth-floor terrace (family rooms, some view rooms, air-con, elevator, wheelchair-accessible, cheap parking, Via Capo d'Africa 47, tel. 06-7045-0615, www.lance lothotel.com, info@lancelothotel.com).

$$$$ Nerva Boutique Hotel is a snazzy slice of tranquility with 20 small, stylish, and often discounted rooms (RS%—use code "RICKSTEVES," air-con, elevator, Via Tor de' Conti 3, tel. 06-678-1835, www.hotelnerva.com, info@hotel nerva.com, Antonio and Paolo).

$$$ Nicolas Inn Bed & Breakfast, a delightful little four-room place with thoughtful touches, is spacious and bright, and right on busy Via Cavour. Staying here can make you feel like you have caring friends in Rome (RS%, cash only, air-con, Via Cavour 295, mobile 328-555-3004,

www.nicolasinn.it, info@nicolasinn.it).

$$$ Hotel Paba is homey, choco-late-box tidy, and lovingly cared. You'll take a vintage elevator to reach the seven rooms (RS%, email reservations preferred, big beds, breakfast served in room, air-con, elevator, Via Cavour 266, second floor, tel. 06-4782-4497, www.hotelpaba. com, info@hotelpaba.com).

$$$ Casa Il Rosario is a peaceful, well-run Dominican convent renting 40 rooms with monastic simplicity to both pilgrims and tourists in a steep but pleasant corner of the Monti neighborhood. Doubles have two single beds which can be pushed together (RS%—use code "ricksteves," cheaper single rooms with shared bath, reserve several months in advance, air-con, elevator, small garden and rooftop terrace, midnight curfew, near bottom of Via Nazionale at Via Sant'Agata dei Goti 10, bus #40 or #170 from Termini, tel. 06-679-2346, www.casailrosarioroma.it, info@casailrosarioroma.it).

$$ Hotel Antica Locanda is a gem on a small street in the heart of the Monti neighborhood. While there are four floors and no elevator, the 15 rooms with roman-tically rustic, stylish furnishings (air-con, no elevator, Via del Boschetto 84, tel. 06-484-894, www.anticalocandaroma.it, anticalocandaroma@gmail.com).

$ Hotel Rosetta, a homey and family-run *pensione* in the same building as Nicolas Inn, rents 15 simple rooms. It's pretty minimal, with no lounge and no breakfast, but its great location makes it a fine budget option (air-con, up one flight of stairs, Via Cavour 295, tel. 06-4782-3069, www.rosettahotel.com, info@rosetta hotel.com, Antonietta and Francesca).

Pantheon Neighborhood

This part of Rome still feels like a village, and as in a real village, buses and taxis are the only practical way to connect with other destinations.

Hotels & Restaurants near Ancient Rome

To Pantheon — PLEBISCITO — BATT.

Piazza Venezia

To Ghetto

GESÚ

Piazza Madonna di Loreto

VICTOR EMMANUEL MONUMENT

Piazza Campidoglio

CAPITOLINE MUSEUMS

TRAJAN'S COLUMN

TRAJAN'S FORUM

TRAJAN'S MARKET

Largo Magnanapoli

VIA NAZIONALE

V. 4 NOV.

VIA ALESSANDRINA

VIA BACCINA

MADONNA

CAPITOLINE HILL

ROMAN

EXIT ONLY

VIA DEI FIENILLI

VIA SAN TEODORO

ACCESS BETWEEN FORUM & PALATINE HILL

PALATINE HILL

Accommodations
1. Hotel Lancelot
2. Nerva Boutique Hotel
3. Nicolas Inn B&B & Hotel Rosetta
4. Hotel Paba
5. Casa Il Rosario
6. Hotel Antica Locanda

Eateries
7. Barzilai Bistrot
8. Taverna Romana
9. Taverna dei Fori Imperiali
10. Alle Carrette Pizzeria
11. Trattoria da Valentino
12. Trattoria Luzzi
13. Ristorante Pizzeria Naumachia
14. Li Rioni

Near Largo Argentina and Campo de' Fiori

$$$$ Relais Teatro Argentina, a six-room gem, is steeped in tasteful old-Rome elegance, but has all the modern comforts (air-con, 3 flights of stairs, breakfast in room or on balcony, Via del Sudario 35, tel. 06-9893-1617, www.relaisteatroargentina.com, info@relaisteatroargentina.com, kind Paolo).

$$$ Arch Rome Suites rents 12 spacious, modern, and cozy rooms—some with balconies and views (family rooms, air-con, elevator, Via dell'Arco della Ciambella 19, tel. 06-4549-8947, www.archromesuites.it, info@archromesuites.com, friendly Marika and Omar).

$$$ Casa di Santa Brigida has soft-spoken sisters gliding down polished hallways. You won't have a double bed

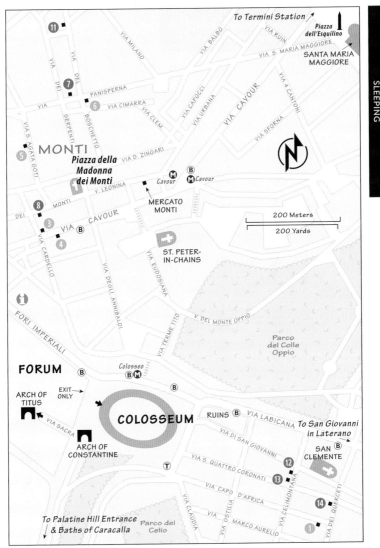

To Termini Station

Piazza dell'Esquilino

SANTA MARIA MAGGIORE

VIA MILANO

VIA DEL

VIA BALBO

VIA RUIN

VIA S. MARIA MAGGIORE

VIA 4 CANTONI

VIA DEI

PANISPERNA

VIA CIMARRA

VIA CAPOCCI

VIA URBANA

VIA CAVOUR

VIA SFORNA

VIA CLEM

VIA S. AGATA GOTI

SERPENTI

BOSCHETTO

MONTI

Piazza della Madonna dei Monti

VIA D. ZINGARI

V. LEONINA

Ⓜ Cavour Ⓑ Ⓜ Cavour

MERCATO MONTI

DEI

MONTI

VIA CAVOUR

Ⓑ

VIA CARDELLO

ST. PETER-IN-CHAINS

VIA EUDOSIANA

200 Meters

200 Yards

Ⓘ

FORI IMPERIALI

VIA DEGLI ANNIBALDI

VIA TERME TITO

V. DEL MONTE OPPIO

Parco del Colle Oppio

FORUM Ⓑ

Colosseo Ⓑ Ⓜ

Ⓑ

ARCH OF TITUS

EXIT ONLY

COLOSSEUM

RUINS Ⓑ VIA LABICANA **To San Giovanni in Laterano**

VIA SACRA

VIA DI SAN GIOVANNI

ARCH OF CONSTANTINE

Ⓣ

VIA S. QUATTRO CORONATI

SAN CLEMENTE Ⓑ

⑫

⑬

VIA CAPO D'AFRICA

VIA CELIMONTANA

⑭

VIA DEI QUERCETI

To Palatine Hill Entrance & Baths of Caracalla

VIA CLAUDIA

VIA OSTILIA

VIA MARCO AURELIO

Parco del Celio

⑪ ⑦ ⑥ ⑤ ⑧ ③ ④

or a TV, but you can luxuriate in the inn's public spaces or on its lovely roof terrace (book well in advance, air-con, elevator, tasty €25 dinners—reserve ahead, roof garden, plush library, Via di Monserrato 54, tel. 06-6889-2596, www.brigidine.org, casabrigidaroma@brigidine.org).

$$$ Hotel Smeraldo, with 66 rooms, is clean and a reasonable deal in a good location (air-con, elevator, roof terrace, midway between Campo de' Fiori and Largo Argentina at Via dei Chiavari 20, tel. 06-687-5929, www.smeraldoroma.com, info@smeraldo roma.com, Massimo and Walter).

Close to the Pantheon

$$$$ Hotel Nazionale, a four-star landmark, is a big, stuffy hotel, but it's a worthy splurge if you want security, comfort, and the heart of Rome at your doorstep

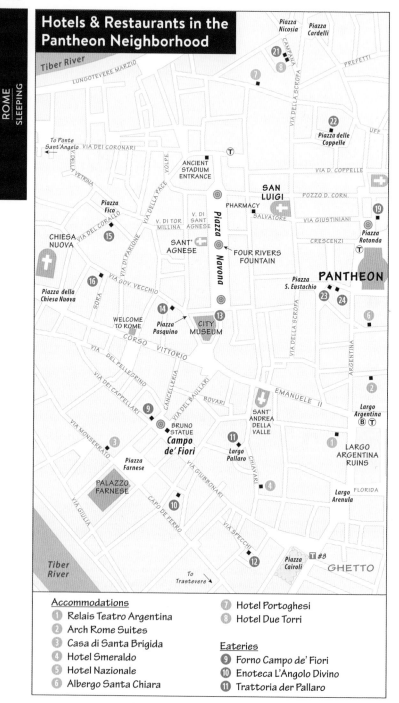

Hotels & Restaurants in the Pantheon Neighborhood

Accommodations

1. Relais Teatro Argentina
2. Arch Rome Suites
3. Casa di Santa Brigida
4. Hotel Smeraldo
5. Hotel Nazionale
6. Albergo Santa Chiara
7. Hotel Portoghesi
8. Hotel Due Torri

Eateries

9. Forno Campo de' Fiori
10. Enoteca L'Angolo Divino
11. Trattoria der Pallaro

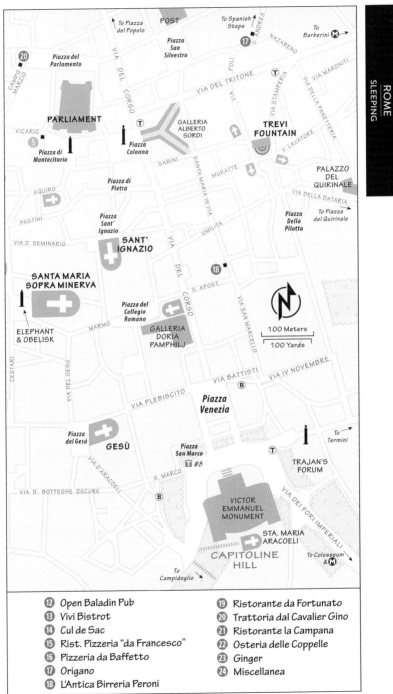

To Piazza del Popolo

POST

To Spanish Steps

To Barberini Ⓜ→

Piazza del Parlamento

Piazza San Silvestro

S. ANDREA

NAZARENO

CAMPO MARZIO

⑳

VIA DEL CORSO

VIA DEL TRITONE

VIA POLI

VIA STAMPERIA

VIA MAKONITI

VIA DELLA PANETTERIA

PARLIAMENT

⑰

Ⓣ

GALLERIA ALBERTO SORDI

TREVI FOUNTAIN

VICARIO

⑤

Ⓣ

SABINI

SANTA MARIA IN VIA

MURATTE

V. LAVATORE

Piazza di Montecitorio

Piazza Colonna

PALAZZO DEL QUIRINALE

AQUIRO

Piazza di Pietra

VIA DELLA DATARIA

To Piazza del Quirinale

PASTINI

Piazza Sant' Ignazio

UMILTA

Piazza Della Pilotta

VIA D. SEMINARIO

SANT' IGNAZIO

VIA DEL CORSO

SANTA MARIA SOPRA MINERVA

Piazza del Collegio Romano

S. APOST.

⑱

N

VIA SAN MARCELLO

100 Meters

100 Yards

ELEPHANT & OBELISK

MARMO

GALLERIA DORIA PAMPHILJ

CESTARI

VIA DEL GESÙ

VIA BATTISTI

VIA IV NOVEMBRE

Ⓑ

VIA PLEBISCITO

Piazza Venezia

To Termini

Piazza del Gesù

GESÙ

Piazza San Marco

Ⓣ

VIA D'ARACOELI

Ⓣ #8

TRAJAN'S FORUM

VIA D. BOTTEGHE OSCURE

Ⓑ

S. MARCO

VICTOR EMMANUEL MONUMENT

VIA DEI FORI IMPERIALI

STA. MARIA ARACOELI

CAPITOLINE HILL

To Colosseum & Ⓜ

To Campidoglio

⑫	Open Baladin Pub	⑲	Ristorante da Fortunato
⑬	Vivi Bistrot	⑳	Trattoria dal Cavalier Gino
⑭	Cul de Sac	㉑	Ristorante la Campana
⑮	Rist. Pizzeria "da Francesco"	㉒	Osteria delle Coppelle
⑯	Pizzeria da Baffetto	㉓	Ginger
⑰	Origano	㉔	Miscellanea
⑱	L'Antica Birreria Peroni		

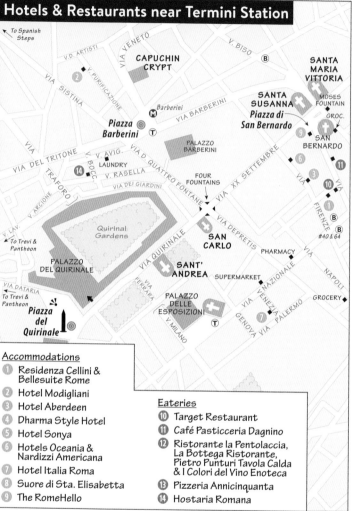

Hotels & Restaurants near Termini Station

Accommodations

1. Residenza Cellini & Bellesuite Rome
2. Hotel Modigliani
3. Hotel Aberdeen
4. Dharma Style Hotel
5. Hotel Sonya
6. Hotels Oceania & Nardizzi Americana
7. Hotel Italia Roma
8. Suore di Sta. Elisabetta
9. The RomeHello

Eateries

10. Target Restaurant
11. Café Pasticceria Dagnino
12. Ristorante la Pentolaccia, La Bottega Ristorante, Pietro Punturi Tavola Calda & I Colori del Vino Enoteca
13. Pizzeria Annicinquanta
14. Hostaria Romana

(RS%—use code "RICK," family rooms, air-con, elevator, Piazza Montecitorio 131, tel. 06-695-001, www.hotelnazionale.it, info@hotelnazionale.it).

$$$$ Albergo Santa Chiara is big, solid, and hotelesque. Its ample public lounges are dressy and professional, and its 96 rooms are quiet and spacious (RS%—use code "RICK," family rooms, air-con, elevator, Via di Santa Chiara 21, tel. 06-687-2979, www.albergosantachiara. com, info@albergosantachiara.com).

$$$$ Hotel Portoghesi is a classic hotel with 27 colorful rooms. It's peaceful, quiet, and comes with a delightful roof terrace (family rooms, breakfast on roof, air-con, elevator, Via dei Portoghesi 1, tel. 06-686-4231, www.hotelportoghesiroma. it, info@hotelportoghesiroma.it).

$$$ Hotel Due Torri feels professional yet homey, with an accommodating staff, generous public spaces, and 26 rooms (family rooms, air-con, elevator, Vicolo del Leonetto 23, tel. 06-6880-6956, www.

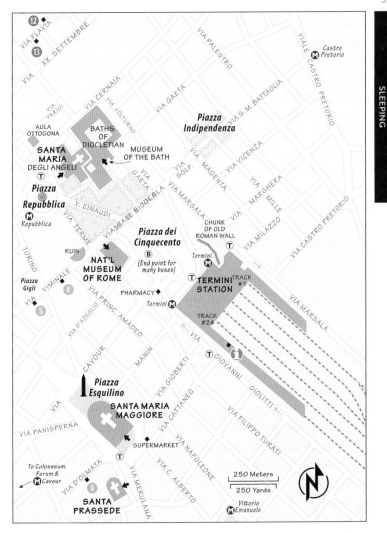

hotelduetorriroma.com, info@hoteldue
torriroma.com, Cinzia and her daughter
Giorgia).

Near Termini Station

While this neighborhood is not as atmospheric as other areas of Rome, some
hotels near Termini train station are less
expensive, and the Metro and buses link
you easily to the rest of the city.

$$$$ Residenza Cellini feels like a
gorgeous Neoclassical palace. It offers 13
rooms, four-star comforts and service,
and a small, breezy terrace (RS%, breakfast extra, air-con, elevator, Via Modena
5, third floor, tel. 06-4782-5204, www.
residenzacellini.it, info@residenzacellini.it;
Barbara, Gaetano, and Donato).

$$$$ Hotel Modigliani, a delightful
23-room place, has a vast and plush
lounge, a garden, and a newslet-
ter introducing you to each of the
staff (RS%, air-con, elevator; Via della
Purificazione 42; tel. 06-4281-5226,

www.hotelmodigliani.com, info@hotel modigliani.com, Giulia and Marco).

$$$$ Hotel Aberdeen, combines quality and friendliness. The 37 comfy rooms, on the ground floor and one floor up, are a fine value (RS%—use "Rick Steves reader reservations" link, family rooms, air-con, Via Firenze 48, tel. 06-482-3920, www.hotelaberdeen.it, info@hotelaberdeen.it).

$$$ Dharma Luxury Hotel spreads its 40 stylish rooms and suites across a few floors of a big palazzo, with elegant furnishings and room to breathe (RS%, family rooms, air-con, elevator, Via del Viminale 8, reception at #10, tel. 06-482-4460, www.dharmagroup.it/hotel/dharma-luxury, booking@dharmaluxuryhotel.it.).

$$$ Hotel Sonya offers 40 well-equipped rooms in varied sizes, a hearty breakfast, and decent prices (RS%—see the "Special Offers" page, family rooms, air-con, elevator, Via Viminale 58, tel. 06-481-9911, www.hotelsonya.it, info@hotelsonya.it, Francesca and Simone).

$$$ Hotel Oceania is a peaceful slice of air-conditioned heaven. The 24 rooms are spacious, quiet, and tastefully decorated, and the elegant sitting room has a manor-house feel (RS%—use code "RICKSTEVES," family rooms, elevator, TV lounge, Via Firenze 38, third floor, tel. 06-482-4696, www.hoteloceania.it, info@hoteloceania.it; Anna, Kira, and Roberto round out the staff).

$$ Bellesuite Rome offers seven small but nice rooms that are worth considering for the location—in the same fine building as Residenza Cellini and Target Inn (family rooms, air-con, elevator, Via Modena 5, third floor, tel. 06-9521-3049, www.bellesuiterome.com, mail@bellesuiterome.com, Martina).

$$ Hotel Nardizzi Americana, with a small rooftop terrace, 40 standard rooms, and a laid-back atmosphere, is another decent value (RS%—email reservation for discount, family rooms, air-con, elevator, Via Firenze 38, fourth floor, tel. 06-488-0035, www.hotelnardizzi.it, info@

hotelnardizzi.it; friendly Stefano, Fabrizio, Mario, and Giancarlo).

$$ Hotel Italia Roma, in a busy and handy locale, has 35 modest but comfortable rooms plus four newer, more expensive "residenza" rooms on the third floor (RS%, family rooms, air-con, elevator, Via Venezia 18, just off Via Nazionale, tel. 06-482-8355, www.hotelitaliaroma.it, info@hotelitaliaroma.it; Andrea, Sabrina, Abdul, and Eleonora).

$ Suore di Santa Elisabetta is a heavenly Polish-run convent with a serene garden, roof terrace with grand views, and 37 rooms (family rooms, cheaper rooms with shared bath, fans but no air-con, elevator for top floors, guest kitchen, Wi-Fi in lounge only, 23:00 curfew; Via dell'Olmata 9, Metro: Termini or Vittorio Emanuele; tel. 06-488-8271, www.csse-roma.com, select "Casa per ferie" for English, ist.it.s.elisabetta@libero.it).

¢ The RomeHello hostel is, as their slogan brags, "more than just a bed." Recently opened, it's a modern, quiet, and friendly hostel run with a mission to employ locals and provide a comfortable home for travelers (Via Torino 45, tel. 06-9686-0070, www.theromehello.com, ciao@theromehello.com).

EATING

Romans take great pleasure in dining well. Embrace this passion over a multicourse meal at an outdoor table, watching a parade of passersby while you sip wine with loved ones.

sine in a snug interior that bustles with energy (Wed-Mon 12:30-15:00 & 19:30-22:30, closed Tue, reserve for dinner, Via della Madonna dei Monti 9, tel. 06-679-8643, www.latavernadeiforiimperiali.com).

$$ Alle Carrette Pizzeria—simple, rustic, and family-friendly—serves great wood-fired pizza just 200 yards from the Forum. It's cheap and fast (daily 12:00-15:30 & 19:00-24:00, Vicolo delle Carrette 14, tel. 06-679-2770).

$ Trattoria da Valentino is a classic time warp specializing in *scamorza* (grilled cheese with various toppings; about €10), pastas, and a variety of meat dishes (Mon-Sat 13:00-14:45 & 19:30-23:00, closed Sun, Via del Boschetto 37, tel. 06-488-0643).

Behind the Colosseum

$ Trattoria Luzzi is a well-worn, no-frills eatery serving simple food in a high-energy—sometimes chaotic—environment, so reserve ahead (Thu-Tue 12:00-24:00, closed Wed, Via Celimontana 1, tel. 06-709-6332).

$$ Ristorante Pizzeria Naumachia is a good second bet if Trattoria Luzzi next door is jammed up. It's a bit more upscale and serves good-quality pizza and pastas at decent prices (Via Celimontana 7, tel. 06-700-2764).

$$ Li Rioni, a pizzeria, is open only for dinner, when the busy chef plunges dough into its wood-fired oven, then pulls out crispy-crust Roman-style pizzas (Wed-Mon 19:30-24:00, closed Tue, Via dei SS. Quattro 24, tel. 06-7045-0605).

Pantheon Neighborhood
On and near Campo de' Fiori

In the evening, Campo de' Fiori offers a characteristic setting—although it can be overrun by tourists out drinking.

$$ Enoteca L'Angolo Divino is an inviting little wine bar. With tiny tables, a tiny menu, and more locals than tourists, this place can leave you with a lifelong

---

Eating Tips: Kitchens close at most restaurants between lunch and dinner; if it's a quality restaurant, it won't reopen before 19:00. If a smaller restaurant is booked up later in the evening (from 20:30 or so), they may accommodate walk-ins if you're willing to eat quickly.

Rome's fabled squares—most notably Piazza Navona, near the Pantheon, and Campo de' Fiori—are lined with the outdoor tables of touristy restaurants with enticing menus and formal-vested waiters. The atmosphere is super romantic. But restaurants in these areas are notorious for surprise charges, forgettable food, microwaved ravioli, and bad service. I enjoy the view by savoring just a drink or dessert on a famous square, but I dine with locals on nearby low-rent streets.

Ancient Rome

For locations, see the map on page 368.

Monti District

$$ Barzilai Bistrot, a wine bar with a kitchen under stout timbers, is family-run, with a fun menu ranging from pastas to burgers (daily, no reservations, Via Panisperna 44, tel. 06-487-4979).

$$ Taverna Romana is small, simple, and a bit chaotic. This family-run eatery's *cacio e pepe* (cheese-and-pepper pasta) is a favorite. Arrive early, as they take no reservations (daily 12:30-14:45 & 19:00-22:45, Via della Madonna dei Monti 79, tel. 06-474-5325).

$$ Taverna dei Fori Imperiali serves typical, slightly higher-priced Roman cui-

Roman Cuisine

For more on Italian food, see the "Eating" section of the Practicalities chapter.

Antipasti (Appetizers)

Antipasto misto: Marinated or grilled vegetables (eggplant, artichokes, peppers, mushrooms), cured meats, cheeses, or seafood (anchovies, octopus)

Bruschetta: Toasted bread brushed with olive oil and garlic, topped with chopped tomatoes, mushrooms, or other tidbits.

Fritti: Battered or breaded fried snacks—often olives stuffed with meat, potato croquettes, or mozzarella balls. Other classics are *supplí* (rice balls with mozzarella) and *fiori di zucca* (squash blossoms filled with mozzarella and anchovies).

Prosciutto e melone: Cantaloupe wrapped in thin-sliced ham

Primo Piatto (First Course)

Bucatini all'amatriciana: Thin pasta tubes with a sauce of tomatoes, onion, pancetta, and pecorino cheese

Gnocchi alla romana: Semolina dumplings baked with butter and cheese

Penne all'arrabbiata: Spicy tomato sauce with chili peppers (*peperoncini*) and garlic over penne

memory (daily 17:00-24:00, also Tue-Sat 11:00-14:00, Via dei Balestrari 12, tel. 06-686-4413).

$$ Trattoria der Pallaro, an eccentric and well-worn eatery that has no menu, has a slogan: "Here, you'll eat what we want to feed you." You have three menu choices: €25 for the works; €20 for appetizers, *secondi,* and dessert; or €16 for appetizers and pasta (daily 12:00-16:00 & 19:00-24:00, reserve if dining after 20:00, cash only, Largo del Pallaro 15, tel. 06-6880-1488).

$$ Open Baladin is a busy, modern, and spacious brewpub featuring a few dozen Italian craft beers and a menu of burgers, salads, and freshly cooked potato chips (daily 12:00-24:00, Via degli Specchi 5, tel. 06-683-8989).

Near Piazza Navona

$$ Vivi Bistrot is in the Museum of Rome building at the south end of Piazza Navona. This cheery and modern little restaurant serves salads, pastas, and burger plates with a focus on organic ingredients (Tue-Sun 10:00-24:00, closed Mon, Piazza Navona 2, tel. 06-683-3779).

$$ Cul de Sac, a long and skinny trattoria lined with wine bottles, is packed with an enthusiastic crowd enjoying a wide-ranging menu, from pasta to homemade pâté. They don't take reservations—come early (daily 12:00-24:00, Piazza Pasquino 73, tel. 06-6880-1094).

$$$ Ristorante Pizzeria "da Francesco," bustling and authentic, has a hardworking young waitstaff, great indoor seating, and a

Rigatoni con la pajata: Pasta topped with a stew of calf intestines

Spaghetti alla carbonara: Eggs, pancetta or *guaniciale* (cured pork cheek), cheese (*pecorino romano* or *parmigiano reggiano*), and black pepper over pasta

Spaghetti alle vongole veraci: Pasta served with small clams in the shell

Stracciatella alla romana: Meat broth with whipped eggs, topped with parmesan

Secondo Piatto (Second Course)

Abbacchio alla scottadito: Baby lamb chops grilled and eaten as finger food

Anguillette in umido: Stewed baby eels from Lake Bracciano

Coda alla vaccinara: Oxtail braised with garlic, wine, tomato, and celery

Filetti di baccalà: Battered and fried salt cod fillets (like fish-and-chips minus the chips)

Involtini di vitello al sugo: Veal cutlets rolled with prosciutto, celery, and cheese in a tomato sauce

Saltimbocca alla romana: "Jump-in-the-mouth"—thinly sliced veal layered with prosciutto and sage, then lightly fried

Trippa alla romana: Tripe braised with onions, carrots, and min.

Contorni (Side Dishes)

Carciofi: Artichokes served either *alla romana* (simmered with garlic and mint) or *alla giudia* (flattened and fried)

Fave al guanciale: Fava beans simmered with cured pork cheek and onion

Misticanza: Mixed green salad of arugula (*rucola*) and curly endive (*puntarelle*)

few tables stretching along the quiet street (daily 12:00-15:30 & 19:00-24:00, Piazza del Fico 29, tel. 06-686-4009, www.dafrancesco.it). Reservations are required for evening seatings at 19:00, 20:30, or 22:00.

$ Pizzeria da Baffetto is famous and therefore generally comes with a ridiculous line. The pizzas are great, the service is surly, and the tables are tightly arranged (daily 12:00-15:30 & 18:30-late, cash only, order "M" or "D"—medium or large, Via del Governo Vecchio 114, tel. 06-686-1617).

Near the Trevi Fountain

$$$ Origano is a bustling, modern bistro located three blocks away from the Trevi Fountain. It serves well-priced traditional Roman specialties and wood-fired pizza in an often chaotic setting (daily 12:00-24:00, Via di Sant'Andrea delle Fratte 25/26, tel. 06-699-20907).

$$ L'Antica Birreria Peroni is Rome's answer to a German beer hall, the place is a hit with Romans for a cheap night out (Mon-Sat 12:00-24:00, closed Sun, a block off Via del Corso at Via di San Marcello 19, tel. 06-679-5310).

Near the Pantheon

$$$$ Ristorante da Fortunato is an Italian classic, with white-coated, black-tie career waiters politely serving good meat and fish to politicians, foreign dignitaries, and well-heeled tourists (figure €50/person, daily 12:30-16:00 & 18:30-23:30, Via

Restaurants near Vatican City

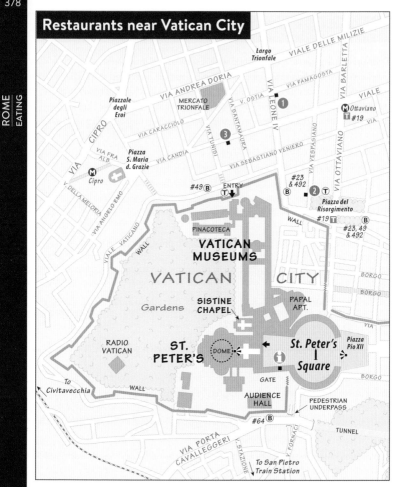

del Pantheon 55, tel. 06-679-2788, www. ristorantefortunato.it).

$$ Trattoria dal Cavalier Gino, tucked away on a tiny street behind the Parliament, has English-speaking siblings Carla and Fabrizio serve up traditional Roman favorites. They offer four seatings a day: 13:00, 14:30, 20:00, and 22:00. Reserve ahead (Mon-Sat, closed Sun, behind Piazza del Parlamento and just off Via di Campo Marzio at Vicolo Rosini 4, tel. 06-687-3434).

$$$ Ristorante la Campana is a classic—an authentic slice of old Rome appreciated by well-dressed locals. It serves typical Roman dishes and daily specials, plus it

has a self-service *antipasti* buffet, which makes a nice €12 lunch (Tue-Sun 12:30-15:00 & 19:30-23:00, closed Mon, Vicolo della Campana 18, tel. 06-687-5273, www. ristorantelacampana.com).

$$ Osteria delle Coppelle, a slapdash, trendy place, serves traditional dishes to a local crowd and a fun selection of €3 *cicchetti*—small plates (daily 12:30-15:30 & 19:00-late, Piazza delle Coppelle 54, tel. 06-4550-2826).

$$ Ginger is a crisp, modern restaurant one block from the Pantheon, with a menu selection—pastas, *panini,* salads, and smoothies—that is healthy, organic,

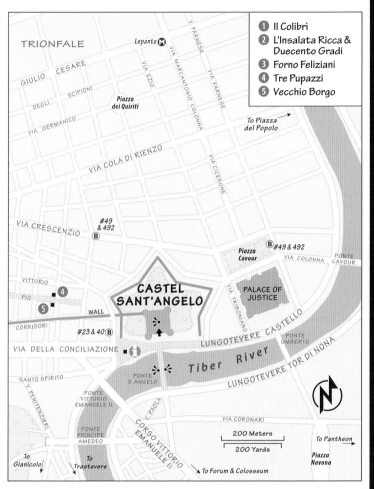

To Piazza
del Popolo

Map Legend:

1. Il Colibrì
2. L'Insalata Ricca & Duecento Gradi
3. Forno Feliziani
4. Tre Pupazzi
5. Vecchio Borgo

and a bit pricey (daily 8:00-23:00, Piazza di S. Eustachio 54, tel. 06-6830-8559).

$$ Miscellanea, run by much-loved Miki, offers €4 sandwiches, pizza-like bruschetta, and a long list of hearty salads, along with pasta and other staples (daily 9:00-24:00, Via della Palombella 37, tel. 06-6813-5318).

Near Vatican City

As in the Colosseum area, some eateries near the Vatican prey on exhausted tourists. Instead, tide yourself over with a slice of pizza or at any of these places, and save your euros for a better meal elsewhere.

Handy Lunch Places near Piazza Risorgimento

$$ Il Colibrì, run by the Ricci brothers, has noisy streetside seating and a quiet interior (daily 10:30-15:30 & 17:00-24:00, at corner of Via Leone IV and Via Famagosta 69, tel. 06-3751-4767).

$ L'Insalata Ricca is a branch of the popular chain that serves hearty salads and pastas (daily 12:00-23:30, across from the Vatican walls at Piazza Risorgimento 5, tel. 06-3973-0387).

$ Duecento Gradi is a good bet for fresh and creative sandwiches—though at €5-8 they're expensive by Roman standards. Munch your lunch sitting down (€1 extra) or take it away (daily 11:00–24:00, Piazza Risorgimento 3, tel. 06-3975-4239).

Other Options in the Vatican Area

Viale Giulio Cesare and **Via Candia:** These streets are lined with cheap *pizza rustica* shops and self-serve places. **$ Forno Feliziani** (closed Sun, Via Candia 61) is a fancy version with nicely presented pizza by the slice and simple cafeteria-style dishes that you can eat in or take out.

Close to St. Peter's: The pedestrian-only Borgo Pio—a block from Piazza San Pietro—has restaurants worth a look, such as the traditional **$$ Tre Pupazzi** (Mon-Sat 12:00–15:00 & 19:00–23:00, closed Sun, at corner of Via Tre Pupazzi and Borgo Pio, tel. 06-6880-3220). At **$ Vecchio Borgo,** across the street, you can get pasta, pizza by weight, and veggies to go or to eat at simple tables (daily 9:30–22:30, Borgo Pio 27a).

North Rome

To locate these restaurants, see the map on page 370.

$$$$ Ristorante il Gabriello is inviting and small—modern under medieval arches. Gabriello cooks creative Roman cuisine using fresh, organic products from his wife's farm. While you're likely to dine surrounded by my readers here, the atmosphere is fun and convivial (dinner only, Mon-Sat 19:00–23:00, closed Sun, reservations smart, air-con, dress respectfully—no shorts, 3 blocks from Spanish Steps at Via Vittoria 51, tel. 06-6994-0810, www.ilgabriello.com).

$$ Ginger, four blocks in front of the Spanish Steps, is modern and bright, with an emphasis on sustainable and healthy ingredients (daily 8:00–23:00, Via Borgognona 43, tel. 06-9603-6390). A sister location near the Pantheon is described earlier.

$$$ Caffè Vitti, delightfully set on a fine traffic-free square, has been serving its neighborhood for over a century. The food won't win any awards—and you pay for the location—but it offers a delightful chance to enjoy a meal (good salads, pizza) or a cocktail on a quiet and characteristic square (daily 6:30–24:00, Piazza San Lorenzo in Lucina 33, tel. 06-687-6304).

Near Termini Station

For locations, see the map on page 372.

Around Via Firenze

$$$ Target Restaurant has a sleek and dressy ambience, capable service, and food that's reliably good, but pricey (free *aperitivo* with this book, daily 12:00–15:30 & 19:00–24:00, closed Sun at lunch, reserve to specify seating outside or inside—avoid getting seated in basement, Via Torino 33, tel. 06-474-0066, www.targetrestaurant.it).

$$ Café Pasticceria Dagnino, a time-warp from the 1960s, is known for its fine pastry section and Sicilian treats from *arancini* to cannoli. It's fast, reasonably priced, and reliable, with good seating inside, upstairs, and outside in the mall (daily 7:00–23:00, Galleria Esedra, enter at Via Torino 95, tel. 06-481-8660).

Around Via Flavia

$$$ Ristorante la Pentolaccia, upscale and romantic, is a dressy but still tourist-friendly place with tight seating and traditional Roman cooking—reservations are smart (daily 12:00–15:00 & 18:00–23:00, a block off Via XX Settembre at Via Flavia 38, tel. 06-483-477, www.lapentolaccia-restaurant.it).

$$$ La Bottega Ristorante is a bright, contemporary, and easygoing place serving Roman and Mediterranean cuisine, and good wine by the glass (nightly from 17:00, Via Flavia 46, tel. 06-487-0391). They run the adjacent pizzeria.

$ Pietro Punturi Tavola Calda is a *rosticceria* cooking up super casual dishes sold by weight and eaten on plastic at its fast-food-type seating (Mon-Sat 8:30-20:30, closed Sun, Via Flavia 46).

$$ Pizzeria Annicinquanta, big and modern, is a neighborhood fixture serving Neapolitan-style pizzas in a calm ambience with outdoor seating (daily 12:00-15:30 & 19:30-24:00, Via Flavia 3, tel. 06-4201-0460).

$$$ I Colori del Vino Enoteca is a classy wine bar with a creative menu of *affettati* (cold cuts) and cheeses, and a great list of fine wines by the glass (Mon-Sat 12:00-15:00 & 18:00-23:00, closed Sun, Via Aureliana 15 at corner of Via Flavia, tel. 06-474-1745).

Between Piazza Barberini and Trevi Fountain

$$$ Hostaria Romana is a busy bistro with a hustling and fun-loving gang of waiters. Its menu specializes in traditional Roman dishes such as *saltimbocca alla romana* (Mon-Sat 12:30-15:00 & 19:15-23:00, closed Sun and Aug, reservations smart, Via del Boccaccio 1, tel. 06-474-5284, www.hostariaromana.it).

TRANSPORTATION

Getting Around Rome

Rome's public transportation system is cheap and efficient, but also confusing and crowded. The three Metro lines are relatively sane and straightforward, but serve a limited area. Buses are more chaotic—there are no posted timetables or maps, and stop names are announced only in the newest vehicles. But they run frequently and go everywhere. The website www.atac.roma.it has a **journey planner** in English that will help you sort through the thicket of routes.

Buying Tickets: All public transportation uses the same ticket. It costs €1.50 and is valid for one Metro ride—including

transfers underground—plus unlimited city buses and trams during a 100-minute period. Passes good on buses and the Metro are sold in increments of 24 hours (€7), 48 hours (€12.50), 72 hours (€18), one week (€24—about the cost of three taxi rides), and one month (€35, valid for a calendar month).

You can purchase tickets and passes from machines at Metro stations and a few major bus stops (cash/coins only), and from some newsstands and tobacco shops (*tabacchi,* marked by a black-and-white *T* sign). Tickets are not sold on board.

Validate your ticket by sticking it in the Metro turnstile (magnetic strip-side up, arrow-side first) or in the machine when you board the bus (magnetic strip-side down, arrow-side first)—watch others and imitate. It'll return your ticket with your expiration time printed. To get through a Metro turnstile with a transit pass, press the card to the turnstile's electronic sensor pad. On buses and trams, you need to validate your pass only your first time using it.

By Metro

The Roman subway system (Metropolitana, or "Metro") is simple, clean, cheap, and fast. The two lines you need to know—A and B—intersect at Termini Station. The Metro runs from 5:30 to 23:30 (Fri-Sat until 1:30 in the morning). The subway's first and last compartments are generally the least crowded, and the least likely to harbor pickpockets.

By Bus

The Metro is handy, but it won't get you everywhere—you often have to take the bus (or tram). Route and system maps aren't posted, but with some knowledge of major stops, you can wing it without one. (The ATAC website has a PDF bus map that you can download, bookstores sell paper transport maps, and the ATAC journey planner is helpful.) Rome's few

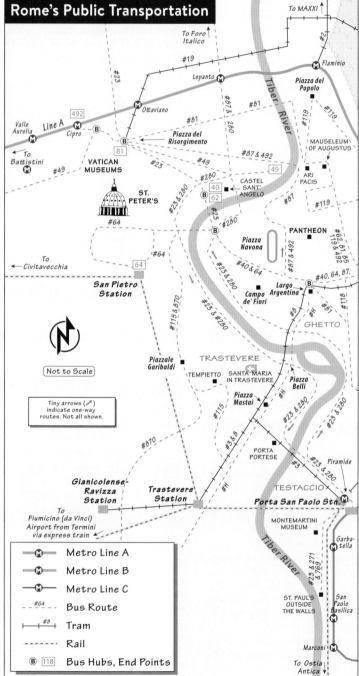

Rome's Public Transportation

To MAXXI

To Foro Italico

#19

#2

Flaminio

Lepanto

Piazza del Popolo

#23

Ottaviano

Tiber River

#87 & 280

#81

#81

#119

#119

Line A

492

Valle Aurelia

Cipro

B

Piazza del Risorgimento

#87 & 492

MAUSELEUM OF AUGUSTUS

To Battistini

81

#49

#23

#49

49

ARI PACIS

VATICAN MUSEUMS

#280

CASTEL SANT' ANGELO

#87

#119

ST. PETER'S

B 40
62

#87 & 492

PANTHEON

#64

#25 & 280

B

#25 & 280

Piazza Navona

#62, 81, 85
119 & 492

#64

64

San Pietro Station

#115 & 870

#23 & 280

#40 & 64

Campo de' Fiori

Largo Argentina

#40, 64, 87,

B

#8

#81

#118

To Civitavecchia

GHETTO

Not to Scale

Tiny arrows (↗) indicate one-way routes. Not all shown.

Piazzale Garibaldi

TRASTEVERE

#23 & #280

#115

TEMPIETTO

SANTA MARIA IN TRASTEVERE

Piazza Belli

#H

#23 & 280

#23 & 280

Piazza Mastai

#870

#115

#3 & 8

PORTA PORTESE

#H

#3

#23 & 280

Piramide

#23 & 280

Gianicolense-Ravizza Station

Trastevere Station

Porta San Paolo Stn.

TESTACCIO

To Fiumicino (da Vinci) Airport from Termini via express train

MONTEMARTINI MUSEUM

Garba-tella

#23 & 271
& 769

ST. PAUL'S OUTSIDE THE WALLS

San Paolo Basilica

Tiber River

Marconi

To Ostia Antica

	Metro Line A
	Metro Line B
	Metro Line C
#64	Bus Route
#8	Tram
	Rail
B 118	Bus Hubs, End Points

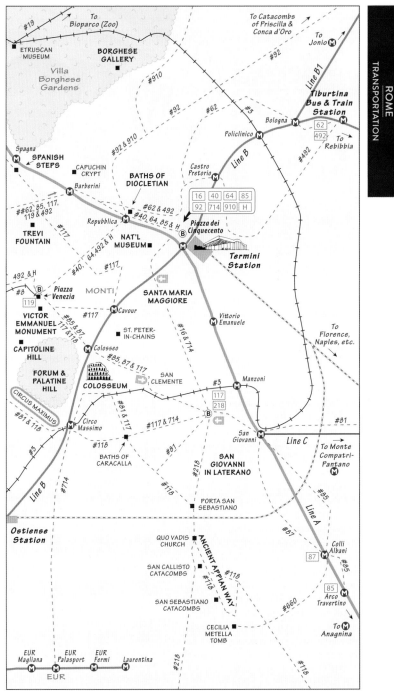

tram lines function for all intents and purposes identically to buses. Frustratingly, the exact frequency of various bus routes is difficult to predict (and not printed at bus stops). At major stops, an electronic board shows the number of minutes until the next buses arrive.

Rick's Tip: Buses #64 and #40 *are popular with tourists and* **pickpockets.** *If one bus is packed, there's likely a second one on its tail with fewer crowds and thieves.*

These are the most important bus routes for tourists:

Bus #64: This bus links Termini Station with the Vatican, stopping at Piazza della Repubblica (sights), Via Nazionale (recommended hotels), Piazza Venezia (near Forum), Largo Argentina (near Pantheon and Campo de' Fiori), St. Peter's Basilica (get off just past the tunnel), and San Pietro Station.

Bus #40: This express bus, which mostly follows the #64 route (but ends near the Castel Sant'Angelo on the Vatican side of the river), is especially helpful—fewer stops and (somewhat) fewer crowds.

Other useful routes include:

Bus #49: Piazza Cavour/Castel Sant'Angelo, Piazza Risorgimento (Vatican), and Vatican Museums.

Buses #85 and #87: Piazza Navona (#87 only), Pantheon, Via del Corso (#85 only), Piazza Venezia, Forum, and Colosseum.

Bus #492: Travels east-west, connecting Tiburtina (train and bus stations), Largo Santa Susanna (near Piazza della Repubblica), Piazza Barberini, Piazza Venezia, Largo Argentina (near Pantheon and Campo de' Fiori), Piazza Cavour (Castel Sant'Angelo), and Piazza Risorgimento (St. Peter's Basilica and Vatican).

Elettrico **Minibuses:** Cute electric minibuses take circular routes past major sights (small, so hard to find a seat). They run weekdays 7:15-20:15. *Elettrico* #117 connects San Giovanni in Laterano, Colosseo, Via Cavour, Via Nazionale, and Trevi Fountain. *Elettrico* #119 connects Piazza Venezia, Via del Corso, Trevi Fountain, Piazza di Spagna, Piazza del Popolo, and Piazza Augusto Imperatore.

By Taxi

I use taxis in Rome more often than in other cities. They're reasonable and useful for efficient sightseeing in this big, hot metropolis. Three or four companions with more money than time should taxi almost everywhere. Taxis start at €3, then charge about €1.50 per kilometer (surcharges: €1.50 on Sun, €3.50 for nighttime hours of 22:00-6:00, one regular suitcase or bag rides free, tip by rounding up—€1 or so). Sample fares: Termini area to Vatican—€15; Termini area to Colosseum—€7; Termini area to the Borghese Gallery—€9; Colosseum to Trastevere—€12 (or look up your route at www.worldtaximeter.com).

You can hail a cab on the street, but Romans generally walk to the nearest taxi stand (many are marked on this book's maps). Or have your hotel or restaurant call a taxi for you. The meter starts when the call is received. To call a cab on your own, dial 06-3570, 06-4994, or 06-6645, or use the official city taxi line, 06-0609; they'll likely ask you for an Italian phone number (give them your mobile number or your hotel's).

You can also use the Free Now app, which orders an official white taxi at regular taxi rates, with the convenience of paying via the app.

Beware of corrupt taxis. First, only use official Rome taxis. They're white, with a taxi sign on the roof and a maroon logo on the door that reads *Roma Capitale.* When you get in, make sure the meter (*tassametro*) is turned on (you'll see the meter either on the dashboard or up by the rearview mirror). You'll rarely pay more than €12 for a ride in town. Keep an eye on the fare on the meter as you near your destination; some cabbies turn the meter off instantly when they stop and tell you a higher price.

By law, every cab must display a multilingual official price chart—usually on the back of the seat in front of you. If the fare doesn't seem right, point to the chart and ask the cabbie to explain it.

Uber works in Rome as it does in the US, but only at the more expensive Uber Black level.

Arriving and Departing
By Plane
Rome's two airports—**Fiumicino** (a.k.a. Leonardo da Vinci, code: FCO) and the small **Ciampino** (code: CIA)—share the same website (www.adr.it).

FIUMICINO AIRPORT
Rome's major airport is manageable. Terminals T1, T2, and T3 are all under one roof—walkable end to end in 20 minutes. T5 is a separate building requiring a short shuttle trip. (T4 is still being built.) The T1-2-3 complex has ground transport, a TI (in T3, daily 9:00-17:30, longer in summer), ATMs, banks, luggage storage, shops, and bars. For airport information, call 06-65951.

Getting Between Fiumicino Airport and Downtown Rome: In either direction, give yourself plenty of time to allow for traffic delays, finding your train or bus, and walking to the terminal.

By Train: Trenitalia's slick, direct, first-class-only Leonardo Express train connects the airport train station (called Fiumicino Aeroporto) and Rome's central Termini Station in 32 minutes for €14. At either station, buy your ticket from a Trenitalia machine, a ticket office (*biglietteria*), or a newsstand near the platform. You must validate your ticket before boarding by stamping it in a green-and-gray machine near the track. Be aware that people offering help are likely pickpockets: Watch your belongings. Trains run at least twice hourly in both directions from roughly 6:00 to 23:00 (up to 4/hour in busy times). Make sure the train you board is going to the central "Roma Termini" station.

Returning from Termini train station *to* the airport, trains usually depart from track 23 or 24. Check the departure boards for "Fiumicino Aeroporto" and confirm with an official or a local on the platform that the train is indeed going to the airport.

You can access most of the airport's

terminals from the airport train station. If your flight leaves from terminal T5 (where most American air carriers flying direct to the US depart), catch the T5 shuttle bus (*navetta*) on the sidewalk in front of T3—it's too far to walk with luggage.

By Bus: Four bus companies—Terravision (www.terravision.eu), SIT (www.sitbusshuttle.com), T.A.M. (www.tambus.it), and Schiaffini (www.romeair portbus.com)—connect Fiumicino and Termini train station. While cheaper than the train (about €7 one-way), buses take twice as long (about an hour, depending on traffic). At the airport, the bus station is at the far end of terminal T3.

By Airport Shuttle: Shared shuttle van services can be economical for one or two people. Consider Rome Airport Shuttle (€25 for one person, extra people–€6 each, by reservation only, tel. 06-4201-4507 or 06-4201-3469, www.airportshuttle.it).

By Taxi: A taxi between Fiumicino and downtown Rome takes 45 minutes in normal traffic and by law costs exactly €48. (Establish the price when you get in; add a €2-5 tip for good service.) From the airport, be sure to catch an official Rome city taxi at the taxi stand (see "Getting Around Rome, By Taxi," above).

CIAMPINO AIRPORT
Rome's smaller airport (tel. 06-6595-9515) handles charter flights and some budget airlines (including most Ryanair flights).

Getting Between Ciampino Airport and Downtown Rome: Bus companies Terravision, Schiaffini, and SIT will take you to Rome's Termini train station (about €5, 2/hour, 45 minutes). Atral runs a quicker route (25 minutes, www.atral-lazio.com) to the Anagnina Metro stop, where you can connect to the stop nearest your hotel (departs every 40 minutes). City bus #520 runs from Ciampino to the Subaugusta Metro stop for a single transit ticket. The fixed price for any official **taxi** (with the maroon *Roma Capitale* logo on the door) is €30 to downtown (within the old city walls, including most of my recommended hotels).

Rome Airport Shuttle also offers shared van rides to and from Ciampino (€25 for one person, listed earlier).

By Train
Rome's primary train station, centrally located **Termini,** has high-speed connections to other Italian cities and fast trains to the airport. Rome's other major station is called **Tiburtina.**

TERMINI STATION
Termini, Rome's main train station (www.romatermini.com), is a buffet of tourist services. For security, entry to the train platforms themselves is restricted to ticketholders. Entrances are from the inner atrium and from the halls to the sides of the tracks. You may need to show your ticket, but there are no metal detectors and lines are generally short.

In the hall along Via Giovanni Giolitti, on the southwest side of the station (near track 24), you'll find the TI (daily 8:00-18:45), a travel agency, a car-rental desk, a medical center, and baggage storage (*deposito bagagli;* paying €12 daily rate rather than hourly allows you to skip the line; daily 6:00-23:00). The Leonardo Express train to Fiumicino Airport runs from track 23 or 24 on this side of the station (see "Getting Between Fiumicino Airport and Downtown Rome," earlier). Pay WCs are down the escalators from the inner atrium and inside the Mercato Centrale (near track 24).

The Termini Metro station, where Metro lines A and B intersect, is beneath the station. City buses leave from the square directly in front of the outer atrium. Buses to the airport leave from the streets on both sides of the station.

TRAIN CONNECTIONS
Unless otherwise specified, the following connections are for Trenitalia.

From Termini by Train to: Fiumicino Airport (Leonardo Express; 2/hour, 32 minutes), **Venice** (hourly, 4 hours, 1 direct night train, 7 hours; Italo: 4/day, 3.5 hours), **Florence** (2-3/hour, 1.5 hours; Italo: 2/hour, 1.5 hours), **Siena** (1-2/hour, 1 change, 3-4 hours), **Orvieto** (every 1-2 hours, 1.5 hours; regional trains are half the price and only slightly slower than Intercity trains), **Assisi** (4/day direct, 2 hours; more with change in Foligno), **Pisa** (1-2/hour, 3 hours, some change in Florence), **Milan** (1-3/hour, 3.5 hours; Italo: 11/day nonstop, 3 hours, more with stops), **Naples** (1-4/hour, 1 hour on Frecciarossa, 2 hours on Intercity, 2.5 hours and much cheaper on regional trains; Italo: hourly, 70 minutes), **Sorrento** (Italo train/bus combination, 2/day, 3.5 hours).

Rick's Tip: **Shady characters** *linger around the station, especially* **near ticket machines.** *Some offer help for a "tip"; others have official-looking business cards.* **Avoid anybody selling anything** *unless they're in a legitimate shop at the station. There are no official porters;* **carry your own bags.**

TIBURTINA STATION AND AUTOSTAZIONE TIBURTINA

Tiburtina, Rome's second-largest train station (www.stazioneromatiburtina.it), sits next to the Tiburtina Metro station in the city's northeast corner. Across the road is Rome's long-distance bus station, Autostazione Tiburtina. To reach the bus station from the train station, don't follow the *Bus* signs, which lead to the city bus stop. Instead, exit the station, cross the street under the elevated freeway, and look for the fenced-in area with bus platforms. The bus station is chaotic and crowded, so buy your ticket online in advance, if possible.

From Tiburtina by Bus to: Siena (9/day, 3 hours, https://global.flixbus.com), **Sorrento** (1-2/day, 4 hours; this is a cheap and easy way to go straight to Sorrento, buy tickets at www.marozzivt.it—in Italian only, at the Tiburtina ticket office, travel agencies, or on board for a €3.50 surcharge).

Rick's Tip: *A car is a worthless headache in Rome, If Rome is the first stop of your trip,* **enjoy the city car-free,** *then take the train to Orvieto and rent a car there.*

By Car

If you absolutely must drive and park a car in Rome, there's a large underground garage at the Villa Borghese Gardens near the Spagna Metro station, just outside the restricted downtown zone (€18/day, Viale del Galoppatoio 33, www.sabait.it). Alternatively, use one of the more than two-dozen park-and-ride lots at Rome's outlying Metro stations (€5/24 hours). These vary in size and convenience; one of the largest is at the Anagnina Metro station, just inside Rome's ring expressway along the Via Tuscolana (southeast of downtown). For details, search for "park and ride" *(parcheggi di scambio)* at www.atac.roma.it.

Naples
& the Amalfi Coast

taly intensifies as you plunge deeper. If you like Italy as far south as Rome, keep going—it gets better. If Italy is getting on your nerves, don't go farther. Naples is Italy in the extreme—its best (the birthplace of pizza and Sophia Loren) and its worst (home of the Camorra, Naples' "family" of organized crime).

Naples is also the springboard for a region full of varied, fascinating sights. Just beyond Naples are the ancient Roman ruins of Pompeii, in the shadow of the brooding volcano, Mount Vesuvius. A few more miles down the road is the pleasant resort town of Sorrento and the island of Capri. And plunging farther south, you'll reach the dramatic scenery of the Amalfi Coast.

NAPLES & THE AMALFI COAST IN 3 DAYS

Naples, with its incomparable Archaeological Museum, makes a memorable half-day stop between Rome and Sorrento. The resort town of Sorrento is a pleasant home base with easy transit connections to the surrounding sights: Pompeii, Capri, and the Amalfi Coast.

The following plan assumes you're heading south to Naples (from Rome, Orvieto, or Florence), but it also works if you fly into Naples to start your trip.

Day 1: For a quick stop in Naples, visit the Archaeological Museum (closed Tue), follow my self-guided Naples walk, and eat a pizza. Then head to Sorrento, your home base.

Day 2: Choose between busing along the Amalfi Coast or boating to Capri. Or add another day to fit in both.

Day 3: See the unforgettable ruins of Pompeii as a day trip from Sorrento, or en route heading north (to Rome or beyond).

Getting Around the Region

To connect Naples, Sorrento, and the Amalfi Coast, you can travel by bus, train, and taxi, but consider taking a boat—it's faster, cooler, and more scenic. Here's an overview; for some destinations more specifics are provided later in this chapter.

By Bus: CitySightseeing's fleet of bright red shuttle buses with audio commentary offer easy trips from Naples to Pompeii, along the popular Amalfi Coast, and even up to the town of Ravello (www.city-sightseeing.it). Crowded SITA buses also traverse the Amalfi Coast.

By Train: The dingy, crowded **Circumvesuviana** commuter train links Naples, Pompeii, and Sorrento. The Circumvesuviana station in Naples (called "Garibaldi") is underneath Centrale station. To find it, follow the signs downstairs to *Statione Garibaldi* and then *Circumvesuviana* signs down the corridor to the Circumvesuviana ticket windows and turnstiles. Buy your ticket, confirm time

NAPLES & THE AMALFI COAST AT A GLANCE

▲▲**Naples** Lively, gritty port city featuring vibrant street life and a top archaeological museum with treasures from Pompeii. See page 395.

▲▲▲**Pompeii** Famous ruins of the ancient Roman town, stopped in its tracks by the eruption of Mount Vesuvius. See page 418.

▲▲**Sorrento** Seaside resort port and transit hub, serving as a good home base for the region. See page 430.

▲▲**Capri** Island getaway boasting the Blue Grotto, a short cruise from Sorrento. See page 445.

▲▲▲**The Amalfi Coast** String of seafront villages linked by a scenic, cliff-hanging road, overlooking the shimmering Mediterranean Sea. See page 453.

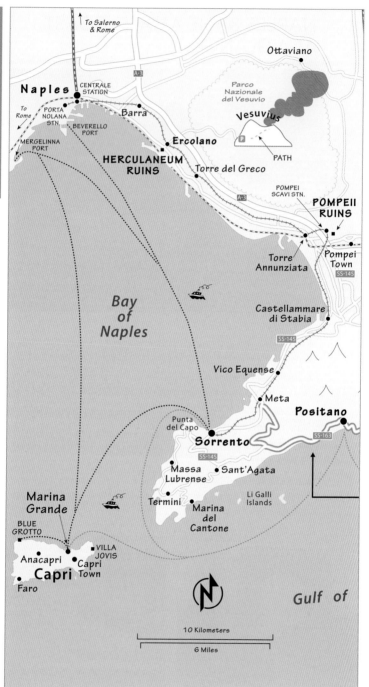

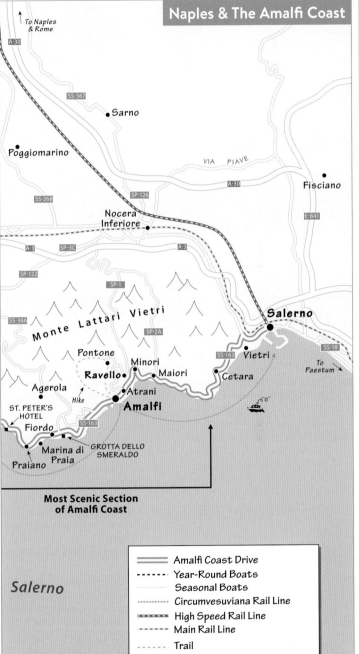

Naples & The Amalfi Coast

To Naples & Rome

A-30

SS-367

Sarno

Poggiomarino

VIA PIAVE

A-30

Fisciano

SS-268

SP-126

Nocera Inferiore

E-841

A-3

SP-3C

A-3

SS-18

SP-122

SP-1

To Paestum

SS-366

Monte Lattari Vietri

SP-2A

Salerno

Pontone

Minori

SS-163

Vietri

Ravello

Maiori

Cetara

Agerola

Atrani

ST. PETER'S HOTEL

Hike

Amalfi

Fiordo

SS-163

Marina di Praia

GROTTA DELLO SMERALDO

Praiano

Most Scenic Section of Amalfi Coast

Salerno

	Amalfi Coast Drive
	Year-Round Boats
	Seasonal Boats
	Circumvesuviana Rail Line
	High Speed Rail Line
	Main Rail Line
	Trail

and track, insert your ticket at the turnstiles, and head down another level to the platforms.

The Circumvesuviana is covered by the Campania ArteCard (see page 396), but not by rail passes. If you're heading to Pompeii, take any Circumvesuviana train marked *Sorrento*—they all stop at both (usually depart from platform 3). Sorrento-bound trains depart twice hourly, and take about 35 minutes to reach Pompei Scavi-Villa dei Misteri (for the Pompeii ruins, €2.90 one-way), and 60 minutes to reach Sorrento, the end of the line (€3.60 one-way). Express trains to Sorrento marked *DD* (6/day) reach Sorrento 15 minutes sooner, and also stop at Herculaneum and Pompeii. For schedules, see www.eavsrl.it.

On the platform, double-check with a local that the train goes to Sorrento (avoid lines that branch out to other destinations). Perhaps your biggest risk of theft is while catching or riding the Circumvesuviana commuter train. You won't be mugged—but you may be conned or pickpocketed. Wear your money belt, and avoid the Circumvesuviana late at night.

Pricier **Campania Express trains,** operated by Circumvesuviana, use the same tracks and stops. They run only four times a day, but are much less crowded—and they have air-conditioning (€6 one-way to Pompeii, 30 minutes; €8 one-way to Sorrento, 1 hour; trains run mid-March-Oct only, not covered by Campania ArteCard or TIC ticket, online sales at http://ots.eavsrl.it or buy at the station).

By Taxi: For €110, you can take a 30-mile taxi ride from Naples directly to your Sorrento hotel (ask the driver for the nonmetered *tariffa predeterminata*). You can hire a cab on Capri for about €70/hour. Taxis on the Amalfi Coast are generally expensive, but they can be convenient, especially with a larger group.

By Boat: Major companies include Caremar (www.caremar.it), SNAV (www.snav.it), Gescab (a.k.a. NLG Jet, www.gescab.it), Navigazione Libera del Golfo (www.navlib.it), Alilauro (www.alilauro.it), Travelmar (www.travelmar.it), and Alicost (www.alicost.it). Some lines (like Sorrento-Capri) run all year; others (on the Amalfi Coast, for example) only in summer. Trips can be cancelled in bad weather. A hydrofoil, sometimes called a "jet boat," skims between Naples and Sorrento—it's swifter, safer from pickpockets, more scenic, and more expensive than the Circumvesuviana train.

For schedules, check online (www.capritourism.com; click "Shipping Timetable"), or ask at any TI or at Naples' Molo Beverello boat dock (departure board on rooftop of Molo Beverello terminal shows upcoming departures). Most boats charge €2 or so for luggage. Note return times—the last boat usually leaves before 19:00. The preset price for a taxi between Naples' Centrale train station and its port (Molo Beverello) is €11, or you can take Metro line 1 to the Municipio stop and walk to the port.

Shared Tours

If you want to take a tour of all or part of this region, consider Naples-based **Mondo Guide**'s shared tours for Rick Steves readers. These allow you the luxury of a private, professional guide at a fraction of the usual cost, because you'll be sharing the expense with other travelers using this book. Tours run from April through October, and include **Pompeii,** a walking tour of **Naples,** and two longer-distance trips from Sorrento: an **Amalfi Coast** van tour and a private boat to the **isle of Capri.** The Pompeii and Naples tours are timed so you can do both on the same day.

Reservations are required. For specifics and to sign up, go to www.sharedtours.com (Mondo tel. 081-751-3290, mobile 340-460-5254, www.mondoguide.com, info@mondoguide.com). On the website, use your credit-card number to reserve a spot. You'll then pay cash for the tour. If you must cancel, email more than three days in advance or you'll be billed.

Each tour requires a minimum of six participants. You'll be sent an email confirmation as soon as they're sure your tour will run. If there's not enough demand to justify the trip, they'll notify you three days before the departure date (giving you time to come up with an alternative plan). Confirmed departures are continually updated on the website.

NAPLES

Naples is southern Italy's leading city, the third-largest city in Italy, and Europe's most densely populated city, with more than one million people and few open spaces or parks. While in many ways it feels like an urban jungle, Naples surprises the observant traveler with its impressive knack for living, eating, and raising children with good humor and decency. Overcome your fear of being run down or ripped off long enough to enjoy a few smiles and jokes with the people you meet.

The pulse of Italy throbs in Naples. Like Cairo or Mumbai, it's shocking and captivating at the same time, the closest thing to "reality travel" that you'll find in Western Europe. But this tangled mess still somehow manages to breathe, laugh, and sing—with a joyful Italian accent. Thanks to its reputation as a dangerous place, Naples doesn't get nearly as many tourists as it deserves. While the city has its problems, it has improved a lot in recent years. And even though it remains a bit edgy, I feel comfortable here. Naples richly rewards those who venture in.

Orientation

Naples is set deep inside the large, curving Bay of Naples, with Mount Vesuvius looming just five miles away. Although Naples is a sprawling city, its fairly compact core contains the most interesting sights. The tourist's Naples is a triangle, with its points at the Centrale train station

in the east, the Archaeological Museum to the west, and Piazza del Plebiscito (with the Royal Palace) and the port to the south. Steep hills rise above this historic core, including San Martino, capped with a mighty fortress.

On a quick visit, start with the Archaeological Museum, follow my self-guided Naples Walk, and celebrate your survival with pizza.

Tourist Information

Central Naples has multiple small TIs, none of them particularly helpful—just grab a map and browse the brochures. The handiest one is in **Centrale train station** (daily 8:30-19:30, in the main lobby, tel. 081-268-779). Two others are by the entrance to the **Galleria Umberto I** shopping mall, across from Teatro di San Carlo (Mon-Sat 9:00-17:00, Sun until 13:00, tel. 081-402-394), and on Spaccanapoli, across from the **Church of Gesù Nuovo** (same hours as Galleria Umberto I TI, tel. 081-551-2701). For information online, the best overall website is www.inaples.it.

Helpful Hints

Theft Alert: While most travelers visit Naples safely, err on the side of caution. Be aware that thieves and con artists hang out close to where travelers tumble into Naples: the train station and the port. Don't let your first impression of the station area get in your way of enjoying Naples—the city changes drastically as you move further away. Touristy Spaccanapoli, Capodimonte, and the posh Via Toledo shopping boulevard are more upscale, but you may still see panhandlers.

Stick to busy streets and beware the odd gang of hoodlums. As in most big cities, consider any jostle or commotion a possible thief-team smokescreen. Keep a low profile and carry only the bare minimum.

Traffic Safety: In Naples, red lights are timed short, and pedestrians need to be wary, particularly of motor scooters that zip among the cars and even on "pedestrian" streets.

Sightseeing Pass: The **Campania ArteCard** regional pass may save you a few euros if you're here for two or three days, use public transportation, and visit multiple major sights (such as Pompeii, Naples' Archaeological Museum, and several other museums in Naples). The **three-day Campania** version (€32) is good if you'll be visiting both Naples and Sorrento; it includes free entry to two sights, a 50 percent discount off others, and transportation within Naples, on the Circumvesuviana train (but not the Campania Express), and on Amalfi Coast buses. The **seven-day Campania** version (€34) covers five sights and discounts on others, but no transportation. If you're focusing on Naples, the **three-day Napoli** version (€21) covers transportation within Naples and three city sights, plus discounts on others, but doesn't cover outlying ancient sites. The card is sold at participating sights and some Naples TIs (cards activate on first use, expire 3 or 7 days later at midnight, www.campania rtecard.it).

Free Days: Some state museums in Italy (including Naples' Archaeological Museum) are free to enter once or twice a month, usually on a Sunday. Free days are actually bad news—they attract crowds. Check sight websites in advance.

Laundry: A block from the Università Metro stop, **Lavasciuga** is convenient but has just three washing machines (Mon-Sat 9:00-19:00, closed Sun, Via Sedile di Porto 54, mobile 327-754-6639).

Tours
LOCAL GUIDES

For private walking and driving tours of Naples and the region, try **Pina Esposito** (€60/hour, 2-hour minimum, RS%—10 percent off with this book, additional discounts for full-day tours, mobile 338-763-4224, annamariaesposito1@virgilio.it) or **Mondo Guide** (€120/2-hour Archaeological Museum tour, €240/4-hour city tour, tel. 081-751-3290, www.mondoguide.it, sharedtours@mondoguide.com). For more on Mondo's offerings, see "Shared Tours" on page 394.

HOP-ON, HOP-OFF BUS TOURS

CitySightseeing Napoli tour buses make two different hop-on, hop-off loops through the city. The red line, which loops around the historical center and stops at the Archaeological Museum and Capodimonte, is best (€23, ticket valid 24 hours, 2/hour, buy from driver or from kiosk at Piazza Municipio in front of Castel Nuovo near the port, scant recorded narration, tel. 081-551-7279, www.city-sightseeing.it). The same company offers a handy shuttle from the city center to the Capodimonte Museum and shuttles to Pompeii.

Piazza Bellini

Archaeological Museum

Galleria Principe di Napoli

Piazza Dante

🔊 Naples Walk

This self-guided walk, worth ▲▲▲, takes you from the Archaeological Museum through the heart of town and back to Centrale station. Visit the museum first (see page 403), then allow at least two hours for the full walk, plus time for pizza and sightseeing stops. If your time is short, you can end the walk at Piazza Carità and take the Metro back to the station. If you're overnighting in Naples, you could split the walk over two days.

🎧 Download my free Naples City Walk **audio tour.**

From the Archaeological Museum to Piazza Carità

Start at the Archaeological Museum, at the top of Piazza Cavour (Metro: Cavour or Museo). From here, we'll ramble down a fine boulevard before cutting into the medieval heart of the city.

Archaeological Museum: The palatial building, built in the mid-1700s, captures the glory of Naples at its peak, when the city was rich from sea trade and home to erudite nobles from abroad. They built a magnificent capital of buildings like this one.

• *From the door of the Archaeological Museum, cross the street, veer right, and enter the arched doorway of the beige-colored Galleria Principe di Napoli mall. (If the entrance is blocked, simply loop around the block to another entrance or pick up our walk behind the Galleria.)*

Galleria Principe di Napoli: There's no better example of Naples' grandeur—and decline—than this elegant 19th-century shopping mall. You'll enjoy a soaring skylight, carved woodwork, ironwork lanterns, playful cupids, an elegant atmosphere... and empty shops. In the US, we call this decorative style Art Nouveau; in Italy it's "Liberty Style," named for a British department store that was in vogue at a time when Naples was the "Paris of the South." Despite its grandeur, the mall never took off. Ambitious renovations in recent years have failed to attract much business, leaving the mall in a state of disrepair.

• *Leaving the gallery through the opposite end, walk one block downhill. At Via Conte*

Naples

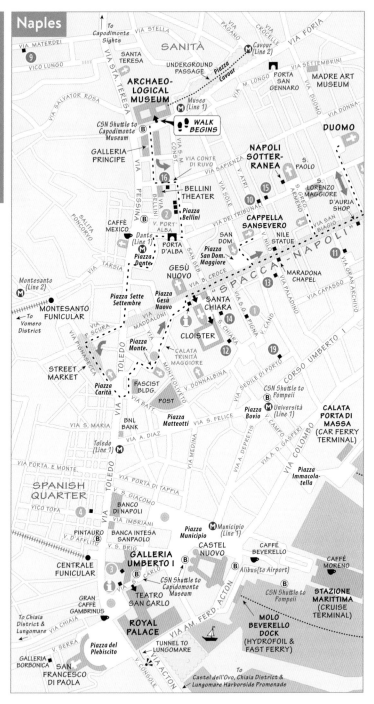

To Capodimonte Sights

VIA MATERDEI

VICO LUNGO

VIA STELLA

VIA PAGANO

VIA CROCELLE

VIA FORIA

SANITÀ

SANTA TERESA

Cavour (Line 2)

VIA SETTEMBRINI

UNDERGROUND PASSAGE

Piazza Cavour

PORTA SAN GENNARO

MADRE ART MUSEUM

VIA SALVATOR ROSA

VIA STA. TERESA

ARCHAEO-LOGICAL MUSEUM

Museo (Line 1)

DUOMO

CSN Shuttle to Capodimonte Museum

WALK BEGINS

NAPOLI SOTTER-RANEA

S. PAOLO

GALLERIA PRINCIPE

VIA CONTE DI RUVO

S. LORENZO MAGGIORE

SALITA PONCORVO

BELLINI THEATER

D'AURIA SHOP

CAFFÉ MEXICO

Piazza Bellini

CAPPELLA SANSEVERO

Dante (Line 1)

PORTA D'ALBA

SAN DOM.

NILE STATUE

Piazza Dante

Piazza San Dom. Maggiore

Montesanto (Line 2)

VIA TARSIA

GESÙ NUOVO

MARADONA CHAPEL

MONTESANTO FUNICULAR

Piazza Sette Settembre

Piazza Gesù Nuovo

SANTA CHIARA

To Vomero District

Piazza Monte.

CLOISTER

STREET MARKET

CALATA TRINITÀ MAGGIORE

CORSO UMBERTO I

Piazza Carità

FASCIST BLDG.

POST

CSN Shuttle to Pompeii

CALATA PORTA DI MASSA (CAR FERRY TERMINAL)

BNL BANK

Piazza Matteotti

Piazza Bovio

Università (Line 1)

Toledo (Line 1)

VIA A. DIAZ

VIA MEDINA

Piazza Immacola-tella

VIA PORTA E. MONTE

SPANISH QUARTER

VIA PORTA DI TAPPIA

VICO TOFA

BANCO DI NAPOLI

Piazza Municipio

Municipio (Line 1)

PINTAURO

BANCA INTESA SANPAOLO

CASTEL NUOVO

CAFFÉ BEVERELLO

CAFFÉ MORENO

CENTRALE FUNICULAR

GALLERIA UMBERTO I

Alibus (to Airport)

CSN Shuttle to Capidomonte Museum

CSN Shuttle to Pompeii

STAZIONE MARITTIMA (CRUISE TERMINAL)

GRAN CAFFÉ GAMBRINUS

TEATRO SAN CARLO

ROYAL PALACE

MOLO BEVERELLO DOCK (HYDROFOIL & FAST FERRY)

To Chiaia District & Lungomare

GALLERIA BORBONICA

SAN FRANCESCO DI PAOLA

Piazza del Plebiscito

TUNNEL TO LUNGOMARE

To Castel dell'Ovo, Chiaia District & Lungomare Harborside Promenade

STREET MARKET

VIA SANT' ANTONIO ABATE

VIA ROSARELLI

VIA CARBONARA

WALL

PORTA CAPUANA

Piazza Capuana

REGINA

VIA CASANOVA

CORSO GARIBALDI

VIA MILANO

VIA TORINO

VIA BOLOGNA

VIA AQUILA

CORSO NUOVA

VIA VENEZIA

VIA PALERMO

VIA FIRENZE

CORSO MERIDIONALE

6

5

To Salerno & Palermo

VICO FERROVIA

NAPLES CENTRALE STATION

VIA DEI TRIBUNALI

PIO MONTE MISERICORDIA

VIA DE MADDALENA

GARIBALDI STATUE

VIA MANCINI

WALK ENDS

Piazza Garibaldi

Airport Ⓑ

Ⓣ

ⓘ

UNDER-GROUND MALL

Garibaldi (Line 1)

CSN Shuttle to Pompeii

Centrale (Line 2)

UNDERGROUND PASSAGE

VIA PICA

Ⓜ

To Herculaneum, Pompeii & Sorrento

VIA VICARIA VECCHIA

V. COLLETTA

Piazza V. Calenda

FORCELLA

UMBERTO I

FISH MARKET

V. NOLANA

Ⓑ

18

8

Piazza Nolana

17

GARIBALDI CIRCUM-VESUVIANA STATION

VIA G. FERARIS

To A-3 Autostrada

7

SERSALE

CORSO

PORTA NOLANA

VIA SAN COSMO

VIA DUOMO

STREET MARKET

VIA SOPRAMURO

CORSO GARIBALDI

PORTA NOLANA CIRCUMVESUVIANA STATION

CORSO LUCCI

MERCATO

Piazza Amore

Ⓜ Duomo (Line 1) (May be closed for renovation)

Piazza del Mercato

Piazza Pepe

Piazza Carmine

VIA DUOMO

VIA NUOVA MARINA

VIA VESPUCCI

RESTRICTED AREA

Port

Ⓝ

400 Meters

400 Yards

To Capri, Sicily & Sardinia

To Capri & Sorrento

Bay of Naples

- - - - NAPLES WALK

Accommodations

1. Decumani Hotel de Charme
2. Hotel Piazza Bellini & La Stanza del Gusto
3. Art Resort Galleria Umberto
4. Hotel Il Convento
5. Hotel Stelle
6. Grand Hotel Europa

Eateries & Other

7. Antica Pizzeria da Michele
8. Pizzeria Trianon da Ciro
9. Pizzeria Starita
10. Gino Sorbillo
11. La Figlia del Presidente
12. Ecomesarà
13. Tandem Ragù
14. Taverna a Santa Chiara
15. Trattoria Campagnola
16. Osteria da Carmela
17. Da Donato
18. Polo Nord Gelateria
19. Laundry

"Spaccanapoli" street

Via Pignasecca Market

*di Ruvo, turn left, passing the fine **Bellini Theater** (also in Liberty Style). After one block, turn right on Via Santa Maria di Costantinopoli. Walking between two grand churches, continue directly downhill to a small park with a statue in the center called...*

Piazza Bellini: Suddenly you're in neighborhood Napoli. The statue honors the opera composer Vincenzo Bellini, whose career was launched in Naples in the early 1800s, when opera itself was being born. Just past the statue, peer down into the sunken area to see Naples' ancient origins as a fifth-century BC Greek colony called Neapolis—"the new city." You can see how the street level has risen from the rubble of centuries.

• *Walk 30 yards downhill on the right. Stop at the horseshoe-shaped **Port'Alba gate.** Spin slowly 360 degrees and take in the scene. The proud tile across the street (upstairs, between the two balconies) shows Piazza Bellini circa 1890. Pass through the gate, down Via Port'Alba, and stroll through this pleasant passage lined with book stalls. You emerge into a big square called...*

Piazza Dante: This square is marked by a statue of Dante, the medieval poet. Fittingly, half the square is devoted to bookstores. Old Dante looks out over an urban area that was once grand, then chaotic, and is now slowly becoming grand again.

• *Before moving on, note the red "M" that Dante seems to be gesturing to. This marks the **Dante Metro station,** the best of Napoli's art-splashed Metro stations. (To take a look, go down three flights of escalators and then back up; you'll need a ticket, unless you can sweet-talk a guard.) Then, exit Piazza Dante at the far end, walking downhill on...*

Via Toledo: The long, straight street heading downhill from Piazza Dante is Naples' principal shopping drag. It originated as a military road built by the Spanish viceroys who made Naples great in the 16th century. Back then, Via Toledo skirted the old town wall to connect the Spanish military headquarters (now the museum where you started this walk) with the Royal Palace (down by the bay).

After a couple hundred yards, you'll reach the triangular **Piazza Sette Settembre.** This public space recalls the event that precipitated Naples' swift decline. On September 7, 1860, from the white marble balcony of the Neoclassical building overlooking the square, the revolutionary Giuseppe Garibaldi declared Italy united and Victor Emmanuel II its first king. And a decade later, that declaration became reality when Rome also fell to unification forces. It was the start of a glorious new era for Italy, Rome, and the Italian people. But not for Naples.

Naples' treasury was confiscated to subsidize the industrial expansion of the north, and its bureaucrats were transferred to the new capital in Rome. Within a few decades, Naples went from being a thriving cultural and political capital to a provincial town, with its economy in shambles and its dialect considered backward.

Piazza Gesù Nuovo

Chapel of the Maradona

• *Continue straight on Via Toledo. A block past Piazza Sette Settembre you'll come to Via Maddaloni, which marks the start of the long, straight, narrow street nicknamed...*

Spaccanapoli: Via Maddaloni is the modern name for the beginning of this thin street that, since ancient times, has bisected the city. The name Spaccanapoli translates as "split Naples." Look left down the street (toward the train station), and right (toward San Martino hill), and you get a sense of how Spaccanapoli divides this urban jungle of buildings.

• *At the Spaccanapoli intersection, go right (toward the church facade on the hill), heading up Via Pasquale Scura. After about 100 yards, you hit a busy intersection. Stop. You're on one of Naples' most colorful open-air market streets...*

Via Pignasecca: Take in the colorful scene at the intersection. Then, turn left down Via Pignasecca and stroll this colorful market strip. You'll pass fish and meat stalls, produce stands, street-food vendors, and much more. This is a taste of Naples' famous **Spanish Quarter** (its center is farther down Via Toledo but this area provides a good sampling).

• *Turn left and follow Via Pignasecca as it leads back to Via Toledo at the square called...*

Piazza Carità: This square, built for an official visit by Hitler to Mussolini in 1938, is full of stern, straight, obedient lines. The modern memorial statue in the center of this square celebrates Salvo d'Acquisto, a rare hometown hero. In 1943, he was

executed after falsely confessing to sabotage...saving 22 fellow Italian soldiers from a Nazi revenge massacre.

• *From Piazza Carità, veer northwest (past more fascist-style architecture) on Via Morgantini through Piazza Monteoliveto. Cross the busy street, then angle up Calata Trinità Maggiore to the fancy column in the piazza at the top of the hill.*

From Piazza Gesù Nuovo to Centrale Station

• *You're back on the straight-as-a-Greek-arrow Spaccanapoli, formerly the main thoroughfare of the Greek city of Neapolis. (Spaccanapoli changes names several times: Via Maddaloni, Via B. Croce, Via S. Biagio dei Librai, and Via Vicaria Vecchia.) Linger on...*

Piazza Gesù Nuovo: This square is marked by a towering 18th-century Baroque monument to the Counter-Reformation. Although the Jesuit order was powerful in Naples because of its Spanish heritage, locals never attacked Protestants here with the full fury of the Spanish Inquisition. If you'd like, you can visit the two bulky old churches— the dark, fortress-like, 17th-century **Church of Gesù Nuovo** and the simpler **Church of Santa Chiara** (described later, under "Sights").

• *Continue along the main drag for another 200 yards. Since this is a university district, you may see students and bookstores. As this neighborhood is also famously superstitious, look for incense-burning women with carts full of good-luck charms for sale.*

Passing Palazzo Venezia—the embassy of Venice to Naples when both were independent powers—you'll emerge into the next square...

Piazza San Domenico Maggiore: It's marked by another ornate 17th-century monument built to thank God for ending the plague. From this square, detour left along the right side of the castle-like church, then follow yellow signs, taking the first right and walking one short block to the remarkable Baroque **Cappella Sansevero** (described later, under "Sights in Naples").

• *Return to Via B. Croce (a.k.a. Spaccanapoli), turn left, and continue your cultural scavenger hunt. At the intersection of Via Nilo, find the...*

Statue of the Nile (on the left): A reminder of the multiethnic makeup of Greek Neapolis, this statue is in what was the Egyptian quarter. Locals like to call this statue *The Body of Naples,* with the overflowing cornucopia symbolizing the abundance of their fine city. This intersection is considered the center of old Naples.

• *Directly opposite the statue, inside of Bar Nilo, is the...*

"Chapel of Maradona": The small "chapel" on the right wall is dedicated to Diego Maradona, a soccer star who played for Naples in the 1980s. Locals consider soccer almost a religion, and for a time this guy was practically a deity. Unfortunately, his reputation has since been sullied by problems he's had with organized crime, drugs, and police. To take a photo, buy coffee first.

• *Continue to a tiny square at the intersection with Via San Gregorio Armeno.*

Via San Gregorio Armeno: Stroll up this tiny lane toward the fanciful tower that arches over the street. The street is lined with stalls selling lots of souvenir kitsch, as well as some of Naples' most distinctive local crafts. Among the many figurines on sale, find items relating to **presepi** (Nativity scenes). Just as many

Presepi *nativity scenes*

Americans keep an eye out year-round for Christmas-tree ornaments, Italians regularly add pieces to the family *presepe,* the centerpiece of their holiday decorations. You'll see elaborate manger scenes made of bark and moss, with niches to hold Baby Jesus or the Virgin Mary. You'll also see lots of jokey figurines caricaturing local politicians, soccer stars, and other celebrities. (Some of the highest-quality *presepi* pieces are sold at the D'Auria shop, a little farther down Spaccanapoli, on the right at #87. They even sell the classy *campane* version, under a glass bell.)

Another popular Naples souvenir sold here—and all over—is the **corno,** a skinny, twisted, red horn that resembles a chili pepper. The *corno* comes with a double symbolism for fertility: It's a horn of plenty, and it's also a phallic symbol turned upside-down. Neapolitans explain that fertility isn't sexual; it provides the greatest gift a person can give—life.

• *Continue down Spaccanapoli another 100 yards until you hit busy Via Duomo. Consider detouring five minutes north (left) up Via Duomo to visit Naples' **Duomo;** just around the corner from that is the **Pio Monte della Misericordia Church,** with a fine Caravaggio painting. But for now, continue straight, crossing Via Duomo. Here, Spaccanapoli is named...*

Via Vicaria Vecchia: Along this stretch, street scenes intensify. The area is said to be a center of the Camorra (the Naples-based version of the Sicilian Mafia), but as a tourist, you won't notice.

Naples has the most intact street plan of any surviving ancient Greek or Roman city. Imagine this city during those times (and retain these images as you visit Pompeii), with streetside shop fronts that close up after dark, and private homes on upper floors. What you see today is just one more page in a 2,000-year-old story of a city: all kinds of meetings, beatings, and cheatings; kisses, near misses, and little-boy pisses.

You name it, it occurs right on the streets today, as it has since ancient times. People ooze from crusty corners. Black-and-white death announcements add to the clutter on the walls. Widows sell cigarettes from buckets. The neighborhood action seems best at about 18:00.

At the tiny fenced-in triangle of greenery, hang out for a few minutes to just observe the crazy motorbike action and teen scene.
• *From here, veer right onto Via Forcella. You emerge into Piazza Vincenzo Calenda. Hungry? Turn right here, on Via Pietro Colletta, and close out the walk with three typical Neapolitan...*

Eateries: Step into the North Pole at the recommended **Polo Nord Gelateria** (at #41). The oldest *gelateria* in Naples has had four generations of family working here since 1931. Before you order, sample a few flavors, including their *bacio*, or "kiss," flavor (chocolate-and-praline)—all are made fresh daily.

Two of Napoli's most competitive **pizzerias** are nearby. **Trianon da Ciro** (across the street from Polo Nord) has been serving them up hot and fast for almost a century. A half-block farther, on the right, is the place where some say pizza was born—at **Antica Pizzeria da Michele.** (For more on both, see "Eating," later.)
• *Our walk is over. It's easy to return to Centrale station. Continue straight ahead, downhill, until you hit the grand boulevard, Corso Umberto I. Turn left here, and it's a straight 15-minute walk to Centrale station. (Or cross the street and hop on a bus; they all go to the station.) You'll pass a gauntlet of purse/CD/sunglasses salesmen and shady characters hawking stolen mobile phones. You'll soon reach the vast **Piazza Garibaldi,** with a modern canopy in the middle. On the far side is the station. You made it.*

Sights
Near Piazza Cavour
▲▲▲ARCHAEOLOGICAL MUSEUM
Naples' Archaeological Museum (*Museo Archeologico*) boasts supersized statues as well as art and decorations from Pompeii and Herculaneum, the two ancient burgs that were buried in ash by the eruption of Mount Vesuvius in AD 79. For lovers of antiquity, this museum alone makes Naples a worthwhile stop. When Pompeii was excavated in the late 1700s, Naples' Bourbon king bellowed, "Bring me the best of what you find!" The finest art and artifacts ended up here.

🎧 Download my free Archaeological Museum **audio tour.**

Cost and Hours: €18, sometimes more for temporary exhibits; Wed-Mon 9:00-19:30, closed Tue, some rooms closed July-Aug; buy tickets online to avoid lines; decent audioguide-€5, Metro: Piazza Cavour, tel. 081-442-2149, www.museo archeologiconapoli.it.

⊙ SELF-GUIDED TOUR
Enter the museum and stand at the base of the grand staircase. To your right, on the ground floor, are the larger-than-life statues of the Farnese Collection, starring the *Toro Farnese* and the *Farnese Hercules.* Up the stairs on the mezzanine level are mosaics and frescoes from Pompeii, including the Secret Room of erotic art. On the top floor are more artifacts from Pompeii, a scale model of the doomed city, and bronze statues from Herculaneum. WCs are behind the staircase.
• *From the base of the ❶ grand staircase, turn right through the door marked Collezione Farnese and head for the far end, walking through a rich collection of ancient portrait ❷ busts. Jog right, then left, entering Room 13.*

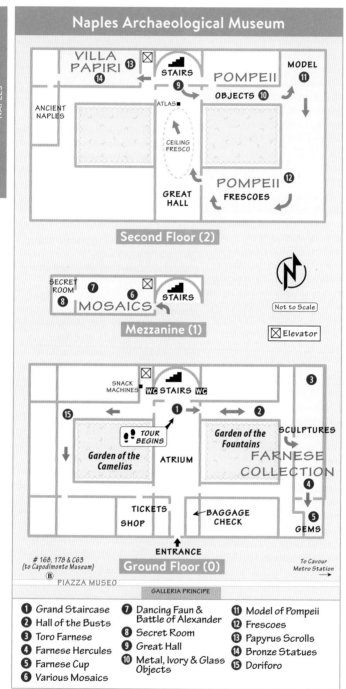

Naples Archaeological Museum

Second Floor (2)

VILLA PAPIRI ⑬ ⑭

STAIRS ⑨

POMPEII

MODEL ⑪

OBJECTS ⑩

ANCIENT NAPLES

ATLAS

CEILING FRESCO

POMPEII ⑫

GREAT HALL

FRESCOES

Mezzanine (1)

SECRET ROOM ⑦ ⑧

⑥ MOSAICS

STAIRS

N

Not to Scale

⊠ Elevator

Ground Floor (0)

SNACK MACHINES

WC STAIRS WC

⑮

❶

❷

❸

TOUR BEGINS

Garden of the Camelias

ATRIUM

Garden of the Fountains

SCULPTURES

FARNESE COLLECTION

❹

❺ GEMS

TICKETS

SHOP

BAGGAGE CHECK

ENTRANCE

168, 178 & C63 (to Capodimonte Museum)

Ⓑ PIAZZA MUSEO

To Cavour Metro Station →

GALLERIA PRINCIPE

❶ Grand Staircase
❷ Hall of the Busts
❸ Toro Farnese
❹ Farnese Hercules
❺ Farnese Cup
❻ Various Mosaics
❼ Dancing Faun & Battle of Alexander
❽ Secret Room
❾ Great Hall
❿ Metal, Ivory & Glass Objects
⑪ Model of Pompeii
⑫ Frescoes
⑬ Papyrus Scrolls
⑭ Bronze Statues
⑮ Doriforo

GROUND FLOOR: THE FARNESE COLLECTION

The Farnese Collection statues were dug up in the 1540s from Rome's Baths of Car-acalla at the behest of Alessandro Farnese (by then Pope Paul III) while he was building the family palace on the Campo de' Fiori. His main purpose in excavating the baths was to scavenge quality building stone. The sculptures were a nice extra and helped the palace come in under budget on decorations. In the 1700s, the collection ended up in the hands of Charles, the Bourbon king of Naples (whose mother was a Farnese). His son, the next king, had it brought to Naples.

• *Quick—look down to the left end of the hall. There's a woman being tied to a snorting bull.*

The tangled ❸ *Toro Farnese* tells a thrilling Greek myth. At 13 feet, it's the tallest ancient marble group ever found, and the largest intact statue from antiquity. A third-century AD copy of a lost bronze Hellenistic original, it was carved out of one piece of marble. Michelangelo and others "restored" it at the pope's request—meaning that they integrated surviving bits into a new work. Some pieces were actually carved by Michelangelo: the head of the woman in back, the torso of the aunt under the bull, and the dog.

Here's the tragic story behind the statue: Once upon an ancient Greek time, King Lycus was bewitched by Dirce. He abandoned his pregnant wife, Antiope (standing regally in the background). The single mom gave birth to twin boys. When they grew up, they killed their deadbeat dad and tied Dirce to the horns of a bull to be bashed against a mountain. Captured in marble, the action is thrilling: cape flailing, dog snarling, hooves in the air. You can almost hear the bull snorting.

At the opposite end of the hall stands the ❹ *Farnese Hercules.* The great Greek hero leans wearily on his club (draped with his lion skin) and bows his head. He's just finished the daunting Eleventh Labor, having traveled the world, fought men and gods, freed Prometheus from his rock, and carried Atlas' weight of the world on his shoulders. Now he's returned with the prize: the golden apples of the gods, which he cups behind his back.

Toro Farnese

Farnese Hercules

The 10-foot colossus is a third-century AD Roman marble copy (signed by "Glykon") of a fourth-century BC Greek bronze original (probably by Lysippos). The statue was enormously famous in its day. Dozens of copies—some marble, some bronze—have been found in Roman villas and baths. This version was unearthed in Rome's Baths of Caracalla in 1546, along with the *Toro Farnese.*

• *Behind Hercules is a doorway into the impressive Farnese gem collection (Rooms 9 and 10). You'll see the ancient cereal bowl-shaped* ❺ *Farnese Cup, which features a portrait thought to be of Cleopatra. Now backtrack to the main entry hall with its grand staircase and head up to the mezzanine level (turn left at the lion and go under the Mosaici sign), and enter Room 57.*

MEZZANINE: POMPEIIAN MOSAICS AND THE SECRET ROOM

These ❻ **mosaics**—mostly of animals, battle scenes, and geometric designs—were excavated from the walls and floors of Pompeii's ritzy villas. The *Chained Dog* once graced a home's entryway. The colorful mosaic columns (to your right in adjoining Room 58) shaded a courtyard, part of an ensemble of wall mosaics and bubbling fountains. In Room 59, admire the realism of the tambourine-playing musicians, the drinking doves, and the skull—a reminder of impending death.

Continue a few steps into Room 60, with objects taken from one of Pompeii's greatest villas, the House of the Faun. The 20-inch-high statue was the house's delightful centerpiece, the ❼ *Dancing Faun.* This rare surviving Greek bronze statue (from the fourth century BC) is surrounded by some of the best mosaics of that age.

A museum highlight, just beyond the statue, is the grand ***Battle of Alexander,*** a second-century BC copy of the now-lost original Greek fresco, done a century earlier. It decorated a floor in the House of the Faun and was found intact. Alexander (left side of the scene, with curly hair and sideburns) is about to defeat the Persians under Darius (central figure, in chariot with turban and beard). This pivotal victory allowed Alexander to quickly overrun

Dancing Faun

Battle of Alexander mosaic (detail)

much of Asia (331 BC). Alexander is the only one without a helmet...a confident master of the battlefield.

Farther on, the ❽ **Secret Room** (Gabinetto Segreto, Room 65) contains a sizable assortment of erotic frescoes, well-hung pottery, and perky statues that once decorated bedrooms, meeting rooms, brothels, and even shops at Pompeii and Herculaneum. These bawdy statues and frescoes—many of them once displayed in Pompeii's grandest houses—were entertainment for guests. The Roman nobles commissioned the wildest scenes imaginable. Think of them as ancient dirty jokes.

At the entrance, you're enthusiastically greeted by big stone penises that once projected over Pompeii's doorways. A massive phallus was not necessarily a sexual symbol, but a magical amulet used against the "evil eye." It symbolized fertility, happiness, good luck, riches, straight A's, and general wellbeing.

The back room is furnished and decorated the way an ancient brothel might have been. The 10 frescoes on the wall functioned as both a menu of services offered and as a kind of *Kama Sutra* of sex positions.

• *So, now that your travel buddy is finally showing a little interest in art...finish up your visit by climbing the stairs to the top floor.*

At the top of the stairs, pause and get oriented to our final sights. Directly ahead is a doorway (marked Salone Meridiana) that leads into a big, empty hall. To the left of this grand hall is a series of rooms with more artifacts from Pompeii. To the right are rooms of statues from Herculaneum.

TOP FLOOR: FRESCOES, STATUES, ARTIFACTS, AND A MODEL OF POMPEII

First, step into the Salone Meridiana. This was the ❾ **great hall** of the university (17th and 18th centuries) until the building became the royal museum in 1777. Walk to the center. The sundial (from 1791) still works. Look up to the far-right corner of the hall and find the tiny pinhole. At noon

(13:00 in summer), a ray of sun enters the hall and strikes the sundial, showing the time of the year...if you know your zodiac.

Now enter the series of rooms to the left of the grand hall, with ❿ **Metal, Ivory, and Glass Objects** found in Pompeii. You enter through a doorway marked *Vetri e Avori,* which leads into Room 89. Browse your way to the far end, with the stunning *Blue Vase* (Room 85), decorated with cameo Bacchuses harvesting grapes. Turn left, then right, to find the huge, room-filling ⓫ **model of Pompeii,** a 1:100 scale model of the ruins (Room 96).

Continue on (through Rooms 83-80) and enter Room 75 (marked *affreschi*) to see the museum's impressive collection of (nonerotic) ⓬ **frescoes** taken from the walls of Pompeii villas. Pompeiians loved to decorate their homes with scenes from mythology (Hercules' labors, Venus and Mars in love), landscapes, everyday market scenes, and faux architecture. To the left (in Room 78), find the famous dual portrait of baker Terentius Neo and his wife—possibly two of the 2,000 victims when Vesuvius erupted.

• *Eventually, you end up back near the great hall. From here (facing the hall entrance), turn right and find the entrance to the wing labeled La Villa dei Papiri.*

These artifacts came from the Herculaneum holiday home of Julius Caesar's father-in-law. ⓭ In Room 114, find the glass cases holding two blackened examples of the 2,000 **papyrus scrolls** that gave the villa its name. The half-burned scrolls were unrolled and (with luck) read after excavation in the 1750s.

Continuing into Room 116, enjoy some of the villa's ⓮ **bronze statues.** Look into the lifelike blue eyes of the intense *Corridore* (runners), bent on doing their best. The *Five Dancers,* with their inlaid-ivory eyes and graceful poses, decorated a portico. The next room (117) has more fine works: *Resting Hermes* (with his tired little heel wings) is taking a break. Nearby, the *Drunken Faun* (singing and snapping his

fingers to the beat, a wineskin at his side) is clearly living for today—true to the *carpe diem* lifestyle of the Epicurean philosophy.
• *Return to the ground floor. To reach the exit, circle around the museum courtyard to the gift shop. As you circle the courtyard toward the exit, find* ❶ *Doriforo. This seven-foot-tall "spear-carrier" is a Roman-made marble replica of one of the most-copied statues of antiquity, a fifth-century BC bronze Greek original by Polyclitus. This copy once stood in a Pompeii gym.*

Churches on or near Spaccanapoli

▲CHURCH OF GESÙ NUOVO

This church's unique pyramid-grill facade survives from a fortified 15th-century noble palace. Step inside for a brilliant Neapolitan Baroque interior. The second chapel on the right features a much-adored **statue of St. Giuseppe Moscati** (1880-1927), a Christian doctor famous for helping the poor. In 1987, Moscati became the first modern doctor to be canonized.

Continue on to the third chapel (past his vertical tombstone) and enter the **Sale Moscati.** Look high on the walls of this long room to see hundreds of ex-votos—tiny red-and-silver plaques of thanksgiving for prayers answered with the help of St. Moscati (each has a symbol of the ailment cured). As you leave the Sale Moscati, notice the big bomb casing that hangs high in the left corner. It fell through the church's dome in 1943, but caused almost no damage...yet another miracle.

Cost and Hours: Free, daily 6:45-13:00 & 16:00-19:30, Piazza del Gesù Nuovo, www.gesunuovo.it.

CHURCH OF SANTA CHIARA

Dating from the 14th century, this church is from a period of French royal rule under the Angevin dynasty. Consider the stark contrast between this church (Gothic) and the Gesù Nuovo (Baroque), across the street. Inside, look for the faded Trinity on the back wall (on the right as you face the door, under the stone canopy), which shows a dove representing the Holy Spirit between the heads of God the Father and Christ (c. 1414). The altar is adorned with four finely carved Gothic tombs of Angevin kings. A chapel stacked with Bourbon royalty is just to the right.

Cost and Hours: Free, daily 7:30-13:00 & 16:30-20:00, Piazza del Gesù Nuovo, www.monasterodisantachiara.it. Its tranquil cloistered courtyard, around back, is not worth its €6 entry fee.

▲▲CAPPELLA SANSEVERO

This small chapel is a Baroque explosion mourning the body of Christ, who lies on a soft pillow under an incredibly realistic veil. It's also the personal chapel of Raimondo de Sangro, an eccentric Freemason, scientist and inventor, and patron of the arts. His chapel—filled with Masonic symbolism—contains his tomb and the tombs of his family.

Study the incredible *Veiled Christ* in the center. Carved out of marble (by Giuseppe "Howdeedoodat" Sammartino, 1753), it combines a Christian message (Jesus died for our salvation) with

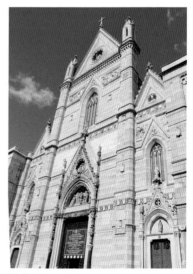

Naples Duomo

a Masonic message (the veil represents how the body and ego are obstacles to real spiritual freedom). As you walk from Christ's feet to his head, Jesus' expression goes from suffering to peace. Downstairs are two mysterious **skeletons**—the inventor's work with artificial veins to illustrate the circulatory system.

Cost and Hours: €7, buy tickets at office at the corner—or skip the long ticket-buying line by reserving ahead online (€2 fee); open Wed-Mon 9:30-18:30, closed Tue; Via de Sanctis 19, tel. 081-551-8470, www.museosansevero.it. The least crowded time to visit is after 16:00—the later the better. Pick up the free floor plan, which identifies each of the statues lining the nave.

▲DUOMO

Naples' historic cathedral, built by imported French Anjou kings in the 14th century, boasts a breathtaking Neo-Gothic facade. Step into the vast interior to see the mix of styles along the side chapels—from pointy Gothic arches to rounded Renaissance ones to gilded Baroque decor. Explore the two largest side-chapels (flanking the nave, about halfway to the transept). Each is practically a church in its own right. On the right is the **Chapel of San Gennaro**—dedicated to the beloved patron saint of Naples—decorated with silver busts of centuries of bishops, and six paintings done on bronze (skip the €3 chapel audioguide). On the left, the **Chapel of Santa Restituta** stands on the site of the original, early Christian church that pre-dated the cathedral (at the far end, you can pay a small fee to see its sixth-century baptismal font under mosaics and go downstairs to see its even earlier foundations; shorter hours than cathedral). The cathedral's **main altar** at the front is ringed by carved wooden seats, filled three times a year by clergy to witness the Miracle of the Blood, when two tiny vials of the dried blood of St. Gennaro temporarily liquefy before their eyes. Thousands of Neapolitans cram into the church to watch. They believe that if the blood remains solid, it's terrible luck for the city. The stairs beneath the altar lead to a **crypt** with the relics of St. Gennaro.

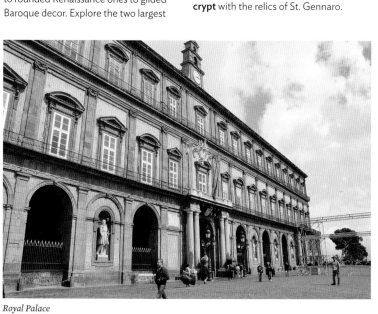

Royal Palace

Cost and Hours: Free, Mon-Sat 8:30-13:30 & 14:30-20:00, Sun 8:30-13:30 & 16:30-19:30, Via Duomo.

In the City Center

This cluster of important sights can be found between the big ceremonial square, Piazza del Plebiscito, and the cruise ship terminal. If touring the entire neighborhood, I'd see it in this order.

▲PIAZZA DEL PLEBISCITO

This square celebrates the 1861 vote (*plebiscito,* plebiscite) in which Naples chose to join Italy. Dominating the top of the square is the Church of San Francesco di Paola, with its Pantheon-inspired dome and broad, arcing colonnades. If it's open, step inside to ogle the vast interior—a Neoclassical re-creation of one of ancient Rome's finest buildings.

• *Opposite is the...*

ROYAL PALACE (PALAZZO REALE)

From the square in front of the palace, look for eight kings in the niches, each from a different dynasty (left to right): Norman, German, French, Spanish, Spanish, Spanish, French (Napoleon's brother-in-law), and, finally, Italian—Victor Emmanuel II, King of Savoy. The statues were done at the request of V. E. II's son, so his dad is the most dashing of the group. As far as palaces go, the interior is relatively unimpressive.

Cost and Hours: €6, skip the dry €3 audioguide—each room has excellent descriptions in English; Thu-Tue 9:00-20:00, closed Wed, last entry one hour before closing; tel. 848-082-408, www. coopculture.it).

• *Continue 50 yards past the Royal Palace (toward the trees) to enjoy a...*

FINE HARBOR VIEW

While boats busily serve Capri and Sorrento, Mount Vesuvius smolders ominously in the distance. Look back to see the vast "Bourbon red" palace—its color inspired by Pompeii. The hilltop above

Piazza del Plebiscito is San Martino, with its Carthusian monastery-turned-museum and Castle of St. Elmo. The promenade you're on continues to Naples' romantic harborfront—the fishermen's quarter (Borgo Marinaro)—a fortified island connected to the mainland by a stout causeway.

• *Head back through the piazza and pop into...*

GRAN CAFFÈ GAMBRINUS

This coffeehouse, facing the piazza, takes you back to the elegance of 1860. It's a classic place to sample a crispy *sfogliatella* pastry, or perhaps the mushroom-shaped, rum-soaked bread-like cakes called *babà* (daily 7:00-24:00, Piazza del Plebiscito 1, tel. 081-417-582).

• *A block away, tucked behind the palace, you can peek inside the Neoclassical...*

TEATRO DI SAN CARLO

Built in 1737, 41 years before Milan's La Scala, this is Europe's oldest opera house and Italy's second most-respected (after La Scala). Guided 35-minute visits in English basically just show you the fine auditorium with its 184 boxes—each with a big mirror to reflect the candlelight (€6; tours Mon-Sat at 10:30, 11:30, 12:30, 14:30, 15:30, and 16:30; Sun at 10:30, 11:30, and 12:30; tel. 081-797-2331, www.teatrosancarlo.it).

• *Beyond Teatro di San Carlo and the Royal Palace is the huge, harborfront...*

CASTEL NUOVO

This imposing castle now houses government bureaucrats and the **Civic Museum.** It feels like a mostly empty shell, with a couple of dusty halls of Neapolitan art, but the views over the bay from the upper terraces are impressive (€6, Mon-Sat 8:30-19:00, closed Sun, last entry one hour before closing, tel. 081-795-7722, www.comune.napoli.it).

• *Head back to Teatro di San Carlo, cross the street, and go through the tall yellow arch into...*

▲GALLERIA UMBERTO I

This Victorian iron-and-glass shopping mall opened in 1890 to reinvigorate the district after a devastating cholera epidemic occurred here. Gawk up, then walk left to bring you back out on Via Toledo.

• *Just up the street and behind Piazza del Plebiscito is an interesting subterranean experience.*

▲GALLERIA BORBONICA

Beneath Naples' Royal Palace was a vast underground network of caves, aqueducts, and cisterns that originated as a quarry in the 15th century. In the mid-1800s, when popular revolutions were threatening royalty across Europe, the understandably nervous king of Naples, Ferdinand II, had this underground world expanded to create an escape tunnel from the palace to his military barracks nearby. In World War II, it was used as an air-raid shelter; after the war, the police used it to store impounded cars and motorcycles. Today, enthusiastic guides take the curious on a fascinating 70-minute, 500-yard-long guided walk through this many-layered world littered with disintegrating 60-year-old vehicles upon which Naples sits.

Cost and Hours: €10 English-language tours leave Fri-Sun at 10:00, 12:00, 15:00, and 17:00, tel. 081-764-5808, www.galleriaborbonica.com. The most convenient entry is just behind Piazza del Plebiscito—up Via Gennaro Serra and down Vico del Grottone to #4 (to avoid that entrance's 90 steep steps, enter at Via Morelli 61).

On Capodimonte

▲▲CAPODIMONTE MUSEUM (MUSEO DI CAPODIMONTE)

This hilltop, about a mile due north from the Archaeological Museum, is home to Naples' top art museum. This pleasant collection has lesser-known (but still masterful) works by Michelangelo, Raphael, Titian, Caravaggio, and other huge names. It fills the Bourbons' cavern-

Raphael, Cardinal Farnese

ous summer palace, set in the midst of a sprawling hilltop park overlooking Naples, and part of the museum showcases the palace's history and furnishings.

Cost and Hours: €12, Thu-Tue 8:30-19:30, closed Wed, last entry one hour before closing, avoid lines by purchasing your ticket online (€2 fee), fine audioguide-€5 (bring earbuds for better sound), café, Via Miano 2, tel. 081-749-9111, www.museocapodimonte.beniculturali.it.

Getting There: It's easiest by taxi (figure €15 from the city center). You can also catch the CitySightseeing shuttle bus that runs from Teatro San Carlo and Piazza Municipio directly to the museum (€8 round-trip, tel. 081-551-7279, www.napoli.city-sightseeing.it).

Nearby: The expansive **Capodimonte Park** surrounding the museum, once a hunting ground for royalty, the park is now a pleasure garden—beloved by Neapolitans—with elegant paths and lovely gardens sprouting trees and exotic plants from around the world. If you've planned ahead, this is a lovely spot for a picnic.

Porta Nolana fish market

South of Spaccanapoli
PORTA NOLANA OPEN-AIR FISH MARKET

Of Naples' many boisterous outdoor markets, its centuries-old fish market will net you the most photos, memories—and smells. From Piazza Nolana, wander under the medieval gate (Porta Nolana) and take your first left down Via Sopramuro, to enjoy an edible scavenger hunt (Tue-Sun 8:00-14:00, closed Mon).

▲▲HARBORSIDE PROMENADE: THE LUNGOMARE *PASSEGGIATA*

Each evening, relaxed and romantic Neapolitans in the mood for a scenic harborside stroll do their *vasche* (laps) along the inviting Lungomare harborside promenade. To join in this elegant people-watching scene (best after 19:00), stroll down to the waterfront from Piazza del Plebiscito and then along Via Nazario Sauro to the beginning of a delightful series of harborside promenades that stretch romantically all the way out of the city. Along the way, you'll enjoy views of Mount Vesuvius and the Bay of Naples. The entire route is crowded on weekends and lively any evening of the week with families, amorous couples, and friends hanging out.

On San Martino

The ultimate view overlooking Naples, its bay, and the volcano is from San Martino hill, just above (and west of) the city center. Up top the mighty but empty **Castel Sant'Elmo** fortress offers the best views (€5, half-price after 16:15, open Wed-Mon 9:00-19:00, closed Tue, last entry one hour before closing, Via Tito Angelini 22, tel. 081-229-4401, www.polomusealecampania.beniculturali.it).

Nearby, the ▲▲ **San Martino Carthusian Monastery and Museum** features a beautiful Baroque-explosion church and a variety of exhibits, art, and sculpture, including giant ceremonial gondolas used by royalty and an excellent collection of *presepi* (Nativity scenes; €6, Thu-Tue 8:30-19:30, closed Wed, last entry one hour before closing, audioguide-€5, Largo San Martino 5, tel. 081-229-4502). Cheapskates can enjoy the views for free from the benches on the square in front of the monastery.

Getting There: Three different funicular lines lead from lower Naples to the hilltop (departures every 10 minutes): the Centrale line from near the bottom of Via Toledo; the Montesanto line from the Metro stop of the same name (near the top end of Via Toledo); and the Chiaia line from farther out, near Piazza Amadeo. All are covered by any regular local transit ticket. Leaving any funicular at the top, head uphill, carefully following brown signs for *Castel S. Elmo* and *Museo di San Martino*. You'll reach the castle with its bronze plaque first, then the monastery/museum (both about a 10-minute walk from Piazza Fuga).

Sleeping

As an alternative to intense Naples, most travelers prefer to sleep in mellow Sorrento, just over an hour away. But, if needed, here are a few good options.

$$$$ Decumani Hotel de Charme is a classy oasis tucked away on a residential lane in the very heart of the city, just off Spaccanapoli. While the street is Naples-dingy, the hotel is an inviting retreat, filling an elegant 17th-century palace with 42 rooms and a gorgeous breakfast room (air-con, elevator, Via San Giovanni Maggiore Pignatelli 15, Metro: Università; if coming from Spaccanapoli, this lane is one street toward the train station from Via Santa Chiara, tel. 081-551-8188, www.decumani.com, info@decumani.com).

$$$ Hotel Piazza Bellini is an artistically decorated hotel with 48 stripped-down, minimalist but comfy rooms surrounding a peaceful and inviting courtyard. Two blocks below the Archaeological Museum and just off the lively Piazza Bellini, it offers modern sanity in the city center (air-con, elevator, Via Santa Maria di Constantinopoli 101, Metro: Dante, tel. 081-451-732, www.hotelpiazzabellini.com, info@hotelpiazzabellini.com).

$$$ Art Resort Galleria Umberto has 17 genteel rooms with older bathrooms in two different buildings inside the Umberto I shopping gallery at the bottom of Via Toledo, just off Piazza del Plebiscito. Consider paying about €20 extra for a room overlooking the gallery (air-con, elevator, Galleria Umberto 83, fourth floor—ask at booth for coin to operate elevator if needed, Metro: Toledo, tel. 081-497-6224, www.artresortgalleriaumberto.com, booking @hotelgalleriaumberto.com).

$$$ Hotel Il Convento, with 14 small but comfortable rooms with balconies, is a good choice for those who want to sleep in the tight tangle of lanes called the Spanish Quarter—quintessential Naples. You're only a couple of short blocks off the main Via Toledo drag, and heavy-duty windows help block out some—but not all—of the scooter noise and church bells (family rooms, top-floor rooms with private garden terrace, air-con, elevator; Via Speranzella 137A, Metro: Toledo—from just below Banco di Napoli entrance, walk two blocks up Vico Tre Re a Toledo; tel. 081-403-977, www.hotelilconvento.com, info@hotelilconvento.com).

$$ Hotel Stelle has 38 sterile, identical, newly remodeled rooms with modern furnishings. It feels sane compared to its hectic surroundings, and a back entrance leads directly into the train station (air-con, elevator, Corso Meridionale 60, exit station near track 5, tel. 081-1889-3090, www.stellehotel.com, info@stellehotel.com).

$ Grand Hotel Europa, across the seedy street right next to Centrale station, has 89 decent rooms and hallways whimsically decorated with not-quite-right reproductions of famous paintings. The hotel is a decent value, and its 1970s-era vibe (including the Kool-Aid and canned fruit at breakfast) makes for fun memories (RS%, family rooms, air-con, elevator, restaurant, Corso Meridionale 14, across street from station's north exit near track 5, tel. 081-267-511, www.grandhoteleuropa.com, info@grandhoteleuropa.com).

Eating

Pizza Places

$ Antica Pizzeria da Michele, filled with locals (and tourists), serves just two varieties: *margherita*—tomato sauce and mozzarella— and *marinara*—tomato sauce, oregano, and garlic, no cheese (Mon-Sat 10:30-24:00, closed Sun; look for the vertical red *Antica Pizzeria* sign at the intersection of Via Pietro Colletta and Via Cesare Sersale at #1).

$ Pizzeria Trianon da Ciro, across the street and left a few doors from da Michele's, offers more choices, higher prices, air-conditioning, and a cozier atmosphere (daily 11:00-15:30 & 19:00-23:00, Via Pietro Colletta 42).

$ Pizzeria Starita, near the Archaeological Museum, has been in business for more than 100 years. This friendly eatery offers both modern and traditional toppings (Tue-Sun 12:00-15:30 & 19:00 until late, closed Mon, from the museum walk 10 minutes up Via Santa Teresa degli Scalzi to the intersection with Via Materdei—the pizzeria is a few steps down on the left at #27, Metro: Museo, tel. 081-557-3682).

$ Gino Sorbillo is a local favorite and is on all the "best pizza in Naples" lists (Mon-Sat 12:00-15:30 & 19:00-24:00, closed Sun, Via dei Tribunali 32, tel. 081-446-643).

$ La Figlia del Presidente updates the Neapolitan classics with abundant and innovative toppings (Tue-Sat 12:00-15:30 & 19:00-23:30, Mon 12:00-15:30, closed Sun, Via Grande Archivio 24—just below Spaccanapoli, tel. 081-286-738).

Restaurants

If you want a full meal rather than a pizza, consider these options.

NEAR SPACCANAPOLI AND VIA TOLEDO

$$$ Ecomesarà serves up quality Neapolitan and *meridionale* (southern Italian) dishes in a modern setting just below the Santa Chiara cloister, a long block south of Spaccanapoli. The atmosphere is mellow, modern, and international (Tue-Sun 13:00-15:00 & 20:00-23:30, closed Mon, Via Santa Chiara 49, tel. 081-1925-9353).

$$ Tandem Ragù Restaurant, tiny with a few charming tables inside and out, features a fun menu specializing in Neapolitan *ragù* (beef, pork, or vegetarian

Fantastic, Famous Pizza

Naples is the birthplace of pizza. Its pizzerias bake just the right combination of fresh dough (soft and chewy, as opposed to Roman-style, which is thin and crispy), mozzarella, and tomatoes in traditional wood-burning ovens. Head for the famous, venerable places, which can have long lines and half-hour waits—or just try the neighborhood pizzeria. An average one-person pie (usually the only size) costs €6-9; most places offer take-out and eat-in, and pizza is often the only thing on the menu.

options). The *scarpetta* (little shoe) dishes are simply various *ragùs* with baskets of bread for dunking (daily from 12:30 and 19:00, Via Giovanni Paladino 51, 50 yards off Spaccanapoli, below the statue of the Nile, tel. 081-1900-2468).

$$ Taverna a Santa Chiara is your classic little eatery buried deep in the old center of Naples. It's convivial, warmly run, and simple. Just 100 yards from the tourist commotion of Spaccanapoli, it provides a fun and easygoing break (daily from 13:00 and 20:00, closed Sun at dinner, Via Santa Chiara 6, tel. 081-048-4908).

$$ Trattoria Campagnola is a traditional family place with a daily home cooking-style chalkboard menu on the back wall, mama busy cooking in the back, and wine on tap. Here you can venture away from pastas, be experimental with a series of local dishes, and not go wrong (daily 12:30-16:00 & 19:30-23:00, opposite the famous pizzerias at Via Tribunali 47, tel. 081-459-034 but no reservations).

NEAR THE ARCHAEOLOGICAL MUSEUM

$$ La Stanza del Gusto, two blocks downhill from the Archaeological Museum, tackles food creatively and injects crusty Naples with a little modern color and irreverence. The ground floor is casual, trendy, and playful, while the upstairs is more refined yet still polka-dotted. A few tables are on the sidewalk (weekday lunch specials, daily 12:00-23:30 except Sun until 17:30, Via Santa Maria di Constantinopoli 100, tel. 081-401-578).

$$ Osteria da Carmela serves up traditional Neapolitan classics only mama could make—like *ragù, polpetti,* and tasty fried fish—with a dash of Old World charm. Affordable house wine and fine cheeses complete the meal. Tables are limited, so reservations are smart (Mon-Sat 12:00-15:00 & 19:00-24:00, closed Sun, Via Conte di Ruvo 11, tel. 081-549-9738, www.osteriadacarmela.it).

NEAR THE STATION

$$ Da Donato, an excellent, traditional, family-run trattoria on a glum street near the station, serves delicious food in an unpretentious atmosphere. The best approach is for two people to share the astonishing *antipasti* sampler—*degustazione "fantasia" della Casa Terra e Mare*—for €25. You'll get more than a dozen small portions, each more delicious than the last (Tue-Sun 12:30-14:30 & 19:30-22:00, closed Mon, two blocks from Piazza Garibaldi—turn down Via Silvio Spaventa to #39, tel. 081-287-828).

Transportation
Getting Around Naples

Most of Naples' public transportation system—Metro, funiculars, and buses—use the same ticket, which must be stamped as you enter (in yellow or blue machines). Tickets are sold at tobacco stores, some newsstands, clunky machines at Metro stations. A €1.10 single ticket *(corsa singola)* covers any ride on bus, funicular, or Metro line 1, with no transfers; for Metro line 2 you need the €1.30 version. A *giornaliero* day pass costs €3.50 (or €4.50 including Metro line 2), and pays for itself quickly, but can be hard to find; many tobacco stores don't sell them. A weekly ticket (Mon-Sun) costs €12.50, or €16 including Metro line 2. Several versions of the Campania ArteCard include public transport in Naples.

By Metro *(Metropolitana):* Naples' subway has three main lines *(linea).* Station entrances and signs are marked by a red square with a white *M.*

Line 1 is very useful for tourists. Starting from the train station (stop name: Garibaldi), it heads to Università (the university), Municipio (at Piazza Municipio, just above the harbor and cruise terminal), Toledo (south end of Via Toledo, near Piazza del Plebiscito), Dante (Piazza Dante), and Museo (Archaeological Museum). Many of line 1's stations are huge and elaborate, designed by prominent artists and architects.

Line 2 (part of the Italian national rail system) is most useful for getting quickly from the train station to Piazza Cavour (a 5-minute walk from the Archaeological Museum) or Montesanto (the top of the Spanish Quarter and Spaccanapoli street).

By Funicular: Central Naples' three funiculars *(funicolare)* carry commuters and sightseers into the hilly San Martino neighborhood just west of downtown.

By Taxi: A short ride in town should cost €10-15. Always ask for the *tariffa predeterminata* (a fixed rate). Your hotel or a TI can tell you the going rate for a given ride. Metered rides have some legitimate extra charges (baggage fees, €2.50 supplement after 22:00, all day Sun, and holidays) but destinations covered in this

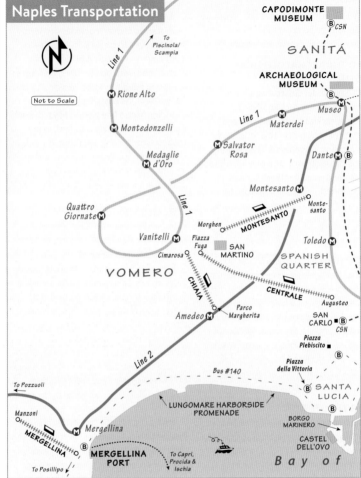

Naples Transportation

chapter are covered by the *tariffa prede-terminata*. Radio Taxi 8888 is one reputable company (tel. 081-8888).

Arriving and Departing

If you're connecting from Naples to a local destination, also see the "Getting Around the Region" section on page 390.

BY TRAIN

All trains coming into town stop at either Napoli Centrale station or Garibaldi station—which are essentially the same place, with Centrale on top of Garibaldi.

Stretching in front of this station complex is the vast Piazza Garibaldi, with an underground shopping mall and Metro entrance.

Centrale, on the ground floor, is the slick, modern main station. It has a small TI (next to the Trenitalia ticket office), a bookstore (near track 24), and baggage check (*deposito bagagli,* near track 2). Pay WCs are down the stairs across from track 13. Shops and eateries are concentrated in the underground level. A good supermarket (Sapori & Dintorni) is out the front door and to the left.

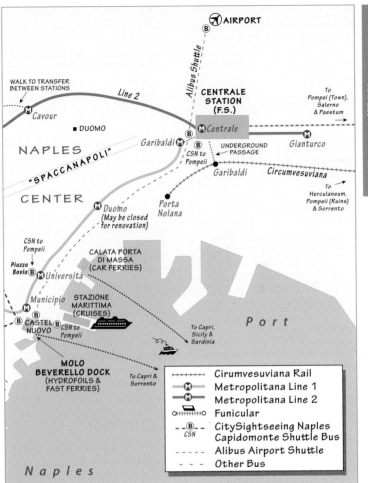

Garibaldi, on the lower level, is used exclusively by the narrow-gauge Circumvesuviana commuter train and the Campania Express (options you can use to connect to Sorrento or Pompeii; for details, see page 419). Note that this is not the terminus for the Circumvesuviana; that's one stop farther downtown, at the station called Porta Nolana.

Getting Downtown from the Station: Arriving at either station, the best bet for reaching most sights and hotels is either the Metro or a taxi. **Metro** lines 1 and 2

are signposted throughout Centrale and Garibaldi. Line 1 is handy for city-center stops, including the cruise port (Municipio), the main shopping drag (Toledo and Dante), and the Archaeological Museum (Museo). Line 2 is slightly quicker for reaching the Archaeological Museum (ride it to the Cavour stop and walk 5 minutes).

Long rows of white **taxis** line up out front. Ask the driver to charge you the fixed rate (*tariffa predeterminata*), which varies from €9 for the old center to €15 for the most distant hotel I list. The TI in the station can tell you the going rate.

From Naples by Train to: Pompeii (Circumvesuviana: 2/hour, 35 minutes; Campania Express: 4/day, 30 minutes; use the Pompei Scavi-Villa dei Misteri stop); **Sorrento** (Circumvesuviana: 2/hour, 70 minutes; Campania Express: 4/day, 1 hour); **Rome** (Trenitalia: 1-5/hour, 70 minutes on Frecciarossa, 2 hours on Intercity, 2.5 hours and much cheaper on regional trains; Italo: hourly, 70 minutes), **Florence** (Trenitalia: at least hourly, 3 hours, most change in Pisa or Rome; Italo: hourly, 3 hours), **Venice** (Trenitalia: almost hourly, 5.5 hours, some change in Bologna or Rome; Italo: 3/day, 5.5 hours, reservations required). Any train listed on the schedule as leaving Napoli PG or Napoli-Garibaldi departs not from Napoli Centrale, but from the adjacent Garibaldi station.

BY BOAT

Naples is a ferry hub with connections to Sorrento, Capri, and other nearby destinations. Cruise ships use the giant Stazione Marittima cruise terminal. Hydrofoils and faster ferries use the Molo Beverello dock (to the west of the terminal). Slower car ferries leave from Calata Porta di Massa, east of the terminal. The entire port area has been under renovation, which may still be ongoing when you visit.

The **taxi** stand is in front of the port area. Expect to pay €12-15 for a ride to the train station or the Archaeological Museum.

Straight ahead across the road from the cruise terminal (on the right side of the big fortress) is Piazza Municipio, with the handy Municipio **Metro** stop. From here, line 1 zips you right to the Archaeological Museum (Museo stop) or, in the opposite direction, to the train station (Garibaldi stop).

On foot, it's a seven-minute **walk**— past the gigantic Castel Nuovo—to Piazza del Plebiscito and the old city center.

From Naples by Boat to: Sorrento (6/day, more in summer, departs roughly every 2 hours starting at 9:00, 40 minutes), **Capri** (roughly hourly, more in summer, hydrofoil: 45 minutes; ferries: 50-80 minutes). For timetables, visit www.capritourism.com and click "Shipping Timetable."

BY PLANE

Naples International Airport (Aeroporto Internazionale di Napoli, a.k.a. Capodichino, code: NAP) is close to town (handy info desk just outside baggage claim to the left, www.aeroportodinapoli.it). Alibus **shuttle buses** zip you in 10 minutes from the airport to Naples' Centrale train station, and then head to the port/Piazza Municipio for boats to Capri and Sorrento (buses run daily 6:00-23:00, 4/hour, 20-30 minutes to the port, €5 on board, stops at train station and port only). If you take a **taxi** to or from the airport, ask the driver for the fixed price (€18 to the train station, €21 to the port, €25 to the Chiaia district near the waterfront).

To reach **Sorrento** from Naples Airport, take the direct Curreri bus (see page 444). A taxi to Sorrento costs about €110.

POMPEII

A once-thriving commercial port of 20,000, Pompeii (worth ▲▲▲) grew from Greek and Etruscan roots to become an important Roman city. Then, on August 24, AD 79, everything changed. Vesuvius erupted and began to bury the city under 30 feet of hot volcanic ash. For the archaeologists who excavated it centuries later, this was a shake-and-bake windfall, teaching them volumes about daily Roman life. Pompeii offers the best look anywhere at what life in Rome must have been like around 2,000 years ago. It's easily reached from Naples by shuttle bus or on the Circumvesuviana commuter (or Campania Express) train. Vesuvius, still smoldering ominously, rises up on the horizon.

Getting to Pompeii

By Shuttle Bus from Naples: CitySightseeing Italy offers a convenient, clean, and stress-free shuttle bus from Naples to Pompeii, with pick-up points at the Molo Beverello boat dock, Piazza Bovio near the Università Metro stop, and Centrale station (stop located across the street and left when exiting, near the Hotel D'Anna).

Tickets can be purchased online, but be aware that each bus has a specific return time about four hours after arrival; no return-trip changes are allowed. Early morning departures beat the heat at Pompeii, but traffic congestion can delay your arrival and cut into your sightseeing time. Departures from Centrale station in summer are at 9:30, 10:15, and 11:15, with corresponding return trips at 13:20, 14:40, and 16:00; fewer departures off-season; 30-minute ride from the train station if traffic is light (€8 one-way, €15 round-trip, tel. 081-551-7279, www.city-sightseeing. it). Skip the option to purchase your Pompeii entrance ticket through CitySightseeing—you'll pay more than buying it yourself online (details later).

By Train from Naples or Sorrento: Pompeii is roughly midway between Naples and Sorrento on the crowded, run-down **Circumvesuviana commuter train** line (2/hour, 35 minutes from Naples, 30 minutes from Sorrento, either trip costs €2.90 one-way, not covered by rail passes, no air-con, Italian-only website: www.eavsrl.it). Get off at the Pompei Scavi-Villa dei Misteri stop; from Naples, it's the stop after Villa Regina. DD express trains (6/day) bypass several stations but do stop at Pompei Scavi, shaving 10 minutes off the trip from Naples. Less-frequent **Campania Express trains** use the same tracks and stops, but are less crowded and have air-conditioning (4/day, 30 minutes from Naples, 25 minutes from Sorrento, either trip costs €6 one-way, mid-March-Oct only, http://ots.eavsrl.it).

From the Pompei Scavi train station, it's just a two-minute walk to the Porta Marina entrance: Leaving the station, turn right and walk down the road about a block to the entrance (on your left).

Pompei vs. Pompei Scavi: Make sure you're taking the Circumvesuviana commuter train or Campania Express to Pompei Scavi (*scavi* means "excavations"), the station right next to the ancient site. Pompei is the name of a separate train station

The Forum at Pompeii

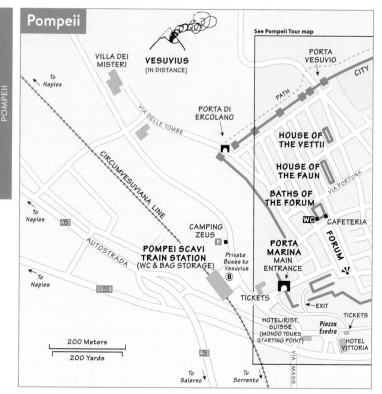

Pompeii

VILLA DEI MISTERI

VESUVIUS (IN DISTANCE)

To Naples

VIA DELLE TOMBE

PORTA DI ERCOLANO

CIRCUMVESUVIANA LINE

To Naples

A-3

AUTOSTRADA

To Naples

SS-18

See Pompeii Tour map

PORTA VESUVIO

CITY

PATH

HOUSE OF THE VETTII

HOUSE OF THE FAUN

VIA FORTUNA

BATHS OF THE FORUM

WC CAFETERIA

CAMPING ZEUS

POMPEI SCAVI TRAIN STATION (WC & BAG STORAGE)

Private Buses to Vesuvius

B

PORTA MARINA MAIN ENTRANCE

FORUM

TICKETS

EXIT

HOTEL/RIST. SUISSE (MONDO TOURS STARTING POINT)

Piazza Esedra

TICKETS

HOTEL VITTORIA

VIA MASS.

200 Meters

200 Yards

A-3

To Salerno

To Sorrento

on the main national rail line that's a long, dull walk from the ruins.

By Car: Parking is available at Camping Zeus, next to the Pompei Scavi train station; several other campgrounds/parking lots are nearby.

Orientation

Cost: €15, includes special exhibits. Consider the Campania ArteCard (see page 396) if visiting other sights in the region.

Hours: Mon-Fri 9:00-19:30, Sat-Sun 8:30-19:30, Nov-March daily until 17:00, last entry 1.5 hours before closing.

Information: Tel. 081-857-5347, general info at www.pompeiisites.org, tickets at www.ticketone.it.

Crowd-Beating Tips: To skip ahead of everyone, purchase your ticket online at www.ticketone.it (€2 surcharge).

If you're buying onsite and there's a very long ticket line at the Porta Marina entrance, continue walking three minutes to the ticket booth near Hotel Vittoria (rarely a line). Buy your ticket, return to Porta Marina, and walk right in.

Some state museums in Italy, including Pompeii, are free to enter once or twice a month, usually on a Sunday. Check in advance and avoid going on a free day, which attracts huge crowds.

Visitor Information: Admission includes a wonderful English guide/booklet and map (be sure to get and use this). Ask for it when you buy your ticket, or check at the info window to the left of the WCs—the maps aren't available within the walls of Pompeii. Ignore the "info point" kiosk at the train station, which is a private agency selling tours.

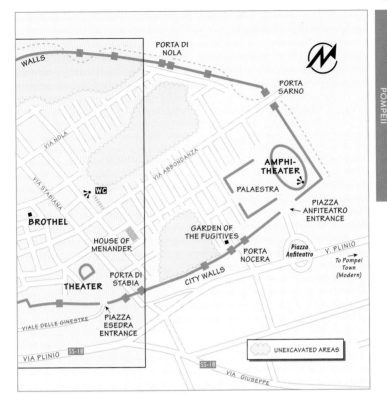

Tours: Simply follow the **self-guided** tour in this chapter (or, better, 🎧 download and enjoy my free Rick Steves **audio tour** version. Both cover the basics and provide a good framework for exploring the site on your own.

Audioguides available from a kiosk near the ticket booth at the Porta Marina entrance (€8, €13 for 2, ID required) offer basically the same info as your free booklet.

Mondo Guide offers shared tours for Rick Steves readers. This is your best budget bet for a tour with an actual guide (€15, doesn't include €15 Pompeii entry, daily at 11:00, reservations required; for details, see page 394). Or hire a guide for a private or shared tour.

Antonio Somma and his team of guides offer good two-hour tours (€120 for up to 6 people, mobile 393-406-3824, tel. 081-850-1992, www.tourspompei-iguide.com, info@pompeitour.com).

Rick's Tip: **Parents** *should note that Pompeii's ancient brothel contains* **sexually explicit frescoes;** *if you're on a tour, let your guide know if you'd rather skip that stop.*

Length of This Tour: Allow two hours, or three if you visit the theater and amphitheater. With less time, focus on the Forum, Baths of the Forum, House of the Vettii, House of the Faun, and brothel.

Baggage Check: Use the free baggage check near the turnstiles at the site entrance (just yards from the station).

The train station also offers pay luggage storage (downstairs, by the WC).

Services: There's a pay WC at the train station. The Pompeii site has three WCs—one near the entrance, one in the cafeteria, and another near the end of this tour, uphill from the theaters.

Eating: These **$** eateries are reasonable, though your cheapest bet may be a discreet picnic. The **Ciao cafeteria,** within the site, serves good sandwiches, pizza, and pasta. **Bar Sgambati,** at the train station, has air-conditioning, Wi-Fi, sandwiches to go, and pastas and pizzas. **Marius Juice Shop** sells sandwiches to go, and is located between Bar Sgambati and the Porta Marina entrance. A second cluster of eateries around the ticket booth near Hotel Vittoria dishes out pizza slices, salads, and pasta.

Background

Pompeii, founded in 600 BC, eventually became a booming Roman trading city. Not rich, not poor, it was middle class—a perfect example of typical Roman life. Most streets would have been lined with stalls and jammed with customers from sunup to sundown. Chariots vied with shoppers for street space. Two thousand years ago, Rome controlled the entire Mediterranean—making it a kind of free-trade zone—and Pompeii was a central and bustling port.

There were no posh neighborhoods in Pompeii. Rich and poor mixed it up as elegant houses existed side by side with sim-

ple homes. Pompeii served an estimated 20,000 residents with more than 40 bakeries, 130 bars, restaurants and hotels, and 30 brothels. With most of its buildings covered by brilliant white ground-marble stucco, Pompeii in AD 79 was an impressive town. As you tour Pompeii, remember that its best art is safeguarded in the Archaeological Museum in Naples.

◕ Self-Guided Tour

• *Just past the ticket-taker, start your approach up to the...*

❶ Porta Marina

The city of Pompeii was born on the hill ahead of you. This was the original town gate. Before Vesuvius blew and filled in the harbor, the sea came nearly to here. Notice the two openings in the gate (ahead, up the ramp). Both were left open by day to admit major traffic. At night, the larger one was closed for better security.

• *Pass through the Porta Marina and continue up to the top of the street, pausing at the three large stepping-stones in the middle.*

❷ Pompeii's Streets

Every day, Pompeiians flooded the streets with gushing water to clean them. These stepping-stones let pedestrians cross without getting their sandals wet. Chariots traveling in either direction could straddle the stones. A single stepping-stone in a road means it was a one-way street, a pair indicates an ordinary two-way, and three (like this) signifies a major thoroughfare. The basalt stones are the original Roman pavement. The sidewalks (elevated to hide the plumbing) were paved with bits of broken pots (an ancient form of recycling) and studded with reflective bits of white marble. These "cats' eyes" helped people get around after dark, either by moonlight or with the help of lamps.

• *Continue straight ahead, don your mental toga, and enter the city as the Romans*

A typical Pompeiian street

Pompeii Tour

1 Porta Marina
2 Pompeii's Streets
3 Forum
4 Basilica
5 Via Abbondanza
6 Forum Granary;
   Plaster Casts of Victims
7 Baths of the Forum
8 Fast-Food Joint
9 House of the Tragic Poet
10 Aqueduct Arch
11 House of the Faun
12 House of the Vettii
13 Bakery & Mill
14 Brothel

once did. The road opens up into the spa-cious main square: the Forum. Stand at the right end of this rectangular space and look toward Mount Vesuvius.

❸ The Forum (Foro)

Pompeii's commercial, religious, and political center stands at the intersection of the city's two main streets. While it's the most ruined part of Pompeii, it's grand nonetheless. Picture the piazza surrounded by two-story buildings on all sides. The pedestals that line the square once held statues of VIPs and gods (now safely displayed in the museum in Naples). Citizens gathered here in the main square to shop, talk politics, and socialize. Business took place in buildings that lined the piazza.

The Forum was dominated by the **Temple of Jupiter,** at the far end (marked by a half-dozen ruined columns atop a stair-step base). Jupiter was the supreme god of the Roman pantheon—you might be able to make out his little white marble head at the center-rear of the temple. To the left of the temple is a fenced-off area, the **Forum granary,** where many artifacts from Pompeii are stored (and which we'll visit later).

At the near end of the Forum (behind where you're standing) is the **curia,** or City Hall. Like many Roman buildings, it was built with brick and mortar, then covered with marble walls and floors. To your left (as you face Vesuvius and the Temple of Jupiter) is the **basilica,** or courthouse.

Pompeii has the same layout and components that you'd find in any Roman city at the time. All power converged at the Forum: religious (the temple), political (the curia), judicial (the basilica), and commercial (this piazza was the main marketplace). Even the power of the people was expressed here, since this is where they gathered to vote.

Look beyond the Temple of Jupiter. Five miles to the north looms the ominous backstory to this site: **Mount Vesuvius.** Mentally draw a triangle up from the

Pompeii's basilica

two remaining peaks to reconstruct the mountain before the eruption. When it blew, Pompeiians had no idea that they were living under a volcano, as Vesuvius hadn't erupted for 1,200 years. Imagine the wonder—then the horror—as a column of pulverized rock roared upward, and then ash began to fall. The weight of the ash and small rocks collapsed Pompeii's roofs later that day, crushing people who had taken refuge inside buildings instead of fleeing the city.

• *As you face Vesuvius, the basilica is to your left, lined with stumps of columns. Step inside.*

❹ Basilica

Pompeii's basilica was a first-century palace of justice. This ancient law court has the same floor plan later adopted by many Christian churches (also called basilicas). The big central hall (or nave) is flanked by rows of columns marking off narrower side aisles. Along the side walls are traces of the original stucco imitating marble.

The columns—now stumps all about the same height—were not ruined by the volcano. Rather, they were left unfinished when Vesuvius blew. Pompeii had been devastated by an earthquake in AD 62, and was just in the process of rebuilding the basilica when Vesuvius erupted, 17 years later. The half-built columns show off the technology of the day. Uniform bricks were stacked around a cylindrical core. Once finished, they would have been coated with marble-dust stucco to simulate marble columns—an economi-

The Eruption of Vesuvius

At about 1:00 in the afternoon on August 24, AD 79, Mount Vesuvius erupted, sending a mushroom cloud of ash, dust, and rocks 12 miles into the air. It spewed for 18 hours straight, as winds blew the cloud southward. The white-gray ash settled like a heavy snow on Pompeii, its weight eventually collapsing roofs and floors, but leaving walls intact. And though most of Pompeii's 20,000 residents fled that day, about 2,000 stayed behind.

That night, the type of eruption changed. The mountain let loose a superheated avalanche of ash, pumice, and gas that flowed eastward (away from Pompeii). This red-hot "pyroclastic flow" sped down the side of the mountain at nearly 100 miles per hour, engulfing everything in its path. Around 7:30 in the morning, another pyroclastic flow headed south and struck Pompeii, snuffing out all life.

cal construction method found throughout Pompeii (and the Roman Empire).

Besides the earthquake and the eruption, Pompeii's buildings have suffered other ravages over the years, including Spanish plunderers (c. 1800), 19th-century souvenir hunters, WWII bombs, creeping and destructive vegetation, another earthquake in 1980, and modern neglect. The fact that the entire city was covered by the eruption of AD 79 actually helped preserve it, saving it from the sixth-century barbarians who plundered many other towns into oblivion.

• *Exit the basilica and cross the short side of the square to where the city's main street hits the Forum. Stop at the three white stones that stick up from the cobbles.*

❺ Via Abbondanza

Glance down Via Abbondanza, Pompeii's main street. Lined with shops, bars, and restaurants, it was a lively, pedestrian-only

zone. The three "beaver-teeth" stones are traffic barriers that kept chariots out. On the corner at the start of the street (just to the left), take a close look at the dark travertine column standing next to the white one. Notice that the marble drums of the white column are not chiseled entirely round—another construction project left unfinished when Vesuvius erupted.

• *Our tour will eventually end a few blocks down Via Abbondanza after making a big loop. But now, head toward Vesuvius, cutting across the Forum. To the left of the Temple of Jupiter is the...*

❻ Forum Granary

A substantial stretch of the west side of the Forum was the granary and ancient produce market. Today, it houses thousands of artifacts excavated from Pompeii. You'll see lots of crockery, pots, pans, jugs, and containers used for transporting oil and wine. You'll also see casts of a couple of Pompeiians eerily captured in their last moments, hands covering their mouths as they gasped for air. They were quickly suffocated by a superheated avalanche of gas and ash, and their bodies were encased in volcanic debris. While excavating, modern archaeologists detected hollow spaces underfoot, created when the victims' bodies decomposed. By gently filling the holes with plaster, the archaeologists created molds of the Pompeiians who were caught in the disaster.

A few steps to the left of the granary is a tiny alcove that contained the Mensa Ponderaria, a counter where standard units (such as today's liter or gallon) were used to measure the quantities of liquid and solid food that were sold. And just to the right of the granary is the remains of a public toilet. You can imagine the many seats, lack of privacy, and constantly flushing stream running through the room.

• *Exit the Forum by crossing it again in front of the Temple of Jupiter and turning left. Go under the arch. In the road are more "bea-*

Plaster cast of victim

Baths of the Forum

ver-teeth" traffic blocks. On the pillar to the right, look for the pedestrian-only road sign (two guys carrying an amphora, or ancient jug; it's above the REG VII INS IV sign). The modern cafeteria (on the left) is the only eatery inside the archaeological site. Twenty yards past the cafeteria, on the left-hand side at #24, is the entrance to the...

❼ Baths of the Forum (Terme del Foro)

Pompeii had six public baths, each with a men's and a women's section. You're in the men's zone. The leafy courtyard at the entrance was the gymnasium. After working out, clients could relax with a hot bath (*caldarium*), warm bath (*tepidarium*), or cold plunge (*frigidarium*).

The first big, plain room you enter served as the **dressing room.** Holes on the walls were for pegs to hang clothing. High up, the window (with a faded Neptune underneath) was originally covered with a less-translucent Roman glass. Walk over the nonslip mosaics into the next room.

The **tepidarium** is ringed by mini statues or *telamones* (male caryatids, figures used as supporting pillars), which divided the lockers. Clients would undress and warm up here, perhaps relaxing on one of the bronze benches near the bronze heater while waiting for a massage. Look at the ceiling—half crushed by the eruption and half intact, with its fine blue-and-white stucco work.

Next, admire the engineering in the steam-bath room, or **caldarium.** The double floor was heated from below—so it was nice for bare feet (look into the grate across from where you entered to see the brick support towers). The double walls with brown terra-cotta tiles held the heat. Romans soaked in the big tub, which was filled with hot water. Opposite the big tub is a fountain, which spouted water onto the hot floor, creating steam. The lettering on the fountain reminded those enjoying the room which two politicians paid for it...and how much it cost them. (On the far right, Roman numerals indicate they paid 5,250 *sestertii*). To keep condensation from dripping from the ceiling, fluting was added to carry water down the walls.

• *Today's visitors exit the baths through the original entry (at the far end of the dressing room). Immediately across the street is an ancient...*

❽ Fast-Food Joint

After a bath, it was only natural to want a little snack. So, just across the street is a fast-food joint, marked by a series of rectangular marble counters. Most ancient Romans didn't cook for themselves in their tiny apartments, so to-go places like this were commonplace. The holes in the counters held the pots for food. Each container was like a thermos, with a wooden lid to keep the soup hot, the wine cool, and so on. You could dine in the back or get your food to go. Notice the groove in the front doorstep and the holes out on the curb. The holes likely accommodated cords for stretching awnings over the sidewalk to shield the clientele from the hot sun, while the grooves were for the shop's folding accordion doors.

• Just a few steps uphill from the fast-food joint, at #5 (with a locked gate), is the...

❾ House of the Tragic Poet (Casa del Poeta Tragico)

This house is typical Roman style. The entry is flanked by two family-owned shops (each with a track for a collapsing accordion door). The home has an atrium (with skylight and pool to catch the rain), den (where deals were made by the shop-keeper), and garden (with rooms facing it and a shrine to remember both the gods and family ancestors). In the entryway is the famous "Beware of Dog" (*Cave Canem*) mosaic.

When it's open, today's visitors enter the home by the back door (circle around to the left). The richly frescoed dining room is off the garden. Diners lounged on their couches (the Roman custom) and enjoyed frescoes with fake "windows," giving the illusion of a bigger and airier room. Next to the dining room is a humble BBQ-style kitchen with a little closet for the toilet (the kitchen and bathroom shared plumbing).

• Return to the fast-food place and continue about 10 yards downhill to the big intersection. From the center of the intersection, look left to see a giant arch, framing a nice view of Mount Vesuvius.

❿ Aqueduct Arch

This arch was part of Pompeii's water-delivery system. A 100-mile-long aqueduct carried fresh water down from the hillsides to a big reservoir perched at the highest point of the city wall. Since overall water pressure was disappointing, Pompeiians built arches like the brick one you see here (originally covered in marble) with hidden water tanks at the top. Located just below

the altitude of the main tank, these smaller tanks were filled by gravity and provided each neighborhood with reliable pressure. Look closely at the arch and you'll see 2,000-year-old pipes (made of lead imported all the way from Cornwall in Britannia) embedded deep in the brick.

If there was a water shortage, democratic priorities prevailed: First the baths were cut off, then the private homes. The last to go were the public fountains, where all citizens could get drinking and cooking water.

• If you're thirsty, fill your water bottle from the modern fountain. Then continue straight downhill one block (50 yards) to #2 on the left.

⓫ House of the Faun (Casa del Fauno)

Stand across the street and marvel at the grand entry with *"HAVE"* (hail to you) as a welcome mat. Go in. Notice the two shrines above the entryway—one dedicated to the gods, the other to this wealthy family's ancestors. (Contemporary Neapolitans still carry on this practice; you'll notice little shrines embedded in walls all over Naples.)

House of the Faun

You are standing in Pompeii's largest home, where you're greeted by the delightful small bronze statue of the *Dancing Faun,* famed for its realistic movement and fine proportion. (The original is in Naples' Archaeological Museum.) With 40 rooms and 27,000 square feet, the House of the Faun covers an entire city block. The next floor mosaic, with an intricate diamond-like design, decorates the homeowner's office. Beyond that, at the far end of the first garden, is the famous floor mosaic of the *Battle of Alexander.* (The original is also at the museum in Naples.) In 333 BC, Alexander the Great beat Darius and the Persians. Romans had much respect for Alexander, the first great emperor before Rome's. While most of Pompeii's nouveau riche had notoriously bad taste and stuffed their palaces with over-the-top, mismatched decor, this guy had class. Both the faun (an ancient copy of a famous Greek statue) and the Alexander mosaic show an appreciation for history.

The house's back courtyard is lined with pillars rebuilt after the AD 62 earthquake. Take a close look at the brick, mortar, and fake-marble stucco veneer.

• *Leave the House of the Faun through its back door in the far-right corner, past a tiny guard's station. (If closed, exit out the front and walk around to the back.) Turn right and walk about a block until you see metal cages over the sidewalk protecting exposed stretches of ancient lead water pipes. Con-* *tinue east and take your first left, walking about 20 yards to the entrance (on your left) to the...*

⑫ *House of the Vettii*

This is Pompeii's best-preserved home, retaining many of its mosaics and frescoes. The House of the Vettii was the bachelor pad of two wealthy merchant brothers. In the entryway, it's hard to miss the huge erection. This was not pornography. This was a symbol of success: The penis and sack of money balance each other on the goldsmith scale above a fine bowl of fruit. Translation? Only with a balance of fertility and money can you enjoy true abundance.

Step into the atrium with its replica wooden ceiling open to the sky and a lead pipe to collect water for the house cistern. The pool was flanked by two large moneyboxes (one survives, the footprint of the other shows how it was secured to the ground). The brothers wanted all who entered to know how successful they were. A variety of rooms give an intimate peek at elegant Pompeiian life. The dark room to the right of the entrance (as you face out) is filled with exquisite frescoes. Notice more white "cat's eye" stones embedded in the floor. Imagine these glinting like little eyes as the brothers and their friends wandered around by oil lamp late at night, with their sacks of gold, bowls of fruit, and enormous...egos.

Fresco in the House of the Vettii

Fresco in the Brothel

• *Our next stop, the bakery, is located about 150 yards south (downhill) from here. To get there, return to the street in front of the House of the Vettii. Walk downhill along Vicolo dei Vetti. Go one block, to where you dead-end at a T-intersection with Via della Fortuna. Go a few steps left and then right at the first corner. Continue down this gently curving road to #22.*

⑬ Bakery and Mill

The stubby stone towers are flour grinders. Grain was poured into the top and donkeys or slaves, treading in a circle, pushed wooden bars that turned the stones that ground the grain. The powdered grain dropped out the bottom as flour—flavored with tiny bits of rock. Nearby, the thing that looks like a modern-day pizza oven was...a brick oven. Each neighborhood had a bakery just like this.

• *Continue down the curvy road to the next intersection. As you walk consider the destructive power of all the plants and vines that you see. Also, notice the chariot grooves worn into the pavement. When the curvy road reaches the intersection with Via degli Augustali, turn left. Ahead, in 50 yards, at #44, is the Taberna Hedones, an ancient tavern with an original floor mosaic still intact. A few steps past that, turn right and walk downhill to #18—one of many Pompeii brothels.*

⑭ Brothel (Lupanare)

You'll find the biggest crowds in Pompeii at a place that was likely also quite popular 2,000 years ago—the brothel. Prostitutes were nicknamed *lupe* (she-wolves), alluding to the call they made when attracting business. The brothel was a simple place, with beds and pillows made of stone and then covered with mattresses. The ancient graffiti includes tallies and names of the women, indicating the prostitutes came from all corners of the Mediterranean (it also served as feedback from satisfied customers). The faded frescoes above the cells may have been a kind of menu for services offered.

Note the idealized women (white, which was considered beautiful; one wears an early bra) and the rougher men (dark, considered horny). The bed legs came with little disk-like barriers to keep critters from crawling up, the tiny rooms had curtains for doors, and the prostitutes provided sheepskin condoms.

• *Leaving the brothel, go right, then take the first left, and continue going downhill two blocks to return to Via Abbondanza. This walk is over. The Forum—and exit—are to the right. If you exit now, you'll be routed through the exhibition rooms— where you'll find a scale model of the city, an interesting video, some artifacts—and the gift shop.*

But before you leave, consider these extra stops—all worth the time and energy (if you have any left). To locate them, refer to your map.

Temple of Isis

This temple served Pompeii's Egyptian community. The little white stucco shrine with the modern plastic roof housed holy water from the Nile. Isis, from Egyptian myth, was one of many foreign gods adopted by the eclectic Romans. Pompeii must have had a synagogue, too, but it has yet to be excavated.

Theater

Originally a Greek theater (Greeks built theirs with the help of a hillside), this was the birthplace of the Greek port here in 470 BC. During Roman times, the theater sat 5,000 people in three sets of seats, all with different prices: the five marble terraces up close (filled with romantic wooden seats for two), the main section, and the cheap nose-bleed section (surviving only on the high end, near the trees). The square stones above the cheap seats once supported a canvas rooftop. The high-profile boxes, flanking the stage, were for guests of honor. From this perch, you can see the gladiator barracks—the colonnaded courtyard beyond the theater. They lived in tiny rooms, trained in the courtyard, and fought in the nearby amphitheater. Check out the adjacent and well-preserved smaller Teatro Piccolo.

House of Menander (Casa di Menandro)

Once owned by a wealthy Pompeiian, this house takes its current name from a fresco of the Greek playwright Menander on one of the walls. Admire the grand atrium (with frescoes depicting scenes from Homer's *Iliad* and *Odyssey,* and an altar to the family gods), the wall frescoes, and the mosaics. The cloister-like back courtyard leads to a room with skeletons (not plaster casts) of eruption victims from this house. Farther back, a passage leads to the servants' quarters.

Viewpoint

You're at ground level—post eruption. To the right (inland), the farmland shows how locals lived on top of the ruins for centuries without knowing what was underneath. To the left, you can see the entire ancient city of Pompeii spread out in front of you and appreciate the magnitude of the excavations.

Garden of the Fugitives

Archaeologists identified this house as belonging to a middle-class merchant family. Plaster casts of this fleeing ("fugitive") family are placed exactly as the bodies were found after the eruption: lined up in single file as they attempted to escape several cubic feet of already fallen ash. Their exit was stopped by a sudden wave of hot gas and volcanic material, likely traveling over 100 miles per hour. Frozen in time, servants cannot be distinguished from their masters.

Amphitheater

If you can, climb to the upper level of the amphitheater (though the stairs are often blocked). Mentally replace the tourists below with gladiators and wild animals locked in combat. Walk along the top of the amphitheater and look down into the grassy rectangular area surrounded by columns. This is the **Palaestra,** an area once used for athletic training. (If you can't get to the top of the amphitheater, you can see the Palaestra from outside—in fact, you can't miss it, as it's right next door.) Facing the other way, look for the bell tower that tops the roofline of the modern city of Pompei, where locals go about their daily lives in the shadow of the volcano, just as their ancestors did 2,000 years ago.

• *If it's too crowded to bear hiking back along uneven lanes to the entrance, you can slip out the site's "back door," which is next to the amphitheater. Exiting, turn right and follow the site's wall all the way back to the entrance.*

SORRENTO

Spritzed by lemon and olive groves, Sorrento is an attractive resort of 20,000 residents and, in summer, just as many tourists. Just an hour south of Naples but without a hint of big-city chaos, serene Sorrento makes an ideal home base for exploring the entire region. This gateway to the Amalfi Coast has a pedestrianized old quarter, lively shopping streets, and a spectacular cliffside setting.

Serene Sorrento

Relaxed Sorrento is well located for sightseeing—and a fine place to stay and stroll.

Orientation

Downtown Sorrento is long and narrow. Piazza Tasso marks the town's center. The main drag, Corso Italia, runs parallel to the sea through Piazza Tasso and then out toward the cape, where the road's name becomes Via Capo. Nearly everything mentioned here (except Marina Grande and the hotels on Via Capo) is within a 10-minute walk of the station. The town is perched on a cliff (some hotels have elevators down to sundecks on the water); the best real beaches are a couple of miles away.

Sorrento has two separate port areas. Marina Piccola is a functional harbor with boats to Naples and Capri, as well as cruise-ship tenders. Despite its name, Marina Grande, below the other end of downtown, is a little fishing enclave, with recommended restaurants and more charm.

Sorrento is busiest in summer and hibernates in winter (Nov-March).

Rick's Tip: *Sorrento makes a great home base because all of the* **key destinations are within an hour or so:** *Naples (by train or boat), Pompeii (by train), the Amalfi Coast (by bus), and the island of Capri (by boat).*

Tourist Information

The helpful regional TI (labeled Azienda di Soggiorno)—located inside the Foreigners' Club—hands out a great city map and schedules for boats and buses (Mon-Sat 9:00-19:00, Sun until 18:00 except closed Sun April-May; Nov-March Mon-Fri 8:30-16:00, closed Sat-Sun; Via Luigi de Maio 35, tel. 081-807-4033, www.sorrentotourism.com).

Small "Info Points" are conveniently located around town, where you can get answers to basic questions (open in warm months only). Find them just outside the train station in the green caboose; near Piazza Tasso at the corner of Via Correale (under the yellow church); at Marina Piccola; and at the Achille Lauro parking garage.

Helpful Hints

Baggage Storage: Store bags at the underground parking lot **Parcheggio de Curtis,** downhill from the train station (daily 7:30-23:30, Via E. de Curtis 5, just before Corsa Italia). Another option with pick-up and drop-off service is **Sorrento Luggage** (mobile 338-431-7323, www.sorrentoluggage.com).

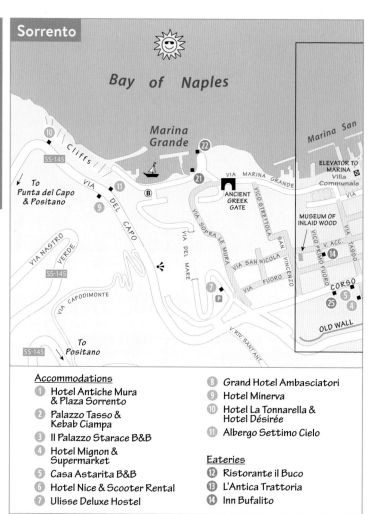

Sorrento

Bay of Naples

Marina Grande

Marina San

ELEVATOR TO MARINA
Villa Communale

To Punta del Capo & Positano

ANCIENT GREEK GATE

MUSEUM OF INLAID WOOD

VIA MARINA GRANDE
VICO STRETTOLA
SAN VINCENZO
VIA SAN NICOLA
VIA FUORO
VICO PRIMO FUORO
V. ACC
VIA TASSO
CORSO

OLD WALL

To Positano

SS-145

VIA DEL CAPO
VIA DEL MARE
VIA SOPRA LE MURA
VIA NASTRO VERDE
VIA CAPODIMONTE

Cliffs

V. RIV SANT'ANT

Accommodations

1. Hotel Antiche Mura & Plaza Sorrento
2. Palazzo Tasso & Kebab Ciampa
3. Il Palazzo Starace B&B
4. Hotel Mignon & Supermarket
5. Casa Astarita B&B
6. Hotel Nice & Scooter Rental
7. Ulisse Deluxe Hostel
8. Grand Hotel Ambasciatori
9. Hotel Minerva
10. Hotel La Tonnarella & Hotel Désirée
11. Albergo Settimo Cielo

Eateries

12. Ristorante il Buco
13. L'Antica Trattoria
14. Inn Bufalito

Laundry: Handy 24-hour self-service **Rosy Laundry** is a couple of blocks past the station (daily, Corso Italia 321, mobile 331-912-1122).

Shared Tours: Naples-based **Mondo Guide** offers my readers special shared tours of Pompeii, Naples, the Amalfi Coast (starting in Sorrento), and Capri. For details, see page 394.

Local Guide: For tours of Sorrento, Capri, and Amalfi, try **Giovanna Donadio** (€100/half-day, €180/day, mobile 338-466-0114, giovanna_dona@hotmail.com).

⊙ Sorrento Walk

This lazy self-guided town stroll that ends down by the waterside at the small-boat harbor, Marina Grande (to trace the walk, see the map on page 434).

• *Begin on the main square. Stand under the flags between the sea and the town's main square...*

❶ **Piazza Tasso:** This piazza is Sorrento's living room. Noisy and congested, it's where the action is. The most expensive apartments and top cafés are on or near this square.

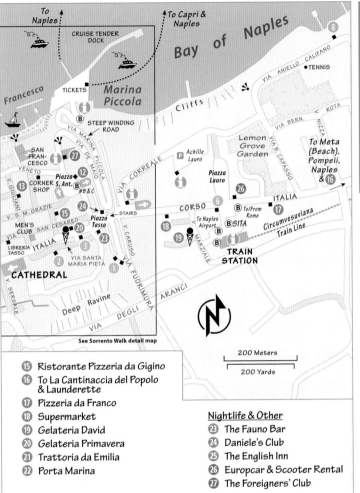

Map labels:

To Naples

To Capri & Naples

CRUISE TENDER DOCK

Bay of Naples

VIA ANIELLO CALIFANO

TENNIS

TICKETS

Marina Piccola

Francesco

Cliffs

VIA BERN.

NIZZA

ROTA

STEEP WINDING ROAD

VIA MARINA PICCOLA

VIA DE MAIO

SAN FRAN-CESCO

VIA CORREALE

Lemon Grove Garden

VIA B. CAPASSO

To Meta (Beach), Pompeii, Naples & ⑯

VENETO

Piazza S. Ant. ⑫ #B & C

⑬ CORNER SHOP

Achille Lauro

Piazza Lauro

⑯

V. GIULIANI

V. S. M. GRAZIE

ITALIA

⑮

STAIRS

CORSO ⑥

⑯

To/From Rome

Circumvesuviana Train Line

MEN'S CLUB

SAN CESAREO

⑳

Piazza Tasso

⑰

SITA

LIBRERIA TASSO

ITALIA

⑲

V. CARUSO

To Naples Airport

MARINELLE

TRAIN STATION

CATHEDRAL

V. SERSALE

VIA SANTA MARIA PIETÀ

VIA FUORIMURA

Deep Ravine

VIA DEGLI

ARANCI

VIA

See Sorrento Walk detail map

200 Meters

200 Yards

Legend:

⑮ Ristorante Pizzeria da Gigino

⑯ To La Cantinaccia del Popolo & Launderette

⑰ Pizzeria da Franco

⑱ Supermarket

⑲ Gelateria David

⑳ Gelateria Primavera

㉑ Trattoria da Emilia

㉒ Porta Marina

Nightlife & Other

㉓ The Fauno Bar

㉔ Daniele's Club

㉕ The English Inn

㉖ Europcar & Scooter Rental

㉗ The Foreigners' Club

A statue of St. Anthony the Abbot, patron of Sorrento, is surrounded by traffic. He faces north as if greeting those coming from Naples (he's often equipped with an armload of fresh lemons and oranges).

This square bridges the gorge that divides downtown Sorrento. The newer section (to your left) was farm country just two centuries ago. The older part (to your right) retains its ancient Greek gridded street plan.

For a better glimpse of the city's gorge-gouged landscape, consider this quick detour: With the water to your back, cross through the square and walk straight ahead a block inland, under a canopy of trees and past a long taxi queue. Belly up to the green railing in front of Hotel Antiche Mura and look down to see steps that were carved centuries before Christ. The combination of the gorge and the seaside cliffs made Sorrento easy to defend. A small section of wall closed the landward gap in the city's defenses (you can still see a surviving piece of it a few blocks away, near Hotel Mignon).

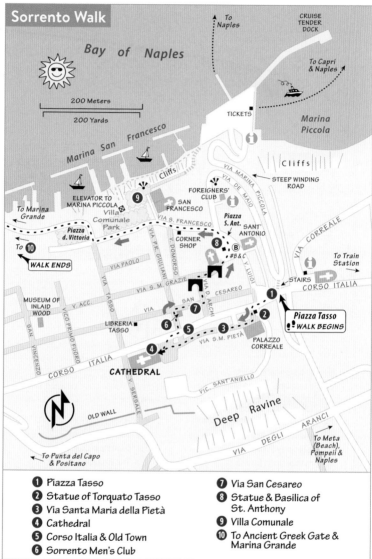

Sorrento Walk

1 Piazza Tasso
2 Statue of Torquato Tasso
3 Via Santa Maria della Pietà
4 Cathedral
5 Corso Italia & Old Town
6 Sorrento Men's Club
7 Via San Cesareo
8 Statue & Basilica of St. Anthony
9 Villa Comunale
10 To Ancient Greek Gate & Marina Grande

Sorrento's name may come from the Greek word for "siren," the legendary half-bird, half-woman that sang an intoxicating lullaby. According to Homer, the sirens lived on an island near here. All who sailed by the sirens succumbed to their musical charms...and to death. But Homer's hero Ulysses was determined to hear the song and restrain his manhood. He put wax in his oarsmen's ears and had himself lashed to the mast of his ship and survived their song. The sirens, thinking they had lost their powers, threw themselves into the sea. Ulysses' odyssey was all about the westward expansion of Greek culture; to the ancient Greeks, Sorrento was the wild west.

Sorrento Cathedral

• *Back at Piazza Tasso, head to the far-left inland corner of the square. You'll find a...*

❷ **Statue of Torquato Tasso:** The square's namesake, a Sorrento native, was a lively Renaissance poet—but today he seems only to wonder which restaurant to choose. Directly behind the statue, pop into the **Fattoria Terranova** shop, one of many fun, family-run, and touristy boutiques. They sell regional goodies and offer free biscuits and tastes of liqueurs, and the shop makes all of its organic products on an *agriturismo* outside the city. The gifty edibles spill into the courtyard of **Palazzo Correale,** which gives you a feel for an 18th-century aristocratic palace's courtyard. Its patio walls are lined with characteristic tiles from 1772.

• *As you're leaving the courtyard, on your immediate left you'll see the narrow...*

❸ **Via Santa Maria della Pietà:** Here, just a few yards off the noisy main drag, is a street that goes back centuries before Christ. About 100 yards down the lane, at #24 (on the left), find a 13th-century palace (no balconies back then...for security reasons), now an elementary school. A few steps farther on, you'll see a tiny shrine across the street. Typical of southern Italy, it's where the faithful pray to their saint, who contacts Mary, who contacts Jesus, who contacts God. This shrine is a bit more direct—it starts right with Mary.

• *Continue down the lane to reach the delightful...*

❹ **Cathedral:** Walk through the wrought-iron gate, which leads to the church patio. The church is free to enter (daily 8:00-12:30 & 16:30-21:00). Step inside the main door and examine the impressive *intarsio* (inlaid-wood) interior doors. They show religious scenes and depict this very church. Take a cool stroll down the right-hand side of the nave, checking out the intricate inlaid Stations of the Cross. Notice the fine inlaid-marble seat of the bishop and how the church's elegance matches the town's. Before exiting, on the right find the *presepe* (manger scene) with its lovingly painted terra-cotta figures, each with an expressive face. This first Christmas is set in Sorrento—with pasta, salami, local lemons, and even Mount Vesuvius in the background.

• *Cross the open plaza—where the end of the narrow street you just walked down meets the main drag.*

❺ **Corso Italia and the Old Town:** In the summer, this stretch of road is closed to traffic each evening, when it hosts a wonderful *passeggiata*. Look at the bell tower, with the scavenged ancient Roman columns at its base. Now go left down

Corso Italia passeggiata

Via P. Reginaldo Giuliani, following the old Greek street plan. Locals claim the ancient Greeks laid out the streets east-west for the most sunlight and north-south for the prevailing and cooling breeze. Pause at the poster board on your right to see who's died lately.

• *One block ahead, on your right, the 14th-century loggia (called Sedil Dominova) is home to the...*

❻ Sorrento Men's Club: Once the meeting place of the town's nobles, it's now a retreat for retired working-class men. Strictly no women—and no phones.

Italian men venerate their mothers. (Italians joke that Jesus must have been a southern Italian because his mother believed her son was God, he believed his mom was a virgin, and he lived at home with her until he was 30.) But Italian men have also built into their culture ways to be on their own. Here, men play cards and gossip under an historic emblem of the city and a finely frescoed 16th-century dome, with its marvelous 3-D scenes.

• *Turn right for a better view of the Men's Club and a historical marker describing the building. Then continue along...*

❼ Via San Cesareo: This touristy pedestrian-only shopping street leads back to Piazza Tasso. It's lined with shops where you can sample lemon products. Notice the huge ancient doorways with their tiny doors—to let the right people in, carefully, during a more dangerous age.

Sorrento Men's Club

• *After a block, take a left onto Via degli Archi, go under the arch, and then hang a right (under another arch) to the square with the...*

❽ Statue and Basilica of St. Anthony: Sorrento's town saint humbly looms among the palms, facing the Basilica of St. Anthony. Step inside and descend into the crypt (free, stairs beside main altar), where you'll find a chapel and reliquary containing a few of Anthony's bones surrounded by lots of votives. Locals have long turned to St. Anthony when faced with challenges and hard times. Exploring the room, you'll find countless tokens of appreciation to the saint for his help. Before tourism, fishing was the big employer. The back walls feature paintings of storms with Anthony coming to the rescue. Circle behind the altar with Anthony's relics and study the shiny ex-votos (religious offerings) thanking the saint for healthy babies, good employment, surviving heart attacks and lung problems, and lots of strong legs.

• *Follow the road that skirts the piazza with St. Anthony's statue (don't go down the street with the line of trees and Porto signs). Watch on the left for The Corner Shop, where Giovanni sells a wide variety of wines, limoncello, pastas, and other foods. Soon after, on the right you'll see the trees in front of the Imperial Hotel Tramontano, and to their right a path leading to the...*

❾ Villa Comunale: This fine public park overlooks the harbor. Belly up to the banister to enjoy the view of Marina Piccola and the Bay of Naples. Notice Naples' skyline and the boats that commute from here to there in 35 minutes. Imagine the view in AD 79 when Vesuvius blew its top and molten mud flowed down the mountain, burying Pompeii. From here, steps zigzag down to the harbor (there's also the elevator to the harbor). The Franciscan church fronting this square faces a fine modern statue of Francis across the street.

The view from Villa Comunale

Next to the church is a dreamy little **cloister.** Pop inside to see local Gothic—a 13th-century mix of Norman, Gothic, and Arabic styles, all around the old pepper tree. This is an understandably popular spot for weddings and concerts.

At the far side of the cloister, stairs lead to a **photo exhibit:** *The Italians* shows off the work of local photographer Raffaele Celentano, who artfully captures classic Italian scenes from 1990 to 2016 in black and white (€2.50, daily 10:00-22:00, great prints for sale, fun photo-op through the grand tree on their deck, adjacent music box exhibit is free).

• From here, you can quit the walk and stay in the town center, or continue another few minutes downhill to the waterfront at Marina Grande.

❿ *To continue to **Marina Grande,** return to the road and keep going downhill. At the next square (Piazza della Vittoria, with a dramatic WWI memorial and another grand view), cut over to the road closest to the water. After winding steeply down for a few minutes, it turns into a wide stairway, then makes a sharp and steep switchback (take the right fork to continue downhill). Farther*

down, just before reaching the waterfront, you pass under an...

Ancient Greek Gate: This gate fortified the city of Sorrento. Beyond it was Marina Grande, technically a separate town with its own proud residents—it's said that even their cats look different.

• Now go all the way down the steps into Marina Grande, Sorrento's "big" small-boat harbor.

Marina Grande: Until recently, this little community was traditional, with its economy based on fishing. Locals recall when women wore black when a relative died (1 year for an uncle, aunt, or sibling; 2-3 years for a husband or parent). Men got off easy, just wearing a black memorial button.

Two recommended restaurants are on the harbor. **Trattoria da Emilia** and, at the far-right end of the harbor, **Porta Marina**—smaller, less fancy, and more local but with food every bit as tasty as that of its competition.

• From here, where the road hits the beach, minibus #D returns to the center at Piazza Tasso every hour (pay the driver). Or you can walk back up.

Lemon Grove Garden

Experiences
Lemon Grove Garden

This lemon-and-orange grove (*agrumi-nato*, rated ▲) is lined with shady, welcoming paths and dotted with benches, tables, and an inviting little tasting (and buying) stand. You'll get a chance to sniff and taste the varieties of lemons and enjoy free samples of *limoncello* along with other homemade liqueurs made from mandarins, licorice, or fennel. Check out how they've grafted orange-tree branches onto a lemon tree so that both fruits grow on the same tree.

Cost and Hours: Free, daily April-Sept 10:00-21:00, shorter hours off-season, closed in rainy weather, tel. 081-878-1888, www.igiardinidicataldo.it. Enter the garden on Corso Italia (100 yards north of the train station—where painted tiles show lemon fantasies) or at the intersection of Via Capasso and Via Rota (next to Hotel La Meridiana).

Nearby: A small "factory"—where you can see how the operators use the lemons, and buy a tasty gelato, *granita,* or lemonade—is just past the parking garage along the road below the garden (Via Correale 27). They also have a small shop across from the Corso Italia entrance (at #267).

Swimming and Sunbathing

There are no great beaches in Sorrento—the gravelly, jam-packed private beaches of **Marina Piccola** are more for partying

Lemons

Around here, *limoni* are ubiquitous: adorning items from dishtowels to ceramics and providing distinctive flavor to edibles from liqueurs to desserts.

The Amalfi Coast and Sorrento area produce several kinds of lemons. The gigantic, bumpy "lemons" are actually citrons, called *cedri,* and are more for show—they're pulpier than they are juicy, and make a good marmalade. The juicy *sfusato sorrentino,* grown only in Sorrento, is shaped like an American football, while the *sfusato amalfitano,* with knobby points on both ends, is less juicy but equally aromatic. These two kinds of luscious lemons are used in sweets such as *granita* (shaved ice doused in lemonade), *limoncello* (a candy-like liqueur with a big kick, called *limoncino* on the Cinque Terre), *delizia al limone* (a dome of fluffy cake filled and slathered with a thick whipped lemon cream), *spremuta di limone* (fresh-squeezed lemon juice), and, of course, gelato or sorbetto *al limone.*

than pampering, and there's just a tiny spot for public use. The elevator in Villa Comunale city park (next to the Church of San Francesco) gets you down for €1. There's another humble beach at **Marina Grande.**

The classic, sandy Italian beach two miles away at **Meta** is generally overrun with teenagers from Naples. Bus #A goes from Piazza Tasso to Meta beach (last stop, schedule posted for hourly returns; you can also get there on the Circumvesuviana but the Meta stop is a very long walk from the beach). At Meta, you'll find pizzerias, snack bars, and a little free section of beach, but the place is mostly dominated by several sprawling private-beach complexes—if you go, pay for a spot in one of these, such as Lido

Metamare (lockable changing cabins, lounge chairs, tel. 081-532-2505). It's a very Italian scene—locals complain that it's "too local" (that is, inundated with riffraff)—with light lunches, a playground, a manicured beach, loud pop music...and no international tourists.

More relaxing beaches are west of Sorrento. Tarzan might take Jane to the wild and stony beach at **Punta del Capo,** a 15-minute bus ride from Piazza Tasso (the same bus #A explained earlier, but in the opposite direction from Meta; 2/hour, get off at stop on Via Capo just after the Maxim Gorky house, then walk 10 minutes down Calata Punta del Capo, past ruined Roman Villa di Pollio).

Another good choice is **Marina di Puolo,** a tiny fishing town popular in the summer for its sandy beach, surfside restaurants, and beachfront disco (to get here, stay on bus #A a bit farther beyond the Punta del Capo stop above—ask driver to let you off at Marina di Puolo— then follow signs and hike down about 15 minutes).

Food Tour

Sorrento Food Tours, run by a US expat, offers an information-filled, fast-paced food tour. Tamara and colleagues dish up a parade of local edibles interspersed with lots of food history, stopping at eight places in three hours (€75, RS%—15 percent discount, use code "ricksteves"; departures at 10:30 and 16:00 with demand, maximum 12 people; mobile 331-304-5666, www.sorrentofoodtours.com).

Snorkeling and Scuba Diving

To snorkel or scuba dive in the Mediterranean, contact **Futuro Mare** for details on a one-hour boat ride to the protected marine zone between Sorrento and Capri (options for snorkelers, beginners, and experienced certified divers; about 3 hours round-trip, call 1-2 days in advance to reserve, mobile 349-653-6323, www. sorrentodiving.it, info@futuromare.it).

Motorboat Rental

You can rent motorboats big enough for four people (with your back to the ferry-ticket offices, it's to the left around the corner at Via Marina Piccola 43; tel. 081-807-2283, www.nauticasicsic.com).

Nightlife

The Fauno Bar dominates Piazza Tasso with tables spilling onto the square.

Daniele's Club is run by DJ Daniele, who tailors music to the audience (including karaoke). The scene, while sloppy, is generally comfortable for the 30- to 60-year-old crowd (no cover charge, try their signature cocktail, "Come Back to Sorrento," a mojito made with *limoncello;* no food, nightly from 21:30, down the steps from the flags at Piazza Tasso 10).

The English Inn offers both a street-side sports pub and a more refined-feeling garden out back—at least until the evening, when the music starts blaring. English vacationers come to Sorrento in droves (many have holidayed here annually for decades). The menu includes fish-and-chips, all-day English breakfast, baked beans on toast, and draft beer (daily, Corso Italia 55, tel. 081-878-2570).

The Foreigners' Club (known in Italian as the **Terrazza delle Sirene**) offers live Neapolitan songs, Sinatra-style classics, and jazzy elevator music nightly at 20:00 throughout the summer. It's just right for old-timers feeling frisky (Via Luigi de Maio 35, entrance just past the TI).

Theater

At **Armida Theater Cinema,** a hardworking troupe puts on *The Sorrento Musical,* a folk-music show with schmaltzy Neapolitan Tarantella music and dance—complete with "Funiculì Funiculà" and "Santa Loo-chee-yee-yah." The 75-minute Italian-language extravaganza features a cast playing guitar, mandolin, saxophone, and tambourines, and singing operatically from Neapolitan balconies. Your €25 ticket includes a preshow drink (€50 with

4-course dinner at Basilico Italia restaurant; RS%—€5 discount if you buy directly at the box office and show this book, 2 tickets/book; shows run 3-5 nights/week mid-April-Oct at 21:00, bar opens 30 minutes before show, dinner starts at 20:00 and must be reserved in advance—in person or by email; box office open long hours daily, about halfway between Piazza Tasso and the train station at Corsa Italia 219, tel. 081-878-1470, www.cinema teatroarmida.it, booking@cinemateatro armida.it).

Sleeping

Hotels here often have beautiful views, and many offer balconies. At hotels that offer sea views, ask for a room *"con balcone, con vista sul mare"* (with a balcony, with a sea view).

The spindly, more exotic, and more vertical Amalfi Coast town of Positano (described later) is also a good place to spend the night.

In the Town Center

$$$$ Hotel Antiche Mura, with 50 rooms and four stars, is sophisticated, elegant, and plush. It offers all the amenities, including an impressive breakfast buffet. Surrounded by lemon trees, the pool and sundeck are a peaceful oasis. Just a block off the main square, it's quieter than some central hotels because it's perched on the ledge of a dramatic ravine (RS%, some rooms with balconies, family rooms, air-con, elevator, pay parking, closed Jan-Feb, a block inland from Piazza Tasso at Via Fuorimura 7, tel. 081-807-3523, www. hotelantichemura.com, info@hotelan tichemura.com, Michele).

$$$$ Palazzo Tasso, nicely located near the center, has 11 small, sleek, fashionably designed modern rooms; there's no public space except for the breakfast room (some rooms with balconies, air-con, elevator, Via Santa Maria della Pietà 33, tel. 081-878-3579, www.palazzotasso. com, info@palazzotasso.com, Elena).

$$$$ Plaza Sorrento is a contemporary-feeling, upscale refuge in the very center of town (next door to Antiche Mura but not as elegant). Its 65 rooms mix mod decor with wood grain, and the rooftop swimming pool is inviting (RS%, some rooms with balconies, air-con, elevator, closed Jan-Feb, Via Fuorimura 3, tel. 081-878-2831, www.plazasorrento.com, info@ plazasorrento.com).

$$$ Il Palazzo Starace B&B, conscientiously run by Massimo, offers seven tidy, modern rooms in a little alley off Corso Italia, one block from Piazza Tasso (RS%—use code "RSWEL," some rooms with balconies, family room, air-con, lots of stairs, luggage dumbwaiter and no elevator, ring bell around corner from Via Santa Maria della Pietà 9, tel. 081-807-2633, mobile 366-950-5377, www.palazzo starace.com, info@palazzostarace.com).

$$$ Hotel Mignon rents 22 soothing blue rooms with beautiful, tiled public spaces, a rooftop sundeck, and a small garden surrounded by a lemon grove (RS%—email for discount code, most rooms have balconies but no views, air-con, closed in Jan-Feb; from the cathedral, walk a block farther up Corso Italia and look for the hotel up a small gated lane to your left; Via Sersale 9, tel. 081-807-3824, www.sorrentohotel mignon.com, info@sorrentohotelmignon. com, Paolo).

$$$ Casa Astarita B&B, hiding upstairs in a big building facing the busy main street, has a crazy-quilt-tiled entryway and eight bright, tranquil, creatively decorated rooms (three with little balconies). Thin doors, echoey tile, and a buzzing location can result in noise… bring earplugs (air-con, open year-round, 50 yards past the cathedral on Corso Italia at #67, tel. 081-877-4906, www. casastarita.com, info@casasastarita.com, Annamaria and Alfonso). If there's no one at reception, ask at Hotel Mignon (described above)—the same family runs both hotels.

$$ Hotel Nice rents 27 simple, cheap rooms with high ceilings 100 yards in front of the train station on the main drag. This last resort is worth considering only for its very-handy-to-the-train-station location. Alfonso promises a quiet room—double-paned windows help dim the hum of its busy location—if you request it when you book by email (RS%, air-con, elevator, sundeck terrace, closed Nov-March, Corso Italia 257, tel. 081-878-1650, www. hotelnice.it, info@hotelnice.it).

$ Ulisse Deluxe Hostel is the best budget deal in town. This "hostel" is actually a hotel, with 56 well-equipped, marble-tiled rooms and elegant public areas, but it also has two single-sex dorm rooms with bunks (RS%, family rooms, breakfast buffet extra, air-con, elevator, spa and pool use extra, pay parking, closed Jan-mid-Feb, Via del Mare 22, tel. 081-877-4753, www.ulissedeluxe. com, info@ulissedeluxe.com, Chiara). It's a five-minute walk from the old-town action: From Corso Italia, walk down the stairs just beyond the hospital (*ospedale*) to Via del Mare. Go downhill along the right side of the big parking lot to find the entrance.

At the East End of Town

$$$$ Grand Hotel Ambasciatori is a sumptuous five-star hotel with 100 rooms, a cliffside setting, a sprawling garden, and a pool. This is Humphrey Bogart land, with plush public spaces, a relaxing stay-awhile ambience, and a free elevator to its "private beach"—actually a sundeck built out over the water (RS%, some view rooms, balconies in all rooms, air-con in summer, elevator, pay parking, closed Nov-March, Via Califano 18, tel. 081-878-2025, www. ambasciatorisorrento.com, ambasciatori@ manniellohotels.com). It's a short walk from the town center (10-15 minutes from the train station or Piazza Tasso).

With a View, on Via Capo

These cliffside hotels are outside of town, toward the cape of the peninsula (from the train station, go straight out Corso Italia, which turns into Via Capo). Once you're set up, commuting into town by bus or on foot is easy.

Getting to and from Via Capo: From the city center, it's a gradually uphill 15-minute walk (20 minutes from train station, last part is a bit steeper), a €20 taxi ride, or a cheap bus ride. If you're arriving with luggage, you can wait at the train station for one of the long-distance SITA buses that stop on Via Capo on their way to Massa Lubrense (about every 40 minutes; some buses heading for Positano/Amalfi also work—check with the driver). Frequent Sorrento city buses leave from near Piazza Tasso in the city center (go down a block and turn left on Corso Italia; from far side of the piazza, look for bus #A, about 2-3/hour). Get off at the Hotel Belair stop for the hotels listed here. To reach downtown Sorrento from Via Capo, catch any bus heading downhill from Hotel Belair.

$$$$ Hotel Minerva is a sun-worshipper's temple. The road-level entrance (on a busy street) leads to an elevator that takes you to the fifth-floor reception. Getting off, you'll step onto a spectacular terrace with outrageous Mediterranean views. Bright common areas, a small rooftop swimming pool, and a cold-water whirlpool tub complement 60 large, tiled, colorful rooms with views, some with balconies (3-night peak-season minimum, air-con, pay parking, closed Nov-March, Via Capo 30, tel. 081-878-1011, www.minervasorrento.com, info@minervasorrento.com).

$$$$ Hotel La Tonnarella is an old-time Sorrentine villa-turned-boutique-hotel, with several terraces, stylish tiles, and indifferent service. Eighteen of its 24 rooms have views of the sea, and you can pay extra for a terrace (air-con, pay parking, small beach with private elevator access, closed Nov-March, Via Capo 31, tel. 081-878-1153, www. latonnarella.it, info@latonnarella.it).

$$$ Albergo Settimo Cielo ("Seventh Heaven") is an old-fashioned, family-run cliffhanger sitting 300 steps above Marina Grande. The reception is just off the waterfront side of the road, and the elevator passes down through four floors with 50 clean but spartan rooms—all with grand views, and many with balconies. The rooms feel dated for the price—you're paying for the views (family rooms, air-con in summer, parking, inviting pool, sun terrace, closed Nov-March, Via Capo 27, tel. 081-878-1012, www.hotelsettimo cielo.com, info@hotelsettimocielo.com; Giuseppe, sons Stefano and Massimo, and daughter Serena).

$ Hotel Désirée is a modest affair, with reasonable rates, humbler vistas, and no traffic noise. The 22 basic rooms have high, ravine-facing or partial-sea views, and half have balconies (all the same price). There's a fine rooftop sunning terrace and a lovable cat, Tia. Owner Corinna (a committed environmentalist), daughter Cassandra, and receptionist Antonio serve an organic breakfast and are helpful with tips on exploring the peninsula (family rooms, most rooms have fans, lots of stairs and no elevator, laundry services, free parking, shares driveway and beach elevator with La Tonnarella, closed early Nov-Feb except open at Christmas—rare for this area, Via Capo 31, tel. 081-878-1563, www.desireehotelsorrento.com, info@ desireehotelsorrento.com).

Eating
Gourmet Splurges Downtown

$$$$ Ristorante il Buco is a small, dressy restaurant that serves delightfully presented and creative modern Mediterranean dishes. Peppe holds a Michelin star, and he and his staff love to explain their sophisticated dishes with an emphasis on seafood, with a good vegetarian selection. They offer lots of fine wines by the glass. Reserve ahead (extravagant-tasting €75-100 fixed-price meal, RS%—10 percent discount with this book, Thu-Tue 12:30-14:30 & 19:30-22:30, closed Wed and Jan; just off Piazza Sant'Antonino—facing the basilica, go under the grand arch on the left and immediately enter the restaurant at II Rampa Marina Piccola 5; tel. 081-878-2354, www.ilbucoristorante.it).

$$$$ L'Antica Trattoria enjoys a sedate, *romantico,* candlelit ambience. The cuisine is traditional with modern flair, and the inviting menu is fun to peruse (though pricey). Reservations are smart (RS%—show this book to choose a 10 percent discount on a fixed-price meal or a free *limoncello* if ordering à la carte, good vegetarian options, daily 12:00-23:30, closed Jan-Feb, air-con, Via Padre R. Giuliani 33, tel. 081-807-1082, www. lanticatrattoria.it).

Midpriced Restaurants Downtown

$$$ Inn Bufalito specializes in all things buffalo: *mozzarella di bufala* (and other buffalo-milk cheeses), steak, sausage, salami, carpaccio, and buffalo-meat pasta sauce on homemade pasta. The smartly designed space has a modern, casual atmosphere (don't miss the seasonal specialties on the blackboard, Wed-Mon 12:00-23:00, closed Tue and Jan-March, Vico I Fuoro 21, tel. 081-365-6975).

$$ Ristorante Pizzeria da Gigino, lively and congested with a sprawling interior and tables spilling onto the street, makes huge, tasty Neapolitan-style pizzas in their wood-burning oven (daily 12:00-24:00, closed Jan-Feb, just off Piazza Sant'Antonino at Via degli Archi 15, tel. 081-878-1927, Antonino).

$$ La Cantinaccia del Popolo draws a spirited crowd anxious to taste Annalisa's cooking. Peruse the counter of antipasti displayed under hanging prosciutto, but save room for delicious pasta that's stylishly served in large metal skillets (Tue-Sun 12:00-15:30 & 16:45-23:30, closed Mon, no reservations but free homemade wine while you wait, a couple of blocks past the train station at Vico Terzo Rota 3, mobile 349-955-6574).

Cheap Eats

$ Pizzeria da Franco is Sorrento's favorite place for basic, casual pizza in a fun, untouristy atmosphere. Join the locals on benches eating hot sandwiches and great pizzas served on waxed paper in a square tin (daily 8:00-late, just across from Lemon Grove Garden on busy Corso Italia at #265, tel. 081-877-2066).

$ Kebab Ciampa serves the best cheap, non-Italian meal in town. Choose beef or chicken—locals don't go for pork—and garnish with fries and/or salad (Thu-Tue from 17:00, closed Wed, before the cathedral off Via Santa Maria della Pietà, at Vico il Traversa Pietà 23, tel. 081-807-4595).

Picnics: Get groceries at the large **Decò** supermarket (Mon-Sat 8:30-20:00, shorter hours Sun, Corso Italia 223) or at the **Carrefour** supermarket underneath Hotel Mignon (daily 8:00-22:00).

Gelato: Near the train station, **Gelateria David** has many repeat customers. Before choosing a flavor, sample *Profumi di Sorrento* (an explosive sorbet of mixed fruits), "Sorrento moon" (white almond with lemon zest), or lemon crème (daily 9:00-24:00, shorter hours off-season, closed Dec-Feb, Via Marziale 19, tel. 081-807-3649). Mario also offers gelato-making classes (€12/person, 5-person minimum, 1 hour, call or email ahead to reserve, www.gelateriadavidsorrento. itinfo@gelateriadavidsorrento.it). Don't mistake this place for the similarly named Gelateria Davide, in the town center.

At **Gelateria Primavera,** Antonio and Alberta whip up 70 exotic flavors... and still have time to make pastries for the pope and other celebrities—check out the nostalgic photos in their inviting back room (daily 9:00-24:00, just west of Piazza Tasso at Corso Italia 142, tel. 081-807-3252).

Harborside in Marina Grande

For a decent lunch or dinner *con vista,* head down to either of these restaurants by Sorrento's small-boat harbor, Marina Grande. To get there, follow the directions from Villa Comunale on my self-guided Sorrento walk, earlier. You can also take minibus #D from Piazza Tasso. Be prepared to walk back (last bus leaves at 20:00) or spring for a pricey taxi.

$$ Trattoria da Emilia, at the city-side end of the Marina Grande waterfront, is good for straightforward, typical Sorrentine home-cooking, including fresh fish, lots of fried seafood, and *gnocchi di mamma*—potato dumplings with meat sauce, basil, and mozzarella (daily 12:00-15:00 & 18:30-22:00, closed Nov-Feb, no reservations taken, indoor and outdoor seating, tel. 081-807-2720).

$$ Porta Marina serves fresh-as-can-be seafood in a modest location at the end of the port, with views every bit as good as more expensive places nearby. Servers will tell you the catch of the day—always the best option—but if grilled octopus is on the menu then think no more (daily, 12:00-21:30, Via Marina Grande 25, tel. 081-877-4781).

Transportation
Getting Around Sorrento

By Bus: City buses all stop near the main square, Piazza Tasso, and run until at least 20:00 (3/hour, www.eavsrl.it). Bus #A takes a long route parallel to the coast, heading east to Meta beach or west to the hotels on Via Capo before continuing to Massa Lubrense; buses #B and #C loop up and down, connecting the port (Marina Piccola) to the town center; and minibus #D heads to the fishing village (Marina Grande). The trip between Piazza Tasso and Marina Piccola (or Marina Grande) costs €1.30 (buy tickets at tobacco shops and newsstands). Stamp your ticket upon entering the bus. The €10, 24-hour Costiera SITA Sud pass, good for the entire Amalfi Coast, also covers Sorrento city buses.

Bus stops can be tricky to find. Buses #A and #D generally stop near where Corso Italia passes through Piazza Tasso.

Buses #B and #C stop at the corner of Piazza Sant'Antonino, just down the hill toward the water.

By Scooter: Several places near the station rent motor scooters for about €35 per day, including **Europcar** (Corso Italia 210p, tel. 081-878-1386, www.sorrento. it) and **Autoservizi De Martino,** in Hotel Nice (Corso Italia 259, tel. 081-878-2801, www.admitaly.com). Don't rent a vehicle in summer unless you enjoy traffic jams.

By Taxi: Taxis charge an outrageous €15 for the short ride from the station to most hotels (more for Via Capo). If you do use a taxi, agree to a set price and be sure it has a meter (all official taxis have one).

Rick's Tip: Within Sorrento, **taxis can be a huge rip-off.** *Because of heavy traffic and the complex one-way road system, you can often walk faster than you can ride.*

Arriving and Departing
BY TRAIN
Sorrento is the last stop on the Circumvesuviana train line from Naples. In front of the train station is the town's main bus stop, as well as taxis waiting to overcharge you (€15 minimum). All recommended hotels—except those on Via Capo—are within a 10-minute walk.

From Sorrento by Train to Naples and Pompeii: The run-down **Circumvesuviana commuter train** runs twice hourly between Naples and Sorrento with crowds, pickpockets, and no air-conditioning (Italian-only website at www. eavsrl.it). The schedule is available at the TI: Pompeii (30 minutes, €2.40); Naples (70 minutes, €3.90). If there's a line at the train station, you can also buy tickets at the snack bar (across from the main ticket office) or downstairs at the newsstand.

A more comfortable but less frequent alternative to the Circumvesuviana commuter train, the tourist-oriented **Campania Express train** runs from mid-March to October. It's less crowded, has air-conditioning, and provides some space for luggage (4/day, €6 one-way to Pompeii, 25 minutes; €8 one-way to Naples, 1 hour; online sales at http://ots.eavsrl.it or buy at the station).

BY BUS
Curreri buses run daily to the airport (€10, purchase online or pay driver, 8/day from 6:30-16:30, no service Dec 25 and Jan 1, a long 1.5 hours on winding roads, departs from in front of train station, tel. 081-801-5420, www.curreriviaggi.it). From Naples Airport to Sorrento, eight buses depart between 9:00 and 19:30.

From Sorrento by Bus to Rome: Most people ride the Circumvesuviana or Campania Express to Naples, then catch the Frecciarossa or Italo express train to Rome. Italo also offers a nifty but infrequent bus/trail connection ("Italobus" from Sorrento to Naples, then train to Rome, 2/day, 3.5 hours, www.italotreno.it).

BY BOAT
Passenger boats and cruise-ship tenders dock at Marina Piccola. As you walk toward town from the marina, go up the big staircase where the pier bends. Standing on the promenade and facing town, you'll see the bus stop directly ahead; a TI kiosk and ticket windows for boats to Capri and Naples in the lower area to your left; and the elevator up to town to the right, about a five-minute walk along the base of the cliff (follow *lift/acensore* signs).

The elevator (€1, ; faster, cheaper, and more predictable than a bus) takes you to the Villa Comunale city park. From there, exit through the park's iron gate and bear left; Piazza Tasso is about four blocks away. Buses take you to Piazza Tasso (city bus #B or #C, buy €1.20 ticket at newsstand or tobacco shop).

Boat Connections: The number of boats that run per day varies: The frequency indicated here is for roughly mid-May through mid-October, with more boats per day in the peak of summer and fewer off-season. The specific companies operating each route also tend to change from season to season. Check all schedules locally with the TI, your hotel, or online (use the individual boat-company websites—see below—or visit www.capritourism.com, select English, and click "Shipping timetable"). Although some ferry-company websites sell tickets online, buying tickets at the port is easy (and keeps your departure options open, especially valuable if you're watching the weather); next-day tickets typically go on sale starting the evening before. All boats take several hundred people each and (except for the busiest days) rarely fill up.

From Sorrento by Boat to Capri: Boats run at least hourly. Your options are a fast **ferry** (*traghetto* or *nave veloce,* takes cars, 4/day, 30 minutes, Caremar, tel. 081-807-3077, www.caremar.it) or a slightly faster and pricier **hydrofoil** (*aliscafi,* over 20/day, 25 minutes, Gescab, tel. 081-807-1812, www.gescab.it). To visit Capri when it's least crowded, it's best to buy your ticket at 8:00 and take the 8:30 hydrofoil (try to depart by 9:45 at the very latest). If you make a reservation, it's not changeable. These early boats can be jammed, but it's worth it once you reach the island.

From Sorrento by Boat to Other Points: Naples (6/day, more in summer, departs roughly every 2 hours starting at 7:20, few or no boats on winter weekends, arrives at Molo Beverello, 35 minutes), **Amalfi** (mid-April-mid-Oct only, 4-6/day, 1 hour).

BY CAR

The Achille Lauro underground parking garage is centrally located, just a couple of blocks in front of the train station (€2/hour, €24/12 hours, €40 overnight, on Via Correale).

CAPRI

The island of Capri is just a short cruise from Sorrento. It was the vacation hideaway of Roman emperors Augustus and Tiberius and, in the 19th century, the haunt of Romantic Age aristocrats.

About 12,000 people live on Capri (although many winter in Naples) and during any given day in high season, the island hosts another 20,000 tourists. The "Island of Dreams" is a zoo in July and August—overrun with tacky, low-grade group tourism at its worst. At other times of year, though still crowded, it can provide a relaxing and scenic break from the cultural gauntlet of Italy. Even with its crowds, commercialism, fame, and glitz, Capri is a flat-out gorgeous place: Chalky white limestone cliffs rocket boldly from the shimmering blue-and-green surf, and the Blue Grotto sea cave glows with reflected sunlight.

Rick's Tip: *A cheap day trip to Capri is tough. But if you picnic and ride buses rather than enjoying restaurants and taxis, you'll find your time on the island itself to be relatively inexpensive.* **Many of Capri's greatest pleasures are free.**

Day Plan

This is the best see-everything-in-a-day plan from Naples or Sorrento:

Take an early hydrofoil to Capri (from Sorrento, buy ticket at 8:00, boat leaves around 8:30 and arrives around 8:50). You'll land at Marina Grande (Capri's port has the same name as the small-boat harbor at Sorrento).

At the port, select from three boating options: Enjoy the scenic circle-the-island tour with a visit to the Blue Grotto (1.5-2 hours); circle the island without Blue Grotto stop (1 hour); or just visit the Blue Grotto. (There are generally spaces available for departures every few minutes.)

Arriving back at Marina Grande, catch a bus to Anacapri, which has two or three hours' worth of sightseeing. See the town, ride the chairlift to Monte Solaro and back (or hike down), stroll out from the base of the chairlift to Villa San Michele for the view, and eat lunch. Afterward, catch a bus to Capri town, which is worth an hour of browsing.

Finally, ride the funicular from Capri town down to the harbor and laze on the free beach or wander the yacht harbor while waiting for your boat back to Sorrento.

Rick's Tip: If you're heading to Capri specifically to see the **Blue Grotto,** *be sure to check the weather and sea conditions. If the tide is too high or the water too rough, the grotto can be closed.*

Ticketing Tips: If you buy a one-way boat ticket to Capri, you'll have maximum schedule flexibility and can take any convenient hydrofoil or ferry back. (Check times for the last return crossing upon arrival with any TI on Capri, or at www. capritourism.com; the last return trips usually leave between 18:30 and 19:30.) During July and August, however, it's wise to get a round-trip ticket (ensuring you a spot). On busy days, be 20 minutes early for the boat, or you can be bumped.

Orientation

Pronounce it right: Italians say KAH-pree, not kah-PREE like the song (or the pants). The island is just four miles by two miles, separated from the Sorrentine Peninsula by a five-mile strait. Get oriented on the boat before you dock, as you near the harbor with the island spread out before you. The port is a small community of its own, called **Marina Grande,** connected by a funicular and buses to the rest of the island. **Capri town** fills the ridge high above the harbor. The ruins of Emperor Tiberius' palace, **Villa Jovis,** cap the peak on the left. To the right, the dramatic *"Mamma mia!"* road arcs around the highest mountain on the island **(Monte Solaro),** leading up to **Anacapri** (the island's second town, just out of sight). Notice the old zigzag steps below that road. Until 1874, this was the only connection between Capri and Anacapri. The white house on the ridge above the zigzags is **Villa San Michele** (where you can go later for a grand view).

Capri's Marina Grande, with the Sorrento Peninsula in the distance

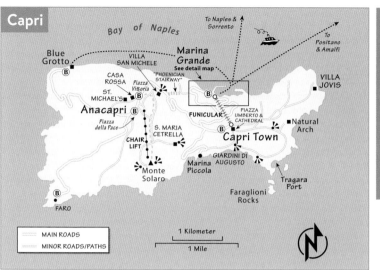

Tourist Information

Capri's efficient English-speaking TI has three branches (www.capritourism.com). The **Marina Grande TI** is by the Motoscafisti Capri tour-boat dock (Mon-Sat 8:30-18:15, Sun 9:30-17:15, shorter hours off-season, tel. 081-837-0634). The **Capri town TI** fills a closet under the bell tower on Piazza Umberto I and is less crowded than its sister at the port (same hours as Marina Grande TI, WC and baggage storage downstairs behind TI, tel. 081-837-0686). The tiny **Anacapri TI** is on the main pedestrian/shopping street, Via Orlandi, at #59 (Mon-Sat 8:30-16:15, closed Sun, shorter hours Nov-Easter, tel. 081-837-1524).

Helpful Hints

Baggage Storage: At the port, the fourth souvenir shop to the right of the funicular stores bags (€3/bag, look for awning sign, daily 9:00-18:00, tel. 081-837-4575, shorter hours or closed in winter).

Free Beach: Marina Grande has a free pebbly beach (pay at the bar for a shower).

Local Guides: Anna Bilardi Leva guides on Capri around the region (groups of 2-15: €150/half-day, €230/day, mobile 339-712-7416, www.capritourinformation.com, annaleva@hotmail.it).

Sights
On the Water

You have three boat-tour options: circle the island with a stop at the Blue Grotto, circle only, or Blue Grotto only.

▲▲▲CAPRI BOAT CIRCLE (GIRO DELL' ISOLA)

For me, the best experience on Capri is to take the scenic boat trip around the island. It's cheap, comes with good narration and lots of curiosities, and there are plenty of departures from Marina Grande.

Both **Laser Capri** and **Motoscafisti Capri** run trips that circle the island and pass stunning cliffs, caves, and views that most miss when they go only to the Blue Grotto (€18, no one-way discount; Motoscafisti Capri—tel. 081-837-7714, www.motoscafisticapri.com; Laser Capri—tel. 081-837-5208, www.lasercapri.com). The circular tour comes with a live guide and takes about an hour (1.5-2 hours with Blue Grotto stop). As you circle the dramatic limestone rock called Capri, you'll see quirky sights (a solar-powered lighthouse, tiny statues atop desolate rocks, holes in the cliffs with legends going back to Emperor Tiberius' times), pop into various caves and inlets, power through a tiny hole in the famed Faraglioni Rocks, hear stories of celebrity-owned villas, and marvel at a nonstop parade of staggering cliffs.

With both companies, you can combine the boat trip with a stop at the Blue Grotto at no extra charge (this adds about an hour; check schedules to find out which tours include the optional Blue Grotto stop). As the 10-minute ride just to the grotto costs €15 (no one-way discount), the island circle is well worth the extra three euros.

All boats leave daily from 9:00 until at least 13:00 (or later, depending on when the Blue Grotto rowboats stop running—likely 16:00 in summer).

▲▲BLUE GROTTO

Thousands of tourists a day visit Capri's Blue Grotto (Grotta Azzurra). I did—early (when the light is best), without the frustration of crowds, and with choppy waves nearly making entrance impossible...and it was great.

The actual cave experience isn't much: a short dinghy ride through a three-foot-high entry hole to reach a 60-yard-long cave, where the sun reflects brilliantly blue on its limestone bottom. But the experience—getting there, getting in, and getting back—is a scenic hoot. You get a fast ride and scant narration on a 30-foot boat partway around the gorgeous island; along

Blue Grotto

the way, you see bird life and dramatic limestone cliffs. You'll understand why Roman emperors appreciated the invulnerability of the island—it's surrounded by cliffs, with only one good access point, and therefore easy to defend.

Just outside the grotto, your boat idles as you pile into eight-foot dinghies that hold up to four passengers each. Next, you'll be taken to a floating ticket counter to pay the grotto entry fee. From there, your ruffian rower will elbow his way to the tiny hole, then pull fast and hard on the cable at the low point of the swells to squeeze you into the grotto (keep your head down and hands in the boat). Then your man rows you around, spouting off a few descriptive lines and singing "O Sole Mio." Depending upon the strength of the sunshine that day, the blue light inside can be brilliant.

The grotto was actually an ancient Roman *nymphaeum*—a retreat for romantic hanky-panky. Many believe that, in its day, a tunnel led here directly from the palace, and that the grotto experience was enlivened by statues of Poseidon and company, placed half-underwater as if emerging from the sea. It was ancient Romans who smoothed out the entry hole that's still used to this day.

When dropping you off, your boatman will fish for a tip—it's optional, and €1 is enough.

Cost: The €14 entry fee (separate from the €15 ride from Marina Grande and back) includes €10 for the rowboat service plus €4 for admission to the grotto itself. Though some people swim in for free from the little dock after the boats stop running (about 17:00), it's illegal and can be dangerous.

Timing: When waves or high tide make entering dangerous, the grotto can close without notice, sending tourists home disappointed. If this happens to you, consider the one-hour boat ride around the island instead.

If you're coming from Capri's port

(Marina Grande), allow 1-2 hours for the entire visit, depending on the chaos at the caves. Going with the first trip (around 9:00) will get you there at the same time as the boatmen in their dinghies—who hitch a ride behind your boat—resulting in less chaos and a shorter wait at the entry point.

If you arrive on the island later in the morning—when the Blue Grotto is already jammed—try visiting about 15:00, when most of the tour groups have vacated. This may only work by bus (not boat). Confirm that day's closing time with a TI before making the trip.

Getting There: You can take the **boat** from Marina Grande (either as part of a longer circle-the-island tour—€18 or directly—€15, 10 minutes; described earlier), as most people do, or save money by taking the **bus** via Anacapri. You'll save almost €8, lose time, and see a beautiful, calmer side of the island (roughly 3/hour, 10 minutes; buses depart only from the Anacapri bus station at Piazza della Pace—not from the bus stop at Piazza Vittoria 200 yards away). If you're coming from Marina Grande or Capri town and want to transfer to the Blue Grotto buses, don't get off when the driver announces "Anacapri." Instead, ride one more stop to Piazza della Pace. At the Piazza della Pace bus station, notice the two lines: "Grotta Azzurra" for the Blue Grotto, and "Faro" for the lighthouse.

Getting Back: You can take the boat back or ask your boatman to drop you off on the small dock next to the grotto entrance (for a small tip), from there you climb up the stairs to the stop for the bus to Anacapri (if you came by boat, you'll still have to pay the full round-trip boat fare).

Rick's Tip: *The scenic three-hour* **Fortress Hike** *takes you under ruined forts along the rugged coast, from the Blue Grotto to the faro (lighthouse). From there, you can take a bus back to Anacapri (3/hour). The TI has a fine map/brochure.*

Anacapri Town and Nearby

Anacapri has two or three hours' worth of sights. Though Anacapri sits higher up on the island than Capri town, there are no sea views at street level in the town center.

There are two bus stops: **Piazza Vittoria,** in the center of town at the base of the Monte Solaro chairlift; and 200 yards farther along at **Piazza della Pace** (pronounced "PAH-chay"), a larger bus station near the cemetery. Piazza Vittoria gets you closer to the main sights (chairlift and Villa San Michele), while Piazza della Pace is where you transfer to the Blue Grotto bus. When leaving Anacapri for Marina Grande, buses can be packed. Your best chance of getting on board is to catch the bus from Piazza della Pace (the first stop). Another option is to catch a bus to Capri town, visit sights there, then take the funicular down to Marina Grande. Bus tickets can be purchased at the "Moda Mare" souvenir store directly opposite the bus stop in Piazza Vittoria.

Anacapri's pedestrianized main drag, **Via Orlandi,** is just a block or so from either bus stop. From Piazza Vittoria, the street is right there—just go down the lane to the right of the Anacapri statue. From Piazza della Pace, cross the street and go down the small pedestrian lane called Via Filietto. The **TI** is at Via Orlandi 59, near Piazza Vittoria.

To see the town, stroll along Via Orlandi for a few minutes. Signs propose a quick circuit that links the Casa Rossa, St. Michael's Church, and peaceful side streets. You'll also find shops and eateries, including good choices for quick, inexpensive pizza, *saltimbocca* (prosciutto and mozzarella on baked pizza bread—great for a filling picnic), *panini,* and other goodies. These two **$** options are both open daily in peak season: **Sciué Sciué** (same price for informal seating or takeaway, 50 yards below the TI at #73, tel. 081-837-2068) and **Pizza e Pasta** (takeaway only, lots of benches nearby, just before the church at #157, tel. 328-623-8460).

Tile floor at the Church of San Michele

▲ CHURCH OF SAN MICHELE

This Baroque church in the village center has a remarkable majolica floor showing paradise on earth in a classic 18th-century Neapolitan style. The entire floor is ornately tiled, featuring an angel (with flaming sword) driving Adam and Eve from paradise. The devil is wrapped around the trunk of a beautiful tree. For the best view, climb the spiral stairs from the postcard desk.

Cost and Hours: €2, daily 9:00-19:00, Nov and mid-Dec-March usually 10:00-14:00, closed late Nov-mid-Dec, in town center just off Via Orlandi—look for *San Michele* signs, tel. 081-837-2396, www. chiesa-san-michele.com.

▲ VILLA SAN MICHELE AND GRAND CAPRI VIEW

This is the 19th-century mansion of Axel Munthe, Capri's grand personality, an idealistic Swedish doctor who lived here until 1946 and whose services to the Swedish royal family brought him into contact with high society. Munthe was gay at a time when that could land you in jail. He enjoyed the avant-garde and permissive scene at Capri, during an era when Europe's leading artists and creative figures could gather here and be honest about their sexual orientation.

Walk the path from Piazza Vittoria past the villa to a superb, free viewpoint over Capri town, Marina Grande, and—in the distance—Mount Vesuvius and Sorrento. Paying to enter the villa lets you see a few rooms with period furnishings (follow the one-way route, good English descriptions); an exhibit on Munthe; and one of this region's most delightful gardens, with a chapel and the Olivetum (a tiny museum of native birds and bugs). A view café serves affordable sandwiches.

Cost and Hours: €8, daily 9:00-18:00, closes earlier Oct-April, tel. 081-837-1401, www.villasanmichele.eu.

Getting There: From Piazza Vittoria, walk up the grand staircase and turn left onto Via Capodimonte.

▲▲ CHAIRLIFT UP TO MONTE SOLARO

You can ride the chairlift (*seggiovia*) to the 1,900-foot summit of Monte Solaro for a commanding view of the Bay of Naples. Work on your tan as you float over hazelnut, walnut, chestnut, apricot, peach, kiwi, and fig trees, past a montage of tourists. Prospective smoochers should know that the lift seats are all single. The ride takes 13 minutes each way, and you'll want at least 30 minutes on top, where there are picnic benches and a café with WCs.

Cost and Hours: €9 one-way, €12 round-trip, daily 9:30-17:00, last run down at 17:30; March-April until 16:00, Nov-Feb until 15:30, tel. 081-837-1438, www.

Chairlift to Monte Solaro

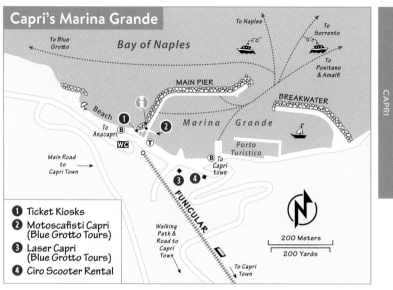

Capri's Marina Grande

Bay of Naples

To Naples

To Sorrento

To Positano & Amalfi

To Blue Grotto

MAIN PIER

BREAKWATER

Beach

To Anacapri

Marina Grande

Porto Turistico

Main Road to Capri Town

To Capri town

Walking Path & Road to Capri Town

To Capri Town

FUNICULAR

N

200 Meters

200 Yards

❶ Ticket Kiosks
❷ Motoscafisti Capri (Blue Grotto Tours)
❸ Laser Capri (Blue Grotto Tours)
❹ Ciro Scooter Rental

capriseggiovia.it. Note that the lift gets more crowded with tour groups in the afternoon.

Getting There: From the Piazza Vittoria bus stop, just climb the steps and look right.

At the Summit: Enjoy the panorama of lush cliffs. Find the Faraglioni Rocks. The pink building nearest the rocks was an American R&R base during World War II. On the peak closest to Cape Sorrento are the distant ruins of Emperor Tiberius' palace. The Galli Islands mark the Amalfi Coast in the distance. Cross the bar terrace for views of Mount Vesuvius and Naples.

Hiking Down: A highlight for hardy walkers (provided you have strong knees and good shoes) is the 40-minute downhill hike from the top of Monte Solaro, through lush vegetation and ever-changing views, past the 14th-century Chapel of Santa Maria Cetrella (at the trail's only intersection, it's a 10-minute detour to the right), and back into Anacapri. The trail starts downstairs, past the WCs (last chance). Down two more flights of stairs, look for the sign to *Anacapri e Cetrella*—you're on

your way. While the trail is well-established, you'll encounter plenty of uneven steps, loose rocks, and few signs.

Capri Town and Nearby

This cute but extremely clogged and touristy shopping town is worth a brief visit, if only for window shopping.

PIAZZA UMBERTO I

If you arrive by the funicular, it drops you just around the corner from Piazza Umberto I, the town's main square. With your back to the funicular, the bus stop is 50 yards straight ahead down Via Roma. The **TI** is under the bell tower on Piazza Umberto.

Capri town's multidomed Baroque **cathedral,** which faces the square, is worth a quick look. Its multicolored marble floor at the altar dates from the first century AD—it was scavenged from Emperor Tiberius' villa.

The lane to the left of the cathedral (past Bar Tiberio, under the wide arch) is a fashionable shopping strip that's justifiably been dubbed **"Rodeo Drive"** by residents. Walk a few minutes down the street (past Gelateria Buonocore at #35, with its fresh waffle cones) to Quisisana Hotel, the island's top old-time hotel. From there, head left for fancy shops and villas, and right for gardens and views.

To the right and downhill, a five-minute walk leads to **Giardini di Augusto,** a lovely public garden (€1, daily 9:00-19:30, Nov-March until 17:30, free to enter off-season, no picnicking). It boasts great views over the famous Faraglioni Rocks—handy if you don't have the time, money, or interest to access the higher vantage points near Anacapri (Monte Solaro, Villa San Michele).

One of the most historic buildings on the island is the **Monastery of San Giacomo**—a.k.a. Certosa di San Giacomo (€4, €3 combo-ticket with Giardini di Augusto at the garden entry, Tue-Sun 10:00-17:00, later in summer, closed Mon). The stark monastery has an empty church and sleepy cloister. But the finest piece of art on Capri is over the church's front entrance: an exquisite 14th-century fresco of Mary and the Baby Jesus by the Florentine Niccolo di Tommaso. Today, the monastery hosts the **Museo Diefenbach,** a small collection of dark and moody paintings by eccentric German artist Karl Wilhelm Diefenbach.

Transportation
Getting Around Capri
By Public Transportation: Tickets for the island's **buses and funicular**—available at newsstands, tobacco shops, and official ticket offices—cost €2 per ride. The €10 all-day pass (available only at official ticket offices) isn't a good value for most visitors. Validate your ticket when you board.

Schedules are clearly posted at all bus stations. Public buses are orange, while gray and blue buses are for private tour groups. Public buses from the port to Capri town, and from Capri town to Anacapri, are frequent (4/hour, 10 minutes). The direct bus between the port and Anacapri runs less often (2/hour, 25 minutes). From Anacapri, branch bus lines run to the parking lot above the Blue Grotto and to the Faro lighthouse (3/hour). Buses are teeny (because of the island's narrow roads) and often packed, the aisles filled with people standing. At most stops, you'll see ranks for passengers to line up in (locals feel free to cut the line). If the driver changes the bus's display to read *completo* (full), you'll need to wait for the next one. Cut your wait times by combining my recommended bus trips with the funicular at the end of your visit.

By Taxi: Taxis have fixed rates, listed at www.capritourism.com (Marina Grande to Capri town—€17; Marina Grande to Anacapri—€28). You can hire a taxi for about €70 per hour—negotiate.

By Scooter: Capri's steep and narrow roads aren't a good place for novices to learn. **Capri Scooter** rents bright-yellow scooters with 50cc engines—strong enough to haul couples. Rentals come with a map and instructions with parking tips and other helpful information (€15/hour, €55/day, RS%—10 percent discount on rentals of 2 hours or more with this book; includes helmet, gas, and insurance; daily April-Oct 9:30-18:00, may open in good weather off-season, at Via Don Giobbe Ruocco 55, Marina Grande, mobile 338-360-6918, www.capriscooter.com).

Arriving and Departing
From Capri's Marina Grande by Boat to: Sorrento (ferry: 4/day, 30 minutes, www.caremar.it; hydrofoil: up to 20/day, 20 minutes, www.gescab.it), **Naples** (roughly hourly, more in summer, hydrofoil: 50 minutes, arrives at Molo Beverello; ferries: 50-80 minutes, arrive at Calata Porta di Massa), **Positano** (mid-April-mid-Oct, 6/day, 30 minutes). Confirm the schedule carefully at TIs or www.capritourism.com (under "Shipping Timetable")—the last boats back to the mainland usually leave around 18:00-20:00. For a steep price, you can always hire a water taxi (weather permitting).

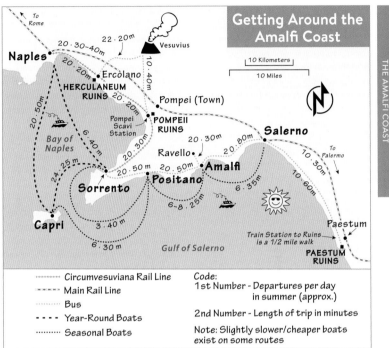

Getting Around the Amalfi Coast

10 Kilometers

10 Miles

.... Circumvesuviana Rail Line
- - - - Main Rail Line
.... Bus
- - - - Year-Round Boats
.... Seasonal Boats

Code:
1st Number - Departures per day
  in summer (approx.)

2nd Number - Length of trip in minutes

Note: Slightly slower/cheaper boats
exist on some routes

THE AMALFI COAST

With its stunning scenery, hill- and harbor-hugging towns, and historic ruins, Amalfi is Italy's coast with the most. The trip from Sorrento to Salerno is one of the world's great bus or taxi rides. Cantilevered garages, hotels, and villas cling to the vertical terrain, and beautiful but out-of-reach coves tease from far below. As you hyperventilate, notice how the Mediterranean, a sheer 500-foot drop below, really twinkles. Over the centuries, this landscape has lured Roman Emperor Tiberius, Richard Wagner, Sophia Loren, and Gore Vidal, to enjoy *la dolce vita.*

Amalfi Coast towns are pretty, but they're also touristy, congested, and overpriced. Most beaches here are private, pebbly, and expensive. Check and understand your bills in this greedy region.

Getting Around the Amalfi Coast

The scenic Amalfi drive is thrilling, but treacherous; even if you have a car, consider taking the bus or hiring a driver out of Sorrento.

Many travelers take a round-trip bus tour, though you could go one way by bus and return by boat. For example, take the bus along the coast from Sorrento to Positano and/or Amalfi, then catch the ferry back. This works best in summer, because ferries run less often in spring and fall; some don't run at all off-season (mid-Oct-mid-April); and they don't run in stormy weather at any time of year. If boats aren't running between Amalfi and Sorrento, you can change boats in Capri.

By Bus

From Sorrento by Public Bus: SITA buses to Amalfi, via Positano, are the most common, inexpensive way to see the coast (for schedules, see www.sitabus.it or—easier to read—www.positano.com). In Sorrento, buses depart from in front of the train station beginning at 6:30; from 8:30 they run roughly every half hour until 17:00, then hourly until 22:00 in summer, until 20:00 in winter (50 minutes to Positano; another 50 minutes to Amalfi). To reach Ravello (the hill town beyond Amalfi) or Salerno (at the far end of the coast), transfer in Amalfi.

Individual tickets are inexpensive (€2-4). All rides are covered by the 24-hour Costiera SITA Sud pass (€10), which may not save you money but does save time buying tickets. Tickets are sold at tobacco shops and newsstands, not by drivers.

Line up under the *Bus Stop SITA* sign across from the train station (10 steps down, look for the sales desk under an umbrella). When checking the schedule, note that *Giornaliero (G)* means daily, *Scolastico (S)* means school bus, *Feriale (F)* denotes Monday-Saturday, and *Festivo (H)* is for Sundays and holidays.

Avoiding Crowded Buses: Amalfi Coast public buses are routinely unable to handle demand during summer months and holidays. Generally, if you don't get on one bus, you're well-positioned to catch the next one. From Sorrento, aim to leave on the 8:30 bus at the latest—earlier if possible. Departures between 9:00 and 11:00 can be frustratingly crowded.

Note that an eight-seater minibus and driver costs about €300 for the day: If you can organize a small group, €40 per person is a very good deal. (For options, see "By Taxi," later.)

From Sorrento by Tour Bus: City-Sightseeing's bright red hop-on, hop-off buses travel from Sorrento to Positano to Amalfi and back. While more expensive than public buses, they can be much less crowded and come with a recorded commentary. You'll pay €10 for your outgoing ride (buy tickets onboard), then €6 for the return trip (on the same day). Buses run hourly all day April-October, leaving the Sorrento train station at :45 past each hour starting at 8:45. Return trips from Amalfi leave at :15 past each hour (until 19:15—confirm locally). The trip takes about 1.5 hours, with a stop in Positano each way. Check out www.city-sightseeing.it (but don't be confused by their "two bays" tour of the Cape of Sorrento, which is not worth considering).

Rick's Tip: Summer congestion can be so bad that return buses don't even stop in Positano (because they filled up in Amalfi). Those trying to get back from Positano to Sorrento are stuck with taking an extortionist taxi or hopping a boat...if one's running. If touring the coast by bus, **stop in Positano first and come home from Amalfi,** *where the bus originates.*

By Boat

A few passenger boats per day link Positano and Amalfi with Sorrento, Capri, and Salerno (generally April-Oct only). The last daily departure can be as early as midafternoon and is never much later than 18:00. Check schedules carefully: Frequency varies from month to month, and boats may be cancelled in bad weather (especially at Positano, where there's no real pier). The companies operating each route change frequently, compete for passengers, and usually claim to know nothing about their rivals' services. The best sources for timetables are www.capritourism.com (under "Shipping Timetable") and www.positano.com (under "Ferry Schedules"). You can also check individual company websites (such as www.travelmar.it, www.alicost.it, and www.gescab.it). It's smartest to confirm locally: The region's TIs hand out flyers with current schedules. Buy tickets on the dock. For a summary of sample routes, frequencies, and travel times, see the "Getting Around the Amalfi Coast" map on page 453.

If you're going to Capri from Positano or Amalfi, save time and money by finding a boat that goes directly to the Blue Grotto (rather than dropping you in the port in Capri to catch another boat from there). Here's another useful trick: If no boats are going directly between Sorrento and Positano/Amalfi, you can usually still connect the two sides of the peninsula via Capri.

By Taxi

Given the hairy driving, impossible parking, crowded public buses, and potential fun, you might consider splurging to hire your own car and driver for your Amalfi day.

The **Monetti family** car-and-driver service—Raffaele, daughter Carolina, cousin Tony, and Gianpaolo—have taken excellent care of my readers' transit needs for decades. Sample trips and rates: all-day Amalfi Coast (Positano, Amalfi, Ravello), 8 hours, €300; Amalfi Coast and Paestum, 10 hours, €450; transfer to Naples airport or train station to Sorrento, €130. These prices are for up to three people; you'll pay more for a larger eight-seater van. Though based in Sorrento, they also do trips from Naples. Payment is cash only (as with most of the car services listed). Their reservation system is simple and reliable (Raffaele's mobile 335-602-9158 or 338-946-2860, "office" run by his English-speaking Finnish wife, Susanna, www.monettitaxi17. com, monettitaxi17@libero.it). Don't just hop into any taxi claiming to be a Monetti—call first. If you get into any kind of serious jam in the area, you can call Raffaele for help.

Francesco del Pizzo is another smooth and honest Sorrento-based driver who offers commentary in English (9 hours or so in a car with up to 4 passengers, €300; up to 8 passengers in a minibus, €340; mobile 333-238-4144, francescodelpizzo@ yahoo.it).

Anthony Buonocore, an Amalfi native, specializes in cruise shore excursions, as well as transfers anywhere in the region in his eight-person Mercedes van (rates vary, special deals for early booking and in low season, tel. 349-441-0336, www. amalfitransfer.com, buonocoreanthony@ yahoo.it).

Rides Only: If you're hiring a cabbie off the street for a ride and not a tour, here are sample fares from Sorrento to Positano: up to four people one-way for about €80 in a car, or up to six people for €90 in a minibus. Figure on paying 50 percent more to Amalfi. While taxis must use a meter within a city, a fixed rate is OK elsewhere. Negotiate—ask about a round-trip.

By Shared Minibus

Naples-based **Mondo Guide** offers a nine-hour minibus trip that departs from Sorrento and heads down the Amalfi Coast, with brief stops in Positano, Amalfi, and Ravello, before returning to Sorrento (€55/person). They also offer Rick Steves readers shared tours in Pompeii and Naples. For details, see page 394.

Amalfi Coast Tour

The wildly scenic Amalfi Coast drive from Sorrento to Salerno, worth ▲▲▲, is one of the all-time great white-knuckle rides, whether you tackle it by bus, taxi, or shared minibus.

Traffic is so heavy that private tour buses are only allowed to go in one direction (southbound from Sorrento). Summer traffic is infuriating. Fluorescent-vested police are posted at tough bends during peak hours to help fold in side-view mirrors and keep things moving. This loose, self-guided tour is organized from west to east.

Rick's Tip: *For the* **best views of the Amalfi Coast,** *sit on the right when leaving from Sorrento and on the left returning to Sorrento. Sit toward the front to* **minimize carsickness.**

◉ **Self-Guided Tour:** Leaving **Sorrento,** the road winds up into the hills past lemon groves and hidden houses. The gray-green trees are olives. (Notice the green nets slung around the trunks; these are unfurled in October and November, when the ripe olives drop naturally, for an easy self-harvest.) Dark, green-leafed trees planted in dense groves are the source of the region's lemons. The black nets over the orange and lemon groves create a greenhouse effect, trapping warmth and humidity for maximum tastiness, while offering protection from extreme weather.

Atop the ridge outside Sorrento, look to your right: The two small islands are the **Li Galli Islands.** The largest of these islands was once owned by the famed ballet dancer Rudolf Nureyev; it's now a luxury residence.

When Nureyev bought the island, the only building standing was the stony watchtower—the first of many you'll see all along the coast. These were strategically placed within sight of one another so that a relay of rooftop bonfires could quickly spread word of a pirate attack.

The limestone cliffs that plunge into the sea were traversed by a hand-carved trail that became a modern road in the mid-19th century. Fruit stands sell produce from farms and orchards just over the hill. Limestone absorbs the heat and rainwater, making this south-facing coastline a fertile suntrap, with temperatures as much as 10 degrees higher than in nearby Sorrento. The chalky, reflective limestone, which extends below the surface, accounts for the uniquely colorful blues and greens of the water. With the favorable climate, bougainvillea, geraniums, oleander, and wisteria grow like weeds here in the summer. Notice the nets pulled tight against the cliffs—they're designed to catch rocks that often tumble loose after heavy rains.

Dramatic **Positano** is the main stop along the coast. The town is built on a series of man-made terraces, which were carefully carved out of the steep rock, then filled with fertile soil carried here from Sorrento on the backs of donkeys.

If you're getting off here, stay on through the first stop by the round-domed yellow church (Chiesa Nova), which is a very long walk above town. Instead, get off at the second stop, Sponda, then head downhill toward the start of my self-guided Positano Walk (described later). Sponda is also the best place to catch the onward bus to Amalfi. If you're coming on a smaller minibus, you'll twist all the way down—seemingly going in circles—to the start of the walk.

The next town you'll see is **Praiano.** Less ritzy or charming than Positano or Amalfi, it's notable for its huge Cathedral of San Gennaro, with a characteristic majolica-tiled roof and dome. Most of the homes are accessible only by tiny footpaths and staircases. Near the end of town, just before the big tunnel, watch on the left for the big *presepe* (manger scene) embedded into the cliff face. This Praiano-in-miniature was carved by one local man over several decades. At Christmas-

Positano overview

Marina di Praia

time, each house is filled with little figures and twinkle lights.

Just past the tunnel, look below and on the right to see another Saracen watchtower. (Yet another caps the little point on the horizon.)

A bit farther along, look down to see the fishing hamlet of **Marina di Praia** tucked into the gorge between two tunnels. If you're driving, consider a detour down here for a coffee break or meal. This serene nook has its own little pebbly beach with great views of the stout bluffs and watchtower that hem it in. A seafront walkway curls around the bluff all the way to the tower.

Just after going through the next tunnel, watch for a jagged rock formation on its own little pedestal. Locals see the face of the Virgin Mary in this natural feature and say that she's holding a flower (the tree growing out to the right). Also notice several caged, cantilevered parking pads sticking out from the road. This stretch of coastline is popular for long-term villa rentals.

Look down and left for the blink-or-you'll-miss-it fishing village that's aptly named **Fiordo** ("fjord"), filling yet another gorge. Humble homes burrowed into the cliff face, tucked so far into the gorge that they're entirely in shadow for much of the year. Today these are rented out to vacationers; the postage-stamp beach is uncrowded and inviting.

After the next tunnel, in another hamlet, keep an eye out for donkeys with big baskets on their backs; they're the only way to make heavy deliveries to homes high in the rocky hills.

Soon you'll pass the big-for-Amalfi parking lot of the **Grotta dello Smeraldo** (Emerald Grotto), a cheesy roadside attraction that wrings the most it can out of a pretty, seawater-filled cave. Passing tourists park here and pay to take an elevator down to sea level, pile into big rowboats, and get paddled around a genuinely impressive cavern. Unless you've got time to kill, skip it.

Now you're approaching what could be the most dramatic watchtower on the coast, which guarded the harbor of the Amalfi navy until the fleet was destroyed in 1343 by a tsunami caused by an earthquake, which also led to Amalfi's decline.

Around the next bend you're treated to stunning views of the coastline's namesake town—**Amalfi.** The white villa sitting on the low point between here and there (with another watchtower at its tip) once belonged to Sophia Loren. Now look up to the very top of the steep, steep cliffs overhead to see the hulking former Monastery of Santa Rosa. Locals proudly explain that the beloved *sfogliatella* dessert was first created there. (Today it's a luxury resort, where you can pay a premium to sleep in a former monk's cell.)

The most striking stretch of coastline ends where the bus pulls to a halt—at the end of the line, the waterfront of Amalfi town. Spend some time enjoying the city.

From Amalfi, you can transfer to another bus to head up to **Ravello** (described later), capping a cliff just beyond Amalfi, or onward to the big city of **Salerno.** Alternatively, buses and boats take you back to Positano and Sorrento.

POSITANO

Specializing in scenery and sand, Positano hangs halfway between Sorrento and Amalfi town on the most spectacular stretch of the coast. The town flourished as a favorite under the Bourbon royal family in the 1700s, when many of its fine mansions were built. Until the late 1800s, the only access was by donkey path or by sea. In the 20th century, Positano became a haven for artists and writers escaping Communist Russia and Nazi Germany. In 1953, American writer John Steinbeck's essay on the town popularized Positano among tourists, and soon after it became a trendy Riviera stop. The town gave the world "Moda Positano"—a leisurely *dolce vita* lifestyle of walking barefoot; wearing

Positano, on the Amalfi Coast

bright, happy, colorful clothes; and sporting skimpy bikinis.

Today, the village is a pleasant gathering of cafés and expensive stores draped over an almost comically steep hillside. Terraced gardens and historic houses cascade downhill to a stately cathedral and a broad, pebbly beach.

The "skyline" looks like it did a century ago. Notice the town's characteristic rooftop domes. There's little to do here but eat, window shop, and enjoy the beach and views...hence the town's popularity.

While Positano has 4,000 residents, an average of 12,000 tourists visit daily from Easter through October. But because hotels don't take large groups (bus access is too difficult), this town—unlike Sorrento—has been spared the worst ravages of big-bus tourism. In winter, hotels shut down and the town once again belongs to the locals.

Consider seeing Positano as a day trip from Sorrento: Take the bus out and the afternoon ferry home, but be sure to check boat schedules when you arrive—the last ferry often leaves before 18:00.

Orientation

Squished into a ravine, with narrow alleys that cascade down to the harbor, Positano requires you to stroll, whether you're going up or heading down. The center of town has no main square (unless you count the beach).

Tourist Information

The TI is a block from the beach, in the red building a half-block beyond the bottom of the church steps (Mon-Sat 9:00-19:00, Sun until 14:00, shorter hours off-season, Via Regina Giovanna 13, tel. 089-875-067, www.aziendaturismopositano.it).

Helpful Hints

Baggage Storage: Neither bus stop has baggage storage. **Positano Porter** can meet you at the Sponda bus stop and watch your bags for €5 apiece; call in advance (tel. 089-875-310).

Local Guide: Positano native **Lucia Ferrara** leads guided hiking tours (up to 10 people, about 4 miles, 5 hours, €55/person, includes picnic)town walks (3 hours, departs at 17:00, €30/person); and food tours (mobile 339-272-0971, www.zialucy.com).

◗ Positano Walk

This short, self-guided stroll downhill will help you get your bearings.
* Start at...

Piazza dei Mulini: This is as close to the beach as vehicles can get—and the lower stop for the little shuttle bus. **Collina Bakery** is a local hangout (older people gather inside, while the younger crowd congregates on the wisteria-draped terrace across the street).

Dip into the little yellow **Church of the Holy Rosary** (by the road), with a serene 12th-century interior. Up front, to the right of the main altar, find the delicately carved fragment of a Roman sarcophagus (first century BC). Positano sits upon the site of a sprawling Roman villa.

At the top of the town lane (across from the church) is a popular *granita stand,* where the family has been following the same secret lemon slush recipe for generations.

Now continue downhill into town, passing a variety of **shops**—many selling linen and ceramics. These industries boomed when tourists discovered Positano. The beach-inspired Moda Positano fashion label was born as a break from the rigid dress code of the 1950s. You'll also see many **galleries** featuring the work of area artists.
* Wander downhill to the "fork" in the road (stairs to the left, road to the right). You've reached...

Midtown: At **Enoteca Cuomo** (#3), butchers Pasquale and Rosario stock fine local red wines and make homemade sausages, salami, and *panini*—good for

a quick lunch. The smaller set of stairs leads to the recommended **Delicatessen grocery,** where Emilia can fix you a good picnic.

La Zagara (across the lane from the steps, at #10) is a pricey pastry shop by day and a cocktail bar by night (music nightly in summer). Tempting pastries such as the rum-drenched *babà* (a southern Italian favorite) fill the window display. A bit farther downhill, **Brunella** (on the right, at #24) is respected for linens.

Across the street, **Hotel Palazzo Murat** fills what was once a grand Benedictine monastery. Napoleon, fearing the power of the Church, had many such monasteries closed during his rule here. This one became a private palace, named for his brother-in-law, who was briefly the king of Naples. Step into the plush courtyard to enjoy the scene, with great views of the cathedral's majolica-slathered dome below. Continuing on, under a fragrant wisteria trellis, you'll pass "street merchants' gulch," where artisans display their goodies.
* Continue straight down. You'll run into a fork at the big church. For now, turn right and go downstairs to Piazza Flavio Gioia, facing the big...

Church of Santa Maria Assunta: Set upon Roman ruins, this was once the abbey of Positano's 12th-century Benedictine monastery. Originally Romanesque, in the 18th century, it was given an extreme Baroque makeover.

Inside, the first chapel on the left is a fine manger scene *(presepe).* Its original 18th-century figurines give you an idea of the folk costumes of the age. Above the main altar is the Black Madonna, a Byzantine painting likely brought here from Constantinople by monks in the 12th century. To the right of the altar, a small freestanding display case holds a silver-and-copper bust of St. Vitus (along with his bones, now holy relics). He's the town patron, who brought Christianity here in about AD 300. In the adjacent

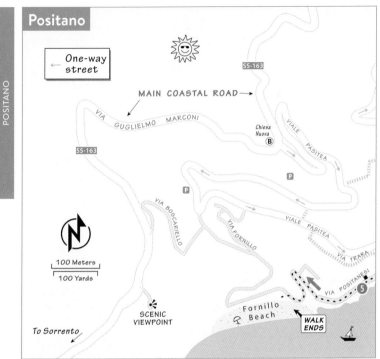

niche (on the right) is a rare 1599 painting by Fabrizio Santafede of Baby Jesus being circumcised.

Back outside, you'll see the **bell tower,** dating from 1707. Above the door, it sports a Romanesque relief scavenged from the original church. The scene—a wolf mermaid with seven little fish—was a reminder to worshippers of how integral the sea was to their livelihood.

Church of Santa Maria Assunta

• *Backtrack up the steps, circling around the church. You'll likely see the entry to an underground Roman exhibit.*

The entire town center of today's Positano—from this cathedral all the way up to the Piazza dei Mulini, where we started this walk—sits upon the site of a huge **Roman villa complex,** buried when Mount Vesuvius erupted in AD 79. Positano excavated one small part of the villa, and a small museum provides views of a surviving fragment of a large Roman fresco.

• *Descend the steps to the right (following beach/spiaggia signs). You'll eventually come to the little square with concrete benches facing the beach.*

Piazzetta: This is the town gathering point in the evening, as local boys hustle tourist girls into the nearby nightclub. Step down to beach level. Residents traded their historic baptistery font with Amalfi town for the two iron lions you see facing the beach. Around the staircase, you'll also

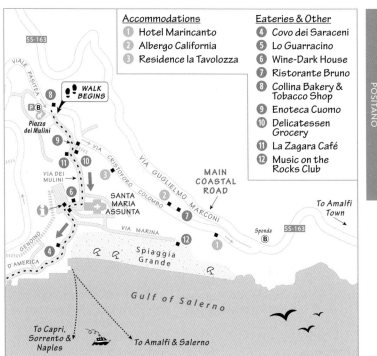

Accommodations
1. Hotel Marincanto
2. Albergo California
3. Residence la Tavolozza

Eateries & Other
4. Covo dei Saraceni
5. Lo Guarracino
6. Wine-Dark House
7. Ristorante Bruno
8. Collina Bakery & Tobacco Shop
9. Enoteca Cuomo
10. Delicatessen Grocery
11. La Zagara Café
12. Music on the Rocks Club

see some original Roman columns, scavenged from the buried villa. Look up and admire the colorful majolica tiles so typical of church domes in this region.

Big Beach: Called Spiaggia Grande, it's half public (straight ahead) and half private (to the left, behind the little fence). The big kiosk sells excursions to Capri and elsewhere.

From the beach you can see three of the **watchtowers** built centuries ago to protect the Amalfi Coast from Saracen pirates: one on the far-left horizon, just below Praiano; one on the Li Galli Islands, ahead and right; and the rectangular one far to the right, marking the far end of Fornillo Beach. Defenders used these towers—situated within sight of each other—to relay smoke signals. In more recent times, the tower on the right (near Fornillo Beach) was a hangout for artists, who holed up inside for inspiration.

As you face out to sea, on the far-left side of the beach (below Rada Restaurant) is **Music on the Rocks,** a chic club that's the only remaining piece of the 1970s scene. While it's dead until very late, you're welcome to peek in at the cool troglo-disco interior, or go upstairs to the Fly Bar for the priciest cocktails in town.

• *Now turn right and wander across the beach. Behind the kiosks that sell boat tickets, find the steps to the **path** that*

Spiaggia Grande Beach, Positano

climbs up and over, past a 13th-century lookout fort from pirate days, to the next beach. It's a worthwhile five-minute walk through a shady ravine to...

Fornillo Beach: This is where locals go to swim (and escape tourists).

• *Our walk is over. Time to relax.*

Shopping

Linen garments are popular. To find a good-quality piece that will last, look for "Made in Positano" (or at least "Made in Italy") on the label, and check the percentage of linen; 60 percent or more is good quality and 100 percent is best. **Brunella** and **Pepito's** have top reputations and multiple outlets.

For **handmade sandals** crafted to your specifications while you wait (at prices starting at about €50), try **La Botteguccia,** facing the tranquil little square just up from the TI, or **Carmine Todisco** around the corner.

Sleeping

These hotels are all on or near Via Cristoforo Colombo, which leads from the Sponda bus stop down into the village. They close in the winter (Dec-Feb or longer). Expect to pay more than €20 per day to park, except at Albergo California.

$$$$ Hotel Marincanto is a somewhat impersonal four-star hotel with 32 beautiful rooms and a bright breakfast terrace practically teetering on a cliff. Suites seem to be designed for a *luna di miele*—honeymoon (air-con, elevator, pool, stairs down to a private beach, pay parking, closed Nov-March, 50 yards below Sponda bus stop at Via Cristoforo Colombo 50, reception on bottom floor, tel. 089-875-130, www.marincanto.it, info@marincanto.it).

$$$ Albergo California has 15 spacious rooms (all with lofty views), a grand terrace draped with vines, and full breakfasts (air-con, free parking, closed Nov-Easter, Via Cristoforo Colombo 141, tel. 089-875-382, www.hotelcaliforniapositano.it, info@hotelcaliforniapositano.it).

$$ Residence la Tavolozza is an attractive six-room hotel, warmly run by Celeste (cheh-LEHS-tay) and daughters Francesca (who speaks English) and Paola. Each cheerily tiled room comes with a view, a terrace, and silence (lavish à la carte breakfast extra, families can ask for sprawling "Royal Apartment," air-con, confirm by phone if arriving late, closed Dec-Feb, Via Cristoforo Colombo 10, tel. 089-875-040, www.latavolozzapositano.it, info@latavolozzapositano.it).

Eating

At the waterfront, several interchangeable restaurants with view terraces leave people fat and happy, albeit with skinnier wallets (figure €15-20 pastas and *secondi,* plus pricey drinks and sides, and a cover charge).

$$$ Covo dei Saraceni offers the best value on the beach, with good pizza and tables overlooking the action (daily, on the far right as you face the sea, where Via Positanesi d'America starts).

Near the Beach: A local favorite for its great views, **$$$ Lo Guarracino** is on the path to Fornillo Beach, with good food at prices similar to the beachfront places (daily 12:00-15:30 & 18:00-22:30, closed Nov-March, follow path behind the boat-ticket kiosks 5 minutes to Via Positanesi d'America 12, tel. 089-875-794).

$$ Wine-Dark House, tucked around the base of the stairs near the beach (and the TI), fills a cute little piazzetta at the start of Via del Saracino. They serve good pastas and *secondi,* have a respect for wine (several excellent local wines), and are popular with Positano's youngsters for their long list of sandwiches (Wed-Mon 10:00-15:30 & 18:30-22:30, closed Tue, Via del Saracino 6, tel. 089-811-925).

"Uptown": The unassuming, family-run **$$$ Ristorante Bruno** is handy to my listed hotels on or near Via Cristoforo Colombo. While expensive, it has nice views and is worth considering if you want a meal without hiking down into the town center (daily 12:30-23:00, closed Nov-Easter, near the top of Via Cristoforo Colombo at #157, tel. 089-875-179).

Transportation

The main coastal highway winds above the town. Regional SITA buses stop at two scheduled bus stops located at either end of town: **Chiesa Nuova** (at Bar Internazionale, near the Sorrento end of town) and **Sponda** (nearer Amalfi town). Although both stops are near roads leading downhill through the town to the beach, Sponda is closer and less steep; from this stop, it's a scenic 20-minute downhill stroll/shop/munch to the beach (and TI).

The SITA bus from Positano leaves from the Sponda stop, sometimes up to five minutes before the printed departure time. In case the driver is early, you should be, too. Buy tickets at the tobacco shop in the town center (on Piazza dei Mulini).

Shuttle buses (marked *Interno Positano*), connect the lower town with the highway's two bus stops (2/hour, €1.30 at tobacco shop on Piazza dei Mulini, €1.80 on board, convenient stop at the corner of Via Colombo and Via dei Mulini, heads up to Sponda). Collina Bakery, located off Piazza dei Mulini is just across from the shuttle bus stop, with a fine, breezy terrace to enjoy while you wait.

Drivers must go with the one-way flow, entering the town only at the Chiesa Nuova bus stop (closest to Sorrento) and exiting at Sponda. Driving is a headache here. Parking is even worse.

AMALFI TOWN

After Rome fell, the town of Amalfi was one of the first to trade goods—coffee, carpets, and paper—between Europe and points east. Its heyday was the 10th and 11th centuries, when it was a powerful maritime republic that rivaled Venice. Amalfi established "rules of the sea"—the basics of which survive today.

In 1343, this little powerhouse was suddenly destroyed by a tsunami caused by an undersea earthquake. That disaster, compounded by devastating plagues, left Amalfi a humble backwater. Today its 5,000 residents live off tourism. The coast's namesake is not as picturesque as Positano or as well-connected as Sorrento, but it has a real-life feel and a vivacious bustle.

Amalfi's one main street runs up from the waterfront through a deep valley, with stairways to courtyards and houses on either side. It's worth walking uphill to the workaday upper end of town. Super-atmospheric, narrow, stepped side lanes branch off, squeezing between hulking old buildings.

Orientation

Amalfi's waterfront is the coast's biggest transport hub. Right next to each other are the bus station, ferry docks, and a parking lot (€5/hour). Venture into town, and you'll quickly come to Piazza Duomo, the main square, with the cathedral and a statue of St. Andrew.

Tourist Information

The **TI** is about 100 yards from the bus station and ferry dock, next to the post office (Mon-Sat 9:00-14:00 & 15:00-18:30, Nov-March Mon-Sat 9:00-14:00, closed Sun year-round, pay WC in same courtyard, Corso della Repubbliche Marinare 27; tel. 089-871-107, www.amalfitouristoffice.it).

Helpful Hints

Baggage Storage: You can store your bag safely at the **Divina Costiera Travel Office** facing the waterfront square, across from the bus parking area (€5/4 hours, daily 8:00-20:00, closed Feb, tel. 089-871-181).

Speedboat Charters: Consider **Charter La Dolce Vita** (mobile 335-549-9365, www.amalficoastyacht.it).

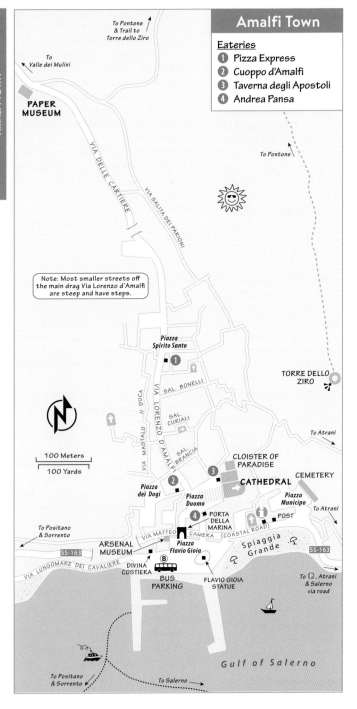

Amalfi Town

Eateries
1. Pizza Express
2. Cuoppo d'Amalfi
3. Taverna degli Apostoli
4. Andrea Pansa

Note: Most smaller streets off the main drag Via Lorenzo d'Amalfi are steep and have steps.

Rick's Tip: Don't get stranded! *The* **last bus from Amalfi back to Sorrento** *leaves in the evening (in winter this can be as early as 19:00). Don't plan to leave on the last bus of the day; if that bus is full, your only option might be a €100 taxi ride.*

Sights

CATHEDRAL

This church is a mix of Moorish and Byzantine flavors, built c. 1000-1300). Its imposing stairway functions as a hangout zone and outdoor theater. The 1,000-year-old bronze door at the top was given to Amalfi by a wealthy local merchant who had it made in Constantinople. The courtyard of 120 graceful columns—the "Cloister of Paradise"—was the cemetery for nobles in the 13th century. Don't miss the fine view of the bell tower and its majolica tiles. The original ninth-century

Amalfi Cathedral

church, known as the Basilica of the Crucifix for its 13th-century wooden crucifix, today is a museum filled with the cathedral's art treasures. Down the stairs to the right of the basilica's altar is the Crypt of St. Andrew. Under the huge bronze statue, you'll see a reliquary holding what are believed to be Andrew's remains (€3, daily 10:00-17:00, tel. 089-871-324, www. parrocchiaamalfi.com). A free WC is at the top of the steps (through unmarked green door, just a few steps before ticket booth, ask for key at desk).

▲PAPER MUSEUM (MUSEO DELLA CARTA)

Paper has been an important industry here since Amalfi's glory days in the Middle Ages. At this cavernous, cool 13th-century paper mill-turned-museum, a guide recounts the history and process of papermaking and turns on the museum's vintage machinery (€4.50; daily 10:00-18:30; Nov-Jan Tue-Sat until 15:30, closed Mon; a 10-minute walk up the main street from the cathedral—follow signs to *Museo della Carta* at Via delle Cartiere 23; tel. 089-830-4561, www. museodellacarta.it).

Eating

Quick Bites: Walk five minutes up the main drag; on the right, past the first archway, is **$ Pizza Express,** with honest pies, calzones, and heated sandwiches to go (Mon-Sat 9:00-21:00, closed Sun, Via Capuano 46, mobile 339-581-2336). The **Cuoppo d'Amalfi** fried-fish stand at Piazza dei Dogi is another good option.

On the Main Square, Piazza Duomo: Tucked just around the left side of the grand staircase, up a smaller flight of stairs is **$$ Taverna degli Apostoli,** with colorful outdoor tables and cozy upstairs dining room in what was once an art gallery. The menu is brief but thoughtful, going beyond the old standbys, and everything is well-executed (daily 12:00-16:00 & 19:00-24:00, Supportico San Andrea 6, tel. 089-872-991). For dessert, the **Andrea Pansa** pastry shop and café, to the right as you face the cathedral steps, is the most venerable place in town—a good spot to try *sfogliatella* (the delicate pastry invented at a nearby monastery) and other desserts popular in southern Italy (daily 7:30-24:00).

RAVELLO

Ravello sits atop a lofty perch 1,000 feet above the sea, with breathtaking views that have attracted celebrities for generations. Gore Vidal, Richard Wagner, D. H. Lawrence, M. C. Escher, Henry Wadsworth Longfellow, Tennessee Williams, and Greta Garbo have all called it home.

The town is like a lush and peaceful garden floating in a world all its own. It seems to be made entirely of cafés, stonework, old villas-turned-luxury hotels, tourists, and grand views. Ravello feels like a place to convalesce.

Sights

The town's entry tunnel deposits you on the main square, **Piazza Duomo.** The **TI** is down the street past the church (TI open daily 10:00-18:00, closes earlier Nov-April, 100 yards from the square—follow signs to Via Roma 18, tel. 089-857-096, www.ravellotime.com).

The **Duomo,** overlooking the main square, feels stripped-down and Romanesque. The front door is locked; to enter, go through the museum on Viale Wagner, around the right side. Its key features are its 12th-century bronze doors; the carved marble pulpit supported by six lions; and the relic of holy blood (left of main altar) (€3, daily 9:00-19:00, Nov-April until 18:00).

Villa Rufolo, **also on Piazza Duomo,** presents wistful gardens among stony walls, with oh-my-God views (€7, daily 9:00-20:00, Oct-April 9:00 until sunset, may close earlier for concerts, tel. 089-857-621, www.villarufolo.it). Enter the villa through the stout watchtower to buy your ticket and pick up the English booklet explaining the sight. Then, walk through part of the sprawling villa ruins. Check out the short video in the tiny theater at the base of the tower and the exhibit upstairs. The palace itself has

Ravello enjoys commanding views.

little to show, but the gardens and views are magnificent and invite exploration. You can enjoy some of the same view, without the entry fee, from the bus parking lot just below the villa.

Eating

Several no-brainer, interchangeable restaurants face Piazza Duomo and line the surrounding streets. To enjoy this fine setting, just take your pick. You can also grab a takeaway lunch at one of the little groceries and sandwich shops that line Via Roma (between Piazza Duomo and the TI). Enjoy your meal at the panoramic benches at the far end of Piazza Duomo (facing the cathedral).

Transportation

Ravello and the town of **Amalfi** are connected by bus along a very windy road. Coming from Amalfi town, buy your bus ticket at the Divina Costiera travel office facing the waterfront square, and ask where the stop for Ravello is (normally by the statue on the waterfront, just to the statue's left as you face the water). When returning from Ravello, line up early, since the buses are often crowded (at least every 40 minutes, 30-minute trip, €1.20, buy ticket in tobacco shop; catch bus 100 yards off main square, by the recommended Ristorante Da Salvatore).

Italian History

Italy has a lot of history, so let's get started.

Origins of Rome
(c. 753 BC-450 BC)

A she-wolf breastfed two human babies, Romulus and Remus, who grew to build the city of Rome in 753 BC—you buy that? Closer to fact, farmers and shepherds of the Latin tribe settled near the mouth of the Tiber River, a convenient trading location. The crude settlement was sandwiched between two sophisticated civilizations—Greek colonists to the south and the Etruscans of Tuscany to the north. Baby Rome was both dominated and nourished by these societies.

In 509 BC the Romans drove out the Etruscan kings and replaced them with elected Roman senators and (eventually) a code of law. The Roman Republic was born.

The Roman Republic Expands
(c. 509 BC-AD 1)

Located at the midpoint of the peninsula, Rome was perfectly situated for trading salt and wine. Roman businessmen, backed by a disciplined army, expanded throughout the Italian peninsula, establishing an infrastructure as they went. Rome soon conquered its northern Etruscan neighbors.

Next, Rome overcame the Greek colonists (c. 275 BC). Rome now ruled a united federation stretching from Tuscany to the tip of the Italian peninsula, with a standard currency, a system of roads, and an army of a half-million ready for the next challenge: Carthage (modern-day Tunisia). Carthage and Rome fought the three bitter Punic Wars for control of the Mediterranean (264-201 BC and 146 BC). The Romans prevailed.

The well-tuned Roman legions easily subdued sophisticated Greece in three Macedonian Wars (215-146 BC). By the first century BC, Rome was master of the Mediterranean. Booty, cheap grain, and thousands of captured slaves poured in, transforming the economic model from small farmers to unemployed city dwellers living off tribute from conquered lands.

Civil Wars and the Transition to Empire
(FIRST CENTURY BC)

With easy money streaming in and traditional roles obsolete, Romans bickered among themselves over their slice of the pie. Wealthy landowners wrangled with the growing population of slaves, and with the middle and working classes, who demanded greater say-so in government.

Amid the chaos of class war and civil war, charismatic generals who could provide wealth and security became dictators. Julius Caesar (100-44 BC) was a cunning politician, riveting speaker, conqueror of Gaul, author of *The Gallic Wars,* and lover of Cleopatra, queen of Egypt. In his four-year reign, he reformed and centralized the government around himself. Disgruntled Republicans feared that he would make himself king. At his peak of power, they surrounded Caesar on the Ides of March (March 15, 44 BC) and killed him.

Julius Caesar died, but the concept of one-man rule lived on in his adopted son, who was proclaimed Emperor Augustus (27 BC). Augustus outwardly followed the traditions of the Republic, while in practice he acted as a dictator with the backing of Rome's legions and the rubber-stamp approval of the Senate. He established his family to succeed him (making the family name "Caesar" a title) and set the pattern of rule by emperors for the next 500 years.

The Roman Empire
(c. AD 1-500)

In his 40-year reign, Augustus ended Rome's civil wars and ushered in the Pax Romana: 200 years of prosperity and relative peace. Rome ruled an empire of 54 million people, stretching from Scotland to northern Africa, from Spain to the Euphrates River. Conquered peoples were welcomed into the fold of prosperity, linked by roads, common laws, common gods, education, and the Latin language. The city of Rome, with more than a million inhabitants, was decorated with statues and monumental structures faced with marble. It was the marvel of the known world, though it prospered on a (false) economy of booty, slaves, and cheap imports.

Decline and Fall
(AD 200-500)

Rome peaked in the second century AD under the capable emperors Trajan (r. 98-117), Hadrian (r. 117-138), and Marcus Aurelius (r. 161-180). For the next three centuries, the Roman Empire declined, shrinking in size and wealth, a victim of corruption, disease, an overextended army, a false economy, and the constant pressure of "barbarian" tribes pecking away at its borders.

Trying to stall the disintegration, Emperor Diocletian (r. 284-305) split the empire into two administrative halves under two equal emperors. Constantine (r. 306-337) moved the capital of the empire from decaying Rome to the new city of Constantinople (330, present-day Istanbul). Almost instantly, the once-great city of Rome became a minor player in imperial affairs. (The eastern "Byzantine" half of the empire would thrive and live on for another thousand years.) Constantine also legalized Christianity (313), and the once-persecuted cult soon became virtually the state religion, the backbone of Rome's fading hierarchy.

By 410, "Rome" had shrunk to just the city itself. Barbarian tribes from the north and east poured in to loot and plunder. The city was sacked by Visigoths (410) and vandalized by Vandals (455), and the pope had to plead with Attila the Hun for mercy (451). Peasants huddled near powerful lords for protection from bandits, planting the seeds of medieval feudalism.

In 476, the last emperor sold his title for a comfy pension, and Rome fell, plunging Europe into a thousand years of darkness. For the next 13 centuries, there would be no "Italy," just a patchwork of rural duke-doms and towns, victimized by foreign powers. Italy lay in shambles, helpless.

Invasions
(AD 500-1000)

In 500 years, Italy suffered through a full paragraph of invasions: Lombards (568) and Byzantines (536) occupied the north. In the south, Muslim Saracens (827) and Christian Normans (1061) established thriving kingdoms. Charlemagne, king of the Germanic Franks, defeated the Lom-bards, and on Christmas Day, AD 800, he knelt before the pope in St. Peter's in Rome to be crowned Holy Roman Emperor, a title meant to resurrect the glory of ancient Rome united with medieval Christianity.

Through all the invasions and chaos, the glory of ancient Rome was preserved in the pomp, knowledge, hierarchy, and wealth of the Christian Church. Strong popes ruled like small-time emperors, governing territories in central Italy called the Papal States.

Prosperity and Politics
(1000-1300)

Sea-trading cities such as Venice, Genoa, Pisa, Naples, and Amalfi grew wealthy as middlemen between Europe and the Orient. During the Crusades (beginning in 1097), Italian ships ferried Europe's Christian soldiers eastward, then returned laden with spices and highly marked-up luxury goods from the Orient. Trade spawned banking, and Italians became capitalists, loaning money at interest to Europe's royalty. The medieval prosper-ity of the cities laid the foundation of the Renaissance to come.

Politically, the Italian peninsula was dominated by two rulers—the pope in Rome and the German Holy Roman Emperor (with holdings in the north).

Italy split into two warring political parties: supporters of the popes (called Guelphs, centered in urban areas) and support-ers of the emperors (Ghibellines, popular with the rural nobility).

The Unlucky 1300s

In 1309, enticed by the fast-rising power of France, the pope moved from Rome to Avignon. At one point, two rival popes reigned, one in Avignon and the other in Rome, and they excommunicated each other. The papacy eventually returned to Rome (1377), but the schism had created a breakdown in central authority that was exacerbated by an outbreak of bubonic plague (Black Death, 1347-1348), which killed a third of the Italian population.

In the power vacuum, new players emerged in the independent cities. Ven-ice, Florence, Milan, and Naples were under the protection and leadership of local noble families, such as the Medici in Florence. Florence thrived in the wool and dyeing trade, which led to dominance in international banking, with branches in all of Europe's capitals. A positive side effect of the terrible Black Death was that the now-smaller population got a bigger share of the land, jobs, and infrastructure. By century's end, Italy was poised to enter its most glorious era since antiquity.

The Renaissance
(1400s– 1600s)

The Renaissance—the "rebirth" of ancient Greek and Roman art styles, knowledge, and humanism—began in Italy (c. 1400) and spread through Europe over the next two centuries. Many of Europe's most famous painters, sculptors, and thinkers—Michelangelo, Leonardo, Raphael, etc.—were Italian.

This cultural boom, financed by thriv-ing trade and lucrative banking, changed people's thinking about every aspect of life. In politics, it meant an eventual rebirth of Greek ideas of democracy. In religion, it meant a move away from

Top 10 Italians

Romulus: Breastfed on wolf milk, this legendary orphan founded the city of Rome (traditionally in 753 BC). Over the next seven centuries, his descendants dominated the Italian peninsula, ruling from Rome as a Republic.

Julius Caesar (100-44 BC): After conquering Gaul (France), subduing Egypt, and winning Cleopatra's heart, Caesar ruled Rome with king-like powers. In an attempt to preserve the Republic, senators stabbed him to death, but the concept of one-man rule lived on.

Augustus (born Octavian, 63 BC-AD 14): Julius' adopted son became the first of the Caesars that ruled Rome during its 500 years as a Europe-wide power. He set the tone for emperors both good (Trajan, Hadrian, Marcus Aurelius) and bad (Caligula, Nero, and dozens of others).

Constantine (c. 280-337 AD): Raised in a Christian home, this emperor legalized Christianity, almost instantly turning a persecuted sect into a Europe-wide religion. With the Fall of Rome, the Church was directed by strong popes and so guided Italians through the next thousand years of invasions, plagues, political decentralization, and darkness.

Lorenzo (the Magnificent) de' Medici (1449-1492): Soldier, poet, lover, and ruler of Florence in the 1400s, this Renaissance Man embodied the "rebirth" of ancient enlightenment. Lorenzo's wealthy Medici family funded Florentine artists who pioneered a new realism in painting and sculpture.

Michelangelo Buonarroti (1475-1564): His statue of David—slayer of an ignorant brute—stands as a monumental symbol of Italian enlightenment. Along with fellow geniuses Leonardo da Vinci and Raphael, Michelangelo mastered the visual arts of the Italian Renaissance: painting, sculpture, and architecture. Their innovations spread northward, influencing the rest of Europe.

Giovanni Lorenzo Bernini (1598-1680): The "Michelangelo of Baroque" kept Italy a major exporter of sophisticated trends. Bernini's ornate statues and architectural projects decorated palaces of the rising power brokers in France, even as Italy was reverting to an economically stagnant patchwork of foreign-ruled states.

Victor Emmanuel II (1820-1878): As the only Italian-born ruler on the peninsula, this king of Sardinia played a central role in Italian unification. Aided by the general Garibaldi, writer Mazzini, and politician Cavour (with a soundtrack by Verdi), he became the first ruler of a united, democratic Italy, in September 1870. (The preceding proper nouns have since come to adorn streets and piazzas throughout Italy.)

Benito Mussolini (1883-1945): An inspiration for Hitler, he derailed Italy's fledgling democracy, becoming dictator of a fascist state and leading the country to defeat in World War II. No public places honor Mussolini, but many streets and piazzas throughout Italy bear the name of Giacomo Matteotti (1885-1924), a politician whose outspoken opposition to Mussolini got him killed.

Federico Fellini (1920-1993): Fellini's films (*La Strada, La Dolce Vita, 8½*) chronicle Italy's postwar years in gritty black and white—the poverty, destruction, and disillusionment of the war followed by the optimism, decadence, and materialism of the economic boom. He captured the surreal chaos of Italy's abrupt social change from traditional Catholicism to a secular, urban world presided over by Mafia bosses and weak government.

Church dominance and toward humanism and a more personal faith. Science and secular learning were revived after centuries of superstition and ignorance. In architecture, it was a return to the balanced columns and domes of Greece and Rome. During the Renaissance, the Italian peninsula once again became the trendsetting cultural center of Europe.

Foreign invasions
(1500s)

In May 1498, Vasco da Gama of Portugal landed in India, having found a sea route around Africa. Italy's monopoly on trade with the East was broken. Portugal, France, Spain, England, and Holland—nation-states under strong central rule—began to overtake decentralized Italy. Italy's once-great maritime cities now traded in an economic backwater, just as Italy's bankers (such as the Medici in Florence) were going bankrupt. While the Italian Renaissance was all the rage throughout Europe, it declined in its birthplace. Italy—culturally sophisticated but weak and decentralized—was ripe for the picking by Europe's rising powers.

Several kings of France invaded (1494, 1495, and 1515)—initially invited by Italian lords to attack their rivals—and began divvying up territory for their noble families. Italy also became a battleground in religious conflicts between Catholics and the new Protestant movement. In the chaos, the city of Rome was brutally sacked by foreign mercenaries (1527).

Foreign Rule
(1600-1800)

For the next two centuries, most of Italy's states were ruled by foreign nobles, who treated them as prizes in Europe's dynastic wars. Italy ceased to be a major player in Europe, politically or economically. Italian intellectual life was often cropped short by a conservative Catholic Church trying to fight Protestantism. Galileo, for example, was forced to renounce his belief that the earth orbited the sun (1633). But Italy did export Baroque art and the budding new medium of opera.

The War of the Spanish Succession (1713)—in which Italy did not participate—gave much of northern Italy to Austria's ruling family, the Habsburgs (who now wore the crown of Holy Roman Emperor). In the south, Spain's Bourbon family ruled the Kingdom of Naples (known after 1816 as the Kingdom of the Two Sicilies), making it a culturally sophisticated but economically backward area, preserving a medieval, feudal caste system.

In 1720, a minor war (the War of Austrian Succession) created a new state at the foot of the Alps, called the Kingdom of Sardinia (a.k.a. the Kingdom of Piedmont, or Savoy). Ruled by the Savoy family, this was the only major state on the peninsula that was actually ruled by Italians. It proved to be a toehold to the future.

Italy Unites—
The Risorgimento
(1800s)

In 1796, Napoleon Bonaparte swept through Italy and changed everything. He ousted Austrian and Spanish dukes, confiscated Church lands, united scattered states, and crowned himself "King of Italy" (1805). After his defeat (1815), Italy's old ruling order (namely, Austria and Spain) was restored. But Napoleon had planted a seed: What if Italians could unite and rule themselves like Europe's other modern nations?

For the next 50 years, a movement to unite Italy slowly grew. Called the Risorgimento ("rising again"), the movement promised a revival of Italy's glory. It started as a revolutionary, liberal movement, but gradually, Italians of all stripes warmed to the idea of unification.

The movement coalesced around the Italian-ruled Kingdom of Sardinia and its king, Victor Emmanuel II. In 1859, Sardinia's prime minister, Camillo Cavour, cleverly persuaded France to drive Austria out of northern Italy, leaving the region in Italian hands. A vote was held, and several central Italian states (including some of the pope's) rejected their feudal lords and chose to join the growing Sardinian kingdom.

After victory in the north, General Giuseppe Garibaldi (1807-1882) steamed south with a thousand of his best soldiers (known as the "Spedizione dei Mille") and marched on the Spanish-ruled city of Naples (1860). The old order simply collapsed. In two short months, Garibaldi had achieved a seemingly impossible victory against a far superior army. Garibaldi sent a one-word telegram to the king of Sardinia: *"Obbedisco"* (I obey). Victor Emmanuel II was crowned "King of Italy." Only the pope in Rome held out, protected by French troops. When the city finally fell—easily—to the unification forces on September 20, 1870, the Risorgimento was complete.

The Risorgimento was largely the work of four men: Garibaldi (the sword), Mazzini (the spark), Cavour (the diplomat), and Victor Emmanuel II (the rallying point). Today, street signs throughout Italy honor them and the dates of their great victories.

Mussolini and War
(1900-1950)

Italy—now a nation-state—entered the 20th century with a progressive government (a constitutional monarchy), a collection of colonies, a flourishing northern half of the country, and an economically backward south. After World War I (1915-1918), being on the winning Allied side, the Italians were granted possession of the alpine regions. But in the swirl of postwar cynicism and anarchy, many radical political parties—Communist, Socialist, Popular, and Fascist—rose up.

Benito Mussolini (1883-1945), a writer for socialist newspapers, led the fascists. In 1922, he seized the government and began his rule as dictator for the next two decades. He struck an agreement with the pope, giving Vatican City to the papacy, while Mussolini ruled Italy with the implied blessing of the Catholic Church.

Mussolini allied his country with Hitler's Nazi regime, drawing an unprepared Italy into World War II (1940). Italy's lame army was never a factor in the war, and when Allied forces landed in Sicily (1943), Italians welcomed them as liberators. The Italians toppled Mussolini's government and surrendered to the Allies, but Nazi Germany sent troops to rescue Mussolini. The war raged on as Allied troops inched their way north against German resistance. Italians were reduced to dire poverty. In the last days of the war (April 1945), Mussolini was killed by the Italian resistance.

Postwar Italy

At war's end, Italy was physically ruined and extremely poor. The nation rebuilt in the 1950s and 1960s with Marshall Plan aid from the US. Italy regained its standing among nations, joining the United Nations, NATO, and what would become the European Union.

However, the government remained weak, changing on average once a year, shifting from right to left to centrist coalitions. Afraid of another Mussolini, the authors of the postwar constitution created a feeble executive branch; without majorities in both houses of parliament, nothing could get done. All Italians acknowledged that the real power lay in the hands of backroom politicians and organized crime. The country remained strongly divided between the rich, industrial north and the poor, rural south.

Italian society changed greatly after the liberal reforms of the Catholic Church at the Vatican II conference (1962-1965). The once-conservative Catholic country legalized divorce and contraception, and the birth rate plummeted. In the 1970s, Italy suffered a wave of violence from left- and right-wing domestic terrorists and organized crime. In the early 1990s, the judiciary undertook a reasonably effective campaign to rid politics of corruption and Mafia ties. Italy entered the 21st century buoyed by a growing economy and living standards nearly on par with its European neighbors.

Italy Today

That turnaround made Italy a magnet for immigration, especially from Albania, North Africa, and Eastern Europe. The influx brought with it cheap labor but also pressures on social services and cultural norms. And then came the global recession. Like other European nations, Italy ran up big deficits, and by the end of 2011, its debt load was the second worst in the euro zone, behind only Greece. Bombastic media tycoon Silvio Berlusconi was forced to resign from his fourth stint as prime minister.

When Italians again went to the polls in 2018, they expressed their frustration with the severe austerity measures enacted to deal with the debt, throwing out the country's traditional centrist parties. The anti-establishment, anti-immigration 5-Star Movement got the largest vote, followed by the far-right, Euroskeptic League party. Political observers compared the election results to populist outcomes elsewhere, such as Brexit and the election of Donald Trump.

After months of haggling, the two parties agreed to a coalition government, but it's unclear how long this political marriage of convenience will last. Italy is used to political merry-go-rounds; it's had 65 governments since World War II. And while Italy remains the third-largest economy in the eurozone (and world's eighth-largest exporter), unemployment seems stuck at about 10 percent—with youth unemployment hovering around 30 percent.

As you travel through Italy today, you'll encounter a fascinating country with a rich history and a per-capita income that comes close to its neighbors to the north. Despite its ups and downs, Italy remains committed to Europe...yet it's as wonderfully Italian as ever.

To learn more about Italian history, consider *Europe 101: History and Art for the Traveler,* written by Rick Steves and Gene Openshaw (available at www.ricksteves.com).

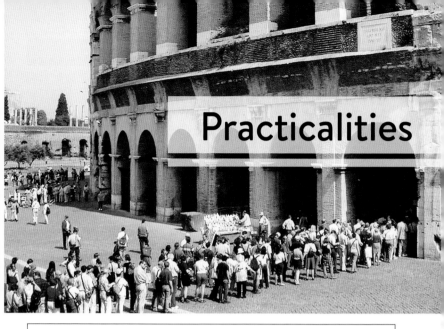

Practicalities

TOURIST INFORMATION

Before your trip, scan the website of the Italian national tourist office (*www.italia.it*). If you have a specific question, try contacting one of their US offices (New York tel. 212/245-5618, *newyork@enit.it*; Los Angeles tel. 310/820-1898, *losangeles@enit.it*).

In Italy, a good first stop in every town is generally the tourist information office (abbreviated **TI** in this book). Swing by to pick up a city map and get information on public transit, walking tours, special events, and nightlife. While Italian TIs are about half as helpful as those in other countries, their information is twice as important.

Avoiding Theft and Scams

Like anywhere in Europe, thieves target tourists, especially in bigger cities and towns. Pickpockets often stage a commotion or a fight to enable them to work unnoticed. Someone in a small group pushing you as you enter or exit a crowded subway car may slip a hand in your pocket or daybag. Thieves snatch purses and break into cars.

Be on guard, and treat any disturbance around you as a smoke screen for theft. Remember to wear a money belt (tucked under your clothes) to keep your cash, credit cards, and passport secure; carry only the money you need for the day in your front pocket.

HELP!

Travel Advisories and Covid-19 Entry Requirements: You'll likely need to present proof of vaccination or a negative Covid-19 test result. For info on this and other health and safety conditions for your destination, check with the US embassy for Italy (see below) and the travel pages of the US State Department (www.travel.state.gov) and Centers for Disease Control and Prevention (www.cdc.gov/travel).

Emergency and Medical Help: For any emergency—ambulance, police, or fire—call **112** from a mobile phone or landline. If you get sick, do as the locals do and go to a pharmacist for advice. Or ask at your hotel for help—they'll know the nearest medical and emergency services.

ETIAS Registration: The European Union may soon require US and Canadian citizens to register online with the European Travel Information and Authorization System (ETIAS) before entering Italy and other Schengen Zone countries (quick and easy process, www.etiasvisa.com).

Theft or Loss: To replace a passport, you'll need to go in person to an embassy (see below). If your credit and debit cards disappear, cancel and replace them (see "Damage Control for Lost Cards" on page 478). File a police report, either on the spot or within a day or two; you'll need it to submit an insurance claim for lost or stolen rail passes or electronics, and it can help with replacing your passport or credit and debit cards. For more information, see www.ricksteves.com/help.

US Embassy in Rome: Tel. 06-46741 for 24-hour emergency line, tel. 06-4674-2420, otherwise by appointment only, Via Vittorio Veneto 121, http://it.usembassy.gov.

US Consulates: Milan tel. 02-290-351, Via Principe Amedeo 2/10; **Florence** tel. 055-266-951, Lungarno Vespucci 38; **Naples** tel. 081-583-8111, Piazza della Repubblica. For all, see http://it.usembassy.gov.

Canadian Embassy in Rome: Tel. 06-854-441, Via Zara 30, www.italy.gc.ca.

TRAVEL TIPS

Time Zones: Italy is generally six/nine hours ahead of the East/West Coasts of the US. The exceptions are the beginning and end of Daylight Saving Time: Europe "springs forward" the last Sunday in March (two weeks after most of North America), and "falls back" the last Sunday in October (one week before North America). For a handy time converter, use the world clock app on your phone or download one (see www.timeanddate.com).

Business Hours: Traditionally, Italy used the siesta plan, with people generally working from about 9:00 to 13:00 and from 15:30-16:00 to 19:00-19:30, Monday through Saturday. Many shops, especially larger stores in tourist areas, stay open through lunch or later into the evening. Shops in small towns and villages are more likely to close during lunch. Stores are usually closed on Sunday, and often on Monday.

Watt's Up? Europe's electrical system is 220 volts, instead of North America's 110 volts. Most electronics convert automatically, so you won't need a converter, but you will need an adapter plug with two round prongs, sold inexpensively at travel stores in the US. Sockets in Italy only accept plugs with slimmer prongs: Don't buy an adapter with the thicker ("Schuko" style) prongs—it won't work.

Discounts: Discounts for sights are generally not listed in this book. However, seniors (age 65 and over), youths under 18, students, and teachers with proper identification cards (obtain from www.isic.org) can get discounts at many sights—always ask. Italy's national museums generally offer free admission to children under 18.

Rick's Tip: *If you aren't sure where to buy something, a **tabacchi** (tobacco shop) is a good place to start. These ubiquitous minimarts are handy places to pay for street parking or purchase transit tickets.*

MONEY

Here's my basic strategy for using money in Europe:

- Upon arrival, head for a cash machine (ATM) at the airport and withdraw some local currency, using a debit card with low international transaction fees.
- In general, pay for bigger expenses with a credit card and use cash for smaller purchases and tips. Use a debit card only for cash withdrawals.
- Keep your cards and cash safe in a money belt.

What to Bring

I pack the following and keep it all safe in my money belt.

Exchange Rate

1 euro (€) = about $1.20

To convert prices in euros to dollars, add about 20 percent: €20 = about $24, €50 = about $60 Like the dollar, one euro (€) is broken into 100 cents. Check Oanda.com for the latest exchange rates.

Debit Card: Use at ATMs to withdraw cash.

Credit Card: Handy for bigger transactions (at hotels, shops, restaurants, car-rental agencies, and so on), payment machines, and online purchases.

Backup Card: Some travelers carry a third card (debit or credit; ideally from a different bank), in case one gets lost, demagnetized, eaten by a temperamental machine, or simply doesn't work.

A Stash of Cash: I carry US $100-200 as a cash backup, which comes in handy in an emergency (such as when the banks go on strike or if your ATM card gets eaten by the machine).

What NOT to Bring: Resist the urge to buy euros before your trip or you'll pay the price in bad stateside exchange rates. I've yet to see a European airport that doesn't have plenty of ATMs.

Before You Go

Know your PIN. Make sure you know the numeric, four-digit PIN for all your cards, both debit and credit. Request it if you don't have one, as it may be required for some purchases in Europe.

Report your travel dates. Let your bank know that you'll be using your debit and credit cards in Europe, and when and where you're headed.

Adjust your ATM withdrawal limit. Find out how much you can take out daily and ask for a higher daily withdrawal limit if you want to get more cash at once.

European ATMs will withdraw funds only from checking accounts; you're unlikely to have access to your savings account.

Ask about fees. For any purchase or withdrawal made with a card, you may be charged a currency conversion fee (1-3 percent) and/or a Visa or MasterCard international transaction fee (less than 1 percent).

In Europe

Using Cash Machines: European cash machines have English-language instructions and work just like they do at home—except they spit out local currency instead of dollars, calculated at the day's standard bank-to-bank rate.

In most places, ATMs are easy to locate—in Italy ask for a bancomat. When possible, withdraw cash from a bank-run ATM located just outside that bank. If your debit card doesn't work, try a lower amount—your request may have exceeded your withdrawal limit or the ATM's limit.

Avoid "independent" ATMs, such as Travelex, Euronet, Moneybox, Your Cash, Cardpoint, and Cashzone. These have high fees, can be less secure than a bank ATM, and may try to trick users with "dynamic currency conversion" (see later).

Exchanging Cash: Avoid exchanging money in Europe; it's a big rip-off. In a pinch, you can always find exchange desks at major train stations or airports—convenient but with crummy rates. Banks generally do not exchange money unless you have an account with them.

Using Credit Cards: Despite some differences between European and US cards, there's little to worry about: US credit cards generally work fine in Europe. I've been inconvenienced only a few times by unattended payment machines (transit-ticket kiosks, parking, self-service gas stations, toll booths) where US cards may not work. Always carry cash as a backup.

Dynamic Currency Conversion: If merchants offer to convert your purchase price into dollars (called dynamic currency conversion, or DCC), refuse this "service." You'll pay extra for the expensive convenience of seeing your charge in dollars. If an ATM offers to "lock in" or "guarantee" your conversion rate, choose "proceed without conversion." Other prompts might state, "You can be charged in dollars: Press YES for dollars, NO for euros." Always choose the local currency.

Damage Control for Lost Cards: If you lose your credit or debit card, report the loss immediately to the respective global customer-assistance centers. With a mobile phone, call these 24-hour US numbers: Visa (tel. +1 303/967-1096), MasterCard (tel. +1 636/722-7111), and American Express (tel. +1 336/393-1111). From a landline, you can call these US numbers collect by going through a local operator. European toll-free numbers can be found at the websites for Visa and MasterCard. You can generally receive a temporary card within two or three business days in Europe (see www.ricksteves.com/help for more).

Tipping

Tipping in Italy isn't as automatic and generous as it is in the US. For special service, tips are appreciated, but not expected. As in the US, the proper amount depends on your resources, tipping philosophy, and the circumstances, but some general guidelines apply.

Restaurants: In Italy, a service charge (servizio) is usually built into your check (look at the bill carefully). If it is included, there's no need to leave an extra tip. If it's not included, it's common to leave about €1 per person (a bit more at finer restaurants) or to round up the bill.

Taxis: For a typical ride, round up your fare a bit (for instance, if the fare is €4.50, pay €5).

Getting a VAT Refund

Wrapped into the purchase price of your Italian souvenirs is a Value-Added Tax (VAT) of about 22 percent. You're entitled to get most of that tax back if you purchase more than €155 (about $185) worth of goods at a store that participates in the VAT-refund scheme.

Get the paperwork. Have the merchant completely fill out the necessary refund document. You'll have to present your passport. Get the paperwork done before you leave the store to ensure you'll have everything you need (including your original sales receipt).

Get your stamp at the border or airport. Process your VAT document at your last stop in the European Union (such as at the airport) with the customs agent who deals with VAT refunds. Some customs desks are positioned before airport security; confirm the location before going through security.

Collect your refund. You can claim your VAT refund from refund companies such as Global Blue or Planet with offices at major airports, ports, or border crossings. These services (which extract a 4 percent fee) can refund your money in cash immediately or credit your card.

Customs for American Shoppers

You can take home $800 worth of items per person duty-free, once every 31 days. Many processed and packaged foods are allowed, including vacuum-packed cheeses, dried herbs, jams, baked goods, candy, chocolate, oil, vinegar, mustard, and honey. Fresh fruits and vegetables and most meats are not allowed, with exceptions for some canned items. As for alcohol, you can bring in one liter duty-free. To bring alcohol (or liquid-packed foods) in your carry-on bag on your flight home, buy it at a duty-free shop at the airport. You'll increase your odds of getting it onto a connecting flight if it's packaged in a "STEB"—a secure, tamper-evident bag.

For details on allowable goods, customs rules, and duty rates, visit http://help.cbp.gov.

SIGHTSEEING

Sightseeing can be hard work. Use these tips to make your visits to Italy's finest sights meaningful, fun, efficient, and painless.

Plan Ahead

Set up an itinerary that allows you to fit in all your must-see sights. Confirm open hours, and don't put off visiting a must-see sight—you never know when a place will close unexpectedly for a holiday, strike, or restoration. Many museums are closed or have reduced hours at least a few days a year. A list of holidays is on page 502; check for possible closures during your trip.

Reservations, Advance Tickets, and Passes

Given how precious your vacation time is, I recommend getting reservations for any must-see sight that offers them. Many popular sights sell advance tickets that guarantee admission at a certain time of

day or allow you to skip entry lines. Either way, it's worth giving up some spontaneity to book in advance. For popular sights, you may need to book weeks or even months in advance. As soon as you're ready to commit to a certain date, book it.

At Sights

Here's what you can typically expect:

Entering: You may not be allowed to enter if you arrive too close to closing time. And guards start ushering people out well before the actual closing time, so don't save the best for last. Many sights have a security check. Allow extra time for these lines. Some sights require you to check daypacks and coats.

Photography: If the museum's photo policy isn't clearly posted, ask a guard. Generally, taking photos without a flash or tripod is allowed. Some sights ban selfie sticks; others ban photos altogether.

Audioguides and Apps: Many sights rent audioguides with excellent recorded descriptions in English. Museums and sights often offer free apps that you can download to your mobile device (check their websites).

Expect Changes: Artwork can be on tour, on loan, out sick, or shifted at the whim of the curator. Pick up a floor plan as you enter, and ask the museum staff if you can't find a particular item.

At Churches: A modest dress code— no bare shoulders or shorts for anyone, even kids—is enforced at larger churches—such as the Duomos in Florence and Siena, Venice's St. Mark's

Basilica, and the Vatican's St. Peter's— but is often overlooked elsewhere. If your heart's set on seeing a certain church, err on the side of caution and dress appropriately.

Some churches have coin-operated boxes that trigger lights to illuminate works of art. I pop in a coin whenever I can, to improve my experience (and photos), as a small contribution to that church.

SLEEPING

Extensive and opinionated listings of good-value rooms are a major feature of this book's Sleeping sections. Rather than list accommodations scattered throughout a town, I choose hotels in my favorite neighborhoods that are convenient to your sightseeing.

Rates and Deals

I've categorized my recommended accommodations based on price, indicated with a dollar-sign rating (see sidebar). The price ranges suggest an estimated cost for a one-night stay in high season in a standard double room with a private toilet and shower, including breakfast, and assume you're booking directly with the hotel (not through a booking site, which extracts a commission).

City hotel taxes vary from place to place in Italy (figure €2-5 per person, per night). Some hoteliers will ask to collect the tax in cash to make their bookkeeping and accounting simpler.

Booking Direct: Once your dates are set, compare prices at several hotels. You can do this by checking hotel websites and booking sites such as Hotels.com or Booking.com. After you've zeroed in on your choice, book directly with the hotel itself. Contact small family-run hotels directly by phone or email. When you go direct, the owner avoids the commission paid to booking sites, thereby leaving enough wiggle room to offer you a dis-

Sleep Code

Hotels are classified based on the average price of a standard double room with breakfast in high season.

$$$$	**Splurge:** Most rooms over €170
$$$	**Pricier:** €130–170
$$	**Moderate:** €90–130
$	**Budget:** €50–90
¢	**Backpacker:** Under €50
RS%	Rick Steves discount

Unless otherwise noted, credit cards are accepted, hotel staff speak basic English, and free Wi-Fi is available. Comparison-shop by checking prices at several hotels (on each hotel's own website, on a booking site, or by email). For the best deal, book directly with the hotel. Ask for a discount if paying in cash; if the listing includes **RS%**, request a Rick Steves discount.

cated in this guidebook by the abbreviation **"RS%."** Discounts vary: Ask for details when you reserve.

Accommodations
Hotels

Italy offers a wide variety of hotels: homey guesthouses, traditional old hotels, impersonal business-class chains, and chic boutiques. Wherever possible, I opt for a family-run hotel.

Arrival and Check-In: Hotels (and B&Bs) are sometimes located on the higher floors of a multipurpose building with a secured door. In that case, look for your hotel's name on the buttons by the main entrance. When you ring the bell, you'll be buzzed in.

Hotel elevators are common, though some older buildings still lack them. You may have to climb a flight of stairs to reach the elevator (if so, you can ask the front desk for help carrying your bags up). Elevators are typically very small—you may need to send your bags up without you.

The EU requires that hotels collect your name, nationality, and ID number. When you check in, the receptionist will normally ask for your passport and may keep it for anywhere from a couple of minutes to a couple of hours. If you're not comfortable leaving your passport at the desk for a long time, ask when you can pick it up. Or, if you packed a color copy of your passport, you can generally leave that rather than the original.

count, a nicer room, or a free breakfast (if it's not already included). If you prefer to book online or are considering a hotel chain, it's to your advantage to use the hotel's website.

Getting a Discount: Some hotels extend a discount to those who pay cash or stay longer than three nights. And some accommodations offer a special discount for Rick Steves readers, indi-

Using Online Services to Your Advantage

From booking services to user reviews, online businesses play a greater role in travelers' planning than ever before. Take advantage of their pluses—and be wise to their downsides.

Booking Sites

Booking websites Booking.com and Hotels.com offer one-stop shopping for hotels. To be listed, a hotel must pay a sizeable commission. When you use an online booking service, you're adding a middleman. To support small, family-run hotels whose world is more difficult than ever, book direct.

Short-Term Rental Sites

Rental juggernaut Airbnb and other short-term rental sites allow travelers to rent rooms and apartments directly from locals. Airbnb fans appreciate feeling part of a real neighborhood as "temporary Europeans."

Critics view Airbnb as creating unfair competition for established guesthouse owners. As a lover of Europe, I share the worry of those who see residents nudged aside by tourists. But as an advocate for travelers, I appreciate the value and cultural intimacy Airbnb provides.

User Reviews

User-generated review sites and apps such as Yelp and TripAdvisor can give you a consensus of opinions about everything from hotels and restaurants to sights and nightlife. But a user-generated review is based on the limited experience of one person, while a guidebook is the work of a trained researcher who visits many restaurants and hotels year after year.

Both types of information have their place, and in many ways, they're complementary. If something is well reviewed in a guidebook and it also gets good online reviews, it's likely a winner.

Bed-and-Breakfasts

B&Bs can offer good-value accommodations in excellent locations. Usually converted family homes or apartments, they can range from humble rooms with communal kitchens to high-end boutique accommodations with extra amenities. Boutique B&Bs can be an especially good option, as they are typically less expensive than a big hotel, but often newer and nicer, with more personal service. Because the B&B scene is constantly changing, it's smart to supplement this book's recommendations with your own research.

Short-Term Rentals

A short-term rental—whether an apartment, house, or room in a local's home—is an increasingly popular alternative, especially if you plan to settle in one location for several nights. For stays longer than a few days, you can usually find a rental that's comparable to—and even cheaper than—a hotel room with similar amenities. Websites such as Airbnb, FlipKey, Booking.com, and the HomeAway family of sites (HomeAway, VRBO, and VacationRentals) let you browse a wide range of properties. Alternatively, rental

Making Hotel Reservations

Requesting a Reservation: For family-run hotels, it's generally best to book your room directly via email or phone. For business-class and chain hotels, or if you'd rather book online, reserve directly through the hotel's official website (not a booking website).

Here's what the hotelier wants to know:
- Type(s) of rooms you want and size of your party
- Number of nights you'll stay
- Your arrival and departure dates, written European-style as day/month/year (18/06/23 or 18 June 2023)
- Special requests (en suite bathroom, cheapest room, twin beds vs. double bed, quiet room)
- Applicable discounts (such as a Rick Steves reader discount, cash discount, or promotional rate)

Confirming a Reservation: Most places will request a credit-card number to hold your room. If you're using an online reservation form, make sure it's secure by looking for *https* or a lock icon at the top of your browser. If the website isn't secure, it's best to share that confidential info via a phone call.

Canceling a Reservation: If you must cancel, do so with as much notice as possible, especially for smaller family-run places. Cancellation policies can be strict; read the fine print before you book. Many discount deals require prepayment, with no cancellation refunds

Reconfirming a Reservation: Always call or email to reconfirm your room reservation a few days in advance. For B&Bs or very small hotels, I call again on my day of arrival to tell my host what time to expect me (especially important if arriving late—after 17:00).

Phoning: For tips on how to call hotels overseas, see page 490.

agencies such as InterhomeUSA.com or RentaVilla.com, which list more carefully selected accommodations that could cost more, can also provide more personalized service.

Agriturismi

Agriturismi—working farms that double as countryside B&Bs—make a peaceful home base for those exploring rural Italy, and are ideal for those traveling by car—especially families. It's wise to book several months in advance for high season (late May-mid-Oct). In addition to my listings, local TIs can give you a list of places in their area. For a sampling, visit AgriturismoItaly.it.

Hostels

A hostel provides cheap beds in dorms where you sleep alongside strangers for about €25-30 per night. Travelers of any age are welcome if they don't mind dorm-style accommodations and meeting other travelers. Most hostels offer kitchen facilities, guest computers, Wi-Fi, and a self-service laundry. Family and private rooms are often available.

Independent hostels tend to be easy-going, colorful, and informal (no membership required; www.hostelworld.com). You may pay slightly less by booking directly with the hostel. **Official hostels** are part of Hostelling International (HI) and share a booking site (www.hihostels.com). HI hostels typically require that you be a member or else pay a bit more per night

EATING

The Italians are masters of the art of fine living. That means eating long and well. Lengthy, multicourse meals and endless hours sitting in outdoor cafés are the norm. Americans eat on their way to an evening event and complain if the check is slow in coming. For Italians, the meal is an end in itself, and only rude servers rush you.

In general, Italians eat meals a bit later than we do. They have a light breakfast (coffee and a pastry, often standing up at a café). For lunch (between 13:00 and 15:00), they grab a quick meal or buy a sandwich. Italians eat a late dinner around 20:00-21:30 (maybe earlier in winter). To bridge the gap, people drop into a bar in the late afternoon for a spuntino (snack) and aperitif.

Breakfast

Italian breakfasts, like Italian bath towels, can be small: The basic, traditional version is coffee and a roll with butter and marmalade. Many places have yogurt and juice (the delicious red orange juice—*spremuta d'arancia rossa*—is made from Sicilian blood oranges), and possibly also cereal, cold cuts and sliced cheese, and eggs (typically hard-boiled; scrambled or fried eggs are less common). Small budget hotels may leave a basic breakfast in your room (stale croissant, roll, jam, yogurt, coffee).

Italian Restaurants

When restaurant-hunting, choose a spot filled with locals. Venturing even a block or two off the main drag leads to higher-quality food for less than half the price of the tourist-oriented places. Locals eat better at lower-rent locales.

Most restaurant kitchens close between their lunch and dinner service. Good restaurants don't reopen for dinner before 19:00. Small restaurants with a full slate of reservations for 20:30 or 21:00 often will accommodate walk-in diners willing to eat a quick, early meal, but you aren't expected to linger.

When you want the bill, mime-scribble on your raised palm or request it: *"Il conto, per favore."* You may have to ask more than once. If you're in a hurry, request the check when you receive the last item you order.

Cover and Tipping

Avoid surprises when eating out by familiarizing yourself with two common Italian restaurant charges: *coperto* and *servizio*. You won't encounter them in all restaurants, but both charges, if assessed, by law must be listed on the menu.

The *coperto* (cover), sometimes called *pane e coperto* (bread and cover), is a minor fee (€1.50-3/person) covering the cost of the typical basket of bread, oil, salt, cutlery, and linens found on your table. It's not negotiable, even if you don't eat the bread.

The *servizio* (a 10- to 15-percent service charge) is similar to the mandatory gratuity that American restaurants often add for groups of six or more. You can consider it a "tourist tax," as you're most likely to encounter it in locations with lots of tourists. Because the service charge is sometimes built into your bill, look carefully at your check to see if you've already paid a tip. If there is no *servizio* on the bill, a common **tip** at a simple restaurant or pizzeria is €1 per person at the table (or simply round up the bill). At a finer restaurant, leave a few euros per person.

Italian Menu Courses

A full Italian meal consists of multiple courses (all described below). To avoid overeating (and to stretch your budget), share dishes. A good rule of thumb is for each person to order any two courses. For example, a couple can order and share one *antipasto,* one *primo,* one *secondo,* and one dessert; or two *antipasti* and two *primi;* or whatever combination appeals.

Antipasto: An appetizer such as bruschetta, grilled veggies, deep-fried tasties, thin-sliced meat (prosciutto or carpaccio), or a plate of olives, cold cuts, and cheeses.

Primo piatto: A "first dish" generally consisting of pasta but also rice or soup.

Secondo piatto: A "second dish," equivalent to our main course, of meat or fish/seafood.

Contorno: A vegetable side dish may come with the *secondo* but more often must be ordered separately. Typical *contorni* are *insalata mista,* spinach, roasted potatoes, or grilled veggies.

Dolce: On most menus you'll find typical Italian desserts such as tiramisu and *panna cotta* as well as local favorites.

Ordering Tips

Seafood and steak may be sold by weight and priced by the *etto* (100 grams, 3.5 ounces) or the *kilo* (1,000 grams, 2.2 pounds). The abbreviation *s.q. (secondo quantità)* indicates an item is priced by weight (often used at antipasto buffets). Unless the menu indicates a fillet *(filetto),* fish is usually served whole with the head and tail. However, you can always ask your server to select a small fish and fillet it for you.

Some special dishes come in larger quantities meant to be **shared by two people.** The shorthand way of showing this on a menu is "X2" (for two).

In a traditional restaurant, if you order a pasta dish and a **side salad**—but no main course—the server will bring the salad after the pasta. If you want the salad with your pasta, specify *insieme* (een-see-EH-meh; together).

You can save by getting a **fixed-priced meal.** Avoid the cheapest ones (often called a *menù turistico*). Look instead for a genuine *menù del giorno* (menu of the day), which offers diners a choice of appetizer, main course, and dessert.

Budget Eating
Pizzerias

Pizza is cheap and readily available. Stop by a pizza shop for stand-up or takeout (many pizza places sell whole pies meant for one person; *pizza al taglio* means "by the slice"). Supermarkets usually have a pizza counter, too.

Some shops feature *pizza rustica*—thick pizza baked in a large rectangular pan and sold by weight. Clearly indicate how much you want: 100 grams, or *un etto,* is a hot and cheap snack; 200 grams, or *due etti,* makes a light meal. Or show the size with your hands—*tanto così* (TAHN-toh koh-ZEE; this much).

Bars/Cafés

Italian "bars" are not taverns, but inexpensive cafés. These neighborhood hangouts serve coffee, mini pizzas *(pizzette)*, sandwiches, and drinks from the cooler. This budget choice is the Italian equivalent of English pub grub.

Many bars are small—if you can't find a table, you'll need to stand or find a ledge to sit on outside. Most charge extra for table service. To get food to go, say, *"da portar via"* (for the road). All bars have a WC *(toilette, bagno)* in the back, and customers—and the discreet public—can use it.

Prices and Paying: Drinking a cup of coffee while standing at the bar is cheaper than drinking it at an indoor table (you'll pay still more at an outdoor table). Many places have a *lista dei prezzi* (price list) with two columns—*al bar* and *al tavolo* (table)—posted somewhere by the bar or cash register. If you're on a budget, don't sit down without first checking out the financial consequences. Throughout Italy, you can get cheap coffee at the bar of any establishment, no matter how fancy, and pay the same low, government-regulated price (generally about a euro if you stand).

Tavola Calda Bars and Rosticcerie

For a fast and cheap lunch, find an Italian variation on the corner deli: a *rosticceria* (specializing in roasted meats and accompanying *antipasti*) or a *tavola calda* bar (a "hot table" point-and-shoot cafeteria with a buffet spread of meat and vegetables). With a pointing finger, you can assemble a fine meal. If something's a mystery, ask for *un assaggio* (oon ah-SAH-

joh) to get a little taste. To have your choices warmed up, ask for them to be heated (*riscaldare;* ree-skahl-DAH-ray).

Wine Bars

Wine bars (*enoteche*) are a popular, fast, and inexpensive option for lunch. Surrounded by the office crowd, you can get a salad, a plate of meats (cold cuts) and cheeses, and a glass of good wine (see blackboards for the day's selection and price per glass). A good *enoteca* aims to impress visitors with its wine and will generally feature excellent-quality ingredients for the simple dishes it offers with the wine (though the prices add up—be careful with your ordering to keep this a budget choice).

Aperitivo Buffets

The Italian term *aperitivo* means a predinner drink, but it's also used to describe their version of what we might call happy hour: a light buffet that many bars serve to customers during the predinner hours (typically around 18:00 or 19:00 until 21:00). The drink itself may not be cheap (typically around €8-12), but bars lay out an enticing array of meats, cheeses, grilled vegetables, and other *antipasti*-type dishes, and you're welcome to nibble to your heart's content while you nurse your drink. Bars advertising *"apericena"* (*cena* means dinner) tend to have buffets hearty enough to pass as dinner.

Markets, Groceries, and Delis

Picnicking saves lots of euros and is a great way to sample regional specialties. For the most colorful experience, gather your ingredients in the morning at a **produce market.** Towns big and small have markets selling everything imaginable for a fantastic picnic, including cheese, meat, bread, sweets, and prepared foods.

Another budget option is to visit a **supermarket** (look for the Conad, Carrefour, and Co-op chains), *alimentari* (neighborhood grocery), or *salumeria* (del-

icatessen) to pick up cold cuts, cheeses, and other picnic supplies.

At a market or a grocery, use gestures to show exactly how much you want. The word *basta* (BAH-stah; enough) works as a question or as a statement. Shopkeepers are happy to sell small quantities of produce, but it's customary to let the merchant choose for you.

Gelato

Most *gelaterie* clearly display prices and sizes. Point to the price or say what you want—for instance, a €3 cup: *"Una coppetta da tre euro"* (OO-nah koh-PEH-tah dah tray eh-OO-roh).

The best *gelaterie* display signs reading *artigianale, nostra produzione,* or *produzione propria,* indicating that the gelato is made on the premises. Seasonal flavors are also a good sign, as are mellow hues (avoid colors that don't appear in nature). Gelato stored in covered metal tins (rather than white plastic) is more likely to be homemade. Gourmet gelato shops are popping up all over Italy, selling exotic flavors.

Gelato variations or alternatives include *sorbetto* (sorbet—made with fruit, but no milk or eggs); *granita* or *grattachecca* (a cup of slushy ice with flavored syrup); and *cremolata* (a gelato-*granita* float).

Beverages

Italian bars serve great drinks—hot, cold, sweet, caffeinated, or alcoholic.

Water, Juice, and Cold Drinks

Italians are notorious water snobs. At restaurants, your server just can't understand why you wouldn't want good water to go with your good food. It's customary and never expensive to order a *litro* or *mezzo litro* (half-liter) of bottled water. *Acqua leggermente effervescente* (lightly carbonated water) is a mealtime favorite. Or simply ask for *con gas* if you want fizzy water and *senza gas* if you prefer still water. You can ask for *acqua del rubinetto* (tap water) in restaurants, but your server may give you a funny look. Chilled bottled water—still *(naturale)* or carbonated *(frizzante)*—is sold cheaply in stores.

Juice is *succo,* and *spremuta* means freshly squeezed. Order *una spremuta* (don't confuse it with *spumante,* sparkling wine). In grocery stores, you can get a liter of O.J. for the price of a Coke or coffee. Look for *100% succo* or *senza zucchero* (without sugar) on the label.

Tè freddo (iced tea) is usually from a can—sweetened and flavored with lemon or peach. Lemonade is *limonata.*

Coffee

The espresso-based style of coffee so popular in the US was born in Italy. If you ask for *"un caffè,"* you'll get a shot of espresso in a little cup—the closest thing to American-style drip coffee is a *caffè americano.* Most Italian coffee drinks begin with espresso, to which they add varying amounts of hot water and/or steamed or foamed milk. Milky drinks, like cappuccino or *caffè latte,* are served to locals before noon and to tourists any time of day. If they add any milk after lunch, it's just a splash, in a *caffè macchiato.* Any coffee drink is available decaffeinated—ask for it *decaffeinato* (deh-kah-feh-NAH-toh).

Cappuccino: Espresso with foamed milk on top (*cappuccino freddo* is iced)

Caffè latte: Espresso mixed with hot milk, no foam, in a tall glass (ordering just a "latte" gets you only milk)

Caffè macchiato: Espresso "marked" with a splash of milk, in a small cup

Latte macchiato: Layers of hot milk and foam, "marked" by an espresso shot, in a tall glass.

Caffè corto/lungo: Concentrated espresso diluted with a tiny bit of hot water, in a small cup

Caffè americano: Espresso diluted with even more hot water, in a larger cup

Caffè corretto: Espresso "corrected" with a shot of liqueur (normally grappa, *amaro,* or *sambuca*)

Marocchino: "Moroccan" coffee with espresso, foamed milk, and cocoa powder; the similar *mocaccino* has chocolate instead of cocoa

Caffè freddo: Sweet and iced espresso

Caffè hag: Instant decaf

Alcoholic Beverages

Beer: While Italy is traditionally considered wine country, in recent years there's been a huge and passionate growth in the production of craft beer *(birra artigianale).* You'll find local brews (Peroni and Moretti) as well as imports such as Heineken. Italians drink mainly lager beers. Beer on tap is *alla spina.* Get it *piccola* (33 cl, 11 oz), *media* (50 cl, about a pint), or *grande* (a liter). A *lattina* (lah-TEE-nah) is a can and a *bottiglia* (boh-TEEL-yah) is a bottle.

Cocktails and Spirits: Italians appreciate both *aperitivi* (palate-stimulating cocktails) and *digestivi* (after-dinner drinks designed to aid digestion). Popular *aperitivo* options include Campari (carmine-red bitters with herbs and orange peel), Americano (vermouth with bitters, brandy, and lemon peel), Cynar (bitters flavored with artichoke), Aperol (bright orange bitters with herbal, citrusy undertones) and Punt e Mes (sweet red

Ordering Wine

To order a glass of red or white wine, say, *"Un bicchiere di vino rosso/bianco."* House wine comes in a carafe; choose from a quarter-liter (8.5 oz, *un quarto*), half-liter (17 oz, *un mezzo*), or one-liter pitcher (34 oz, *un litro*). *Salute!*

English	Italian
wine	*vino* (VEE-noh)
house wine	*vino della casa* (VEE-noh DEH-lah KAH-zah)
glass	*bicchiere/calice* (bee-kee-EH-ray/ KAH-lee-chay)
bottle	*bottiglia* (boh-TEEL-yah)
carafe	*caraffa* (kah-RAH-fah)
red	*rosso* (ROH-soh)
white	*bianco* (bee-AHN-koh)
rosé	*rosato* (roh-ZAH-toh)
sparkling	*spumante / frizzante* (spoo-MAHN-tay / freed-ZAHN-tay)

vermouth and red wine). Widely used vermouth brands include Cinzano and Martini.

Digestivo choices are usually either strong herbal bitters or something sweet. Many restaurants have their own secret recipe for a bittersweet herbal brew called *amaro;* popular commercial brands are Fernet Branca and Montenegro. If your tastes run sweeter, try any of these flavored liqueurs: *amaretto* (almond), Frangelico (hazelnut), *limoncello* (lemon), *nocino* (walnut), *sambuca* (anise), or a sweet Marsala wine. Grappa is a brandy distilled from grape skins and stems; *stravecchio* is an aged, mellower variation.

Wine: Even if you're clueless about wine, the information on an Italian wine label can help you choose something decent. Terms you may see on the bottle

include *classico* (from a defined, select area), *annata* (year of harvest), *vendemmia* (harvest), and *imbottigliato dal produttore all'origine* (bottled by producers).

In general, Italy designates its wines by one of four official categories:

Vino da Tavola (VDT) is table wine, the lowest grade, made from grapes grown anywhere in Italy. It's often inexpensive, but Italy's wines are so good that, for many people, a basic *vino da tavola* is just fine with a meal.

Denominazione di Origine Controllata (DOC) meets national standards for high-quality wine made from grapes grown in a defined area.

Denominazione di Origine Controllata e Guarantita (DOCG) wines, the highest grade, can be identified by the pink or green label on the neck of the bottle...and the scary price tag on the shelf. They're generally a good bet if you want a quality wine. (*Riserva* indicates a DOC or DOCG wine that's been aged for even longer than required.)

Indicazione Geografica Tipica (IGT) is a broad group of wines that don't meet the standard for DOC or DOCG status, but have been designated as "typical" of a particular region.

STAYING CONNECTED

One of the most common questions I hear from travelers is, "How can I stay connected in Europe?" The short answer is: more easily and cheaply than you might think. The simplest solution is to bring your own device—mobile phone, tablet, or laptop—and use it just as you would at home (following the money-saving tips below). For more details, see *RickSteves.com/phoning.* For a very practical one-hour talk covering tech issues for travelers, see *RickSteves.com/ mobile-travel-skills.*

How to Dial

To make an international call, follow the dialing instructions below. Drop an initial zero, if present, when dialing a European phone number—except when calling Italy. I've used the telephone number of one of my recommended Rome hotels as an example (tel. 06-482-8334).

From a Mobile Phone

It's easy to dial with a mobile phone. Whether calling from the US to Europe, country to country within Europe, or from Europe to the US—it's all the same. Press zero until you get a + sign, enter the country code (39 for Italy), then dial the phone number.

▶ To call the Rome hotel from any location, dial +39 06 482 8334.

From a US Landline to Europe

Dial 011 (US/Canada access code), country code (39 for Italy), and phone number.

▶ To call the Rome hotel from your home phone, dial 011 39 06 482 8334.

From a European Landline to the US or Europe

Dial 00 (Europe access code), country code (1 for the US, 39 for Italy), and phone number.

▶ To call my US office from Italy, dial 00 1 425 771 8303.
▶ To call the Rome hotel from Germany, dial 00 34 06 482 8334.

For a complete list of European country codes and more phoning help, see HowToCallAbroad.com.

Using a Mobile Phone in Europe

Sign up for an international plan. To stay connected at a lower cost, sign up for an international service plan through your carrier. Most providers offer a simple bundle that includes calling, messaging, and data. Your normal plan may already include international coverage (T-Mobile's does).

Use free Wi-Fi whenever possible. Unless you have an unlimited-data plan, you're best off saving most of your online tasks for Wi-Fi. You can access the internet, send texts, and even make voice calls over Wi-Fi.

Minimize the use of your cellular network. The best way to make sure you're not accidentally burning through data is to put your device in "airplane" mode (which also disables phone calls and texts), turn your Wi-Fi back on, and connect to networks as needed. When you need to get online but can't find Wi-Fi, simply turn on your cellular network (or turn off airplane mode) just long enough for the task at hand. Disable automatic updates so your apps will update only when you're on Wi-Fi.

Use Wi-Fi calling and messaging apps. Skype, WhatsApp, FaceTime, and Google Hangouts are great for making free or low-cost calls or sending texts over Wi-Fi worldwide. Just log on to a Wi-Fi network, then connect with any of your friends or family members who use the same service.

Tips on Internet Security

Make sure that your device is running the latest versions of its operating system, security software, and apps. Next, ensure that your device and key programs (like email) are password-protected. On the road, use only secure, password-protected Wi-Fi. Ask the hotel or café staff for the specific name of their network, and make sure you log on to that exact one.

If you must access your financial info online, use a banking app rather than accessing your account via a browser, and use a cellular connection, not Wi-Fi. Never log on to personal finance sites on a public computer. If you're very concerned, consider subscribing to a VPN (virtual private network).

Buy a European SIM Card. If you anticipate making a lot of local calls or need a local phone number, or if your provider's international data rates are expensive, consider buying a SIM card in Europe to replace the one in your (unlocked) US phone or tablet.

In Italy, buy SIM cards at mobile-phone shops. You'll be required to register the SIM card with your passport as an anti-terrorism measure. There are no roaming charges when using a European SIM card in other EU countries, though to be sure you get this "roam-like-at-home" pricing, ask if this feature is included when you buy your SIM card.

TRANSPORTATION

Figuring out how to get around in Europe is one of your biggest trip decisions. **Cars** work well for two or more traveling together (especially families with small kids), those packing heavy, and those delving into the countryside. **Trains** and **buses** are best for solo travelers, blitz tourists, city-to-city travelers, and those who want to leave the driving to others. Smart travelers can use short-hop **flights** within Europe to creatively connect the dots on their itineraries.

If your itinerary mixes cities and countryside, my advice is to connect cities by train or bus and to explore rural areas by rental car. Arrange to pick up your car in the last big city you'll visit, then use it to lace together small towns and explore the countryside. For more detailed information on transportation throughout Europe, see RickSteves.com/transportation.

Trains

To travel by train affordably within Italy, you can simply buy tickets as you go. For travelers ready to lock in dates and times weeks or months in advance, buying nonrefundable tickets online can cut costs in half (note that the Italy rail pass is generally not a good value). For advice on figuring out the smartest train-ticket or rail-pass options for your trip, visit the Trains & Rail Passes section of my website at RickSteves.com/rail.

Types of Trains

Most trains in Italy are operated by the state-run **Trenitalia** company (www.trenitalia.com, a.k.a. Ferrovie dello Stato Italiane, abbreviated FS). Ticket prices depend on the speed of the train, so it helps to know the different types of trains: pokey Regionale (R or REG); medium-speed Regionale Veloce (RV); fast InterCity (IC) and EuroCity (EC); and super-fast Frecce trains. All Frecce trains, many EuroCity and InterCity trains, and most international trains require reservations.

Regional trains offer only open seat-

Rail Pass or Point-to-Point Tickets?

Will you be better off buying a rail pass or point-to-point tickets? It pays to know your options and choose what's best for your itinerary.

Rail Passes

A Eurail Italy Pass lets you travel by train in Italy for three to eight days (consecutively or not) within a one-month period. Italy is also covered (along with most of Europe) by the classic Eurail Global Pass.

Discounted rates are offered for seniors (age 60 and up) and youths (ages 12-27). Up to two kids (ages 4-11) can travel free with each adult-rate pass (but not with senior rates). All rail passes offer a choice of first or second class for all ages.

Rail passes are best purchased outside Europe (through travel agents or Rick Steves' Europe). For more on rail passes, including current prices, visit Rick Steves.com/rail.

Point-to-Point Tickets

Italian train tickets are relatively cheap, and most include seat reservations, making them the best deal for most travelers. Use this map to add up approximate pay-as-you-go fares for your itinerary, and compare that to the price of a rail pass plus reservations. Keep in mind that significant discounts on point-to-point tickets may be available with advance purchase.

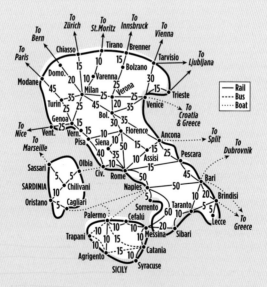

Map shows approximate costs, in US dollars, for one-way, second-class tickets on faster trains.

ing (no assigned seats); all other classes of service come with an assigned seat. If you're traveling with a rail pass, you'll need to reserve a seat for any service but regional trains (see below under "Rail Passes," later).

The private train company called **Italo** (www.italotreno.it) runs fast trains on major routes in Italy. Italo is focused on two corridors: Venice-Padua-Bologna-Florence-Rome-Salerno and Turin-Milan-Bologna-Florence-Rome-Naples. They also run a useful Milan-Venice train. Italo has fewer departures than Trenitalia but offers discounts for tickets booked well in advance. In Naples, Milan, and Rome, some departures use secondary stations—pay attention to which station you need. Italo does not accept rail passes.

Schedules

Check schedules at Trenitalia.it and ItaloTreno.it (domestic journeys only) or use their apps; for international trips, use Bahn.com (Germany's excellent all-Europe schedule website). At the train station, the easiest way to check schedules is at a ticket machine. Enter the desired date, time, and destination to see all your options. Printed schedules are also posted at the station (yellow posters show departures—partenze; white posters show arrivals).

Buying Point-to-Point Tickets

You can buy tickets online, with a smartphone app, at train station ticket windows, from ticket machines, or at travel agencies. For long-haul runs or travel on a busy weekend or holiday, it can be cheaper to buy tickets in advance. But because most Italian trains run frequently and there's no deadline to buy tickets, for the most part I prefer to keep my travel plans flexible by purchasing tickets as I go.

It's easy to buy tickets **online** at Treni-talia.com or ItaloTreno.it. On either website, choose English and be sure to read the pricing info, as many of the cheaper tickets are not refundable or changeable. You can keep the ticket on your mobile device (either as a PDF or in a "ticketless" format with a booking code), or you can print it out.

Or download the Trenitalia or Italo app to your **phone**—both have English versions. If using the Trenitalia app to buy tickets, do so as a guest (a log-in isn't necessary—or possible—if you don't live in Italy).

At the train station, use the **ticket machines** in station halls. You'll be able to easily purchase tickets for travel within Italy, make seat reservations, and even book a cuccetta (koo-CHEH-tah; overnight berth). If you do use the **ticket windows** (e.g., to buy international tickets), be sure you're in the correct line. Key terms: biglietti (general tickets), prenotazioni (reservations), nazionali (domestic), and internazionali.

To buy tickets at the station for **Italo** trains, look for a dedicated service counter (in most major stations) or a red ticket machine labeled Italo.

Some **international tickets** can't be bought online or from machines; for these tickets and anything else that requires a real person, you must go to a ticket window at the station. A good alternative, though, is to drop by a local travel agency. Agencies sell domestic and international tickets and make reservations. They charge a small fee, but the language barrier (and the lines) can be smaller than at the station's ticket windows.

Rail Passes

The single-country Eurail Italy Pass may save you money if you take several long train rides or prefer first-class travel, but for most people it's not a good value. Most train travelers in Italy take relatively short rides on the Milan-Venice-Florence-Rome

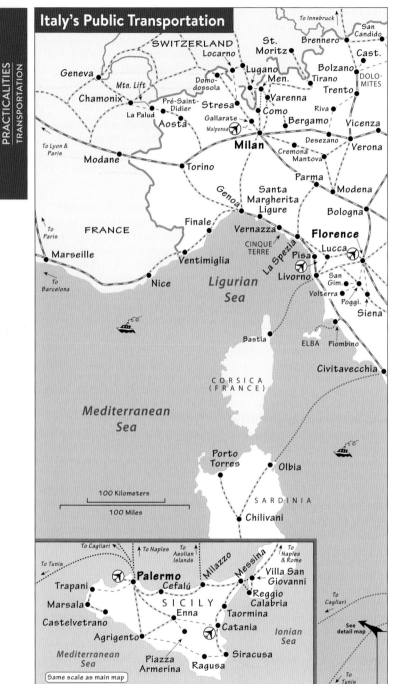

Italy's Public Transportation

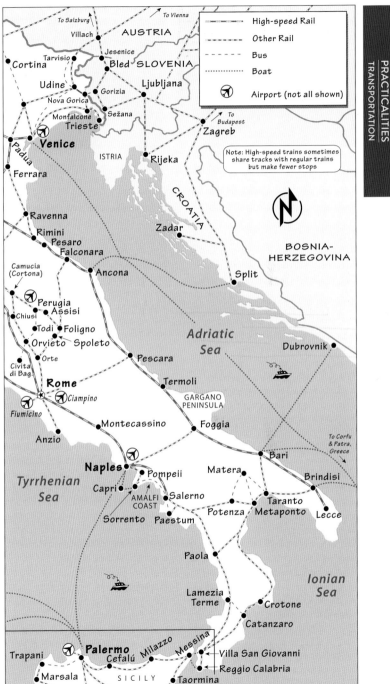

circuit. For these trips, it can be cheaper to buy point-to-point tickets. Remember that rail passes are valid only on Trenitalia trains (not on Italo trains).

Train Tips

Validating Tickets: If your ticket includes a seat reservation on a specific train (*biglietto con prenotazione*), you're all set and can just get on board. The same is true for any ticket bought online or with the Trenitalia or Italo apps (whether open or reserved seating); these tickets are considered already validated.

An open ticket (generally for a *regionale* train) bought from a ticket desk or machine must be validated (date-stamped) before you board (the ticket may say *da convalidare* or *convalida*). To validate it, before getting on the train, stamp your ticket in the machine near the platform (usually marked *convalida biglietti* or *vidimazione*). Once you validate a ticket, you must complete your trip within the stamped timeframe (usually about four hours).

Baggage Storage: Many Italian stations have *deposito bagagli* where you can safely leave your bag for a standardized but steep price (€6/5 hours, €12/12 hours, €17/24 hours, payable when you pick up the bag, double-check closing hours; they may ask to photocopy your passport). Due to security concerns, no Italian stations have lockers.

Theft: In big cities, exercise caution and prudence at train stations to avoid thieves and con artists. If someone helps you to find your train or carry your bags, be aware that they are not an official porter; they are simply hoping for some cash. And if someone other than a uniformed railway employee tries to help you use the ticket machines, politely refuse.

Italian trains are famous for their thieves. Never leave a bag unattended. Police do ride the trains, cutting down on theft. Still, for an overnight trip, I'd feel safe only in a *cuccetta* (a bunk in a special sleeping car with an attendant who keeps track of who comes and goes while you sleep—approximately €40 or more).

Strikes: Strikes, which are common, generally last a day (often a Friday). Train employees will simply explain, *"Sciopero"* (SHOH-peh-roh, strike). But in actuality, a minimum amount of "essential" main-line service is maintained (by law) during strikes. When a strike is pending, travel agencies, savvy hoteliers, and remaining station personnel can check to see when the strike will go into effect and which trains will continue to run. Revised schedules may be posted online and in Italian at stations. Visit *Trenitalia.com*, choose English, then "Information and Contacts," and then "In Case of Strike."

Buses

You can usually get anywhere you want in Italy by bus, as long as you're not in a hurry and plan ahead (pick up bus schedules at local TIs or bus stations). For reaching small towns, buses are sometimes the only option if you don't have a car. In many hill towns, trains leave you at a station in the valley far below, while buses more likely drop you right into the thick of things. (If the bus stop or station is below town, sometimes an escalator or elevator helps get you up into town.)

Long-distance buses are catching on in Italy as an alternative to the train. Some of the operators you'll see are Megabus (www.megabus.com), Flixbus (http://global.flixbus.com), and Marozzi (www.marozzivt.it).

Larger towns have a (usually chaotic) long-distance bus station (*stazione degli autobus*), with ticket windows and several stalls (usually labeled *corsia, stallo,* or *binario*)—but to save time, buy your ticket at a travel agent or online, and print it out. Smaller towns—where buses are more useful—often have a central bus stop (*fermata*), likely along the main road or on the main square, and maybe several more scattered around town. In small towns, buy bus tickets at newsstands or tobacco shops (with the big T signs). When buying your ticket, confirm the departure point (*"Dov'è la fermata?"*).

Taxis and Ride-Booking Services

Most Italian taxis are reliable and cheap. In many cities, two people can travel short distances by cab for little more than the cost of bus or subway tickets. If you like ride-booking services such as Uber, their apps usually work in Europe just like they do in the US. In Italy, however, Uber faces legal challenges, and may not be consistently available (for instance, Uber does not operate in Florence).

Renting a Car

It's cheaper to arrange most car rentals from the US, so research and compare rates before you go. Most of the major US rental agencies (including Avis, Budget, Enterprise, Hertz, and Thrifty) have offices throughout Europe. Also consider the two major Europe-based agencies, Europcar and Sixt. Consolidators such as Auto Europe (www.autoeurope.com—or the sometimes cheaper www.autoeurope.eu) compare rates at several companies to get you the best deal.

Rental Costs and Considerations

Figure on paying roughly $250 for a one-week rental for a basic compact car. Allow extra for supplemental insurance, fuel, tolls, and parking. To save money on fuel, request a diesel car.

Manual vs. Automatic: Almost all rental cars in Europe are manual by default—and cars with a stick shift are generally cheaper. If you need an automatic, request one in advance.

Age Restrictions: Some rental companies impose minimum and maximum age limits. Young drivers (25 and under) and seniors (69 and up) should check the rental policies and rules section of car-rental websites.

Choosing Pick-Up/Drop-off Locations: Always check the hours of the locations you choose: Many rental offices close from midday Saturday until Monday morning and, in smaller towns, at lunchtime. Be aware that most Italian cities have a "ZTL" (limited traffic zone) that's carefully monitored by cameras. If your drop-off point is near this zone, get clear directions on how to get there to avoid getting a big fine.

Have the Right License: If you're renting a car in Italy, bring your driver's license. You're also technically required to have an International Driving Permit—an official translation of your license (sold at AAA offices for about $20 plus the cost of two passport-type photos; see www.aaa.com). While that's the letter of the law, I generally rent cars without having this permit. How this is enforced varies from country to country: Get advice from your car-rental company.

Picking Up Your Car: Before driving off in your rental car, check it thoroughly and make sure any damage is noted on your rental agreement. Rental agencies in Europe tend to charge for even minor damage, so be sure to mark everything. Find out how your car's gearshift, lights, turn signals, wipers, radio, and fuel cap function, and know what kind of fuel the car takes (diesel vs. unleaded). When you return the car, make sure the agent verifies its condition with you. Some drivers take pictures of the returned vehicle as proof of its condition.

Car Insurance Options

When you rent a car in Europe, the price typically includes liability insurance, which covers harm to other cars or motorists—but not the rental car itself. To limit your financial risk in case of damage to the rental, choose one of these options: Buy a Collision Damage Waiver (CDW) with a low or zero deductible from the car-rental company (roughly 30-40 percent extra), get coverage through your credit card (free, but more complicated), or get collision insurance as part of a larger travel-insurance policy. For more on car-rental insurance, see RickSteves.com/cdw.

Navigation Options

Your Mobile Phone: If you'll be navigating using your phone, remember to bring a car charger and device mount. Driving all day can burn through a lot of very expensive data. The economical work-around is to use map apps that work offline. By downloading in advance from Google Maps, City Maps 2Go, Apple Maps, Here WeGo, or Navmii, you can still have turn-by-turn voice directions and maps that recalibrate even though they're offline.

You must download your maps before you go offline—and it's smart to select large regions. Then turn off your data connection so you're not charged for roaming. This option is great for navigating in areas with poor connectivity.

GPS Devices: If you want the convenience of a dedicated GPS unit, consider renting one with your car ($10-30/day). These units offer real-time turn-by-turn

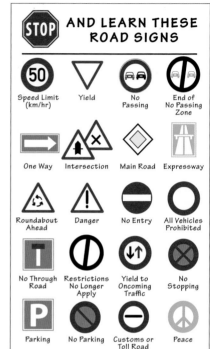

directions and traffic without the data requirements of an app.

Paper Maps and Atlases: Even when navigating primarily with a mobile app or GPS, I always make it a point to have a paper map, ideally a big, detailed regional road map (easy to buy locally at bookstores or gas stations). It's invaluable for getting the big picture, understanding alternate routes, and filling in if my phone runs out of juice.

Driving

Driving in Italy can be scary—a video game for keeps, and you only get one quarter. Locals drive fast and tailgate as if it were required. They pass where Americans are taught not to—on blind corners and just before tunnels. Roads have narrow shoulders or none at all. Driving in the countryside is less stressful than driving through urban areas or on busy highways, but stay alert.

Driving in Italy

AUSTRIA

Brenner Pass

SWITZERLAND

Villach

Dolomites (Bolzano)

Mt. Blanc Tunnel

Lake Como (Varenna)

SLOVENIA

70m·2h

260m·5h

160m·4.5h (via Cortina)

155m·2.5h

Trieste

95m·1.75h

145m·2.5h

110m·2.5h

100m·1.5h

30m·.75h

100m·1.75h

Venice

Milan

Verona

80m·1.5h

200m·4h

185m·3.25h

225m·4h

155m·3h

85m·2.5h

Ravenna

CROATIA

175m·2.75h

135m·2.5h

155m·2.5h

115m·2h

Adriatic Sea

160m·2.75h

90m·1.75h

Florence

FRANCE

Cinque Terre (La Spezia)

50m·1h

70m·1.5h

100m·2h

125m·2.25h

Ligurian Sea

Pisa

45m·1h

80m·2h

Venti-miglia

Siena

100m·1.75h

Assisi

115m·2.25h

75m·1.5h

55m·1.5h

m = miles h = hours
Note: Your times may vary based on traffic, construction, and road conditions.

Orvieto

2·10m·4h

75m·1.5h

Rome

Mediterranean Sea

155m·2.5h

SARDINIA (ITALY)

Tyrrhenian Sea

Naples

35m·1h

Salerno

30m·.75h

30m·1h

Sorrento

30m·1.5h

Paestum

Road Rules: Car traffic is restricted in many city centers. Don't drive or park in any area that has a sign reading *Zona Traffico Limitato* (ZTL, often shown above a red circle—see image). If you do, your license plate will likely be photographed and a hefty (€80-plus) ticket mailed to

your home. Bumbling in and out of these zones can net you multiple fines. If your hotel is within a restricted area, ask your hotelier to direct you to parking.

Be aware of typical European road rules; for example, many countries require headlights to be turned on at all times, and you're not allowed to turn right on a red light unless a sign or signal specifically authorizes it. Ask your car-rental company about these rules, or check the "International Travel" section of the US State Department website (www.travel. state.gov, search for your country in the "Learn about your destination" box, then click "Travel and Transportation").

Tolls: You'll pay tolls for some stretches of freeway (autostrada; for costs, use the trip-planning tool at www.autostrade.it or search "European Tolls" on www.theaa. com). When approaching a tollbooth, skip lanes marked Telepass; for an attended booth, choose a lane with a sign that shows a hand or coins.

Fuel: Fuel is expensive—often about $6.50 per gallon for unleaded and a bit less for diesel. Diesel cars are more common in Europe than back home, so be sure you know what type of fuel your car takes before you fill up. Gas pumps are color-coded: green for unleaded (*senza piombo*); black for diesel (*gasolio*). You'll also see the term *benzina,* which is standard fuel. If you are unsure or need help, stop for full-service gas (*servito*). To fill up, say *"Pieno"* (pee-EH-noh). Autostrada rest stops can have full- or self-service stations (open daily without a siesta break). Many 24-hour stations are entirely automated.

Maps and Signage: Learn the universal road signs (see illustration). Although roads are numbered on maps, actual road signs give just a city name (for example, if you were heading west out of Venice, the map would be marked "route S-11"—but you'd follow signs to Padua, the next town along this road). Signs are inconsistent: They may direct you to the nearest big city or simply the next town along the route.

Theft: Cars are routinely vandalized and stolen. Thieves easily recognize rental cars and assume they are filled with a tourist's gear. Be sure all of your valuables are out of sight and locked in the trunk, or even better, with you or in your room.

Parking: White lines generally mean parking is free. Yellow lines mean that parking is reserved for residents only (who have permits). Blue lines mean you'll have to pay.

Zona disco has nothing to do with dancing. Italian cars come equipped with a time disc (a cardboard clock), which you can use in a *zona disco*—set the clock to your arrival time and leave it on the dashboard. (If your rental car doesn't come with a *disco*, pick one up at a tobacco shop

or just write your arrival time on a piece of paper and place it on the dashboard.) These are generally used in areas where parking is free but has a time limit.

Garages are safe, save time, and help you avoid the stress of parking tickets. Take the parking voucher with you to pay the cashier before you leave.

Flights

To compare flight costs and times, begin with an online travel search engine: Kayak is the top site for flights to and within Europe, easy-to-use Google Flights has price alerts, and Skyscanner includes many inexpensive flights within Europe. To avoid unpleasant surprises, before you book be sure to read the small print about refunds, changes, and the costs for "extras" such as reserving a seat, checking a bag, or printing a boarding pass.

Flights to Europe: Start looking for international flights about four to six months before your trip, especially for peak-season travel. Depending on your itinerary, it can be efficient and no more expensive to fly into one city and out of another. If your flight requires a connection in Europe, see my hints on navigating Europe's top hub airports at RickSteves. com/hub-airports.

Flights Within Europe: Flying between European cities is surprisingly affordable. Before buying a long-distance train or bus ticket, check the cost of a flight on one of Europe's airlines, whether a major carrier or a no-frills outfit like Easyjet or Ryanair. Be aware that flying with a discount airline can have drawbacks, such as minimal customer service and time-consuming treks to secondary airports.

Flying to the US and Canada: Because security is extra tight for flights to the US, be sure to give yourself plenty of time at the airport. Charge your electronic devices before you board in case security checks require you to turn them on (see www.tsa.gov for the latest rules).

Resources from Rick Steves

Begin Your Trip at RickSteves.com

My mobile-friendly website is the place to explore Europe in preparation for your trip. You'll find thousands of fun articles, videos, and radio interviews; a wealth of money-saving tips for planning your dream trip; travel news dispatches; a video library of my travel talks; my travel blog; tips on finding the right rail pass for your itinerary and budget, and our latest guidebook updates (www.ricksteves.com/update).

Our **Travel Forum** is a well-groomed collection of message boards where our travel-savvy community answers questions and shares personal travel experiences—and our well-traveled staff chimes in when they can be helpful.

. Our **online Travel Store** offers bags and accessories designed to help you travel smarter and lighter. These include my popular carry-on bags (which I live out of four months a year), money belts, totes, toiletries kits, adapters, and guidebooks.

Rick Steves' Tours, Guidebooks, TV Shows, and More

Small Group Tours: We offer more than 40 itineraries reaching the best destinations in this book...and beyond. You'll enjoy great guides and a fun bunch of travel partners. For all the details and to get a tour catalog, visit RickSteves.com/tours or call us at 425/608-4217.

Books: This book is just one of many in my series on European travel, which includes country and city guidebooks, Snapshots (excerpted chapters from bigger guides), Pocket guides (full-color little books on big cities), and my budget-travel skills handbook, *Rick Steves Europe Through the Back Door*. A complete list of titles appears near the end of this book.

TV Shows and Travel Talks: My public television series, *Rick Steves' Europe*, covers Europe from top to bottom with over 100 half-hour episodes (watch them at the website). My free online video library, Rick Steves Classroom Europe, offers a searchable database of short video clips on European history, culture, and geography. And, to raise your travel I.Q., check out the video versions of our popular classes (covering most European countries as well as travel skills).

Audio Tours on My Free App: I've produced dozens of free, self-guided audio tours of the top sights in Europe. For those tours and other audio content, get my free **Rick Steves Audio Europe app,** an extensive online library organized by destination. For more on the app, see page 28.

Radio: My weekly public radio show, *Travel with Rick Steves,* features interviews with travel experts from around the world. It airs on 400 public radio stations across the US, or you can hear it as a podcast. A complete archive of programs is available on my website.

Podcasts: You can enjoy my travel content via several free podcasts, including my radio show, clips from my public television show, my audio tours of Europe's top sights, and my travel classes.

HOLIDAYS AND FESTIVALS

This list includes selected festivals in major cities, plus national holidays observed throughout Italy (when many sights and banks close). Before planning a trip around a festival, verify the dates with the festival website, the national tourist office (www.italia.it), or RickSteves.com.

Jan 1	New Year's Day
Jan 6	Epiphany
Late Jan/early Feb	Carnevale, Venice (Mardi Gras, www.carnevale.venezia.it)
March/April	Easter weekend; Scoppio del Carro fireworks in Florence on Easter Sunday
April	Vinitaly wine festival, Verona (www.vinitaly.com)
April 25	Italian Liberation Day; Feast of St. Mark, Venice
May 1	Labor Day
May (third Sun)	Monterosso Lemon Festival, Cinque Terre
May 21	Ascension Day
June 2	Anniversary of the Republic
June	Feast of Corpus Christi
June 24	St. John the Baptist Day, Florence (parades, dances, and boat races)
June 29	Sts. Peter and Paul Day, most fervently celebrated in Rome
June-Aug	Verona opera season
July 2	Palio horse race, Siena
July (third weekend)	Feast and Regatta of the Redeemer, Venice
Aug 15	Feast of the Assumption (Ferragosto)
Aug 16	Palio horse race, Siena
Early Sept (first weekend)	Historical Regatta, Venice
Sept 19	St. Januarius Day, Naples
Sept-Oct	Chestnut festivals, mainly towns north of Rome (chestnut roasts)
Late Sept/early Oct	Musica dei Popoli Festival, Florence (folk music and dances)
Nov 1	All Saints' Day
Dec	Christmas market, Rome, Piazza Navona
Dec 8	Feast of the Immaculate Conception
Dec 25	Christmas
Dec 26	St. Stephen's Day

CONVERSIONS

Numbers and Stumblers

- Europeans write a few of their numbers differently than we do. 1=1, 4 = 4, 7 =7.
- In Europe, dates appear as day/month/year, so Christmas 2023 is 25/12/23.
- Commas are decimal points and decimals commas. A dollar and a half is $1,50, one thousand is 1.000, and there are 5.280 feet in a mile.
- When counting with fingers, start with your thumb. If you hold up your first finger to request one item, you'll probably get two.
- What Americans call the second floor of a building is the first floor in Europe.
- On escalators and moving sidewalks, Europeans keep the left "lane" open for passing. Keep to the right.

Metric Conversions

A **kilogram** equals 1,000 grams (about 2.2 pounds). One hundred **grams** (a common unit at markets) is about a quarter-pound. One **liter** is about a quart, or almost four to a gallon.

Clothing Sizes

Women: For pants and dresses, add 36 in Italy (US 10 = Italian 46). For blouses and sweaters, add 8 for most of Europe (US 32 = European 40). For shoes, add 30-31 (US 7 = European 37/38).

Men: For shirts, multiply by 2 and add about 8 (US 15 = European 38). For jackets and suits, add 10. For shoes, add 32-34.

Children: Clothing is sized by height—in centimeters (2.5 cm = 1 inch), so a US size 8 roughly equates to 132-140. For shoes up to size 13, add 16-18, and for sizes 1 and up, add 30-32.

ITALY'S CLIMATE

First line, average daily high; second line, average daily low; third line, average days without rain. For more detailed weather statistics for destinations in this book (as well as the rest of the world), check www.wunderground.com.

Rome

J	F	M	A	M	J	J	A	S	O	N	D
55°	57°	63°	68°	75°	84°	90°	86°	81°	73°	64°	59°
37°	37	43°	46°	55°	63°	66°	64°	61°	54°	46°	39°
24	22	24	21	24	26	28	31	24	23	22	22

Florence

J	F	M	A	M	J	J	A	S	O	N	D
54°	54°	59°	66°	75°	82°	88°	88°	81°	70°	59°	52°
37°	39°	43°	48°	55°	63°	66°	64°	61°	54°	45°	39°
25	21	24	23	24	23	27	26	22	22	21	23

Venice

J	F	M	A	M	J	J	A	S	O	N	D
42°	46°	53°	62°	70°	76°	81°	80°	75°	65°	53°	46°
33°	35°	41°	49°	56°	63°	66°	65°	61°	53°	44°	37°
25	21	24	21	23	22	24	24	25	24	21	23

Naples

J	F	M	A	M	J	J	A	S	O	N	D
54°	56°	59°	65°	73°	79°	85°	85°	79°	71°	63°	57°
39°	40°	43°	47°	54°	60°	64°	64°	60°	53°	46°	41°
21	18	21	21	25	26	29	27	24	23	19	20

Packing Checklist

Whether you're traveling for five days or five weeks, you won't need more than this. Pack light to enjoy the sweet freedom of true mobility.

Clothing

- ❑ 5 shirts: long- & short-sleeve
- ❑ 2 pairs pants (or skirts/capris)
- ❑ 1 pair shorts
- ❑ 5 pairs underwear & socks
- ❑ 1 pair walking shoes
- ❑ Sweater or warm layer
- ❑ Rainproof jacket with hood
- ❑ Tie, scarf, belt, and/or hat
- ❑ Swimsuit
- ❑ Sleepwear/loungewear

Money

- ❑ Debit card(s)
- ❑ Credit card(s)
- ❑ Hard cash (US $100-200)
- ❑ Money belt

Documents

- ❑ Passport
- ❑ Tickets & confirmations: flights, hotels, trains, rail pass, car rental, sight entries
- ❑ Driver's license
- ❑ Student ID, hostel card, etc.
- ❑ Photocopies of important documents
- ❑ Insurance details
- ❑ Guidebooks & maps

Toiletries Kit

- ❑ Basics: soap, shampoo, toothbrush, toothpaste, floss, deodorant, sunscreen, brush/comb, etc.
- ❑ Medicines & vitamins
- ❑ First-aid kit
- ❑ Glasses/contacts/sunglasses
- ❑ Sewing kit
- ❑ Packet of tissues (for WC)
- ❑ Earplugs

Electronics

- ❑ Mobile phone
- ❑ Camera & related gear
- ❑ Tablet/ebook reader/laptop
- ❑ Headphones/earbuds
- ❑ Chargers & batteries
- ❑ Phone car charger & mount (or GPS device)
- ❑ Plug adapters

Miscellaneous

- ❑ Daypack
- ❑ Sealable plastic baggies
- ❑ Laundry supplies: soap, laundry bag, clothesline, spot remover
- ❑ Small umbrella
- ❑ Travel alarm/watch
- ❑ Notepad & pen
- ❑ Journal

Optional Extras

- ❑ Second pair of shoes (flip-flops, sandals, tennis shoes, boots)
- ❑ Travel hairdryer
- ❑ Picnic supplies
- ❑ Water bottle
- ❑ Fold-up tote bag
- ❑ Small flashlight
- ❑ Mini binoculars
- ❑ Small towel or washcloth
- ❑ Inflatable pillow/neck rest
- ❑ Tiny lock
- ❑ Address list (to mail postcards)
- ❑ Extra passport photos

Italian Survival Phrases

English	Italian	Pronunciation
Good day.	Buon giorno.	bwohn **jor**-noh
Do you speak English?	Parla inglese?	**par**-lah een-**gleh**-zay
Yes. / No.	Sì. / No.	see / noh
I (don't) understand.	(Non) capisco.	(nohn) kah-**pees**-koh
Please.	Per favore.	pehr fah-**voh**-ray
Thank you.	Grazie.	**graht**-see-ay
You're welcome.	Prego.	**preh**-go
I'm sorry.	Mi dispiace.	mee dee-spee-**ah**-chay
Excuse me.	Mi scusi.	mee **skoo**-zee
(No) problem.	(Non) c'è un problema.	(nohn) cheh oon proh-**bleh**-mah
Good.	Va bene.	vah **beh**-nay
Goodbye.	Arrivederci.	ah-ree-veh-**dehr**-chee
one / two	uno / due	**oo**-noh / **doo**-ay
three / four	tre / quattro	tray / **kwah**-troh
five / six	cinque / sei	**cheeng**-kway / **seh**-ee
seven / eight	sette / otto	**seh**-tay / **oh**-toh
nine / ten	nove / dieci	**noh**-vay / dee-**ay**-chee
How much is it?	Quanto costa?	**kwahn**-toh **koh**-stah
Write it?	Me lo scrive?	may loh **skree**-vay
Is it free?	È gratis?	eh **grah**-tees
Is it included?	È incluso?	eh een-**kloo**-zoh
Where can I buy / find...?	Dove posso comprare / trovare...?	**doh**-vay poh-soh kohm-**prah**-ray / troh-**vah**-ray
I'd like / We'd like...	Vorrei / Vorremmo...	voh-**reh**-ee / voh-**reh**-moh
...a room.	...una camera.	**oo**-nah **kah**-meh-rah
...a ticket to _____	...un biglietto per _____	oon beel-**yeh**-toh pehr _____
Is it possible?	È possibile?	eh poh-**see**-bee-lay
Where is...?	Dov'è...?	doh-**veh**
...the train station	...la stazione	lah staht-see-**oh**-nay
...the bus station	...la stazione degli autobus	lah staht-see-**oh**-nay **dehl**-yee ow-toh-boos
...tourist information	...informazioni per turisti	een-for-maht-see-**oh**-nee pehr too-**ree**-stee
...the toilet	...la toilette	lah twah-**leh**-tay
men	uomini / signori	**woh**-mee-nee / seen-**yoh**-ree
women	donne / signore	**doh**-nay / seen-**yoh**-ray
left / right	sinistra / destra	see-**nee**-strah / **deh**-strah
straight	sempre dritto	**sehm**-pray **dree**-toh
What time does this open / close?	A che ora apre / chiude?	ah kay **oh**-rah ah-**pray** / kee-**oo**-day
At what time?	A che ora?	ah kay **oh**-rah
Just a moment.	Un momento.	oon moh-**mehn**-toh
now / soon / later	adesso / presto / tardi	ah-**deh**-soh / **preh**-stoh / **tar**-dee
today / tomorrow	oggi / domani	**oh**-jee / doh-**mah**-nee

In an Italian Restaurant

English	Italian	Pronunciation
I'd like...	Vorrei...	voh-**reh**-ee
We'd like...	Vorremmo...	vor-**reh**-moh
...to reserve...	...prenotare...	preh-noh-**tah**-ray
...a table for one / two.	...un tavolo per uno / due.	oon **tah**-voh-loh pehr **oo**-noh / **doo**-ay
Is this seat free?	È libero questo posto?	eh **lee**-beh-roh **kweh**-stoh **poh**-stoh
The menu (in English), please.	Il menù (in inglese), per favore.	eel meh-**noo** (een een-**gleh**-zay) pehr fah-**voh**-ray
service (not) included	servizio (non) incluso	sehr-**veet**-see-oh (nohn) een-**kloo**-zoh
cover charge	pane e coperto	**pah**-nay ay koh-**pehr**-toh
to go	da portar via	dah **por**-tar **vee**-ah
with / without	con / senza	kohn / **sehnt**-sah
and / or	e / o	ay / oh
menu (of the day)	menù (del giorno)	meh-**noo** (dehl **jor**-noh)
specialty of the house	specialità della casa	speh-chah-lee-**tah deh**-lah **kah**-zah
first course (pasta, soup)	primo piatto	**pree**-moh pee-**ah**-toh
main course (meat, fish)	secondo piatto	seh-**kohn**-doh pee-**ah**-toh
side dishes	contorni	kohn-**tor**-nee
bread	pane	**pah**-nay
cheese	formaggio	for-**mah**-joh
sandwich	panino	pah-**nee**-noh
soup	zuppa	**tsoo**-pah
salad	insalata	een-sah-**lah**-tah
meat	carne	**kar**-nay
chicken	pollo	**poh**-loh
fish	pesce	**peh**-shay
seafood	frutti di mare	**froo**-tee dee **mah**-ray
fruit / vegetables	frutta / legumi	**froo**-tah / lay-**goo**-mee
dessert	dolce	**dohl**-chay
tap water	acqua del rubinetto	**ah**-kwah dehl roo-bee-**neh**-toh
mineral water	acqua minerale	**ah**-kwah mee-neh-**rah**-lay
milk	latte	**lah**-tay
(orange) juice	succo (d'arancia)	**soo**-koh (dah-**rahn**-chah)
coffee / tea	caffè / tè	kah-**feh** / teh
wine	vino	**vee**-noh
red / white	rosso / bianco	**roh**-soh / bee-**ahn**-koh
glass / bottle	bicchiere / bottiglia	bee-kee-**eh**-ray / boh-**teel**-yah
beer	birra	**bee**-rah
Cheers!	Cin cin!	cheen cheen
More. / Another.	Di più. / Un altro.	dee pew / oon **ahl**-troh
The same.	Lo stesso.	loh **steh**-soh
The bill, please.	Il conto, per favore.	eel **kohn**-toh pehr fah-**voh**-ray
Do you accept credit cards?	Accettate carte di credito?	ah-cheh-**tah**-tay **kar**-tay dee **kreh**-dee-toh
tip	mancia	**mahn**-chah
Delicious!	Delizioso!	day-leet-see-**oh**-zoh

INDEX

MAP INDEX

NAPLES & THE AMALFI COAST

PRACTICALITIES

Start your trip at

ricksteves.com

your travel dreams into affordable reality

Radio Interviews

Enjoy ready access to Rick's vast library of radio interviews covering travel tips and cultural insights that relate specifically to your Europe travel plans.

Travel Forums

Learn, ask, share! Our online community of savvy travelers is a great resource for first-time travelers to Europe, as well as seasoned pros.

Travel News

Subscribe to our free Travel News e-newsletter, and get monthly updates from Rick on what's happening in Europe.

Classroom Europe®

Check out our free resource for educators with 500+ short video clips from the *Rick Steves' Europe* TV show.

Audio Europe™

Rick's Free Travel App

Get your FREE Rick Steves Audio Europe™ app to enjoy…

- Dozens of self-guided tours of Europe's top museums, sights and historic walks
- Hundreds of tracks filled with cultural insights and sightseeing tips from Rick's radio interviews
- All organized into handy geographic playlists
- For Apple and Android

With Rick whispering in your ear, Europe gets even better.

Find out more at ricksteves.com

Pack Light and Right

Gear up for your next adventure at ricksteves.com

Light Luggage

Pack light and right with Rick Steves' affordable, custom-designed rolling carry-on bags, backpacks, day packs and shoulder bags.

Accessories

From packing cubes to moneybelts and beyond, Rick has personally selected the travel goodies that will help your trip go smoother.

Shop at ricksteves.com

Rick Steves has

Experience maximum Europe

Save time and energy

This guidebook is your independent-travel toolkit. But for all it delivers, it's still up to you to devote the time and energy it takes to manage the preparation and logistics that are essential for a happy trip. If that's a hassle, there's a solution.

Rick Steves Tours

A Rick Steves tour takes you to Europe's most

with minimum stress

interesting places with great guides and small groups of 28 or less. We follow Rick's favorite itineraries, ride in comfy buses, stay in family-run hotels, and bring you intimately close to the Europe you've traveled so far to see. Most importantly, we take away the logistical headaches so you can focus on the fun.

nearly half of them repeat customers—along with us on four dozen different itineraries, from Ireland to Italy to Athens.

Is a Rick Steves tour the right fit for your travel dreams? Find out at ricksteves.com, where you can also request Rick's latest tour catalog.

Join the fun

This year we'll take 33,000 free-spirited travelers—

Europe is best experienced with happy travel partners. We hope you can join us.

See our itineraries at ricksteves.com

A Guide for Every Trip

BEST OF GUIDES

*Full color easy-to-scan format,
focusing on Europe's most
popular destinations and sights*

Best of England
Best of Europe
Best of France
Best of Germany
Best of Ireland
Best of Italy
Best of Scotland
Best of Spain

COMPREHENSIVE GUIDES

*City, country, and regional guides
with detailed coverage for a
multi-week trip exploring the
most iconic sights and venturing
off the beaten track*

Amsterdam & the Netherlands
Barcelona
Belgium: Bruges, Brussels,
  Antwerp & Ghent
Berlin
Budapest
Croatia & Slovenia
Eastern Europe
England
Florence & Tuscany
France
Germany
Great Britain
Greece: Athens & the Peloponnese
Iceland
Ireland
Istanbul
Italy
London
Paris
Portugal
Prague & the Czech Republic
Provence & the French Riviera
Rome
Scandinavia
Scotland
Sicily
Spain
Switzerland
Venice
Vienna, Salzburg & Tirol

THE BEST OF ROME

ome, Italy's capital, is studded with
ncient ruins and floodlit-fountain
uares. From the Vatican to the Col-
seum, with crazy traffic in between,
me is wonderful, huge, and exhaust-
  The crowds, the heat, and the

weighty history of the Eternal City where
Caesars walked can make tourists wilt.
Recharge by taking siestas, gelato breaks,
and after-dark walks, strolling from one
atmospheric square to another in the
refreshing evening air.

nired **Pantheon**—which
rgest dome until the
arly 2,000 years old
day over 1,500).

ol of Athens in
ums embodies the
of the Renaissance.

n, gladiators fought
e another, entertaining
0.

POCKET GUIDES

Compact, full color city guides with the essentials for shorter trips

Amsterdam	Munich & Salzburg
Athens	Paris
Barcelona	Prague
Florence	Rome
Italy's Cinque Terre	Venice
London	Vienna

SNAPSHOT GUIDES

Focused single-destination coverage

Basque Country: Spain & France
Copenhagen & the Best of Denmark
Dublin
Dubrovnik
Edinburgh
Hill Towns of Central Italy
Krakow, Warsaw & Gdansk
Lisbon
Loire Valley
Madrid & Toledo
Milan & the Italian Lakes District
Naples & the Amalfi Coast
Nice & the French Riviera
Normandy
Northern Ireland
Norway
Reykjavík
Rothenburg & the Rhine
Sevilla, Granada & Southern Spain
St. Petersburg, Helsinki & Tallinn
Stockholm

CRUISE PORTS GUIDES

Reference for cruise ports of call

Mediterranean Cruise Ports
Scandinavian & Northern European
Cruise Ports

Complete your library with...

TRAVEL SKILLS & CULTURE

Study up on travel skills before visiting "Europe through the back door" or gain insight on European history and culture

Europe 101
Europe Through the Back Door
Europe's Top 100 Masterpieces
European Christmas
European Easter
European Festivals
For the Love of Europe
Travel as a Political Act

PHRASE BOOKS & DICTIONARIES

French
French, Italian & German
German
Italian
Portuguese
Spanish

PLANNING MAPS

Britain, Ireland & London
Europe
France & Paris
Germany, Austria & Switzerland
Iceland
Ireland
Italy
Spain & Portugal

PHOTO CREDITS

Avalon Travel
Hachette Book Group
1700 Fourth Street
Berkeley, CA 94710

Text © 2020 by Rick Steves' Europe, Inc. All rights reserved.
Maps © 2020 by Rick Steves' Europe, Inc. All rights reserved.

Printed in China
Third Edition. Fourth printing March 2023.
ISBN 978-1-64171-273-6

For the latest on Rick's talks, guidebooks, tours, public television series, and public radio show, contact Rick Steves' Europe, 130 Fourth Avenue North, Edmonds, WA 98020, 425/771-8303, www.ricksteves.com, rick@ricksteves.com.

RICK STEVES' EUROPE
Managing Editor: Jennifer Madison Davis
Assistant Managing Editor: Cathy Lu
Special Publications Manager: Risa Laib
Editors: Glenn Eriksen, Tom Griffin, Suzanne Kotz, Rosie Leutzinger, Teresa Nemeth, Jessica Shaw, Carrie Shepherd, Meg Sneeringer
Editorial & Production Assistant: Megan Simms
Graphic Content Director: Sandra Hundacker
Maps & Graphics: David C. Hoerlein, Lauren Mills, Mary Rostad
Digital Asset Coordinator: Orin Dubrow

AVALON TRAVEL
Editorial Director: Kevin McLain
Senior Editor and Series Manager: Madhu Prasher
Associate Managing Editors: Jamie Andrade, Sierra Machado
Copy Editor: Kelly Lydick
Indexer: Stephen Callahan
Cover Design: Kimberly Glyder Design
Interior Design: McGuire Barber Design
Interior Production: Tabitha Lahr, Rue Flaherty, Jane Musser
Maps & Graphics: Kat Bennett

Let's Keep on Travelin'

Your trip doesn't need to end.

Follow Rick on social media!